The
HEDGEHOG REVIEW
READER

The fox knows many things,
but the hedgehog knows one big thing.

—Archilochus

The
HEDGEHOG REVIEW
READER
Two Decades of Critical Reflections on Contemporary Culture

Edited, with an introduction, by Jay Tolson

Preface by James Davison Hunter

Published by the Institute for Advanced Studies in Culture
Distributed by the University of Virginia Press

Institute for Advanced Studies in Culture
Publisher of *The Hedgehog Review*
P.O. Box 400816
Charlottesville, Virginia 22904

Printed in the United States of America.
Designed by Branner Graphic Design, LLC.
Art direction: Leann Davis Alspaugh.

Cover: *Blue Rail* (detail), 1969, by Helen Frankenthaler (1928–2011); acrylic on canvas,
106 15/16 x 93 3/4 inches; Museum of Fine Arts, Houston, Texas, National Endowment for
the Arts and Friends of Modern Art/Bridgeman Images; © 2019 Helen Frankenthaler
Foundation, Inc./Artists Rights Society (ARS), New York.

HedgehogReview.com

Contents

PREFACE

On the Priority of Culture / **9**
James Davison Hunter

INTRODUCTION

In Pursuit of One Big Thing / **13**
Jay Tolson

I.   POLITICS AND CULTURE

The New Ruling Class / **19**
Helen Andrews

Democratic Authority at Century's End / **32**
Jean Bethke Elshtain

Liberal Democracy and the
Unraveling of the Enlightenment Project / **43**
James Davison Hunter

Technocratic Vistas: The Long Con of Neoliberalism / **58**
T.J. Jackson Lears

Not Melting into Air / **66**
John M. Owen IV

Europe and the New Democracy / **77**
Philippe Bénéton

Cosmopolitanism and Democracy:
Affinities and Tensions / **83**
Seyla Benhabib

Two Liberalisms of Fear / **94**
John Gray

Civil Society and Democracy:
A Conversation with Michael Walzer / **105**
Talbot Brewer

II. KNOWLEDGE AND TECHNOLOGY

On Not Being There:
The Data-Driven Body at Work and at Play / **117**
Rebecca Lemov

Intellectuals and Their Discontents / **128**
Russell Jacoby

Why Google Isn't Making Us Stupid...or Smart / **140**
Chad Wellmon

Under the Sign of Satan:
William Blake in the Corporate University / **157**
Mark Edmundson

How We Lost Our Attention / **165**
Matthew B. Crawford

When Science Went Modern / **174**
Lorraine Daston

Digital Metaphysics:
The Cybernetic Idealism of Warren McCulloch / **187**
Leif Weatherby

The University in Question:
A Conversation with Martha C. Nussbaum / **201**
Jennifer L. Geddes

III. ECONOMY AND WORK

Temps, Consultants, and
the Rise of the Precarious Economy / **213**
Louis Hyman

Poverty and Paradox / **227**
Alice O'Connor

Falling / **236**
William McPherson

Saving the Soul of the Smart City / **242**
Joshua J. Yates

The New Political Economy and Its Culture / **258**
Richard Sennett

Seeing the Invisible Poor:
A Conversation with Mike Rose / **270**
Jay Tolson

IV. RELIGION AND SOCIETY

We Have Never Been Disenchanted / **277**
Eugene McCarraher

Globalization and Religion / **291**
Peter L. Berger

The Witness of Literature: A Genealogical Sketch / **302**
Alan Jacobs

The Protestant Structure of American Culture / **317**
Robert N. Bellah

The Theological Roots of Liberalism in Turkey:
"Muslimism" from Islamic Fashion to Foreign Policy / **333**
Neslihan Cevik

Religion and Violence:
A Conversation with Veena Das / **340**
Thomas Cushman

V. THE SELF AND SELF-MAKING

Get a Life: Illusions of Self-Invention / **351**
Wendy Kaminer

The Strange Persistence of Guilt / **362**
Wilfred M. McClay

Moodiness: The Pathos of Contemporary Life / **376**
Harvie Ferguson

Ladies in Waiting / **387**
Becca Rothfeld

On Being Midwestern: The Burden of Normality / **398**
Phil Christman

Love and Its Discontents: Irony, Reason, Romance / **411**
Eva Illouz

Adolescents and the Pathologies of the Achieving Self / **425**
Joseph E. Davis

Evil, Pain, and Beauty:
A Conversation with Elaine Scarry / **438**
Jennifer L. Geddes

CONTRIBUTORS / 447

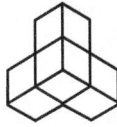

On the Priority of Culture

James Davison Hunter

The subtext of much of what appears in the news media these days implies the priority of politics to…well, everything. Politics has priority not only in the sense of what is prior and determinative but also in the sense of what is of foremost importance. So the principal way to make sense of, for example, contemporary economics—whether the issue is international trade, income inequality, labor, finance, the monetary system, or corporate responsibility—is through the prism of political conflict and the mobilization of resources by different factions and interests. So it is with climate change, health care, immigration, science and technology, education, and even the most intimate of matters, sexuality. This way of seeing things has become commonplace to the point of banality.

One would imagine that in a world that prizes intricacy and complexity, one would find in academia a counter-sensibility—a sensitivity at the least, if not a dogged commitment, to the multiple dimensions, causes, and layers of reality. But as is well known, the *reductio ad potentia* casts a fixed and perhaps permanent shadow over every field in the humanities and social sciences. The principles for interpreting texts, biographies, historical events, and social life in general are invariably traced back to the dynamics of race, class, and gender—and to the power relations among these paramount identities. In the competition for attention, the studies of identity politics are what stand out and matter most. It is no surprise, then, that the politics of recognition profoundly influences the actual organization of academic life in colleges and universities themselves—and, indeed, of most other organizations in contemporary society, from the military to the large corporation.

Even in the way we understand and relate to each other, and not only in more distant relationships, political ideology becomes a prism through which we understand who is good and who is bad, who is safe and who is unsafe, who is in the tribe and who is outside, and whom we take seriously and whom we can just ignore. We hear all the time, even if it is not our personal experience, how ideological harmony, or its absence, can cause the bonds of friendship and family to strengthen, or fray—even sever.

The priority of politics to everything ultimately implies an ontology: that what is most real and most basic about our world is power. To understand the root of most things, go to power and the interests that drive it.

Within this framing, culture is merely the sum of those artifacts derived from or reflecting the struggle for power and privilege. The symbolic and expressive dimensions of social life and the institutions that sustain it are, in the materialist epistemology that funds it, basically epiphenomenal. Culture is worth paying attention to when we understand how it serves to legitimate—or in the case of a counterculture, to challenge—the power dynamics at play.

There is no question that seeing everything in terms of power relations is appealing. It is, on the surface, easy to grasp its logic, and it makes for a coherent story. What is more, the appeal is seemingly universal. High born, middle born, low born, men, women, Black, White, Asian, Hispanic, the religiously faithful, the secular, the Left and the Right, indeed, the extreme Left and the extreme Right—all can use the idiom of power and the resentments it invariably engenders. It is a language game everyone can play, most effectively against one another.

To be sure, it would be foolish to deny the importance of power and politics to human affairs. Both are constitutive of human relations. But to make these the only or principal things that count is simply inadequate to the reality we inhabit, and to the social and historical factors that have brought us where we are.

Indeed, the prioritization of politics distracts us from more fundamental cultural dynamics and the many challenges they present in the late-modern world. Among these are the instrumentalization of social relations in virtually every sphere of human activity, even the most intimate; the progressive emptying of historical and human particularity, and thus the reduction of complexity to superficiality; the flattening of value and quality; and the tendency toward dehumanization that all of these imply. Politicization itself is just one expression of our current cultural impoverishment.

The human consequences of such cultural developments are far reaching, whether in the functioning of the state, the workings of the market, the delivery of health care, or the goals and processes of education. And while there are efforts in various countercultural redoubts to resist the formative influences of the dominant culture, the totalizing tendencies of the latter are difficult to resist. The very embeddedness of the dominant cultural norms, values, and meanings in the most powerful institutions of late-modern societies tells us that they are not going away anytime soon.

For better and worse, then, culture is determinative. The dynamics of power in society, and of politics itself, always operate against a symbolic backdrop that frames the meaning of institutions and actors and, of course, the actions that take place among them. At the most basic level, language—the very heart of that symbolic frame—gives articulate form to the social world in all of its complexity, including its politics. Accordingly, the most materially "real" phenomena in human experience—not least, a society's political economy—are themselves culturally constituted: They are underwritten by a culture's symbolically formulated assumptions, and they grow, ramify, and find sustenance through cultural resources. As the old poststructuralist dictum has it, there is no "outside" of culture. Culture is determinative precisely because it is definitional.

Unlike the facile binaries of power in its prevailing conception (e.g., ideological polarization and extreme partisanship), the dynamics of culture are irreducibly complex. Culture informs and encompasses all that we understand and imagine, what matters, what is good and bad, right and wrong, and what we hope for and fear. Woven together, the symbolic expressions of a culture depict the way the world is; they shape the structures that make that culture distinct, the logics by which it works, and thus the structure within which action is framed, interpreted, and taken. In short, this symbolic structure provides the context within which all human thought and action take place.

It is important to note that these elemental features of culture—these structures and systems of knowledge, meaning, normativity, and teleology—are never fully articulable, but, rather, take shape as dispositions and sensibilities about the nature of reality. As such, they are generally taken for granted: understood, simply, as *the way things are*. These deep structures of culture that define reality are so deeply rooted in the discourse of everyday life and the suppositions of our most prominent institutions that we often fail to see their profound, enduring, and indeed determinative force. They are what make culture the central and defining feature of every human social arrangement.

Which means that the news media, much of academia, most social movements, and, indeed, most denizens of the modern world get it all backward. Culture is prior to politics, and prior to everything else as well. Until we grasp that and begin to understand the subtle, mostly hidden ways that culture frames the problems we face, we have no hope of addressing the matters we care most about in this troubled world.

It is this conviction about the priority of culture, in its thickest and richest conception, and the ethical imperative to attend critically to its workings, that animate *The Hedgehog Review*, and that provide its distinctive voice.

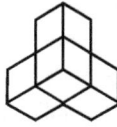

INTRODUCTION

In Pursuit of One Big Thing

Jay Tolson

In the fall of 1999, the inaugural issue of *The Hedgehog Review* introduced itself to readers as an interdisciplinary journal "offering critical reflections on contemporary culture." The editors went on to explain that each issue would address a single theme from different vantage points, through essays, reviews, and interviews. The journal's title derived from an aphorism attributed to the ancient Greek poet Archilochus ("The fox knows many things, but the hedgehog knows one big thing"), and the journal in turn would strive, as the editors put it, "for the breadth of the fox and the depth of the hedgehog."

The "one big thing" alluded to something more than each issue's thematic focus. It also signaled a larger ambition, one reflecting the intellectual agenda of the Institute for Advanced Studies in Culture, the University of Virginia–based research institute out of which the journal grew, and particularly of the Institute's founder and longtime director (and current executive director), James Davison Hunter. That agenda is the investigation of cultural change in modernity, culture being understood as the symbolic system of meanings and values underlying and orienting any human society.

Well before 1999, the resilience of the modern project was coming into question. Despite its great promise and achievements—political and moral as well as economic, scientific, and technological—that project appeared to be unraveling at its deep cultural core. Shaped, variously, by religious reformation and the subsequent wars of religion, the inductive, empirical methods and mentality fostered by the New Science, the philosophical, political, and moral elaborations of Enlightenment rationalism, the institutionalization of liberal, democratic, and increasingly secularist principles during more than a century of political revolutions, the culture of modernity began its self-questioning, self-doubting turn almost as soon as it reached its zenith, in the late nineteenth and early twentieth centuries. At least among intellectual elites—the clerisy of High Modernity—it was becoming evident that the promise of progress on all human fronts was, at best, problematic.

Science, for example, once thought to be the unitary, demystifying, and all-powerful force behind such progress, was showing its own internal inconsistences, contradictions, and limitations. Instead of building truth upon truth, successive discoveries were dismantling previous ones, raising fundamental questions about the once-assumed relationship between science and truth (a development acutely explored by historian Lorraine Daston in her essay in this volume). The implications of such instability were ramifying through the broader culture, manifest in a new suspicion of reason and "common sense" as adequate guides to understanding the human predicament, whether individual, social, or political. The Great War, in addition to consuming the flower of a generation, proved that the sleep of reason was not the only thing that produced monsters.

Even as confidence in science and reason was faltering, the "disenchantment" of the world continued apace, further eroding the more traditional sources of spiritual and moral authority, leaving the late-modern individual alternately liberated or adrift, empowered or despairing, free but never wholly at ease with the burdens of growing autonomy. As older sources of identity lost their purchase—religion and a whole set of feudal ties and obligations—new or refashioned older ones emerged (including highly racialized forms of nationalism), sometimes with militant ferocity, often supporting or giving rise to the totalizing ideologies of Nazism, fascism, and communism that vexed the twentieth century and sparked the most cataclysmic war in human history.

Questions that were being asked even before World War II were asked with heightened urgency in its aftermath. Was truth reducible to power? Did humans control technology, or vice versa? Were alienation and despair the conditions of people without the supports of tradition, community, and faith? Was the human person reducible to *Homo economicus*; the good life, to the maximization of utility and profit? Did unbridled capitalism lead to unbearable inequalities and even the distortion of supposedly free markets? Would rampant consumerism and the commodification of everything distort human relations even while despoiling the earth? Were liberal democracies resilient political arrangements, or fragile structures fated to recurrent crises of authority and legitimacy?

Among those asking such questions most directly were the thinkers associated with the Frankfurt School—philosophers, sociologists, psychologists, political theorists, and historians who had personally witnessed the rise of Nazism and worried, often in Freudian-inflected Marxist (or at least Left Hegelian) terms, about how the dynamics of modernization could lead again to such horrors. Taking refuge in the United States during Hitler's Third Reich, the Frankfurt thinkers elaborated and disseminated their brand of dialectical critical theory, with some of the major figures (including Herbert Marcuse and Erich Fromm) remaining in America after the war and others (Max Horkheimer and Theodor Adorno) returning to Germany, cultivating new intellectual acolytes such as Jürgen Habermas who extended and advanced critical theory into our time.

Resistance to the scientism and positivism that are still regnant in the West—as well as to the facile postmodernism that played fool to both—was one of the lasting legacies of the Frankfurt School. And though the Institute for Advanced Studies in Culture (IASC) embraced thinkers influenced more by Max Weber than by Karl Marx, it modeled itself in part after the Frankfurt School, taking on the same broad scope of study and combining social research, philosophy, political theory, religious studies, and literary criticism, among other disciplines, to advance a morally engaged critique of the crisis of modernity. In its Weberian turn, the Institute differs from the Frankfurt School by taking religion seriously, as a still-vital cultural force even if institutionally fragmented in a decidedly postreligious world. Yoking ontologically serious if largely postreligious thinkers with those who credit religion's continuing relevance (including, among the latter, Charles Taylor, Jean Bethke Elshtain, Alasdair MacIntyre, Marilynne Robinson, Peter Berger, Walker Percy, and Robert Bellah) has become one of the trademark pursuits of Institute scholars, and one that has shed light on many of the seminal questions relating to cultural change and the increasingly divisive culture wars. Taking the Frankfurt critique of modernity's technocratic imperative as a starting point, the Institute's research has gone even further, critiquing the broader effects of modernity's tendency to instrumentalize human relations and even the self-conceptions of the late-modern person. While not denying the power of economic and political dynamics, Institute research, as James Davison Hunter affirms in the preface to this volume, has been dedicated to studying the primacy of culture in human affairs.

Reflecting this dedication, *The Hedgehog Review* has consistently sought to showcase the work not only of its own fellows and affiliated scholars but also of a wide range of like-minded scholars, public intellectuals, and authors who share a similar concern with cultural change and the broad crisis of modernity. In its earliest years, *THR* drew directly from Institute-hosted symposia on themes ranging from "Identity," "Evil," and "Democracy" to "Living with Our Differences," "Religion and Globalization," and "Technology and the Human Person."

In addition to Hunter's scholarly interest in the deep currents of the culture wars, the challenges of pluralism and diversity, and questions of character and formation, *THR* benefited hugely from the intellectual concerns of its other founding editors, Jennifer L. Geddes and Joseph E. Davis. Currently an associate professor in religious studies at the University of Virginia and a fellow of IASC, Geddes brought her interest in the interplay of the arts, literature, and religion directly to bear on shaping the contents of many of *THR*'s stronger issues, including "Meditations on Exile and Home," "Religion and Violence," "The Uses of the Past," and the enduringly apposite "Celebrity Culture." Deeply influenced by the thought of Hannah Arendt and Emmanuel Levinas, Geddes made ethics and memory (and the ethics of memory) an abiding concern of *THR*, and her deep and wide-ranging intellect made her the ideal interlocutor in her illuminating interviews with leading scholars.

Equally crucial in instilling intellectual rigor and scope in *THR* were Davis's editorial direction and his many and varied contributions to the journal. A research associate professor in the University of Virginia's department of sociology, Davis has taken many leadership roles at the Institute since its founding, currently chairing its Colloquy on Picturing the Human and directing the IASC Culture Lab. His interests in identity and social change, medicalization and the reductive tendencies of modern medicine, emotional control and manipulation, the changing nature of work, the rise of the post-psychological subject, suffering, and other topics directly bearing on the human person in modernity have shaped the themes of numerous distinctive issues such as "Illness and Suffering," "The Phantom Economy," "The Shifting Experience of Self," "Humanism amidst Our Machines," "Work and Dignity," and "Science and Moral Life." Having also edited the Institute's popular newsletter (*InSight*, renamed *Culture* in 2006), he merged elements of that publication with *THR* in 2009, when he began his tenure as coeditor and, later, editor and publisher of the journal.

With the help of our longtime circulation manager Monica Powell and designer Beth Branner and a cast of outstanding managing, senior, and copy editors that has included Emily Gum, Brianne Warner Alcala, Leann Davis Alspaugh, B.D. McClay, and Vincent Ercolano, the founding editors created and shepherded a prize-winning publication aimed at readers both inside and beyond the academy, a publication over which I assumed editorial guidance only in recent years, with the intent not to change but to hone its well-established editorial agenda.

This anthology offers a representative sampling of what *THR* has tackled in its first twenty years. The essays and interviews are grouped in five sections: "Politics and Culture," "Knowledge and Technology," "Economy and Work," "Religion and Society," and "The Self and Self-Making." This arrangement reflects less a Procrustean ambition to force things to fit within restrictive categories than a desire to show how and why various crucial precincts of our social existence relate indispensably to culture.

Our world abounds with challenges so severe that they might justifiably be called crises. Ranging from the political to the environmental, these will grow only more acute, we contend, unless humankind comes directly to terms with a crisis within and among ourselves, in the meanings we live by and for, meanings that are found and made in culture—that, indeed, *are* culture, in the deepest sense of the word. Call this anthology a summary report on the culture of late modernity at a time when human mastery over the world has never been more determinative of either its flourishing or its devastation. An optimism born of learning, experience, and perhaps even inclination (though tempered by a tragic awareness of human frailty) compels us to believe that we will come through this crisis as more mindful custodians of our cultural ecology, with a wiser sense of the ends and means of the human project. It is to that fundamental optimism that we dedicate this anthology.

I.
Politics and Culture

The New Ruling Class

Helen Andrews

Last fall, Toby Young did something ironic. Toby is the son of Michael Young, the British sociologist and Labour life peer whose 1958 satire *The Rise of the Meritocracy* has been credited with coining the term. Toby has become an education reformer in his own right, as founder of the West London Free School, after a celebrated career as a journalist and memoirist (*How to Lose Friends and Alienate People*). In September, he published an 8,000-word reconsideration of his father's signature concept in an Australian monthly. The old man was right that meritocracy would gradually create a stratified and immobile society, he wrote, but wrong that abolishing selective education was the cure. "Unlike my father, I'm not an egalitarian," Young wrote. If meritocracy creates a new caste system, "the answer is more meritocracy." To restore equality of opportunity, he suggested subsidies for intelligence-maximizing embryo selection for poor parents "with below-average IQs."[1] The irony lay in the implication that Young, because of who his father was, has special insight into the ideology that holds that it shouldn't matter who your father is.

His outlandish resort to eugenics suggests that Toby Young found himself at a loss for solutions, as all modern critics of meritocracy seem to do. The problems they describe are fundamental, but none of their remedies are more than tweaks to make the system more efficient or less prejudicial to the poor. For instance, in *Excellent Sheep*, William Deresiewicz accuses the Ivy League of imposing a malignant ruling class on the country, then meekly suggests that elite universities might solve the problem by giving greater weight in admissions to socioeconomic disadvantage and less to "résumé-stuffing."[2] In *The Tyranny of the Meritocracy*, Lani Guinier belies the harsh terms of her title by advising that we simply learn to reward "democratic rather than testocratic merit."[3] Christopher Hayes subtitled his debut book *Twilight of the Elites* "America after Meritocracy," but the remedies he prescribes are all meant to preserve meritocracy by making it more effective.[4] In his latest book, *Our Kids*, Robert Putnam proves that American social mobility is in crisis, then reposes his hopes in such predictable nostrums as housing vouchers and universal pre-kindergarten.[5]

When an author caps two hundred pages of rhetorical fire with fifteen pages of platitudes or utopian fantasy, that is called "the last chapter problem." When every author who takes up a question finds himself equally at a loss, that is something else. In this case, our authors fail as critics of meritocracy because they cannot get their heads outside of it. They are incapable of imagining what it would be like not to believe in it. They assume the validity of the very thing they should be questioning.

But what would it be like not to take meritocracy for granted? The basic idea—that we should rank candidates for power according to some desirable quality, then pick the best of them—seems too obvious to have needed inventing, but invented it was, and (at least in the West) not so long ago. If we go back to the occasion of its first appearance in the English-speaking world, we will find a group of men who opposed it, not just because they did not think it would work in practice, but because they disagreed with it in principle. Meritocracy had a beginning and a middle and may yet have an end, and the beginning is exactly where the man who coined the term said it was on the very first page of his book: the Northcote-Trevelyan Report of 1854.[6]

A Tale of Two Reformers

King George III is said to have remarked that any man was fit to occupy any government post he could manage to get. That is about as far as someone of his generation was likely to go in justifying patronage. Mostly it was accepted as a fact of politics. A party democracy required political workers, and without civil service jobs to distribute to the faithful, how could parties persuade anyone to work for them? Patronage was seen then as cash donations are now: seedy, no doubt, and definitely vulnerable to corruption, but not illegitimate. Benjamin Disraeli, in this as in so much else, formed a bridge between Georgian laxity and Victorian moral justification, writing in 1858, "Patronage is the outward and visible sign of an inward and spiritual grace, and that is Power."[7]

This sacramental reasoning meant nothing to the Protestant reformers then coming of age, and certainly not to Sir Charles Trevelyan. Thomas Babington Macaulay is today considered the archetype of liberal Clapham Sect self-satisfaction, and even he thought his brother-in-law was a prig. "His mind is full of schemes of moral and political improvement," Macaulay wrote of Trevelyan when they were in India together. "His topics even in courtship are steam navigation, the education of the natives, the equalization of sugar duties."[8] This did not prevent Macaulay from using his influence to have Trevelyan appointed senior

permanent secretary to the Treasury in 1840, although he never told him of this intervention. History might have turned out differently if he had. As it was, Trevelyan thought his
promotion was a case of virtue rewarded, and he returned to England more convinced than
ever of the merit principle.[9]

So when William Gladstone needed a second chairman for his inquiry into civil-service
reform, in addition to Sir Stafford Northcote, his own former private secretary, he knew that
Charles Trevelyan was someone he could rely on to return the answer he wanted. A consensus
had arisen that something ought to be done about the civil service, which had become disorga-
nized, unaccountable, and inefficient—Tite Barnacle of the Circumlocution Office made his
appearance in Charles Dickens's *Little Dorrit* around this time. Gladstone's particular concern,
as Chancellor of the Exchequer, was the expense of maintaining hacks and protégés in their
sinecures, and his innate moral prissiness inclined him toward competitive examination as a
way of removing all discretion, and thus temptation, from ministers at a single stroke.

It took less than eight months for Northcote and Trevelyan to complete their report,
which is only twenty-three pages long. Fortunately for them, it appeared just as the Crimean
War debacles were arousing public clamor for administrative reform. (No one seems to have
noted that the military commissary system, as part of the Treasury, was under Trevelyan's
supervision.) The report recommended that all new recruits to the government service be
subject to some form of examination by a central civil-service commission. At minimum,
a *qualifying* examination in basic spelling and arithmetic would keep out obvious incom-
petents. Better would be a *competitive* examination of university-level difficulty, to be conducted on a set date each year, in a handful of locations, in a range of available subjects
from Greek to chemistry. Anyone could take the test, no sponsorship required. However
many vacancies there were in the civil service that year, exactly that many names would be
accepted from the top of the list of scores.[10]

Public reaction was divided. Like most reform-minded liberals, John Stuart Mill was
exultant: "Competitive examination appears to me to be one of those great public improvements the adoption of which would form an era in history."[11] The headmaster of Harrow
admitted that beneficiaries of the status quo might make reform difficult to enact, but, he
said, "I can scarcely understand the existence of two opinions as to its abstract desirable-
ness."[12] But for the bulk of Englishmen who were not yet accustomed to test taking as a
feature of life outside the schoolroom, it seemed (in the words of a later historian) "like the
intrusion into the world of politics of a scheme of cause and effect derived from another
universe—as if one should propose to the Stock Exchange that the day's prices should be
fixed by prayer and the casting of lots."[13]

Trevelyan canvassed opinions of the finished report from headmasters, professors, and
mandarins, and it is remarkable how unanimously the educators favored the plan and how
unanimously the mandarins opposed it. The report's finely phrased ideas would collapse
in practice, the latter warned. For instance, replacing promotion by seniority with more

subjective "promotion according to merit" would give free rein to favoritism. In departments that had experimented with qualifying exams, supervisors found that the tests put money in the pockets of "crammers" but did little for productivity. To its opponents, the whole thing smelled like a schoolmasters' scheme. In Anthony Trollope's *The Three Clerks*—the first and as far as I know the only satirical novel written against the Northcote-Trevelyan reforms— the character modeled on Oxford don and reform booster Benjamin Jowett fantasizes about the day when "every man in England should…be made to pass through some 'go.' The green-grocer's boy should not carry out cabbage unless his fitness for cabbage-carrying had been ascertained."[14] As a civil servant himself, Trollope suspected that this proliferation of examinations would benefit no one but the examiners.

There was also worry about what throwing competition open to all comers would do to the service's social tone. "The more the civil service is recruited from the lower classes, the less it will be sought after by the higher," warned the MP Edward Romilly.[15] This was not mere snobbery. If the government wanted civil servants who could stand up to MPs, financiers, and foreign statesmen, it had to recruit men of comparable social standing. Robert Lowe, who as Gladstone's chancellor did more than anyone to put the Northcote-Trevelyan reforms into practice, nevertheless thought the service ought to remain at least partly aristocratic, because although class was no guarantee of merit, it constituted "a sort of freemasonry among men which is not very easy to describe but which everybody feels."[16] Perhaps Lowe was thinking of his schooldays at Winchester and the famous "fags' rebellion" of 1829, which was sparked when the school decided to appoint the top scholars in the senior class as prefects, instead of the "haughty heroes of the playing field" who had always been appointed before.[17] Underclassmen revolted, and Lowe (one of the unathletic prefects deposed) had an early lesson that people will decide for themselves what kinds of authority they will recognize.

Other objections approached closer to the principle. There were, first of all, questions of democratic accountability. Civil servants who felt they owed their jobs to no one and nothing but their own merit would be independent, which was also to say impervious to checks and balances. They would not derive their power from the people even by so remote a means as a parliamentary patron. Ralph Lingen of the Education Office begged Trevelyan to remember that the voters of England were used to treating office as among "the legitimate prizes of war" after elections, "not merely for its emoluments, but also for the sake of influencing administration."[18] It was almost a kind of direct democracy.

Transforming the Spirit of Government

A greater concern was that meritocracy would produce an overweening centralized state. The Prussian precedent left Walter Bagehot wary of "establishing, virtually for the first time in England, an organized Bureaucracy."[19] On the floor of the House of Commons, MPs brandished warnings from Tocqueville and Montalembert against following imperial France's example, which would inevitably lead to administrative tyranny, the creation of a political clerisy, and "a venal and servile humor" to supplant the English spirit of liberty.[20] Gladstone replied that such worries were "idle, pusillanimous, and womanish," since Parliament could be trusted to keep the civil service in its place. "In certain continental states the experiment may be perilous, but in England you may make the Civil Service as strong as you please."[21]

Hearing this, Robert Cecil (later Lord Salisbury) rose to say that "he did not regard that fear as so groundless and unfounded as the right honorable Gentleman appeared to do."[22] Salisbury's comprehensive case against Northcote-Trevelyan was dismissed by Gladstone biographer John Morley as "the lazy doctrine that men are much of a muchness," and no doubt this was Salisbury's starting point.[23] Beyond ensuring that candidates could spell and add, he thought that selecting the most intelligent men you could find was unnecessary—even positively harmful. Such men would be arrogant and argumentative, and would "look upon their duties as beneath their abilities." This was not mere speculation, but the attested experience of their supervisors in departments where examination had been implemented. One bitter customs officer cited by Salisbury complained of "a self-sufficiency and presumption, from an imagined superiority in having undergone such examination, and a desire for literature in business, which I have been obliged to check." This arrogance was bad enough around the office, Salisbury believed, but to the extent that it encompassed the public, it was a threat to their liberties.[24]

More generally, Salisbury predicted that competitive examination would dangerously transform the spirit of government. As he saw it, reformers were seeking to automate the art of politics in a way "manifestly repugnant to the commonest and not the worst feelings of our nature." Rattling off instances of patronage exercised nobly by Sir Walter Scott, Samuel Johnson, and Robert Peel, Salisbury asked whether it was worth abjuring such acts merely to keep out a handful of slow-witted copyists: "Why should favour and friendship, kindness and gratitude, which are not banished by men from private life, be absolutely excluded from public affairs?" And in the effort to eliminate all unmathematical considerations from the exercise of power, what other human qualities might not be driven out? Mercy? Flexibility? Loyalty to country? It was a dangerous and metastatic idea, this notion that statesmen could govern by formula.[25]

Then again, Salisbury was a reactionary who never had a good word for progress of any kind. The same could not be said of open competition's other vocal opponent, Sir James Stephen, whose credibility as a liberal was matched only by his reputation as an administrator of genius. His long experience in Whitehall had led him to believe, like Salisbury, that "the man whose name stood half way down the examinations list of merit would probably make a better clerk than he whose name stood first"—not as good a clerk, but *better*.[26] Working for the government did not offer enough scope for the talents and ambitions of the men at the top of the list. Nor should it, a small-government man like Salisbury would have added.

But like a good Victorian liberal, Stephen objected mainly on humanitarian grounds. According to the findings of the Northcote-Trevelyan Report, the civil service deserved its reputation as a stashing place for crippled, blind, deaf, and sickly clerks (some of whom, it neglected to add, were highly competent). Stephen admitted the charge with pride. "Patronage exercised in the spirit of nepotism is made the shelter of the weak and otherwise helpless," he wrote to Trevelyan. "Those whom nature or training have made strong can usually help themselves." Worse, if the meritocratic principle were widely adopted, Stephen suspected that a surprising number of men would discover to their dismay that they stood in relation to the talented minority as cripples and deaf-mutes stood in relation to themselves. "A *detur digniori* world [one in which merit decides] would, I imagine, be a world made up of despots and slaves."[27]

Out with the Old Grandees, in with the New Men

So who turned out to be right, merit's boosters, or its naysayers? The boosters made surprisingly few specific predictions, apart from asserting that, in general, men chosen on a more rational basis would be superior. It is thus hard to tell whether appointment by merit fulfilled their expectations for it. "The adoption of open competition in 1870 seemed to obviate any necessity for further consideration not only of the method by which officials were appointed but also of the system under which they did their work," reflected a Fabian progressive in 1908. Competitive examination, "like the wedding in a middle-Victorian novel, was to be the end of the story."[28]

There is no question that the size of government did explode. The staff of the civil service tripled in fifty years and then doubled in ten, hitting 281,000 on the eve of World War I. Obviously, this was mainly because the government had taken on so many more tasks—but one reason for *that* was that the public had come to trust that the government was full of people who knew what they were doing. Interference that would have never been tolerated in the bad old days of jobbery was now justified by the national government's (largely meretricious) mystique as a repository of intelligence. Usually a great fan of competition, Herbert Spencer complained that under competitive examination "men who might otherwise reprobate further growth of officialism are led to look on it with tolerance, if not favourably."[29] It was a self-perpetuating dynamic, too. A complicated budget like Lloyd George's demanded more intelligence to implement than the straightforward arithmetic of the Victorian tax system—and once you've hired a cadre of clever men, why not get the most out of them?

Bagehot had warned that the smart young men ensnared by open competition would "only mope, wither, and blaspheme in the Public Departments."[30] If only he had been right. Alas, Bagehot forgot that intelligent people who are bored by their jobs will *make their jobs interesting* as far as possible—which, when civil servants do it, is not necessarily to the public good. The domestic departments began hunting around for problems to solve, whether anyone wanted their solutions or not, and the Colonial Office started meddling even more in the decisions of local officials. Anytime a district officer cabled home about a dispute, headquarters would examine the question from every angle with lingering attention, rummaging for precedents and murmuring "Most intriguing!" Meanwhile, the man on the spot was desperate to make a decision, any decision, regardless of whether it was consistent with what had been done under Shippard in Bechuanaland in 1885.

The Colonial Office became especially notorious for its highhandedness, probably because the rough, active men it supervised had in many cases gone abroad in the first place from a lack of prospects at home. Permanent Undersecretary Robert Meade's comment in 1892 that colonial governors were "very inferior persons" was typical.[31] But this was emphatically not the old arrogance of the landed aristocracy. (Meade himself was a meritocrat of unimposing background.) The debate in the days of Northcote-Trevelyan had been over whether open competition would benefit the middle class or the upper class. Gladstone and Trevelyan both thought the latter, and they considered this a mark in its favor. In the event, neither side in that debate turned out to be correct. Meritocracy called into being an entirely new class, partly taken from the old gentry, partly from the new commercial class, and loyal to neither. Between 1870 and World War I, this new class took possession of all the former pillars of the old aristocracy's power, not just the civil service but the army, the bar, local government, party associations, and the church.

This was the significance of Northcote-Trevelyan. The merit principle was like a virus in the code of the British polity; the class it created was perfectly designed to sweep all before it. In the same way that religious fanatics and nationalists can sometimes defeat ordinary soldiers from sheer fervor of belief, so the meritocrats prevailed by being more convinced of their own superiority than the old grandees had ever been, with none of that *deo gratias* nonsense to keep them humble, either. Another battlefield advantage of the meritocrats was mobility. A good way to measure their takeover of national politics is to look at the percentage of rural MPs who were born in their constituencies—the sharp decline in Cheshire, from 70 percent (1832–85) to 25 percent (1885–1918), was not unusual. The new men, as David Cannadine writes in *The Decline and Fall of the British Aristocracy*, were primarily "outsiders, professionals, and trade-union leaders, men with no local links or of limited standing in the community."[32]

Local government went the same way, as its responsibilities became too much for the amateur mayors and magistrates of the local gentry, and professionals had to be imported. As Cannadine explains, "The patrician element on the county councils had not been undermined by the lower-class democrats, as had been feared initially, so much as by the upstart bureaucrats."[33] Therein lies the essence of the story. The purpose of the old aristocracy, in its own mind, had been to act as a counterweight to the plutocracy on one hand and the impulsive common masses on the other. It turned out the aristocrats had more to fear from the bureaucratic class than from either of these. In their responsibility to prevent that class from dominating the state, the aristocrats failed utterly. This defeat was not just the replacement of one ruling class by another, but the end of the venerable system of social checks and balances that not even monarchs and Chartists had been able to upset. This made the meritocracy's victory in England almost more impressive than its later, more comprehensive victory in the United States.

Aristocracy—Embrace It!

Meritocracy began by destroying an aristocracy; it has ended in creating a new one. Nearly every book in the American anti-meritocracy literature makes this charge, in what is usually its most empirically reinforced chapter. Statistics on the decline of social mobility are not lacking. In 1985, less than half of students at selective colleges came from families in the top income quartile; in 2010, 67 percent did.[34] For those authors brave enough to cite Charles Murray (as Robert Putnam, for one, was not), *Coming Apart* documents quantitatively the growing tendency of the members of America's cognitive elite to marry each other, live near each other in "Super Zips," and launch their children into the same schools, and thence onto the same path to worldly success.[35] Deresiewicz puts this betrayal of the democratic impulse neatly: "Our new multiracial, gender-neutral meritocracy has figured out a way to make itself hereditary."[36]

But the solutions on offer never rise to the scale of the problem. Authors attack the meritocratic machine with screwdrivers, not sledgehammers, and differ only in which valve they want to adjust. Some think the solution is to tip more disadvantaged kids over the lip of the intake funnel, which would probably make things worse. If more people start competing for a finite number of slots, slim advantages like those that come from having grown up with two meritocrats for parents will only loom larger. And has anyone asked working-class families if being sucked into a frantically achievement-obsessed rat race is a benefaction they are interested in?

Others favor the slightly more radical solution of redefining our idea of merit, usually in a way that downplays what Guinier calls "pseudoscientific measures of excellence."[37] She even has a replacement in mind, the Bial-Dale College Adaptability Index, the testing of which involves Legos. (Why are you laughing? It is backed by a *study*.) This is even less likely to work than fiddling with the equality-of-opportunity end. For one thing, the minority of families willing to do whatever it takes to get into Harvard will still do whatever it takes to get into Harvard. They have adapted to new admissions criteria before, and they will do so again. Furthermore, unless families are abolished, successful parents will always pass on advantages to their children, which will compound with each generation. It does not matter how merit is defined; the *dynamic* of meritocracy remains the same, its operations inexorable.

My solution is quite different. The meritocracy is hardening into an aristocracy—so let it. Every society in history has had an elite, and what is an aristocracy but an elite that has put some care into making itself presentable? Allow the social forces that created this aristocracy to continue their work, and embrace the label. By all means this caste should admit as many worthy newcomers as is compatible with their sense of continuity. New brains, like new money, have been necessary to every ruling class, meritocratic or not. If ethnic balance is important to meritocrats, they should engineer it into the system. If geographic diversity strikes them as important, they should ensure that it exists, ideally while keeping an eye on the danger of hoovering up all of the native talent from regional America. But they must give up any illusion that such tinkering will make them representative of the country over which they preside. They are separate, parochial in their values, unique in their responsibilities. That is what makes them aristocratic.

A tough sell, I realize. Not since the Society of the Cincinnati has a ruling elite so vehemently disclaimed any resemblance to an aristocracy. The structure of the economy abets the elite in its delusion, since even the very rich are now more likely to earn their money from employment than from capital, and thus find it easier to think of themselves basically as working stiffs.[38] As cultural consumers they are careful to look down their noses at nothing except country music. All manner of low-class fare—rap, *telenovelas*, Waffle House—is embraced by what Shamus Rahman Khan calls the "omnivorous pluralism" of our elite. "It is as if the new elite are saying, 'Look! We are not some exclusive club. If anything, we are the most democratized of all groups.'"[39]

Khan's *Privilege: The Making of an Adolescent Elite at St. Paul's School* is a fascinating document, because he seems to have been genuinely surprised by what he found when he returned to his old boarding school to teach for a year. Khan, the grandson of Irish and Pakistani peasants, worked his way to a Columbia University professorship in sociology via St. Paul's and Haverford College. So he thought he knew meritocrats—but today's breed gave him a bit of a fright. For one thing, they proved to be excellent haters. Consider how they talk about a legacy student whose background can be inferred from the pseudonym Khan gives him, "Chase Abbott":

> After seeing me chatting with Chase, a boy I was close with, Peter, expressed what many others would time and again: "that guy would never be here if it weren't for his family.... I don't get why the school still does that. He doesn't bring anything to this place." Peter seemed annoyed with me for even talking with Chase. Knowing that I was at St. Paul's to make sense of the school, Peter made sure to point out to me that Chase didn't really belong there.... Faculty, too, openly lamented the presence of students like Chase.[40]

"Openly lamented"! Poor Chase. This hatred is out of all proportion to the power still held by the Chases of the school, which is almost nil. Khan discovers that the few legacy WASPs live together in a sequestered dorm, just like the "minority dorm" of his own schooldays, and even the alumni "point to students like Chase as examples of what is wrong about St. Paul's."[41] No, the hatred of students like Chase feels more like the resentment born of having noticed an unwelcome resemblance. It is somehow unsurprising to learn that Peter's parents met at Harvard.

Of course, Peter is not at St. Paul's because his parents went to Harvard; as he makes clear to Khan, he is there because of his hard work and academic achievement. Here we have the meritocratic delusion most in need of smashing: the notion that the people who make up our elite are especially smart. They are not—and I do not mean that in the feel-good democratic sense that we are all smart in our own ways, the homely-wise farmer no less than the scholar. I mean that the majority of meritocrats are, on their own chosen scale of intelligence, pretty dumb. Grade inflation first hit the Ivies in the late 1960s for a reason. Yale professor David Gelernter has noticed it in his students: "My students today are…so ignorant that it's hard to accept how ignorant they are…. [I]t's very hard to grasp that the person you're talking to, who is bright, articulate, advisable, interested, and doesn't know who Beethoven is. Had no view looking back at the history of the twentieth century—just sees a fog. A blank."[42] Camille Paglia once assigned the spiritual "Go Down, Moses" to an English seminar, only to discover to her horror that "of a class of twenty-five students, only two seemed to recognize the name 'Moses'…. They did not know who he was."[43]

Once again, Khan uncovers the clue to this phenomenon by letting his St. Paul's students speak for themselves:

> "I don't actually know much," an alumnus told me after he finished his freshman year at Harvard. "I mean, well, I don't know how to put it. When I'm in classes all these kids next to me know a lot more than I do. Like about what actually happened in the Civil War. Or what France did in World War II. I don't know any of that stuff. But I know something they don't. It's not facts or anything. It's how to think. That's what I learned in humanities."
>
> "What do you mean, 'how to think'?" I asked.
>
> "I mean, I learned how to think bigger. Like, everyone else at Harvard knew about the Civil War. I didn't. But I knew how to make sense of what they knew about the Civil War and apply it. So they knew a lot about particular things. I knew how to think about everything."[44]

"How to think bigger" is indeed a fine quality for a governing class to have, but this young man was cheated if his teachers tried to cultivate it as a skill in isolation and not via the discipline of learning "particular things." It was the meritocratic ideology that paved this road to ignorance. Being open to all comers, with intelligence the only criterion, meant that no particular body of knowledge could be made mandatory at an institution like St. Paul's, lest it arbitrarily exclude students conversant only with their own traditions. This has predictably yielded a generation of students who have no body of knowledge at all—not even "like about what actually happened in the Civil War."

Unlike meritocracies, aristocracies can put actual *content* into their curricula—not just academically, but morally. Every aristocracy has an ethos, and a good ethos will balance out the moral faults to which that aristocracy is prone. The upper-class WASPs who constituted "the Establishment" in twentieth-century America were very rich; so they instilled in their children a Puritan asceticism. The Whig grandees of eighteenth-century Britain, who were the opposite of ascetic, cultivated a spirit of *usefulness* to check their tendency toward idleness. The besetting sin of the current elite seems to be arrogance, both moral and intellectual, with humorlessness a close second. To address the first, their acculturating institutions might try putting greater emphasis on humility—and they may find that learning how to laugh at themselves is one way this virtue can be acquired.

There is a wonderfully sad anecdote about Kingman Brewster, the man who as president of Yale did more than any other individual to create the modern meritocracy. In his first portentous strike at the WASP elite that reared him, he turned down his Skull and Bones tap on anti-elitist grounds. He then hopped on his bicycle and rushed to boast of his principled stand to A. Whitney Griswold, his ultra-WASPy but reform-minded mentor, whom he would succeed as Yale president two decades later. Far from being impressed, Griswold was not even home to receive him—he was across town at his own secret society, Wolf's Head, for its Tap Night ceremonies.[45] The poignancy of this story lies in the realization that, for all his *Mayflower* pedigree, Brewster really did not understand at all the class he would destroy. In retrospect, it seems likely that Brewster could have achieved all he desired—a more diverse student body, a more rigorous academic curriculum, a more liberal general atmosphere—by building upon the existing virtues of Old Yale, its sense of public duty and fair play. Unfortunately, he was blind to these virtues. So he did the only thing contempt can do: He destroyed.

The task of reforming our present elite ought to be entrusted to someone with a feeling for what is good in it. For all its flaws, this elite does have many virtues. Its moral seriousness contrasts favorably with the frivolousness of certain earlier generations, and its sense of pragmatism, which can sometimes be reductive, can also be admirably brisk and hard-nosed. What is needed is someone who can summon a picture of the meritocratic elite's best selves and call others to meet the example. But this process can begin only when this new ruling class finally owns up to the only name for what it already undeniably is.

(Summer 2016, 18.2)

Notes

1 Toby Young, "The Fall of the Meritocracy," *Quadrant*, September 2015, https://quadrant.org.au/magazine/2015/09/fall-meritocracy/.

2 William Deresiewicz, *Excellent Sheep: The Miseducation of the American Elite and the Way to a Meaningful Life* (New York, NY: Free Press, 2014), 235.

3 Lani Guinier, *The Tyranny of the Meritocracy: Democratizing Higher Education in America* (Boston, MA: Beacon Press, 2015), 1.

4 Christopher Hayes, *Twilight of the Elites: America after Meritocracy* (New York, NY: Crown, 2012).

5 Robert Putnam, *Our Kids: The American Dream in Crisis* (New York, NY: Simon & Schuster, 2015).

6 Michael Young, *The Rise of the Meritocracy, 1870–2033: An Essay on Education and Equality* (London, England: Thames & Hudson, 1958), 1. The Northcote-Trevelyan Report was published in 1854, but its recommendations were not fully implemented until 1870; hence the first date in the book's title.

7 Quoted in Robert Blake, *Disraeli* (London, England: Eyre & Spottiswoode, 1966), 388.

8 George Otto Trevelyan, *The Life and Letters of Lord Macaulay* (New York, NY: Harper, 1876), 1: 341.

9 Laura Trevelyan, *A Very British Family: The Trevelyans and Their World* (London, England: I.B. Tauris, 2006), 36.

10 The full report is available in *Papers on the Re-organisation of the Civil Service, Presented to Both Houses of Parliament by Command of Her Majesty* (London, England: Eyre & Spottiswoode, 1855). The best summary of the report and its background is in W.H. Greenleaf, *The British Political Tradition. Volume 3, A Much Governed Nation: Part 1* (New York, NY: Routledge, 1983), chap. 3, "In Dark Wonder."

11 *Papers on the Re-organisation of the Civil Service*, 92.

12 Ibid., 87.

13 Graham Wallas, *Human Nature in Politics* (London, England: Archibald Constable, 1908), 252.

14 Anthony Trollope, *The Three Clerks, a Novel* (London, England: Richard Bentley, 1858), 1: 233.

15 *Papers on the Re-organisation of the Civil Service*, 289.

16 Quoted in David William Sylvester, *Robert Lowe and Education* (Cambridge, England: Cambridge University Press, 1974), 202.

17 "Haughty heroes" is from John Chandos's summary of the rebellion in *Boys Together: English Public Schools 1800–1864* (London, England: Hutchison, 1984), 101.

18 *Papers on the Re-organisation of the Civil Service*, 104.

19 Walter Bagehot, "Tests for the Public Service," *National Review* 24 (January 1861): 143.

20 George Cornewall Lewis, speech to the House of Commons, April 24, 1856, *Hansard Parliamentary Debates*, vol. 141, cc. 1418–20. The man Lewis describes as "another French statesman whose name, if I were to disclose it, would command the instant respect of the House of Commons," is identified as Tocqueville in John Roach, *Public Examinations in England 1850–1900* (Cambridge, England: Cambridge University Press, 1971), 193.

21 William E. Gladstone, speech to the House of Commons, April 24, 1856, *Hansard Parliamentary Debates*, vol. 141, cc. 1423.

22 Lord Robert Cecil, speech to the House of Commons, April 24, 1856, *Hansard Parliamentary Debates*, vol. 141, cc. 1437.

23 John Morley, *The Life of William Ewart Gladstone*, vol. 1, 1809–1859 (Cambridge, England: Cambridge University Press, 2011), 511. First published 1903.

24 Lord Salisbury, "Competitive Examination," *Quarterly Review* 108 (October 1860): 595–96.

[25] Ibid., 569–72.

[26] *Papers on the Re-organisation of the Civil Service*, 76.

[27] Ibid., 78.

[28] Wallas, *Human Nature in Politics*, 261.

[29] Herbert Spencer, "The Coming Slavery" in *Spencer: Political Writings*, ed. John Offer (Cambridge, England: Cambridge University Press, 1994), 91.

[30] Bagehot, "Tests for the Public Service," 136.

[31] Quoted in Martin J. Wiener, A*n Empire on Trial: Race, Murder, and Justice under British Rule, 1870–1935* (Cambridge, England: Cambridge University Press, 2009), 14.

[32] David Cannadine, *The Decline and Fall of the British Aristocracy* (London, England: Vintage, 1999), 149, 153. First published 1990.

[33] Ibid., 166.

[34] Deresiewicz, *Excellent Sheep*, 205.

[35] Charles Murray, *Coming Apart: The State of White America 1960–2000* (New York, NY: Crown Forum, 2012).

[36] Deresiewicz, *Excellent Sheep*, 210.

[37] Guinier, *The Tyranny of the Meritocracy*, 22.

[38] Thomas Piketty and Emmanuel Saez, "Income Inequality in the United States: 1913–1998," *Quarterly Journal of Economics* 118 (2003): 1–39. Quoted in Shamus Rahman Khan, *Privilege: The Making of an Adolescent Elite at St. Paul's School* (Princeton, NJ: Princeton University Press, 2011), 17.

[39] Khan, *Privilege*, 135.

[40] Ibid., 3–4.

[41] Ibid., 4.

[42] David Gelernter, interviewed on *Conversations with Bill Kristol*, July 6, 2015, http://conversationswith-billkristol.org/.

[43] Emily Esfahani Smith, "My Camille Paglia Interview: The Outtakes," *Acculturated*, December 17, 2012, http://acculturated.com/my-camille-paglia-interview-the-outtakes/.

[44] Khan, *Privilege*, 141.

[45] Geoffrey Kabaservice, *The Guardians: Kingman Brewster, His Circle, and the Rise of the Liberal Establishment* (New York, NY: Henry Holt, 2004), 155.

Democratic Authority at Century's End

Jean Bethke Elshtain

T here is widespread agreement that American democracy is in trouble. Social scientists offer up a mountain of data showing that we are civically depleted, politically cynical and rootless, socially mistrustful, and personally fearful. This is a strange turn of events for a country associated with can-do optimism, with a robust democratic faith—indeed, a country once quite confident about its institutions and its ability to transmit them intact over time. An anemic and faltering democratic faith—a decline of confidence in our basic institutions—threatens to render us incapable of sustaining these institutions over the long haul.

The Crisis of Democratic Authority

One can approach this matter—this concern—from a number of angles. Social scientists who have tracked the sharp decline in associational life in America argue that the evidence points to nothing less than a crisis in "social capital formation," by which they mean the forging of bonds of social and political trust and competence. Political and social theorists, of whom I am one, evoke Tocqueville and speak of the thinning out of that dense fabric—that social ecology—that historically did much of the hands-on work of democracy. Certainly the debilitating effects of rising mistrust, privatization, and anomie are many. For example: there is overwhelming empirical support for the popularly held view that where neighborhoods are intact, drug and alcohol abuse, crime, and teen-age childbearing diminish. Because families and neighborhoods are less and less likely to be intact, all forms of socially-and self-destructive behavior are on the rise among children and young people. The list goes on and on. For every Panglossian optimist there are, at present, a dozen with far gloomier assessments of our prospects. All of this suggests that the buoyant confidence that long sustained democratic prospects, especially the notion that human beings are capable of self-limiting freedom and sturdy self-government, is badly battered, and our public culture shows considerable signs of wear and tear.

I will focus on but one dimension of our discontents: the crisis in democratic authority. I am convinced that our collective decline of confidence flows, in part, from a general crisis of authority. That crisis cuts across all formative institutions: religion, education, families, and government. And it raises questions about the continuing power of what political theorists call "foundings" or founding moments.

Much overshadowed by the epistemological debate over foundationalism, a concern with specifically political foundings has faded. But it is worth recalling what such moments were about and what they set in motion. Imagine the following: a new civic order comes into being. Certain questions must be asked: What is the nature of this new order? How is it to be instituted among men and women? Where does authority reside? For no exercise of political power is legitimate without a general sharing of certain authoritative norms, standards, documents, institutions, even cultural narratives, stories, and songs. The democratic story added the following: Through pledges and promises—a social contract or covenant—persons throw in their fortunes with one another. They seek not a perfect world, but a better one. And authority is necessary to its realization.

But perhaps we have lost this understanding of authority. At least so Hannah Arendt believed. Among the many strong claims lodged by Arendt, one must include the following: Authority, she claimed, "has vanished from the modern world. Since we can no longer fall back upon authentic and undisputable experiences common to all, the very term has become clouded by controversy and confusion."[1] We will return to this strong argument below and consider whether it is, in fact, necessary as a precondition for a defensible account of authority. But, for now, it is important to note that Arendt here seems to suggest that we need the deep and wide sharing of an overarching, as well as grounding, set of experiences of labor, work, and action to fall back upon, and if we don't have this, authority "vanishes."

She continues: We late moderns "are no longer in a position to know what authority really is." What we have lost, Arendt adds rather elliptically, is not "'authority in general,' but rather a very specific form which had been valid throughout the Western World over a long period of time."[2] Arendt doesn't note, though she might have, that much of that history of the Western World was not democratic—did not take shape as a democratic polity in the form we now honor and recognize. Perhaps, we might reply by way of rejoinder, if Arendt had limited her lament to traditional pre-democratic authority, she wouldn't have wound up with such a mordant conclusion.

But Arendt is cutting deeper than that. Democratic authority, too, she would argue, depends on taking certain truths as self-evident, certain things for granted. The sovereignty of the people is never absolute but checked, shaped, and reformulated in practice through a variety of institutions that help to modulate the passions and to give shape and form to democratic interests. And these institutions, in turn, have always taken a good bit of their legitimating force from some point outside themselves—in nature or "nature's God," for example. In a sense, democrats historically worried that the self-sovereignty of the people might become an absolute principle, a tyranny in practice. So it could never be a law simply unto itself. Hence constitutionalism, with its long, complex history—a history far too vast to go into in any detail here. The American Constitution's legitimacy derived, in part, from the nobility and right reason of its founders—consider here the American reverence, until recently, for the Founding Fathers. But that "right reason" wasn't simply theirs, a product of their own self-confirming ratiocinations; rather, it was "right reason" as discernment of a certain kind, discovering (not inventing) certain perduring principles that pre-dated (at least in situ) the lives of Jefferson, Franklin, Madison, Hancock, Hamilton, and the others.

Let's return to Arendt's account. If she is correct, the brief narrative just recalled of America's founding no longer holds water or, rather, it is water dripping rapidly through the holes of a sieve called "late modernity." The problem with our inability to distinguish authority from other human possibilities and enactments generates and perpetuates a terrible mistake, indeed, a base confusion—namely, the tendency to conflate power, coercion, even violence with authority. Mao did this most famously, of course, with his statement: "Power grows out of the barrel of a gun." No niceties about authority here. Just brute force and legitimation will follow once the enemies are vanquished. Arendt blasted Mao for this. What grows out of the barrel of a gun is violence, not power. Failing to distinguish between different modalities and ways of being in a political world, we fall into something akin to the abyss, conceptually and even politically. We lose the past as "the permanence and durability" of the world melts away. This loss is tantamount to the loss of the groundwork of the world, which indeed since then has begun to shift, to change and transform itself with ever-increasing rapidity from one shape into another, as though we were living and struggling with a Protean universe where everything at any moment can become almost anything else.[3]

Arendt singles out for critical fire tendencies within philosophic liberalism, by which she refers to that mode of thought most deeply implicated in the conflation of coercion and authority. (Were she alive today, she would no doubt find other targets.) This conflation, in turn, spawns political actors who similarly disdain any distinction between authoritarianism, on the one hand, and authoritative rule of governance, on the other. But authority is not tyranny; indeed, the resort to tyranny is a sign that legitimate authority has broken down and given way to violence.

Historically the legitimate authoritative figure was one who was bound. He or she was bound by law, bound by tradition, and bound by the force of past example and experience. Being bound in particular ways guaranteed a framework for action and helped to create and to sustain particular public spaces—whether of church, polity, or other institutions of social life. The bound authority figure was, therefore, not free to do just anything, to make just any claim and to make it stick. That was the lawlessness of the tyrant, whether the King who had become tyrannical and might, therefore, be killed as a scourge to his people and a rebel against God (here John of Salisbury's Politicraticus is my touchstone); or the twentieth-century tyrant, a Hitler or a Stalin, who knows and recognizes neither the laws of God, nor of nature, nor of human decency (a "common sense," in Arendt's formulation) and makes himself a law unto himself, hence an enactor of capricious terror and violence. To see this sort of thing as an instance of unusually harsh authority is, for Arendt, to vulgarize; it is to do violence to the truth, to what she unabashedly called the stubborn fact of the matter. Authority and obedience or faithfulness are twins. But in obeying—in offering fealty to a tradition that is shared, constitutive of the self and of a world—one remains free, free yet bound. This bounded freedom is the only way to guarantee creation of a common space, simultaneously to constrain yet to nurture and to make possible human action.

Authority in the Political Realm

Arendt was most concerned with a political world constituted by authority—a world, therefore, that rejected despots as unfit to rule. For the power to coerce is incompatible with the freedom of others and "his [the tyrant's] own freedom as well. Wherever he ruled there was only one relation, that between masters and slaves."[4] Between masters and slaves (or so the Greeks thought) there was no possibility of commonality or a common tradition; the gulf was impassable. All of subsequent political thought, at least until late modernity, is an attempt to establish "a concept of authority in terms of rulers and the ruled. and there is no philosopher-king to regulate human affairs once and for all."[5] This, then, involves a search for a community of equals who share ruling and being ruled and share as well a mutual commitment to authoritative rules and norms.

For the life of the polity was not just about life but about the "good life." This good life plays a formative and educative role. It inducts the next generation into a way of being in the world made possible only when free people submit to authority mutually—the sort of authority created when citizens pledge themselves to something, hold one another accountable, keep their promises. As well, in Arendt's account, authority is natural in the pre-political realm of necessity. (This is where she located the family, for example.) But authority takes on something—only something—of a volitional dimension in that sphere of action we call politics. The word auctoritas, deeded to us by those most indefatigable of antique law-givers, the Romans, derives from augere, to augment, to deepen. What is deepened is an authoritative moment of political birth or founding. Without such an authoritative moment, there is only violence or a rampant antinomianism.

Fast forward to the present moment. It seems that we have arrived at a point where our options get cast either as a desperate attempt to reaffirm and reassert traditional modes of authoritative determination of the sort Arendt argues modernity has shattered, on the one hand, or, on the other, as participation in a kind of political and epistemological free-for-all. We are, then, stuck increasingly in a political realm in which, lacking either recognition of, or commitment to, an awareness that "the source of authority transcends power," we are confronted daily "by the elementary problems of human living-together."[6] Because we place so little confidence in authoritative norms and claims, nearly everything at every moment is up for grabs. By Arendt's reckoning we aren't doing a very good job of confronting this crisis of authority. If we see the world as a series of volitional acts, as if anything that "I" affirm marks a new beginning, we are in a world of radical antinomianism and romantic flailing that all too easily fuels cries of "oppression" whenever any constraint is put on the self, whenever the self is called upon to bend the knee or to bow the head before the authority of God within a religious tradition or, in politics, to aver the legitimacy of a constitutional regime even if we disagree with it in particulars. One effect of the crisis of authority, then, is that all institutional rules of the sort needed to define institutions, to hold them intact in order that they might create space within which individuals can act and react, can be formed and re-formed, are construed as tyranny.

It seems to be the case that, traditional belief over time growing less reliable as an authoritative standard, human beings in Western democracies turned to constitutionalism and adherence to certain fundamental laws and rules. Initially, these were not merely or simply procedural but exuded a strong normative content, an image of what citizens might aspire to, what a democracy should live up to. This dense latticework of laws is now under assault, condemned as nothing but the window dressing for the power machinations of a narrow-minded, self-serving elite. And there is just enough truth in this charge that we all feel the sting. The upshot is that cynicism is deepened. If one sees nothing but coercion and arbitrariness in any proclamation of "self-evident truths," there is nowhere to repair to. If all is power and violence, one grabs as much for oneself as one can. This helps to account for the fear and worry, even despair, surrounding American democratic life at century's end. We are unable to justify authority in any robust sense, but without justifiable authority we flounder and flail politically. Why should anyone be obliged to adhere to law if all that one is confronted with is so many arbitrary injunctions dressed up as natural law or right or the good opinion of humankind?

Democracy and Commonality

Let's dig a little deeper. Remember that Arendt spoke both of the "groundwork of the world" and of "experiences common to all" as what we have lost and yet what we cannot do without if authority, including democratic authority, is to endure or to revive. And remember that the alternative to authority is not some free-form utopia but coercion, domination, violence, and unaccountable methods and systems of manipulating persons. Let's begin with the standard that Arendt argues we can no longer live up to, or perhaps even aspire to, namely, "experiences common to all." One wonders if Arendt could have meant this in the strong sense. Even in a relatively self-contained Greek polis of the sort Arendt much admires and in which authority, presumably, was intact, experiences weren't "common to all," as she herself notes when she mentions that between masters and slaves there can be no commonality. But there is another sense, a more American sense, if you will, that goes like this: Democracy requires laws, constitutions, and authoritative institutions. But it also depends on democratic dispositions, those habits of the heart that are formed and forged within the framework such institutions provide. The ever-prescient Tocqueville, in Democracy in America, offered foreboding thoughts along these lines. He warned of a world very different from the robust democracy he surveyed. He urged Americans to take to heart a possible corruption of their way of life. In his worst-case scenario, narrowly self-involved individualists—radically voluntaristic and disarticulated from the saving constraints and nurture of overlapping associations of social life and the horizon of an authoritative set of laws with extra-legal justification—would require more and more controls from above to muffle at least somewhat the disintegrative effects of what Tocqueville called "bad egoism."

Should this world of associational life, a world in which citizens were both free and bound, weaken, bad egoism and the isolation that resulted from it would, in turn, generate new forms of domination: democratic despotism. The social webs that once held individuals intact having disintegrated, the individual would find himself or herself isolated, impotent, exposed, and unprotected. Into this power vacuum would move a centralized, top-heavy state or other centralized and organized forces (the maw of consumerist society comes to mind) that would, so to speak, push social life to its lowest common denominator. For Tocqueville, religious belief "was inseparable from free government and free public life because it was the channel of a self-imposed moral restraint that shaped and, in so doing, liberated the individual for participation in the republic."[7] The collapse of religious authority necessary to sustain the institutions that engage in ethical formation fuels a political crisis in turn. That crisis helps to generate a deepening crisis in self-formation, in the very standing of the self itself. And so on.

Arendt, too, saw this coming, or some version of it. She detected it in the assault on authority in every arena—including the family and the school. She saw it in the attack on truth, the "blurring of the dividing line between factual truth and opinion."[8] Knowing, as she did, how totalitarian societies can simply make embarrassing facts disappear down the memory hole, she embraced factual truth as the last redoubt of political possibility, by which she meant the need to have a record, to begin from some common understanding. But common understanding is not the same as "experiences common to all." I agree with Arendt that liars have an easier time of it than truth-tellers in this world, and that plausibility may even be on their side because they can concoct tight systems that appear to contain everything and control for every contingency. But I am not so much concerned with that as with the continuing possibility of "common understanding" despite vastly different experiences. For this is the democratic wager. To cast it epistemologically: You cannot found and sustain a democratic society if you presume experiences are so vastly different for distinct categories and groups of people that the gulf thus created is, in principle, unbridgeable. A likely scenario in such a situation is that any possibility of a rough and ready sharing of moral norms and aspirations goes out the window. Some might argue that this isn't necessarily devastating because it leaves political authority, including the legitimacy of certain procedural norms, intact. But that doesn't seem a viable option over the long run. Procedures themselves are substantive and reflect a moral vision. We must have enough trust and confidence in the propositions that ground a democratic experiment, and that give rise to legal and political procedures and regularities (a system of criminal justice, for example) that we know we can repair to these propositions, whether in solidarity or in opposition. The matter can be cast rather starkly: Unless citizens or would-be citizens are able to repair to some shared political and normative vocabulary, a democratic society cannot sustain itself over time.

Frederick Douglass: An Appeal to Commonality

Let's consider this claim through a concrete example of solidarity and opposition. I will draw upon Frederick Douglass's oration delivered on July 5, 1852, at Rochester, New York, on "What to the Slave is the Fourth of July?" He begins by asking: "Are the great principles of political freedom and of natural justice, embodied in that Declaration of Independence, extended to us? and am I, therefore, called upon to bring our humble offering to the national altar...?"[9] His answer is not in the affirmative: "I am not included within the pale of this glorious anniversary! Your high independence only reveals the immeasurable distance between us. The blessings in which you this day rejoice are not enjoyed in common." You cannot drag a man forward in fetters before the temple of liberty and call him to join you in a "joyous anthem." God does not take such mockery lightly. And he will smite the nation that does. Note that Douglass can here draw upon a common religious and civic idiom to drive home his point to his listeners. The nations are under God's judgment: woe and behold!

Above all the joy, Douglass hears the "mournful wail of millions." And he will not forget them, these bleeding "children of sorrow." For his subject is "American Slavery." And when you see things from the slaves' point of view, why do they look differently? What you see is an America "false to the past, false to the present," and binding herself "to be false to the future." Following his thundering exposé and denunciation, Douglass begins to build toward common understanding. And, he insists, there already is a base to build on. We don't have to prove that slaves are men: "That point is conceded already. Nobody doubts it. The slaveholders themselves acknowledge it in the enactment of laws for their government. They acknowledge it when they punish disobedience on the part of the slave." This is a brilliant move on Douglass's part, for he shows the ways in which, through their incorporation into a legal and constitutional system, the status of the slave here affirmed runs counter to the degraded status slavery presupposes: "What is this but the acknowledgment that the slave is a moral, intellectual, and responsible being." So, affirming that equal "manhood of the Negro race," looking at the hundreds of tasks Negroes are called upon to do and are, in fact, doing in slavery and in freedom, they have nothing more to prove. And because your founding documents argue "that man is entitled to liberty? that he is the rightful owner of his own body?" where can you go to justify slavery? You must repair to a bad theology, but that is blasphemous on its face.

So: "What to the American slave is your Fourth of July? I answer, a day that reveals to him, more than all other days in the year, the gross injustice and cruelty to which he is the constant victim." In "revolting barbarity and shameless hypocrisy, America reigns without a rival." Douglass can make this argument—and he knows that he can make this argument—because he has access to certain standards, norms, and "self-evident truths," constitutional and sacred, that his own countrymen are flouting and, in so doing, they are violating their own civic temple and poisoning their own political well. Douglass bridges the gap that separates the experiences of slave and free by appealing to understanding common to all—even, he insists, the slaveholder himself. Authority is alive and well in this account because certain shared norms and idioms, a language of denunciation and affirmation, is sturdy and reliable. Douglass knows he can count on it. Most of our great democratic reformers knew they could count on it. It was possible to move from vastly different experiences to common understanding, because there was a common understanding on some deep level already—else the slave, the disenfranchised woman, and the disempowered factory worker wouldn't have a language of protest available that called those with different experiences to account. In fact, one can presuppose certain commonalties.

Immanence: The Loss of Democratic Authority

Let's take up Arendt's other reason for claiming that authority has simply disappeared from modernity. It was, you will recall, that the "groundwork of the world" itself has shift-ed and become uncertain. The permanence and durability of the world has melted, or is melting, before our eyes. I can't be certain what all Arendt has in mind here, so I will give her insight a twist that I owe to Charles Taylor in his essay, "The Immanent Counter-Enlightenment."[10] Denying transcendence "means denying that human life finds any point beyond itself." The twentieth-century process of denying transcendence has been powerful and effective. It means that man really has become his own measure. We find no meaning in anything above or beyond ourselves. Lived life exhausts itself; it is self-encapsulated. This doesn't mean we accept what is given. It means that, increasingly, we reject the whole idea that anything is given; rather, we presume anything and everything is constructed. We are the masters of our own fate and so on. But the upshot, over time, is a kind of flattening out of human possibility and a deep sense of emptiness. People yearn for meaning. But the prevailing climate of opinion dictates that they must find it immanently, so to speak. (Taylor writes of a "metaphysics of immanence.") Small wonder we have become so fascinated with end-things, with death and violence and experiences on the edge: they alone promise to deliver much needed relief from the self circling endlessly round itself.

In this world of absolute immanence, where all is flattened out and no standards can be upheld, authority simply cannot survive. For authority is about distinctions and account-ability; it is about norms and standards and trying to live up to them; it is about seeing oneself in a long stream of life; it is about being able to utter the ancient prayer, "That I may see my children's children and peace upon Israel." Our humanism has become anti-hu-manistic without at least some sort of transcendental aspiration, without some notion of a higher, a beyond, a "something more," a solidarity that is not reducible to the concatena-tion of all our private interests. Perhaps one acknowledges a groundwork—a grounding—a notion that "here I stand" on this ground, only if one acknowledges the possibility of some sort of "greater than" or "higher" or "above." I don't know. But it surely isn't merely historic fortuity that democracy's trials and the further erosion of democratic legitimacy go hand-in-hand with the loss of common understandings or, perhaps better put, with our insistence that there are no common understandings to be found and, as well, that our own ends and purposes are ultimate, that there is no authority, human or divine, who can judge us.

What moves can we possibly make to restore some of the texture of a world in which authority makes claims on us and we, in turn, on it? For authority helps to solidify the world, indeed, helps to make a world out of what would otherwise be William James's "blooming, buzzing confusion." Given our current dilemma, we seem to seek more of what ails us by hobbling ourselves in advance when it comes to robust arguments about this important matter. If we talk "rights talk," we can say pretty much anything we want. But if we start to talk "norm talk," we are accused of wanting to start a new civil war. We are urged to retreat where we should advance, and we advance where we would be well advised to retreat.

False Pride and Democratic Demise

A recuperative project must preserve our commitment to the dignity of the human person, to democracy under law, and to traditions of political and religious faith in a world in which each is under assault. No one thinker or book or conference can offer a definitive statement as to the shape and scope of such a project. But I am obliged, in light of my call for a renewal of democratic authority or, perhaps better put, for a deeper recognition that authority still makes claims on us, to offer a set of necessary recognitions—necessary in the logical sense and necessary in the historical sense, in a world in which experiences "common to all" seems an impossible standard. But that depends, in part, on how one thinks about what we might have "in common." In arguing that we do, perhaps, have more in common than we may believe—for we all breathe the rarefied air of self-overcoming and putative mastery so characteristic of late modernity—I will turn to St. Augustine's brilliant unpacking of false pride.[11] For that seems to me to lie at the heart of much of our current trouble. It is pridefulness that holds up as normative a view of the self constructed in such a way that she is immunized from the claims made on her by others. False pride is the presumption that we are the sole and only ground of our own being. False pride lies behind much of the contemporary assault on all authoritative claims and traditions. We deny our birth from the body of a woman. We deny our dependence on her and others to nurture and to tend us. We deny our dependence on friends and family to sustain us. We most certainly deny what Frederick Douglass so fervently believed—that the nations are under God's judgment. This false pride is the name Augustine gives to a particular form of corruption and deformation.

Pridefulness denies our multiple and manifold dependencies—and authority, in fact, is one way we have devised to recognize such dependencies. Those who refuse to recognize dependence are those most overtaken by an urge to dominate, or "the need to secure the dependence of others," an observation from Peter Brown, who goes on to argue that "first the Devil, then Adam, chose to live on their own resources; they preferred their own fortitudo, their own created strength, to acknowledging their dependence upon God."[12]

Augustine writes, every "proud man heeds himself, and he who pleases himself seems great to himself. But he who pleases himself pleases a fool, for he himself is a fool when he is pleasing to himself."[13]

In late modernity we have all become self-pleasers and self-pleasers cannot sustain institutional forms, for that seems nothing but the imposition of unacceptable constraint on a subject deemed sovereign. So we are in the soup. We lament that the center does not hold. But we will not permit ourselves to be "held," so to speak. Our political commitments are thin. Our religious commitments increasingly chafe under any constraint. Thus, we daily surrender a bit more of the pluralistic, communal, formative dimension of that world known as the American democracy—one that requires institutional robustness of considerable variety. We are all alone with our freedom and coerced in ways beyond our imaginings.

We may well and truly be approaching the moment Hannah Arendt dreaded—the moment when the actions of free citizens and the power they create when they come together is a frozen tableau from a lost time and place, rather than an ever present possibility.

(Spring 2000, 2.1)

Notes

[1] Hannah Arendt, "What is Authority?," *Between Past and Future* (Baltimore, MD: Penguin, 1980), 91.

[2] Ibid., 92. Portions of this discussion of Arendt and authority are drawn from my essay "The Question Concerning Religious Authority," prepared for a conference at Notre Dame. This paper, along with the other conference papers, was published in *Religion and Contemporary Liberalism*, ed. Paul Weithman (Notre Dame, IN: University of Notre Dame Press, 1997). The primary question taken up by participants at the Notre Dame event had to do with the inclusion or exclusion of "religious language" from political life.

[3] Ibid., 95.

[4] Ibid., 105.

[5] Ibid., 116.

[6] Ibid., 141.

[7] George Armstrong Kelley, *Politics and Religious Consciousness in America* (New Brunswick, NJ: Transaction, 1974), 47. This summary of Tocqueville's position is drawn from Kelley's wonderful book.

[8] Hannah Arendt, "Truth and Politics," *Between Past and Future*, 250.

[9] Frederick Douglass, *Autobiographies* (New York, NY: The Library of America, 1994). The great Fourth of July Oration, from which all quotations are drawn, appears as an Appendix to the first "Narrative" and can be found on pages 431–435.

[10] Charles Taylor, "The Immanent Counter-Enlightenment," unpublished essay.

[11] Here I draw upon my book *Augustine and the Limits of Politics* (Notre Dame, IN: University of Notre Dame Press, 1996).

[12] Peter Brown, "Political Society," *Augustine: A Collection of Critical Essays*, ed. Robert Markus (Garden City, NY: Doubleday Anchor, 1972) 320–321.

[13] Augustine, "Psalm 122: God is True Wealth," *Selected Writings, Homilies on the Psalms* (New York, NY: Paulist, 1984), 250.

Liberal Democracy and the Unraveling of the Enlightenment Project

James Davison Hunter

How do we make sense of our political moment?

There has been no dearth of commentary on the meaning of the 2016 American presidential election and its political aftermath. Pundits, scholars, and others have expressed alarm about the degree of fragmentation and polarization, the increase in vulgarity in political discourse and the loss of political civility, the weakening of traditional international alliances, the abuse of basic ethics in governing, and the resurgence of nativism, populism, isolationism, and nationalism, all of which could encourage authoritarian behavior among those in or seeking power. There are good reasons to be uneasy.

Yet beyond a pervasive sense of panic, one invariably encounters the belief that whatever problem we face, it is, in the end, fixable. Yes, our republic is deeply fractured and Washington is profoundly dysfunctional. Yes, there is a vast depletion of social capital. Yes, our public discourse is debased. Yes, for all of its power, late-modern capitalism has failed to maintain a steadily rising living standard for average people, making them fearful and politically angry. And yes, the *culture* of democracy, which has long been the glue holding Americans together, has begun to dissolve. But if we eschew the ideologies of left and right and focus instead on pragmatic solutions to core problems, we can find a way forward.

So, whether from the left, right, or center, the various analyses of contemporary political life unfailingly offer practical, sensible-sounding, step-by-step suggestions for *fixing* the problems: "If we just try harder, we can set things aright." Such pragmatic optimism is, of course, a widely acknowledged American trait. As the historian Arthur Mann observed forty years ago, the people of the United States have long had confidence that American know-how can always convert problems into opportunities.

Nevertheless, while institutions tend to be stable and enduring, even as they evolve, no institution is permanent or indefinitely fixable. The question now is whether contemporary American democracy can even be fixed. What if the political problems we are rightly worried about are actually symptoms of a deeper problem for which there is no easy or obvious remedy?

These are necessarily historical questions. The democratic revolutions of the eighteenth and nineteenth centuries in Europe and North America were largely products of the Enlightenment project, reflecting all of its highest ideals, contradictions, hopes, and inconsistencies. It underwrote the project of modern liberalism, which, for all of its flaws and failures, can still boast of some of the greatest achievements in human history. As the first president of Czechoslovakia, Tomáš Garrigue Masaryk, observed, democracy is the political form of the humane ideal.

Yet with the advantage of twenty-first-century hindsight, we can now see that the Enlightenment project has been unraveling for some time, and that what we are witnessing today are likely the political consequences of that unraveling. Any possibility of "fixing" what ails late-modern American democracy has to take the full measure of this transformation in the deep structures of American and Western political culture. While politics can give expression to and defend a particular social order, it cannot direct it. As Michael Oakeshott famously said, "Political activity may have given us Magna Carta and the Bill of Rights, but it did not give us the contents of these documents, which came from a stratum of social thought far too deep to be influenced by the actions of politicians."[1]

What I am driving at is made clearer by the distinction between the politics of culture and the culture of politics. The *politics of culture* refers to the contestation of power over cultural issues. This would include the mobilization of parties and rank-and-file support, the organization of leadership, the formation of special-interest coalitions, and the manipulation of public rhetoric on matters reflecting the symbols or ideals at the heart of a group's collective identity. This is what most people think about when they use the term *culture war*. In this case, culture war is the accumulation of political conflicts over issues like abortion, gay rights, or federal funding of the humanities and arts. Though culture is implicated at every level, the politics of culture is primarily about politics.

The *culture of politics*, by contrast, refers to the symbolic environment in which political institutions are embedded and political action occurs. This symbolic environment is constituted by the basic frameworks of implicit meaning that make particular political arrangements understandable or incomprehensible, desirable or reprehensible. These frameworks constitute a culture's "deep structure." Absent a deep structure, certain political institutions and practices simply do not make any sense.

This distinction is essential to making sense of our political moment.

The Question of the "Center"

In this light, one can see that however factionalized, any kind of meaningful democratic politics presupposes certain shared understandings and commitments that exist prior to political action. These may or may not represent a social or political consensus on a range of policy issues. More fundamentally, they define the arena in which legitimate political discourse and action take place. This shared cultural space can range widely. At one end of a continuum, it might include a binding consensus on certain ideals that define the identity and aspirations of the political regime. At the other end are agreements usually concerning the administrative processes and procedures that mediate political action. However thick or thin, the social and political solidarity upon which democratic life unfolds is formed through these agreements.

In America, this set of understandings and commitments held in common has been talked about in a variety of ways. In symbolic terms, it has been referred to as the "*unum*" of the national motto, *E pluribus unum*. In popular terms, it has been referred to as "the American dream." In scholarly treatises, it has been framed as "the American creed," America's "civil religion," its "public philosophy," or its "vital center." In legal-rational terms, it has been discussed in terms of the binding power of the Constitution.

In political theory, the question of the "center" or "*unum*" has been framed in terms of a perennial debate between the theoretical antinomies of foundationalism and proceduralism. Foundationalists, as a rule, argue that the legitimacy of any democratic regime depends upon a generally held commitment to a higher normative standard of justice or the common good that looms over the political process, policing its decisions and even its standards of reason. It is a thick prior consensus on the values and ideals of a shared way of life that is essential to a vibrant democracy. Proceduralists, by contrast, argue that there are no higher laws or transcendent values and that democratic order depends exclusively on recognition of the intrinsically rational character of a democratic process grounded in the presumption of rational outcomes. In social theorist Jürgen Habermas's version, reason resides in the formal pragmatic conditions that facilitate deliberative politics.[2]

In truth, the opponents in the debate are much closer to each other than they imagine, and the supposedly clear lines of difference between foundationalism and proceduralism are deceptive. No one disputes that there have to be *some* shared understandings, *some* agreements. However thin or thick, those agreements and commitments provide a framework within which legitimate democratic power is contained and managed and form the cultural substructure of a democratic polity: a "center" that defines the boundaries of national identity, collective recognition, and individual right.

It is important to emphasize that the agreements upon which the deep cultural center of liberal democracy is based are fundamentally normative in character—and authoritatively so. When thick, the bonds people share are *explicitly moral* in nature. When thin, they are nonetheless capable of *generating the moral.*

The real debate between the foundationalists and the proceduralists is over how thick the agreements and commitments that underwrite a democracy need to be to sustain democracy and to make it vital. All of the democratic revolutions of the eighteenth and nineteenth centuries were premised upon a commitment to a social order rooted in the accessibility and reasonableness of truth, the possibility of genuine human justice, the guarantee of individual freedom, and the protection of tolerance. But whose truth? Whose justice? Tolerance of whom? And where lay the boundaries between individual freedom and the public good?

Those questions have always been contested, but within an epistemological and ethical framework that constituted a legitimate authority for working through such conflict. *Any* legitimate exercise of political power has depended upon *some* shared authoritative institutions—elections, legislatures, courts—and undergirding these, some more-or-less authoritative values, standards, and narratives.

The efficacy of that authority is measured by the degree to which the claims made by those in power and the justifications given for the use of power are received as self-evidently real and true. When citizens regard the political system as legitimate, public and political stability follows. There may be irritability, complaint, and protest, but citizens will generally consent to and comply with decisions made. Things still get done. When citizens distrust their government, are cynical about their leaders' motives, or feel alienated from the political system that rules them, it becomes difficult to address basic political problems, and conflict often ensues.

Only on the surface, then, is the question of the "center" or an "*unum*" a question of public opinion. At its deepest levels, it is a question of authority, and less formal authority than informal authority, less the formal structures of authority (although these matter greatly) than the framework of reality and moral good upon which those structures are based.

In all of this, the difference between leaders and publics is important. Popular sovereignty, resting on the doctrine of consent, presupposes at least some shared values and a common narrative. It is only out of those values embedded in a common story that a common good is defined, a common good for which people are willing to endure sacrifice. Yet historically, it is the intellectual who articulates the reasons for granting or withholding legitimacy to the powers that be. Authority, as the historian John Patrick Diggins put it, represents the intellectual expression of power, and the problem of authority remains the problem of the men and women of ideas.[3]

The Enlightenment Project

It was, of course, the Enlightenment, broadly understood, that formed the cultural substructure of the democratic revolution. In America, the Enlightenment project was moderate, rather than radical, and not one thing but rather a cluster of embryonic, historically provisional, and sometimes inconsistent ideas and convictions. These drew from many and assorted sources, but, most prominently, from biblical, classical, and Whiggish tributaries that were synthesized philosophically, in large part, by the common-sense realists of the Scottish Enlightenment. Within that complex and fragile collection of beliefs we find the animating cultural logic of a new social and political order. A liberal and democratic regime, it celebrated above all the ideals of freedom, tolerance, and equality, providing a foundation upon which people and associations with different interests and vantage points could contest each other's claims.[4]

The cultural logic of the Enlightenment project also provided the foundation of a form of authority to adjudicate disputes and dilemmas of every kind, the central ideas for collective identity, the boundaries by which claims and actions could be deemed legitimate or illegitimate, and the ground rules for political engagement. "Right Reason" would be the final arbiter of ethical and moral dilemmas.

John Locke was the key transitional theorist in the early development of this cultural logic. The ontological status of the rights and privileges that were at the basis of his conception of civil society derived not only from the traditions of natural law but from a Christian reading of the relationship of humankind to God. As Locke put it in his *Two Treatises of Government*,

> The state of nature has a law of Nature to govern it, which obliges every one, and reason, which is that law, teaches all mankind who will but consult it, that being all equal and independent, no one ought to harm another in his life, health, liberty, or possessions; for men being all the workmanship of one omnipotent and infinitely wise Maker; all the servants of one sovereign Master, sent into the world by His order, and about His business; they are His property, whose workmanship they are made to last during His, not one another's pleasure. And being furnished with like faculties, sharing all in one community of Nature, there cannot be supposed any such subordination among us.[5]

Thus, equality, as the sociologist Adam Seligman put it, is not rooted in "a psychological, historical, or logical *a priori* but in a Christian, and more particularly Calvinist, vision of a community of individuals under God's dominion."[6]

For Locke, all authority in this world was derived ultimately from God. The different structures of political authority found in the world were all derived from the individual's own executive and legislative authority in the state of nature, which individuals held in their "capacity of agents of God." Instead of a community of saints, there was a community of individualized moral agents pursuing the social good in conformity to the "will of God."

By the eighteenth century, according to Seligman's account, the transcendent aspects of the Lockean vision were being replaced by the ideas of moral sentiments and natural sympathy (reason and the passions) as the source of the moral order. [7] In an intellectual climate defined by deism, the transcendent grounding of the social order had lost credibility. Now, the dictates of "Right Reason" were understood to be in accord with the laws of nature. As such, Reason embodied universal principles that were valid for all people at all times. The universality of Reason would bridge the distinction between private and public, between the individual and the collective, between egoism and altruism, between the ever-perplexing relationship of personal interests and the social good. How so?

In terms of the private interests of individuals, Reason offered certain universally applicable rules of conduct. By following these rules, the individual would be able to ascertain his or her own benefit. Among these benefits, the three most important for the working of society were the stability of possessions, their transfer by consent, and the fulfillment of promises. Whatever else the rules of Reason might mean and whatever else they might accomplish, individuals would follow these rules if only to maximize their self-interest.

Reason both governed the passions and guided them toward the public good. For some, Reason brought us to a true understanding of the providential designs for the world. For others, Reason was itself an element of the natural affections, the combined effect of which always led to mutuality and cooperation. Reason was thought to be the source of our common and inalienable rights—the rights to freedom, equality, and justice. Reason and nature made these rights, and the ideals they represented, coherent to all men and provided the means by which they could be achieved.

The fragile synthesis of the Reformed and Enlightenment traditions depended upon a shared epistemology of transcendence. As a concept and even as a felt reality, transcendence was capacious enough to absorb many views, opinions, and traditions. As such, it provided a common framework for understanding the significance of the individual in the world, offered a common grammar for recognizing the natural affections and moral sentiments shared by all humanity, grounded Reason within nature (which was read by Calvinists as expressive of the will of God), and universalized the principles and ideals to which Reason pointed. Though plagued by internal contradictions, this was a transcendent moral order that embraced both individual and collective spheres equally and reconciled one to the other. The seeds of social solidarity could be found in human sentiments, the public good within private interests, the universal within the individual.

This synthesis represented a radical departure from traditional providentialist accounts of the ancien régime in which all authority in public and private life was mediated by the ritual practices, hierarchical structures, and institutional processes of Roman Catholicism or

Anglicanism. This was a new model of the moral order in which authority was now grounded in a society of individuals (the meaning of popular sovereignty) who, in principle, shared the moral ties of sentiments and sympathy as well as a vision of universal truths. This applied as much to the strident Calvinist whose individuality (his life and conscience) was defined in an unmediated relationship to God as it did to the most skeptical freethinking deist, whose individuality was measured by the dictates of conscience and Right Reason. Not only was the status of the individual transformed by imbuing him or her with a new autonomy and agency, but the nature of the ties between individuals, that is, the nature of society itself, was also transformed. These ties were no longer defined by an ascriptive membership defined by geography, family, and the faith one was born into (as they had been in the ancien régime), but by the ties of moral sentiment, reason, and the common, though voluntary, belief in shared ideals.

This new kind of moral order was not a spineless civil religion based on a least-common-denominator faith arrived at through compromise for the purposes of political legitimacy. It was a synthesis informed by rich traditions of thought and practice. Drawing as much from the Bible as from the philosophical traditions of natural law and owing as much to Revelation as to Reason, this synthesis provided the framework for the emergence of democratic life in America that was quite different from anything seen before. What also made it singular was that this synthesis was broad enough and inclusive enough that nearly everyone—from the privileged and powerful to the impoverished, from every faith tradition to deism to no faith at all—could read himself or herself into it. While the class, ethnic, and faith factions that constituted American pluralism could remain separated by their own interests and sense of superiority over others, they were nevertheless brought together in its common language and symbolism.

Institutionalizing Enlightenment

It was in America that this unique and fragile configuration of the cultural logic of the Enlightenment was institutionalized. When Henry Steele Commager gave his 2000 book *The Empire of Reason* the subtitle *How Europe Imagined and America Realized the Enlightenment*, he may have overstated the case, but the point had ample merit. Self-consciousness of something new against the backdrop of an old world was pervasive. The motto on the Great Seal of the United States, *Novus ordo seclorum* ("A new order of the ages"), gave expression to a widely shared sensibility that marked the beginning of the new era in the human drama.

Americans hadn't inherited the traditional preconditions of nationhood—they didn't possess a common language, common legends, common rituals or traditions, a common church, or even a bounded territory. Rather, they asserted a national identity rooted in a public philosophy. As Richard Hofstadter famously observed, "It has been our fate as a nation not to have ideologies but to be one."[8] The French immigrant and agriculturalist Crèvecoeur described the American as "a new man, who acts upon new principles...new ideas…new opinions."[9] Indeed, at least compared to the Old World—and however imperfectly—America stood for political freedom, equality before the law, economic opportunity, religious tolerance, and popular sovereignty through representative government.

The Enlightenment project also found fertile soil in America because of the vitality of popular religion not only in the exiled Puritan communities of colonial New England but in the various communities of ascetic Protestantism that predominated throughout the colonies in the eighteenth century and in the new republic in the first half of the nineteenth century. Though the political philosophy of the founders was post-Lockean, large swaths of the American people were still operating within the providentialist sensibilities of the Lockean world. Thus, within the habitus of these faith communities, authority in worldly affairs, no less than in the churches they inhabited, largely remained rooted in a particular model of communal identity based on covenantal commitments to church, community, and nation.[10]

No one would make the case that a thick conception of moral and political authority, and, upon that, a consensus of constitutive ideas and ideals, would alone provide the solidarity upon which the experiment in democracy could be sustained. From the outset, the founders were skeptical of that. Early in his life, for example, John Adams held out the hope that America would be a "Republic of Virtue," a nation in which the baser tendencies of humankind could be tempered by the higher ideals of virtue, benevolence, and duty. But after the Revolution, he realized that neither the people nor their leadership "could be trusted as guardians of the republic."[11] Elites were driven by ambition, the masses were driven by their appetites, all were guided by self-interest, and none possessed the virtue for self-rule. As Adams put it in a letter to Jefferson in 1781, "I have been long settled in my opinion, that neither Philosophy, nor Religion, nor Morality, nor Wisdom, nor Intellect, will ever govern nations or Parties, against their Vanity, Pride, Resentment or Revenge, or their Avarice or Ambition. Nothing but Force and Power and Strength can restrain them."[12] In *The Federalist*, Alexander Hamilton echoed the point. "Why has government been instituted at all?" he asked. "Because the passions of men will not conform to the dictates of reason and justice, without constraint."[13] Adams and Hamilton were right—a common agreement upon institutional procedures and constraints through a dispersion of powers would have to do its work.

That said, no one would dispute how important the ideas of freedom, equality, and tolerance at the heart of the Enlightenment conception of civil society would continue to be for national identity and purpose. For ordinary Americans, this was the meaning of the American dream: The freedom, equality of opportunity, and high valuation of diligent effort and talent that it offered meant that someone could start from almost anywhere and become anything. It was a narrative that made sense of sacrifice, self-denial, hard work, and a willingness to play by the rules. Intellectually and ideologically, as Arthur Mann wrote, "the United States has been the land of the enduring Enlightenment."[14]

Enduring, yes, but far from static.

In the Face of Failure

The copious bloodshed of two world wars and the enslavement and annihilation of millions of Jews in the Holocaust, not to mention the imprisonment of millions of dissidents in the Gulag, brought home the epic failure of the Enlightenment project to deliver on its claims of a just, tolerant, and humane social order rooted in "Reason." This was not just a realization by the post-Marxist theorists of the Frankfurt School. Intellectuals of wide-ranging political commitments came to this recognition.

As Hannah Arendt observed, the moral and political authority of the Enlightenment project and the Western tradition more extensively was simply too frail to counter the challenge of totalitarianism.[15] The remnants of ascetic Protestantism, not to mention Christianity more broadly, as well as the Jewish faith, continued to endure over generations in the personal lives of individuals and the bounded lives of local communities, but as a cultural logic of the public sphere, these attenuated faith traditions were mostly discredited intellectually and marginalized culturally. Their conceptions of the good and the just became associated not with a healthy morality but with small-minded and mean-spirited moralism; their conceptions of legitimate authority, with authoritarianism. As to reason, for all of the remarkable discoveries of science, science itself failed spectacularly to deliver a grounding for a common ethics and everyday morality. Neither faith nor reason, nor their early Enlightenment synthesis, could make sense of the horrors of two world wars or the very real possibility of nuclear annihilation. Neither faith nor reason could resolve the concrete political questions made pressing by the advance of modernity: Who can enjoy the benefits of freedom? Equality for whom? What are the limits of tolerance? And, hovering above all the others, On what grounds do we reconcile various personal and private interests with the public good?

What followed were successive attempts to rework the Enlightenment project for a world it no longer accounted for and for which it had less and less credibility. On what foundation could cultural and civic authority be established? On what grounds could any solidarity in a contentious, fragmented population be found? On what basis could civil society, upon which democratic life is built, be renewed?

Among intellectuals and other elites, attempts to hold to a thicker conception of civil society ranged widely. Even before the totalitarian challenges of the twentieth century, Americans from Walt Whitman to John Dewey sought to refashion the American creed through a secular romanticism.[16] No less than the most ardent of patriots, they viewed America as an exceptional nation, not least in its potential for fraternity, love of neighbor, and social justice. But they sought to ground its exceptionalism in what America was by itself, rather than in reference to any transcendent authority. To search for its ideals of justice, equality, and fraternity in the authority of God or Reason was, in effect, a quest for a certainty that did not exist. Like the idea of an antecedent universal truth, authority was not something given to consciousness, but was, rather, produced by the human mind in interaction with others. America's civil religion was America itself.

For the progressive journalist Walter Lippmann, writing in the mid-twentieth century, the vitality of democracy depended upon the explicit renewal of the "public philosophy" that undergirded it. For Lippmann, "public philosophy" was just another label for the natural law tradition that posits a rational order to the universe "upon which all rational men of good will, when fully informed, will tend to agree." What makes it "natural," he wrote, is that it "can be discovered by any rational mind." "Rational procedure is the ark of the covenant of the public philosophy." Though its roots are classical, it is a tradition that has been revived through the ages, most recently in the Enlightenment and the democratic revolutions it spawned. Indeed, it has been the "premise of the institutions of the Western society," and "liberal democracy," in particular, "is not an intelligible form of government and cannot be made to work except by men who possess the philosophy in which liberal democracy was conceived and founded." Lippmann wrote that "the modern democracies [had] abandoned the main concepts, principles, precepts, and the general manner of thinking" that characterized the public philosophy, yet the revival and adaptation of its "common and binding principles was more necessary than it had ever been."[17]

This effort to rework and revivify the Enlightenment project was not unique to a few intellectuals operating in isolation from the broader intellectual community. The burden of reanimating the cultural center of democratic life in the post–World War II period preoccupied public intellectuals everywhere, on both the left and right. It was especially felt by the professional humanities. This was a period that has recently been described as "the age of the crisis of man," a crisis in the ethics of a universalizing humanism—of the meaning of "man," per se. This burden was reflected in midcentury fiction, as Mark Greif has so carefully elucidated.[18] It was also reflected in a range of thoughtfully crafted and broadly disseminated committee reports on the humanities written over the second half of the twentieth century and into the early twenty-first.[19] These reports collectively press an argument about the humanities as the home of a uniquely American civic humanism that was understood to be crucial to the future of democracy. This broad, perhaps nebulous civic humanism would find expression *in* and be underwritten *by* the humanistic disciplines.

In one of these reports, the 1945 Harvard "Red Book," (as *General Education in a Free Society* was dubbed), James Bryant Conant argued that "whatever one's views, religion is not now for most colleges a practicable source of intellectual unity." The only thing that could replace it, Conant wrote, was a common, humanistic education. The purpose of the humanities was to enable "man to understand man in relation to himself, that is to say, in his inner aspirations and ideals." The "main problem" of education and the humanities, in particular, was "not with the thousand influences dividing man from man, but with the necessary bonds and common ground between them"—those common "aspirations and ideals" that would join people together. Indeed, the future of democracy depended on our discovering "a common heritage and…a common citizenship," and from these, "the binding ties of common standards"[20] that would allow us to discover common ground. As the authors of the *Red Book* and other similar reports believed, only the humanities had the capability to recover and maintain common assumptions and traditions central to civic trust, vibrant public debate, and strong democratic institutions.[21]

In the decades that followed, the various humanities reports made similar appeals. As recently as 2013, in *The Heart of the Matter*, the American Academy of Arts and Sciences asked the portentous question "Who will lead America into a bright future?" and suggested that the humanities would be central to this endeavor.[22]

Lippmann believed that there was an urgency to the revival of the public philosophy, without which free and democratic nations would be unable to "face the totalitarian challenge." Yet he also recognized that the obstacles to its recovery were formidable. The masses had become a mob with strong consumer appetites and too much power, and were untrained in the traditions of civility. They were, as a result, constitutively incapable of self-rule. As for the leadership class, "the public philosophy was in a large measure intellectually discredited among contemporary men." Certainly, it seemed to Lippmann, the drift of modern philosophy did not portend any hope of scholarly renewal. As a sign of what was to come, he asserted, Jean-Paul Sartre had done away not only "with God the Father, but with the recognition that beyond our private worlds there is a public world to which we belong. If what is good, what is right, what is true, is only what the individual 'chooses' to 'invent,' then we are outside the traditions of civility. We are back in the war of all men against all men."[23]

The "age of the crisis of man" came to an end in the failed effort to revive an Enlightenment humanism capable of responding to the various threats to human existence posed by war and the instrumentalities of a world dominated by technology. It aspired to universality, yet was incapable of acknowledging irreducible human particularities and the conflicts based upon them, not least, of course, the particularities of race and gender. Yet even as the humanities—the carrier of this humanism—sought to provide a corrective to the hegemonic discourses and master canons, it left the *human* of the humanities an all-but-empty category.

The Unraveling

The problems were there from the beginning. Even at its founding, the architects of the new republic wondered what hope there was for popular sovereignty when individuals failed to act within the dictates of Reason, pursued nothing but their own interest, and failed to serve the common good. What happens when the laws of nature and the will of God become unclear? What does authority mean when individuals and groups offer competing reasons and pursue competing notions of the social good in such a way as to generate deep social divisions?

Despite efforts to revive it and despite the general peace that characterized the West in the second half of the twentieth century, the tensions and contradictions inherent in the Enlightenment project only deepened. How is political equality possible in a world of growing economic and enduring racial inequality? Given the seemingly infinite expansion of pluralism, including moral pluralism, are there any limits to tolerance? On what basis can private interests, often incorporated into influential, highly factional special-interest organizations and powerful corporations, be reconciled with the public good? What is the public good, anyway? The forces that were unraveling the Enlightenment project have since only intensified.

The record of intellectual life during the past half century is, in part, the record of those often brilliant minds who found the cultural logic of the Enlightenment project and its aspirations to a liberal democratic order vacuous. Yet the ability to interrogate and highlight the imperfections and hypocrisies of that order were a luxury that intellectuals could enjoy only so long as the rest of the citizenry did not. So long as the majority of Americans—even if some of them were "deplorable" or "clinging to their guns and religion"—continued to believe in the project, there would be relative political stability.

But now, the skepticism of intellectuals has percolated into the general public. Now, everyone is a postmodern skeptic. Now, everyone sees the hypocrisy, questions the efficacy of the government, doubts the goodwill and competence of their leaders. This widespread suspicion and, often, cynicism is in large measure what is so distinctive about our political moment.

Indeed, the record of popular political opinion over the past half century is the record of a citizenry losing confidence, not so much in the ideals of liberal democracy per se or in the idea of America, but in the government that enacts those ideals. The failed war in Vietnam went far toward undermining peoples' trust in the government to make wise decisions and speak for the interests of the nation. So did the failed war on poverty. So did decades of gridlock in which the government failed to get much of anything done.

Reams of data collected over nearly six decades have demonstrated beyond doubt that the electorate's disaffection with the political establishment—what scholars have called the legitimation crisis—continues to spread, and even to harden into a central feature of our national political consciousness.

Today, the majority of Americans have little to no confidence that "the government in Washington" will actually solve the problems it sets its mind to. Indeed, the majority of Americans now believe that what the country really needs is a new political party because the current two-party system isn't working.[24]

Here, the special ire of the American public is directed toward the political leaders in the power centers of government. Vast majorities of citizens have little or no confidence that the people who run our government will tell the truth to the public, but, rather, believe that most politicians are more interested in winning elections than in doing what is right. Most Americans consider their leaders not only venal but utterly incompetent.

While these patterns of public opinion have been in place for decades, skepticism toward the political establishment is now more obdurate, and indifference to the political theater of our leadership class more reflexive. Indeed, disaffection with the governing class may be the one thing American citizens hold in common. The resulting alienation is unevenly distributed through the population, but it is still broadly formative. The majority of Americans agree that most elected officials don't care what ordinary citizens think and that ordinary citizens "don't have any say" about what the government does.

Furthermore, whatever else the culture war of the last four decades has accomplished, it unquestionably intensified America's legitimation crisis. For decades now, the ideals each side of that struggle cherishes have been the very reasons each side deems the other illegitimate. Back and forth it has gone in a contest that has been less about persuasion than about denigration of the opposition. The cycle has repeated itself with great predictability on every issue: reproduction, sexuality, family life, education, immigration, the relationship between church and state, government funding of the humanities and the arts, and so on. This animus, and the challenge to legitimacy it presents, extends to the parties in power and those who sit in the seats of power. Thus, a toxic Clinton-hatred gave way to an equally noxious Bush-hatred, and eventually to an equally venomous Obama-hatred. Should we be surprised at its latest manifestation, a pervasive disdain for Donald J. Trump, who himself has perfected a toxic form of preemptive attack? This cycle will certainly continue into the future, regardless of who holds the office.

An Altered Arc of History

The cultural logic of the Enlightenment project has lost credibility, and the liberal—genuinely liberal—regime it inspired is collapsing. The institutional structures we have built remain intact and they continue to give stability to the regime. But while the procedural republic can address certain matters of power, it cannot address matters of identity and collective purpose. It cannot tell a compelling story that binds a community in common purpose. The cultural logic that underwrote liberalism exists only in fragments, and it is not likely to come together again in any coherent way.

A common cultural logic is unlikely to return because there is no credible foundation of authority upon which to rebuild it. For all of its continued vitality in personal lives and local communities, religious faith has been thoroughly weaponized on behalf of partisan interests. In the civic or political realm, it speaks no universal truths. And for all of the achievements of science in so many different realms of inquiry, the credibility of science as an enterprise has been undermined by both the skepticism of postmodern theory and the weaknesses of "peer review." Even in the popular mind, many believe that science itself is biased toward personal and political interests—that facts don't matter.

Nor can we look to the media, the institution whose civic purpose is to educate the public with accurate information. Long before accusations of "fake news" were flung from the White House, popular trust in the media to report the news fully, accurately, and fairly had been declining. Most Americans agree that "you can't believe much of what you hear from the mainstream media."[25]

An attitude of mistrust extends to other powerful institutions—nearly all Americans believe that Wall Street and big businesses in our country often profit at the expense of ordinary Americans. Significant majorities believe that the "system is rigged in favor of the wealthiest Americans," that "the leaders in American corporations, media, universities, and technology care little about the lives of most Americans," and that "the most educated and successful people in America are more interested in serving themselves than in serving the common good."[26]

Leaders and elites in America, whether in politics, business, education, or the media, have become cut off from ordinary Americans by virtue of their affluence, their education, their neighborhoods, and a range of class markers, not least of which are speech codes. The elites live in the same nation, but in a different universe. Is it any wonder we are seeing populist disdain for elites and their culture?

The antiestablishment candidates in the 2016 election made their name by repudiating the long-standing party institutions. They didn't emerge and gain a broad public platform in a vacuum. They represented a rebuke to the parties and leaders who failed to tell a believable story of common dreams.

So while it tempting to imagine Trump as sui generis—and no doubt he is in many ways—he has almost certainly established new and troublingly low standards for how to acquire and maintain political power. His incivility, boorishness, and willingness to denigrate the reputation of opponents, not to mention the superficiality of his thinking and absence of experience, may be extreme, but these attributes also model a new kind of cultural logic that is already well established in contemporary American democratic practice. It is a cultural logic that, if followed, will likely bend the arc of history *away* from justice, freedom, truth, tolerance, and unity, not toward them.

Can the cultural logic underwriting late-stage democracy be fixed? Maybe, but not easily and not anytime soon.

(Fall 2017, 19.3)

Notes

[1] Michael Oakeshott, *Religion, Politics, and the Moral Life*, ed. Timothy Fuller (New Haven, CT: Yale University Press, 1993), 93.

[2] Jürgen Habermas, *Between Facts and Norms: Contributions to a Discourse Theory of Law and Democracy*, trans. William Rehg (Cambridge, MA: MIT Press, 1996), 285.

[3] John P. Diggins, "Authority in America: The Crisis of Legitimacy," in Diggins and Mark E. Kann, *The Problem of Authority in America* (Philadelphia, PA: Temple University Press, 1981), 6.

[4] The account in this section draws heavily from Adam B. Seligman's masterwork, *The Idea of Civil Society* (New York, NY: Free Press, 1992).

[5] John Locke, *Two Treatises of Government* (1690), essay 2, ch. 2, sect. 6, 107. Retrieved from York University (Toronto), http://www.yorku.ca/comninel/courses/3025pdf/Locke.pdf.

[6] Seligman, *The Idea of Civil Society*, 23.

[7] Ibid., chapter 1, "The Modern Idea of Civil Society."

[8] Quoted in Hans Kohn, *American Nationalism: An Interpretive Essay* (New York, NY: Collier Books, 1957), 13.

[9] J. Hector St. John de Crèvecoeur, *Letters from an American Farmer*, letter 3 (1782). Retrieved from University of Tennessee, Knoxville, http://web.utk.edu/~mfitzge1/docs/374/creve.pdf.

[10] Seligman, *The Idea of Civil Society*, 74.

[11] John P. Diggins, "The Three Faces of Authority," in Diggins and Kann, *The Problem of Authority in America*, 35.

[12] Quoted in Lester J. Cappon, ed., *The Adams-Jefferson Letters* (Chapel Hill, NC: University of North Carolina Press, 1988), xlii.

[13] Alexander Hamilton, "Concerning the defects of the present constitution...," *The Federalist* 15.11 (Clark, NJ: The Lawbook Exchange, Ltd., 2008), 95.

[14] Arthur Mann, *The One and the Many: Reflections on the American Identity* (Chicago, IL: University of Chicago Press, 1979), 68.

[15] Hannah Arendt, "What Is Authority?," in *Between Past and Future* (Baltimore, MD: Penguin, 1980), 91.

[16] Richard Rorty, *Achieving Our Country: Leftist Thought in Twentieth-Century America* (Cambridge, MA: Harvard University Press, 1998), 15–18.

[17] Walter Lippmann, *The Public Philosophy* (Boston, MA: Little, Brown, 1955), 107, 109, 133, 160–61.

[18] Mark Greif, *The Age of the Crisis of Man* (Princeton, NJ: Princeton University Press, 2016).

[19] These include *General Education in a Free Society* (1945), *One Great Society: Humane Learning in the United States* (1959), the *Report of the Commission on the Humanities* (1964), *The Humanities in American Life: Report of the Commission on the Humanities* (1980), *A Report to the Congress on the State of the Humanities and the Reauthorization of the National Endowment for the Humanities* (1985), *Reinvigorating the Humanities* (2004), and *The Heart of the Matter* (2013). The sponsors of these reports were august, to say the least: respectively, Harvard University, the American Council of Learned Societies, Phi Beta Kappa, the Rockefeller Foundation, the Association of American Universities, and American Academy of Arts and Sciences.

[20] Harvard University, *General Education in a Free Society*, 5.

[21] "A Humanities for Our Time," *The New Humanities Working Group*, draft, 2017, http://iasculture.org/events/humanities-our-time.

[22] American Academy of Arts and Sciences, *The Heart of the Matter*, 2013, https://www.humanitiescommission.org/_pdf/hss_report.pdf.

[23] Lippmann, *The Public Philosophy*, 161, 176, 179.

[24] See, for example, James Davison Hunter and Carl Desportes Bowman, *The Vanishing Center of American Democracy: The 2016 Survey on American Political Culture* (Charlottesville, VA: Institute for Advanced Studies in Culture, 2016), 18.

[25] Ibid., 22.

[26] Ibid., 20.

Technocratic Vistas
The Long Con of Neoliberalism

T.J. Jackson Lears

Liberal democracy is one of those formulaic terms that all too easily evaporate into the realm of grand abstractions: the American Dream, the Free World, the Right Side of History. Yet those two words succinctly capture the tension between individual freedom and communal well-being that has animated American politics since the nation's founding. Various ways of balancing that tension have surfaced throughout US history: legal principles and practices, lists of inalienable rights, government structures and procedures, legislation in response to civil war and social upheaval.

Since World War II and the Cold War, *liberal democracy* has described the package of balances most appealing to transatlantic elites. The term has served as an authentic conceptual counter to the spurious "people's democracies" spawned by dictatorships of right and left, as well as a handy label for the kind of society anyone would (allegedly) want, if given the opportunity—pluralistic, formally democratic, open for business. The end of the Cold War and the collapse of the Soviet Union only reinforced the common assumption among foreign policy elites that longings for liberal democracy were universal and irresistible.[1]

By now, most Americans know how mistaken that assumption turned out to be. The dream of a global liberal order is being challenged at every turn—not only by jihadists and white nationalists, but by libertarians, social democrats, and even democratic socialists. Liberal intellectuals have responded by assuming that the barbarians are at the gate—lumping Bernie Sanders with Marine Le Pen, Syriza with Brexit—striking a heroic posture, vowing their hatred of populism (which they conflate with fascism) and their fealty to freedom.[2]

Sustaining this heroic liberal persona requires a refusal to recognize that what is called liberal democracy has taken a sharp and disturbing turn in recent decades. What many defenders of liberal democracy fail to realize is that they are no longer defending either liberalism or democracy; the forms of elite rule that provoke popular anger are merely the husk of liberal democracy. The once-vital discourse of liberal democracy has been hollowed out and transformed into a language of managerial technique—a technocratic jargon used to legitimate the spread of free-flowing capital. Within this discourse, freedom has been reduced to market behavior, citizenship to voting, efficiency for the public good to efficiency for profit. The rich civic culture that gave rise to popular American politics in the past— unions, churches, local party organizations—has been largely replaced, in both parties, by elites who have benefited from the technocratic turn.

Reviving liberal democracy requires remembering what preceded it: the melding of liberal and republican ideals that animated American civic culture at the local level, well into the twentieth century. The recovery of liberal democracy also requires recognizing that what calls itself liberal democracy these days is often a poor pretender to that title or—even worse—a diabolically thorough counterfeit.

Seeking Equipoise

Down to the 1910s or even later, liberal individualist ideals were counterbalanced less by a democratic rhetoric of equality than by a republican one of commonweal. Many Americans were democrats who remained attached to republican idioms. They often sought to negotiate conflicts between the liberal pursuit of private interest and the republican commitment to the public good; these terms dominated debate from the Jacksonian assault on the second Bank of the United States to the Populist critique of monopolistic corporate power. As the nineteenth century became the twentieth, the acquisition of overseas colonies combined with an unprecedented merger wave on Wall Street to create a new imperial state with a new public discourse, better suited to a dawning era of monopoly capital and overweening military power than to the mix of settler colonialism and entrepreneurial capitalism that had characterized the nineteenth century.

The liberal versus republican split began to seem outdated as the republic became an empire and liberal individualism appeared trapped in a corporate cage of its own making. "Every spirit makes its house," Ralph Waldo Emerson had written prophetically in 1851, "but afterward the house confines the spirit." William James and Mark Twain bemoaned the triumph of mere bigness and the tarted-up piracy of overseas land grabs, but to John Hay, Theodore Roosevelt, and other prophets of empire, imperial expansion was "the large policy" national greatness required.[3] During the early decades of the twentieth century, republican idioms gradually disappeared from polite conversation, surviving mainly in the speeches of conservative constitutionalists and Hoosier socialists; *liberalism* became a word less associated with economic than with civil liberty, especially after the Wilson administration's suppression of dissent made protection of minority points of view seem more urgent.

The national conversation emerging in the United States in the early twentieth century was dominated by admiration, blustering or decorous, of imperial greatness. Still the unruly stepson democracy—the bumptious lad in knickers who always seemed to wandering in from a Frank Capra movie—was also allowed a place at the table of public discourse. Woodrow Wilson wanted to make the world safe for him; John Dewey wanted to permeate the workplace with his presence; Reinhold Niebuhr wanted Christians to abandon their pacifism to fight for him.

The rise of totalitarian states made democracy seem the only sane, humane alternative to misery and madness. World War II and the Cold War charged the very word *democracy* with unprecedented emotional urgency. Twice in a generation, Americans defined their polity against monstrous, implacable alternatives that also claimed to represent "the people." In an era of people's democracies and national socialism, terminological ambiguities abounded. Rhetoricians in the West needed concepts and categories that seemed as clear-cut as the morality of world war and cold war.

By midcentury, *liberal democracy* was beginning to fill the bill. It distinguished Western democracies, with their concern for individual rights, from dictatorial pretenders, left and right; it also exorcised the more diffuse specter of "the tyranny of the majority"[4] that Tocqueville had warned against and that was reappearing in popular American journalism and social science, in a spate of postwar screeds against lonely crowds, organization men, and suburban captivity.

Liberal democracy was the perfect rhetorical trope to underwrite an emerging ideological consensus as elites sought equipoise after the ravages of depression and war. The word *liberal* vaccinated the polity against the plagues of totalitarian and majoritarian rule, protecting the vital freedoms of speech and religion; the word *democracy* applied balm to the wounds inflicted by capitalist individualism, tempering freedom with equality. This was the midcentury agenda of policy elites in the postwar Atlantic world: Besides countering communism abroad, they contained the rule of socially irresponsible capital at home by creating welfare states. Progressive taxation, strong unions, and social security all salved the abrasions of unregulated enterprise, helped create a broad middle class, and balanced the inherent conflict between liberalism and democracy.

The US welfare state was always a jury-rigged affair, committed to minimizing government oversight and preserving opportunities for private profit wherever possible; "liberal democracy" described the US system better than "social democracy," with its Euro-style connotations of five-week vacations and midafternoon wine. But ultimately, on both sides of the Atlantic, the post–World War II decades were the moment of liberal democracy—the moment of equipoise, the ascendance of a "mixed economy" that appeared to have abolished the conflict between capital and labor, that led sociological soothsayers to announce, as Daniel Bell put it, "the end of ideology."[5]

Neoliberalism Rises

Reports of ideology's death were greatly exaggerated. Since the 1970s we have seen a resurgent reactionary ideology used to justify the systematic dismantling of the welfare state—a process organized by right-wing elites who, for example, seek to enact policies that have the effect of defunding the public schools, then use allegations of incompetence as an excuse to privatize education. The assault on the public sector, the celebration of markets as the solution to all problems, the underwriting of free-market ideology by government policy— these tendencies reacquired legitimacy and centrality in the 1980s and have maintained their hegemony ever since. In less than four decades, the ship of state and the conversation on its bridge have steered away from the midcentury idiom of liberal democracy and toward... what? New times, alas, demand neologisms. The return of nineteenth-century slogans and pieties, combined with a twenty-first-century veneer of technocratic expertise, has inspired many observers to call this new ideological consensus "neoliberalism."

The term grates on some ears. To civilians outside Fort Academe, it smacks of leftist jargon; to unreconstructed New Dealers, it associates a good thing (liberalism) with mean-spirited policies; to political historians, it resurrects a label briefly pinned on Bill Clinton, Gary Hart, and other technocratically minded Young Turks in the Democratic Party of the 1980s. None of these objections are mistaken, but none have stopped the use of the term. So far there is simply nothing else as succinct and precise to describe the seismic shift that has occurred in the world political economy since the 1970s.

Neoliberalism's chief semantic competitor is *globalization*, which almost from its introduction into public discourse has been little more than a euphemism deployed by apologists for free-flowing capital. For examples, see almost any *New York Times* column written by Thomas Friedman since the 1990s. *Globalization* has been used to describe a process that is inevitable and beneficent: We are all going to love doing what we have to do anyway. In any case, we have no choice—the abstract, reified force of globalization has decreed the shape of our present and future. Devotees of globalization deliver deterministic homilies in a bland and upbeat tone, always implying the same conclusion: Resistance is futile. For Friedman and friends, there is simply no point in asking the fundamentally political question *Is this what we want?*—a question one would have thought central to liberal democracy. *Globalization*, in short, is a word that facilitates the forgetting of history and the end of politics—or at least of democratic politics, which depends on open debate and public choice.

Neoliberalism, by contrast, is a term grounded in historical contingency and human agency; it describes an ideology that is nothing if not political, created by specific human beings for specific purposes. The cover of David Harvey's *Brief History of Neoliberalism* portrays a veritable rogues' gallery: Ronald Reagan, Margaret Thatcher, Augusto Pinochet, and Deng Xiaoping—the founders of neoliberalism, whose successors came from both sides of the aisle: Republicans and Democrats, Tories and Labourites, the Clintons, the Bushes, Blair, Cameron, Obama. One could, of course, go on. The rise of neoliberal politics was neither an abstract project nor a secret one. Promoters of neoliberal policies were clear on what they were about— the end of welfare as we know it (in Bill Clinton's words); the deregulation of capital; the transfer of political authority from government and other public entities to "free markets" or their representatives; and, at least in the United States, a commitment to policing the shambles created by "creative destruction" with an increasingly militarized carceral state.

The role of the state is a crucial part of the distinction between nineteenth-century liberalism and the version currently on offer. "Part of what makes neoliberalism 'neo' is that it depicts free markets, free trade, and entrepreneurial rationality as achieved and normative, as promulgated through law and through social and economic policy—not simply as occurring by dint of nature," the political theorist Wendy Brown writes. The free-market rhetoric of the Republican right (and much of the center as well) conceals the interdependence of a supposedly free market and a state dedicated to promoting and serving it.[6]

The electorate may be finally getting wise to this long con, as the campaigns of Bernie Sanders and Donald Trump suggest, but neoliberalism has survived thus far in part due to its exceptionally flexible, porous, and pervasive ideology—a mobilized worldview that redefines the self as "human capital." This self has become the stuff of commencement oratory: "Each of you starts the next portion of your life's journey with the tremendous benefit of a Cornell education. I hope that you'll carry with you…a continuing commitment to build human capital so that more will have opportunities to pursue their dreams," David Skorton, president of Cornell University, told the graduating class there in 2014.[7]

The sentimental language of "pursuing your dream" sugarcoats the neoliberal restructuring of the self. Redefined as "human capital," each person becomes a little firm with assets, debts, and a credit score anxiously scrutinized for signs of success or failure, much as the Calvinist scrutinized his soul for evidence of salvation or damnation. The neoliberal self seeps instrumentalist market assumptions into every corner of human experience. Institutions like hospitals and schools that had been thought to serve the commonweal, and therefore to deserve public support and public access, are now routinely turned into profit-making ventures. The pricing of everyday life has been underway for centuries, as the historian Eli Cook has recently shown, but until quite recently it had been the domain of mavericks like Irving Fisher, who in 1910 priced a healthy newborn baby at $362 a pound. What was eccentric has now become mainstream. As Brown writes, "The vanquishing of homo politicus by contemporary neoliberal rationality, the insistence that there are only rational market actors in every sphere of human existence, is novel, indeed, revolutionary, in the history of the West."[8]

The Neoliberal Self and Its Rhetoric

The capitalization of the self has wide and deep impact. Consider the eagerness with which homebuyers embraced predatory mortgage schemes during the housing bubble of the early 2000s. For the new forms of indebtedness to work, Philip Mirowski speculates, "the personal identity of the consumer had to have been first turned topsy-turvy [so] that the grand sausage-grinder of securitization could have chewed up such a vast swath of individually-owned owner-occupied real estate." By recasting the self as a firm, managing its own spending and borrowing to enhance its asset value, neoliberal ideologues popularized indebtedness as just another entrepreneurial venture. But the universal celebration of risk obscured a double standard: Borrowers inhabited a world of unsecured debt, while lenders regimented, reinterpreted, and repackaged that debt to ensure themselves dependable profits. Risk varied dramatically, dependent on power relations.[9]

The impact of the neoliberal self went far beyond promoting susceptibility to predatory lenders. An hour's worth of sponsor advertising on National Public Radio suggests the emergence of a new model psyche, reflected in the current obsession with behavioral economics and neuroscience generally. The enterprises at its vanguard purport to point the way beyond old, static, rational-actor models while at the same time encouraging self-modification to conform to the ever more pervasive and relentless demands of market rationality. The cultivation of expertise becomes essential—not merely to the management of corporations and governments but also to the management of personal identity.

It remains to be seen how deeply these tendencies penetrate into the mentalities of most people, who have preserved various resources for resistance and have even begun to deploy them in protest movements of varying efficacy. Still, there is no denying the ideological power of neoliberal market worship, especially when there are so few alternatives in public debate—and when they are so easily caricatured and dismissed by custodians of conventional wisdom, as the Sanders and Trump campaigns were. This is not to imply any fundamental similarity between the social democrat Sanders and the demagogic mountebank Trump (except that they both embodied protest against the Washington consensus). It is, rather, to suggest how neoliberal ideologues have made their worldview our dominant discourse—by patrolling the boundaries of permissible dissent, trying to make any real challenge appear ridiculous. The resulting reign of "responsible opinion" has been catastrophic for liberal democracy.

Neoliberalism has impoverished fundamental conceptions of freedom by reducing them to market choice. The impoverishment is especially apparent in public discussions of higher education. The idea that a liberal arts education might provide the "priceless" opportunity to pose ultimate questions about oneself and one's relation to the world is disappearing as college becomes reduced to job training. The "culture wars" that roiled higher education in the 1980s and '90s have come to seem quaint today. In those days, conservatives and liberals shared a faith in the foundational importance of the humanities tradition; the debate was about how that tradition should be defined and who should be included in it—John Locke or Frantz Fanon, Ernest Hemingway or Toni Morrison (or all of the above). How times have changed. Now the "conservative" governors of Wisconsin and Florida want to abolish or at best marginalize humanities education altogether, while a "liberal" president (Obama—himself the beneficiary of a superb liberal arts education) mocked the uselessness of art history and promoted a database that allows prospective applicants to calculate the monetary value of various college degrees. Both sides, at the highest levels of mainstream partisan debate, now apparently agree that a college degree is little more than a meal ticket.

This narrowing of human horizons has political as well as educational effects. As humans become "human capital"—for themselves, for a firm, for a state—investment value trumps all other values; moral autonomy fades, and with it the very notion of a sovereign individual; citizenship shrivels to the mere ritual of casting a vote. Beneath the all-seeing gaze of the omnipotent market, the sovereignty of the state (like the sovereignty of the individual) shrinks to the vanishing point. Amid chants about freedom, the very basis of freedom (at least in the liberal and republican traditions)—individual and state sovereignty—is undermined and ultimately destroyed.

The consequences for democratic discourse are disastrous: "Public life is reduced to problem solving and program implementation, a casting that brackets or eliminates politics, conflict, and deliberation about values or ends," Wendy Brown observes.[10] In lieu of substantive debate, we are left with the antipolitical language of open markets and open sources. Yet the rhetoric of openness obscures the actuality of a closed system, committed to market discipline as the primary mechanism for maintaining social order.

The neoliberal conception of politics is perfectly consistent with the clamor against "partisan bickering" that has echoed through official Washington and its media for decades. To be sure, partisanship can be mindless and can obstruct the business of government, but expertise is never neutral, efficiency is not always compatible with democracy, and bipartisan problem solving (when it occurs) invariably reaches neoliberal solutions—ignoring public sentiment in support of such programs as single-payer health care, starving whatever is left of the public sector by ever more stringent austerity. Such policies are justified with reference to expert consensus on the need for market solutions to social problems. The technocratic idiom makes profoundly political decisions appear to be neutral problem solving, adjustments to the reality of market discipline. Nothing could be more insidiously threatening to liberal democracy.

Still, in recent years, on both sides of the Atlantic, popular discontent with top-down governance by managerial elites has become impossible to ignore. Such protest occasionally takes grotesque form, but liberals make a profound mistake when they dismiss this unrest as childish antics (as they did with the Sanders campaign) or try to tar it with the brush of protofascism (as they did with Trump and Brexit). The pain beneath the protest is pervasive; the anger is rooted in real grievances against the technocratic consensus that rules Brussels as well as Washington. The crisis of liberal democracy can be met only by unmasking its neoliberal counterfeit.

(Fall 2017, 19.3)

Notes

[1] A graphic representation of publications using the term *liberal democracy* may be found in Google Books' Ngram Viewer at https://books.google.com/ngrams/graph?content=liberal+democracy&year_start=1800&year_end=2000&corpus=15&smoothing=0&share=&direct_url=t1%3B%2Cliberal%20democracy%3B%2Cc0. The graph clearly shows that appearances of the term increased steadily throughout the second half of the twentieth century, and especially sharply in its last several decades. I am grateful to my research assistant Michael Van Unen for locating this information for me.

[2] For an example of this posture, see Timothy Garton Ash's review essay "Is Europe Disintegrating?," *New York Review of Books*, January 29, 2017, http://www.nybooks.com/articles/2017/01/19/is-europe-disintegrating/.

[3] Ralph Waldo Emerson, "Fate," (1851), *Arisbe: The Peirce Gateway*, http://www.iupui.edu/~arisbe/menu/library/aboutcsp/emerson/fate.htm. The best recent survey of the debate over American empire is Stephen Kinzer, *The True Flag: Theodore Roosevelt, Mark Twain, and the Birth of the American Empire* (New York, NY: Henry Holt, 2017).

[4] Alexis de Tocqueville, *Democracy in America* (1835), vol. 1, ch. 15, http://xroads.virginia.edu/~HYPER/DETOC/1_ch15.htm.

[5] Daniel Bell, *The End of Ideology: On the Exhaustion of Political Ideas in the Fifties* (Glencoe, IL: Free Press, 1960).

[6] Wendy Brown, "American Nightmare: Neoliberalism, Neoconservatism, and De-democratization," *Political Theory* 34 (2006): 690–714.

[7] David Skorton quoted in Wendy Brown, *Undoing the Demos: Neoliberalism's Stealth Revolution* (Brooklyn, NY: Zone Books, 2015), 175.

[8] Eli Cook, *The Pricing of Progress* (Cambridge, MA: Harvard University Press, 2017), and "The Neoclassical Club: Irving Fisher and the Progressive Origins of Neoliberalism," *Journal of the Gilded Age and Progressive Era* 15 (2016): 246–62; Brown, *Undoing the Demos*, 99.

[9] Philip Mirowski, *Never Let a Serious Crisis Go to Waste: How Neoliberalism Survived the Financial Meltdown* (London, England: Verso, 2013), 122.

[10] Brown, *Undoing the Demos*, 127.

Not Melting into Air

John M. Owen IV

Marxism failed years ago, but in our time of rapid global change, Karl Marx is as quotable as ever. "All fixed, fast-frozen relations, with their train of ancient and venerable prejudices and opinions, are swept away, all new-formed ones become antiquated before they can ossify"—shave that, from the *Communist Manifesto*, down to 140 characters, and you have learned-sounding retweetable material. Read on in Marx's 1848 pamphlet, and you find a familiar engine behind all of the change: the bourgeoisie or owning class—our own One Percent—with its "naked, shameless, direct, brutal exploitation."[1]

Are we back in 1848, then, except with better technology? In a sense we are, and ironically that makes Marx a better analyst than prophet. His depiction of Victorian-era global political economy is strikingly familiar—"In place of the old local and national seclusion and self-sufficiency, we have intercourse in every direction, universal inter-dependence of nations,"[2] he went on to write—but Marx expected that revolution soon would knock the global system off course and redirect it into history's final phase of communism. The revolution did come, but it took nearly seven decades, and occurred in Russia rather than the expected birthplace, Germany. And far from breaking the proletariat's chains, the revolution produced a cruel and imperialist regime that the workers of the communist world united to throw off another seven decades later.

Marx's ability to predict was hobbled by mistakes that Marxism's liberal adversaries often repeat today. They, like him, have underestimated the robustness of two particular obstacles to universal market logic. One is the nation-state; the other, traditional cultures. The nation-state's resistance is manifest in the form of a rising, ambitious, and decidedly nonliberal China. Traditional cultures' defiance is manifest in Western movements chafing against the homogenizing ways of global elites and finding articulation in populism.

"All that is solid melts into air, all that is holy is profaned," Marx wrote in another tweetable aphorism.[3] Here, at the close of the second decade of the twenty-first century, old solid particularisms are not melting away, and the sacred is having its revenge. Liberal internationalism has warded off acute threats before—fascism and communism, among others—albeit at high cost. Today, Chinese and Western variants of populism threaten not so much the violent destruction of liberal internationalism, but its atrophy; in the end, they may succeed where older grand ideologies failed.

The Resistance

We can think of liberal internationalism as the scaling up of liberal principles to the global level. The project began in earnest two centuries ago, as liberal thinkers, politicians, merchants, bankers, and other elite groups in Great Britain and elsewhere opened national markets and accelerated technological innovation. Ever since, in a cluster of countries that has grown in fits and starts, jobs have been created and destroyed, societies homogenized, power shifted around. Now, as in 1848, there is resistance; now as then, the resisters can precisely agree neither on what they are resisting nor on what ought to replace it. Some participants in the revolutions that erupted as Marx's tract went to press were early communists, but more prevalent on the streets of Paris and Vienna were guildsmen, heirs of the traditional economy, who wanted to preserve their jobs and way of life against the Industrial Revolution. Conservatives, in other words.

In another parallel with 1848, it is not only antiquated jobs and ways of production that are disappearing. Old and local cultures are giving way to new and universal ones. Marx wrote that traditional social relations, beliefs, literature, even the "holy," were being consigned to history's ash heap. These nonmaterial things were important to Marx, even though for him they were mere epiphenomena, products of what for him was *real*, the capitalist mode of production. Here may be where the old materialist started to go wrong. A certain type of mind, fond of a certain notion of rigor, reflexively reduces the cultural to the (ostensibly) material. Causality can run only one way, from matter to thought and practice. For all of his breathtaking ability to make a coherent whole of disparate elements, Marx had such a mind, and he did not see that beliefs, language, social relations, and ways of life affect the material as much as the material affects them.

"The working men have no country," yet another aphorism from *The Communist Manifesto*, follows directly from this mistake.[4] Scholars have frequently pointed out that July 1914 put paid to that audacious claim, as socialist parties all over Europe, putatively representing the working men, supported appropriations to fund their respective nations' militaries as they careened into war. The Soviet Union would soon enough become one country among many, its state not "withering away" but growing and thickening over time. The Soviet Union was able to vanquish Nazi Germany in World War II because it resorted to old-fashioned appeals to Mother Russia.

One difference between our time and Marx's is that today it is not only the bourgeoisie that is attacking the old particularities: It is also foundations, nongovernmental organizations, Western militaries, scientific networks—entities sometimes working at cross-purposes in an immediate sense, but all of which carry with them a recognizable set of liberal practices and ideas and that provoke both cultural homogenization and the rise of political and cultural counterforces.

Those counterforces were not supposed to be so defiant, so capable at this late date of gathering strength and pushing back. Liberal internationalism's designers through the centuries thought to replace an old system of war and injustice with one of peace and justice. They had plans to make the world smarter through creative destruction. Free markets went hand in glove with liberal democracy; the glove fit the hand because personal liberty would enable individuals to do what they do naturally—engage in voluntary, mutually beneficial transactions—and these autonomous agents would demand and inevitably get political freedom. Liberal internationalism was supposed to be self-perpetuating and self-expanding.

A Potted History of Liberal Internationalism

The liberal internationalist project has evolved over time, but it has a recognizable core that it shares with liberalism in general. We can do no better than adopt the abstract notion of liberalism attributed to the eighteenth-century German philosopher Immanuel Kant: It is a doctrine designed to uphold the autonomy ("self-law") of each individual. "Autonomy" did not mean, originally, self-sufficiency (that would be "autarchy") or antisociality. It meant the ability of each to accept for him- or herself what is true, good, and right. (For many, "accept" has shifted to "invent," a point to which we shall return later.) Securing individual autonomy requires certain institutions and laws, generally captured in liberal democracy's civil rights and commitment to regular free elections.

Liberalism was never a project simply for individual countries. The body of political theory developed by Locke, Smith, Kant, Mill, and others saw all men (later, persons) as fundamentally the same, and hence equally deserving of autonomy. Individual liberal writers and statesmen may have been nationalistic, tribal, sexist, or racist, but the theory itself was not. Liberalism's central tendency was toward cosmopolitanism, because if one state set up a liberal regime but remained surrounded by despotic states threatening war, the liberal state could not guarantee its citizens' autonomy. But as Kant himself recognized, a cosmopolis was unachievable: Rulers of states would mightily resist it, and the resulting wars would be even worse than the status quo. Thus, the compromise of liberal *internationalism*: not a single world state, but the liberalization of existing states and their relations.

Kant's plan, *Toward Perpetual Peace* (1795), called for a league of republics, roughly what we would now call liberal democracies. These republics would not necessarily be morally superior to despotic states; they would simply pursue their interests through smarter means. They would fight wars only when truly threatened, and they would not threaten one another because their international trade would make war too expensive. Because their governments were ultimately accountable to their citizenries, republics would follow their true interests in peace and commerce.

Kant was part of a general Enlightenment project to overcome the expensive European system of zero-sum acquisition and war. In his 1776 book *Wealth of Nations*, Scottish Enlightenment thinker Adam Smith had already launched a broadside against the mercantilist trading system, in which states intervened in the national and international economy to enrich the powerful rather than the nation as a whole. Anglo-American activist Tom Paine wrote in *The Rights of Man* (1791) that republican principles, if applied universally, would bring universal peace. Swiss activist Benjamin Constant carried the work into the early nineteenth century.

A generation later came the first actual existing version of liberal internationalism. Under the influence of Manchester School figures Richard Cobden and John Bright, Great Britain, the world's most powerful country, began eliminating barriers to trade in the 1840s. Other countries began to follow suit, international trade grew sharply, and industrialization accelerated. This is the world Marx saw in 1848.

The 1870s, however, brought two events that slowed and eventually reversed liberal internationalism. In 1871, having humiliated France in a quick war, Prussia reconstituted the German Empire. Modern Germany, now continental Europe's strongest state, had the form of a constitutional monarchy, but Kaiser Wilhelm I and his chancellor, Otto von Bismarck, held the real power. Then in 1873 the stock market in Vienna crashed, pulling the industrial world down into what became known as the Long Depression. The losses of wealth and jobs led most states to erect new trade barriers. As liberals narrate the subsequent decades, the contraction of international commerce and the rise of German power led to European imperial competition in Africa and Asia, the polarization of Europe into two alliances, and ultimately the catastrophic Great War of 1914–18. Thus ended the first version of liberal internationalism.

President Woodrow Wilson led the United States into that war in 1917 explicitly to "make the world safe for democracy." Wilson, a prominent political scientist, had in mind restoring and improving liberal internationalism through the breakup of formal empires (at least those of America's enemies); the creation of new self-determining democracies; free trade; and the League of Nations, an approximation of Kant's league of republics. This second manifestation of liberal internationalism had some successes in the 1920s, but ultimately failed as well, not least because Wilson could not convince his own Senate to ratify the league's enabling document, the Treaty of Versailles. Wilsonianism drew fire from realists, such as Carl Schmitt in Germany and Edward Carr in Britain, who saw it as nothing more than a cleverly disguised power play by the Anglo-Saxon powers to keep second-tier countries in their place. In the 1930s, another global economic depression and a resentful Germany—this time much more malignant and authoritarian, and joined by Japan and Italy—propelled the world into another war.

In 1945, a smart investor might have sold liberal internationalism short: two abortive tries over the preceding century, both ending in world wars. But the United States and Britain were victorious in World War II, and their leaders drew from the awful 1930s the lesson that the problem was not liberal internationalism but its abandonment. In particular, the Anglo-Americans decided that US leverage was needed to help smooth out the boom-bust cycles that had produced devastating depressions and to defend liberal democracies from despotic great powers. With help from its democratic friends, the United States built an interlocking set of global institutions to regulate international trade and monetary relations.

But looming over the horizon was a new kind of antiliberal threat: the totalitarian Soviet Union, now no longer a brooding, self-weakening oddity but a fellow victor in the recent war and a model for rapid industrialization. It was the other superpower, evidently bent on expanding its empire as far as it could. Washington protected its democratic partners, and other countries besides, with a set of military alliances guaranteeing them against Soviet attack and coercion.

Political scientist G. John Ikenberry calls this US strategy self-binding: Through international institutions, America rendered itself more predictable and restrained, and in return its allies agreed not to challenge its hegemony.[5] A new theory of international relations, "hegemonic stability," grew out of the Western postwar order. Notwithstanding inevitable frictions and hypocrisies, this third try at liberal internationalism worked brilliantly. The Europeans and the Japanese lost their empires for good, but were compensated with steady economic growth through trade and monetary stability. The rich democracies grew richer together, American power was maintained and extended, and the probability of another war in Western Europe approached zero.

Liberal internationalism peaked in the early 1990s. The exhausted Soviet Union, unable to reform itself out of its downward economic and political spiral, broke into pieces, and most of the pieces sought to join the US-sponsored system. China was still ruled by a communist party, but market economics were pulling it into the system as well, and Western experts doubted that Beijing could resist the pull of liberal democracy for long. Democratic India and Brazil were setting aside their long-standing objections to capitalism, as were smaller countries the world over. Following the 1991 Gulf War, even the Middle East looked to be joining up.

"Globalization" was liberal internationalism stretched to fit over virtually the entire planet. World trade grew as Third World countries became "emerging markets," each of which followed the Washington Consensus directives from the International Monetary Fund on restructuring their political and economic systems. Marx's description of 1848—"In one word, [the bourgeoisie] creates a world in its own image"[6]—was closer than ever to realization. A few holdouts excepted—Cuba, Iran, Burma, North Korea—the countries of the world were moving through a liberal matrix they had, in Kantian fashion, accepted for themselves. With a tint of regret, and with prescient qualifications usually forgotten, Francis Fukuyama declared that history, the millennia-old struggle over the best way to order society, was over.[7]

But it was not so, of course. In 2001, transnational Islamist terrorism showed that liberal internationalism, at least for now, had its geographic limits. The 2008 financial collapse traumatized the Western institutions at the heart of the globalization project and was exploited by populist parties of left and right. Still, the liberal-internationalist program always has generated resistance among those it does not co-opt or dissolve. It has seen off this resistance before, and has learned from that history. Are today's threats really more serious than those of the past?

Perhaps. What is casting doubt on the project's future brings us back to Marx's underestimation of both the nation-state and traditional culture. The old ideologies of fascism and communism sought to destroy liberalism. Today's threats operate more gradually, and from within the system. The threat is one of atrophy rather than violent death.

Internationalism with Chinese Characteristics

Today, authoritarian great powers, resentful of the power and arrogance of the liberal hegemon, bully their neighbors and appear interested in acquiring some of their territory. Russia steadily moves into a new yet old despotism, and China continues to benefit from the global economy while obstinately refusing to follow the Kantian plan and become a constitutional republic. Russia, which retains formidable assets and under the Putin regime is bidding to restart history, must not be underestimated. But China's sustained economic growth and proven ability to adjust to new challenges make it more consequential than Russia in the long term.

China's leaders know that their country owes its spectacular economic growth to its qualified participation in liberal internationalism. By contrast, in the 1930s, Nazi Germany, fascist Italy, and imperial Japan sought autarchy: specifically, independence from the liberal order through conquest and empire. Today, China's biggest customers are the United States, Japan, Germany, and South Korea, and China in addition holds roughly $1 trillion in US debt. This is not a country preparing to pull the cloth off the dining room table.

It may, however, want to change the menu. What does China want, then? More precisely, what do the leaders of the Chinese Communist Party, preeminently general secretary and national president Xi Jinping, want? What will their successors want?

China's leaders embrace commerce, but are far from being fervent liberal internationalists. Indeed, party leaders have encouraged nationalism among China's citizenry, most strikingly by periodically stirring up fears that Japan, a liberal-democratic and virtually pacifistic country since 1955, has the same malevolent intentions as it had in the 1930s. Opinion polls show that the Chinese public is resentful as well of enduring American power and influence in East Asia.

Chairman Mao, like Marx, could turn a memorable aphorism. ("A revolution is not a dinner party,"[8] he once declared.) His famous "socialism with Chinese characteristics" was not his best material, but that characterization has proved politically astute over the years. "Internationalism with Chinese characteristics" seems to be what the Chinese Communist Party seeks today. Sensibly enough, the party wants to continue to broaden and deepen Chinese economic interaction with the rest of the world. But we should not expect China's internationalism to be *liberal*. Liberal internationalism is designed to safeguard the autonomy of individuals. The party is determined precisely that Chinese citizens not enjoy autonomy, for that would end its prized monopoly on power. For that matter, China's leaders associate liberalism with American or Western power, and they are not crazy to do so. Liberals throughout the world generally want their countries to align with the West, and the West clearly would prefer a China in which the Communist Party lost its monopoly—yielding a weakened, fissiparous state facing an even more powerful West.

There are clear signs that the party wants to remove the liberal bias the West has built into international institutions. Loans from the new Asian Infrastructure Investment Bank, China's answer to the World Bank, are not contingent upon democratic and free-market reforms, unlike World Bank and International Monetary Fund loans. Andrew Nathan notes that Beijing has labored to weaken human rights monitoring by the United Nations, with all its attendant publicity, and has opposed US-sponsored universal rules for Internet freedom.[9] None of this is surprising; China has long considered human rights advocacy nothing more than imperialism with Western characteristics.

At the same time, China is hedging by investing in infrastructure to its west, along the old Silk Road, in the so-called One Belt, One Road initiative. One Belt, One Road is designed to ensure that China will be able to feed its voracious and growing appetite for energy and food. There are actually two "roads," one over water (through the South China Sea and Indian Ocean) and—the sea route being vulnerable to disruption by the US Navy—one over land (through Central Asia and the Middle East). China cuts deals with governments and companies in the countries along the two routes without pestering them about human rights. This is Chinese internationalism: enrichment through foreign commerce but without the familiar liberal accent.

The difficulty for liberal internationalism is clear. Depending on how we measure national economies, China's either should surpass America's during the next decade or it has already done so. The People's Liberation Army is far weaker than America's armed forces, and its reach is limited to China's immediate vicinity, but the growth of Chinese military spending has outpaced the country's impressive economic expansion for several years. Money and guns do not exhaust the sources of international power, but countries with plenty of both generally shape international society. If China wants the internationalism without the liberalism, it may get it, little by little.

The Changing Content of Liberalism

Were global power not shifting to China, liberal internationalism would still be in trouble in its own homelands. It would be easy to blame the trouble wholly on the economic disruptions open markets always bring. As surely as night follows day, free trade eliminates inefficient firms and hence jobs; foreign investment relocates jobs; immigration generally lowers wages. Creative destruction brings new winners and new losers, who find the autonomy promised by liberalism to be beside the point, and the losers will always resist and be ripe for political mobilization.

The material losses that many suffer from globalization do explain some of the opposition. But scholars who have studied the data closely report a curious finding: A stronger force is cultural resistance to the entire package that liberal internationalism now offers.[10] In Europe and North America, many people who are not suffering from the effects of imports, offshored factories, and immigration are nonetheless souring on liberal internationalism. Understanding cultural resistance in the West requires understanding that the content of liberalism itself has changed over the decades, to the point where many in its countries of origin no longer recognize it.

I have argued elsewhere that, since its emergence in the eighteenth century, liberalism has passed through two historical stages and is in the middle of a third.[11] Liberalism has been committed to an abstraction, namely, individual autonomy or self-legislation. What has changed is the content that fills that form—what is meant by autonomy, and hence what most threatens it.

In the first-stage liberalism of Kant's time, the chief threat to autonomy was the despotic state, in which coercive power over people and groups was intimate with religious authority—thus the constitutional republic, with its limits on state power, and the liberal internationalism of Marx's time. By the late nineteenth century, the rise of the working class and socialism had prodded leading liberal thinkers and politicians into seeing capital, or unchecked capitalism, as the main obstacle to individual autonomy. Left-of-center parties began to recruit the now liberal state to tame markets. Among the results were the

Progressive movement in the United States and the liberal internationalism of Wilson. In the 1960s, leading liberals began seeing that women, racial minorities, and other groups were not enjoying full liberal autonomy. The source of the trouble was traditional norms and institutions—tribalism, racism, sexism, and then localism, the traditional family, and orthodox religious beliefs and institutions—and liberals recruited both the liberal state and now-liberalized capital to shrink the scope of these entities.

The autonomy safeguarded by third-stage liberalism has shifted what Kant had in mind. For him, morality was already "out there," and the autonomous individual discovered and owned it but did not create it. Today's autonomy-seeking liberal finds that stance still too "heteronomous," too beholden to what is external to the self. Today, the good life is understood to be one of what the sociologist Robert Bellah termed "expressive individualism," in which individuals create and enact their own values (so long as these values do not entail coercion of others).[12]

Twenty-first-century political, economic, and cultural elites are pressing third-stage liberalism downward into societies attached to older liberalisms. First-stage liberalism still exists, and has its champions in free-market, small-government political parties of the right. Some parties of the left and center-left continue to be organized around second-stage liberalism. Elites try to hold all of these liberalisms together, but tensions are inevitable and seem more and more to be resolved in favor of third-stage liberalism. In 2012 a German higher regional court ruled traditional Jewish circumcision illegal because "a child's right to self-determination superseded his parents' right to freedom of religion." (The following year, the German parliament passed a law allowing certain exceptions.) In the United States, bakers adhering to conservative Christianity have been fined for refusing to cater same-sex weddings. Citizens who have chosen traditional beliefs and communities—Christian, Jewish, and Muslim—doubt that the liberal state and progressive big corporations are protecting their autonomy.

Third-stage liberal internationalism has a different shape from that of its predecessors. Local cultures as sources of art and food remain acceptable—at least as raw material for "fusion cuisine" and "world music"—but as shapers of norms they must give way. And progressive states and corporations help here as well, by moving money, goods, and people so freely across national borders. These movements begin to dissolve local cultures into a more general whole that its mandarins present as universal but that seems simply elitist to many.

Cultural confrontation in North America and Europe is channeled through democratic politics and is in some ways augmented by it. It interacts with the resurgence of the nation-state, less in the case of China than in those of Hungary, Poland, Turkey, and especially Russia, where Vladimir Putin is a virtuoso in exploiting reactions to third-stage liberalism, in his country and in the West. The revenge of the particular and traditional is now enervating liberal internationalism itself. No matter that many of the besieged ways of life are themselves not so old, and indeed that the modern factory, the newspaper, and the supermarket originated in the very dynamics that are now destroying them.

Third Stage or End Stage?

Liberal internationalism is in trouble because it has gotten wrong what Marx got wrong. Liberalism, in the form of open markets and societies, human rights, and democracy, can dissolve many things. The result, however, is not a universal whole, but just another particular culture, less tied to place than to class, carried by a transnational meritocracy to which it is suited, and resisted by people who like the local and particular. Populism, of right or left, has emerged as the only viable resistance many of the latter can find. The chorus that mocks Fukuyama's 1992 "end of history" declaration has either forgotten, or never read, his speculations that liberal democracies could find post-history unsatisfying and lurch toward megalothymia, or assertions of superiority. That is one plausible reading of the phenomenon of Donald Trump, whose assertions of superiority, whether in reference to himself or the nation, appealed to enough Americans in 2016 to put him in the White House. Meanwhile, elsewhere in the world, liberal culture's propensity to dissolve whatever it touches also has about it, for many, the odor of overweening American or Western influence and power vis-à-vis non-Western states. Thus the Chinese challenge.

Liberal internationalism, at its best, is worth saving, not least because its historical alternatives have proved much worse. It needs reforming, however, and reform can begin with a recollection of liberalism's pragmatic turn from cosmopolitanism toward internationalism more than two centuries ago. Then, Kant saw that the radical cosmopolitan cure for particularism would be worse than the disease. The good news is that liberalism is elastic by nature, and has shown itself capable of adapting to new circumstances. Third-stage liberalism can meet the populist challenge in the West by losing its militant edge and finding ways to coexist with liberalism's earlier stages. The challenge from China is going to be harder.

(Fall 2017, 19.3)

Notes

[1] Karl Marx and Friedrich Engels, *The Communist Manifesto*, ed. Jeffrey C. Isaac (New Haven, CT: Yale University Press), 7. First published 1848. Engels was officially Marx's coauthor, but the weight of scholarly opinion holds that Marx wrote most if not all of the tract.

[2] Ibid.

[3] Ibid.

[4] Ibid., Part 2, 18.

[5] G. John Ikenberry, *After Victory: Institutions, Strategic Restraint, and the Rebuilding of Order after Major Wars* (Princeton, NJ: Princeton University Press, 2001).

[6] Marx and Engels, *Communist Manifesto*, 8.

[7] Francis Fukuyama, *The End of History and the Last Man* (New York, NY: Free Press, 1992). Fukuyama noted a few ways that liberal democracies might restart history, one of which I shall come to later in the present essay.

[8] Mao Zedong, *Report on an Investigation of the Peasant Movement in Hunan* (1927), https://www.marxists.org/reference/archive/mao/selected-works/volume-1/mswv1_2.htm.

[9] Andrew J. Nathan, "China's Challenge," *Journal of Democracy* 26, no. 1 (2015): 156–70.

[10] Ronald Inglehart and Pippa Norris, "Trump and the Populist Authoritarian Parties: The Silent Revolution in Reverse," *Perspectives on Politics* 15, no. 2 (2017): 443–54.

[11] John M. Owen IV, "Anti-Liberalism Pushes Back," *Global Policy* 8, no. 54 (2017): 73–84.

[12] Bellah and his colleagues coined "expressive individualism" in their classic book *Habits of the Heart: Individualism and Commitment in American Life* (Berkeley, CA: University of California Press, 1985).

Europe and the
New Democracy

Philippe Bénéton

The project of creating a unified Europe, which began in earnest a half century ago, has been a great adventure, and partly a great success. The European "civil war," which began in the sixteenth century and went on for hundreds of years, has finally ended. Peace is firmly established within the European borders. In this respect, the founders of Europe, and especially the architects of the Franco-German reconciliation, made history. And they knew the history they were making.

Apart from that signal achievement, the adventure of unification gives the appearance of groping in the dark. The general reason is clear: Europe is a powerful idea, but it is also an indeterminate idea. Gradually, from about the 1970s, the procedures of unification took the place of the project. Now official Europe is thought of as a process. European issues are reduced to taking the next step. Any pause will ruin the undertaking. The obligation to walk together and the obsession with compromise prevent serious debate. The process governs.

As a result, the primary questions remain unanswered: Europe no doubt, but which Europe? For what purpose? In what form? With whom? Things are unclear. Those who make the history appear not to understand the history they make.

The process took a new direction in the 1980s. Accelerating as new members were brought on, it culminated in the drafting of the "European Constitution" of 2005 (which was signed by the heads of states but fell short of ratification chiefly because the French and Dutch publics rejected it in national referendums). Since then, Europe has entered a slow-boil crisis.

So what is this new Europe that is being made through a kind of blind groping? At the time when there was a clear disagreement about the nature of the European project, the debate pitted the idea of a Europe of nation-states (the plan of General de Gaulle) against a conception of a United States of Europe (the federal idea of Europe as a new nation). Unless a sudden and surprising change occurs, the plan of de Gaulle has lost. But the idea of Europe as a new nation has not prevailed. Instead, another Europe has come into being, a postnational Europe. And, in a sense, a postpolitical Europe.

Postpolitical Europe

A postpolitical Europe is one in which European democracy has assumed a new meaning, characterized by three features: It is a Europe without history or geography, and therefore without substance. It is a Europe that works to reduce the scope of politics. And it is a Europe that regulates extensively, but generally fails to act as a political unit.

The new Europe breaks with its history. The preamble to the 2005 constitution was silent on the Christian roots of Europe and on many other things. According to that document, the European adventure is not rooted in a common history and a particular civilization; it is something new, based on modern and universal values. Heritage is treated accordingly, with the preamble's first clause beginning as follows: "Drawing inspiration from the cultural, religious and humanist inheritance of Europe, from which have developed the universal values of the inviolable and inalienable rights of the human person, freedom, democracy, equality and the rule of law…" As these lofty words would have it, Europe is based only on universal principles, having thrown away its particular historical experience. Indeed, its aim is a kind of transcendence. Europe is to be the vanguard of a new humanity.

It follows logically from this that Europe refuses to fix borders. All European treaties have that in common: the territory to which the treaties apply is never specified. Europe is defined no more by its geography than by its history. The 2001 declaration of the European Council, issued in Laeken, Belgium, states that "the European Union's one boundary is democracy and human rights." That idea had already been expressed at the Council's 1978 summit in Copenhagen, and was confirmed by all subsequent treaties. Any country that respects democracy and human rights can apply for membership. The Europe of rights is without borders.

Consequently, Europe is expected not to form a great nation but to leave the idea of the nation behind altogether. The "values" by which Europe is defined should be the common denominator of the emerging global civil society, governed by judges and experts. In early 2002, Romano Prodi, the president of the European Commission, declared before the Convention on the Future of Europe that the Union represented "the only real attempt to achieve democratic globalization." The vision is that of a postnational humanity. Ultimately, the future of Europe is not its construction but its disappearance.

In practice, what has happened? The European Union has expanded, again and again, and it is intended to expand further. The founding members were six. The number of members rose to nine in 1973, to twelve in 1980, to fifteen in 1995, to twenty-five in 2004, and to twenty-seven in 2007. Since then, crisis has slowed things down, but the principle of enlargement has not changed. Turkey remains at the threshold. But the reasons it has not yet been admitted—at least the official reasons—are those of the new Europe: at issue is not the fact that Turkey belongs to another continent, to another history, to another civilization, but that it falls short of embracing all of the "universal values" of the Union.

Enlargement has led to endless institutional adjustments, but it has not led to a discussion of the nature of the European project. According to champions of the new Europe, the number of members doesn't matter. The goal is not to achieve a substantive unity of the people; a formal unity is enough. It is not to generate a common will; it is to establish uniform rules.

A Society of Individuals

In some ways, the new Europe neutralizes politics and reduces society to a conglomerate of individuals who agree only on respecting the rules. Europe "depoliticizes" the common life. It reduces the sphere of politics to make greater room for the imperatives of human rights and a market economy. It exempts from political debate all rules deriving from individual rights and free market competition. It creates a supranational and suprapolitical law. Consequently, more and more issues have been removed from genuine democratic discussion. The democracy "Eurocrats" speak of in Brussels is not the democracy of citizens; it is the democracy of rights holders and consumers. The new Europe is working to build a society of individuals. Autonomy is the first of virtues, and free competition and diversity are considered unquestioned goods. As a result, many things tend to disappear: civic participation, shared commitment, common decency.

Basically, there are only two legitimate categories: the individual and humanity. Those who love their fellow citizens betray the rights of those who are not fellow citizens. The attachment to the nation is somehow suspect. It is assumed that the "values" of the new Europe are enough to attach people politically. The good citizen of former times was attached to his flag, to his land, to his native tongue, to his history. The good European of today should be committed to equality, tolerance, diversity, pluralism, individual rights. To be sure, these formal "values," rightly understood, are important. They are part of liberal democracy. But can they be enough? What do they give to love? If a Swede is no different from a Greek, or a European from a Japanese, the ideal is to be a citizen of the world, that is to say, a person who comes from nowhere in particular.

The new Europe regulates extensively, but it is deficient as a meaningful political unit. Such is the consequence of the withdrawal of politics. In a world of individual rights and free concurrence, regulations increase but "common policies" are rare. Regulations aim at uniformity. The rules for hunting must be the same in Denmark as in Italy; bulbs or lawn mowers must be the same from Vilnius to Athens; university degrees must be identical whether one has studied at Oxford, Berlin, or the Sorbonne. On the other hand, where European countries have an interest in acting together, things don't work. The examples are numerous: there is no real industrial policy, no energy policy, no real foreign policy at the European level. Among the reasons are the decline of politics and the divisions among the nation-states. The situation is this: Europe hampers the member states, and the member states hinder Europe. In others words, the cooperative Europe works badly, but the regulating Europe works only too well.

The crisis besetting Europe has obvious economic sources in the general financial crisis of the West and the specific crisis of the euro. It also has a political source: a growing number of European citizens have lost confidence in Europe. Yet the official principles remain the same. The tone has changed from triumphant to anxious, but within the European institutions, no one questions the direction that has been taken.

The main "generative principle" behind the process of unification is the principle of equality, in the sense intended by Alexis de Tocqueville—that is, the idea of the sovereignty of the individual. But it does not follow that the main actor behind the new Europe was the common man. In his works, Tocqueville tended to underestimate the role of minorities. In the case of Europe, the march of history is above all the work of political and intellectual elites with the support of the media. People have occasionally been called upon to ratify choices that were made without their real input. And if they did not ratify, they were compelled to reconsider their choice, as the Danes were in 1992 and the Irish in 2008. In 2005, the French and Dutch publics said "no" to the European Constitution. So in the Treaty of Lisbon of 2007, the constitution's institutional arrangements were ratified by the parliaments of France and the Netherlands.

A Procedural Democracy

The regime in place in Europe is a procedural democracy. It is defined exclusively by formal rules: human rights, a free market, majority rule in the political arena. Liberal democracy is a machine in working order as long as everyone respects the rules of the game. The qualities of the participants matter little. In the world of modern equality, each individual is judge of his own behavior. A substantial interpretation of liberal democracy does not deny the importance of the rules of the game—the regime has by nature a procedural dimension—but it interprets them differently. The essential point is this: *The rules of the game are not sufficient.* They are sufficient neither to forge a true political society nor to make a liberal-democratic regime a good regime. No system suffices by itself. Much depends on the conduct of participants and on the relationships between them.

Procedural politics founded on modern equality benefits from the appeal of simple ideas, but it ignores a number of essential (or substantial) distinctions: the distinction between a "society" and a "community," the distinction between a corrupt and a healthy people, and those other important distinctions between a demagogue and a statesman, between passions and reason, between procedures and forms.

An agreement on the rules of the game does not suffice to make a strong society. Who would risk his life to defend procedures, either those of the political regime or those of the market? And can this agreement itself be solid if the members of the society have nothing in common? According to a more substantial definition, political society cannot be reduced to a mere association. In particular, it cannot be established successfully except in the kind of community that was forged in the modern era: the nation-state. Liberal democracy and the nation-state can be separated only at great risk.

Why is this bond so important? The essential reason is that liberal democracy honors discord and establishes majority rule as the principle of decision making in the political sphere. In order to sustain this institutionalization of conflict, there must be a strong sense of common belonging. There are costs inherent in this regime, a big one being the willingness of minorities to recognize the legitimacy of decisions made by the representatives of their adversaries. This cost is bearable, and is borne in Western regimes for two reasons: first, because these democratic regimes are also liberal (and liberal rule limits the scope and the cost of democratic rule); second, because national unity forges communitarian bonds.

If this analysis is correct, liberal democracy requires a substance beyond itself: a common memory, shared references, awareness of a common destiny. To seek to go beyond the nation and forge a postnational Europe on the basis of a "constitutional [i.e., procedural] patriotism" is to advocate weak citizenship and a political society without substance. It is also to risk undermining certain foundations of liberal democracy.

When liberal democracy is considered to be a machine, respect for procedures is supposed to suffice, and citizens and leaders are relieved of all other obligations. The system, it is thought, can do without the civic virtue of its participants. Yet the rules of the game cannot themselves function in the complete absence of feelings of civic obligation. Electoral results never come down to one person's vote. A purely selfish and rational citizen would never vote, since he would know that his vote would not change the outcome at the polls. Moreover, respect for formal rules in no way guarantees good government: it is a matter of indifference, formally speaking, whether the officeholder is an honest person or a scoundrel, a statesman or a demagogue. But the good functioning of the regime depends upon a shared sense of responsibility concerning the common destiny.

This necessity becomes plainly apparent in extreme situations. In wartime, if individual aims prevail over the common interest, what becomes of the country's defense? Extreme situations remind us that politics is not just one activity among others and that the common interest can go so far as to require that citizens risk their lives. But if the sense of political obligation weakens or even disappears in ordinary times, what strength will it have in those dramatic moments when much more is expected? Procedural democracy navigates well enough in calm waters, but it may be vulnerable when the wind begins to blow.

These effects are now visible in Europe. In many countries, the political elites are discredited as a result of various scandals. Partisanship wreaks havoc, and the sense of common interest loses its force. With regard to international affairs, Europe as such is unable to act. It confusedly aspires to get out of history.

In short, liberalism pushed to the point of relativism and utmost individualism creates a moral and political crisis. It is a crisis Tocqueville partly anticipated when he wrote that democracy was constantly engaged in the process of democratizing itself, extending and expanding the sovereignty of the individual. To him, of course, America was the avant-garde of democracy. But since the moral revolution of the 1960s, the conquest of humankind by democracy has gone beyond anything Tocqueville foresaw. The result, though now more advanced in Europe than in America, has been the transformation of democracy as a political regime, a transformation that eliminates everything (including most substantive politics) in the march toward "equality of conditions." It can only be hoped, for Europe's sake, that Tocqueville was wrong when he saw that march as irreversible.

(Spring 2014, 16.1)

Cosmopolitanism and Democracy
Affinities and Tensions

Seyla Benhabib

Cosmopolitanism has become a much-evoked term in contemporary debates across a variety of fields, ranging from law to cultural studies, from philosophy to international politics. For me, cosmopolitanism involves the recognition that human beings are moral persons entitled to legal protection in virtue of the rights that accrue to them not as nationals, or members of an ethnic group, but as human beings as such. Cosmopolitanism acknowledges human interdependence and maintains that borders in the twenty-first century have become increasingly porous and that justice inside borders and justice across borders are interconnected even if they can be, and often are, in tension as well.

Understood thus, however, cosmopolitanism seems hardly reconcilable with democracy. Democracy is about defining the boundaries of a political entity; democracy means constituting oneself as a political unit with clear rules governing the relations between the inside and the outside. In a democracy, the constitution derives its legitimacy from the united and collective will of this people. A democratic people recognizes the rule of law over itself because it views itself both as subject, that is, as the originator of the law, and as its object, that is, as the one to whom the law applies. The citizen of a democracy is not a citizen of the world but a citizen of this well-demarcated unit—whether this be a unitary or a federal state, whether this be a "European Union" or a nation-state. How is this compatible with the cosmopolitan vision of justice *across* borders? Or with the vision of *porous borders* over which the people's representatives have little control? Isn't "the right to have rights," in Hannah Arendt's words, always the right of the human being to be a member in an organized political community? Shouldn't the title of this essay then be not "Cosmopolitanism *and* Democracy" but rather "Cosmopolitanism *or* Democracy"?

In this essay[1] I would like to explore the relationship between cosmopolitan norms and aspirations, understood in the broadest sense as relations of right and justice across borders, and democratic constitutionalism. Modern constitutions incorporate universalistic cosmopolitan ideals in the form of a list of basic rights. But there can often be a tension between the moral and legal principles articulated in these basic rights and other articles of the same constitution, or between the interpretation of these basic rights by judicial instances and their concretization by legislatures in the form of specific laws. A great deal of constitutional debate, though not all, concerns this legal hermeneutic task. The interpretation of the meaning of basic rights is also a political project, in the sense that such interpretations concern how a people wishes to live abiding by certain principles both in the light of its own changing self-understanding and in the light of its wishes for the future.

In addition to the tension between basic rights and other aspects of democratic constitutions both in theory and practice, today most states operate in an increasingly transformed international legal environment with many intergovernmental organizations, nongovernmental organizations, and new postnational reconfigurations of sovereignty, such as the European Union, emerging and proliferating. Cosmopolitan norms also structure this international environment through many international treaties, such as the Universal Declaration of Human Rights. In this respect as well, the democratic will of the people has to bind itself in accordance with these international covenants. How can we understand the conflicts that may arise through these various norms incorporated in various treaties?

I wish to begin with a brief historical overview of cosmopolitanism in the history of political thought and then move to a systematic analysis of democratic constitutionalism in the age of legal cosmopolitanism. In conclusion I return to the problem of constituting the *demos* as one domain in which the tension between cosmopolitanism and democracy is most palpable and which still requires to be addressed—politically as well as legally.

The word "*Kosmopolitismus*" is composed of *kosmos* (the universe) and *polites* (citizen). And the tension between these perspectives is significant.[2] "Socrates was asked," writes Montaigne, where he came from. He replied not "Athens," but "the world." He, whose imagination was fuller and more extensive, embraced the universe as his city, and distributed his knowledge, his company, and his affections to all mankind, unlike us who look only at what is underfoot.[3]

Whether or not Socrates said anything of this kind is in dispute, but the story of Socrates is repeated by Cicero in *Tusculum Disputationes*, by Epictetus in his *Discourses*, and by Plutarch in *De Exilio*, who praises Socrates for saying that "he was no Athenian or Greek, but a Cosmian."[4]

What does it mean to be a Cosmian and how can a Cosmian be a democrat, when democracy could only be realized in the city? To live outside the boundaries of the city, said Aristotle, one needed to be either a beast or a God, but since men were neither and since the *Kosmos* was not the *polis*, the *kosmopolites* was not really a citizen at all but some other kind of being. Cynics like Diogenes Laertius agreed with this conclusion and claimed that rather than being at home in *every* city, they were *indifferent* to them *all*. The *kosmopolites* was a nomad without a home, at peace with nature and the universe but not with the human city, from whose follies she distanced herself. Some of the negative connotations of the term with which we are familiar from subsequent history, such as "rootless cosmopolitanism," are already present in this early period.

As opposed to this negative version of cosmopolitanism as nomadism without the city, there is also the more elevated Stoic doctrine that holds that what humans share is not just the *nomoi*—the laws of their individual cities—but *logos*, that in virtue of which they are capable of reason. In his *Meditations* Marcus Aurelius writes,

> If we have intelligence in common, so we have reason (logos)…. If so, then
> the law is also common to us and, if so, we are citizens. If so we share a
> common government. And if so, the universe is, as it were, a city.[5]

The idea of an order, transcending the differences among the human laws of different cities and rooted instead in the rationally comprehensible order of nature, as formulated by the Stoics, converges with the Christian doctrine of universal equality in the centuries that follow. The Stoic doctrine of natural law inspires the Christian ideal of *the city of God versus the city of men*, and eventually finds its way into the natural law theories of modern political thought with Thomas Hobbes, John Locke, Jean-Jacques Rousseau, and Immanuel Kant.

These negative and positive valences that attach to the word *kosmopolites* and that we first encounter in Greek and Roman thought remain throughout the centuries: a *kosmopolites* is one who distances him or herself either in thought or in practice from the habits or laws of his city and who judges them from the standpoint of a higher order that is considered to be identical with reason. The thinker who resuscitates the Stoic meaning of cosmopolitanism and who gives the term a new turn such as to make it compatible with the demands of a modern state based on the rule of law is Immanuel Kant. With Kant, we also begin to see that cosmopolitanism and democracy, as embedded in a republican constitution, are not incompatible but may in fact require each other.

From Cosmopolitanism to World Citizenship—Immanuel Kant

Written in 1795, upon the signing of the Treaty of Basel by Prussia and revolutionary France, Kant's essay on "Perpetual Peace" has enjoyed considerable revival of attention in recent years. What makes this essay particularly interesting under the current conditions of political globalization is the visionary depth of Kant's project for perpetual peace among nations. Kant formulates three "definitive articles for perpetual peace among states." These read: "The Civil Constitution of Every State should be Republican," "The Law of Nations shall be founded on a Federation of Free States," and "The Law of World Citizenship Shall be Limited to Conditions of Universal Hospitality."[6]

Regarding the Third Article of perpetual peace, Kant himself notes the oddity of the locution of "hospitality" in this context, and therefore remarks that "it is not a question of philanthropy but of right." In other words, hospitality is not to be understood as a virtue of sociability, as the kindness and generosity one may show to strangers who come to one's land or who become dependent upon one's act of kindness through circumstances of nature or history; hospitality is a "right" that belongs to all human beings insofar as we view them as potential participants in a world republic. But the "right" of hospitality is odd in that it does not regulate relationships among individuals who are members of a particular civil entity and under whose jurisdiction they stand; this "right" regulates the interactions of individuals who belong to different civic entities yet who encounter one another at the margins of bounded communities. Kant writes:

> Hospitality [*Wirtbarkeit*] means the right of a stranger not to be treated as an enemy when he arrives in the land of another. One may refuse to receive him when this can be done without causing his destruction; but, so long as he peacefully occupies his place, one may not treat him with hostility. It is not the right to be a permanent visitor [*Gastrecht*] that one may demand. A special beneficent agreement would be needed in order to give an outsider a right to become a fellow inhabitant [*Hausgenossen*] for a certain length of time. It is only a right of temporary sojourn, a right to associate, which all men have. They have it by virtue of their common possession of the surface of the earth, where, as a globe, they cannot infinitely disperse and hence must finally tolerate the presence of each other.[7]

Kant distinguishes the "right to be a permanent visitor," which he calls *Gastrecht*, from the "temporary right of soujourn" (*Besuchsrecht*). The right to be a permanent visitor is awarded through a freely chosen special agreement that goes beyond what is owed to the other morally and what he is entitled to legally; therefore, Kant names this a "contract of beneficence."

Kant's claim that first entry cannot be denied to those who seek it if this would result in their "destruction" has become incorporated into the Geneva Convention on the Status of Refugees of 1951 as the principle of "non-refoulement." This principle obliges signatory states not to forcibly return refugees and asylum seekers to their countries of origin if doing so would pose a clear danger to their lives and freedom. Of course, just as sovereign states manipulate this article to define life and freedom more or less narrowly when it fits their purposes, it is also possible to circumvent the "non-refoulement" clause by depositing refugees and asylees in so-called "safe third countries." Kant's formulations clearly foresaw as well as justified such balancing acts between the moral obligations of states to those who seek refuge in their midst and to their own welfare and interests. The lexical ordering of the two claims—the moral needs of others versus legitimate self-interest—is vague, except in the most obvious cases when the life and limb of refugees would be endangered by denying them the right of entry; apart from such cases, however, the obligation to respect the liberty and welfare of the guest can permit a narrow interpretation on the part of the sovereign to whom it is addressed and need not be considered an unconditional duty.

Kant's legacy is ambiguous: On the one hand, he wanted to justify the expansion of commercial and maritime capitalism in his time insofar as these developments brought the human race into closer contact; on the other hand, he did not support or encourage European imperialism. The cosmopolitan right of hospitality gives one the right of peaceful temporary sojourn, but it does not entitle one to plunder and exploit, conquer and overwhelm by superior force, those peoples and nations among whom one is seeking sojourn, as Kant's comments on European attempts to penetrate into Japan and China make clear.

While the distinction between the permanent visitor and the temporary sojourner in the context of eighteenth-century developments of European maritime imperialism was a progressive one, it no longer is. The claim of the foreigner to citizenship rights must be guaranteed by the Constitution itself, and it can no longer be considered a beneficent contract. The entitlement to citizenship itself will of course depend upon the fulfillment of certain conditions, as defined by each democratic sovereign more or less narrowly. But the right to naturalization is a human right that is guaranteed by Article 15 of the Universal Declaration of Human Rights.

We owe Kant the distinction between relations of law and justice between persons within a state and such relations between states, and the distinction between those and "the Right for all nations," or "cosmopolitan Right," which deals with relations of law and justice between persons viewed not as citizens of determinate human communities but as members of a world civil society. In claiming that relevant actors in the international domain were not only states and heads of states but also civilians and their various associations that themselves could be subject to a new sphere of law, Kant gave the term "cosmopolitan" the new meaning of world citizen. World citizenship involves a utopian anticipation of world peace to be attained as a consequence of increased communication between human beings, including "le doux commerce." Through increased human contact, "the injustices done in one part of the world would be felt by all." Cosmopolitan citizenship means first and foremost a new world legal order in which the human being would be entitled to rights in virtue of her humanity alone.

From World Citizenship to Cosmopolitan Law

It is now widely accepted that since the U.N. Declaration of Human Rights in 1948, we have entered a phase in the evolution of global civil society that is characterized by a transition from *international* to *cosmopolitan* norms of justice. While norms of international law emerge through treaty obligations to which states and their representatives are signatories, cosmopolitan norms accrue to individuals considered as moral and legal persons in a worldwide civil society. Even if cosmopolitan norms also originate through treaty-like obligations, such as the U.N. Charter, and the various human rights covenants can be considered to be for their member states, their peculiarity is that they bind states and their representatives, sometimes against the will of the signatories themselves. This is the uniqueness of the many human rights agreements concluded since World War II.

The 1948 Universal Declaration of Human Rights and the succeeding era of international rights declarations reflect the moral learning experiences not only of western humanity but of humanity at large. The World Wars were fought not only in the European continent but also in the colonies, in the Middle East, Africa, and Asia. The national liberation and anti-colonization struggles of the post–World War II period deeply inspired principles of self-determination enshrined in these rights documents. These public law documents have introduced a crucial transformation in international law. While it may be too utopian to name them steps toward a "world constitution," they are certainly more than mere treaties among states. They are constituent elements of a global civil society. In this global civil society, individuals are rights-bearing not only in virtue of their citizenship within states but in the first place in virtue of their humanity. Although states remain the most powerful actors, the range of their legitimate and lawful activity is increasingly limited. We need to rethink the law of peoples against the background of this newly emergent and fragile global civil society, which is always being threatened by war, violence, and military intervention. These transformations in law have consequences for how we conceptualize the relationship of cosmopolitanism and democracy in the contemporary period. Our question no longer is: cosmopolitanism *and* democracy, nor simply cosmopolitanism *or* democracy, but rather *democracy in the age of legal cosmopolitanism.* The spread of a cosmopolitan legal order brings with it its own problems.

The most important objections to legal cosmopolitanism are twofold: What sense does it really make to defend such a position when to be a rights-bearing person means first and foremost to be a member of a sovereign polity in which one's "right to have rights" (Hannah Arendt) is protected? Furthermore, how is legal cosmopolitanism to be reconciled with the diversity of the world's governments and regimes that consider the individual first and foremost as a being embedded in specific moral, religious, ethical, and linguistic contexts? Doesn't legal cosmopolitanism amount to a justification of moral interventionism and moral imperialism? Certainly, some of the recent critiques in contemporary discourse about the universalist justification of human rights can be traced back to their instrumentalization for political ends by some and to fear on the part of others that the robust language of human rights can usher in moral imperialism.

A very good example of this slippery slope from the *responsibility* to protect all human beings in accordance with cosmopolitan law to the duty to intervene, by military force if necessary, occurred during the great typhoon that hit Myanmar-Burma in Spring 2008. Bernard Kouchner, the former President of Medecins Sans Frontières, now foreign minister of France, argued that the nations of the world had a duty to intervene even against the will of the secretive Myanmar military junta. Robert Kaplan, the conservative American thinker, concurred and suggested that the U.S. Navy could move up the river delta to Myanmar and that once it did so, the mission of humanitarian aid to the victims of the cyclone could easily morph into one of "nation-building." Only this time, one would be self-conscious about this task and apply the Crate and Barrel principle outright: "if you break it, you own it"![8]

I do not wish to deny, therefore, the many ambivalences, contradictions, and treacherous double meanings of world citizenship and the current world situation, which often transforms cosmopolitan intents into hegemonic nightmares. However, I do wish to claim that some of these general assertions and criticisms derive from a faulty understanding of legal cosmopolitanism, in that they view the new international legal order as if it were a smooth "command structure" emanating from a hegemonic source—whether this be global capitalism, the modern nation-state as complicit in the spread of global capitalism, or the Security Council itself. In all these diagnoses, little attention is paid to the interplay between legal cosmopolitanism and constitutionalism and the *social dissemination* of human rights norms throughout member states and to the legal, social, cultural, and political institutions through which this takes place. But the distinguishing feature of the period we are in cannot be captured through the *bon mots* of "globalization" and "empire"; rather, we are facing the rise of an international human rights regime and the spread of cosmopolitan norms, while the relationship between state sovereignty and such norms is becoming more contentious and conflictual.

Such conflicts of norms are indicative of the completely altered relationship between cosmopolitanism and democracy today: cosmopolitanism means upholding the dignity of human beings as rights-bearing persons in a global civil society, but only within the limits of democracy's constitutions can these rights assume concrete justiciable form. Human rights instruments can empower democracies by creating new vocabularies for claim-making for citizens in signatory states as well as opening new channels of mobilization for civil society actors who then become part of transnational networks of rights activism and hegemonic resistance.

Democratic Iterations

To conceptualize the relationship between cosmopolitan norms, the individual constitutions of democratic polities, and democratic will-formation, I want to introduce a concept I have discussed in previous writings as well: *democratic iterations*. By *democratic iterations* I mean complex processes of public argument, deliberation, and exchange through which universalist rights claims are contested and contextualized, invoked and revoked, posited and positioned throughout legal and political institutions as well as in the associations of civil society.[9]

Every iteration transforms meaning, adds to it, enriches it in ever so-subtle ways. The iteration and interpretation of norms and of every aspect of the universe of value, however, is never merely an act of repetition. Every iteration involves making sense of an authoritative original in a new and different context. The antecedent thereby is reposited and resignified via subsequent usages and references. Meaning is enhanced and transformed; conversely, when the creative appropriation of that authoritative original ceases to have meaning for us, then the original loses its authority upon us as well. Through such iterative acts, a democratic people that considers itself bound by certain guiding norms and principles reappropriates and reinterprets these, thus showing itself to be not only the *subject* but also the *author of the laws.*

Natural right doctrines assume that the principles that underline democratic politics are impervious to transformative acts of will. Legal positivism identifies democratic legitimacy with the correctly posited norms of a sovereign legislature; by contrast, democratic iterations signal a space of interpretation and intervention between context-transcendent norms and the will of democratic majorities. The rights claims that frame democratic politics, on the one hand, must be viewed to transcend the specific enactments of democratic majorities in specific polities; on the other hand, such democratic majorities *re-iterate* these principles and incorporate them into the democratic will-formation process of the people through argument, contestation, revision, and rejection.

Democratic iterations take place in overlapping communities of conversation between all those who are formal citizens and residents of a jurisdictional system, and other more fluid and unstructured communities of conversation that can involve international and transnational human rights organizations such as Amnesty International, various U.N. representative and monitoring bodies, global activist groups such as Medecins Sans Frontières, and the like. Democratic iterations are not concerned with the question, "which norms are valid for human beings at all times and in all places?," but rather with questions such as, "in view of our moral, political, and constitutional commitments as a people, our international obligations to human rights treaties and documents, what collective decisions can we reach that would be deemed both just and legitimate?" Democratic iterations aim at democratic justice.[10] They mediate between a collectivity's constitutional and institutional responsibilities, and the context-transcending universal claims of human rights to which such a collectivity is equally committed. Democratic iterations help us think of the interaction between legal cosmopolitanism and constitutionalism as a process of mutual adjustment and convergent as well as divergent interpretations.

Conclusion

In conclusion I would like to briefly address two issues. First there is a great deal of reductionism in thinking about the complexities of legal cosmopolitanism. Defenders of economic globalization, such as Thomas Friedman (at least in his earlier work, *The World Is Flat*), reduce cosmopolitan norms to a thin version of the human rights to life, liberty, equality, and property that are supposed to accompany the spread of free markets and trading practices. In this respect, neoliberal theorists of globalization join hands with neo-Marxist theorists of "empire," most notably, Tony Negri and Michael Hardt. As is well-known, Hardt and Negri distinguish between *imperialism* and *empire* in order to capture the novel logic of the international order. While imperialism refers to a predatory, extractive, and exploitative order through which a sovereign power imposes its will upon others, "empire" refers to an anonymous network of rules, regulations, and structures that entrap one in the system of global capitalism. Global capitalism requires the protection of the rights of the individual to freely exchange goods and services in the market place; above all global capitalism demands that contracts be upheld (*pacta sunt servanda*), that they be predictable and capable of execution. Empire is the ever-expanding power of global capital to bring farther and farther reaches of the world into its grip.[11]

In the period of the greatest economic turmoil in the world since the Great Depression of the 1920s, the neo-Marxist critique of global capitalism will find new audiences. Ironically, however, this is a period when even the purported empire, that is, the U.S., has lost its way, and the market has overwhelmed the empire. We need to rethink the rules and regulations of global markets from the bottom up, and we need to extend legal cosmopolitan norms into the sphere of the economy as well. Today cosmopolitanism must involve new, multiple, overlapping projects of global governance for a world economy run amok, caused in large part by the free market ideologies of the Bush years; the egotism and greediness of the financial sector; and the breakdown of social trust and public care which were already manifest through the disastrous reaction to Hurricane Katrina.

This era of selfishness within capitalist countries has been reduplicated at the world level. The contribution of major industrial nations to development in poorer countries has declined and the withdrawal of the state from protecting its citizens in large parts of Africa, Afghanistan, Central America, and Burma is proceeding apace. "Failed states" are yielding their place either to warring ethno-religious tribes or to *maquilladoras* or to free-economic zones in which the human as well as civil and socio-economic rights of workers and peasants are suspended. In the desperate straits that the current world economic crises will generate in many developing countries, it is likely that these rights will be further suspended in a Faustian bargain to keep foreign direct investment coming and the economies growing.

It is not only increased regulation of financial markets, stricter controls over free-growth and trade-zones to comply with international labor laws, human rights, and ecological standards that are needed but a fundamental rethinking of the meaning of global distributive justice will be required. And for this task, we need a reconfiguration of the world-map in our minds such that economic and ecological interdependence are understood to be not episodic aspects of the life of nations but crucial building blocks of the formation of modernity as global human history. In other words, we need to remind ourselves of what Kant, with his limited knowledge in the eighteenth century, could already see as the double-edged sword of western imperial expansion, namely the increase of unequal exchange between the West and the "rest" on the one hand, and the intensification of human contact and interdependence on the other.

Second, the legacy of cosmopolitanism requires us to rethink the famous boundary problem in democratic theory, sometimes also referred to as "the problem of constituting the *demos*."[12] If in the eighteenth century, it was the West that colonized the rest, today the rest of the world has come to the metropolis in patterns of predictable migratory flows between center and periphery. This means that the boundaries of the demos can no longer be taken as if they were given by ancient history; world migratory patterns, as they ebb and flow, make it very clear that people are constituted and reconstituted historically.

I would like to quote here my eminent Yale colleague, Robert Dahl, who writes: Strange as it may seem…how to decide who legitimately makes up "the people"…and hence are entitled to govern themselves…is a problem almost totally neglected by all the great political philosophers who write about democracy. I think this is because they take for granted that a people has already constituted itself…. The polis is what it is; the nation-state is what history has made it. Athenians are Athenians. Corinthians are Corinthians, and Greeks are Greeks.[13]

We can no longer believe this; however, there is no democratic procedure for deciding democratically who should or should not be part of the *demos*, since every such decision already involves a distinction between those who are entitled to decide and those who are not. We face an inevitable circularity. Yet although this logical problem of circularity cannot be avoided, there are more or less just, and more or less intelligent solutions to the problem of constituting the *demos*. In our age, the legacy of cosmopolitanism involves treating the guest not as a guest but as a potential citizen and political consociate.

Cosmopolitan norms then pose challenges to contemporary democracies to reevaluate and reshape their own practices in accordance with the universalistic ideals that are already embodied in their own constitutions. While we can never eliminate the distinction between human rights and citizens' rights, and I for one would not wish to do so, as citizens who are also aspiring to be citizens of the world, we should take our obligations of "solidarity with the other," whether they be within or outside our borders, with utmost seriousness.

(Fall 2009, 11.3)

Notes

1 This article is based on a lecture to the German Bundestag (Parliament), which the author was invited to deliver on March 13, 2009, by the German Green Party upon the occasion of the 60th anniversary celebrations of the German Constitution (*Grundgesetz*).

2 Darrin M. McMahon, "Fear and Trembling: Strangers and Strange Lands," *Daedalus* 137.3 (Summer 2008): 5–17; A. A. Long, "The Concept of the Cosmopolitan in Greek and Roman Thought," *Daedalus* 137.3 (Summer 2008): 50–8.

3 Michel de Montaigne, "Education of Children," *The Complete Essays of Montaigne*, trans. Donald M. Frame (Stanford, CA: Stanford University Press, 1965) 116.

4 Montaigne, 7.

5 As quoted in McMahon, 9.

6 Immanuel Kant, "Zum Ewigen Frieden. Ein philosophischer Entwurf," (1795) *Immanuel Kants Werke*, ed. A. Buchenau, E. Cassirer, and B. Kellermann (Berlin, Germany: Verlag Bruno Cassirer, 1923), 434–6, my translation.

7 Ibid., 443.

8 Seth Mydans, "Myanmar Faces Pressure to Allow Major Aid Effort," *The New York Times* (8 May 2008); and Robert Kaplan, "Aid at the Point of a Gun," *The New York Times* (14 May 2008).

9 See Seyla Benhabib, with commentaries by Jeremy Waldron, Bonnie Honing, and Will Kymlicka, *Another Cosmopolitanism*, The Berkeley Tanner Lectures, ed. Robert Post (Oxford, England: Oxford University Press, 2006) 45ff.

10 See Ian Shapiro, *Democratic Justice* (New Haven, CT: Yale University Press, 1999).

11 Although first translated into English in 2001, the Italian version of Michael Hardt and Antonio Negri's *Empire* (Cambridge, MA: Harvard University Press, 2001) was written in the period between the Persian Gulf War of 1991 and the Yugoslav Civil War of 1994. Its view of US power is more benevolent than the subsequent work by Hardt and Negri, *Multitude: War and Democracy in the Age of Empire* (New York, NY: Penguin, 2004).

12 See Frederick G. Whelan, "Democratic Theory and the Boundary Problem," *Nomos XXV: Liberal Democracy*, ed. J. R. Pennock and J. W. Chapman (New York, NY: New York University Press, 1983), 13–47; Robert Goodin, "Enfranchising All Affected Interests, and Its Alternatives," *Philosophy and Public Affairs* 35.1 (2007): 40–68.

13 Robert Dahl, *After the Revolution?: Authority in a Good Society* (New Haven, CT: Yale University Press, 1970), 60–1.

Two Liberalisms of Fear

John Gray

The root of liberal thinking is not in the love of freedom, nor in the hope of progress, but in fear—the fear of other human beings and of the injuries they do one another in wars and civil wars. A liberal project that seeks to diminish the fear that humans evoke in one another is open and provisional in its judgments as to the institutions that best moderate the irremovable risk of social and political violence. It does not imagine that any one regime is the only legitimate form of rule for all humankind, and it does not assess political regimes by the degree to which they conform to any doctrine of universal human rights or theory of justice. It rejects the view—which in the United States is treated as an axiom of political discourse—that democratic institutions are the only basis for legitimate government. It views democracy as only one among a range of legitimate regimes in the late modern world and does not subscribe to the Enlightenment hope—revived recently by Francis Fukuyama—that peoples everywhere will converge on democracy as a political ideal.

The original and best exemplar of this liberalism of fear is Thomas Hobbes. In Hobbes, the principal obstacle to human well being is war. Wars arising between practitioners of different religions are to be feared the most. They are the most destructive of the human good and generate a war of all against all in which no sovereign power exists to keep the peace.

Writing in a time of religious civil wars, Hobbes was clear that, aside from the human passion of vainglory or pride, the chief impediment to a *modus vivendi* was the claim to truth in matters of faith. On no account should the sovereign make or act upon any such claim. The sovereign does not hold to any worldview but seeks to craft terms of peaceful coexistence among the divergent worldviews that society harbors. Here the liberal project is not a plan for universal progress, but a search for peace. In this liberalism of fear, the

94

institutions of the state are not what is most terrifying. What is most to be feared is the condition of anarchy in which human life is ruled by the *summum malum*—death at the hands of one's fellows. A liberal state is one that aims to deliver its subjects from this evil. Today, there will be many who deny that such a project could embody liberal thought in any of its many varieties. Yet a reasonable argument can be made that *this* liberalism of fear is, in fact, liberalism in its most primordial form.

Such a liberalism of fear may seem to late moderns unambitious and timid, lacking in noble hopes for the species. For that very reason, it is the liberalism that speaks most cogently and urgently to us, that addresses the needs of a time whose ruling project is peaceful coexistence among diverse and potentially antagonistic communities and regimes. This Hobbesian liberalism of fear is inherently tolerant of diversity in polities and communities, because of its indifference to private belief. The authority of a Hobbesian state does not derive from its embodying any doctrine or creed, but only from its efficacy in promoting peace. In early modern times, this meant ruling without partisan regard to the religious beliefs of subjects. A Hobbesian state is not bound to attempt to disestablish or to privatize religious practice.

In a late modern context, the Hobbesian indifference to private belief has an application to ideological commitments. In our historical context, a Hobbesian state does not make allegiance to political authority conditional on subscription to any creed. A peace-making state can hope to command the allegiance of the religious and the irreligious, those who share Enlightenment hopes and those who do not. It can be accepted as legitimate by communities and cultural traditions that are not, and will never be, "liberal." The original liberalism of fear does not aim to subject the late modern world to democratic institutions. It recognizes a democratic regime as one among many devices, potential and actual, for containing and moderating conflict, but it denies that democracy has any universal authority.

Hobbes's liberalism of fear can be contrasted sharply with a second fearful liberalism—the anti-statist liberalism, grounded in theories of universal human rights or justice, which is the ruling orthodoxy of contemporary political philosophy. Nearly all liberal theory today is a program for limiting the state. Yet, in the conditions of late modern societies, anti-statist liberalism is bound to issue in a significant enhancement of the state's most purely repressive functions—without, however, significantly enhancing the security of the citizenry. Conversely, regimes that aim for peace and are not burdened by an agenda of anti-statism may be better able to assure their subjects security without enhancing the state's repressive role. The demonization of the state may have been unavoidable during the totalitarian period that spanned much of this century. As we near the century's end, it has become unreasonable.

This second liberalism of fear—the liberalism of Rawls, Dworkin, Nozick, Hayek, and many others—which is a liberalism of fear of the state, does not serve our needs in a time in which the state is a desperately fragile and often inefficacious institution. The state must be rehabilitated as an instrument of individual well being and the common good. We must not look to the institutions of the state for universal rights, strong communities, or moral regeneration. To do so risks some of the worst evils of the age. Neither should we regard it with such suspicion that we strive to limit it by foolish doctrines of minimum government. We must rehabilitate the state as a protective institution. This rehabilitation, Hobbesian liberalism, duly amended, may be able to achieve.

Hobbesian Liberalism vs. Liberal Imperialism

Hobbes's liberalism of fear rejects, as anachronistic and indefensible, the Enlightenment philosophy in which *we* are the *telos* of history. Perceiving the dilemmas of modernity from a standpoint near the beginning of the modern age as acutely as Weber and Nietzsche did towards its end, Hobbes remains an instructive critic of the conception of progress with which liberal thought came later to be identified. Hobbes's thought shares with that of other early modern, proto-Enlightenment thinkers, such as Spinoza, an underestimation of the cultural variability of human motives; lacks altogether the insight of Herder that individual well being requires participation in strong communities; and shares with later Enlightenment thinkers, such as Hume, the illusion that civilized human beings have every-where the same values.

Even so, unlike later liberal theory, Hobbes's thought is not committed, essentially and inescapably, to the "hubristic" and dangerous project of deploying the power of the state to promote a universal civilization. It sees the institutions of the state as indispensable—variable and alterable instruments for the achievement of security against the chief evils of human life. In this Hobbesian account, the state is not the embodiment of a civil religion or a philosophy of history, nor the vehicle of a project of world-transformation, nor a means of recovering a lost cultural unity, but rather an artifice whose purpose is peace.

Hobbesian liberalism rejects the other liberalism of fear—the dominant liberalism of our time, which responds to evidence of deep cultural differences in the relations of liberal democracies with nonliberal regimes and a fundamentalist reassertion of "Western values" and which understands the state as a vehicle for the defense of these threatened values. At present, liberal political philosophy in all its standard varieties is fundamentalist in style and apologetic in strategy. Its goal is a transcendental deduction of western institutions as the only legitimate form of government.

The political consensus, which conventional liberal political philosophy articulates, asserts the universal authority of liberal human rights, individualist ethical life, and (more often than not) free market capitalism. In the context of international relations, it is a late blossoming species of liberal imperialism. It is a triumphal reassertion of the western project at just the historical moment when non-Occidental peoples are demonstrating that westernization and modernization are not one and the same, but different and sometimes conflicting paths of development. In domestic political practice in the United States, this other liberalism of fear is a *project of return*—an attempt to recover "traditional values," forms of family life, of law, and of national sovereignty that belong to early rather than late modernity.

If the Hobbesian liberalism of fear can reasonably claim a universal root in the generic human evil of civil war, this latter-day liberalism of fear is evidently an historically highly specific phenomenon. Its aggressive affirmation of universality ties and dates it irrevocably to the loss of American ideological identity that has followed the Soviet collapse.

The fearful reality that the dominant contemporary liberalism screens from the perceptions of western societies is the polycentric diversity of the post-totalitarian world. In the late modern world all western ideologies are of declining global significance, and western institutions no longer function as the cutting edge of modernity. Indeed, for parts of the world—the societies of East Asia, for example—further westernization could mean a retreat from late modernity. The perception that this other liberalism of fear is meant to occlude is a perception of western decline.

If, in international relations, this other liberalism of fear is a reaction against the passing of western global hegemony, in domestic political life, it is an attempt to recover a national culture that has irretrievably vanished. That is the significance of the cultural preoccupation with relativism. The neoconservative discourse of "relativism" is not used to conduct a debate in moral philosophy.

"Relativism" signifies views of which neoconservatives disapprove in a dispute about American identity. This is a debate that has arisen with multiculturalism and the erosion of popular confidence in American exceptionalism. It is a local affair. The discourse of relativism is not a moment in the history of philosophy. It is an episode in the dissolution of American global hegemony.

The centrality and power in contemporary American political discourse and practice of this other liberalism of fear is a perilous dominance. No universalist political project can do without enemies. In an incorrigibly plural world, they are soon found. The imagined threat to "the West" emanating from Soviet Communism—itself pre-eminently an artifact of western Enlightenment ideology—has been swiftly supplanted, in the writings of Samuel Huntington and elsewhere, by a discourse of "civilizational conflict." Now, if it means anything, "civilizational conflict" means that cultural differences of themselves occasion war. Yet this is a dangerously unhistorical claim.

In the longer perspective of history, "multiculturalism" does not denote one moment in a local debate about American identity; it signifies the normal condition of humankind. Most polities of which there is historical record, and all empires, have been "multicultural," and the destruction of multicultural human settlements in our century—such as the destruction of the city of Alexandria by Nasserist nationalism—has typically been the work of decidedly modernist nation-building movements. Huntington's polemic against multi-culturalism in the United States is not a contribution to historical inquiry or to political theory, but rather a move in a campaign to recover an early modern culture of nationhood that is foredoomed by the conditions of late modernity.

In this climate of debate, it is unsurprising that longer historical perspectives are foreshortened and distorted. The diverse cultural traditions of Confucianism, Islam, and Christianity—which until quite recently had coexisted for long periods in the Ottoman Empire, the Hapsburg Empire, and the British Raj—are perceived as inherently rivalrous. The very existence of cultures that have not embraced westernization is perceived as a danger to peace, particularly if—like the present regime in mainland China—these cultures reject the universal authority of liberal rights. The existing reality in some East Asian contexts (such as Singapore, Malaysia, and Japan) of societies that have modernized without westernizing, that have matched or surpassed western levels of prosperity without importing an individualist culture of capitalism, and that have assured low levels of crime-related insecurity for their citizens without adopting a western culture of rights is comprehensively denied.

The most feared and repressed possibility is that these achievements were possible only because such countries have rejected or limited westernization. For if this possibility were allowed, the Enlightenment philosophy of history and the civil religion of American exceptionalism—in which the creation of wealth depends on institutions that embody a culture of individualism, progress, and rights—would be falsified. In domestic contexts, this other liberalism of fear is expressed in the poisonous politics of "family values," in the atavistic legalist reduction of all policy issues to questions in the arbitration of (supposedly) Lockean rights, and in the recuperation of an early modern understanding of national sovereignty. This liberalism supports "welfare reform," whose effect is social exclusion, and penal policies in which mass incarceration is adopted as a central institution of social control.

This other liberalism of fear cannot yield a modus vivendi of any kind in the late modern societies in which it has arisen. It is, on the contrary, an ideological rationale for social division and cultural warfare. The history of the abortion issue in the United States may be a marker for a future in which a legalist culture of unconditional rights becomes an arena of political conflict where compromise—and therefore politics, considered as an abatement of war—is impossible. Indeed, in its combustible fusion of a legalist culture of non-negotiable rights with a repressive culture of mass incarceration and radically exclusionary social policies, the new liberalism of fear is a recipe for low-intensity civil war.

Hobbes's Abstract Individualism and Anti-Political Liberalism

In our historical context, the Hobbesian liberalism of fear has many decisive advantages over the conventional liberal philosophies of the late modern period. Yet it cannot be adopted unamended. I will in the last section of this paper comment on the respects in which

Hobbes's thought requires most radical revision. Here I note, first, that Hobbes's thought belongs to the early modern period in its abstract individualism and its proto-Enlightenment project of deriving political obligation from a rational choice of individual advantage. No doubt it is immeasurably closer to political realities than most subsequent liberalisms, but its individualist philosophical anthropology is ill suited to thinking about how communities and cultures can coexist in peace. As the author of one of the great neglected twentieth-century classics of political thought, *Crowds and Power*, has observed in a different work:

> Hobbes explains everything through selfishness, and while knowing the crowd (he often mentions it) he really has nothing to say about it. My task, however, is to show how complex selfishness is: to show how what it controls does not belong to it, comes from other areas of human nature, the ones to which Hobbes is blind.[1]

Second, Hobbes's thought has in common with the dominant Rawlsian liberalism of our time the illusion that the principal impediment to peace is the rivalrous diversity of individual purposes. The banal Rawlsian pluralism of individual life-plans, each expressing a specific conception of the good, lacks the stark realism of Hobbes's insistence on the insatiability of human desires, but these very different liberalisms share in common a neglect of rivalrous cultural identities as a cause of social conflict and—in the worst case—war. Rawls is right in seeing the liberal problematic as the search for peaceful coexistence that issued from the Wars of Religion and the Reformation, but he is mistaken in supposing that, in late modern conditions, peace can be pursued by relegating worldviews, conceptions of the good, and cultural identities to the sphere of voluntary association. Liberal institutions in which divisive commitments are privatized are successful as devices for promoting peace only when the background moral culture of society is already individualist. Where it is not—as in most of the world—the search for terms of peace leads not to liberal civil society, but to various kinds of pluralist institutions.

Third, Hobbes's seeming hope that a form of rule can be constructed in which *politics* has been marginalized links him with that tradition of legalist utopianism that has had so paralyzing an effect on liberal thought in our own time. Commonly, Hobbes is criticized for his illiberal unconcern with the limits of state power, and his apparent approval of tyranny, and it is true that we who know, as he could not, the evils that go with totalitarian states cannot rest content with his account of the sovereign's powers. What is wrong with Hobbesian thought is not, however, its neglect of constitutional limitations on governments, but its attempt to render political life redundant—a project it shares with today's anti-political liberalisms. In our conditions, peace cannot be the construction of a sovereign, if indeed any such thing still exists in late modern contexts; it must be an artifact of political activity. This is not to say that a *modus vivendi* can be achieved in the late modern world only through democratic institutions. It means that in societies that already possess a highly developed tradition of political activity, peace cannot be secured by trying to suppress politics.

In arguing that Hobbes's thought has an application to the conditions of late modernity, I am not meaning to pass over those aspects of Hobbesian liberalism that belong with a superseded Enlightenment project. Hobbes's Cartesian understanding of political reasoning, the unyielding universalism and individualism of his philosophical outlook, together with his conception of political obligation as arising from a calculus of rational advantage, all tie his thought irrevocably to the Enlightenment project and cannot speak to us today. The aspect that does speak to us—that must inform the attempt to articulate a postliberal pluralism—aims to identify universal and generically human evils and understands political life as an enterprise of moderating and mitigating these evils. This aspect of Hobbes's thought is far removed from the unrestricted cultural relativism (such as Richard Rorty's) that animates most attempts at formulating a postmodern liberalism.

Prospects for a Postliberal, Postmodern Pluralism

Thinking about the future roles of the two liberalisms of fear begins with the recognition that there is no single trajectory of modernity on which diverse societies stand at earlier and later points. Our world contains pre-modern, early modern, late modern, and post-modern states.[2] In much of post-imperial Africa, in parts of post-communist Russia, and perhaps in some areas of China, there is nothing that resembles the institutions of a modern state. Economic and social life goes on, but in a context of near-anarchy where the protective functions of the state are lacking or are exercised by local military production centers.

The disappearance in many parts of the world of effective state institutions of any kind is one of the most important but least considered developments of the past decade. It represents an acceleration in the declining leverage of the modern state that has led prominent theorists of strategy to argue that along with the decline of the modern sovereign state, which was inaugurated with the treaty of Westphalia in 1648, we are now witnessing the disappearance of Clausewitzian war.[3] Considered as military conflict conducted between agents of sovereign states, Clausewitzian war appears to have been largely supplanted by intractable low-intensity conflicts in which the principal actors are not states and their agents, but political organizations, clans, and ethnic groups. Clausewitzian war has not disappeared, as the Falklands War and the Gulf War testify, but the ability of states or associations of states to direct organized violence has declined dramatically in many parts of the world. The control of war, taken in modern times to be the central constitutive power of sovereign states, has slipped from states' grasp.

Where this has happened, the result has been the emergence of something not far from a Hobbesian state of nature. At the same time, late modern societies are imbued by post-military cultures. It is hard to mobilize democratic publics in support of any interventionist policy that threatens to be risky, costly, and protracted. In these circumstances, the anarchic, pre-modern conditions of some post-communist countries may persist indefinitely. Alternatively, these countries may attempt to reinvent their imperial traditions—an option particularly attractive in Russia, which has never been a modern nation-state. There is no reason to think that states in such circumstances will be forced towards modernity in their political institutions.

The first signs of postmodern political institutions are most clearly observable in Europe. The institutions of the European Union are not the institutions of a modern state writ large. The EU is not, and will not become, a modern federal state. It is an association of nation states that have embarked on a common project of shedding much of the sovereignty that distinguished the modern, "Westphalian" state. This project embodies the wager that nineteenth-century balance-of-power relations between the Union's nation-states can be rendered redundant in the context of the EU's common institutions.

The wager this project entails is on the possibility of enduring and stable political institutions that do not presuppose a common political culture and are not legitimated by a unifying ideology. This is the postmodern dimension of the European project. It is the attempt to found political institutions whose cultural identities are not singular, comprehensive, or exclusive (after the fashion of nineteenth-century nationalism and twentieth-century *weltanschauung*-states), but complex, plural, and overlapping.

This is *not* the project of privatizing cultural identity in the realm of voluntary association that is advanced in the standard liberalisms of today. That project, in practice, can only entrench the dominant cultural identity of a generation or more ago. This project instead attempts to enable plural identities to find collective expression in overlapping political institutions. The institutions of the European Union constitute the single most convincing exemplar thus far of the postmodern project of founding political legitimacy not on a common national culture or on any universalist ideology, but on a common acceptance of cultural difference. In East Asia, the fascinating experiment that is underway in Singapore may amount to an exercise in postmodern state-building and the conditions of post-modernity may have been present for generations in Japan. There may be a future for postmodernity in East Asia by virtue of the fact that some of its diverse cultures have modernized very successfully without thereby accepting any Enlightenment ideology.

It is in this historical context that an amended Hobbesian liberalism of fear may be salient. The animating interest of European institutions, as they have developed over the past 30 years or so, is an interest in peaceful coexistence without loss of cultural diversity. This points to the first radical revision that is needed in the Hobbesian view—namely, an acknowledgment of the political relevance of the human need for strong and deep forms of common life. Hobbes's thought needs to be fertilized with the insights of Herder. The abridgment of Hobbesian individualism that this entails is plainly considerable and necessitates consideration of how participation in common cultural forms can find political expression.

The second large revision to the Hobbesian account is to provide for the permanent necessities of politics. Unlike later anti-political liberals, Hobbes never supposed that the institution of law could secure the conditions of peace. Such an unreasonable optimism about law was alien to the spirit of his thought and foreign to his experience of the fragility of legal orders. Yet, aside from his insistence on the necessity of unfettered judgment by the sovereign, there is little in Hobbes's thought that acknowledges the role of political practice in negotiating the terms of peace—a lack that derives from its debts to an early modern rationalist project of conferring Cartesian certainty on thinking about politics. Hobbes's thought must be modified to accommodate Machiavelli's perception that politics is an ineradicable activity in common life.

This postmodern Hobbesian view does not hold that a condition of postmodernity is the fate of all societies. That is only the illusive Enlightenment idea of a universal history refracted through a late modern prism, a kind of Enlightenment fideism. It may well be that only a few societies will ever enter a postmodern condition, and that, even for them, it may not be irreversible. We need to learn to think of a world, integrated by innumerable economic and technological linkages, which nevertheless contains societies, cultures, and polities that are set on radically divergent developmental paths.

The alteration in thinking that goes with such a postmodern perspective is substantial and requires adopting an instrumental, rather than doctrinal, view of state and market institutions. At the same time, it means accepting that the institutions that best serve human needs will vary quite radically over time and in differing cultural contexts. This is partly because the role served by social institutions is never entirely instrumental; it is also always expressive. The cultural forms that economic and political institutions express are changeable, diverse, and complicated; and the development of social or political institutions does not conform to any universal laws. Much in the application of this Hobbesian view will depend on highly contingent circumstances. In our present historical context, however, the postmodern view I have sketched will tend to undermine the vast claims made on behalf of the social institutions of law and the market and to focus on the indispensable place of the state and of the practice of politics among the conditions of a peaceful *modus vivendi*.[4]

Postmodern Politics: Searching for a Modus Vivendi

An amended Hobbesian liberalism repudiates the Enlightenment expectation that the world's peoples and cultures will converge in a universal civilization and accepts cultural difference to be a permanent feature of the human condition. It conceives political life as the search, never completed, for a *modus vivendi* in which the human goods of cultural diversity can be harvested, while the unavoidable evils arising from the conflict of evils are tempered and moderated. Among the diverse and changeable forms that such a *modus vivendi* can take, democratic institutions are only one; they have no special privileges of the sort conferred on them in recent versions of the Enlightenment project.

The dominant fearful liberalism of today is part of the problem, not the solution. By making the legitimacy of political institutions dependent on ephemeral and contested ideologies—hubristic theories of rights and discredited Enlightenment expectations of a universal civilization—it works to exclude all those who do not subscribe to an early modern worldview in which these beliefs were central. For the majority of humankind today, such beliefs are not credible. Like all western secular faiths, they have a declining leverage on human allegiance throughout the world. The coming century may be no better, or even worse, than the one that is ending, but it will be profoundly different in that its central conflicts will not be family arguments amongst western political faiths.

For the United States, there is no alternative to liberal democracy. Its traditions and present circumstances do not allow the luxury, or tragedy, of radical political experiment. It would be alien to the spirit of the present argument to engage in prescription. But there are clear implications of the argument I have developed: the legalist cult of unconditional rights must be moderated; the suspicion of the state, and of politics, with which the current liberalism of fear is imbued is intemperate; and the evangelical faith in the free market as the only acceptable mode of economic organization is a danger both to domestic social peace and to international order. America's present public philosophy and policies need some large revisions.

The present argument suggests that more weight must be given to political practice, less to the arbitration of rights; more emphasis given to collective choices, and less to free markets. The faith that law can supplant the murky compromises of politics, that societies that lack a moral consensus can cohere through the practice of rights, that the legitimacy of a democratic state must depend on its embodying universal principles—these beliefs are poor guides to the world in which Americans, along with the rest of humankind, must henceforth live. Clearing away the debris of today's fearful liberalism may contribute modestly to the large changes in public philosophy and public policy that will be unavoidable in the United States in the coming years.

(Spring 2000, 2.1)

Notes

1. Elias Canetti, *The Human Province* (London, England: Picador, 1986) 115–6.

2. On this point, see Robert Cooper, *The Post-Modern State and the World Order* (London, England: Demos, 1996).

3. See Martin van Craveld, *On Future War* (London, England and Washington, DC: Brassey's, 1991).

4. I have considered what such a shift in our evaluation of state and market institutions might mean, primarily in the context of Britain today, in my monograph *After Social Democracy* (London, England: Demos, 1996) republished in my book *Endgames: Questions in Late Modern Political Thought* (Cambridge, MA: Polity, 1997).

Civil Society and Democracy
A Conversation with Michael Walzer

Talbot Brewer

Talbot Brewer (TB): In your early book, *Obligations*, you argue that the ideal of citizenship portrays our highest political possibility, the possibility of obeying only laws of our own making. You note, however, that this ideal is often invoked as if it were already realized, and then it becomes the worst sort of ideological mystification. Still you find something redeeming in this ideology. As you put it, "Ideology is the social element in which ideals survive, and this may well be true even when the ideology is perfectly hypocritical. For if hypocrisy is the tribute that vice pays to virtue, then it serves at least to sustain the social recognition of virtue." What sort of political potency do you think the ideal of citizens as self-rulers has today?

Michael Walzer (MW): It's not so easy to talk about those ideals and to talk about citizenship in a country where, in the last presidential election, less than half the people bothered to vote, and where rates of political participation in state and local and municipal elections run even lower. The old democratic vision, the Rousseauian vision, of a society of active citizens where people "fly" to the assemblies, where as Rousseau says, they derive a larger proportion of their happiness from their public commitments and activities than from any private concerns—that vision of democratic self-rule just doesn't seem evocative now in an American setting.

And maybe it's worth speculating on the different meanings of "democracy" in a society that is also as committed as we are to liberal and individualistic values and to the pursuit of happiness or the development of private life. It may be that American citizenship is going to involve a fairly low scale of routine political activity interrupted occasionally by upsurges of popular feeling like the civil rights movement of the '60s, and that we can't hope within a liberal and individualistic environment to sustain the upsurges, so the aim should be to keep the routine engagement as high as you can and then to cultivate the opportunities for participatory eruptions on specific issues when those seem urgently necessary or simply properly motivated.

Some people thought that environmentalism and feminism, the new social movements of the '70s and '80s, would produce a sharp increase in participation of the kind we saw in the '60s and the '30s. So far they haven't, but they have sustained themselves above the routine of citizen engagement and so they have also sustained the possibility of a larger-scale engagement on specific sets of issues. But the Rousseauian ideal, I think, is lost to us and I'm not sure that an effort to reproduce it—that is, to get 85 percent of the people to "fly" to the assemblies and to vote—is at all the right thing to do.

When you get sudden increases in participation that don't arise out of new organizations and movements, then you have a dangerous influx of—I'm not sure what the right word is—of uneducated voters. The role of parties, movements, and the associations of civil society is to educate and to produce competent citizens. If you don't have organizations of that sort and you get an upsurge of new people who haven't voted before, who haven't participated before, the outcomes are more likely to be ugly than democratically beneficial. I think, for example, of the Nazi vote in the early '30s as the product of lots of new voters, people who hadn't voted before and hadn't worked through the union movement and the Social Democratic party or the Catholic parties, but were raw and open to demagogic appeals. The best protection against demagogy in democratic life is associational richness, and if you're lacking that, then it's not clear to me that your goal should be very high levels of participation.

TB: Perhaps our ideal of citizenship is different from Rousseau's ideal—more like citizen as recipient of benefits from the state—and the aspiration to self-rule has dropped out of our picture of what the status of citizen involves. Or, perhaps the public holds on to the aspiration to self-rule, but finds current political practices and structures resistant to their influence or will in a politically de-energizing way. It sounds as if you're favoring the first diagnosis.

MW: I think both are true, which isn't a very bold statement. Certainly the sense of citizenship as entitlement is now very powerful in American life. But the fact is that we still have a fairly large-scale engagement in the associations of civil society and in various kinds of single-issue political movements and organizations that come out of civil society, right now many of them on the right—anti-abortion, pro-capital punishment, prayer in the schools. These are issues around which people do mobilize, and even someone who disagrees with their goals has to recognize that those mobilizations are acts of engagement. So, the question is: Why isn't there more citizen engagement of that sort across the political spectrum, and particularly—where it used to be so strong—on the left?

The standard response is the one you gave: Well, nobody is giving them something to vote for. That may be true, but it can't be the whole story because there are, in fact, organizers out there, some of them left over from the '60s, some of them newly mobilized by the revivalist leadership of the AFL-CIO; there are organizers in the field, and they are encountering a degree of resistance among people who "objectively"—as we used to say—need to organize themselves. Why that is so is not at all clear to me.

TB: Hasn't the mobility of capital and the globalization of the economy objectively reduced the bargaining power of labor workers in this country to a degree where there may be some rational basis for being suspicious of organization as a strategy? Could that be part of an account of demobilization on the left?

MW: Economists disagree fairly radically about the impact of globalization, and the extent to which it undermines sovereignty and the ability of a single government to shape its own economy. Of course, I would like to believe those economists who say that it's still possible for a political movement in a country as powerful as the United States to shape the economy significantly. I hope they're right. But the most successful strike in the last couple of years was a strike in a non-globalizable industry, that is, UPS. They can't deliver packages in Mexico City. They've got to deliver them in New York. So that was an industry that couldn't threaten to leave, and it did produce the biggest union victory in recent years. Whereas in industries that are more mobile and more globally organized, unions have so far been less successful.

Still, a stronger AFL-CIO would have produced a different NAFTA Treaty, and one which would have served the interests of both the American workers and Mexican workers better than the actual Treaty. So I'm not sure the rationale is gone, but something is gone. I think the factors are, in part, historical and cultural. The old working class was culturally distinct—perhaps less so in the United States than in Europe but here too—in its language, in its dress, in the cohesiveness of its neighborhoods, in the patterns of self-help, in the religious culture. There was a working class world, and it was the often-unacknowledged foundation of a great deal of political activity. That seems to have disintegrated with the impact of mass culture, of a certain degree of affluence, of geographic even more than social mobility.

TB: In your book, *On Toleration*, you lament the fact that the poorest and politically weakest members of our polity have, as you say, "come to be spoken for and also exploited by a growing company of racial and religious demagogues and tin-horn charismatics." I wonder if you could say a bit more about how this has come to be, and what the prospects for improvement might be.

MW: I probably wrote those lines in the aftermath of the so-called Million Man March organized by Farrakhan and the Nation of Islam. Since I grew up politically in part with the civil rights movement in this country, and went South a number of times to write about it in 1960, I have a vision of what the mobilization of Americans committed to racial justice ought to be like—in part because I have a sense of what it was like. Now, what caused the collapse of the civil rights movement in the '60s? Some people on the right say its success caused its collapse. It achieved much of what it aimed for and so it slowly disappeared, which is the right thing for political movements to do after they have achieved most of what they aimed for. There is a grain of truth, but only a grain of truth, in that. The more visible legal forms of discrimination were eliminated from American life, and we see the beginnings of a black middle class of a different kind than existed before. But in fundamental ways the movement didn't achieve what it aimed for. It didn't produce the mobilization among black Americans that it aimed for, or it didn't sustain that mobilization. It didn't produce the multiplicity of organizations that were a feature of working class mobilization in the nineteenth century.

I think there was a clear aim of sustaining a whole organizational structure alongside the churches out of which many of the civil rights leaders came. They wanted better schools, they wanted newspapers of their own, they wanted magazines, they wanted drama societies, they wanted summer camps, they wanted athletic associations—the same kind of richness that social democracy produced for the European working class. They wanted all of that for black Americans and didn't achieve it. And the result was an increasingly radical polarization among black Americans between those who made it into the new middle class, and the larger mass, especially of urban blacks, and the emergence of new patterns of alienation from whites, which only looked like they were being overcome in the '60s movements.

So it's in that context—it's in the context of the decline of cities; of black political leaders taking over cities at the depth of their decline, so that they were without the resources that office is supposed to bring and did bring to successive generations of ethnic immigrant politicians; the rise in crime; the drug culture; the weakening of the hold of the black churches in many communities—all this produced the situation that I described in the quotation with which you began. And I thought that there was an obligation on the part of black intellectuals to talk about what had happened, to acknowledge the failures, to speak out against some of the visible consequences of those failures, like Farrakhan, and to search for ways of redeeming the '60s vision.

TB: At the beginning of *On Toleration*, you write that toleration is "the work of democratic citizens." But on completing the book, it seemed to me at least that you were calling for something more demanding than toleration. You believe that we ought to use political means self-consciously to reinvigorate a diverse civil society. This involves not merely toleration of diverse political voices but an active effort to promote associational membership, ethnic and religious affiliation, unions, neighborhood groups, youth centers, charter schools, community arts, and so forth—many of the things that you just named as original goals of the civil rights movement. I can imagine some critics objecting that this would represent a deep strain on the public political culture, not to mention an abandonment of the liberal ideal of neutrality. What do you think of such worries?

MW: Let's begin with the worry that led to this argument before we get to the worries produced by the argument. Toleration is supposed to be the solution to a problem posed by seemingly irreconcilable differences—religious, cultural, ethnic, whatever. So the original structure of the argument is: "difference requires toleration." I have, so to speak, been born into a highly successful regime of toleration, within which difference has begun to be blurred, and the argument now takes not the form "difference requires toleration" but "toleration requires difference." If you're to have a liberal regime of toleration, there have to be diverse groups—with significantly different conceptions of the world, the good life and the good society—to be tolerated. If the regime of toleration is so bland that it blurs all the differences, or if difference comes to name individual idiosyncrasy rather than group culture, then there's nothing to tolerate.

I think the ideal of a liberal regime of toleration, one that makes it possible to live with significant differences and in a single political community, is very attractive. And looking at the decline of difference, and the decline of the organizations—cultural and religious—that have sustained it, I'm led to the proposal that you just described: Maybe we need now consciously to support difference, and to support the organizations that sustain it.

Take, for example, the argument of Robert Putnam's very famous article—every American social scientist dreams of writing an article that becomes that famous—"Bowling Alone," a description of associational life in the United States. Many of its details are disputed quite fiercely, and it's possible he got some things wrong. But it's a description of associational life accompanied by a series of graphs, and all the graphs have the same straight line moving down from left to right on the page. There are something like 16 graphs and they all look the same. They describe membership in unions, attendance at meetings of parent-teacher associations, participation in the old fraternal organizations—Kiwanis, Lions, Elks, and those kinds of groups—reading a daily newspaper, voting; and it's the same line. A study of that sort simply documents the anxiety that I was feeling that the kind of associational life that sustains cultural difference and gives it potency is in decline. Now, exactly how radical a decline we can argue about, but it's in decline.

It seemed to me that there were already some precedents for remedies. The public subsidy of the civil/social realm, the public subsidy of associational life, including religious life, in the United States (despite the so-called wall between church and state) is already very well advanced. It provides, in fact, a model for what we should be doing, but doing more extensively and more self-consciously, because there is so much denial in the United States, so much pretending.

When the Republicans came to power in 1994 and started cutting the welfare budget, the loudest screams of protests went up from the religious organizations—the Catholic charities, the Jewish federations, and so on—and *The New York Times* ran an extraordinary article with graphs showing the portion of the budget of Catholic charities and of Jewish and Lutheran charities that came from tax money, and the percentages were very high. I think close to 60 percent of the money Catholic charities spend is tax money, and it comes in all kinds of ways. For example, we have a voucher plan for nursing homes. We've rejected vouchers so far for parochial schools, but we have vouchers for parochial nursing homes. My wife's mother is in a Jewish nursing home near Trenton. The budget must be 60 percent tax money because people bring in Medicare benefits, and Medicare entitlement is a voucher. You can bring it to a Jewish or a Catholic or a Lutheran nursing home, and it's perfectly all right that a rabbi comes on Saturday, and they celebrate the Jewish holidays, and there's a kosher kitchen. The tax money flows in. I think it does mean you couldn't turn away a non-Jewish applicant, but you don't get many non-Jewish applicants for a nursing home of that kind. So in effect, we are sponsoring, with federal money, religious welfare organizations.

Now, if you look closely, you will immediately see that the communities that get the most federal money are the best organized, already the strongest politically in the United States. Black Baptists get some federal money and run some programs, but they get a lot less than white Lutherans, say, because they are politically weaker and have fewer trained professionals who know how to get at the available money. So if you want a vibrant associational life, and one that sustains cultural difference—that means it also has to provide life-cycle services, because that's the crucial way that you sustain cultural difference, from day care centers to nursing homes. They have to be provided in a universal fashion for everybody. But there also has to be a capacity within civil society to provide them in a more particular way. And this has to be subsidized. In a society where all of the communities are dispersed and lack the coercive power to tax—and they also lack, because of their dispersion, the forms of social pressure that once existed within these communities—they have to be helped, and I don't see anything wrong with helping them.

TB: I want to talk in general terms about the liberal-communitarian debate in which you've been a key figure for many years. One way to characterize the wellspring of this controversy is as a conflict of intuitions about what is most to be feared. The primary fear of communitarians seems to be that we might lose our capacity for worthy and life-animating convictions in a swamp of consumerism, careerism, television addiction, etc. The primary liberal fear seems to be that our life-animating convictions might be so thoroughly at odds with those of others, and have such a strong grip on us, that we'll be unable to sustain any common life at all, or to find any common ground for political decisions. If we view the debate in this way, it does alter what some have taken to be its fixed points, since it portrays the communitarians as rebels against an increasingly wide-

ly-shared but debased common culture, rather than as champions of a common culture, and it portrays liberals as would-be forgers of a not-yet-established political community, even though this would be a very thin one.

You seem to understand both of these fears and to have an interest in both of these projects. I have a nest of questions here. Do you think that the liberal/communitarian categorizations are useful? Where would you locate yourself in the context of these debates?

MW: I'm sympathetic to both of these anxieties, and I feel them differently in different times and places. The issue, exactly the way you posed it, was best expressed for me by an Israeli friend at a conference in Jerusalem, who said to an American communitarian political theorist (not me but a friend): "For you community is a dream; for us it is a trauma." Living in Israel with ultra-orthodox political parties—not just religious communities but politically mobilized religious communities—I think the vision that you attributed to liberals, the fear of the loss of any kind common culture, is very powerful. And there's another fear that liberals also express, which is also justified, that communities of that kind (I've just spent six months in Jerusalem, so I have a very vivid conception of a mobilized ultra-orthodox hard-core fundamentalist community) are not only a threat to the unity or the civic culture of the country; they are also oppressive to the weakest of their own members, and above all to women. So, many liberal critics of communitarianism are simply supporters of the individual rights that these communities trample on. And increasingly feminist critics of communitarianism are, so to speak, driven to where perhaps they didn't want to be—that is, to a liberal politics—in order to defend women who have no chance to defend themselves in these communities. So those fears are very real.

One of the questions that any communitarian has to address, and many of them don't, is the question: "At what point do you call for state intervention to protect individual rights?" It's a small version of the larger question of intervention in international society, and I would not want to turn away from that question. I think that at a minimum—maybe we should not stay at the minimum, but at a minimum—you've got to preserve the right of exit from these communities. I'm not exactly sure how to do that, but there has to be a way of getting out.

TB: Would you say further that the way of getting out has to be relatively palatable or not very costly? I take it you don't think it's sufficient for apostasy not to be a crime.

MW: No, that's not sufficient. Since leaving these communities commonly means a complete break with family and friends, you can't make it costless. It'll always be costly, but you have to make sure that there are no civil penalties, no disabilities, no discrimination after the fact of leaving—in all those ways you've got to protect the people who break away.

Now the harder questions—we've so far avoided these—are the questions of schools. You can protect people who leave, but those are going to be grown-ups or at least adolescents. But what about children? There are some of these communities that teach the boys how to pray and something of the religious culture, but teach the girls nothing at all. So what do you do? Do you refuse to pay for the schools? Do you insist on regulating the schools? Do you enforce a certain curriculum? You can prescribe a curriculum, but if you don't go in and teach it, it will be taught with a nod and a wink.

In the Israeli case, the religious schools do not teach secular history. They don't teach anything about democratic government, although these kids are going to grow up to vote. They are taught nothing about democratic values or the right of opposition. That's where the hardest questions arise, it seems to me, in the degree of control over cultural reproduction that the state is going to exercise, or parents are going to exercise.

TB: This issue is addressed in the Supreme Court case *Wisconsin v. Yoder*, where Justice Burger argues that Amish children ought to be exempted from certain mandatory school requirements, in part because of the distinctiveness of the Amish belief system and the presence in the public schools of an "hydraulic pressure towards conformity" with an alien mass culture. Increasingly, it seems, this is becoming not merely an Amish problem but a general problem: mass culture has a grip on the socialization of our children that significantly infringes on the capacities of parents to shape their children's conception of the good.

MW: I'm sympathetic to that Supreme Court decision. I think that was an example of judicial wisdom, though possibly not of principle. It may be that they effected a compromise, which is not what courts are supposed to do, on the Dworkin model that distinguishes what courts do from what the legislatures do. But it was a wise decision. One of the things that made it possible is the general Amish withdrawal from political life. It's much safer to accept the exemption in the case of the Amish because these children are not going to vote in our elections. They're not going to determine, along with our children, the general fate of the country. If they were, we might be a little more insistent on shaping their education and making sure that they know at least some of the things that we think citizens ought to know.

Now, the general weakness of American cultural communities is partly a consequence of liberal culture, and of social and geographic mobility, and of the nature of immigrant communities cut off from the territorial base that turns out to be very important in sustaining a common culture. The weaknesses of these communities are, I think, a peculiar feature of American life. It's not a universal feature. It's a particular problem, it seems to me, of immigrant societies and of large-scale states spread across vast distances. This gives rise to the communitarian anxiety about the loss of cultural particularity and the thinness of the common culture.

What young people educated in this world of mass culture, commercial culture—what they're going to be like is unclear to me. I think that the short-term impacts are probably exaggerated. We have good reason to believe in the capacity of families to sustain religious and other particularist cultures over very long periods of time, without the support or even against the pressure of mass media and commercialism. So I just don't know how great the danger is.

But what we see is weakness in cultural communities, high levels of intermarriage, low levels of participation in the core activities of the communities. You may know John Higham's image of the ethnic communities in the United States as having a core and kind of spreading periphy. The core struggles to hold the periphery. The periphery rides free on the work of the core. The core will often sustain, for example, religious services that people on the periphery will use at birth and death and maybe once or twice in between; they count on the core to provide those services, but they're not willing to pay for them. Participation in the core seems to be less than it used to be. More and more people live on the periphery, and the peripheries are spread wide and they overlap with the peripheries from other cores. And there's general confusion about identity.

All that leads me to look for some sort of remedy in the strengthening of associational life—and because of the free-rider problem, in subsidizing the cores. But exactly how great the danger is, and what's really happening out on the peripheries, where the peripheries overlap, I don't know.

TB: You've used the phrase "the post-modern self " as a place-holder for whatever's happening on the peripheries. And this idea of free ridership surfaces in your discussion of the rise of post-modern selves. You argue that it can be fulfilling for isolated individuals to pick and choose amongst elements of cultures that aren't their own, incorporating bits of cultures into a cosmopolitan identity, but that cosmopolitanism can only be vibrant where it is free riding. That is, the elements that the cosmopolitan self picks out of traditional cultures would be pallid if the cores weren't holding. So universal cosmopolitanism is not nearly as attractive as isolated cases of cosmopolitanism.

MW: Right. I was once involved in a public debate with a strong defender of cosmopolitanism, who described his own life. He was a cosmopolitan intellectual, born in one place, educated in another, now living in a third, and continuing to visit the three places and celebrating his peripheral engagement in all three—and, it seemed to me, forgetting that his peripheral engagement in all three was dependent, was parasitic, on other people sitting still in each. He could not enjoy his cosmopolitanism without the parochialism of some other people. There's a lot that is very attractive in cosmopolitan intellectual life, but I find it less attractive when it doesn't acknowledge the value of the particularisms that make it possible.

TB: So when it celebrates itself as an exemplar of autonomy and denigrates embedded-ness in traditional ways of life as instances of failure to be autonomous or something of that sort, then this is when you find it unpalatable?

MW: Right. I become most communitarian in the face of that version of cosmopolitanism.

(Spring 2000, 2.1)

II.
Knowledge and Technology

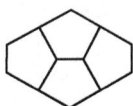

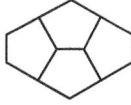

On Not Being There
The Data-Driven Body at Work and at Play

Rebecca Lemov

The protagonist of William Gibson's 2014 science-fiction novel *The Peripheral*, Flynne Fisher, works remotely in a way that lends a new and fuller sense to that phrase. The novel features a double future: One set of characters inhabits the near future, ten to fifteen years from the present, while another lives seventy years on, after a breakdown of the climate and multiple other systems that has apocalyptically altered human and technological conditions around the world.

In that "further future,"[1] only 20 percent of the Earth's human population has survived. Each of these fortunate few is well off and able to live a life transformed by healing nano-bots, somaticized e-mail (which delivers messages and calls to the roof of the user's mouth), quantum computing, and clean energy. For their amusement and profit, certain "hobbyists" in this future have the Borgesian option of cultivating an alternative path in history—it's called "opening up a stub"—and mining it for information as well as labor.

Flynne, the remote worker, lives on one of those paths. A young woman from the American Southeast, possibly Appalachia or the Ozarks, she favors cutoff jeans and resides in a trailer, eking out a living as a for-hire sub playing video games for wealthy aficionados. Recruited by a mysterious entity that is beta-testing drones that are doing "security" in a murky skyscraper in an unnamed city, she thinks at first that she has been taken on to play a kind of video game in simulated reality. As it turns out, she has been employed to work in the future as an "information flow"—low-wage work, though the pay translates to a very high level of remuneration in the place and time in which she lives.

What is of particular interest is the fate of Flynne's body. Before she goes to work she must tend to its basic needs (nutrition and elimination), because during her shift it will effectively be "vacant." Lying on a bed with a special data-transmitting helmet attached to her head, she will be elsewhere, inhabiting an ambulatory robot carapace—a "peripheral"—built out of bio-flesh that can receive her consciousness.

Bodies in this data-driven economic backwater of a future world economy are abandoned for long stretches of time—disposable, cheapened, eerily vacant in the temporary absence of "someone at the helm." Meanwhile, fleets of built bodies, grown from human DNA, await habitation.

Alex Rivera explores similar territory in his Mexican sci-fi film *The Sleep Dealer* (2008), set in a future world after a wall erected on the US-Mexican border has successfully blocked migrants from entering the United States. Digital networks allow people to connect to strangers all over the world, fostering fantasies of physical and emotional connection. At the same time, low-income would-be migrant workers in Tijuana and elsewhere can opt to do remote work by controlling robots building a skyscraper in a faraway city, locking their bodies into devices that transmit their labor to the site. In tank-like warehouses, lined up in rows of stalls, they "jack in" by connecting data-transmitting cables to nodes implanted in their arms and backs. Their bodies are in Mexico, but their work is in New York or San Francisco, and while they are plugged in and wearing their remote-viewing spectacles, their limbs move like the appendages of ghostly underwater creatures. Their life force drained by the taxing labor, these "sleep dealers" end up as human discards.

Flickering In and Out

What is surprising about these sci-fi conceits, from "transitioning" in *The Peripheral* to "jacking in" in *The Sleep Dealer*, is how familiar they seem, or at least how closely they reflect certain aspects of contemporary reality. Almost daily, we encounter people who are there but not there, flickering in and out of what we think of as presence. A growing body of research explores the question of how users interact with their gadgets and media outlets, and how in turn these interactions transform social relationships. The defining feature of this heavily mediated reality is our presence "elsewhere," a removal of at least part of our conscious awareness from wherever our bodies happen to be. As MIT psychologist Sherry Turkle has shown in pioneering work that extends from *The Second Self* (1984) to *Alone Together* (2012), the social ramifications of these new disembodied (or semi-disembodied) arrangements are radical. They introduce a "new kind of intimacy with machines," a "special relationship" in the space beyond the screen, and a withering away of once-central, physically mediated social bonds. Turkle's focus, and the focus of much literature on video-game playing and online behavior, is on these engrossing relationships between humans (particularly children) and computers, the social fallout of those relationships, and the resulting effects on self-formation, as hauntingly described in an early work by Turkle on "computer holding power":

> The [thirteen-year-old] girl is hunched over the console. When the tension momentarily lets up, she looks up and says, "I hate this game." And when the game is over she wrings her hands, complaining that her fingers hurt. For all of this, she plays every day "to keep up my strength." She neither claims nor manifests enjoyment in any simple sense. One is inclined to say she is more "possessed" by the game than playing it.[2]

The young teens Turkle watched playing Asteroids and Space Invaders are now in their mid-forties, and the dynamic of absorption, tension, possession, and disappearance is, of course, no longer confined to games. Much discussion of data-gathering technologies in daily domains focuses on their inescapability, as Tom McCarthy recently pointed out: "Every website that you visit, each keystroke and click-through are archived: even if you've hit delete or empty trash it's still there, lodged within some data fold or enclave, some occluded-yet-retrievable avenue of circuitry."[3]

Self-Knowledge Through Numbers

But seemingly undaunted by the extent to which we are now routinely subjected to the data gathering of others, many people are now driven to accumulate endless quantities of data about themselves, their bodies, their activities, their moods, even their thoughts and reveries. The "most connected human on earth," Chris Dancy, a former information technology specialist who took to gathering data about himself after being laid off from his job, bills himself as a "Data Exhaust Cartographer," "The Versace of Silicon Valley," and "Cyborg."[4] He bedecks his body with myriad wearables and promotes himself as the locus of up to 700 devices or online services that collect, crunch, save, and collate the data he generates. The metrics he tracks include pulse, REM sleep, skin temperature, and mood, among others. Perhaps not surprisingly, all of this self-tracking eventually led Dancy to a crisis of alienation. He became increasingly aware that his intense connection was also a form of disconnection: "I was coming slightly unhinged with the amount of information I had about myself. It started to make me feel slightly detached from reality." As a result, he says, he was "almost waterboarded with awareness. It's one thing to Google yourself. It's another to Google…your life. I could see too much."[5]

Despite his discomfort, Dancy seems unable to disconnect, unhook, or go offline. He is not alone. The focus of much recent interest in the entrance of tracking technology, counting devices, and calculation strategies into the domain of self-understanding is the Quantified Self (QS) movement. Founded in 2007 through the efforts of Kevin Kelly, then of *Wired* magazine, and Gary Wolf, a Bay Area writer, the movement brought together self-trackers ranging from the ardent to the merely curious. Under the banner of "self-knowledge through numbers"—those numbers gathered through biometrics, sociometrics, and psychometrics—enthusiasts combine platforms and tools to find new ways of gathering data and teasing out correlations. "Once you know the facts, you can live by them" is another guiding principle of the movement, and QS-ers continue to form groups across the United States and in thirty other countries, meeting weekly to share results. During the week of March 15, 2015, for example, groups came together in London, Washington, St. Louis, Denton, Texas, and Thessaloniki, Greece. Typically, such gatherings report on their tracking of a range of phenomena from the mundane (cups of coffee drunk per day, pulse rate, sleep hours) to the more esoteric ("spiritual well-being," scores on personality tests or a "narcissism index," or a repository of "all the ideas I've had since 1984") via devices that might be attached to the wrist (Fitbit), the lower back (UpRight), the chest (Spire), or eating utensils (HAPIfork), if not stowed away in one's pockets (as smartphone apps).

The movement marked its arrival in the cultural mainstream with the publication in 2010 of Wolf's manifesto, "The Data-Driven Life," in the *New York Times Magazine*. His fascination with the obsessively self-regarding project came through most clearly in his example of the tracker who had kept all of his ideas for the past several decades:

> Mark Carranza—[who] makes his living with computers—has been keeping a detailed, searchable archive of all the ideas he has had since he was 21. That was in 1984. I realize that this seems impossible. But I have seen his archive, with its million plus entries, and observed him using it.... Most thoughts are tagged with date, time, and location. What for other people is an inchoate flow of mental life is broken up into elements and cross-referenced.[6]

Wolf went on to describe how numbers inexorably enter the domain of the personal, insisting that no place should be considered sacrosanct or beyond the probing sensors of quantification.

Wolf was so surprised, he later told me, by the contempt and mockery he and his fellow self-trackers came in for after the article appeared that he almost came to regret writing it. Much of the online comment focused on the atrophied selves and dehumanizing effects seemingly produced by the self-tracking enterprise: "These unfortunate people spend so much time with computers they have begun thinking about their own person as a machine," wrote one reader. Another comment was even more barbed: "This tracking seems like taking self-centeredness to the nth degree. It is basically OCD [obsessive-compulsive disorder] behavior with a fancy title. How about 'tracking outward,' seeing how much time we spend on being with and helping others? Perhaps that is the secret to a longer, healthier life."

Those and other critics clearly saw the self-tracking obsession as navel-gazing, inward-turning, computer-oriented geek behavior, typical of those who have lost contact with the external world, with other human beings, and with "what matters," in their eagerness to render the world knowable, computable. At stake, it seems, is nothing less than the transformation or deformation of the "human." Writing in the monthly magazine *Prospect*, literature scholar and psychoanalyst Josh Cohen raised the pertinent question:

> Sifting through the talks, blog posts, and articles daily uploaded by Quantified Self disciples, you soon become aware of an anxious insistence on numbers as a means rather than an end. All this data is meant to spur us to love ourselves better and run our lives more efficiently. And yet it's hard not to hear, lurking in this promise of self-possession, the threat of numbers dispossessing us, of becoming a feverish addiction we can't kick. Can even the most adept multi-tasker really live the life they're simultaneously tracking?[7]

Other critics see the QS movement as part of information technology's more widespread induction of people into "a perpetual state of shallow performativity."[8]

What is neglected or bracketed in both the criticism and the celebration of self-tracking is the curious status of the body that serves as the passively patient platform for a self's "remote" activity or as the hooked-up object of endless measurement and observation—or indeed as both. Critics and enthusiasts of this strange reality both neglect the peculiar Möbius-strip form taken by the body as the increasingly phantom-like self flickers in and out of its confines. The status of the body that holds these devices, the body as platform—the body that is vacated—is curiously invisible.

Clickworkers, Gold Farmers, Porn Zappers

Where the body *can* be seen, I believe, is in the menial, low-wage, data-driven labor that is created at the downtrodden edges of expanding economies where virtual domains meet brick-and-mortar enterprises. One clear picture of the simultaneously abandoned and surveilled body emerges in research on the most menial work: collective labor markets harnessing human computing abilities. "Clickwork" is the mass labor of many hands on many keyboards, their collective output aggregated by means of Internet tools such as Amazon Mechanical Turk. Through AMT, individuals and businesses (known as Requesters) can crowdsource complex tasks that computer intelligence is currently unequipped to complete.

Amazon and other companies cannot afford to regulate this labor through traditional means; instead, administrators filter it through "light" automated management rather than top-down, heavy-handed control. Microwork ethnographer Lilly Irani describes how, for example, management of a work force of 10,000 to 60,000 for a particular project can never affordably be handled by means of Foucauldian "disciplinary" techniques, which carefully mold individual workers physically and mentally for their tasks. Rather, management must operate automatically, with a light touch: Instead of using surveillance to assess performance, "requesters sort desirable workers through faint signals of mouse clicks, text typed, and other digital traces read closely as potential indicators."[9] Most often, workers work alone at home on their own computers.

Repetitive work in the virtual sphere, in addition to being isolating, often necessitates less attention to bodily postures and needs, and may promote ongoing abuse of the body by motivating the worker to conform to algorithmically defined productivity goals that affect the body at its performance limits. Two examples are China-based World of Warcraft "gold farmers" and content moderators in the Philippines who zap porn and disturbing images from social media sites for cash.

Many of them based in suburban Manila in former elementary schools and other unlikely sites, the content moderators perform the unsavory job of repeatedly adjudicating whether images posted to Twitter feeds, Facebook pages, or other social networking sites are sufficiently offensive to be eliminated from view. Moderators at PCs sit at long tables for hours, an "army of workers employed to soak up the worst of humanity in order to protect the rest of us." By some estimates, the content-moderating army is 100,000 strong, twice the size of Google's labor pool, and many of its members have college degrees. Such workers suffer both physical pain and psychological distress. Jane Stevenson, of the British organization Workplace Wellbeing, which supports traumatized workers in high-pressure digital jobs, says that even after a worker has quit such a job, he or she may continue to be haunted by disturbing images. Looking for hours at YouTube videos of unspeakable abuse, many become paranoid and uneasy about leaving their children with sitters.[10]

In a profile of other potentially abusive digital-work environments, technology writer Julian Dibbell emphasizes their "surreal" quality.[11] One such workplace is that of Chinese "gold farmers," who participate in multiplayer online role-playing games, known as MMOs. In these games, which can involve thousands of participants, players advance by earning extra powers and levels of play not only through hard hours at the keyboard but also (particularly among Europeans and Americans who can pay real money for virtual gold or game goods) by buying them online. In the early years of MMOs, these transactions took place on eBay, but now there are "high-volume online specialty sites like the virtual-money superstores IGE, BroGame, and Massive Online Gaming Sales—multimillion-dollar businesses [that] offer one-stop, one-click shopping and instant delivery of in-game cash." Gold farmers work shifts in "sweatshops," advancing through MMOs so that richer players can jump effortlessly to higher levels. Such digital toil is not so different from that of Chinese laborers who work long hours to produce cheap real-world products for the global market. Yet the alienation of the body is perhaps more extreme because it is more unaccounted for. Dibbell describes the common condition of such laborers, exemplified by the routine of one particular gold farmer:

> Consider, for example, a typical interlude in the workday of the 21-year-old gold farmer Min Qinghai. Min spends most of his time within the confines of a former manufacturing space 200 miles south of Nanjing in the midsize city of Jinhua. He works two floors below the plywood bunks of the workers' dorm where he sleeps. In two years of 84-hour farming weeks, he has rarely stepped outside for longer than it takes to eat a meal. But he has died more times than he can count. And last September on a warm afternoon, halfway between his lunch and dinner breaks, it was happening again.[12]

What was happening again was that Min was being "exterminated" online, within the confines of the game. Although the Chinese gold farmers sit relatively motionless in their rows of chairs facing screens in nondescript rooms, they are frequently subjected to targeted "kills" by Western players who, playing purely for "fun," regard the Chinese players as mercenaries. Each time they "die" (in World of Warcraft or other games), their pace of play slows down and they lose money rebooting their characters.[13] Art imitates life in *The Peripheral*, where Flynne Fisher does online gaming for hire and endures similar abuse: A rich man who played the game himself instead of outsourcing got a charge from killing the avatars of people like Flynne because "it really cost them.... People on her squad were feeding their children with what they earned playing, and maybe that was all they had."[14]

Economic inequality, whether in fictional 2030 or actual 2015, plays out in online spaces and even extends to forced labor. *Forbes* magazine recently reported that Chinese prisons forced inmates to gold-farm in twelve-hour shifts without pay.[15] The coercive element highlights arrangements that also exist in the putatively voluntary forms of loot farming.

Extensive digital tracking of workplace activity adds to bodily stresses. An American Management Association survey found that 66 percent of US-based employers monitor the Internet use of their employees, 45 percent track employee keystrokes, and 43 percent monitor employee e-mail. UPS uses a system, Kronos, under which each of its delivery trucks is equipped with 200 sensors, which feed information back to headquarters about driving speed, seatbelt use, and delivery efficiency. Even trying to cheat the system can hurt the worker. Drivers commonly evade the seatbelt sensor by keeping the seatbelt locked but not strapping themselves in. UPS can claim higher safety compliance even though workers are actually more endangered. A driver recently described cutting corners, slapping delivery slips on doors, and sprinting from site to site to keep up with impossibly demanding quotas. (After eight years, he sustained such extensive spinal damage that his doctor told him it would be impossible to treat.)[16] Work-force management systems such as Kronos and "enterprise social" platforms like Microsoft's Yammer, Salesforce's Chatter, and (coming soon) Facebook at Work operate on similar principles of efficiency and maximization.[17] With the emergence of "flexible," short-term regimes of service-based labor and the eclipse of social welfare programs, the self can increasingly be seen as an entrepreneurial project and a risk-taking device.[18] If the self is risk taking, the body is risk absorbing.

New labor forces of clickworkers, gold farmers, porn zappers, Starbucks flextimers, and Amazon warehouse fulfillers bring to light more clearly the consequences of both the abandonment and extreme monitoring of the body. At the same time, because such workers are often desperate for work and less picky about conditions, they are less likely to incorporate practices or technologies that are becoming increasingly common among upper management as methods of counteracting the physical toll of excessive "screen time" and "chair time": exercise regimes such as yoga or extreme fitness, or office equipment such as "stand-up desks."[19]

The Detachable Body and the Mobile Self

Despite the fact that the vacant or overly tracked body is increasingly the condition of people at play, and (especially) at certain kinds of repetitive and exploitative work, the body remains in the background of our awareness. It is perhaps no coincidence that both Gibson and Rivera focus on situations of wrenching economic inequality across globalized domains of capital transfer. At this level and scale of human activity, the strangeness of bodily conditions becomes more obvious through a kind of exaggeration that de-familiarizes what we have come to take for granted. It is not that we are completely unaware of real stories of warehouse workers in companies such as Amazon who are digitally tracked and prodded as they go about the work of fulfilling online orders. Dystopian fiction only amplifies and catalogs the indignities of existing dehumanizing practices. "They're Watching You at Work," declares an *Atlantic* headline, while a public radio report on "the data-driven workplace of the future" describes employees who ruin their bodies keeping up with "telematic" surveillance devices that track every keystroke they make, every latte they whip, every package they deliver.[20]

These conditions are moving inexorably up the corporate ladder and economic strata, even as they dissolve ordinary hierarchies. The Quantified Self, once seen as a respite from work, is arriving in the workplace in the form of perpetual self- and management-imposed surveillance. (As mentioned above, the quality of this surveillance is "lighter" and more flexible than traditional panoptical oversight.) Among higher-wage workers, the Quantified Self at work takes the form of socially networked goal setting, in which workers prod each other or companies target "millennials" (who are thought to respond more readily to these new forms of what could be called cheerful tracking). Santa Monica-based Enkata, for example, a human resources firm that hires out data-driven platforms to prod claims and sales workers into higher productivity, explicitly eschews keystroke monitoring in favor of "meaningful data" and "predictive analytics to help all members of the sales organization work smarter and close more deals."[21]

The body of today's digitally driven worker evokes those images of bodies stored in suspended animation in various movies from the 1970s onward, including *Coma* (1978) and *Altered States* (1980). A number of films explored the horrifying possibility of human bodies being used as food (*Soylent Green*, 1973), batteries (*The Matrix*, 1999), or intelligence systems drained in the process of use (*Minority Report*, 2002). By contrast, James Cameron's *Avatar* (2009), itself the product of the work of thousands of animators and digital engineers, strikes a more hopeful, even utopian note. It is a film in which a disabled vet is enabled by technological prostheses to inhabit a mythical world while leaving his wired-up body behind. The shocking vulnerability of his temporarily discarded physical form becomes all too evident in the climactic battle, but the hero ultimately prevails by sundering the connection to the body and living on in the fantastic realm of the Na'vi, who have their own, organic way of "plugging in"—inserting their braids into the neural cords of horse-like animals and operating them through their thoughts. To be more fully human, or post-human, will mean finding a new way of plugging in, jacking in, or transmitting.

Whether fantastic or horrifying, the picture presented in these films is that of a body increasingly detached—or made detachable—from a mobile self. This body, because of the systemic shocks it bears, its use as a platform or a source of energy, and even its inescapable mortality, exemplifies what political scientist Timothy Pachirat in *Every Twelve Seconds*, an ethnographic study of work in a Nebraska slaughterhouse, calls the politics of sight.

Exploring the conditions of a low-wage job typically sought by criminals, undocumented workers, or other desperate souls, Pachirat finds that the slaughterhouse operates to make the repetitive acts of killing—which take place "every twelve seconds," hence the title—invisible even to 99 percent of those who work there. Only one out of 280 workers is responsible for firing the fatal shot into the head of the cow. The shooter's work is visible to only one or two others on the killing floor, and he becomes the subject of mythology throughout the abattoir. (A common rumor is that the shooter undergoes constant psychotherapy to fend off work-produced psychosis.) Workers stationed throughout the rendering process, who spend hours each day repetitively detaching the limbs and extracting the livers and other viscera of the recently executed creatures, suffer difficult work conditions and marginalization that mirror the unseen suffering of the slaughtered animals. In the end, Pachirat argues, this cultivated "invisibility" (which, in a sense, is the main service offered by the modern slaughterhouse and its disassembly lines) is supremely necessary social and political labor. It allows most people in the "outside world" to act without knowing the consequences, to consume without knowing the cost, and to benefit from others' work without knowing the source.

It is, in fact, on such exquisitely chosen "invisibilities" that the collective delusions and collusions of the modern economy run, particularly as that economy merges with the virtual realm. To extend the analogy, just as there is a public need for packaged meat that does not bear the evidence of its origins or even of the fact that it once lived, there is likewise a public desire for products (be they iPhones or UPS packages) that sleekly obscure the conditions under which they were made or made possible. Pachirat tells of "work that remains hidden from the majority of those who literally feed off such labor."[22] As literary scholar Katherine Hayles recently remarked, the body "has an inability to lie" in the way thoughts can and do: "This is exactly what consciousness lacks."[23] The body offers a kind of resistance and testimony to realities that some would like us simply to ignore. We need to heed the body.

(Summer 2015, 17.2)

Notes

[1] Gibson describes it in an interview with Karin L. Kross posted at Tor.com, "William Gibson on Urbanism, Science Fiction, and Why *The Peripheral* Weirded Him Out," October 29, 2014; http://www.tor.com/blogs/2014/10/william-gibson-the-peripheral-interview. Spoiler alert: please skip the next three paragraphs if you would rather not know some of the plot details of *The Peripheral*.

[2] Sherry Turkle, "Video Games and Computer Holding Power," *The New Media Reader* (Cambridge, MA: MIT Press, 2003), 500. Originally published 1984; http://www.newmediareader.com/book_samples/nmr-34-turkle.pdf.

[3] Tom McCarthy, "The death of writing—if James Joyce were alive today he'd be working for Google," *The Guardian.com*, March 7, 2015; http://www.theguardian.com/books/2015/mar/07/tom-mccarthy-death-writing-james-joyce-working-google.

[4] Chris Dancy website; http://www.chrisdancy.com. Accessed April 24, 2015.

[5] Ibid.

[6] Gary Wolf, "The Data-Driven Life," *New York Times Magazine*, April 28, 2010; http://www.nytimes.com/2010/05/02/magazine/02self-measurement-t.html?_r=0.

[7] Josh Cohen, "Quantified Self: The Algorithm of Life," *Prospect*, February 5, 2014; http://www.prospect-magazine.co.uk/arts-and-books/quantified-self-the-algorithm-of-life.

[8] Dennis Tenen, "Writing Technology," *Public Books blog*; http://www.publicbooks.org/fiction/writing-technology. Accessed April 24, 2015.

[9] Lilly Irani, "Microworking the Crowd," *Limn*, no. 2, March 2012; http://limn.it/microworking-the-crowd/.

[10] Adrien Chen, "The Workers Who Keep Dick Pics and Beheadings Out of Your Facebook Feed," *Wired*, October 23, 2014; http://www.wired.com/2014/10/content-moderation/.

[11] Julian Dibbell, "The Life of the Chinese Gold Farmer," *New York Times Magazine*, June 17, 2007; http://www.nytimes.com/2007/06/17/magazine/17lootfarmers-t.html?pagewanted=all.

[12] Ibid. Dibbell adds that "Min would like to explain to 'real' players that he is playing for different stakes: 'I have this idea in mind that regular players should understand that people do different things in the game,' he said. 'They are playing. And we are making a living.'"

[13] Ibid.

[14] William Gibson, *The Peripheral* (New York, NY: G.P. Putnam Sons, 2014), Chapter 13.

[15] Paul Tassi, "Chinese Prisoners Forced to Farm World of Warcraft Gold," *Forbes*, June 2, 2011; http://www.forbes.com/sites/insertcoin/2011/06/02/chinese-prisoners-forced-to-farm-world-of-warcraft-gold/. An estimated 80 percent of all gold farmers are in China, which, according to the CIA World Factbook, has the largest population of Internet users in the world. China is thought to be home to 100,000 full-time gold farmers.

[16] The UPS monitoring system is described by Esther Kaplan in "The Spy Who Fired Me: The Human Costs of Workplace Monitoring," *Harper's Magazine*, March 2015; http://harpers.org/archive/2015/03/the-spy-who-fired-me/.

[17] On the "actuarial self" and "responsibilization," see Nikolas Rose, *Inventing Our Selves*, Chapter 7, "Governing Enterprising Individuals" (Cambridge, England: Cambridge University Press, 1998).

[18] On the calculation of risk as it relates to the definition of self, see ed. Limor Samimian-Darash and Paul Rabinow *Modes of Uncertainty: Anthropological Cases* (Chicago, IL: University of Chicago, 2015).

[19] Evgeny Morozov, "The Mindfulness Racket," *New Republic*, February 23, 2014; http://www.newrepublic.com/article/116618/technologys-mindfulness-racket.

[20] Kai Ryssdal [interviewer], "The Data-Driven Workplace of the Future" *Marketplace* [radio broadcast], March 3, 2015; http://www.marketplace.org/topics/business/data-driven-workplace-future.

[21] "Know More Close More," Enkata website; http://www.enkata.com. Accessed April 14, 2015.

[22] Timothy Pachirat, *Every Twelve Seconds: Industrialized Slaughter and the Politics of Sight* (New Haven, CT: Yale University Press, 2011), Chapter IX.

[23] Hayles made this comment at "The Total Archive," a conference at the Centre for Research in the Arts, Social Sciences and Humanities, Cambridge University, March 19–20, 2015. She has developed these ideas in several publications, in which she figures the body as a site of feedback, not a reified thing. Cf. N. Katherine Hayles, How *We Became Posthuman* (Chicago, IL: University of Chicago Press, 1999).

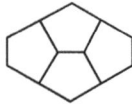

Intellectuals and
Their Discontents

Russell Jacoby

My title, which is pinched from Freud's little book *Civilization and Its Discontents*, is misleading. I should have titled my essay, "Intellectuals and Their Contents." I don't worry that intellectuals are discontented, but rather the reverse: that they are too happy. Intellectuals have settled for too little; they have become too professorial and complacent. I am considering "academics" and "intellectuals" as almost equivalent terms; indeed, part of the story is how this came to be.

Some purchase on the topic of intellectuals (and intellectuals in an academic terrain) can be gained by considering the image of intellectuals and professors in films and novels. Not so long ago the professor was viewed as "absent-minded" and dysfunctional—perhaps as portrayed in the Marx Brothers film *Horse Feathers* or, more grimly, in Heinrich Mann's *Professor Unrat*, which was turned into the movie, *The Blue Angel*. This image, and the reality to which it corresponded, is obsolete. To satirize a professor nowadays one cannot pretend that he or she is sexually repressed or cannot find the classroom door or the keys to the car. Just the opposite—a professor is satirized for being oversexed or too connected. This is the image of the professor that emerges in a host of recent novels, such as those by David Lodge. The fictional portrait resonates because it captures something of the current situation of academic intellectuals.

What might be called the classical image of the intellectual is in eclipse; it was a picture that surfaced in Europe and North America. Intellectuals were seen as subversive, effeminate, disreputable, and elitist.[1] In Milan Kundera's *The Book of Laughter and Forgetting*, when Mirek asked his girlfriend "why she was so withdrawn, she told him she hadn't been satisfied with their lovemaking." She said he made love like an intellectual.

> In the political jargon of the day "intellectual" was an expletive. It designated a person who failed to understand life and was cut off from the people. All Communists hanged at the time by other Communists had that curse bestowed upon them. Unlike people with their feet planted firmly on the ground, they supposedly floated in air.... But what did Zdena mean when she accused him of making love like an intellectual?[2]

In his book *Anti-Intellectualism in American Life*, Richard Hofstadter summarized the 1950s impression of an intellectual:

> A person of spurious intellectual pretensions, often a professor or the protégé of a professor. Fundamentally superficial. Over-emotional and feminine in reactions to any problem...surfeited with conceit and contempt for the experience of more sound and able men. Essentially confused.... A doctrinaire supporter of Middle-European socialism as opposed to Greco-French-American ideas of democracy and liberalism. Subject to the...morality of Nietzsche which frequently leads him into jail or disgrace.... An anemic bleeding heart.[3]

Writing in the late fifties, Hofstadter realized the times had changed. In 1956 *Time* ran a cover story announcing that a new spirit traversed the nation: America now embraced intellectuals. "What does it mean to be an intellectual in the U.S.?" asked *Time*. "Is he really in such an unhappy plight...the ridiculed double-dome, the egghead, the wild-eyed, absent-minded man who is made to feel an alien in his own country?" According to *Time*, Jacques Barzun, the Columbia University professor and writer, represented a new species, "a growing host of men of ideas who not only have the respect of the nation, but who return the compliment."[4]

The shock of a Soviet satellite in 1957 and the onset of Kennedy's presidency in 1961 redoubled the respect. By the early sixties intellectuals were welcomed, sometimes honored in the highest reaches of government. The title of David Halberstam's book on the Kennedy years, *The Best and the Brightest*, partly refers to the intellectual cream that flowed towards Washington. A "new breed of thinkers-doers, half of academe, half of the nation's think tanks" headed to the capital—people like McGeorge Bundy, who was educated at Groton and Yale and had taught at Harvard.[5] The value of knowledge, training, and education rose dramatically. "Intellectuals have come to enjoy more acceptance and, in some ways, a more satisfactory position," stated Hofstadter in his conclusion.[6]

Most intellectuals have embraced the change. Some affect disaffection, claiming a marginality they do not have. To put this sharply, once intellectuals were outsiders who wanted to be insiders. Now they are insiders who pretend to be outsiders—a claim that can be sustained only by turning marginality into a pose. This is not the whole story, but it may be half of it. The other half is the admission, even celebration, of their new insider status as career professionals. These are two responses to the same process. Both signify the eclipse of an older image, which to be sure was always partly mythic, of the independent intellectual.

The old image of intellectuals as marginalized dissenters who attack injustice has not simply vanished. Many of those who bury this image turn about and coolly announce that they themselves are marginalized intellectuals. Edward Said, in his book *Representations of the Intellectual*, advances an idea of the intellectual as a vulnerable critic on the outside. The intellectual, he writes, is "someone whose place it is publicly to raise embarrassing questions, to confront orthodoxy and dogma...to be someone who cannot easily be co-opted by governments or corporations..."[7] The intellectual "always has a choice either to side with the weaker, the less well represented, the forgotten or ignored, or to side with the more powerful."[8]

> And there is something fundamentally unsettling about intellectuals who have neither offices to protect nor territory to consolidate and guard; self-irony is therefore more frequent than pomposity, directness more than hemming and hawing. But there is no dodging the inescapable reality that such representations by intellectuals will neither make them friends in high places nor win them official honors. It is a lonely condition...[9]

This is an engaging portrait, but today what relationship does it bear to reality? No honors? No hemming and hawing? No offices or territory to defend? Lonely existence? Where? Maybe in Egypt or Afghanistan, but hardly in the United States or France. Can we say that Derrida or Said or Henry Louis Gates, Jr., lead unrecognized or marginalized lives? It would be more accurate to state the opposite: they and other oppositional intellectuals hold distinguished positions at major institutions. They are regularly wined and dined, as well as handsomely compensated. Many leading intellectuals like Cornel West or Camille Paglia operate with agents, who arrange fees and schedules for their many speaking engagements. What does this reveal about intellectual life today?

A sign of the times is Stanley Fish's exultation that intellectual life increasingly mimics corporate practices in establishing conferences and travel as the coin of the realm:

> The flourishing of the [conference] circuit has brought with it new sources of extra income, increased opportunities for domestic and foreign travel... an ever-growing list of stages on which to showcase one's talents, and geometric increase in the availability of the commodities for which academics yearn, attention, applause, fame...[10]

* * *

His only regret? The imitation of corporate largesse is only half-hearted and the compensation for professors remains small.

My concern, however, is not with intellectuals in general, but a subset of them: public intellectuals. In *The Last Intellectuals*,[11] I identified Dwight Macdonald and others like Edmund Wilson, Lewis Mumford, and Lionel Trilling—those born around the turn of the century—as classic American intellectuals; and I labeled them *public* intellectuals inas-much as they addressed the educated public. They wrote to be read. To be sure, the term "public intellectual" is not easy to define. I meant roughly an intellectual who uses the vernacular and writes for more than specialists, an intellectual who remains committed to a public.

Some aspects of this topic go far beyond the history of intellectuals. The history of rhetoric illuminates the issue of public intellectuals. Classical thinkers studied and valued rhetoric, in large part, because public life depended on oratory. In Rome, public speaking was a pre-eminent civil occupation. "No pursuit," wrote Cicero in "On the Orator," "has ever flourished with greater vigour than public speaking....almost every ambitious young man felt he ought to bestir himself to the best of his ability to become eloquent."[12] Cicero continued:

> Think, moreover, of the *power* an orator possesses: power to rescue the suppliant, to raise up the afflicted, to bestow salvation, to dispel danger, to preserve citizens' rights; what in the whole world could be more noble, more generous, more princely?[13]

Cicero argued against those who viewed oratory as a specialized field, separate from philosophy and history. In order to be eloquent and convincing, the speaker had to be drenched in knowledge; there was no special "art" of oration. Crassus, who represents Cicero in "On the Orator," is asked at one point whether there is an "art" of oratory:

> "Well, really!," exclaimed Crassus, "Do you imagine I am just one of those idle and talkative Greeks, the sort of little man, no doubt scholarly and erudite enough, whom you can ask trivial questions.... On the contrary, I have always laughed at the impudent characters who sit on their chairs in the schools and call out to the assembled crowds..."[14]

He goes on to say that oratory is more than a specialized "art"; the orator needs broad knowledge, as well as familiarity with the poets and historians:

Indeed he must peruse and scrutinize the writers and experts on every liberal art.... He must know all about our law and our statutes; he must have a thorough understanding of ancient history; he must master the usages of the Senate, the nature of the constitution, the rights of subject allies, our national treaties and agreements...[15]

The Ciceronian model of rhetoric, which inspired Renaissance thinkers, and its idea of "civic humanism" wore the stamp of the city and politics; eloquence was prized in order to convince an audience. And real eloquence depended on wide knowledge and understanding.

Let me jump to the present. Some years ago a professor of writing, Charles Bazerman, published an analysis of an unlikely subject, the *Publication Manual* of the American Psychological Association—that is, the association's guidelines for authors who are preparing scholarly manuscripts for submissions. Bazerman made several telling observations. The guidelines or instructions for the psychologist had expanded tremendously. The first set of instructions, in 1929, was six pages, the most recent edition almost 200.

With this vast enlargement came an increase in the codification of the discipline; only certain kinds of research were possible, and they had to be presented in a single fashion. Articles were no longer meant to be read, but simply to be scanned or indexed; they were broken up into sections: abstract, introduction, method, results, discussion. Each section was to follow a prescribed form. Moreover, a new reference style had been adopted, putting author and date of cited works in parentheses in the text, which implied, according to Bazerman, "the incrementalism of the literature." He continued, "As anyone who has worked with this reference system can attest, it is very convenient for listing and summarizing a series of related findings, but it is awkward for extensive quotation or discussion..."[16] The author of the scholarly psychology piece, he concluded, "must display competence to the audience rather than persuade readers of the truth of an idea."[17] In other words, here was a contemporary discipline that prescribed a narrow scientific approach, both in its research and presentation of research. Scholarly contributions were judged by form; no value was given to readability. The concerns of classical rhetoric had vaporized.

Between Cicero's writings on oratory and the 1983 publication manual of the American Psychological Association, intellectual life changed. For many disciplines, eloquence and wide knowledge were not dismissed for the simple reason that they were never considered. If someone studying to be a psychologist confessed that he or she wanted to study writing and literature or even wanted to write well, he or she would be confessing to a lack of direction, perhaps to instability. This was not always so. The only prize that Freud ever received was a literary prize, the Goethe prize for literature. Certainly much of Freud's impact was due to his greatness as a writer.

In recent years interest in rhetoric has exploded. Oddly this renewed attention has had no effect on how academics write. Indeed, as argued in Brian Vickers's *In Defense of Rhetoric*, the new enthusiasm has abandoned the heart of rhetoric: a commitment to public interventions. In studying the old texts of rhetoric,

> we are not using them for the purposes for which they were designed.... They were "how-to-do-it" manuals, and reading them without the intention of putting their teachings into practice would be as perverse as studying a book on tennis, or bridge, if we never intended to play those games.[18]

He decries the "reductive" use of rhetoric found in Hayden White, who employs four tropes to categorize all literature.[19] Rhetoric gets whittled down to a formalistic analysis of writing. Few, if any, of those who study rhetoric express any desire to participate in public life.

* * *

In the course of the twentieth century, intellectuals have made a progressive retreat from commitment to a public and critical prose. The transition from Lionel Trilling to Fred Jameson, or from Jane Jacobs to younger urbanists like David Harvey, or from William James to younger philosophers, illustrates the cultural shift. The previous generations of intellectuals could be read, and were read, by educated readers; the most recent intellectuals cannot be—nor do they direct themselves to a public audience. They have settled into specialties and sub-specialties. Even as critics have become more sophisticated and daring, they have also become more private and complacent, which belies a critical discourse.

A generational grid used in tracing this evolution—or decline—expresses the real dynamics of intellectual life in the last 50 years. In surveying current intellectual life, I find not a flat-out absence of public intellectuals, but an absence of younger ones—and I am using "younger" in its most expansive meaning: the few public intellectuals are almost all over the age of 50, usually 60. In other words, behind the erosion of public intellectuals, a generational flux is at work. An older generation of intellectuals is passing on, and a new one is not showing up. And this "missing" generation is more or less the sixties generation; they may have been a force for change and ferment, but today they are scarcely present as an intellectual generation. Who are the younger successors to Edmund Wilson or Dwight Macdonald or Lewis Mumford or even Lionel Trilling?

This absence can be explained by looking first at what might be called the cultural geography: the sharp increase in higher education in the post–World War II years and the corresponding increase in academic employment. What is decisive is not simply the growing academic environment but the decline of the alternative environments, and specifically, the decline of the urban bohemias. If the western frontier closed in the 1890s, the cultural frontier closed in the 1950s. For a young writer or artist, out of high school or college, to decide to move to New York City and live in Greenwich Village to begin his or her novel is no longer a possibility. The big cities, mainly New York, but also San Francisco and Chicago, get too difficult and too expensive. Café society gives rise to the essay and aphorism; colleges and colleagues spur the monograph and grant application. Socio-cultural environment gives a cast to intellectuals and ways of thinking and writing. The density and rhythms of thought itself register the environment. And if this environment is one of lectures, seminars, and conferences, it reveals itself in the prose, the approach, and perhaps the content of scholarship. The presupposition might be crudely characterized as materialistic: material circumstances do affect people, and insofar as intellectuals are people, they are affected by their surroundings.

While this presupposition is neither subtle nor original, it proves to be fairly controversial. Left intellectuals, who accent social and economic conditions in their politics, get touchy if it is suggested that their own work must also be situated within the social environment. Several left reviewers of my book *The Last Intellectuals* were scandalized by the notion that anything interesting or important could be said about intellectual work by looking at work conditions. This is apparently true for other kinds of workers—miners, needle workers, autoworkers—but not intellectuals; here we must only consider their ideas. The same people whose scholarship is devoted to documenting how workers live are angered if it is suggested that their ideas may also be related to how they live and work.

To be sure, approached from a different angle, the problem of the increasing professionalization of academic intellectuals has often been broached. For instance, Bruce Kuklick in *The Rise of American Philosophy* states in his last chapter, titled "The Triumph of Professionalism," that while Royce and James assumed two roles—basic research and popular presentations—the next Harvard philosophers

> ignored the public work of Royce and James and centered their attention on logic and epistemology. The order of the day was technical specialized research published for technically competent audiences in technical journals, with popularizations...relegated to hacks, incompetents, and has-beens. The professionalization of philosophy within the American university radically intensified this shift, and philosophy lost its synthesizing, comprehensive function.[20]

Richard Rorty has recalled his days as a graduate student in the early 1950s when analytic philosophers confidently seized the initiative. Prizing technical problems, they derided others who pursued "the history of philosophy, or more generally...the history of thought." He cites from a classic account of scientific philosophy that identified "the philosopher of the old school" as someone "trained in literature and history, who has never learned the precision methods of the mathematical sciences."[21] Thirty years later analytic thinkers staff many departments, but according to Rorty, the philosophical situation is far from favorable. These departments have almost abandoned the humanities (and have not joined the sciences); they produce students who are argumentative logicians, little more. The discipline has no focus. Rorty writes, "the field these days is a jungle of competing research programs, programs which seem to have a shorter and shorter half-life as the years go by."[22]

Many academics and professionals are defensive on the issues of professionalization and surrendering a general audience. I have been accused of being a Luddite, a populist, a romantic, an outsider, and a reactionary. Yet it should be possible to raise the issue of insular specialization without pledging fealty to progress and industrial society. The incarceration of specialists and a return to bloodletting or phrenology is hardly the goal; nor is the point to foster anti-intellectual populism or half-educated generalists. Specialization inheres in industrial society. We need specialists. No one wants to hear a cheery announcement that today your airline pilot will be a family therapist. Nevertheless this truth does not justify every micro-field or subdiscipline or new jargon. Specialization can also be obscurantism, turf building, careerism, and regression, as well as a simple waste of talent and resources.

My concern that humanist studies have evolved into insular activities which have lost contact with the vernacular might be seen as a repressive call for populist intellectuals. I am presumed to wish that intellectuals speak in a uniform language to the great unwashed. Geoffrey Hartman in *Criticism in the Wilderness* complains again and again that some critics allow the creative artist to be involuted or opaque but hold the critics to a single standard of lucidity: "It is as if the literary field were being crassly divided into permissive creativity (fiction) on the one hand, and school masterly criticism on the other."[23] While there is something to this, Hartman's language reveals his real beef: he chafes at being subordinated to literature, at being a servant to it. The critic does not simply want to read texts, he or she wants to be a text or, really, be the center of attention. Yet the objection has some truth. No single standard of lucidity exists; literary criticism must be guided by the subject at hand. And, yes, the interpretation may at times overshadow or surpass that which is interpreted.

Nevertheless, in recent years, we have seen an insistent argument that simplicity in language indicates superficiality, and that complexity denotes subversion. Increasingly in books and articles, "to complicate" is showing up as a virtue. We are told that so-and-so "complicates" our notion of gender or intellectuals. Once upon a time to clarify was considered a goal; now it is assumed to be dangerous, as if there is too much clarity.

In his essay "Persecution and the Art of Writing," Leo Strauss argued that the existence or threat of persecution—past and present—prompted philosophers to develop a peculiar writing technique. Fearful of stating exactly what they thought, they masked their thought, writing as it were "between the lines." This meant that their truths were in fact restricted to a few circles of trustworthy and intelligent readers, for the others would read the lines, not between them. Moreover, it was not simply political fear that encouraged this involuted and dense style; they feared the masses: "They were convinced that philosophy as such was suspect to, and hated by, the majority of men.... They must conceal their opinions from all but philosophers..."[24]

I want to situate Strauss's analysis within the contemporary context. At least in North America, few humanists or critics fear persecution for their thoughts; this is hardly a motive to mask one's writings. But I can less easily dismiss the second reason that Strauss offers: fear of or suspicion of the masses. To be sure, it would not be formulated in these terms; in the contemporary context, it is the fear of being read by a wider public, rather than by the masses. Countless graduate students and younger faculty in numerous fields have recounted that they have been given the friendly and very serious advice by their elders to publish in scholarly and technical journals—not general periodicals of opinion. One of the most damning judgments about a scholar's work is that it is "journalistic." What does this mean? It implies the book is readable, which infers that it is not rigorous and scholarly. We have largely accepted the notion that readability means superficiality, and opacity means profundity.

Often quoted is Fred Jameson's defense of critical theory as requiring complex language rather than the repressive nature of common sense and lucidity. Jameson defended the writing of the German critical Marxists from the charges of obscurity: "It can be admitted that it does not conform to the canons of clear and fluid journalistic writing taught in schools. But what if those ideas of clarity and simplicity have come to serve a very different ideological purpose...?"[25] What if transparency facilitates clichés, but avoids "real thought" requiring effort and time? For Jameson the density of T. W. Adorno's writing exemplified a break with repressive clarity. His "bristling mass of abstractions and cross-references is precisely intended to be read in situation, against the cheap facility of what surrounds it, as a warning to the reader of the price he has to pay for genuine thinking."[26] The point is well taken; but it is also misleading, and not only because the characterization of Adorno's writings as a "bristling mass of abstractions and cross-references" misses the mark—this describes academic writing, not Adorno's. The issue is not the difficulty of writing, but the fetish of difficulty, the belief that fractured English, name dropping, and abstractions guarantee profundity, professionalization, and subversion. With this belief comes the counter-belief: lucidity implies banality, amateurism, and conservatism.

* * *

Loyal to an old-fashioned intellectual style, some conservatives have mounted an effective criticism of professionalization and academization. Distrusting the cost of bureaucratic success, they prize the lucid prose that career professionals often surrender. Partly for this reason they have loomed large in the "cultural wars" that have ebbed and flowed over the last fifteen years. It is easy to list the conservative tracts decrying educational misdeeds (*Illiberal Education, Tenured Radicals, The Closing of the American Mind*),[27] but where are the rejoinders? The liberal professors growl and scowl, but have difficulty answering in limpid English; instead they collect conference papers. When their books finally appear, they lack bite. In the liberal view, education has proceeded swimmingly; it has become more diverse, multicultural, and exciting, which only crabby conservatives fail to fathom. Lawrence Levine's *The Opening of the American Mind* reads like a public relations handout for the contemporary university.[28] A strange inversion has taken place; liberals and leftists, once critics of the establishment, have become its defenders.

But the debate has not stood still; important challenges and contributions have been made to this question of public and university intellectuals. One example: many have suggested that teaching itself is a form of intellectual and political activity. Inasmuch as intellectuals are now professors, and millions go to college, teaching constitutes a public engagement.

Likewise, there are three areas where I see possible change. Driven by academic discontent and boredom, professors might want to reinvent themselves as public writers. To a limited extent in the last ten years, I think this has happened. In the domain of philosophy, for example, Richard Rorty represents an effort to invigorate a public philosophy, and he has been followed by a number of others. Historians and literary critics increasingly try to break out of closed discussions into a larger public. Yet these professionals are not heeding but bucking institutional imperatives that reward technical rather than public contributions. Will they be successful? It is not clear.

In the last decade, the emergence of what has been called the new black public intellectuals has generated much attention. For the first time in many years, a group of African American intellectuals has burst upon the scene—figures like Henry Louis Gates, Jr., Gerald Early, Adolph Reed, Jr., Randall Kennedy, and Cornel West. These are smart, hard-hitting, and (often) graceful writers, who weigh in on public problems of race, sports, politics, law, and culture. They have been both acclaimed as successors to the New York intellectuals and criticized as publicity hounds who ignore earlier black intellectuals such as W.E.B. Dubois and C.R.L. James. The emergence of the new black intellectuals demonstrates that a literate, indeed hungry, public still exists and refutes the claim that there has been an irrevocable demise of a literate public.

Another promising recent development is the increasing importance of what are sometimes called the new science writers, many of whom have been writing for decades. Their growing impact seems to confirm that a public has not disappeared. While scientists are often belittled as technicians and positivists—usually by conformist postmodern theorists—a group of science writers has more or less filled the space vacated by humanists. I am thinking of people such as Stephen Jay Gould, Oliver Sacks, the late Carl Sagan, Jared Diamond, Jonathan Weiner, and Jeremy Bernstein among others. These professionals do not disdain to write with clarity on matters of wide intellectual interest. Their success with a literate public raises numerous questions, among them: What does it mean if humanists lose the ability to think and write lucidly, while scientists become penetrating, engaged, and accessible? "I deeply deplore the equation of popular writing with pap and distortion," says Stephen Jay Gould.[29] Few contemporary humanists or social scientists would agree. Why is that?

What is the situation today? I'm not certain. I would like to see intellectuals reclaim the vernacular and reassert themselves in public life. Some see this as an injunction to sell out to—or just plain sell—an anti-intellectual demand to exchange dense and unpopular work for media coverage. No one can do everything, but intellectual work need not be pitched in a single register. For thinkers and writers it should be possible both to be serious and accessible—not always at the same time, but over time. After all, those thinkers touted as the most original and complex have often sought a broad public. Even the famously difficult Adorno sweated over his radio lectures to ensure they would be clear and understandable. Ultimately, it is not only the larger public that loses when intellectuals turn inward to fetishize their profundity and remain within their university corridors and offices, but also the intellectuals themselves. Not to be overly dramatic, but I sometimes think that the historical break with Latin and the rise of the national vernaculars will be reversed—obviously not everywhere, but within institutional settings. In this sense, we face the rise of a new intellectual class using a new scholasticism accessible only to the mandarins, who have turned their back on public life and letters.

(Fall 2000, 2.3)

Notes

[1] Some of the following remarks are derived from my book, *The End of Utopia: Politics and Culture in an Age of Apathy* (New York, NY: Basic, 1999).

[2] Milan Kundera, *The Book of Laughter and Forgetting*, trans. Michael Henry Heim (New York, NY: Knopf, 1981), 5.

[3] Louis Bromfield as quoted in Richard Hofstadter, *Anti-Intellectualism in American Life* (New York, NY: Vintage/Random House, 1963), 9–10.

[4] "America and the Intellectual," *Time* (11 June 1956): 65.

[5] David Halberstam, *The Best and the Brightest* (New York, NY: Ballantine, 1993), 43.

[6] Hofstadter, *Anti-Intellectualism in American Life*, 393.

[7] Edward W. Said, *Representations of the Intellectual* (New York, NY: Pantheon, 1994), 32.

[8] Ibid., 11.

[9] Ibid., xviii.

[10] Stanley Fish, "The Unbearable Ugliness of Volvos," *English Inside and Out: The Places of Literary Criticism*, ed. Susan Gubar and Jonathan Kamholtz (New York, NY: Routledge, 1993), 103.

[11] Russell Jacoby, *The Last Intellectuals: American Culture in the Age of Academe* (New York, NY: Basic, 1987).

[12] Cicero, "On the Orator," *On the Good Life*, trans. Michael Grant (New York, NY: Penguin, 1971) 240.

[13] Ibid., 246.

[14] Ibid., 272.

[15] Ibid., 289.

[16] Charles Bazerman, "Codifying the Social Scientific Style: The APA Publication Manual as a Behaviorist Rhetoric," *The Rhetoric of the Human Sciences: Language and Argument in Scholarship and Public Affairs*, ed. John S. Nelson, Allan Megill, and Donald M. McCloskey (Madison, WI: University of Wisconsin Press, 1987), 140.

[17] Ibid., 140.

[18] Brian Vickers, *In Defense of Rhetoric* (Oxford, England: Oxford University Press, 1989), 14.

[19] Ibid., 441–42.

[20] Bruce Kuklick, *The Rise of American Philosophy: Cambridge, Massachusetts 1860–1930* (New Haven, CT: Yale University Press, 1977), 565.

[21] Richard Rorty, *Consequences of Pragmatism* (Minneapolis, MN: University of Minnesota Press, 1982), 215.

[22] Ibid., 216.

[23] Geoffrey H. Hartman, *Criticism in the Wilderness: The Study of Literature Today* (New Haven, CT: Yale University Press, 1980), 233.

[24] Leo Strauss, *Persecution and the Art of Writing* (Westport, CT: Greenwood, 1952), 34.

[25] Fredric Jameson, *Marxism and Form* (Princeton, NJ: Princeton University Press, 1971), xiii.

[26] Ibid., xiii.

[27] See Dinesh D'Souza, *Illiberal Education: The Politics of Race and Sex on Campus* (New York, NY: Free, 1991); Roger Kimball, *Tenured Radicals: How Politics Has Corrupted Our Higher Education* (New York, NY: Harper & Row, 1990); and Allan Bloom, *The Closing of the American Mind* (New York, NY: Simon and Schuster, 1987).

[28] See my review of Levine's book: "Pollyanna Goes to College," *Dissent* (Winter 1997): 115–19.

[29] Stephen Jay Gould, *Bully for Brontosaurus: Reflections in Natural History* (New York, NY: Norton, 1991) 11.

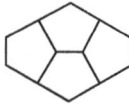

Why Google Isn't Making Us Stupid...or Smart

Chad Wellmon

Last year *The Economist* published a special report not on the global financial crisis or the polarization of the American electorate, but on the era of big data. Article after article cited one big number after another to bolster the claim that we live in an age of information superabundance. The data are impressive: 300 billion emails, 200 million tweets, and 2.5 billion text messages course through our digital networks every day, and, if these numbers were not staggering enough, scientists are reportedly awash in even more information. This past January astronomers surveying the sky with the Sloan telescope in New Mexico released over 49.5 terabytes of information—a mass of images and measurements—in one data drop. The Large Hadron Collider at CERN (the European Organization for Nuclear Research), however, produces almost that much information per second. Last year alone, the world's information base is estimated to have doubled every eleven hours. Just a decade ago, computer professionals spoke of kilobytes and megabytes. Today they talk of the terabyte, the petabyte, the exabyte, the zettabyte, and now the yotta-byte, each a thousand times bigger than the last.

Some see this as information abundance, others as information overload. The advent of digital information and with it the era of big data allows geneticists to decode the human genome, humanists to search entire bodies of literature, and businesses to spot economic trends. But it is also creating for many the sense that we are being overwhelmed by informa-tion. How are we to manage it all? What are we to make, as Ann Blair asks, of a zettabyte of information—a one with 21 zeros after it?[1] From a more embodied, human perspective, these tremendous scales of information are rather meaningless. We do not experience information as pure data, be it a byte or a yottabyte, but as filtered and framed through the keyboards, screens, and touchpads of our digital technologies. However impressive these astronomical scales of information may be, our contemporary awe and increasing worry about all this data obscures the ways in which we actually engage it and the world of which it and we are a part. All of the chatter about information superabundance and overload tends not only to marginalize human persons, but also to render technology just as abstract as a yottabyte. An email is reduced to yet another data point, the Web to an infinite complex of protocols and machinery, Google to a neutral machine for producing information. Our compulsive talk about information overload can isolate and abstract digital technology from society, human persons, and our broader culture. We have become distracted by all the data and inarticulate about our digital technologies.

The more pressing, if more complex, task of our digital age, then, lies not in figuring out what comes after the yottabyte, but in cultivating contact with an increasingly technologically formed world.[2] In order to understand how our lives are already deeply formed by technology, we need to consider information not only in the abstract terms of terrabytes and zettabytes, but also in more cultural terms. How do the technologies that humans form to engage the world come in turn to form us? What do these technologies that are of our own making and irreducible elements of our own being do to us? The analytical task lies in identifying and embracing forms of human agency particular to our digital age, without reducing technology to a mere mechanical extension of the human, to a mere tool. In short, asking whether Google makes us stupid, as some cultural critics recently have, is the wrong question. It assumes sharp distinctions between humans and technology that are no longer, if they ever were, tenable.

Two Narratives

The history of this mutual constitution of humans and technology has been obscured as of late by the crystallization of two competing narratives about how we experience all of this information. On the one hand, there are those who claim that the digitization efforts of Google, the social-networking power of Facebook, and the era of big data in general are finally realizing that ancient dream of unifying all knowledge. The digital world will become a "single liquid fabric of interconnected words and ideas," a form of knowledge without distinctions or differences.[3] Unlike other technological innovations, like print, which was limited to the educated elite, the Internet is a network of "densely interlinked Web pages, blogs, news articles and Tweets [that] are all visible to anyone and everyone."[4] Our information age is unique not only in its scale, but in its inherently open and democratic arrangement of information. Information has finally been set free. Digital technologies, claim the most optimistic among us, will deliver a universal knowledge that will make us smarter and ulti-mately liberate us.[5] These utopic claims are related to similar visions about a trans-humanist future in which technology will overcome what were once the historical limits of humanity: physical, intellectual, and psychological. The dream is of a post-human era.[6]

On the other hand, less sanguine observers interpret the advent of digitization and big data as portending an age of information overload. We are suffering under a deluge of data. Many worry that the Web's hyperlinks that propel us from page to page, the blogs that reduce long articles to a more consumable line or two, and the tweets that condense thoughts to 140 characters have all created a culture of distraction. The very technologies that help us manage all of this information are undermining our ability to read with any depth or care. The Web, according to some, is a deeply flawed medium that facilitates a less intensive, more superficial form of reading. When we read online, we browse, we scan, we skim. The superabundance of information, such critics charge, however, is changing not only our reading habits, but also the way we think. As Nicholas Carr puts it, "what the Net seems to be doing is chipping away my capacity for concentration and contemplation. My mind now expects to take in information the way the Net distributes it: in a swiftly moving stream of particles."[7] The constant distractions of the Internet—think of all those hyperlinks and new message warnings that flash up on the screen—are degrading our ability "to pay sustained attention," to read in depth, to reflect, to remember. For Carr and many others like him, true knowledge is deep, and its depth is proportional to the intensity of our attentiveness. In our digital world that encourages quantity over quality, Google is making us stupid.

Each of these narratives points to real changes in how technology impacts humans. Both the scale and the acceleration of information production and dissemination in our digital age are unique. Google, like every technology before it, may well be part of broader changes in the ways we think and experience the world. Both narratives, however, make two basic mistakes.

First, they imagine our information age to be unprecedented, but information explo-sions and the utopian and apocalyptic pronouncements that accompany them are an old concern. The emergence of every new information technology brings with it new methods and modes for storing and transmitting ever more information, and these technologies deeply impact the ways in which humans interact with the world. Both the optimism of technophiles who predict the emergence of a digital "liquid" intelligence and the pessimism of those who fear that Google is "making us stupid" echo historical hopes and complaints about large amounts of information.

Second, both narratives make a key conceptual error by isolating the causal effects of technology. Technologies, be it the printed book or Google, do not make us unboundedly free or unflaggingly stupid. Such a sharp dichotomy between humans and technology sim-plifies the complex, unpredictable, and thoroughly historical ways in which humans and technologies interact and form each other. Simple claims about the effects of technology obscure basic assumptions, for good or bad, about technology as an independent cause that eclipses causes of other kinds. They assume the effects of technology can be easily isolated and abstracted from their social and historical contexts.

Instead of thinking in such dichotomies or worrying about all of those impending yottabytes, we might consider a perhaps simple but oftentimes overlooked fact: we access, use, and engage information through technologies that help us select, filter, and delimit. Web browsers, hyperlinks, blogs, online newspapers, computational algorithms, rss feeds, Facebook, and Google help us turn all of those terrabytes of data into something more useful and particular, that is, something that can be remade and repurposed by an embodied human person. These now ubiquitous technologies help us filter the essential from the excess and search for the needle in the haystack, and in so doing they have become central mediums for our experience of the world.

In this sense, technology is neither an abstract flood of data nor a simple machine-like appendage subordinate to human intentions, but instead the very manner in which humans engage the world. To celebrate the Web, or any other technology, as inherently edifying or stultifying is to ignore its more human scale: our individual access to this imagined expanse of pure information is made possible by technologies that are constructed, designed, and constantly tweaked by human decisions and experiences. These technologies do not exist independently of the human persons who design and use them. Likewise, to suggest that Google is making us stupid is to ignore the historical fact that over time technologies have had an effect on how we think, but in ways that are much more complex and not at all reducible to simple statements like "Google is making us stupid."

Think of it this way: the Web in its entirety—just like those terrabytes of information that we imagine weighing down upon us—is inaccessible to the ill-equipped person. Digital technologies make the Web accessible by making it seem much smaller and more manageable than we imagine it to be. *The Web* does not exist. In this sense, the history of information overload is instructive less for what it teaches us about the quantity of information than what it teaches us about how the technologies that we design to engage the world come in turn to shape us. The specific technologies developed to manage information can give us insight into how we organize, produce, and distribute knowledge—that is, the history of information overload is a history of how we know what we know. It is not only the history of data, books, and the tools used to cope with them. It is also a history of ourselves and of the environment within which we make and in turn are made by technologies.

In the following sections, I put our information age in historical context in an effort to demonstrate that technology's impact on the human is both precedented and constitutive of new forms of life, new norms, and new cultures. The concluding sections focus on Google in particular and consider how it is impacting our very notion of what it is to be human in the digital age. Carr and other critics of the ways we have come to interact with our digital technologies have good reason to be concerned, but, as I hope to show, for rather different reasons than they might think. The core issue concerns not particular modes of accommodating new technologies—nifty advice on dealing with email or limiting screen time—but our very conception of the relationship between the human and technology.

Too Many Books

As historian Ann Blair has recently demonstrated, our contemporary worries about information overload resonate with historical complaints about "too many books." Historical analogues afford us insight not only into the history of particular anxieties, but also into the ways humans have always been impacted by their own technologies. These complaints have their biblical antecedents: Ecclesiastes 12:12, "Of making books there is no end"; their classical ones: Seneca, "the abundance of books is a distraction";[8] and their early modern ones: Leibniz, the "horrible mass of books keeps growing."[9] After the invention of the printing press around 1450 and the attendant drop in book prices, according to some estimates by as much as 80 percent, these complaints took on new meaning. As the German philosopher and critic Johann Gottfried Herder put it in the late eighteenth century, the printing press "gave wings" to paper.[10]

Complaints about too many books gained particular urgency over the course of the eighteenth century when the book market exploded, especially in England, France, and Germany. Whereas today we imagine ourselves to be engulfed by a flood of digital data, late eighteenth-century German readers, for example, imagined themselves to have been infested by a plague of books [*Bücherseuche*]. Books circulated like contagions through the reading public. These anxieties corresponded to a rapid increase in new print titles in the last third of the eighteenth century, an increase of about 150 percent from 1770 to 1800 alone.

Similar to contemporary worries that Google and Wikipedia are making us stupid, these eighteenth-century complaints about "excess" were not merely descriptive. In 1702 the jurist and philosopher Christian Thomasius laid out some of the normative concerns that would gain increasing traction over the course of the century. He described the writing and business of books as a

> kind of Epidemic disease, which hath afflicted Europe for a long time, and is more fit to fill warehouses of booksellers, than the libraries of the Learned. Any one may understand this to be meant of that itching desire to write books, which people are troubled with at this time. Heretofore none but the learned, or at least such as ought to be accounted so, meddled with this subject, but now-a-days there is nothing more common, it extends itself through all professions, so that now almost the very Coblers, and

Women who can scarce read, are ambitious to appear in print, and then we
may see them carrying their books from door to door, as a Hawker does his
comb cases, pins and laces.[11]

The emergence of a print book market lowered the bar of entry for authors and gradually
began to render traditional filters and constraints on the production of books increasingly
inadequate. The perception of an excess of books was motivated by a more basic assumption
about who should and should not write them.

At the end of the century, even book dealers had grown weary of a market that seemed to
be growing out of control. In his 1795 screed, *Appeal to My Nation: On the Plague of German
Books*, the German bookseller and publisher Johann Georg Heinzmann lamented that "no
nation has printed so much as the Germans."[12] For Heinzmann, late eighteenth-century
German readers suffered under a "reign of books" in which they were the unwitting pawns
of ideas that were not their own. Giving this broad cultural anxiety a philosophical frame,
and beating Carr to the punch by more than two centuries, Immanuel Kant complained
that such an overabundance of books encouraged people to "read a lot" and "superficially."[13]
Extensive reading not only fostered bad reading habits, but also caused a more general
pathological condition, *Belesenheit* [the quality of being well-read], because it exposed readers to the great "waste" [*Verderb*] of books. It cultivated uncritical thought.

Like contemporary worries about "excess," these were fundamentally normative. They
made particular claims not only about what was good or bad about print, but about what
constituted "true" knowledge. First, they presumed some unstated yet normative level of
information or, in the case of a *Bücherseuche*, some normative number of books. There are
too many books; there is too much data. But compared to what? Second, such laments
presumed the normative value of particular practices and technologies for dealing with all
of these books and all of this information. Every complaint about excess was followed by a
proposal on how to fix the apparent problem. To insist that there are too many books was to
insist that there were too many books to be read or dealt with in a particular way and thus
to assume the normative value of one form of reading over another.

Enlightenment Reading Technologies

Not so dissimilar to contemporary readers with their digital tools, eighteenth-century
German readers had a range of technologies and methods at their disposal for dealing with
the proliferation of print—dictionaries, bibliographies, reviews, note-taking, encyclopedias, marginalia, commonplace books, footnotes. These technologies made the increasing
amounts of print more manageable by helping readers to select, summarize, and organize
an ever-increasing store of information. The sheer range of technologies demonstrates that

humans usually deal with information overload through creative and sometimes surprising solutions that blur the line between humans and technology.

By the late seventeenth and early eighteenth centuries, European readers dealt with the influx of new titles and the lack of funds and time to read them all by creating virtual libraries called *bibliotheca*. At first these printed texts were simply listings of books that had been published or displayed at book fairs, but over time they began to include short reviews and summaries intended to guide the collector, scholar, and amateur in their choice and reading of books. They also allowed eighteenth-century readers to avoid reading entire books by providing summaries of individual books.

Eighteenth-century readers also made use of an increasing array of encyclopedias. In contrast to their early modern Latin predecessors that sought to summarize the most significant branches of established knowledge (designed to present an *enkuklios paideia*, or common knowledge), these Enlightenment encyclopedias were produced and sold as reference books that disseminated information more widely and efficiently by compiling, selecting, and summarizing more specialized and, above all, new knowledge. It made knowledge more general and common by sifting and constraining the purview of knowledge.[14]

Similarly, compilations, which date from at least the early modern period, employed cut and paste technologies, rather than summarization, to select, collect, and distribute the best passages from an array of books.[15] A related search technology, the biblical concordance—the first dates back to 1247—indexed every word of the Bible and facilitated its broader use for sermons and, after its translations into the vernacular, even broader audiences. Similarly, indexes became increasingly popular and big selling points of printed texts by the sixteenth century.[16]

All of these technologies facilitated a consultative reading that allowed a text to be accessed in parts instead of reading a text straight through from beginning to end.[17] By the early eighteenth century, there was even a science devoted to organizing and accounting for all of these technologies and books: *historia literaria*. It produced books about books. The technologies and methods for organizing and managing all of these books and information were embedded into other forms and even other sciences.

All of these devices and technologies provided shortcuts and methods for filtering and searching the mass of printed or scribal texts. They were technologies for managing two perennially precious resources: money (books and manuscripts were expensive) and time (it takes a lot of time to read every word).

While many overwhelmed readers welcomed these techniques and technologies, some, especially by the late eighteenth century, began to complain that they led to a derivative, second-hand form of knowledge. One of Kant's students and a key figure of the German Enlightenment, J.G. Herder, mocked the French for their attempts to deal with such a proliferation of print through encyclopedias:

> Now encyclopedias are being made, even Diderot and D'Alembert have
> lowered themselves to this. And that book that is a triumph for the French
> is for us the first sign of their decline. They have nothing to write and, thus,
> produce Abregés, vocabularies, esprits, encyclopedias—the original works
> fall away.[18]

Echoing contemporary concerns about how our reliance on Google and Wikipedia might lead to superficial forms of knowledge, Herder worried that these technologies reduced knowledge to discrete units of information. Journals reduced entire books to a paragraph or blurb; encyclopedias aggregated huge swaths of information into a deceptively simple form; compilations separated readers from the original texts.

By the mid-eighteenth century, the word "polymath"—previously used positively to describe a learned person—became synonymous with dilettante, one who merely skimmed, aggregated, and heaped together mounds of information but never knew much at all. In sum, encyclopedias and the like had reduced the Enlightenment project, these critics claimed, to mere information management. At stake was the definition of "true" knowledge. Over the course of the eighteenth century, German thinkers and authors began to make a normative distinction between what they termed *Gelehrsamkeit* and *Wissen*, between mere pedantry and true knowledge.

As this brief history of Enlightenment information technologies suggests, to claim that a particular technology has one unique effect, either positive or negative, is to reduce both historically and conceptually the complex causal nexus within which humans and technologies interact and shape each other. Carr's recent and broadly well-received arguments wondering if Google makes us stupid, for example, rely on a historical parallel that he draws with print. He claims that the invention of printing "caused a more intensive" form of reading and, by extrapolation, print caused a more reflective form of thought—words on a page focused the reader.[19]

Historically speaking, this is hyperbolic techno-determinism. Carr assumes that technologies simply "determine our situation," independent of human persons, but these very technologies, methods, and media emerge from particular historical situations with their own complex of factors.[20] Carr relies on quick allusions to historians of print to bolster his case and inoculate himself from counter-arguments, but the historian of print to whom he appeals, Elizabeth L. Eisenstein, warns that "efforts to summarize changes wrought by printing in any simple or single formula are likely to lead us astray."[21]

Arguments like Carr's—and I focus on him because he has become the vocal advocate of this view—also tend to ignore the fact that, historically, print facilitated a range of reading habits and styles. Francis Bacon, himself prone to condemning printed books, laid out at least three ways to read books: "Some books are to be tasted, others to be swallowed, and some few to be chewed and digested."[22] As a host of scholars have demonstrated of late, different ways of reading co-existed in the print era.[23]Extensive or consultative forms of reading—those that Carr might describe as distracted or unfocused—existed alongside more intensive forms of reading—those that he might describe as deep, careful, prolonged engagements with particular texts in the Enlightenment. Eighteenth-century German Pietists read the Bible very closely, but they also consistently consulted Bible concordances and Latin encyclopedias.[24] Even the form of intensive reading held up today as a dying practice, novel reading, was often derided in the eighteenth century as weakening the memory and leading to "habitual distraction," as Kant put it.[25] It was thought especially dangerous to women who, according to Kant, were already prone to such lesser forms of thought. In short, print did not cause one particular form of reading; instead, it facilitated a range of ever-newer technologies, methods, and innovations that were deeply interwoven with new forms of human life and new ways of experiencing the world.

The problem with suggestions that Google makes us stupid, smart, or whatever else we might imagine, however, is not just their historical myopia. Such reductions elide the fact that Google and print technology do not operate independently of the humans who design, interact with, and constantly modify them, just as humans do not exist independently of technologies. By focusing on technology's capacity to determine the human (by insisting that Google makes us stupid, that print *makes* us deeper readers), we risk losing sight of just how deeply our own agency is wrapped up with technology. We forego a more anthropological perspective from which we can observe "the activity of situated people trying to solve local problems."[26] To emphasize a single and direct causal link between technology and a particular form of thought is to isolate technology from the very forms of life with which it is bound up.

Considering our anxieties and utopic fantasies about technology or information super-abundance in a more historical light is one way to mitigate this tendency and gain some conceptual clarity. Thus far I have offered some very general historical and conceptual observations about technology and the history of information overload. In the next sections, I focus on one particular historical technology—the footnote—and its afterlife in our contemporary digital world.

The Footnote: From Kant to Google

Today our most common tools for organizing knowledge are algorithms and data structures. We often imagine them to be unprecedented. But Google's search engines take advantage of a rather old technology—that most academic and seemingly useless thing called the footnote. Although Google continues to tweak and improve its search engines, the data that continue to fuel them are hyperlinks, those blue colored bits of texts on the Web that if clicked will take you to another page. They are the sinews of the Web, which is simply the totality of all hyperlinks. The World Wide Web emerged in part from the efforts of a

British physicist working at CERN in the early 1990s, Tim Berners-Lee. Frustrated by the confusion that resulted from a proliferation of computers, each with its own codes and formats, he wondered how they could all be connected. He took advantage of the fact that regardless of the particular code, every computer had documents. He went on to work on codes for html, URLs, and http that could link these documents regardless of the differences among the computers themselves. It turns out that these digital hyperlinks have a revealing historical and conceptual antecedent in the Enlightenment footnote.

The modern hyperlink and the Enlightenment footnote share a logic that is grounded in assumptions about the text-based nature of knowledge. Both assume that documents, the printed texts of the eighteenth century or the digitized ones of the twenty-first century, are the basis of knowledge. And these assumptions have come to dominate not only the way we search the web, but also the ways we interact with our digital world. The history of the footnote is a curious but perspicuous example, then, of how normative, cultural assumptions and values become embedded in technology.

Footnotes have a long history in biblical commentaries and medieval annotations. Whereas these scriptural commentaries simply "buttressed a text" that derived its ultimate authority from some divine source, Enlightenment footnotes pointed to other Enlightenment texts.[27] Footnotes of this sort go back to at least the seventeenth century. John Selden's *History of Tithes* (1618) and Johannes Eisenhart *De fie historica* (1679), which emphasized the importance of citing sources, reveal the process of knowledge production. They highlighted the fact that these texts were precisely not divine or transcendent. They located the work in a particular time and place. The modern footnote anchors a text and grounds its authority not in some transcendent realm, but in the footnotes themselves. Unlike biblical commentaries, modern footnotes "seek to show that the work they support claims authority and solidity from the historical conditions of its creation."[28] The Enlightenment's citational logic is fundamentally self-referential and recursive—that is, the criteria for judgment are always given by the system of texts themselves and not something external, like divine or ecclesial authority. The value and authority of one text is established by the fact that other texts point to it. The more footnotes that point to a particular text, the more authoritative that text becomes by dent of the fact that other texts point to it.

Online newspapers and blogs are central to our public debates, but printed journals were the central medium of the Enlightenment. One of the most famous German journals was the *Berlinische Monatsschrift* published between 1783 and 1811. It published the most important articles to a broad and increasingly diverse reading public. In its first issue, the editors wrote that the journal sought "news from the entire empire [Reich] of the sciences"—ethnographic reports, biographical reports about interesting people, translations, excerpts from texts from foreign lands. The editors envisioned the journal as a central node in the broader world of information exchange and circulation. This editorial plan was then carried out according to a citational logic that structured the entire journal.

The journal's first essay, "On the Origin of the Fable of the Woman in White," centers on a fable "drawn" from another text of 1723. This citation is followed by another one citing another history, published in 1753, on the origins of the fable. The rest of the essay cites "various language scholars and scholars of antiquity" [*Sprach- und Alterthumsforscher*] to authorize its own claims. The citations and footnotes that fill the margins and the parenthetical directives that are peppered throughout the main text not only give authority to the broader argument and narrative, but also create a web of interconnected texts.

Even Kant's famous essay on the question of Enlightenment, which appeared in the same journal in 1784, begins not with a philosophical argument, but with a footnote directly underneath the title, directing the reader to a footnote from another essay published in December of 1783 that posed the original question: "What is Enlightenment?" This essay in turn directs readers to yet another article on Enlightenment from September of that year. The traditional understanding of Enlightenment is based on the self-legislation and autonomy of reason, but all of these footnotes suggest that Enlightenment reason was bound up with print technology from the beginning.

One of the central mediums of the Enlightenment, journals, operated according to a citational logic. The authority, relevance, and value of a text was undergirded—both conceptually and visually—by an array of footnotes that pointed to other texts. Like our contemporary hyperlinks, these citations interrupted the flow of reading—marked as they often were by a big asterisk or a "see page 516." Perhaps most importantly, however, all of these footnotes and citations pointed not to a single divinely inspired or authoritative text, but to a much broader network of texts. Footnotes and citations were the pointing sinews that connected and coordinated an abundance of print. By the end of the eighteenth century, there even emerged a term for all of this pointing: the language of books [*Büchersprache*]. Books were imagined to speak to one another because they constantly pointed to and cited one another. The possibility of knowledge and interaction with the broader world in the Enlightenment rested not only on the pensive, autonomous philosopher, but also within the links from book to book, essay to essay.

Google's Citational Logic

The founders of Google, Larry Page and Sergey Brin, modeled their revolutionary search engine on the citational logic of the footnote and thus transposed many of its assumptions about knowledge and technology into a digital medium. Google "organizes the world's information," as their motto goes, by modeling the hyperlink structure inherent in the document-based Web; that is, it produces search results based on all of the pointing between digital texts that hyperlinks do. Taking advantage of the enormous scaling power afforded by digitization, Google, however, takes this citational logic to both a conceptual and practical extreme. Whereas the footnotes in Enlightenment texts were always bound to particular pages, Google uses each hyperlink as a data point for its algorithms and creates a digitized map of all possible links among documents.

Page and Brin started from the insight that the web "was loosely based on the premise of citation and annotation—after all, what is a link but a citation, and what was the text describing that link but annotation."[29] Page himself saw this citational logic as the key to modeling the Web's own structure. Modern academic citation is simply the practice of pointing to other people's work—very much like the footnote. As we saw with Enlightenment journals, a citation not only lists important information about another work, but also confers authority on that work: "the process of citing others confers their rank and authority upon you—a key concept that informs the way Google works."[30]

With his original Google project, Page wanted to trace all of the links that connected different pages on the Web, not only the outgoing links, but also their backward paths. Page argued that pure computational power could produce a more complete model of the citational structure of the Web—a map of interlinked and interdependent documents by means of tracing hyperlinked citations. He intended to exploit what computer scientists refer to as the Web Graph—the set of all nodes, corresponding to static html pages, with directed hyperlinks from page A to page B. In early 1998 there were an estimated 150 million nodes joined by 2 billion links.[31]

Other search engines, however, had had this modeling idea before. Given the proliferation of Web pages and with them hyperlinks, Brin and Page, like all other search engineers, knew they had to scale up "to keep up with the growth of the web."[32] By 1994 the World Wide Web Worm (WWWW) had indexed 110,000 pages, but by 1997 WebCrawler had indexed over 100 million Web documents. As Brin and Page put it in 1998, it was "foreseeable" that by 2000 a comprehensive index would contain over a billion documents. They were not merely intent on indexing pages or modeling all of the links between documents on the Web, however. They were also interested in increasing the "quality of results" that search engines returned. In order for searches to improve, their search engine would focus not just on the comprehensiveness, but on the relevance or quality of its results.

The insight that made Google Google was the recognition that all links and all pages are not equal. In designing their link analysis algorithm, PageRank, Brin and Page recognized that the real power of this citational logic rested not just in counting links from all pages equally, but in "*normalizing* by the number of links on a page."[33] The key difference between Google and early digital search technologies (like the WWWW and the early Yahoo) was that it did not simply count or collate citations. Other early search engines were too descriptive, too neutral. Brin and Page reasoned that users wanted help not just in collecting but in evaluating all of those millions of webpages. From its beginnings at Stanford, the PageRank algorithm modeled the normative value of one page over another. It was concerned not simply with questions of completeness or managerial efficiency, but of value. It exploited the often-overlooked fact that hyperlinks, like those Enlightenment footnotes, not only connected document to document, but offered an implicit evaluation. The technology of the hyperlink, like the footnote, is not neutral but laden with normative evaluations.

The Algorithmic Self

In conclusion, I would like to forestall a possible concern that in historicizing information overload, I risk eliding the particularity of our own digital world and dismissing valid concerns, like Carr's, about how we interact with our digital technologies. In highlighting the analogies between Google and Enlightenment print culture, I have attempted to resist the alarmism and utopianism that tend to frame current discussions of our digital culture, first by historicizing these concerns and second by demonstrating that technology needs to be understood in deep, embodied connection with the human. Considered in these terms, the question of whether Google is making us stupid or smart might give way to more complex and productive questions. What, for example, is the idea of the human person underlying Google's efforts to organize the world's information and what forms of human life does it facilitate?

In order to address such questions, we need to understand that the Web relies on us as much as we rely on it. Every time we click, type in a search term, or update our Facebook status, the Web changes just a bit. "Google might not be making us stupid but we are making it (and Facebook) smarter" because of all the information that we feed them both every day.[34] The links that make up the Web are evidence of this. They not only point to other pages, but also highlight the contingency of the Web's structure by highlighting how the Web at any given moment is produced, manipulated, and organized by hundreds of millions of individual users. Links embody the contingency of the Web, its historical and ever-changing structure of which humans are an essential element.

Thinking more in terms of a digital ecology or environment and less in a human vs. technology dichotomy, we can understand the Web, as James Hendler, Tim Berners-Lee, and colleagues recently put it, not just as an isolated machine "to be engineered for improved performance," but as a "phenomenon with which we interact." They write, "at the microscale, the Web is an infra-structure of artificial languages and protocols; it is a piece of engineering. However, it is the interaction of human beings creating, linking, and consuming information that generates the Web's behavior as emergent properties at the macro-scale."[35]

It is at this level of analysis, where the human and its technologies are inextricable and together form something like a digital ecology, that we can, for example, evaluate a recent claim of one of Google's founders. Discussing the future of the search firm, Page described the "perfect search engine" as that which would "understand exactly what I mean and give me back exactly what I want."[36] Such an "understanding," however, is a function of the implicit normativity of the citational logic that Google's search engine shares with the Enlightenment footnote. These technologies never leave our desires and thoughts unmediated and unmanipulated. But Google's search engines transform the normativity of the citational logic of the footnote in important and particular ways that have come to distinguish the digital age from the print age. Whereas an Enlightenment reader might have been able to connect four or five footnotes without much effort, Google's search engine follows hundreds of millions of links in a fraction of a second. The embodied human can all too easily seem to disappear at such scales. If, as I have done above, the relevance of technology has to be argued for in the Enlightenment, then the inverse is the case for our digital age—the relevance of the embodied human agent has to be argued for today.

On the one hand, individual human persons play a rather insignificant role in Google's operations. When we conduct a search on Google, the process of evaluation is fundamentally different from the form of evaluation tied to the footnote. Because Google's search engine operates at such massive scales, it evaluates and normalizes links (judges which ones are relevant) through a recursive function. PageRank is an iterative algorithm—all outputs become inputs in an endless loop. The value of something on the Web is determined simply by the history of what millions of users have valued—that is, its inputs are always a function of its outputs. It is a highly scaled-up feedback loop. A Google search can only ever retrieve what is already in a document. It can only ever find what is known to the system of linked documents. The system is defined not by a particular object, operator, or node within the system, but rather by the history of the algorithm's own operations.

If my son's Web page on the construction of his tree house has no incoming links, then his page, practically speaking, does not exist according to PageRank's logic. Google web crawlers will not find it—or if they do, it will have a very low rank—and thus, because we experience the Web through Google, neither will you. The freedom of the Web—the freedom to link and follow links—is a function of the closed and recursive nature of the system, one that includes by necessarily excluding. Most contemporary search engines, Google chief among them, now share the assumption that a "hyperlink" is a marker of authority or endorsement. Serendipity is nearly impossible in such a document-centric Web. Questions of value and authority are functions of and subject to the purported wisdom of the digital crowd that is itself a normalized product of an algorithmic calculation of value and authority.[37]

The normative "I" that Google assumes, the "I" that Page's perfect search engine would understand, is an algorithmic self. It is a function of a citational logic that has been extended to an algorithmic logic. It is an "I" constructed by a limited and fundamentally contingent Web marked by our own history of searches, our own well-worn paths. What I want at any given moment is forever defined by what I have always wanted or what my demographic others have always wanted.

On the other hand, individual human persons are central agents in Google's operations because they author hyperlinks. Columnists like Paul Krugman and Peggy Noonan make decisions about what to link to and what not to link to in their columns. Similarly, as we click from link to link (or choose not to click), we too make decisions and judgments about the value of a link and thus of the document that hosts it.

Because algorithms increase the scale of such operations by processing millions of links, however, they obscure this more human element of the Web. All of those decisions to link from one particular page to the next, to click from one link to the next involve not just a link-fed algorithm, but hundreds of millions of human persons interacting with Google every minute. These are the human interactions that have an impact on the Web at the macro-level, and they are concealed by the promises of the Google search box.

Only at this macro-level of analysis can we make sense of the fact that Google's search algorithms do not operate in absolute mechanical purity, free of outside interference. Only if we understand the Web and our search and filter technologies as elements in a digital ecology can we make sense of the emergent properties of the complex interactions of humans and technology: gaming the Google system through search optimization strategies, the decision by Google employees (not algorithms) to ban certain webpages and privilege others (ever notice the relatively recent dominance of Wikipedia pages in Google searches?). The Web is not just a technology but an ecology of human-technology interaction. It is a dynamic culture with its own norms and practices.

New technologies, be it the printed encyclopedia or Wikipedia, are not abstract machines that independently render us stupid or smart. As we saw with Enlightenment reading technologies, knowledge emerges out of complex processes of selection, distinction, and judgment—out of the irreducible interactions of humans and technology. We should resist the false promise that the empty box below the Google logo has come to represent—either unmediated access to pure knowledge or a life of distraction and shallow information. It is a ruse. Knowledge is hard won; it is crafted, created, and organized by humans and their technologies. Google's search algorithms are only the most recent in a long history of technologies that humans have developed to organize, evaluate, and engage their world.

(Spring 2012, 14.1)

Notes

[1]   Ann Blair, "Information Overload, the Early Years," *The Boston Globe* (28 November 2010).

[2]   Mark N. Hansen, *Embodying Technesis: Technology beyond Writing* (Ann Arbor, MI: University of Michigan Press, 2010), 235.

[3]   Kevin Kelly, "Scan This Book!," *The New York Times* (14 May 2006), http://www.nytimes.com/2006/05/14/magazine/14publishing.html?pagewanted=all.

[4]   Randall Stross, "World's Largest Social Network: The Open Web," *The New York Times* (15 May 2010), http:// www.nytimes.com/2010/05/16/business/16digi.html.

5   The most euphoric among them speak of a coming "singularity" when computer intelligence will exceed human intelligence.

6   For a less utopian and more nuanced account of a posthuman era, see Friedrich Kittler, *Gramophone, Film, Typewriter*, trans. Geoffrey Winthrop-Young and Michael Wutz (Palo Alto, CA: Stanford University Press, 1999).

7   Nicholas Carr, "Is Google Making Us Stupid?: What the Internet Is Doing to Our Brains," *The Atlantic* (July– August 2008), http://www.theatlantic.com/magazine/ archive/2008/07/is-google-making-us-stupid/6868/. See also the expansion of his argument in *The Shallows: What the Internet Is Doing to Our Brains* (New York, NY: Norton, 2010).

8   Quoted in Ann Blair, *Too Much to Know: Managing Scholarly Information before the Modern Age* (New Haven, CT: Yale University Press, 2010), 15.

9   Quoted in Stuart Brown, "The Seventeenth-Century Intellectual Background," *The Cambridge Companion to Leibniz*, ed. Nicholas Jolley (New York, NY: Cambridge University Press, 1995), 61 n28.

10 Johann Gottfried Herder, *Briefe zur Beförderung der Humanität* (Berlin and Weimar, Germany: Aufbau-Verlag, 1971), II: 92–93.

11 A review of Christian Thomasius's *Observationum selectarum ad rem litterariam spectantium* [*Select Observations Related to Learning*], volume II (Halle, 1702), which was published in the April 1702 edition of the monthly British newspaper *History of the Works of the Learned, Or an Impartial Account of Books Lately Printed in all Parts of Europein*, as cited in David McKitterick, "Bibliography, Bibliophily and Organization of Knowledge," The Foundations of Knowledge: Papers Presented at Clark Library (Los Angeles, CA: Willam Andrews Clark Memorial Library, 1985), 202.

12 Johann Georg Heinzmann, *Appell an meine Nation: Über die Pest der deutschen Literatur* (Bern, Switzerland: 1795), 125.

13 Immanuel Kant, *Philosophical Encyclopedia*, 29:30, in Kant's *Gesammelte Schriften*, ed. Königliche Preußische (later Deutsche) Akademie der Wissenschaften (Berlin, Germany: Walter de Gruyter, 1902–present).

14 See Richard R. Yeo, *Encyclopaedic Visions: Scientific Dictionaries and Enlightenment Culture* (Cambridge, England: Cambridge University Press, 2001).

15 Blair, *Too Much to Know*, 34.

16 Ibid., 53.

17 Ibid., 8.

18 Herder quoted in Ernst Behler, "Friedrich Schegels Enzyklopädie der literarischen Wissenschaften im Unterschied zu Hegels Enzyklopädie der philosophischen Wissenschaften," Studien zur Romantik und idealistischen Philosophie (Paderborn, Germany: Schöningh, 1988), 246.

19 From an interview with Nicholas Carr available at http://bigthink.com/nicholarcarr.

20 Kittler, xxxix.

21 Elizabeth L. Eisenstein, *The Printing Revolution in Early Modern Europe* (New York, NY: Cambridge University Press, 2005), 332.

22 Francis Bacon, "On Studies," *Essays with Annotations* (Boston, MA: Lee and Shepard, 1884), 482.

23 Much of this work has been done in German-language scholarship. For an English-language overview, see Guglielmo Cavallo and Roger Chartier, ed., *A History of Reading in the West* (Amherst, MA: University of Massachusetts Press, 1999).

24 See Jonathan Sheehan, *The Enlightenment Bible: Translation, Scholarship, Culture* (Princeton, NJ: Princeton University Press, 2005).

[25] Immanuel Kant, *Anthropologie*, 7:208 in Kant's *Gesammelte Schriften*, ed. Königliche Preußische (later Deutsche) Akademie der Wissenschaften (Berlin, Germany: Walter de Gruyter, 1902–present).

[26] Hansen, 271n8.

[27] Anthony Grafton, *The Footnote: A Curious History* (Cambridge, MA: Harvard University Press, 1997), 32.

[28] Grafton, 32.

[29] John Batelle, *The Search: How Google and its Rivals Rewrote the Rules of Business and Transformed Our Culture* (New York, NY: Portfolio, 2005), 72.

[30] Ibid., 70.

[31] James Glieck, *The Information: A History, a Theory, a Flood* (New York, NY: Pantheon, 2011), 423.

[32] Sergey Brin and Lawrence Page, "The Anatomy of a Large-Scale Hypertextual Web Search Engine," *Computer Networks and ISDN Systems* 30 (1998): 107–17.

[33] Ibid., 214–15.

[34] Siva Vaidhyanathan, *The Googlization of Everything (And Why We Should Worry)* (Berkeley, CA: University of California Press, 2011), 182.

[35] James Hendler, et al., "Web Science: An Interdisciplinary Approach to Understanding the Web," *Communications of the ACM* 51.7 (July 2008): 60–69.

[36] Larry Page, as quoted at http://www.google.com/about/ corporate/company/tech.html.

[37] Critics of Google's document-centric search technologies have long been promising the advent of a semantic web that would "free" data from a document-based web. Some see social media tools like Facebook and Twitter as offering something similar. For an early vision of what this might look like, see Tim Berners-Lee, James Hendler, and Ora Lassila, "The Semantic Web," *The Scientific American* (17 May 2001): 34–43.

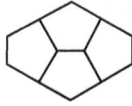

Under the Sign of Satan
William Blake in the Corporate University

Mark Edmundson

"I in my Selfhood am that Satan. I am that Evil One."

—William Blake, "Milton"

1.

Imagine waking up in a world gone wrong. You can feel it: things are out of joint. The center's not quite holding and all the rest. Yet imagine that world as being more agreeable—more secure, more organized, more civilized (in a certain sense)—than any world you had ever imagined inhabiting. One has a wealthy sponsor. One is sheltered, valued. There is the matter of prestige. There is a firm sense of identity, at the very least. One can do one's work. Distractions are few, privileges many. Yet still there is little doubt: one lives in a world gone wrong.

William Blake found himself in such a position when he turned himself over to the protection of his prosperous, kindly friend, William Hayley. Hayley rescued Blake and his wife Catherine from poverty (maybe from financial ruin) and from the neglect that had plagued the poet-painter's work. He brought them out of the blighted, glorious London that Blake loved and into the countryside. (Blake's attitude toward Nature was complex, but overall unfavorable.) Hayley gave Blake time, space, and money; he tried to make the poet into a success.

Blake's grand-sized visionary paintings did not sell? No one wanted to buy his gorgeous, sometimes rather garishly illuminated books? Very well. Hayley wanted Blake to succeed, and Blake did not wish to be dependent on Hayley's charity forever. So Hayley put Blake to work painting miniatures, tiny portraits for broaches and necklaces. Blake, who loved to be expansive, was compelled to do small things. But Hayley loved Blake—Blake knew it. He truly wanted this man of genius to prosper, gain recognition, stand on his own two feet, and all the rest. In a sense, Blake never had a better friend than William Hayley.

2.

No one liked it when Hulk Hogan came to town. At least no one I know did. Hulk came to Charlottesville to perform with his wrestling troupe at the John Paul Jones Arena at the University of Virginia. We had imagined, my faculty friends and I, that the arena would be the site for basketball games and maybe a graduation ceremony or two on rainy days. But not long after the grand opening of the arena, we heard about Hulk and his crew, and then we heard of a performance by something called Monster Trucks. The climax of the Monster Trucks show, I was told, came when a particularly monstrous monster truck, with tires taller than two or three men, rode over the tops of a line of parked vehicles, crushing them into a metal pulp. When the subject of Hulk Hogan and the Monster Trucks arose, my faculty buddies and I looked at each other in exasperated ways and blew out exasperated columns of air, as if to scatter the wrestlers and the steroidal trucks like so many leaves. But we did not say all that much. No, not much at all.

The University of Virginia, like virtually all universities, is a corporation. It requires revenue. It needs to generate funds. There is an operating budget, and expenses must be met, among them the expenses of maintaining me in the English department, and my friends in music, architecture, and religious studies.

That universities are becoming more corporate in orientation and aim is news to no one. We—like every other school that aspires to a certain status, a certain measure of success—have added layer upon layer of administrators. We have brought on no end of fundraisers. More than that, many of the deans once charged with overseeing academic affairs are now also out seeking money from donors. A story in the *New York Times* tells us that over the past two decades, colleges and universities in America have doubled their full-time support staff. Enrollment has increased only 40 percent, full time instructors rose by only fifty, and many of those new instructors are non-tenure-track. The article goes on to say that

> the growth in support staff included some jobs that did not exist 20 years ago, like environmental sustainability officers and a broad array of

information technology workers. The support staff category includes many different jobs, like residential-life staff, admissions and recruitment officers, fund-raisers, loan counselors and all the back-office staff positions responsible for complying with the new regulations and reporting requirements colleges face.[1]

With these changes, a new institutional culture is coming into being. Universities now teem with people who must do what people who work in corporations do: be responsive to their superiors, direct their underlings, romance their Blackberries, subordinate their identities, refrain from making mistakes, keep a gimlet eye always on the bottom line. Organization men and women have come, and they are doing what they can—for an administrator must administer something—to influence the shape of the university. Are they having an influence on the students? Often they don't have to, for many of our students—not all, many—are already organization men and women. Though "organization man" is not the name in favor now; the current term of art is "leader."

How does a young person begin to qualify to become what is now called a leader? The essayist William Deresiewicz talks about the endless series of hoops that students have to jump through now if they hope to get into the right colleges: "Classes, standardized tests, extracurriculars in school, extracurriculars outside of school. Test prep courses, admissions coaches, private tutors." What you get at the end, he says, are "great kids who [have] been trained to be world-class hoop jumpers."[2]

All colleges and universities want leaders. They recruit them from high school. They cultivate them once they have arrived. Colleges are determined to graduate leaders and send them into the world to become prosperous and grateful alumni. But who is a leader? A leader is someone who is drawn to organizations, learns their usages, internalizes their rules. He merges his identity with that of the organization. He always says "we." He starts at the bottom, a leader in training. Then he progresses, always by gradual steps, as close to the top as his powers will allow. He begins "mentoring" other leaders. In his ascent, he is assiduous to get along with people. He blends in like a white moth on a white-washed picket fence. Everyone likes him. He gives no offense, and, where possible, he takes none. He questions the presiding powers, but in the manner of a minor angel, inquiring into the ways of his more opulently fledged brethren.

3.

In "London," perhaps his best-known poem, Blake takes on the role of one of the biblical prophets—Isaiah, Ezekiel, Jeremiah—and rambles through the great city. What he sees stuns him. He is sick to articulate rage about it. The human aspirations to kindliness, community, and gentleness have been drowned in hypocrisy. The little chimney sweeps cry "Every black'ning Church appalls." The sweeps, orphaned, sold into something tantamount to slavery, get no succor from the church. Their cries blacken an already black hulking monolith. The soldier's sigh "Runs in blood down Palace walls." Wars far away—in America, among other places—have sent soldiers off to risk their lives, not for noble ends, but to suppress others' liberty and open up new markets for British merchants.

But perhaps worst of all in Blake's London is the state of love. (Blake greatly values heterosexual love—is in love with it, in fact.) The wandering prophet, edging toward rage, about to go over to Rintrah, as Blake liked to put it, hears "How the youthful Harlot's curse / Blasts the newborn Infant's tear / And blights with plagues the Marriage hearse." Prostitution is to Blake one of the worst human depravities. The man of property, subject to an arranged marriage, flies to the prostitute. She gives him an escape from his loveless marriage; she gives him some measure of intrigue and excitement; she also gives him syphilis, which infects his wife and ruins his marriage.

In Blake's view, the church should engender a community of loving-kindness. The army should encourage bravery in just wars. People should meet and love regardless of finances and social class. Sexual joy should be the culmination of real attraction of body and mind, whether sanctified by marriage or not. Prophets should not be compelled to rage blindly through the streets of London, witnesses to human despair. "I mark," says Blake, "in every face I meet / Marks of weakness, marks of woe." The prophet should offer wise and genial counsel and not be compelled to tremble with rage.

4.

The engineering student sits in the fiction writer's office and asks questions about her craft. This fiction thing, this art thing, what is it about? What is it about exactly? He has read some novels and plans to read many more. His grade point average is high. His SAT scores are also impressive. A nearly perfect score on the verbal test—he makes sure to mention this. He is—he knows—very smart.

But this fiction thing and poetry as well. How does one begin? (The fellow who wrote *The Crying of Lot 49*—what was his name?—he was an engineering student too, right?) There are, he's heard, guidebooks that give step-by-step instructions. Does the teacher advise trying one?

The teacher's way of writing fiction is to find an image, something that lodges in her mind for no reason she can understand. She writes the image down. She describes it as well as she can from a vantage point that is—maybe—not quite her own.

And then what? The student is truly interested.

She waits to see what will happen from there.

And?

Sometimes something happens. Sometimes nothing.

This is writing? This is what you do?

Other people do it differently. But yes. I wait to see what will happen. She tells the student that if she lets her attention float with just the right amount of freedom, she'll eventually go somewhere she's fascinated by going.

Why don't you just start with what fascinates you?

I don't always know, the writer confesses. I don't always really know.

5.

Satan weeps frequently. It's surprising, but true. In Blake's epic, "Milton," Satan is a culti-vated, thoughtful, highly sensitive specimen of what the eighteenth century liked to call a Man of Sensibility. He is not overwhelmingly intellectual. He appears to put feelings before thoughts. Nor is he the fiery, rather charismatic figure that Milton conjures up with a massive more-than-Achillean shield and a spear to which the tallest Norwegian pine tree is but a wand. Blake's Satan has no tail, no claws, no fangs, no cloven foot, not even an odor of pitch on arrival and departure. This Satan is urbanely kind. He is Hayley, the man who brought Blake out of London to Felpham, so Blake the genius might be saved. Of course there are the miniatures, which Blake does not wish to paint. "When Hayley finds out what you cannot do / That is the very thing he'll set you to," Blake complains. There are also some tensions in sensibility: Hayley, who is Satan, is rather on the refined side. "Hayley on his toi-lette seeing the soap / Cries, 'Homer is very much improv'd by Pope.'" Hayley prefers Pope's refined translations of the *Iliad* and the *Odyssey* to Homer's actual unflinching vision. Being on the toilet, close to his odorous humanity, makes Hayley long for purity, long for Pope.

Hayley—and Satan, too—love poetry. They are drawn to poets; they find them mys-terious, alluring, perhaps rather enviable. But then comes the question: why should they, Satan and Hayley, not be poets as well? Already they have succeeded brilliantly at what they have set their hands to do. Hayley is good at business, better than good. As for Satan—here matters get more complicated. Satan has a cosmic role: he presides over time, clock time, ordering, duration. He is the lord of Chronos. All forms of regulation, consistency, and order fall under his power. He grinds time the way a farmer grinds wheat. No sand grain passes through the glass of time without Satan's awareness and approval. He propels the sun punctually through the houses of the zodiac. He measures the shadows on the moon's white face. He is God as a watchmaker, God as a supreme engineer.

But this is not enough for him. Satan also wants to be a poet. He is infatuated with Palamabron, the giant figure who wields the harrow. Palamabron breaks in order to create again; he engraves the soil. His work is sustenance to those who hunger in spirit as well as body. Palamabron concentrates all that Blake feels to be true about true artists. An idealization? Yes, maybe. But Blake deals in giant forms—grand, emblematic concentrations of force.

Finally Satan prevails upon Los, father of the eternals, to let him take Palamabron's harrow from his hands. What happens then? "Satan labour'd all day—it was a thousand years." Or at least it probably feels that way to Blake—the age of Pope and Dryden and Joshua Reynolds and Locke and Hobbes is a desert of tedium to Blake. It probably feels like a millennium. Engineers—people who want to understand art, draw blue prints, and then get to work constructing things—are now the lords of light who live where true thinkers and artists should reside. A mess!

The mess has a double dimension, though. Palamabron's poetic attendants—Blake calls then "gnomes"—take over Satan's time-grinding mills. They get drunk as a tribe of monkeys and stumble around singing the songs of Palamabron. Minutes presumably last hours now; sometimes seconds probably expand into days; some days go blink and are gone. Another mess! The gnomes want to get back to the field, start engraving, start creating again—though getting drunk and messing with temporality is probably diverting to them for a little while.

Satan always wants to grasp the harrow—he wants to be lord high commissioner of everything and creator spirit, all at the same time. He wants to dominate time—as the bureaucrat of the minute—and also to live outside of time where real creation takes place. He wants to engineer odes.

Sometimes Blake loses all of his patience with Satan and wants to purge him out and away. Get thee behind me, and all of that. In "Milton" there is a culminating scene in which Blake, possessed by an apocalyptic fury, goes on about being washed clean in the blood of the lamb and purging away all of the non-human, until "Generation is swallowed up in Regeneration," nature is swallowed up by true human culture. No more Satan then, no more crippling dualisms, just the bliss of ongoing creation, which Blake calls Eden.

6.

Yet at other times one feels that Blake rather likes Satan, much as he rather liked Hayley. "Corporeal friends are spiritual enemies," Blake famously said. Yes, perhaps. But perhaps only to the measure that artists, those spiritual questers, allow them to be. Palamabron could presumably have told Los—the executive faculty of the mind, the spirit of the age, whatever he might be—to Take Off when he demanded the plough for Satan. Artists need Satan to run the world. There must be surgeons and airline pilots and directors of academic fundraising. Satan is after all "Prince of the Starry Hosts / And of the Wheels of Heaven," and in this there is some honor—as long as Satan retains his place and stays off Palamabron's rightful turf.

Artists need a Satanic side sometimes, too. You've got to know how to butter your parsnips, Frost said. ("Provide, provide!," he cries out to his old crone who was once a star of the silver screen and is now scouring the front steps "with pail and rag.") Satan often knows where the butter dish is stored.

It can be tempting for the artist to give up and hand everything over to Satan. Or to be too compliant when Satan asks: Are there books with blueprints for how to write a poem? Of course there are, the weary and neglected writer replies. Good ones, too. She resolves that tonight maybe she will have a peek.

The contemporary artist can be prone to forget what he stands for in a way that Blake never did. Or he can get weary, as Blake surely did, of endorsing his ideals in a culture that cares little for them. Blake knew what he wanted: love that exalted lover and beloved. He knew that the measure of a society is the care, affection, and wisdom that it expends on children. Blake disliked war; he preferred what he called "mental fight." But he surely preferred just wars, like the American Revolution, which gladdened and amazed him, to unjust ones. He wanted poets to be prophets and to call things as they saw them. He told us these things in "London." He seems to have meant them. He left his giant forms to remind us.

Hulk Hogan and those Monster Trucks are giant forms in their own ways. They are, I suppose, Satan's idea of poetry at its very worst: obvious, noisy, and lucrative. They are such gross caricatures that in time even Satan is probably made weary of them. He would dearly love it, I half believe, if Palamabron in his current form would take the harrow out of Satan's hands and tell Hulk, who seems as amiable as Hayley, that it is time to go home. But the contemporary Palamabron has experienced deconstruction and pragmatism and cultural studies, and he knows how to see the world with what Nietzsche called a "perspectival seeing." He doubts his every reflex, Palamabron does. He cannot love what he loves. He cannot believe in eternal truth or everlasting beauty. So now he abides Satan who in his heart probably does not want to be tolerated half so well.

For why did the administrators who seem more and more to dominate the academic scene come to academia in the first place? Why didn't they stay in business where the salaries are higher, the perks cushier, and where everyone seems to receive weekly and gratis a zippy, new, hand-held wireless device? Maybe they came because they wanted to learn things—enduring things, humane things. They wanted to be in a place where people talked about Plato and Blake and Shakespeare and Schopenhauer, rather than exclusively about Hulk Hogan and the bottom line. I sometimes think that there are more *potential* intellectual idealists among the administrators than among the faculty. But as long as we professors can't tell them exactly what is wrong with Hulk Hogan and the Monster Trucks, what are they supposed to do? As long as we can't say why Shakespeare is better than the next episode of *Jersey Shore*, how will they help us and help universities to be enduring centers of learning and of art?

If you do not cultivate (and discipline) Satan, he will grow ever more powerful and ever more pragmatic. He will come to represent worldly values and nothing else, and his confidence in these values will grow and grow. So when Satan in his current guise finally tells Palamabron to fall down and worship him, what will—what can?—Palamabron do?

(Spring 2012, 14.1)

Notes

[1] Tamar Lewin, "Staff Jobs on Campus Outpace Enrollment," *The New York Times* (20 April 2009); http://www.nytimes.com/2009/04/21/education/21college.html.

[2] William Deresiewicz, "Solitude and Leadership," *The American Scholar* (Spring 2010); http://theamericanscholar.org/solitude-and-leadership/. They are, as one member of the generation observes, "excellent sheep."

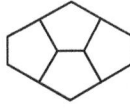

How We Lost Our Attention

Matthew B. Crawford

We are living through a cultural crisis of attention that is now widely remarked upon, usually in the context of some complaint or other about technology. As our mental lives become more fragmented, what is at stake seems to be nothing less than the question of whether one can maintain a coherent self. I mean a self that can act in the world according to settled purposes and ongoing projects, rather than flitting about. The way we tend to view this problem is that our mental autonomy is at risk.

This is all true enough. But I want to suggest that the experience of *attending* to something isn't easily made sense of in the language of autonomy, and that if we want to understand the current crisis, we will have to find another way to think about attention.

Understood literally, *autonomy* means giving a law to oneself. The opposite of autonomy thus understood is *heteronomy*: being ruled by something alien to oneself. In a culture predicated on this opposition (autonomy good, heteronomy bad), it is difficult to think clearly about attention—the faculty that joins us to the world—because everything outside one's skull is regarded as a potential source of heteronomy, and therefore a threat to the self.

If this sounds like an overstatement, that's because it is. It is an extremity that is implicit in the view of the human person that comes to us from certain Enlightenment figures who were working out a new and quite radical notion of freedom. To do justice to the phenomenon of attention, we will have to interrogate that notion of freedom by revisiting the polemical setting in which it was first articulated.

The Underlying Strata

When we talk about freedom, what we are keen to be free *from* is a moving target; it shows up differently at different historical moments. John Locke fleshed out the idea of freedom in a way that was necessary for his political arguments but also required a re-description of the human being, and of our basic situation in the world. Ultimately, it required a new account of how we *apprehend* the world. To anticipate:

- We are enjoined to be free from authority—both the kind that is nakedly coercive and the kind that operates through claims to knowledge. If we are to get free of the latter, we cannot rely on the testimony of others.
- The positive idea that emerges, by subtraction, is that freedom amounts to radical self-responsibility. This is both a political principle and an epistemic one.
- We achieve radical self-responsibility, ultimately, by relocating the standards for truth from outside ourselves to within ourselves. Reality is not self-revealing; we can know it only by constructing mental *representations* of it.
- Attention is thus demoted. Attention is the faculty through which we encounter the world directly. If such an encounter isn't possible, then attention has no official role to play.

My hypothesis in what follows is that Enlightenment epistemology was not the fruit of a serene inquiry into how our minds work. It began as a quarrel about politics, and had a polemical point. The quarrel was "won," as a historical fact, by the party that was animated by a single master principle: to *liberate*—whether from the ancien régime, ecclesiastical authority, or Aristotelian metaphysics. That is why the term *liberalism* is useful for characterizing the big metaphysical and anthropological picture that was established in those revolutionary centuries in which the quarrel played out.

Allow me to sound one further preparatory note before we dive in. I find it instructive to regard our current landscape, and the ideal self who inhabits it, as the sedimented result of a history of forgotten polemics, whose common feature is that they have been animated by this will to liberate. Self-understanding, then, requires digging down into the history of philosophical thinking, for it is in these quarrels that the sediments have been deposited. The point isn't to reach bedrock—some foundational, ahistorical self—but rather to do like a geologist and get a clear sectional view of the strata. If we could do this, I think it would help us to see the topography of current experience a little differently.

Demoting Attention

For John Locke, the main threat against which it was necessary to assert freedom was the arbitrary exercise of coercive power by the political sovereign. The political theory that prevailed in his time (the seventeenth century) legitimized such power by positing a fundamental difference in kind between the sovereign and everyone else. Various arguments tied monarchy to God's will: the sovereign was God's representative on earth, or there was a nested order such that child is to parent as citizen is to the sovereign, and the sovereign is to God. Locke's strategy, however sincere (and scholars disagree on this), was to offer a theological argument of his own: God is so much greater than man, the difference is so unfathomable, that this relation mocks any attempt by one man to claim godlike, coercive power over another.[1] We are all equal in our smallness before God. Therefore, our natural estate is one of freedom in relation to one another.

Locke spelled this out further: once upon a time, we lived in a "state of nature," whose defining feature was the absence of some recognized authority, a third party to arbitrate disputes. At some points in Locke's *Two Treatises of Government* (1690), this appears to be a historical claim about how we once lived; at other points, it is a conceptual device to describe the moral relations that obtain between persons who have not consented to a common government. In the state of nature, the dictates of one's own reason are all that one obeys—there is no such thing as "authority." Political society is instituted in a decisive moment when people give their consent to abide by the rulings of a common judge in whom they invest authority, at which point they acquire political rights and responsibilities. The issue of consent is key: This is the source of the legitimacy of all authority, and of the rights one retains against that authority.

We may allow ourselves to wonder, when does this all-important act of consent happen? I was born into a society that was already up and running, and isn't this the case for almost all of us? Maybe I give my consent to the regime tacitly—for example, by walking on the public road. But I don't have much choice in this, do I? If I veer off the public road and try to bushwhack my way overland, I will quickly encounter "No Trespassing" signs. *Other people* got here first. Locke's theory of legitimate authority founded on consent describes not the normal course of things but a hypothetical moment of political founding. It is not the founding moment of any actual revolution, but of a fable in which there is no already-existing society, and the land is unclaimed. At the foundation of our political anthropology is a creature who comes into existence in a moment of free deliberation (shall I consent to this arrangement?) that occurs in a present unconditioned by the past. The freedom of the liberal self is the freedom of newness and isolation.[2]

Locke's concern with illegitimate authority extends beyond the kind that is nakedly coercive, to the kind that operates through claims to knowledge. His political project is thus tied to an epistemological one. The two are of a piece, because "he is certainly the most subjected, the most enslaved, who is so in his Understanding."[3] Locke does some of his most consequential liberating in his *Essay Concerning Human Understanding* (1690), from which the preceding quote is taken.

Charles Taylor points out that "the whole *Essay* is directed against those who would control others by specious principles supposedly beyond question."[4] These are the priests and the "schoolmen," those carriers of an ossified Aristotelian tradition. The Reformation notwithstanding, political authority and ecclesiastical authority remained very much entwined and co-dependent in Locke's day, and for a century and more thereafter.

Political freedom requires intellectual independence, then. Locke takes this further. Following Descartes, he enjoins us to be free from established custom and received opinions—indeed, from other people altogether, taken as authorities. "We may as rationally hope to see with other Mens Eyes, as to know by other Mens Understandings... The floating of other Mens Opinions in our brains makes us not a jot more knowing, though they happen to be true."[5]

The project for political freedom thus shades into something more expansive: we should aspire to a kind of epistemic self-responsibility. I myself should be the source of all my knowledge; otherwise, it is not knowledge. Such self-responsibility is the positive image of freedom that emerges by subtraction, when you go far enough in pursuit of the negative goal of being free from authority.

But this self-responsibility brings with it a certain anxiety: If I have to stand on my own two feet, epistemically, this provokes me to wonder, how can I be sure that my knowledge really is knowledge? An intransigent stance against the testimony of others leads to the problem of skepticism.

How do we know some evil genius hasn't deceived us? Even our own senses lead us astray—for example, in optical illusions. Descartes took the very existence of an external world as a legitimate problem for philosophy to worry about. He wanted *certainty*, some foundation for knowledge that would be impervious to skeptical challenge. As he thought about this, it occurred to him that this experience itself—"I am thinking"—is beyond doubt. If I am thinking, I must exist. This is the secure beginning point that must serve as the foundation for knowledge altogether. What we need, then, are rules for the conduct of the mind that we can follow from this secure beginning to build up certain knowledge. It is not the content of our thinking that matters now, but how we arrive at that content. This conclusion entails a new conception of what it means to be rational. The standard for rationality is no longer substantive, but procedural, as Taylor points out. And this means that the standard for truth is relocated: It is no longer found out in the world, but inside our own heads.[6]

Attention is therefore demoted. Or, rather, it is redirected. Not by fastening on objects in the world does it help us grasp reality, but by being directed to our own processes of thinking, and making *them* the object of scrutiny. What it means to know, now, is not to encounter the world directly (thinking you have done so is always subject to skeptical challenge), but to construct a mental *representation* of the world, according to canons of correct method.

Another early modern thinker, Giambattista Vico, summed up this view succinctly: *We know only what we make.* This motto well captures the revolution in science accomplished by Galileo and Newton. Natural science became for the first time *mathematical*, relying on mental representations based on idealizations such as the perfect vacuum, the friction-less surface, the point mass, the perfectly elastic collision. What this amounted to, Martin Heidegger said, some three centuries later, is "a project[ion] of thingness which, as it were, skips over the things."[7]

One way to state the conviction that all of these Enlightenment figures shared is that *reality is not self-revealing.* The way it shows up in ordinary experience is not to be taken seriously. For example, we see a blue dress; but "blue" isn't in the dress, it's a mental state. Descartes and Locke both insisted on a distinction between "primary qualities," which are properties of things themselves, and "secondary qualities," which are a function of our own perceptual apparatus. The true description of the dress would refrain from invoking the latter sort of property, and say not that it is blue but that its fabric reflects light of a certain wavelength (as we would now say), which we see as blue. We are to take a detached stance toward our own experience, and subject it to critical analysis from a perspective that isn't infected with our own subjectivity.[8]

Let us pause for a moment to let the weirdness of all this sink in. Notice that we have moved (very quickly, in this compressed treatment) from an argument about the illegitima-cy of certain established political authorities of the seventeenth century to the illegitimacy of the authority of other people in general to the illegitimacy of the authority of our own experience.

In telling the story of the Enlightenment in this sequence, I want to suggest that the last stage (on this telling), the somewhat anxious preoccupation with epistemology, grows out of the enlighteners' political project of liberation, and that we should view it in this light. Their organizing posture against authority compelled the enlighteners to theorize the human per-son in isolation, abstracted from any pragmatic setting in which he might rely on the tes-timony of others, or, indeed, on his own common sense as someone who has learned how to handle things. The pure subject who is posited as the beginning point for the Cartesian/Lockean account of knowledge is a person who has been shorn of those practical and social endowments by which we apprehend the world.[9] If such a creature actually existed, we can well imagine that he would be gripped by the question of how we can know anything.

A residue of the Enlightenment's project of liberation continues to provide the intel-lectual backdrop for contemporary cognitive science. This becomes clear in the discipline's treatment of attention.

Much More Than a Searchlight

One of the persistent claims in cognitive psychology is that attention comes in two flavors: the kind that we direct according to our will, and the kind that is an automatic response to stimuli that are irresistible, such as a loud bang outside the window. This typology maps very neatly onto the autonomy/heteronomy opposition of Enlightenment moral philosophy—so neatly that it raises suspicion that cognitive psychology may be a continuation of moral philosophy by other means, however wittingly.

But I want to focus on another of the enduring tropes in the field, namely, that attention can be understood through an analogy with a searchlight. The point of the analogy is to capture the selectivity of attention, as against the indiscriminateness with which sensual data impinge on us. We actively pick something out from the flux of the available. The analogy is consistent with a more general picture of the human subject as having a certain independence from the surrounding world, which is conceived not as a *situation* that we are bound up in, and that shapes us, but as an "objective," neutral environment, within which we pursue purposes that we generate out of ourselves. A searchlight's beam is the same regardless of what it shines upon; it is unchanged by what it illuminates. In this sense, it captures our notion of mental autonomy.

The attention-as-searchlight metaphor is apt for some specialized mental tasks. It seems to capture pretty well the mental operations that are investigated in "object discrimination" studies, in which one scans a field of objects that hold no intrinsic interest to find one that meets certain criteria. If one is tasked with finding the red object amid a field of blue ones, the red one jumps out immediately; there's no need to scan. Likewise, if one is tasked with picking out circles that are mixed in with a field of squares, they can be found at a glance. But if the objects vary on more than one dimension at once, for example color *and* shape, and one has to find the red circles in a field consisting of circles and squares, both of which may be red or blue, then one scans in the manner of a searchlight.

In a laboratory setting, tasks like this are used because they are easily replicable. The researcher presents meaningless, affect-neutral objects (such as squares) on a computer screen, because in using a computer she can vary the size, shape, color, and location of objects in a controlled manner, arbitrarily according to any hypothesis she might want to investigate, and quickly. Because every variable is *constituted* on the computer, it is already coded, ready to enter into a statistical analysis. This is very convenient. But an unwarranted elision generally follows, whereby such artificial tasks are taken to be paradigmatic of everyday cognition.

It has been said (by the virtual reality pioneer Jaron Lanier) that what makes something real is that it can't be represented to completion. I find this helpful. Conversely, given the methods the discipline of psychology is wed to, what makes something suitable as a stimulus in a psychological study is that it *can* be represented to completion. Yet if the argument I develop in my book, *The World Beyond Your Head* is generally on the right track, then it surely matters that the objects presented in such studies are ones the subject doesn't "have to do with." They are not part of a pragmatic situation the subject finds himself in, other than the meta-situation of the laboratory itself. They have no relevance for him; they are not integrated into a context of meaning; he has no *interests* at stake. This is true even if the subject is motivated to perform well on the task by money or some other reward that is extrinsic to the task itself. In the particular case of object discrimination studies, it is unsurprising that when presented with a field of meaningless objects, one would scan like a searchlight. Such a setting is unworldly in a very definite sense, constructed to reflect some (necessarily) narrow hypothesis under investigation. For the subject, the unworldliness or unrealness of the stimuli means there is nothing to be learned, no prospect of becoming interested. Mechanically scanning is about all one *could* do.

In a more naturalistic setting, closer to the way we actually inhabit the world, the searchlight metaphor for attention seems not quite fitting. It would be more apt to say that a particular thing *pulls us in*, and the character of our regard is altered in accord with its object: a mischievous smile from an alluring stranger, or a car wreck on the shoulder of the road. Things have significance for us, and this significance is not generic, like a quantity of candlepower that has been reflected back. It is qualitative, corresponding to the heterogeneity of the world and of human experience.

The disanalogy with a searchlight holds in the other direction as well, as the particular character of one's attention may alter its object (for example, the alluring stranger) and begin a reciprocal process of mutual attunement that transforms the initial situation. A searchlight illuminates only things that already exist, out there in the darkness, whereas attention can itself be fruitful.

The searchlight metaphor for attention is also hard to square with the experience of learning, in which we are pulled further into some phenomenon and our mental energies are not simply reflected back but refracted. That is, our involvement with the object is often deflected from the agenda we initially brought to it, as we learn more about it. If you have ever raised children, rehabbed an old house, or done a bit of landscaping, then you already know this.

To understand the appeal of the searchlight metaphor, one has to do a bit of genealogy and understand the problem it was initially offered to solve. The notion of attention as free, as unconditioned by its object, was offered as a post hoc attempt to compensate for the subject's *lack* of mental freedom in the basic stimulus notion of perception that was advanced by the school called empiricism. According to this view, sensual data is the sole source of our knowledge. Further, empiricism posits a one-to-one correspondence and constant connection between environmental stimuli and elementary perceptions. This is called the "constancy hypothesis." It seems to over-determine our mental contents; empiricism has to be supplemented with a theory of selective attention if it is to be plausible.

The problem is that, as Maurice Merleau-Ponty wrote, "the empiricist's subject, once he has been allowed some initiative—which is the justification for a theory of attention—can receive only absolute freedom."[10] This is one instance of an oscillation between radical freedom and radical determinism that seems to recur in modern thought. When the subject is conceived as being radically separate from the world he apprehends (Descartes's foundational "I think"), the only possibilities seem to be that he is passively being impinged upon by it, or that he is observing it with the disinterested freedom of a spectator, who already knows what he is looking for. In neither case is he led out of himself.

If empiricism represents a deterministic strand of modern epistemology, the freedomism I sketched above is most evident in rationalism, or intellectualism, as Merleau-Ponty calls it. According to this dispensation, consciousness already possesses the intelligible structure of all its objects. This applies to objects we pay no heed to, no less than to those we are interested in. Whatever intelligibility we find in an object (for example, seeing the form of a circle in a circular plate) was *put* there by consciousness. Therefore, the act of attention "does not herald any new relationship" to the object, as Merleau-Ponty says. Whereas, for empiricism, consciousness is entirely receptive, for intellectualism it constitutes everything. For both, Merleau-Ponty points out, "attention remains an abstract and ineffective power, because it has no work to perform."[11] He further writes,

> Empiricism cannot see that we need to know what we are looking for, otherwise we would not be looking for it, and intellectualism fails to see that we need to be ignorant of what we are looking for, or equally again we would not be searching. They are in agreement in that neither can grasp consciousness in the act of learning, and that neither attaches due importance to that circumscribed ignorance, that still "empty" but already determinate intention which is attention itself.[12]

I think Merleau-Ponty is right to say that attention "has no work to perform" in these founding epistemologies of modern thought. Given the cultural crisis of attention we are now experiencing, it behooves us to get a fuller, more humanistic understanding of attention.

This is a fertile time in the philosophy of mind and cognitive science for thinking about attention. A riot of different theories is on offer. My point in revisiting the Enlightenment has been to suggest that, in going forward, we need to be alert to the intellectual origins of cognitive science in the polemics of centuries ago, and loosen the grip of freedom versus determinism on our thinking.

Getting free of polemics that no longer answer to our circumstances is itself a polemical project, necessarily. But it can take its bearings from our positive intuitions about the good life, and the role that attention might play in it. Consider this article a promissory note along these lines. What I hope to deliver, in my forthcoming book, is a full investigation of those ecologies of attention that are established in skilled practices—the kind that pull us out of ourselves and allow us to join the world in a mood of appreciative discernment.

(Summer 2014, 16.2)

Notes

1   I owe this formulation of Locke's theological argument to Matthew Feeney (personal communication).

2   Ibid. Feeney points out the counterfactual character of state-of-nature theories such as Locke's. "The details of real humans in the real world were [taken to be] *an impediment to understanding.* [It was stipulated that] you can understand man and his moral and practical endowments only in isolation from the settings in which he might realize those endowments or, much less, be endowed with them in the first place."

3   John Locke, *An Essay Concerning Human Understanding* (1690), 4.20.6.

4   Charles Taylor, *Sources of the Self: The Making of the Modern Identity* (Cambridge, MA: Harvard University Press, 1989), 169.

5   Locke, *An Essay*, 1.4.23.

6   Plato's Socrates had, of course, emphasized getting free of mere opinion and convention in order to arrive at the truth. But in principle one could be aided in this by some wise authority. (In the parable of the cave, there is a mysterious stranger who turns one around from the images projected on the wall by the poets, and leads one up to the sun.) The point is to grasp an order that is independent of ourselves. How you get to this point is not the important thing. The important thing is to turn one's attention from ephemeral, material things, and from mere images, to the unchanging Forms—from one set of external objects to another set of external objects. Once again, it is Charles Taylor who has clarified this contrast between ancient and modern thought on the question of where truth is to be found.

7   Martin Heidegger, "Modern Science, Metaphysics, and Mathematics" in *Basic Writings* (San Francisco, CA: Harper and Row, 1977), 267–8.

8   There is an obvious strangeness here: From a beginning point that is radically self-enclosed (Descartes's "I think"), our task is to arrive at "a view from nowhere" (to use the philosopher Thomas Nagel's apt phrase) in which there remains no trace of the knower himself.

9   This way of putting it offers a direct line of contrast with what I call "the situated self" in my book *The World Beyond Your Head*. There I argue that the world—in particular, other people—plays a deep, constitutive role in shaping our cognitive faculties—not least, through the "ecologies of attention" that emerge in skilled practices. (Matthew B. Crawford, *The World Beyond Your Head*, Farrar, Straus & Giroux, 2015).

10   Maurice Merleau-Ponty, *Phenomenology of Perception* (New York, NY: Routledge, 2002), 31.

11   Ibid., 32.

12   Ibid., 32–33.

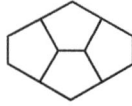

When Science Went Modern

Lorraine Daston

The history of science is punctuated by not one, not two, but three modernities: the first, in the seventeenth century, known as "the Scientific Revolution"; the second, circa 1800, often referred to as "the second Scientific Revolution"; and the third, in the first quarter of the twentieth century, when relativity theory and quantum mechanics not only overturned the achievements of Galileo and Newton but also challenged our deepest intuitions about space, time, and causation.

Each of these moments transformed science, both as a body of knowledge and as a social and political force. The first modernity of the seventeenth century displaced the Earth from the center of the cosmos, showered Europeans with new discoveries, from new continents to new planets, created new forms of inquiry such as field observation and the laboratory experiment, added prediction to explanation as an ideal toward which science should strive, and unified the physics of heaven and earth in Newton's magisterial synthesis that served as the inspiration for the political reformers and revolutionaries of the Enlightenment. The second modernity of the early nineteenth century unified light, heat, electricity, magnetism, and gravitation into the single, fungible currency of energy, put that energy to work by creating the first science-based technologies to become gigantic industries (e.g., the manufacture of dyestuffs from coal tar derivatives), turned science into a salaried profession and allied it with state power in every realm, from combating epidemics to waging wars. The third modernity, of the early twentieth century, toppled the certainties of Newton and Kant, inspired the avant-garde in the arts, and paved the way for what were probably the two most politically consequential inventions of the last hundred years: the mass media and the atomic bomb.

The aftershocks of all three of these earthquakes of modernity are still reverberating today: in heated debates, from Saudi Arabia to Sri Lanka to Senegal, about the significance of the Enlightenment for human rights and intellectual freedom; in the assessment of how science-driven technology and industrialization may have altered the climate of the entire planet; in anxious negotiations about nuclear disarmament and utopian visions of a global polity linked by the worldwide Net. No one denies the world-shaking and world-making significance of any of these three moments of scientific modernity.

Yet from the perspective of the scientists themselves, the experience of modernity coincides with none of these seismic episodes. The most unsettling shift in scientific self-understanding—about what science was and where it was going—began in the middle decades of the nineteenth century, reaching its climax circa 1900. It was around that time that scientists began to wonder uneasily about whether scientific progress was compatible with scientific truth. If advances in knowledge were never-ending, could any scientific theory or empirical result count as real knowledge—true forever and always? Or was science, like the monarchies of Europe's anciens régimes and the boundaries of its states and principalities, doomed to perpetual revision and revolution?

By 1900, when the International Congress of Physics scheduled its inaugural meeting to coincide with the Exposition Universelle in Paris, these anxieties had become acute: The most spectacular recent scientific discoveries, such as x-rays and radioactivity, and theoretical advances, such as the challenges to Newtonian absolute space and the electromagnetic ether, were also experienced by the scientists themselves as dizzying symptoms of malaise—or even of violence. The American historian and statesman Henry Adams, writing about the state of science in 1903, reached for metaphors of anarchist terrorism: "The man of science must have been sleepy indeed who did not jump from his chair like a scared dog when, in 1898, Mme. Curie threw on his desk the metaphysical bomb she called radium."[1] Scientific advances were hurtling forward with the speed and force of a locomotive—but no one knew its final destination, or even whether there was a destination. All one could do was hang on for dear life.[2]

The Great Acceleration

This was the moment when science went modern, when science became not only an active motor of what historian C.A. Bayly has called "the Great Acceleration of 1890–1914,"[3] but also its breathless subject, swept up like everyone and everything else in gale-force winds of change. For the scientists, the realization that progress might have its dark side had been germinating since the mid-nineteenth century, when they noticed with consternation that their publications were no longer read after a decade or so and that it had become necessary to revise university curricula and textbooks several times a generation. Last year's scientific truths, they noted with alarm, were becoming obsolete almost as rapidly as last year's fashion in millinery. By the 1890s, the pell-mell accumulation of novelties on both the theoretical and empirical fronts threatened to bury the scientists like an avalanche and to undermine the foundations of even the most stable sciences, astronomy and physics.

This was also the moment when, as a response to this experience of modernity as acceleration en route to who-knew-where, scientists and later historians of science rethought the relationship of science to history in the broadest sense: not just the past, but also the present and future. As part of a larger effort to explore how the experience of scientific modernity circa 1900 prompted scientists and historians to reimagine the past and the future of science—and indeed the nature of modernity itself—I will here examine the scientists' own disquieting experience of modernity, science in the as-it-is-happening present tense. It was exactly because that experience appeared to trap them in the hurly-burly present, severed from the past and unable to extrapolate into the future, that scientists in the latter half of the nineteenth century began to redirect their energies and resources to building archives for future research, in the hope that at least these would endure long after all other past scientific work was forgotten. By the 1920s, philosophers and historians began to reflect on the significance of science past—since about the seventeenth century—for modernity *tout court*. They concluded that science had made the modern world, and, even more consequentially, had created what they called "the modern mentality." In their view, it was an intellectual revolution of world-shaking dimensions, but one with an ultimately tragic outcome: the loss of lived experience.

Science Under Permanent Construction

A few words about the who, when, and what. First, the who: My materials are drawn from the writings of scientists, historians, and philosophers working in Europe and the United States. Second, the when: The "circa" in my anchor date of "circa 1900" should be interpreted with some latitude. I will on occasion reach as far back as the mid-nineteenth century and as far forward as the mid-twentieth century. And third, the what: Although my focus will be the natural sciences, I will also have occasion to include some of the human sciences, particularly classical philology. This is in part because the scope of the word *science* (as rendered in English and French) and, especially, the German word *Wissenschaft* was wider than it is now, encompassing all branches of learning, but also in part because the experience of galloping scientific modernity was very much shared by the philologists—indeed, in many respects, classical philology was the first discipline to inaugurate modern ideals of research, institutionalize advanced training in university seminars, establish learned journals for the swift publication (and contradiction) of new results, and visit upon its practitioners the anxious sensation of being overtaken by one's own students in an ever-accelerating race to produce new results.

The metaphors the scientists themselves (and not only the scientists) used to describe modernity were architectural: of building upon solid new foundations after tearing down antiquated, dilapidated structures from earlier times. They imagined the modern flourishing of science as Karl Friedrich Schinkel had imagined the efflorescence of ancient Greece in his painting *Blick in Griechenlands Blüte* (A view of Greece in its prime) (1825), as the construction of a new and beautiful city, as *Aufbau*. Conversely, they regarded the outmoded theories and ideas that were flattened by modernity as "ruins": not as romantic, classical ruins, but, rather, as complete devastation. In science as in city planning, modernity was always associated with a kind of violence. The old and new could not coexist peacefully. By the mid-nineteenth century, however, the uncompromising violence of modernity had begun to alarm even the scientists themselves.

These anxieties shaped the *experience* of modernity among scientists, starting in the mid-nineteenth century. In contrast with the intellectual exhilaration associated with the breakthroughs of the three previously delineated moments of modernity in the history of science, the experience of scientific modernity was disorienting, even frightening, for participants. If science was not about the discovery of eternal truths, what then was its raison d'être? If the achievements of one generation would almost certainly be overthrown by the next, and so on ad infinitum (or perhaps ad nauseam), what was the point of dedicating one's life to such a Sisyphean task? These were the questions that haunted the scientists confronted with the specter of their own success, starting circa 1840. Although this moment of self-doubt does not align with any of the three moments of modernity in the history of science, I will argue that it captured a certain melancholy that has tinged our understanding of that term ever since.

It is a cliché of intellectual history that the doctrine of progress emerges in the seventeenth century, and that Francis Bacon was its prophet.[4] For Bacon, it was technology rather than science that was the prototypical progressive enterprise; indeed, he reproached stagnant natural philosophy with the example of the advancing mechanical arts.[5] But by the late eighteenth century, the foremost exemplars of progress had become mathematics and the exact sciences. The French mathematician and philosophe Jean d'Alembert, writing in 1751, held up "geometry, astronomy, and mechanics, which are destined by their nature always to be perfecting themselves."[6] Between about 1750 and 1840, a steady stream of histories of various sciences poured from the presses, all purporting to demonstrate the existence and extent of progress in those disciplines.[7] Some of the publicists of scientific progress, like the Marquis de Condorcet, claimed that it was not only inexorable but contagious, that the "progress of the physical sciences, which neither the passions nor self-interest can disturb," would eventually correct "all errors in politics and morals."[8]

What is striking about late-eighteenth-century and early-nineteenth-century views of scientific progress is not only their buoyant optimism but also their circumscribed understanding of change. Scientific knowledge steadily improved, but it was not renovated. Once the foundations for the new science had been laid in the seventeenth century, so went the standard story, the edifice could be expanded but not remodeled. Certain achievements, Newtonian mechanics being the most often-cited example, were permanent. Even Adam Smith's remarkable history of astronomy, which treated systems of natural philosophy "as mere inventions of the imagination, to connect together the otherwise discordant and disjointed phaenomena of nature," concluded with a tribute to the Newtonian system, "the most universal empire that was ever established in philosophy."[9] Other fields—botany, chemistry, political economy—might await their Newtons, and in this sense scientific progress was open-ended. But the open-endedness was expansionist at the fringes, not transformative at the stable center. To continue Smith's imperial metaphor, new territories awaited scientific conquest, but old victories remained forever safe from reversal.

Such underlying conservatism inspired early-nineteenth-century commentators to contrast scientific progress with more wrenching forms of change in society, politics, and letters. In his famous essay "The Spirit of the Age" (1831), John Stuart Mill located his own era in the sign of Proteus: "The conviction is already not far from being universal, that the times are pregnant with change; and that the nineteenth century will be known to posterity as the era of one of the greatest revolutions of which history has preserved the remembrance in the human mind, and in the whole constitution of society."[10] Mill's was "an age of transition" between periods of stability, an age in which institutions and learning were all in flux, in which "mankind have outgrown old institutions and old doctrines, and have not yet acquired new ones."[11] Although a self-declared political radical, Mill found this vacuum in legitimate authority, intellectual as well as social, more alarming than exciting.

Amid this confusion, Mill made out the physical sciences to be a beacon: "While these two contending parties [past and present] are measuring their sophistries against one another, the man who is capable of other ideas than those of his age, has an example in the present state of physical science, and in the manner in which men shape their thoughts and actions within its sphere, of what is to be hoped for and labored for in all other departments of human knowledge; and what, beyond all possibility of doubt, will one day be attained."[12] In the physical sciences, Mill believed, unanimity had been achieved without recourse, for example, to the nasty inquisitorial methods the medieval Catholic Church had used to persuade heretics. Simply because this unanimity rested upon truth rather than force, it was enduring. Science would never again be shaken to its roots by an age of transition: "The physical sciences, therefore, (speaking of them generally) are continually *growing*, but never *changing*: in every age they receive indeed mighty improvement, but for them the age of transition is past."[13] This was science in permanent *Aufbau*, each generation adding cumulatively to the work already accomplished by its predecessors.

Science was thus the model of the permanent revolution, accomplished only once and once and for all, never undone by reaction, restoration, or new revolutions. The language of "revolution" in fact gradually declined among nineteenth-century scientists, perhaps in self-conscious distinction to multiplying examples of all-too-impermanent political revolutions.[14] Other pundits of the 1830s, such as Auguste Comte and his followers, echoed Mill's optimism about how scientific progress could be the model for orderly, sedate political and social progress, without rupture or violence.[15] But this complacency was short-lived.

It is difficult to date just when the perceived progress of science accelerated to the point of vertigo for its practitioners. Already in 1844 Alexander von Humboldt had concluded the preface to his monumental *Kosmos* with a disquieting reflection on transitory science versus enduring literature:

> It has often been a source of unhappy contemplation that while the purely literary products of the mind are rooted in the depths of emotions and imagination, everything that relates to empiricism and inquiry into natural phenomena and physical laws takes on a different cast in a few decades... indeed, as many say, older works in the natural sciences are consigned to oblivion as unreadable.[16]

Humboldt consoled himself with the familiar credo that many parts of science had, like celestial mechanics, already reached a "firm, not easily shaken foundation," and in 1867 the French astronomer Charles-Eugène Delaunay expressed the view that it was "impossible to imagine a more brilliant proof" for Newtonian astronomical theory than the discovery of the planet Neptune.[17] But by 1892 the French mathematician and physicist Henri Poincaré was calling for ever more precise techniques of approximation in order to test whether Newton's law alone could explain all astronomical phenomena, and was warning that the law of gravitation might hang in the balance of certain divergent series.[18] The great construction of science, the project of many generations, was beginning to look more like the Tower of Babel, ripe for a divine thunderbolt.

The image of the Tower of Babel is used advisedly, for philology was also experiencing the stresses of accelerated advances—and indeed, in this respect and many others, had anticipated developments in the natural sciences by several decades, especially in Germany. Classical philology had pioneered the research-centered institutions of the advanced seminar in Göttingen and Berlin, professional societies that met annually to present papers on the latest results in the field, and journals that published these results speedily—all innovations that were subsequently copied by scientists, first in Germany and then in research-oriented universities all over the world.[19] It was also the classical philologists who in 1850 invented Big Science—both the word and the thing—and thereby once again excited the envy and emulation of the scientists, who fretted that all the money was going to the humanities. It is important to keep in mind that it was the philologists who first defined the ideals of research, created the institutions to train and propel research, persuaded governments to bankroll huge projects, and upheld the cult of specialized methods and exactitude. Not for nothing did the French Orientalist Ernest Renan, writing in 1848, credit philology and physics with dispelling the fantasies of "the primitive dream with the clear views of the scientific age," and praise both disciplines for establishing the "intellectual habits created by modern methods."[20] And the philologists were also the first to experience the obsolescence of their work before their careers had ended, most painfully when their own students wrote scathing reviews criticizing the older generation's outmoded methods.[21]

Scientists like Poincaré had been caught up in what Adams in 1907 called the "vertiginous violence"[22] of late-nineteenth-century scientific progress. Theories succeeded one another at an ever-accelerating pace; facts pointed to contradictory conclusions. There was no firm theoretical ground safe from such upheavals, for even Newtonian celestial mechanics had begun to quake. The history of science would not stay written, for at any moment a theory that had been solemnly pronounced dead might be revived. The expectations for scientific progress voiced in the early nineteenth century had not been disappointed; rather, they had been fulfilled with a vengeance. Never before had science bustled and flourished as it did in the latter half of the nineteenth century.

No one doubted the hurtling progress of science; it was, as Adams shuddered, as real as bombs or wireless telegraphy or airships.[23] But scientists themselves seemed sickened by the speed of it, and to have lost their bearings and their nerve. As Adams remarked of his scientific reading, "Chapter after chapter closed with phrases such as one never met in the older literature: 'The cause of this phenomenon is not understood'; 'science no longer ventures to explain causes'; 'the first step towards a causal explanation still remains to be taken'; 'opinions are very much divided'; 'in spite of the contradictions involved'; 'science gets on only by adopting different theories, sometimes contradictory.'"[24] Adams, like his entire generation, had read his Mill, and trusted scientists to find the truth and point it out at least in their own domain. He was shocked when they defaulted.

Chastened Modernity

As Adams observed, the tone of scientific progress had shifted from confidence to caution. The Berlin physiologist Rudolf Virchow registered the political implications of this change in an 1872 lecture, "*Die Freiheit der Wissenschaften im modernen Staatsleben*" (The freedom of the sciences in the modern life of the state):

> Let us not forget that when a doctrine that had been presented as certain,
> proven, reliable, and with claims to complete generality is [then] shown to
> be fundamentally mistaken...many people will lose their faith in science.
> Then begin the reproaches: You yourselves are not even sure of your doc-
> trines; your truth of today is tomorrow's lie. How can you demand that

your doctrines should become the subject of instruction [in schools] and public knowledge?[25]

This was the nightmare of scientific progress: The truths of today would become the falsehoods—or at least the errors—of tomorrow. Or, in the words of Marx and Engels on the revolutionary impact of the bourgeoisie on European society, "All that is solid melts into air; all that is holy is profaned."

The scientists themselves drew different lessons from this dizzying experience of open-ended progress. Some, like the Austrian physicist Ernst Mach, preached caution and self-restraint: Scientists must confine themselves to what can be observed and stop speculating about merely theoretical entities like forces and atoms. The past success of a theory was no guarantee of its future stability. Mach opposed the kinetic theory of gases not simply because atoms and molecules were unobservable, but because of the historical fragility of the unobservable, writing that the theory "must at every moment reckon with the contradiction of new facts, however much it may have previously contributed to an overview of the properties of gases."[26]

Others, like Max Weber, went even further, from self-restraint to asceticism. In his 1917 lecture *Wissenschaft als Beruf* (Science as vocation), Weber warned all those who contemplated pursuing a career in science that they must resign themselves to the depressing fact that in one or two generations everything they had worked for would be forgotten, left far behind by the inexorable progress of science. He seconded Tolstoy's judgment that modern science was "meaningless" (*sinnlos*) because it could lead us neither to God nor art nor even nature.[27] Those who chose science as a vocation must practice self-denial and resignation on a scale unequaled even by the anonymous builders of medieval cathedrals. The names of the latter might have been forgotten, but they had not labored in vain: Their handiwork still stood and commanded admiration centuries after their deaths. Modern scientists, in contrast, were condemned to oblivion along with everything they had worked for, martyrs to progress.

But no longer martyrs to truth. There had been a minor genre of nineteenth-century literature with titles like *Martyrs of Science* that had celebrated those heroic figures, such as Giordano Bruno and Galileo, who had suffered for the cause of truth, usually at the hands of the benighted and dogmatic Catholic Church.[28] By the late nineteenth century, however, any number of prominent scientists, such as Mach, the German chemist Wilhelm Ostwald, and Poincaré, recommended more modest goals, in light of how quickly scientific truths appeared to change. Mach drew a Heraclitean moral from the history of science: "In science more than in any other domain the words of Heraclitus hold: 'One cannot step twice into the same river'.... One gradually accustoms oneself to the fact that science is unfinished, changeable."[29] Science might be changeable, but could the same apply to truth? The bitter lines in Alfred Tennyson's poem "Locksley Hall Sixty Years After" (1866) must have struck a chord with many scientists: "Truth for truth, and good for good! The Good, the True, the Pure, the Just / Take the charm 'For ever' from them, and they crumble into dust."

This is a chastened modernity, and it stands in stark contrast with the creative furor associated with more familiar moments of scientific modernity. The scientific revolutions of the seventeenth and early nineteenth centuries, like the rise of the new physics in the early twentieth century, were intoxicated with the idea of destroying the old in order to create the new. This was as much an aesthetic as a scientific and philosophical conviction. When in 1637 Descartes wanted to rally support for his radical break with Aristotelian natural philosophy, he chose an architectural metaphor: "Similarly, those ancient towns which were originally nothing but hamlets, and in the course of time have become great cities, are ordinarily very badly arranged compared to one of the symmetrical metropolitan districts which a city planner has laid out in an open plain according to his own designs."[30] According to the modernists, whether in the seventeenth century or the twentieth, innovation means tearing down the old—literally, in the case of cities—in order to make room for the new. Modernism revises everything, fundamentally. *Foundations* is a word borrowed from the modernists' own vocabulary: Because the old has been obliterated, the new must be built upon its own, carefully laid foundations. Modernists are not *bricoleurs*.

Nor do they believe in organic growth—or, indeed, organic anything. Modernists negate the slow accretions of history: They do not want to learn from the past; they want to break with it. This is why the scientific and aesthetic dreams of modernists are so relentlessly radical, whatever their century. For those who want to start afresh, the only possible stance toward the past is rejection. Or, to recur to Descartes's urban planning metaphor, the only way to build the new city is to raze the old one to the ground. But modernist radicalism doesn't stop there. In its purest form, it seeks to annihilate not only the past but the future as well. The new city erected on the smoldering ruins of the old one is intended to stand for all time, perfect and therefore ageless. This is why it is so difficult to locate modernism along the political spectrum of the reactionary right and the progressive left. Both right and left define themselves in relation to an unsatisfactory present: The right wants to return to a better past; the left wants to move on to a better future. The modernists may seem progressive as compared to the right, but they often look reactionary as compared to the left. In truth, they belong to neither party, because they aspire to be the architects of an eternal present. Once modernists have fulfilled their vision, time stops—until the next wave of modernist fervor.

Modernism of a Melancholy Cast

But modernism cannot live with the vision that it comes in recurrent waves. Nothing is more fatal to a movement that seeks to remake art or science or politics from the ground up than to repeat itself. Once-and-for-all is thrilling; twice-and-for-all, embarrassing;

thrice-and-for-all, simply ludicrous. Modernity cannot begin in the seventeenth, the nineteenth, *and* the twentieth century without becoming something like a joke told once too often. This is why the three modernities of the history of science cannot peacefully coexist. There would be no difficulty in characterizing all three as moments of epoch-making change, as indeed all three undoubtedly were. But change, no matter how transformative, falls short of the accolade "modernity." Modernity aims to be the change that is so vehement, so thorough, so fundamental, that no further change thereafter is conceivable. There is thus always a simmering argument among the proponents of each of the three modernities in the history of science as to which is the real one, the implication being that the others are imposters, mere revolutions masquerading as the one and only modernity.

This is also why the prestissimo pace and aimless trajectory of modern science left the political imagination cold. To understand the depth of the disappointment, one must return to Mill's hopeful prophecies of 1831. For Mill, the burning issue of the modern age was legitimate authority, and he found his model in the physical sciences. In contrast with the squabbles of politics, in which everyone felt qualified to voice an opinion, "we never hear of the right of private judgment in science,"[31] he wrote. Of course, one could in principle object to every article of natural philosophy, but the perfection of scientific method and the near-unanimity of scientists combined to silence would-be dissenters. Science ruled in the sign of truth, and was therefore authoritarian but not tyrannical. When society followed science in settling from its present "transitional state" back into a "natural state," the uninstructed would once again defer to those "in whom they trust for finding the right, and for pointing it out."[32]

For Mill, science had disclosed truths that would endure until the end of human history. By the turn of the twentieth century, few scientists could advance such claims so brazenly. Never before had science seemed so successful; never before had scientists been so reluctant to press their claims to truth. This was the paradox of breakneck scientific progress, for truths had become too temporary to merit the name. In the 1830s, Mill had believed scientific truths worthy of an almost religious fervor. In a passage that is all the more telling for being so uncharacteristic, he expressed admiration for the Catholic clergy's passion for its faith. Not that Mill approved of burning heretics; yet he longed for this passion to be transplanted in all its intensity to the truth: "But the deep earnest feeling of firm and unwavering conviction, which [the burning of heretics] pre-supposes, we may, without being unreasonable, lament that it was impossible and could not *but* be impossible, in the intellectual anarchy of a general revolution in opinion, to transfer unimpaired to the truth."[33]

Did the passion, like the authority that once attached to scientific truths, simply evaporate when these truths began to rush past one another at the speed of a landscape viewed from a railcar window? This is the gauntlet modern science flung at the feet of the political imagination: Can passion be harnessed to vision if the vision is not solidified by truth? Or (a still more daunting challenge) can a new ideal of truth be imagined that can encompass the fact that all truths are embedded in time?

Although modern philosophers respect science as the gold standard of rationality, if not of reason, they have been loath to draw the consequences from a concept of truth that dates back millennia, one that yoked the perfect polity to a Platonic heaven of eternal ideas. Enlightenment visions of the perfect polity were anything but Platonic; yet they were still undergirded by allegedly universal, eternal truths, mightier than the powers that be and certain to triumph in the fullness of time. But when scientific progress turned explosionist in the mid-nineteenth century, these foundations of the political imagination melted away. Science had succeeded brilliantly in understanding ever more of the universe, ever more profoundly—but its understanding was a permanent work in progress.

The modernism that overtook the scientists circa 1900 was of a melancholy, less triumphal cast. Their imagination was possessed not by visions of new cities built upon indestructible foundations but by visions of ruins. The scientists did not annihilate time; rather, time annihilated them. Their experience of the modernist predicament was one of evanescence and futility. As Poincaré sighed in *La science et l'hypothèse* (1903), "Every century makes fun of the preceding one, accusing it of having generalized too quickly and too naïvely. Descartes pitied the Ionians; Descartes in his turn makes us smile; doubtless our sons will laugh at us one day."[34] The scientists cultivated an ambivalent modernism, enamored of the new while at the same time nostalgic for the old. Starting in the 1840s, with a crescendo reached in the 1890s, their writings express sadness, yearning, and resignation. This elegiac mood is in some ways paradoxical. During this period, the sciences were by every measure fabulously successful: Brilliant theoretical and experimental breakthroughs in chemistry, bacteriology, and electromagnetism filled learned journals and daily newspapers; science-based technologies boomed; the prestige (and pay) of scientists soared. Yet the victories rang hollow. What was the value of a scientific truth that might last less than the lifetime of a scientist? And if scientific truths were the sturdiest truths of all, what was the value of capital-T Truth?

Very few scientists succumbed to skepticism, but many, if not most, felt obliged to revise their expectations downward. Perhaps science did not seek eternal truths, but something more modest: objectivity, or utility, or precision. Many late-nineteenth-century scientists (and humanists) attempted to salvage something permanent from progress in the form of archives for the future. Whether they succeeded or not is another question. The question of how to reconcile breakneck scientific progress with durable scientific truth is still very much with us, as the confusion surrounding each new medical study that contradicts the recommendations of the previous one shows all too clearly.

But we the public—and, a fortiori, the scientists—have by now become accustomed to the short half-life of scientific truths. For the scientists of the latter half of the nineteenth century, however, the conflict between scientific progress and scientific truth was new and alarming—so alarming that Poincaré tried to replace Descartes's ur-modernist metaphor of ripping up old cities in order to build new ones with something more organic: "We should not compare the advance of science to the transformations of a city, where the old edifices are pitilessly torn down to make room for new constructions, but to the continuous evolution of zoological species that constantly develop and end up by becoming unrecognizable to vulgar eyes, but in which a practiced eye can always find the traces of the earlier work of past centuries."[35] Poincaré did not mention Descartes by name, but no Frenchman drilled on the *Discours de la méthode* in a Troisième République lycée would have missed the allusion. Modern science had seceded from the spirit of modernity.

Notes

[1] Henry Adams, *The Education of Henry Adams: An Autobiography* (Boston, MA: Houghton Mifflin, 1961), 452. First published 1918.

[2] John L. Heilbron, "Fin-de-Siècle Physics," in *Science, Technology, and Society in the Time of Alfred Nobel*, ed. Carl G. Bernhard (Oxford, England: Pergamon, 1982), 51–73; Richard Staley, *Einstein's Generation: The Origins of the Relativity Revolution* (Chicago, IL: University of Chicago Press, 2008).

[3] C.A. Bayly, *The Birth of the Modern World 1780–1914: Global Connections and Comparisons* (Oxford, England: Blackwell, 2004), 456.

[4] J.B. Bury, *The Idea of Progress* (London, England: Macmillan, 1920); Sidney Pollard, *The Idea of Progress* (Harmondsworth, England: Penguin, 1971); Richard Foster Jones, *Ancients and Moderns* (New York, NY: Dover, 1982, first published 1936).

[5] Francis Bacon, *Novum organum* (first published 1620), in *The Works of Francis Bacon, Lord Chancellor of England: A New Edition*, 16 vols., ed. Basil Montagu (London, England: William Pickering, 1825–34), vol. 14, bk. I, aph. 74.

[6] Jean d'Alembert, *Preliminary Discourse to the Encyclopedia of Diderot*, trans. Richard N. Schwab (Indianapolis, IN: Bobbs-Merrill, 1963), 96. First published 1751.

[7] Rachel Laudan, "Histories of Sciences and Their Uses: A Review to 1913," *History of Science* 31 (1993): 1–34.

[8] M.J.A.N. Condorcet, *Sketch for a Historical Picture of the Progress of the Human Mind*, trans. June Barraclough, with an introduction by Stuart Hampshire (London, England: Weidenfeld and Nicolson, 1955), 164, 163. First published 1795.

[9] Adam Smith, *The Principles Which Lead and Direct Philosophical Enquiries: Illustrated by the History of Astronomy* (first published 1795), in *The Works of Adam Smith: With an Account of His Life and Writings* by Dugald Stewart, 5 vols. (London, England: T. Cadell and W. Davies, 1811), vol. 5, 188–89.

[10] John Stuart Mill, "The Spirit of the Age," (first published 1831), in *The Collected Works of John Stuart Mill*, ed. J.M. Robson et al., 33 vols. (Toronto, Canada: University of Toronto Press, 1963–1991), vol. 32, 228–29.

[11] Ibid., 230.

[12] Ibid., 239.

[13] Ibid., 239–40; emphasis in the original.

[14] I. Bernard Cohen, *Revolutions in Science* (Cambridge, MA: Harvard University Press, 1985), 273–80.

[15] Auguste Comte, *Cours de philosophie positive* (Course in Positive Philosophy), 6 vols. (Paris, France: Bachelier, 1830–42), vol. 1, 2–4.

[16] Alexander von Humboldt, *Kosmos* (Cosmos), 4 vols. (Stuttgart, Germany: J.G. Cotta, 1874), vol. 1, xxiv. First published 1845–62. Quoted passage translated by the present author.

[17] Charles-Eugène Delaunay, *Rapport sur le progrès de l'astronomie* (Report on the Progress of Astronomy) (Paris, France: Imprimerie Impériale, 1867), 14.

[18] Henri Poincaré, *Les méthodes nouvelles de la mécanique céleste* (New Methods of Celestial Mechanics), 3 vols. (Paris, France: Gauthier-Villars, 1892–99), vol. 1, 3–4.

[19] William Clark, *Academic Charisma and the Origins of the Research University* (Chicago, IL: University of Chicago Press, 2006); Kathryn Olesko, *Physics as a Calling: Discipline and Practice in the Königsberg Seminar for Physics* (Ithaca, NY: Cornell University Press, 1991); R. Steven Turner, "Historicism, Kritik, and the Prussian Professoriate, 1790–1840," in *Philologie et herméneutique au 19. siècle* (Philosophy and Hermeneutics in the Nineteenth Century), ed. M. Bollack and H. Wismann (Göttingen, Germany: Vanderhoek und Ruprecht, 1983), 450–89.

[20] Ernest Renan, *L'Avenir de la science* (The Future of Science), ed. Annie Petit (Paris, France: Garnier Flammarion, 1995), 114, completed 1848, first published 1890; cp. Friedrich August Wolf, *Darstellung der Alterthumswissenschaft, nebst einer Auswahl seiner kleinen Schriften* (Presentation of the Sciences of Antiquity, with a Selection of Brief Writings), ed. S.F.W. Hoffmann (Leipzig, Germany: Lehhold'sche Buchhandlung, 1839), 25, on the exactitude of philological *Kritik* approximating the certainty of the exact sciences.

[21] Turner, "Historicism," 467.

[22] Adams, *The Education of Henry Adams*, 452, 495.

[23] Ibid., 496.

[24] Ibid., 497.

[25] Rudolf Virchow, "*Die Freiheit der Wissenschaften im Modernen Staatsleben*" (The Freedom of the Sciences in the Modern Life of the State) (1872), *Amtlicher Bericht über die Versammlung Deutscher Naturforscher und Ärtzte* (Official report of the German Association of Scientists and Doctors) 50 (1877): 65–77, 73. Quoted passage translated by the present author.

[26] Ernst Mach, *Die Principien der Wärmelehre: Historisch-kritisch entwickelt* (Principles of the Theory of Heat: Historically and Critically Elucidated) (Leipzig, Germany: Johann Ambrosius Barth, 1896), 115. Quoted passage translated by the present author.

[27] Max Weber, "*Wissenschaft als Beruf*" (Science as Vocation), first published 1918, in *Gesammelte Aufsätze zur Wissenschaftslehre* (Collected Essays on Epistemology), 3rd ed., ed. Johannes Winckelmann (Tübingen, Germany: J.C.B. Mohr, 1968), 524–55, 534–36. Quoted passage translated by the present author.

[28] See, for example, David Brewster, *The Martyrs of Science; or, The Lives of Galileo, Tycho Brahe, and Kepler* (New York, NY: Harper, 1841).

[29] Ernst Mach, *Die Geschichte und die Wurzel des Satzes von der Erhaltung der Arbeit*, (The History and Origins of the Principle of the Conservation of Energy), 2nd ed. (Leipzig, Germany: Verlag von Johann Ambrosius Barth, 1909), 3. First published 1872. Quoted passage translated by the present author.

[30] René Descartes, *Discourse on Method*, in *Discourse on Method and Meditations*, trans. and ed. Laurence J. Lafleur (Indianapolis, IN: Bobbs-Merrill, 1979), Part II, 10. First published 1637.

[31] Mill, "The Spirit of the Age," 239.

[32] Ibid., 304.

[33] Ibid., 305.

[34] Henri Poincaré, *La Science et l'hypothèse* (Science and Hypothesis) (Paris, France: Flammarion, 1968), 157. First published 1903. Quoted passage translated by the present author.

[35] Henri Poincaré, *La Valeur de la science* (The Value of Science) (Paris, France: Flammarion, 1970), 23. First published 1905. Quoted passage translated by the present author.

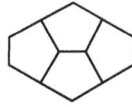

Digital Metaphysics
The Cybernetic Idealism
of Warren McCulloch

Leif Weatherby

I n the autumn of 1948, Warren McCulloch, neurophysiologist, bohemian cold warrior, and a founder of machine learning, stood before a gathering of brain scientists at the California Institute of Technology. The occasion was the inaugural Hixon
Symposium, and the topic, cognitive behavior—more specifically, "Cerebral Mechanisms
in Behavior." John von Neumann, for whom modern computer architecture is named, was
in the audience. Questions about the new digital machines hung in the air, even as the
brain remained the dominant topic. McCulloch decided to talk metaphysics.

He divided the world into "mind" and "body," noting that the physicist claims to study
only the latter, unless we compel him to include himself, as physicist, in his account of
matter. Then he is faced with a choice: refuse, and remain a physicist, or assent, and become
a metaphysician.[1] McCulloch thought he could do this dilemma one better, by developing
what he called an "experimental epistemology." Every path forward, as he would later claim,
lay "through the den of the metaphysician."[2] The physicist, in reality, has no *choice* but to
assent, because the "synthetic *a priori* is the theme of all our physiological psychology,"
McCulloch concluded.[3]

The term "synthetic *a priori*" is taken from the philosophy of Immanuel Kant.[4] To
know something *a priori* is to know it in isolation from experience. The category of "unity,"
for instance, is something we don't derive from experience, but rather take to experience.

(Similarly, we apply *causality* to the world, but can't learn about cause and effect *from* it.) "Synthetic," in Kant's vocabulary, means that what we know does not proceed from its mere concept: This kind of knowledge counts as "about" something outside itself. One example of a synthetic *a priori* judgment would be addition (7 + 5 = 12). Another would be the Newtonian principle that every action causes an equal and opposite reaction.

You'd hardly expect to hear technical terms from Kant's philosophy in a setting like the Hixon Symposium, but McCulloch was telling a roomful of scientists that he was searching for the basis of any possible knowledge that is really informative about the world. Somehow, he was going to do that "experimentally," even mathematically. The "synthetic *a priori*" was to be found somewhere between the brain and the new digital "automata." By placing the physicist's dilemma at the center of his project, McCulloch was reanimating the program of German Idealism—the philosophical movement that began with Kant and ended with Hegel. In doing so, he produced the beginning of a metaphysics we urgently need in the era of Big Data and machine learning, as the digital fades from the horizon of our control, and even our ability to grasp it conceptually.

McCulloch's name is again in the news, in the wake of the recent "explosion" in artificial intelligence. "Machine learning"—in which software programs called "neural nets" (McCulloch had called them "nervous nets") are exposed to millions of iterations of specified processes and build layered "knowledge" of those processes—has moved from twentieth-century fantasy to twenty-first-century fact.[5] The *New York Times Magazine* devoted a cover story to the "new machine learning" last year, recounting parts of this history even while burying McCulloch in a hyperlink.[6] But his influence is felt everywhere, in our artifacts and our algorithms. Hardware and software alike, it turns out, were part of a metaphysics McCulloch drew from German Idealism.

At the beginning of the digital revolution, there existed a speculative energy that we could use now. It was put at the service not of innovation or disruption but of maintenance and politics, of establishing categories to put our digital world on a better course. McCulloch's evocation of Kant can show us a way to think through the balance of the digitization of our world while avoiding the extremes of digital utopianism and digital denialism.

Invasive Bits and Data

In the twenty-first century, bits and data have entered the world in new and increasingly invasive ways. An effusion of new buzzwords—for example, Internet of Things, Big Data, machine learning—underscores this shift. Philosophers and CEOs alike imagine the world as bits and data. The so-called digital philosophy associated with Stephen Wolfram (among others) even maintains that matter itself is digital. Silicon Valley magnate Elon Musk, who runs companies that aim to colonize Mars and to hook brains directly into computers, thinks there is only a vanishingly small chance that we live in "base reality" rather than a computer simulation.[7] We might call this general philosophy "data metaphysics," since it projects the quantifiability and structure of digital data onto being as such.

Even if we don't buy the premise of data metaphysics (and we probably shouldn't), we can no longer imagine the digital through the visual metaphor of the screen, the synecdoche of the computer. In fact, there's no concrete metaphor for the digital at all anymore, not since we entered the "petabyte era," in which the digital forms and guides large-scale social processes. As early as 2008, an article in *Wired* included the assertion that "at petabytes we ran out of organizational analogies."[8] Today, "the digital" is a set of quantities interacting algorithmically at levels of sheer volume and complexity so far outside what we can imagine that size-based metaphors have broken down entirely.[9] We use another cybernetic term, "black box," to denote that we can't see what the digital is even by analogy. Algorithms guide or even dictate social processes like corporate management,[10] medical diagnosis, and infrastructure design.[11] Data, according to this fantasy, are set to replace frameworks, hypotheses, and decisions. But what if, instead of phasing out intellectual labor, the new presence of data is mutating our categories, changing the very way we imagine the world, and ourselves in it?

We should proceed cautiously when we change the terms of our metaphysics, but caution is hardly the watchword of the new style of the digital. Computer scientist Pedro Domingos writes in *Master Algorithm* that machine learning is "the scientific method on steroids."[12] It will change—indeed, has already changed—every field, from health care to politics to journalism. Websites use machine learning to "decide" which headlines to push; political charisma is heavily filtered through individual-level predictions of voting behavior; deep-learning programs can diagnose cancer better than doctors can. The "master algorithm" will create a "perfect" understanding of the world and of society, connecting sciences both to other sciences and to social processes. In other words, the process we have called "automation" since the Industrial Revolution will itself be automated: "The Industrial Revolution automated manual work and the Information Revolution did the same for mental work, but machine learning automated automation itself."[13] In the final clause of this sentence, Domingos imagines society running on the steam of some other intelligence. Automation has been a major force in global history for at least two centuries. To automate automation is to imagine historical causality itself as controlled by artificial intelligence. Domingos is sanguine about automated automation making things better, but it isn't clear why. This kind of thinking leaves us without a conceptual foundation on which to build an understanding of the ubiquitous digital processes in our society, deferring even historical causality to machine learning. McCulloch's group of scientists had a glimmer of such an approach, a way to understand and govern the very machine learning they had set in motion.

Digital processes that can only seem abstract to us are now causal factors in our society; the world itself now features processes that used to be the preserve of the mind. The implicit assumption is that these processes know more or better about the world than we do. Big

Data can target individuals rather than general rules, and thereby forge an unmediated link between data and world. At least at the level of empirical and infrastructural design, Big Data can replace *cause* with *correlation* as the primary means of framing inquiry. The Bigger the Data get, the less we'll have to rely on the "lazy" notion of causality at all.

As Internet researcher Viktor Mayer-Schönberger and journalist Kenneth Cukier write in their book *Big Data*, "In the age of small data, we were driven by hypotheses about how the world worked, which we then attempted to validate by collecting and analyzing data. In the future, our understanding will be driven more by the abundance of data rather than by hypotheses."[14] Big Data will "fundamentally transform the way we make sense of the world," fundamentally altering causality.

When McCulloch turned to Kant, it was precisely to think through digital causality. For Kant, our knowledge of the world could not be derived only from empirical observation. Nature is a composite of the "law" we give to it and a "thing in itself," about which we can know nothing. For our knowledge to be meaningful, it has to be incomplete. This means that "nature" is a composite of mind and world that never touches the "real," or the thing itself. Metaphysics was not about creating a picture of the world the way it "really was"—for example, as data—but instead about the material sites where meaning was generated. For McCulloch, one such site was the digital, where a strange new order of signs was on the rise.

McCulloch never thought the real would yield to data; nor did he ever think humans would defer to their machines. Instead, he saw that the machines would make new principles of abstraction—new kinds of cognition—available. It was a kind of mutated Kantian question. Kant had wanted to know how much mind is in the world, and McCulloch thought the sum might shift. That is, the shape of the relation between abstraction and the real might *change* with the new machines.

Cybernetic Idealism

Before the recent renewal of interest in his work, McCulloch was probably best known for cybernetics, the postwar scientific movement that he founded with mathematician Norbert Wiener and anthropologist Gregory Bateson. Equal parts universal science and pop culture fad, cybernetics (based on the Greek word for "steersman") was a collaboration of machine design, physiology, and philosophical ambition, providing a template for the picture of science and technology we take for granted today.[15] Information theory, feedback loops, and human-machine interfaces were central: Animals and humans, machines and information, were cast in a new vocabulary of communication and control, based on the capacities of new communication technologies. "Information" came to denote the measure of communicated intelligence, increasingly measured in binary digits, or bits. Historian of science Paul Erickson and his colleagues describe this period as a passage from Enlightenment reason to "quantifying rationality,"[16] a shift from a qualitative capacity to judge to an extensive but narrow push to measure. But some Enlightenment notions survived the transition.

Cybernetics, for one, was shot through with German Idealism. Its founders constantly returned to the philosophical trajectory running from Kant to Hegel, extending it back to include Gottfried Wilhelm Leibniz, the Enlightenment polymath who invented the infinitesimal calculus independently from Newton, casually laid out the principles for binary notation as an aid for his own mathematical reasoning, and attempted to construct a machine for computations. Leibniz did all this while conceiving, on a parallel track, the notion of a "universal characteristic," a universal logical language. Leibniz animates, for example, Wiener's best-known philosophical statement about the cybernetics movement:

> The mechanical brain does not secrete thought "as the liver does bile," as the earlier materialists claimed, nor does it put it out in the form of energy, as the muscle puts out its activity. Information is information, not matter or energy. No materialism which does not admit this can survive at the present day.[17]

No materialism without information meant that information was itself material[18]—that messages were not vapor, but something weightier. "Information is...not matter" means that it was not a part of regular physics as it existed before cybernetics. A materialism based in physics would be possible only if physics could be altered to include information, a point Wiener always connected to Leibniz.[19]

Neither matter nor mind survives autonomously in cybernetics. The signature notions of cybernetics—feedback, information, control—could not be described in the language of matter or the language of ideas alone. To speak cybernetics was to abandon the binary built into so many disciplinary vocabularies and to include the physicist himself in physics. That meant employing a "dialectical" form of reasoning that would reverberate through all subsequent digital technologies.

Historian of science Peter Galison has argued that Wiener "vaulted cybernetics into a philosophy of nature,"[20] using Leibniz among other sources. But it was a philosophy of nature striated by information, constituted of cognition, now also to be included in the empire of physics. Leibniz, in other words, authorized the philosophical ambitions of cybernetics to move beyond the binary alternative between material and ideal. Leibniz and Kant were also sources for McCulloch's search for the *conditions* of cognition—the "synthetic *a priori*"—in the digital structure of the brain.

Embodied Computation

With the expanded, supercharged digital regime of the twenty-first century, we have returned to the lexicon of the 1948 Hixon Symposium, using the brain to describe the digital and vice versa. The digital processing of vast amounts of data through "neural nets," crucial software entities in machine learning, is suddenly ubiquitous. The notion that machines might learn or adapt to inputs gained prominence during the 1940s, when digitized data were not so big at all.

Follow the hyperlink to which the 2016 *New York Times Magazine* article on machine learning consigned McCulloch and you can read a 1943 paper by him and his protégé, Walter Pitts, with the curious title "A Logical Calculus of Ideas Immanent in Nervous Activity."[21] In it, McCulloch and Pitts contend that the "all-or-none" character of neurons (excitatory impulses either cause them to fire or not, with no other possible state) means that the brain is a digital computing machine, in the sense that it can encode the propositions of Boolean logic, the flow-chart algebra of propositions developed in the nineteenth century by the mathematician George Boole. To describe this neuronal logic, McCulloch and Pitts introduced the term "nervous nets":

> Because of the "all-or-none" character of nervous activity, neural events and the relations among them can be treated by means of propositional logic. It is found that the behavior of every net can be described in these terms.[22]

Every synapse either fires or does not; it is, like a switch, either "on" or "off." McCulloch saw that this was precisely analogous to the switching boards telephone operators used, and recognized that this switch-like behavior was also a principle for the construction of calculating machines like the ones von Neumann would work on. The infrastructure of our digital machines still relies on the combination of ones and zeroes to code logical propositions like "and" and "or." McCulloch and Pitts were not alone in seeing this point, but they thought it could lead far beyond deterministic calculations.

The nets are by all appearances a characterization of brains, a contribution to neuroscience. The twist, however, is that the nets are not actual neurons at all, but instead a generalized mathematical form for the possibility of embodied computation. Hovering between neurophysiology and the new machine design, McCulloch and Pitts set down principles for digital operation and organization. Their paper not only formed the basis for both dominant contemporary approaches to artificial intelligence (serial and parallel processing)—no mean legacy on its own—but also directly influenced von Neumann. McCulloch and Pitts wrote that this digital activity of the nets would always have a "semiotic" character, giving rise to psychological understanding. Propositions encoded in nets, in other words, were *signs* (in Greek, *semos*) written in the brain.[23] The interface between matter and meaning was limited to the form and order of these signs. Only at this interface could a world come into view; the nets were the premise of any understanding of nature.

Nets operating dynamically should, in principle, be able to "compute" anything any machine could, or possibly anything a mind could "think." Because these nets were not meant to be a representation of the brain itself but only of one of its functions, one could, in principle, design nets that could perform tasks too complex for the brain. It might even be that these nets would begin to make "their own" associative chains. This is what the recent wave of machine learning is now testing, something possible only because of the amount of digitized data available to test the nets, data that did not exist in 1943. The theory remained speculative, building only in fits and starts toward its current success for two generations. Now that its practical implications in machine learning are being felt across the globe, a look at its metaphysics is overdue.

Digital Metaphysics

It was Walter Pitts, according to one of McCulloch's young collaborators, Jerome Lettvin, who brought Leibniz into the working group:

> Walter had read Leibniz, who had shown that any task which can be described completely and unambiguously in a finite number of words can be done by a logical machine. Leibniz had developed the concept of computers almost three centuries back and had even developed a concept of how to program them. I didn't realize that at the time. All I knew was that Walter had dredged this idea out of Leibniz, and then he and Warren sat down and asked whether or not you could consider the nervous system such a device. So they hammered out the essay at the end of '42.[24]

Pitts, who was in his late teens at the time, had run away from home and been taken on as a student by the philosopher Rudolf Carnap at the University of Chicago. McCulloch met Pitts and, enchanted by him, moved him into his home near the University of Illinois. Lettvin's account implies that Pitts and McCulloch used Leibniz to define the question of neuronal-logical activity in the same terms in which Alan Turing had imagined a "universal" machine just a few years before.

As Turing would after him, Leibniz had disaggregated tasks into a finite number of steps, a concept of the algorithm that Pitts and McCulloch would then look for in the brain. As their contemporary and philosopher Paul Schrecker would put it:

If the ultimate aim of Leibniz's efforts were formulated in a very few words, it could be called the invention of a general method of constructing algorisms [sic]. In order to approach this aim he had not only to analyze the formal structure of algorisms, but also to investigate the particular structure of reality which facilitates the reliability and efficacy of this operational procedure. These two inquiries are the task of logic and metaphysics respectively.[25]

To program, in Lettvin's gloss, is to fit the formal structure of algorithms efficaciously into a reliable structure of reality. Although logic and metaphysics remained separate in Leibniz, Pitts and McCulloch saw them as converging in Turing's work and in their own. From that vantage point, the "automata theory" that would then be realized in computers was really a way of testing the boundaries between the material and the logical. This is why McCulloch called it "experimental epistemology." Kant might have called it "metaphysics."[26]

In support of an application for a Guggenheim grant by another member of his research group, McCulloch described their research this way: "What we seek to understand ultimately is what Kant called the transcendental unity of apperception."[27] In late reflections on his work with a group at the Research Laboratory of Electronics at the Massachusetts Institute of Technology, he reiterated this aim, though in slightly different words: "to understand the physiological foundation of perception."[28] To this end, he had worked closely with the neurophysiologist Joannes Gregorius Dusser de Barenne, who in turn had studied with the neo-Kantian Rudolf Magnus, who had sought a "physiological *a priori*," a physical seat of perception. But McCulloch broke with this notion and with his positivist predecessors, reminding readers that Kant himself had "rejected the cerebro-spinal fluid" as the seat of cognition. How can we square "experimental epistemology" with this rejection? If McCulloch et al. were seeking the "synthetic *a priori*" experimentally, how could this be anything other than a physiological basis for perception?

The answer is to be found in the question in the 1961 lecture title that McCulloch set as his life's work as early as 1917: "What is a Number, that a Man May Know it, and What is a Man, that He May Know a Number?" McCulloch wanted to see Kant's principle in numbers and quantity. But this "quantity" was not just a *measure* of mind; it was an original capacity—what Kant called a "faculty"—that transcended any dualism between matter and idea. The digital was a form of cognition, not just a technique of measurement. But it was cognition embedded in material. Every event in the neural net had a "semiotic" character—this meant that the "logical calculus" was the site of the sign, where material organization and meaning coincided before we could pick them apart analytically. This structure was the essence of the digital. Digitally encoded signs constituted the "world" *and* our understanding of it, as irreconcilable but permanently linked aspects of the nets. Kant had allowed McCulloch to make the digital transcendental and real at the same time.

McCulloch was exploiting Kant's argumentative strategy here, not adopting his views.

Kant thought that our tendency to imagine "things" as separate from "ideas" was secondary to the process of judgment, which first produced these elements ("synthetically") before they could be separated.[29] For "judgment" McCulloch substituted "neural propositional logic." The unified source of that synthesis was in the capacity to calculate quantity. That capacity existed because the brain—or at least the formal "net"—was digital.

Even if brains couldn't be entirely described by the theoretical nets, they could compute propositions, manipulate discrete values. This meant that our "contribution to nature," in Kant's sense, was also digital. The new machines that von Neumann and others were designing meant that no obvious limit could be set on what counted as digital embodiment. On the other side of the revolution that McCulloch shepherded into existence, we find ourselves asking his question again: What is the digital? How is it integrated into a nondigital world, and how should we administer that integration? McCulloch's idealism points to the formation of categories—crucially, the category of causality—as the hinge on which the digital-social interface turns.

Toward a Philosophy of the Digital

Kant famously stated that he had "awoken from his dogmatic slumber"[30] by reading the Scottish Enlightenment philosopher David Hume. Hume maintained a bright line between "matters of fact" and "relations of ideas." This meant that mental habit was central. If one wanted to form a meaningful sentence about the world ("this causes that"), then one would have to habituate the mind by noticing common correlations and regularly drawing the conclusion that one thing "caused" another. Kant disagreed. Cause, he reasoned, could not just be a mental habit, because it had a hidden premise: not that one thing followed another in time, but that it *necessarily* did so. To conceive of a necessity in the world was to add something more than habit to observation—to contribute a law to nature.

McCulloch and Pitts concluded their 1943 paper by making this contribution to nature digital. "Causality," they wrote, "which requires description of states and a law of necessary connection relating them, has appeared in several forms in several sciences, but never, except in statistics, has it been as irreciprocal as in this theory."[31] The "state" of a neural net—just like the state of a Turing machine—could be specified at a given time t, and the relation between successive times could provide "the law of necessary connection" that would allow one to "compute from the description of any state that of the succeeding state." But neuronal habits could, they continued, never give rise to the concept of necessity, because "the inclusion of disjunctive relations prevents complete determination" of the preceding state. Knowledge would remain incomplete, abstract, and semiautonomous, just as Kant had claimed:

> Thus our knowledge of the world, including ourselves, is incomplete as to space and indefinite as to time. This ignorance, implicit in all our brains, is the counterpart of the abstraction which renders our knowledge useful. The role of brains in determining the epistemic relations of our theories to our observations and of these to the facts is all too clear, for it is apparent that every idea and every sensation is realized by activity within that net, and by no such activity are the actual afferents fully determined.[32]

In other words, the brain establishes a way to receive and then independently structure impulses from outside itself, which makes its activity autonomous and necessarily "abstract." It realizes states of affairs that are both matters of its logical structure *and* "afferent impulses." The brain, then, is the intersection of *mind* and *world*, and even the source of both of those terms. "Experimental epistemology" confirms this point:

> Thus empiry [empiricism or empirical results] confirms that if our nets are undefined, our facts are undefined, and to the "real" we can attribute not so much as one quality or "form." With determination of the net, the unknowable object of knowledge, the "thing in itself," ceases to be unknowable.[33]

This conclusion appears to be little more than a restatement of Kant's principle in neuro-physiological terms. The problem of real knowledge of the world (the "synthetic *a priori*") is recast as the partial autonomy of neural nets. But McCulloch went one step further.

McCulloch's question, "What is a Man, that He May Know a Number?," places a digital capacity at the apex of his experimental epistemology. McCulloch shifted the Kantian framework from a purely epistemological endeavor into a technological one. The McCulloch-Pitts neuron shows how logical quantities are central to the understanding of embodied cognition, or, in other words, how the digital is real. Even if the paper had not led to the proliferation of actual digital technologies—both mainframe and personal computers, in addition to machine learning techniques—it would still stand as a philosophical achievement. So far from "reducing" human knowledge to number, it made number a dynamic feature of any possible cognition seated at the knife's edge between idea and matter. The digital, we might say, is the specification of the conjunction of these two, the material organization of signs.

Digital embodiment might take any number of forms—in the brain, in the computer, in machine learning processes, or in something as yet unknown. But it can never itself provide its own interpretive framework, because it can never fully "determine" its nets. The digital is a real factor in the way our world is organized—even in the very way we should understand "world" at all—but is still limited to propositions. The digital never exceeds the order of signs; it plays a role in our world in precisely the way that all signs do, giving rise to the world—constituting that world, as Kant had it—and our understanding of it at the same time. McCulloch's insistence on the "semiotic" character of digital embodiment militates against any "data metaphysics"; using Kant to ground a view of the digital limits it to symbols, but also takes the way we use those symbols extremely seriously, as agents in our shared world. The digital is not, for this way of looking at things, anything other than (very) long series of signs. But without signs, we could have no world in the first place. The digital, precisely as a kind of abstraction, constitutes our metaphysics, forcing us to re-evaluate how we deal in even the most basic categories, like that of causality.

McCulloch liked to call causality a "superstition."[34] As sociologist William Davies has recently argued, the shift from traditional statistical methods to data-driven processes abandons causality in favor a deeper and more specific ability to influence and control behavior, like self-care in nutrition and medication, or even how one votes.[35] But Davies is not as sanguine as Domingos in his description of the "master algorithm" about the promises of this new category, and with good reason. When we let data make decisions for us, we confer causality on the digital without participating in the way that causality governs our world. This deferral persists even in the concept of "correlation," which, if anything, harbors an even deeper implicit commitment to the notion that the data and reality are one and the same. But correlations are abstractions, too: The absence of cause doesn't ensure that we are dealing in the real. Kant allowed the McCulloch group to think of the digital as the generative site of meaning, something both abstract and metaphysical, epochal yet not inevitable. We need to regain this sense that the digital is not inevitable, and that means participating in its causal actions in our world. Doing this, in turn, means *understanding it*.

Even the Biggest Data of all is still just a set of interlocking propositions. When we seek correlations in data, we're seeking an understanding of nature that is both encoded in digital nets and, precisely because of that, necessarily incomplete, abstract yet real. This doesn't mean that the new data processing can't be of major importance to our society, as it clearly already is. It does mean, however, that we shouldn't confuse the pragmatic success of algorithms with the structure of reality. A digital metaphysics based on McCulloch's Kantianism reminds us that the size and volume of statements don't change the fact that they *are* abstract. Those abstractions are real, embedded in the materiality of brains and digital machines. They constitute our world, and can't be subtracted from it. But data literally *can't* be promoted to decision makers. Even when we "defer" to machine learning, we're really just deferring to extraordinarily complex sets of inputs—symbolic inputs—conditioned by human-machine interactions in the first place. The digital is causal in the same way any material system of signs is causal: It stabilizes channels of symbolic and other exchange, but can't fully determine the shape that exchange will take. Automation can't be automated, because signs persist as open-ended abstract systems making up our world.

The digital, for McCulloch, was—to repeat—real but not inevitable, as it often seems today. The point was all too obvious in the 1940s, when the first digital computers were still under construction. Now it is virtually impossible to opt out of the digital's causal force field. The digital is part of reality, but it is not the motor of history. McCulloch suggests to us, by way of Kant, that it is not by brute force but by close reading (maybe of some new kind) that we may come to live with the digital.[36] We have to find a way not to defer to a data-based understanding of a world that nevertheless *includes* data. To do that, we have to pay close attention to the way digital processes work as sets of signs—as irreducibly semiotic processes. McCulloch pointed toward a philosophy of the digital that we urgently need to elaborate today.

(Spring 2018, 20.1)

Notes

[1] Warren Sturgis McCulloch, *Embodiments of Mind* (Cambridge, MA: MIT Press, 1965), 73.

[2] Ibid., 156.

[3] Ibid., 74.

[4] Immanuel Kant, *Critique of Pure Reason*, trans. Paul Guyer and Allen W. Wood (Cambridge, England: Cambridge University Press, 1998), 142–43.

[5] Ethem Alpaydin gives an excellent short overview in *Machine Learning: The New AI* (Cambridge, MA: MIT University Press, 2016).

[6] Gideon Lewis-Kraus, "The Great A.I. Awakening," *The New York Times Magazine*, December 14, 2016, https://www.nytimes.com/2016/12/14/magazine/the-great-ai-awakening.html.

[7] Andrew Griffin, "Elon Musk: The Chance We Are Not Living in a Computer Simulation Is 'One in Billions,'" *The Independent*, June 2, 2016, https://www.independent.co.uk/life-style/gadgets-and-tech/news/elon-musk-ai-artificial-intelligence-computer-simulation-gaming-virtual-reality-a7060941.html.

[8] Chris Anderson, "The End of Theory: The Data Deluge Makes the Scientific Method Obsolete," *Wired*, June 23, 2008, https://www.wired.com/2008/06/pb-theory/.

[9] See Frank Pasquale, *The Black Box Society: The Secret Algorithms That Control Money and Information* (Cambridge, MA: Harvard University Press, 2015).

[10] Kathleen O'Toole, "Susan Athey: How Big Data Changes Business Management," *Insights by Stanford Business*, September 20, 2013, https://www.gsb.stanford.edu/insights/susan-athey-how-big-data-changes-business-management.

[11] Keller Easterling, *Extrastatecraft: The Power of Infrastructure Space* (New York, NY: Verso Books, 2014); Orit Halpern, *Beautiful Data: A History of Vision and Research since 1945* (Durham, NC: Duke University Press, 2014); Joshua J. Yates, "Saving the Soul of the Smart City," *The Hedgehog Review* 19, no. 2 (2017): 18–35.

[12] Pedro Domingos, *The Master Algorithm: How the Quest for the Ultimate Learning Machine Will Remake Our World* (New York, NY: Basic Books, 2015), 13.

[13] Ibid., 9.

[14] Viktor Mayer-Schönberger and Kenneth Cukier, *Big Data: A Revolution That Will Change the Way We Live, Work, and Think* (New York, NY: Houghton-Mifflin, 2013), 68–69, 70.

[15] Ronald Kline, *The Cybernetic Moment, or Why We Call Our Age the Information Age* (Baltimore, MD: Johns Hopkins University Press, 2015); N. Katherine Hayles, *How We Became Posthuman: Virtual Bodies in Cybernetics, Literature, and Informatics* (Chicago, IL: University of Chicago, 1999).

[16] Paul Erickson et al., "Enlightenment Reason, Cold War Rationality, and the Rule of Rules," in *How Reason Almost Lost Its Mind: The Strange Career of Cold War Rationality* (Chicago, IL: University of Chicago Press, 2013): 27–50.

[17] Norbert Wiener, *Cybernetics, or Communication and Control in the Animal and the Machine* (Cambridge, MA: MIT Press, 1985), 132. First published 1948.

[18] See Norbert Wiener, *The Human Use of Human Beings* (London, England: Free Association, 1989), 18 ff.

[19] Wiener posited this connection as early as 1932 in a paper titled "Back to Leibniz! Physics Reoccupies an Abandoned Position," *Technology Review* 34 (1932), 201–03, 222–24. See also Wiener, *The Human Use of Human Beings*.

[20] Peter Galison, "The Ontology of the Enemy: Norbert Wiener and the Cybernetic," *Critical Inquiry* 21, no. 1 (1994): 228–66, especially 233.

[21] Warren S. McCulloch and Walter Pitts, "A Logical Calculus of the Ideas Immanent in Nervous Activity," *Bulletin of Mathematical Biology* 52, no. 1/2, 1990, 99–115 (reprint from *Bulletin of Mathematical Biophysics* 5, 115–133 (1943), https://link.springer.com/article/10.1007/BF02478259.

[22] McCulloch, *Embodiments of Mind*, 19. See also Tara Abraham, "(Physio)Logical Circuits: The Intellectual Origins of the McCulloch-Pitts Neural Networks," *Journal of the History of the Behavioral Sciences* 38, no. 1 (2002): 3–25.

[23] McCulloch, *Embodiments of Mind*, 37.

[24] James A. Anderson and Edward Rosenfeld, ed., *Talking Nets: An Oral History of Neural Networks* (Cambridge, MA: MIT, 2000), 3.

[25] Paul Schrecker, "Leibniz and the Art of Inventing Algorisms," *Journal of the History of Ideas* 8, no. 1 (1947): 107–16, especially here 108. Also cited by Lily Kay, "From Logical Neurons to Poetic Embodiments of Mind: Warren S. McCulloch's Project in Neuroscience," *Science in Context* 14, no. 4 (2001), 591–614, here 595, and in Abraham, "(Physio)Logical Circuits."

[26] Here I am building on excellent work done by Michael A. Arbib and Orit Halpern; see Arbib, "Warren McCulloch's Search for the Logic of the Nervous System," *Perspectives in Biology and Medicine* 43k, no. 2 (2000): 193–216; and especially Halpern, "Cybernetic Sense," *Interdisciplinary Science Reviews* 37, no. 3 (2012): 218–36. See also Jean-Pierre Dupuy, *On the Origins of Cognitive Science: The Mechanization of the Mind*, trans. M.B. DeBevoise (Cambridge, MA: MIT, 2009), 93–95.

[27] Warren S. McCulloch Papers, B: M139: III, American Philosophical Society, Philadelphia, PA, Jerome Lettvin, Letter from McCulloch to Henry Moe at the Guggenheim Foundation, December 30, 1959. Also cited in Halpern, "Cybernetic Sense," 232.

[28] Warren S. McCulloch, "Recollections of the Many Sources of Cybernetics," in *The Collected Works of Warren S. McCulloch*, vol. 1, ed. Rook McCulloch (Salinas, CA: Intersystems, 1989), 21–49; also http://www.univie.ac.at/constructivism/archive/fulltexts/2312.html.

[29] Kant, *Critique of Pure Reason*, 245–67.

[30] McCulloch recapitulates this story in *Embodiments of Mind*, 6.

[31] McCulloch, *Embodiments of Mind*, 35. McCulloch also calls Kant's notion of causality one of two "fertile succubi," 297.

[32] Ibid., 35.

[33] Ibid.

[34] Wendy Hui Kyong Chun argues that this delicate relation between knowledge of the unknowable and embodiment is at the root of software in general. See Chun, *Programmed Visions: Software and Memory* (Cambridge, MA: MIT Press, 2011), 153–57.

[35] William Davies, "How Statistics Lost Their Power—and Why We Should Fear What Comes Next," *The Guardian*, January 19, 2017, https://www.theguardian.com/politics/2017/jan/19/crisis-of-statistics-big-data-de.

[36] This point runs parallel to that made by Johanna Drucker for graphical display in the digital: "Thus the *representation* of knowledge is as crucial to its cultural force as any other facet of its production. The graphical forms of display that have come to the fore in digital humanities in the last decade are borrowed from a mechanistic approach to realism, and the common conception of data in those forms needs to be completely rethought for humanistic work." Johanna Drucker, "Humanities Approaches to Graphical Display," *Digital Humanities Quarterly* 5, no. 1 (2011), http://www.digitalhumanities.org/dhq/vol/5/1/000091/000091.html. Accessed November 30, 2017.

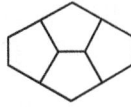

The University in Question
A Conversation with Martha C. Nussbaum

Jennifer L. Geddes

Jennifer L. Geddes (JLG): Your book, *Cultivating Humanity: A Classical Defense of Reform in Liberal Education*, is very optimistic and hopeful about the future of higher education. What sorts of changes have you seen in the university since you began teaching?

Martha C. Nussbaum (MCN): I think there have been tremendous changes. On the whole, they're very much for the good. First of all, there's been a tremendous growth in curiosity about other fields and interdisciplinary cooperation. When people are skeptics about new interdisciplinary scholarship, I always point to Classics, because that's in some ways the most traditional of disciplines, but, of course, it has always contained history, art history, numismatics, philosophy, literary study, technical philology—you could go on and on. The suspiciousness of these new forms of study is often just the irritation of people whose habits are being upset, and what we really need to worry about, if anything, is, first of all, how the cooperation really works. Do we really have enough input from both sides? Is there enough expertise coming from both ways? What we don't want is people who are eclectic, who dabble in another field, but without really consulting with the experts in that field. You have to worry about straying too far from the thing you got started in and love the most.

JLG: Do you think there's a growing concern that scholarship be more relevant to what's going on in the world?

MCN: I think that's true. Of course, history, for example, always had its roots in the world in a way. But even history has expanded, in the sense that it's now taking account of social history, the history of daily life, so that it's not just the narrow swath of high political history,

but the whole of life in periods of history that's of interest. And, philosophy, my own particular love, is much, much more responsive to the world than it used to be.

That struggle began long ago. I've just been teaching [John Stuart] Mill's great essay on
[Jeremy] Bentham, and he quite rightly says that Bentham was the guy who in some ways
began this, in our modern Anglo-American tradition. He said that you can't talk about
rights in a vacuum; you have to look empirically at the world. He set philosophy on a course
that says it has to be responsible to your best take on both human beings and the social
world they live in. He wasn't the first, either; Aristotle did this. So we go in and out of focus
in philosophy, and what I have always loved about the Greeks is that they were out there
in the world. They couldn't hide behind the position of being respected academicians; they
had to justify their whole activity and its worth to people who didn't antecedently care about
that. So that meant they had to be responsible to human beings and their world.

JLG: What other significant changes in the university have you noticed?

MCN: There are two other things that I would single out. The rise of women's studies and
other studies oriented toward the experience of minorities—ethnic studies and race studies
and studies of sexuality—has been a tremendous contributor to the academy on two different levels, because the exclusion of those forms of study was always part and parcel of the
exclusions of the people. Including the people is very much facilitated by giving dignity to
their lives as objects of study. It's improved the culture of the university as a place of fairness
and inclusiveness, but, of course, second, it's also increased our knowledge. There was so
much that had to be learned in all those areas and that had not been studied. It's no surprise
that so many young scholars want to go into those areas, because there's new stuff to do.

I would also say the very great increase in our curiosity about and understanding of
non-Western cultures and people. It's a much bigger part of undergraduate education now
than it used to be. The graduate programs in those areas always existed, but they've grown in
their influence in the university and in their size. I think that's the toughest area of change
because Americans are very lacking in curiosity about the rest of the world. As someone who
does fieldwork in India and who cares a lot about what's happening there and works with
women there, I find that it's extremely hard to get even academic colleagues and students to
be interested enough that they really know something about it. I think that learning about
non-Western cultures and people has to begin earlier in the schools, in the primary and secondary education that people get, because if when they get to college, they don't care about
anything outside America, it's hard to start it at that point.

**JLG: Do you think the contemporary culture is shaping the university and its ideals in
any negative ways?**

MCN: There is an increasing kind of market pressure to produce students who can get jobs and be successful and therefore to teach just those things that are going to produce successful job applicants. The irony is that businesses really don't want that. Typically you ask executives what kind of person they're looking for, and they want someone with a disciplined imagination, like the type of person who's studied philosophy or classics, but it's easy to miss that point and think that the quickest passport to producing successful students is to teach a lot of computer studies or whatever seems to be the hot area in the job market. I don't think that major research universities are succumbing to that at this point. I also think our country's better off than a lot of European countries in this regard because we have a long tradition of liberal education. We have the view—and I think both the Left and the Right share this view—that education is a general preparation for citizenship and the cultivation of life. Whereas in, let's say, Thatcher's Britain, Thatcher asked all the universities and all the departments to demonstrate that they were producing efficient workers in industry. That was her only interest. I remember a very sad document that the Classics department at the University of Birmingham—this great place where Louis MacNeice taught and spent some of his happiest years and where E.R. Dodds taught—had to produce. They wrote about how Classics produces efficient managers for industry. Well, probably it does, but if you have to get to that point, then the game is up.

I'm also worried about the use of adjuncts in teaching. I know that there are not as many jobs as there ought to be. The big reason for this is that people at colleges and universities are employing large numbers of adjuncts to teach in the humanities, and there's not sufficient protest against this. I think we all need to organize to protest against this. And we need to make common cause with those adjuncts to improve their living conditions and their benefits, to get them some benefits. The protest won't come from the consumer side, at least not for a long time. So I think it has to come from us. The Philosophical Association has joined with other professional organizations to pursue that issue, and I think we'd better keep pursuing it.

JLG: What do you think about the growing relationship between universities and corporations, particularly in relation to scientific research?

MCN: I think these connections have always been there. If you look into how science is funded, it's going to come either from a private source or from a public source. When I did look into this at Brown on a committee that I was on, most of the funding, even for basic research, was from the Department of Defense. I'm not sure that that's better than some corporation. But I think it's important that the connection should travel in both directions. That is to say, I think we need to be thinking as scholars and teachers about how we can reach the corporate world and shape its values. For a long time I've thought of my public role in the following way: I teach undergraduates who will go out and play a variety of roles in the world; I also teach law students and interact with law faculty, who will go out and maybe change the culture in certain ways; and then, I do international development work. But I've just realized that if you don't try to reach the corporations, then the game is lost, because, much more than governments, corporations are really setting the agenda for what will happen in developing countries and in our country in the future.

Some of the new executives are actually very interested in ethical issues, so what I've been trying to do recently is to address my teaching, particularly the part that's in the law school, more toward the people who are heading for the corporate world, trying to lure those people in. A colleague and I are creating a new course called "Leadership and Decision Making" to try to get the lawyers to think better about ethical values, without it seeming to be a boring required course in legal ethics, which is a course they always resent. I'm also trying to talk to business people in a variety of different contexts, because I do think that the corporations have to be willing to include human ethical values in their set of goals and priorities when they go abroad. If it's all driven by the profit motive, then international development projects that I care very much about will not get support. Government support alone is not enough for them. Workplace standards have to include building in a role for education, for example. And they can do that. There are plenty of executives who are responsive to that, who understand that it's actually good business to have an educated work force, that it's good business to contribute to the ecology of the area where you're working. But they have to reflect on it in the first place, so I think we all have a role to play here. It would be good if academics did more and more consulting with the corporate world of a sort that doesn't just defer to them and ask them for money, but says: "We have something to offer to you."

JLG: There aren't many scholars doing the kinds of things that you're doing, who are fulfilling the role of public intellectual. You teach, do research, and think about these things in an academic setting, but then you are also very involved in the world, in making practical decisions or in advising people who do. What is the response from your colleagues to this? Do you think that this sort of cross-germination is happening more or will happen more?

MCN: The response varies, and it varies within philosophy so that there would be some philosophers who would think, "Oh, well, that's not serious philosophy any more." But then a lot of philosophers think that about the whole of political philosophy. I think there are public intellectuals who have decided to leave their academic work behind, and they don't interact at a high level of detail and specificity with the work of other scholars in political philosophy. But I love the scholarship in political philosophy. I love to teach the works of John Rawls and all the distinguished people of our time. I'm very much an academic at heart. I would die inside if I left that behind. Whatever I do in public has to bring that with it. There are different levels of detail with which you write, but the core of my work is very academic and will remain so. And I think my colleagues recognize that. I think they think this is somebody who may have these ambitions to change the world for the better, and they sometimes think that that's good and sometimes think that that's naïve and Pollyannaish. But they recognize that I am also a serious scholar.

In the law school, of course, people are doing public work all the time. My colleagues go to Washington all the time. They testify on this and that. They take cases for the city. They take cases for the government. Three of them are federal judges. So, it's a different world in the sense that every legal academic has the potential to be a public intellectual and many, many are.

Do I think more people will do this kind of work? I think there are two obstacles. First of all, it's very hard to do it in America. If I go to Europe and give a talk about human development, let's say, the major newspapers are likely to write it up. In Finland, in Sweden, even if it's not about political things—suppose I talk about grief—it would get written up in the major newspaper. In Holland, it would be on Dutch TV. And I think that's true pretty much throughout Europe. So [Jürgen] Habermas's role is built into the culture. People will come to him. Again, in Finland, they wanted a commission on the spiritual condition of the Finnish nation, and they asked a philosopher to chair it. It just seemed to them the right thing to do. Here, government never comes to the philosopher. So you have to go out and try to create that role, and you have to do it in a world where most of the media are very hostile to that. They really don't want anything in the humanities that's sophisticated. In science, it's different. I think they will come more to the scientists.

It's hard to get the right kind of attention drawn to public work in the humanities in this country. It's really, really a struggle, and then compounding this is the fact that most of the young philosophers I know really don't know very much about the role. I think it is partly our fault. I asked a lot of philosophers to come to the Institute in Finland that [Amartya] Sen and I were consulting on for the United Nations, and a lot of them produced really bad work for that context. That is to say, they talked only to their philosophical colleagues, and they did not know how to write in a jargon-free way, to use examples vividly, to write clearly.

JLG: Why is it that in the United States, if you give a lecture on grief, to use your example, not many of the general public will attend, whereas in Finland, for example, they will?

MCN: Well, I think it's a combination of good and bad. The good is that we're really a much more democratic society than most of the other cultures, in the sense that intellectual elites are not deferred to. People want to make up their own minds about something, and they trust their own judgment and not necessarily the judgment of people who have prestige in the academy. I think that's, on the whole, good. In India, for example, you will have an intellectual elite being called on at every stage, but that's connected with the fact that only 35 percent of women are even literate, so there's a tremendous gulf between the elite and the people for whom, in some way, they're speaking. In Britain, it's still a clubby world, where a very small proportion of people actually go on to higher education, and the ones who do often went to school together. They know each other, so they put each other on commissions.

That's the side where I think we have an advantage—we're much more genuinely pluralistic. We're much more genuinely democratic.

But then, the disadvantage is, I fear, that we're a very sensationalistic country, and we are impatient with complicated ideas. My colleague, Richard Posner, is writing a book about the public intellectual. He did a citation study in connection with this to try to figure out which of the people whom he would classify as public intellectuals are most cited in the American press, ranging from academic journals all the way to popular publications. Well, not one that one would really think of as a serious thinker is on that list. Camille Paglia, for example—at one point she was a serious academic, but she's become a performance artist and a stand up comic. That's the kind of person who really has a public following. They're like media celebrities, like Hollywood celebrities. In that context, if you can't produce those funny sound bites, you're not going to get into it. That's a problem that isn't just caused by the low tastes of the public; it's caused by the media and what they're willing to put up there. The media are much worse than the students that I teach, than the people I talk to. Without very much more public and, let's add, corporate funding, without good, high-level programs in the humanities, we're not going to change that.

JLG: Would funding for certain kinds of programs be the most fruitful avenue that you would see to change the relationship between the media and the public intellectual?

MCN: I really would. It's happened, of course, to some extent on public radio and TV. This past summer the NPR Boston station did a wonderful series on philosophy. They did it because Chris Lydon, who runs the program, "The Connection," is very smart and very good. And then he had this producer named Hitesh Hathi, who is a graduate student in Indian philosophy at Harvard, a very subtle and smart guy. He just started calling around and putting together a program. I was on it twice: once talking about Socrates and the examined life and once talking about love in Plato's Symposium. There were call-ins; it generated a lot of excitement. Bernard Williams was on it talking about justice. Tim Scanlon was on it talking about ethics. The public really loved that, because they love to sit and think about these deep issues of human life. People are thinking about them. And whether it's grief or love or justice, they do have something to say. We got calls from Nebraska, from Cape Cod, from all over the place. But, I think it took those individuals to really go out there and say: "We're going to do this and see what happens." Again, Bill Moyers's "World of Ideas" way back—that had a tremendous public success, but it took Bill Moyers with his clout to get that on there.

I think we American philosophers have a big advantage here over the British and most of the Europeans. We teach undergraduates who are not philosophy majors, and they're never going to be. And if they're not hooked in by the excitement that you generate in the classroom, then you've failed. I think we all have the potential to do that, some better than others, no doubt, and in very different ways. There's an untapped vast group out there.

JLG: That sort of activity is not often rewarded in the academic world, and often it seems, especially to younger scholars, that there's a choice between going a more public or popular route and getting tenure.

MCN: I think that's still really true. Now, I think to some extent it's a false opposition because I've always thought that if you write clearly and use examples vividly, and you're really relating to human experience in all its complexity, then your writing will reach out to other people. I wrote *The Fragility of Goodness* for scholars mostly, but it's been read more than any of my other books. And that's because people care about those topics. I think that a lot of the bad writing that you see in philosophical journals and in dissertations is unnecessarily bad. I think we've gotten into this habit only recently, with the rise of logical positivism. I think we all could do better than we do.

We often assume the validity of two dichotomies in the academy: one is between teaching and research, the other is between the world and the academy. It seems that those are both false dichotomies for you: teaching feeds your research and helps your writing, and your involvement in the world of decisions feeds your research.

One of the things that I've been most critical of in my new university is that I think there is a conception of research there that says: "If you're a serious research person, you don't talk to anyone else outside the university. You certainly don't teach undergraduates." This tremendous resistance that some of my colleagues, not departmental colleagues, but university colleagues, have to teaching more undergraduates comes from a false conception, it seems to me, of research. I've always gotten my best ideas from the thought that tomorrow I have to talk to people who don't care about this text, who've never read it before. I have to lay it on the line and say what I think is exciting and important about it. I think that is what, at its best, undergraduate teaching gives to your research: the sense of why you're in it and what's great in it. The research should feed the teaching.

JLG: In *For Love of Country: Debating the Limits of Patriotism*, you ask the following question: "Should [students] be taught that they are, above all, citizens of the United States, or should they instead be taught that they are, above all, citizens of a world of human beings...?" Your proposal affirms the latter. Might the idea that students be taught to think of themselves as above all world citizens itself be a form of the identity politics that you criticize in the book? There are a number of ways to arrange one's loves and allegiances that would affirm the sorts of ethical ideals for which you are arguing and which most of us would want to affirm. Might there not be a variety of motivations, a variety of self-concep-

tions—not just the understanding of oneself as above all a world citizen—that would lead one to work for justice, mutual respect, the valuing of difference, human rights?

MCN: One place I'm not going to back down is that I think this world that we're in is interlocking and interdependent through and through. It's just wrong, and it's just a mistake, to pretend it isn't. Students have to learn those facts about the world—that their decisions as consumers affect the lives of poor children over in India, that their decisions as lawyers for a corporate law firm are going to affect distant lives, that the way they live their personal lives might affect the air in some other place. They ought to learn the reality of interdependence and interweaving. They all need to learn to think as citizens of the world in the following sense: first, understanding the extent of that interweaving, and, second, understanding the different kinds of lives that are in the world, having some understanding of what it is to live as a woman in rural Bihar, who has never learned to read and who is in a town where the sex ratio is seventy-five women to a hundred men. What is that life like? To have a sense of those complex realities is something that no one should avoid.

Once we have a sense of those realities, you want to know: What are the different priorities among the different allegiances we have, and should we be taught just one set of correct priorities, or should we learn to argue about them? And here I'm altogether with you. I think that the classroom should be a scene of argument. I do have views about which allegiances take priority, but I am also a philosopher. I strongly believe in argument and debate. Various varieties of nationalism, of group identity politics of different kinds, of strong and weak forms of cosmopolitanism—all of these they should understand, and they should learn the arguments for and against each form. But, I think it should be done in a climate of understanding and not in one of sheer ignorance. I think most Americans are chauvinistic not because they've thought it out and decided they're nationalists, but because they don't know a thing. Thinking as citizens of the world, for me, means just that inclusive effort to imagine the lives of others.

JLG: Your idea that universities "produce citizens," and the politicized nature of that phrase, makes some hesitant. Is that the university's primary goal? What about the idea of the university as a place of thinking and discovering and learning, a place of intellectual experimentation?

MCN: I never wanted to say that producing citizens is the only goal. But there is a tradition of liberal education that I'm talking within which says: "We're not in the business simply of producing experts in a single thing; part of education is a general preparation both for citizenship and for life." One could have different views about how those two should be ranked and which is more important. I was once on a panel with my friend Kwame Anthony Appiah, and what astonished me was that he was focusing very much on the preparation for finding your own personal identity: It's a time where you have a break from all these political pressures. You learn to delve into yourself and explore what kind of narrative you want to construct for your own personal life. And, of course, it is that. But, it's also a time—for many American students, it's the first time—when they're interacting with people who are from very different backgrounds. It's a time that is crucial to the formation of democratic citizens.

Our aspiration has been to open college education to anyone who's qualified to receive it. We haven't yet delivered on that promise, but I hope we will increasingly. And I think part of the point of that is that we want a citizenry that's not just going to be at the mercy of sensationalism, of sound bites, of the media, but a critical, hard-headed, curious, skeptical, argumentative citizenry who can really deliberate together. And that means, of course, understanding who the people are with whom we're deliberating, both in the country and in the world. That is a very important aspiration. I don't think democracy will go very far in the next century, if we don't work on that. Every era that has had democracy has also had the tyranny of demagogues, and sensationalism and fads. Ancient Athens was in that way not very different from modern America. And Socrates was put to death and so on. We have to be vigilant. We have to try to create the kind of people who could stand up to Socrates and defend what they want to do and really have an argument, instead of just thinking of political discussion as a place where you show how tough you are. I think that's a very important part of the mission of the university. I don't conceive of it as a place where you're trying to imprint on everyone a certain stamp, but just the reverse. You want to teach them to cultivate their independent ability to deliberate.

JLG: In *Cultivating Humanity* you argue that teaching students about other cultures, different value systems, and different ways of living doesn't lead to cultural relativism, and that it's possible to make cross-cultural judgments and evaluations. How does the study of other cultures help us in making moral judgments? Do you see in your students a reluctance to make judgments, as if the act of judgment itself is a wrong or an evil to be fought against?

MCN: I think this is a real problem. Students have a hands-off attitude to judgments. I think that comes from two confusions that they're inclined to make. One confusion is a confusion between relativism and toleration. They think it is very good to be tolerant. They've heard this. They think deeply that it is true about the relations between religions in America. And then, they somehow think that that requires us not to judge anyone else's way of life. But, of course, you can quickly get them to be a little more puzzled about that by asking them: "What do we think of a society that doesn't practice religious toleration? What do we think of the intolerant culture itself, if toleration requires us to judge it negatively, and yet relativism requires us not to? There's a tension there. Which side are you really on?"

And I think pretty soon they recognize that toleration as a value is really quite at odds with a thorough-going relativism.

The second confusion is a confusion between ignorant judgment and all judgment. They realize quite rightly that a lot of the ways that America has behaved toward other cultures has betrayed a condescension, a chauvinism, and of course, far worse things, for example, the desire to exploit and abuse. And so, quite rightly, instead of approaching a country like India in the way that the British did, thinking that we know what civilized values are and that we're going to see how far they come up to that mark, students say: "It's their culture. Let them figure it out." They don't want to impose their ways. What I think you want to say to those students is, first of all: "Judging and imposing are two very different things. You can have a view about what's right but still believe that because they're a sovereign democratic nation, they better implement it. If anyone's going to implement it, it will be them." And that is, indeed, my view about my universalist proposals, so they build in a very strong role for national sovereignty. But the other thing you want to say is: "The defects of judgment that's ignorant, like the British colonialist judgment, do not attach to all judgment. There's a kind of informed judgment that you hope to make in your own personal lives, that you do make when you choose your friends, your way of life; and, of course, when you're doing that, you're already crossing barriers, often of religion, of ethnicity, or crossing other barriers."

(Fall 2000, 2.3)

III.
Economy and Work

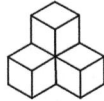

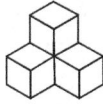

Temps, Consultants, and the Rise of the Precarious Economy

Louis Hyman

In 1967, the celebrated economist and intellectual John Kenneth Galbraith argued in his best-selling book *The New Industrial State* that "we have an economic system which, whatever its formal ideological billing, is in substantial part a planned economy."[1] Though postwar American politicians juxtaposed US free markets to the centrally planned economies of the Soviet bloc, Galbraith recognized that the two were more similar than one might have thought. The private planning of corporations, whose budgets were sometimes bigger than those of governments, defined postwar American capitalism, not markets.[2] Markets meant uncertainty, and postwar corporate planners eschewed risk above all else.[3]

After the chaos of depression and war, corporate planners had worked in conjunction with federal policymakers to make a world that promoted stability. None of the top 100 postwar corporations had failed to earn a profit.[4] This profitability was not an accident. Nor was it the result of seizing every lucrative prospect. Rather, it had come from minimizing risk in favor of long-term certainty.

This postwar economy had allowed employees and employers alike to plan for the future, assuring them steady wages and steady profits. Big business had to be big to contain all the functions it would not entrust to the market. Through their own five-year plans, Galbraith argued, corporations "minimize[d] or [got] rid of market influences."[5] This American planned economy—which had appeared to be the natural future of capitalism in 1967—began to fall apart only two years later, in 1969, nearly twenty years before the fall of the Soviet Union.

The collapse of this postwar economy came from the overreach of its new corporate form—the conglomerate—whose rise was legitimated by the belief in managerial planning. But its essential moral underpinnings—stability for investment and, especially, stability for work—took more of an effort to dislodge. Yet in the 1970s and 1980s, this effort succeeded as corporations began to embrace risk and markets, undoing the stability of the postwar period. By the 1980s, the risk-taking entrepreneur had displaced the safe company man as the ideal employee.

Today, scholars and critics are all abuzz about "precarious" work. Instead of a job for life with General Motors or AT&T, we now have many jobs either in sequence or, increasingly, all at once. Freelancers in the US labor force are estimated to number around fifty-four million, as much as one-third of the work force.[6] "Precarious" has become a catchall term that encompasses everything from day labor to temp work to the gig economy, and denotes flexible work that is insecure, temporary, and generally poorly paid. If the worker in this flexible economy is something new, so too is the firm, which, instead of hiring employees, increasingly outsources its labor needs.

Economists especially like to explain this shift to flexible labor in terms of the reduction of "transaction costs" (the costs of finding and hiring someone).[7] One classic argument proposes that firms arose only because it was too expensive for individuals to transact every obligation. By that logic, the arrival of the Internet—with sites such as Craigslist and Upwork—easily explains the displacement of stable, firm-based jobs by the gig economy. But that explanation is too easy. The origins of precariousness in the rise of temp agencies and the fall of the postwar conglomerate run much deeper than the advent of digital platforms. The shape of our economy is made possible by technology, but it reflects a choice determined more by beliefs about the corporation than by lower transaction costs. Before they outsourced their labor, firms had to overcome old-fashioned shibboleths, such as secure employment for their work force, and they did so during the 1970s, long before the Internet arrived.

Since 1970, temporary labor has become part of the everyday fabric of work across all segments of society, from the bottom to the top. Temps we call "day laborers" linger outside Home Depot waiting in the early morning hours for a contractor's truck while wondering if immigration will be sweeping through. Temps called "light industrial workers" assemble electronic components for Dell or move cardboard packages for Amazon. Temps called "management consultants" fly first-class all over the world to advise CEOs on global strategy. Only the CEO, whose pay has skyrocketed relative to that of frontline workers, has remained essential.

Simply adding up the number of employees of temporary agencies does not do justice to the importance of this new kind of work—the number, even today, amounts to only a small percentage of the work force. Consider, however, that by the 1980s that percentage was already greater than the proportion of workers in private-sector unions—a group we consider central to our economy. By 1989 (long before Craigslist), temps were being used in 97 percent of major US firms.[8] The vast majority of companies had decided that temporary workers should be part of how they ran their business. Flexibility, not stability, became the new ideal against which all decisions were evaluated. The triumph of this new ideal emerged from a crisis in corporate organization and an opportunity in new computer technology. The intersection of these two events would remake the American corporation and the American workplace.

The Rise of the Costocracy

Manpower was launched in 1948 as a service offering temporary secretarial labor—"secretary" being the designation of nearly 10 percent of all women in paid employment—but it would come to provide temps for nearly every kind of work. Like most innovations, the temp agency emerged from a crisis: in this case, a middle-aged attorney named Elmer Winter who found himself unable to find a secretary to type a "long and exacting brief" for the Supreme Court.[9] Winter, who had somehow managed to start a law career in the middle of the Great Depression and then served in the Office of Price Administration during World War II, was by 1948 again in private practice, and he could not type. After calling all the employment agencies (which could provide only permanent staff) and finding no temporary secretaries available, he and his partner, Aaron Scheinfeld, called a "former secretary of ours who had resigned to have her first baby."[10] She came in to type, and the brief was filed. More significantly, Winter and Scheinfeld realized that their need for temporary labor was hardly unique. And so the first temp agency was born.

Manpower's labor model—according to which the temp worked for Manpower and not for the company—was truly novel. It was not an employment agency but a temporary labor agency. Yet expanding Manpower beyond replacement secretaries proved difficult. The challenge was not the transaction costs of supplying workers, but the fixed ideas of management. Temporary workers of all stripes could be had same-day with the ease of a phone call. If you were an oil company drilling off the coast of Texas, for example, a call to Manpower could secure you "30 engineers, purchasing agents, clerks, and roughnecks."[11] If even obscure skills could be found so easily, why did companies persist in hiring permanent staff?

During the 1958 recession, Manpower attempted to introduce the "controlled overhead plan."[12] It was intended to show firms how to use temps to meet peak demand. The most obvious example was the Christmas shopping rush, although the need for seasonal work also challenged florists at Easter and accountancies at tax time. Larger numbers of staff were needed not just to bring in the harvest but also to perform all kinds of service-sector work. Instead of hiring too many employees, or even part-timers, Winter proposed that firms fill such jobs with temps.

"Planned staffing," Winter told a room of management executives at a meeting of the American Management Association, would be as transformational to business as "scientific management." Manpower's job, he believed, was to teach firms that they should not "do it ourselves."[13] But despite the evident savings, few managers were willing to risk their position on some newfangled work scheme when everything worked fine (as it did in the 1960s). Replacing a secretary for a few days when she got sick or went on vacation was one thing; replacing an entire staff was another. Beliefs, not transaction costs, inhibited flexible work forces.

Winter's plan had been implemented only haltingly. Here and there, firms adopted his methods, but mostly they did not. He lamented his difficulties in convincing corporate executives to renounce what they saw as a moral compact with their work force (especially the white-collar work force). Convincing corporate America to outsource its work required a discovery of just how useful temps could be, and that discovery would take place only with the emergence of a new kind of work for which firms could not easily supply sufficient labor: data entry. Data entry would prove to be the opening wedge toward a larger world of flexible labor.[14]

Hiring workers for short-term projects such as data migration could violate corporate policies that guaranteed long-term employment.[15] But at the dawn of the computer age, big companies nevertheless needed to switch record systems.[16] When "Northwestern Mutual Insurance Company decided to convert its [paper] policyholder record to IBM [punch cards]," it used Manpower labor to carry out the task. To ask the permanent staff to do it would have drained morale and taken "about one year." To employ workers just for this task, which was an option, "would have conflicted with a long-established policy of employment security." Instead, the insurance company "lease[d] a crew of experienced key-punch operators to work in the evenings" so that the project could be done faster with more people (who didn't need training). The office space could be used at night so the permanent work staff would not be disrupted.[17] Temps made automation possible not only by running the machines at night but also by providing a feasible way to reconcile corporate employee policies that defended full-time labor with the need for one-time data migration from paper to punch cards.

Northwestern Mutual was not unique. For instance, "a large Milwaukee bank" faced the rising challenge of data entry, but the cost of the machines to enter the data—"Comptometers"—was prohibitive. Instead of hiring more people to work during the day, which would have required more machines, the bank hired "several hundred temporaries [to work] during a short evening shift" doing the data entry on the machines that the permanent staff could not. The hours of expensive overtime became hours of cheaper temporary labor. The temps worked at night, and the bank "got double use out of expensive equipment."[18]

Data migrations would not be one-time events. The migration from cursive to bits became an everyday necessity. Yet even as firms realized the ongoing need for data entry, they would continue to rely on large numbers of temps. In the short term, corporate policy might prevent the shift to temps in the name of "employment security," but such policies could not resist the successful experiences of outsourcing office work. Temps enabled computerization, and Manpower capitalized on the opportunity by offering specialty courses in exactly these skills. Manpower's "business training center" "specializ[ed] in the principles and techniques of operating data processing and other electronic equipment." Despite its name, the business training center was more of a data-processing secretarial school than a true business program. Such electronic skills were in desperate demand in the 1960s as even smaller firms embraced the minicomputer.[19]

Automation had long been the key labor issue for postwar futurists, but they often posited an artificial opposition between machines and people. Arthur Gager in 1952, for instance, the staff director of the National Office Management Association, framed automation as the choice between flexibility and inflexibility, between people and machines. "Machines should be used instead of people whenever possible," he said.[20] Temps would be a kind of employee that would be neither a person (as defined as a worker with privileges) nor a machine. The automated office, even after the first round of data migration, required "human attendants" for the machines, preferably "around the clock."[21] Temporary labor would "be a way to achieve more economical use of the sophisticated electronic machinery that larger offices already are using for accounting, filing, billing, data-control work, etc."[22] As offices migrated their data, a line was drawn between workers who would receive the pay and status of a good job and those who would, literally, toil in the shadows.

As the economic stagnation of the 1970s set in, executives became increasingly receptive to Winter's idea of using flexible labor to contain costs. In the late 1960s, a management consultancy did a study for Manpower that found that "workers were approximately 55 percent productive."[23] "This means," Winter said, "that about half of the time the employee was at his or her desk there was a productive result."[24] The rest of the time the worker was getting paid for doing nothing. Whether or not this "55 percent" was true, the rhetorical effect was real enough. As *Fortune* had noted in 1968, "One of the paradoxical consequences of the private welfare state that unions and management have created to safeguard the permanent worker has been to make his temporary colleague look increasingly attractive."[25] Rather than the "I don't care what it costs" attitude that ruled the 1960s, Winter believed, a new and ascendant "costocracy" would undo the expansion of the corporate bureaucracy.[26]

Winter envisioned a new balance in the work force in which temporary labor would play an essential part: "Many companies will work out a personnel program which will encompass 75 percent full-time permanent employees, 15 percent temporaries, and 10 percent part-time workers."[27] By the end of the 1960s, temporary labor had proved its worth as an alternative to the postwar promise of secure, well-paid work. But selling this new workplace arrangement required a thorough re-imagining not only of work but of the corporation itself.

Conglomerators and Consultants

At the end of World War II, a generation of executives, entranced by the logistical programs of the military and then of the seeming success of Keynesian economic policies, refashioned the American corporation along lines of long-term planning, long-term investment, and well-defined hierarchies. Control seemed possible, and, after the tumult of the Great Depression, necessary. The management whiz kids of the postwar period, including Robert McNamara, rose to power on the promise of total knowledge and perfect planning made possible through quantitative analysis and universal principles of management.[28] The generalists were expected to be able to move from "government agency" to "large corporation" to "university administration" as a matter of course.[29] With an MBA and the ability to conduct computer-driven analysis, these executives would be able to manage nearly any enterprise. Building on the computer's wartime uses, "the new manager" would use it for "planning, control, and financial and personnel management."[30] This ideal of "total management information systems" was the apotheosis of the modernist ideal—at least in business.[31]

Faith in managerial genius, in turn, undergirded the rise of a new form of the corporation: the conglomerate. The conglomerate grew in importance during the postwar period, emerging from the defense economy, the rising stock market, and the strict anti-monopoly laws of the period. Neither horizontally nor vertically integrated, the conglomerate corporation was a hodgepodge of different industries, without any overwhelming domination in any particular product line—evading regulators and investing all of those postwar retained earnings. Because conglomerates were big, but not monopolistic, they created both confusion and fear by disrupting traditional American notions of corporate malfeasance. *Monopolies* had long been how Americans characterized unfree markets. *Monopolists* were the economic equivalent of monarchs—and anathema to capitalist democracy. But in the 1960s, conglomerates were hailed as the future of capitalist organization. Investors admired the "synergies" made possible by the triumph of these men who claimed they could manage anything.[32] Lammot Copeland Sr., president of the Du Pont chemical company, jested that "running a conglomerate is a job for management geniuses, not for ordinary mortals like us at Du Pont."[33] The future belonged to the managers who could run these conglomerates. In only a few years, conglomerators like Charles "Tex" Thornton of Litton Industries and James Ling of LTV had assembled companies that were among the largest in the United States, rewarding shareholders and confounding critics. James Ling, for instance, had needed just a few years to transform his Dallas electrical shop into the conglomerate LTV, at one point the twenty-fifth largest firm in the country.

The best and the brightest flocked to conglomerates to learn their secrets. At the height of the infatuation with them, in 1965, *Time* magazine reported that it was the "hard-driving Litton management" that boosted the value of Thornton's acquisitions. Litton was seen as the best place for young executives to learn the most innovative management techniques. By the late 1960s, less than 10 percent of the *Fortune* 500 corporations remained undiversified. (Standard Oil and US Steel were exceptions.)[34]

But the conglomerators were revealed, through government investigations in 1968 and 1969, to be little more than accounting flim-flam artists. Although the mystique of their management science may have underpinned the conglomerates' rising stock prices, it was clever financial dealings—not operational improvements—that enabled their actual growth. While these firms had grown in size, they had not actually grown in profit.

By 1969 these stock market darlings had disappeared, as a suddenly bearish market undid their leveraged financial schemes. Their apparent genius now suspect, the conglomerate innovators had managed to tarnish all of American big business. Denouncing the conglomerate was tantamount to issuing a blanket denunciation of large firms, since more than 90 percent of them had followed the new conglomerate model to some extent. Suddenly, bigness became weakness. In the aftermath, business experts found themselves searching for a new way to think about the corporation, now that the golden idol had been shown to be made of pyrite.

Conveniently, another model of the corporation had been developing during the mid-1960s at a new kind of management consultancy: Boston Consulting Group (BCG). Its founder, Bruce Henderson, like many early consultants, had a background in engineering. He spent the first decades of his career at Westinghouse, where he rose into senior management. Leaving Westinghouse, he spent a few years at Arthur D. Little (a consulting firm), but left to open his own shop in 1963.[35] BCG began its life focused on strategy. Strategy consulting—which stressed revenue growth and corporate reorganization rather than cost cutting—was just coming into its own. Henderson realized that firms really needed help from consultants in thinking about how to organize their structure to maximize growth. Apocryphally, when batting around ideas for his new firm in the early days, Henderson suggested that it specialize in "business strategy." One of the staff objected that that was "too vague." Henderson, brilliantly, simply replied, "That's the beauty of it. We'll define it."[36] Although BCG led the way, other consultancies, including McKinsey & Company, followed suit, shifting their business away from the old cost-cutting time studies to new growth strategy studies, and in the process began to redraw the boundaries of the firm.

In the form of the "BCG Growth Matrix," the redefinition of the corporation would be an idea that would remake American business. Created in 1968 and first published in 1970 in the form of an essay, "The Product Portfolio,"[37] the Growth Matrix redefined basic corporate strategy by combining growth and cash into one easy-to-understand schema. Imagine a 2 x 2 matrix, with growth on the vertical axis from low to high, and cash generation on the horizontal axis, from high to low.[38] Where the growth is low and the cash flow is high sits the now-commonplace term "cash cow." For Henderson, the cash cow was a mature company that had a large share of the market and generated lots of cash, but whose market was not growing.[39] Henderson's key idea was that the cash generated by this "cow" should not be reinvested in the cow itself, but in new business areas experiencing high growth. Henderson's jargony labels for these two kinds of companies—"stars" (the high-growth, high–cash-creating companies just above the cash cows) and the "problem children" (the high-growth, low–cash-creating companies situated diagonally from the cash cows)—mattered less than the new way of viewing them.

Henderson believed that good management was concerned not just with cash creation in a particular business unit but also with intelligently reinvesting that cash in other business units. Corporate leaders were not managers but investors. For the corporation, Henderson's view demanded that even profitable units should be divested when their capital could be better employed elsewhere. A diversified conglomerate, from this perspective, could have a distinct advantage over single-purpose companies, one that derived not just from being in different sectors but also from operating concerns in different stages of the business life cycle. Postwar conglomerates had reduced risk, but they had not increased profitability, because postwar CEOs had never conceived of their collections of companies as an investment portfolio. They invested for growth, not returns. When viewed through Henderson's matrix, the strategic brilliance of many conglomerates' industrial subsidiaries dimmed. Drawing a 2 x 2 matrix was, nonetheless, easier than reorganizing a conglomerate, which is where BCG and other strategy consultants stepped in.

Corporations reorganized for a variety of reasons, but according to Warren Cannon, McKinsey's director of staff, the first question that needed to be asked would appear at first glance to be an obvious one: "What business(es) are we in?"[40] For many conglomerates, whose interests could span multiple sectors, the answer was not obvious. Luckily, remaking corporations was the bread and butter of the top management consultancies. In 1972, about a third of McKinsey's $45 million in profits came from reorganizing large corporations.[41] The gap between strategy and structure was apparent, and firms turned to consultants for help. In just three years at the end of the 1960s, McKinsey reported that "66 of the nation's top 100 industrial firms reported major organizational realignments."[42] And the bigger the firm, the more likely it was to be reorganized: "9 of the 10 largest companies, 16 of the top 25, 27 of the top 50," were in that group of 66. McKinsey alone was responsible for reorganizing 100 firms, on average, per year.[43] In other words, the multinational conglomerates that had overreached were the firms most in need of the reorganizing guidance of McKinsey and other consultancies.

As the 1960s became the 1970s, the common corporate panacea, at least according to the leading consultancies, was to restructure the firm so that it was smaller, more flexible, and clearly aligned with products. Before this moment, no one would have thought that smaller firms would be better run than large firms. Large firms had resources, economies of scale, professional managers, and many options. But now big business started to seem weak. "As the dinosaur skeletons in museums remind us," McKinsey managing director Gilbert Clee wrote in *McKinsey Quarterly*, "great size has its dangers—the dangers of dulled perceptions, sluggish reflexes, and a fatal loss of rapport with the environment."[44] In this new way of thinking, terms like "small," "efficient," and "flexible" began to seem causally interconnected, as if a smaller enterprise always made for a more efficient business, flexibility required a small enterprise, or flexible firms were more efficient. Consultants and business gurus began to imagine not only a change of degree but also of kind. Rather than trim costs, firms considered eliminating costs entirely—shutting down business units and eliminating workers. Consultants reveled in their radicalism, envisioning nothing less than the end of bureaucracy, and possibly even the boundary between the firm and the market.

Perhaps the most influential synthesis of this line of thinking was Alvin Toffler's best-selling 1970 book *Future Shock*, which, not coincidentally, won a special award from the McKinsey Foundation. For years, *Future Shock* was the touchstone for thinking about how America would change in the coming years, and at its center was a vision of a new workplace. The reprinting of one of the book's chapters, "The Coming Ad-hocracy," in *McKinsey Quarterly* highlighted Toffler's relevance to "top executives."[45] Toffler's work was not only a bestseller. It was also a synthetic account of the ideas about flexibility that had been circulating since the mid-1960s, though presented with far more panache. Toffler rejected the idea of a future dominated by a faceless bureaucracy: "If the orthodox social critics are correct in predicting a regimented, super-bureaucratized future, we should already be mounting the barricades, punching random holes in our IBM cards, taking every opportunity to wreck the machinery of organization."[46] Yet Toffler observed that no one was doing this, because corporate bureaucracy was, he believed, already collapsing of its own dead weight. In Toffler's view, there would soon be a liberation into "a new free-form world of kinetic organizations" that he called, in a horrid neologism, "ad-hocracy."[47] The term didn't catch on, but his vision of the firm did, set in motion by teams of consultants who brought these ideas, and their own way of business, to the core of the firm. While the bureaucracy maintained the line between inside employee and outside contractor, the ad-hocracy would blur those distinctions.

Instead of jobs, there would be projects. Instead of bosses, there would be project managers. Unsurprisingly, this model mimicked the lives of management consultants. In the 1960s, consultants at top firms like Booz, Allen and McKinsey & Company had similar career paths. On average, 17 percent of consultants with an MBA made partner, while 83 percent left their firm within six years.[48] Most of the older consultants, those over thirty-five years old, joined major corporations, while the younger consultants struck out in more entrepreneurial directions. The average tenure at consulting firms was about three years. Few consultants could expect to make a career of consulting. Permanent executives might work on a project for years on end, but consultants measured their projects in terms of days or weeks, only rarely in months. Assembling in teams, they received a problem from the chief executive or one of his lieutenants. Solving this problem, whether by rethinking an organizational chart or re-pricing potato chips, was their only task. These groups might have little specific knowledge of a particular client company or its product, but their expertise, it was believed, consisted in a general ability to ask the right questions and come up with the right answers, filtering the meaningful out of the noise of the known. Management consultants sold themselves as first-rate problem solvers with an institutional memory of the "hundreds, or rather, thousands of companies" they had served, and, as the London director of McKinsey told the BBC, they tried "to make that general experience available to our clients."[49] While consultants had organized themselves this way for decades, for the first time these practices were put at the core of everyday corporate operations.

The company man would soon be dead. The absence of permanent hierarchy, Toffler predicted, would reduce employee "loyalty."[50] Worker identity would become *what* an employee did rather than *where* he or she did it. Employees were not "company men," and they had no commitments other than to their career and the current "problem." This ad-hocracy was remaking not just corporate work but worker identity, fashioning an employee who hopped from project to project instead of making a life in a single corporation. Employees who needed to be kept, who needed be securely held, were those who made decisions in a rapidly changing world—not those that did the same thing, day in, day out. Tasks that remained routine were "such tasks that the computer and automated equipment do far better than men."[51] Computers might not have been able to predict the future, but they could do repetitive work. In this way, the worlds of temps and consultants converged. For more and more executive jobs, consultants—now determining strategy rather than just conducting time studies—acted like high-paid temps.

The boom in consulting fees came from the widespread restructuring in the aftermath of the conglomeration and resurgent globalization of the 1970s.[52] Business leaders, who had become accustomed to decades of an unusually stable, US-centric way of doing things, now confronted a turbulent world market they did not understand. Consultants offered answers. No computer could replace a consultant, even as that consultant installed computers, and temps, to replace the permanent staff.

Toward the Precarious Economy

Temporary workers were not, as temp Annette Hopkins wrote to her state representative in 1975, luxury-seeking hausfraus, but "the victims of 12 percent a year inflation and 10 percent unemployment, [for whom] working for temporary agencies is an alternative to unemployment checks and/or subsistence lifestyle."[53] By 1970, as the growth of the male paycheck began to stall, women's work, even for married women, became less a choice, if it had ever been one. Temporary work was not discretionary, additional income. It was not a flexible alternative to a normal job. Temp work was a job of last resort. Hopkins wrote, "I have been unable to find an entry-level administrative position, and working as a temporary gives me a flexibility in job hunting." These two facts were intertwined. As more women entered the work force, the number of temp firms likewise increased. Women who wanted a "real job" found that many firms were now relying on temps, especially in growing areas like data entry. Hopkins couldn't find a permanent job, and she blamed the existence of temporary firms as part of the reason for the lack of secure work. Temps were not a "small lonely band." In Boston, she wrote, there were more than 100 temporary agencies. Employers had their pick. The flexibility was now one-sided.

While firms had more options, temps did not. "In times of stagflation," Hopkins wrote, "client-companies find contracting with agencies for temporary workers an attractive alternative to hiring permanent employees." Just as the agencies advertised, temps required "no costly benefits package, no paid sick time, no paid vacations, not even paid lunch time." Clients could fire temps at will.

Elmer Winter's dream had finally begun to become a reality. Manpower had fulfilled his ambitions, and it and its many imitators were beginning to remake American work. For Winter, this transformation created his fortune. He sold his majority stake in Manpower in 1976.[54] For the rest of the country, Winter's dream proved less felicitous.

Organizing flexible workers for collective bargaining purposes proved more challenging than organizing regular workers. Reliant on workplace social cohesion, traditional tactics failed. Temps, as second-class outsiders, were never really part of the "family" of a workplace. Even shift work, in which they might be deployed with other temps, was unsteady. As one temp wrote, "I've thought about it some & I don't see anyway you could organize temps— wouldn't they just shit list us? & I need the work to live."[55] The automated office, backed up by windowless caverns full of data entry clerks seated before glowing green screens, was only rarely unionized.

"The office of the future looks very much like the factory of the past," Karen Nussbaum, one of the founders of 9to5 (the most successful of the temp-organizing groups and the inspiration for the 1980 film of the same name) would write in *Computerworld* in 1982. "There's nothing at all new about shift work, piece work, which is what pay per line of information is."[56] Yet there was a difference between temping and "the cottage industries." Between the times of those two forms came the decades when factory work became a path to the middle class. The office had long defined the middle class, but now it had become a path leading back to the working poor. Some temps, of course, were hired into the ranks of permanent employees, but even those felt the pressure of knowing that they could be replaced. The temp agency of the 1970s might have formed a buffer between the workplace "family" and the turbulence of the economy, but it also built a bridge to a new kind of economy, where entire segments of work could be outsourced. Casual laborers could be easily replaced in the early factories, but temp workers were, by design, disposable.

Americans today cannot typically rely on just one job anymore, certainly not over a lifetime, and frequently not even at one time. For some of the new temps, notably the consultants, the work is glamorous and well paid; for others, such as office workers, it is a dead end. Some freelancers might revel in their flexibility, but all wonder and worry about the lack of benefits. The uncertainty of work, not just for office temps but for everyone, is both what is new and what has become normal. Although day laborers, office temps, and management consultants—as well as contract assemblers, Craigslist freelancers, adjunct professors, Uber drivers, Blackwater contractors, and every other kind of worker filing an IRS Form 1099—span the income ranks, they all have one thing in common: They are temporary.

(Spring 2016, 18.1)

Notes

1 John Kenneth Galbraith, *The New Industrial State* (Boston, MA: Houghton Mifflin, 1969), 6. Original work published 1967. Citations refer to the Houghton Mifflin edition.

2 Ibid., 26.

3 Portions of this essay are drawn from Louis Hyman, "Rethinking the Postwar Corporation: Management, Monopolies, and Markets," in *What's Good for Business: Business and American Politics Since World War II*, ed. Kim Phillips-Fein and Julian E. Zelizer (New York, NY: Oxford University Press, 2012): 195–211.

4 Galbraith, *The New Industrial State*, 82.

5 Ibid., 26.

6 According to a joint survey by the Freelancers Union and Upwork, two-thirds of freelancers rely on such work for their primary income. Freelancers Union and Upwork.com, *Freelancing in America: 2015*, 6, accessed December 30, 2015; https://www.upwork.com/i/freelancinginamerica2015/.

7 This line of reasoning began with market theorist Ronald Coase, but his now-famous paper only came to prominence in the 1960s after his later work on the problem of social costs (now called externalities). See Ronald H. Coase, "The Nature of the Firm," *Economica* 4, no. 16 (1937): 386–405.

8 Lawrence Mishel, Jared Bernstein, and John Schmitt, *The State of Working America, 1996–97* (Washington, DC: Economic Policy Institute), 266; http://www.epi.org/publication/books_swa1996_97/.

9 Elmer Winter, *A Woman's Guide to Earning A Good Living* (New York, NY: Simon and Schuster, 1961), 3.

10 Ibid.

11 "Temporary Hiring Climbs Up The Ladder," *Business Week*, July 15, 1961, 17.

12 "To Californian stockbrokers on November 12, 1962," folder 12, box 12, Elmer Winter Papers (EWP), Jewish Museum of Milwaukee, Milwaukee, WI, 9.

13 "Remarks before the New York Society of Security Analysts," November 27, 1962, folder 12, box 12, EWP, 13.

14 An earlier version of this plan was called the "Controlled Overhead Plan." Manpower had been experimenting with this idea as early as 1960. Through the Controlled Overhead Plan, Manpower encouraged firms "to keep their staffs at a level where they can take care of their normal requirements and use Manpower when the peaks or the emergency situations arise." Quoted in "Remarks before the New York Society of Security Analysts," January 26, 1961, folder 5, box 12, EWP, 9–10.

15 *Data migration* is a stunningly anachronistic term, but it is what we are talking about.

[16] Elmer Winter, *Cutting Costs through the Effective Use of Temporary and Part-Time Help* (Waterford, CT: Prentice Hall, 1965), 6–7.

[17] Ibid., 4.

[18] Elmer Winter, *Your Future as a Temporary Office Worker* (New York, NY: Richard Rosens Press, 1968), 29.

[19] Manpower, *Annual Report*, 1961, folder 1, box 11, EWP, 9.

[20] Arthur Gager, "Determining the Need for Office Machines," *Proceedings of the National Office Management Association*, 1952, 27.

[21] Winter, *Your Future*, 90.

[22] Ibid., 126.

[23] "Your Work Force—1976 Style," folder 7, box 13, EWP, 1.

[24] Ibid.

[25] Irwin Russ, "For Rent: Secretaries, Salesmen,Physicists and Human Guinea Pigs" *Fortune*, October 1968, 164.

[26] "Your Work Force—1976 Style," folder 7, box 13, EWP, 1.

[27] Ibid., EWP, 2.

[28] Although a critique of knowledge would not become fashionable in the academy until the 1980s, management consultants such as McKinsey & Company associate Ridley Rhind saw the fissures in this meta-narrative in 1968, about the same time as Michel Foucault.

[29] Gilbert H. Clee, "The New Manager: The Man for All Organizations," *McKinsey Quarterly*, Spring 1968, 11.

[30] Ibid., 8.

[31] C. Ridley Rhind, "Management Information: The Myth of Total Systems," *McKinsey Quarterly* (Summer, 1968), 2–12.

[32] Harvey Segal, "The Urge to Merge: The Time of the Conglomerates," *New York Times*, October 27, 1968, SM32.

[33] Phillips-Fein and Zelizer, *What's Good for Business*, 196.

[34] Bruce R. Scott, "The Industrial State: Old Myths and New Realities," *Harvard Business Review*, March 1973/Summer 1974, 133–48.

[35] Thomas C. Hayes, "Bruce Henderson, 77, Consultant and Writer on Business Strategy," *New York Times*, July 24, 1992; http://www.nytimes.com/1992/07/24/us/bruce-henderson-77-consultant-and-writer-on-business-strategy.html?pagewanted=1.

[36] "Bruce Henderson," Boston Consulting Group, accessed December 29, 2015; https://www.bcgperspectives.com/classics/author/bruce_henderson/; See also Chris McKenna, "Stategy Followed Structure: Management Consulting and the Creation of a Market for 'Strategy,' 1950–2000," in S.J. Kahl, B.S. Silverman & M.A. Cusumano, *Advances in Strategic Management* (Vol 29), (Bingley, United Kingdom: Emerald Group), 153–186.

[37] "The Product Portfolio" is now available at the BCG website; https://www.bcgperspectives.com/content/Classics/strategy_the_product_portfolio/.

[38] The curious inversion of the axes has been maintained by writers on management strategy even though it runs counter to how all other graphs are made.

[39] Bruce Henderson, "The Anatomy of the Cash Cow," in *Perspectives on Strategy from the Boston Consulting Group*, ed. Carl Stern and George Stalk (New York, NY: Wiley, 1998), 200.

[40] Warren Cannon, "Organizational Design: Shaping Structure to Strategy," *McKinsey Quarterly*, Summer 1972, 30.

[41] Figure from "The Consultants Face a Competition Crisis," *Business Week*, November 17, 1973, 70; Warren Cannon, "Organizational Design: Shaping Structure to Strategy," *McKinsey Quarterly*, Summer 1972, 26.

[42] D. Ronald Daniel, "Reorganizing for Results," in *The Arts of Top Management: A McKinsey Anthology*, ed. Roland Mann (New York, NY: McGraw-Hill, 1971), 66.

[43] Ibid.

[44] Clee, "The New Manager," 3.

[45] Alvin Toffler, "The Coming Ad-hocracy," *McKinsey Quarterly* (Summer 1971), 2. Originally published as "Organization: The Coming Ad-hocracy," in Alvin Toffler, *Future Shock* (New York, NY: Random House, 1970).

[46] Ibid., 3.

[47] Ibid., 7.

[48] John Miner, "The Management Consulting Firm as a Source of High-Level Managerial Talent," *Academy of Management Journal* 16, no. 2 (1973), 253.

[49] Michael Barratt, "The Change Makers," *McKinsey Quarterly*, Spring 1969, 27.

[50] Toffler, "The Coming Ad-hocracy," 12.

[51] Ibid., 10.

[52] Interview with Vincent O'Reilly, 3151-1.doc, box 36, PriceWaterhouseCoopers Papers, Rare Book and Manuscript Library, Columbia University, New York, NY, 1–15.

[53] Letter 10.45.28, folder 945, carton 15, 9to5 Papers, Schlesinger Library, Harvard University, Cambridge, MA, 1; names changed to preserve privacy.

[54] Manpower, *Annual Report*, 1976, folder 5, box 11, EWP.

[55] Unnumbered survey document, folder 951, carton 15, 9to5 Papers, Schlesinger Library.

[56] "9to5 President Raps Office Automation, Says It Deskills, Devalues Office Jobs," *Computerworld*, May 3, 1982, 54.

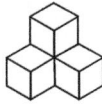

Poverty and Paradox

Alice O'Connor

Fifty years ago this past August, President Lyndon B. Johnson officially launched the War on Poverty by signing the Economic Opportunity Act of 1964. Based on the recommendations of a task force appointed in the wake of Johnson's first State of the Union address, in which he had declared "unconditional war" against economic deprivation, the legislation created the statutory basis for such well-known programs as Job Corps, Head Start, federal legal services, community-based health centers, and, most controversially, the Community Action Program, mandated to assure "maximum feasible participation" of the poor in local program planning. It also established the federal Office of Economic Opportunity (OEO) to run the new programs, and to represent poor people's interests within federal, state, and local government bureaucracies. Although modest in funding in comparison to initiatives run through more established federal agencies, the OEO and its associated programs would serve as both the headquarters of the War on Poverty and an emblem of the Great Society's more expansive and far-reaching social welfare initiatives—including food stamps, Medicare and Medicaid, federal aid to education, housing and urban development, and key provisions in civil rights law. It would also serve as a prime target of political attack for those who, in words made famous by Ronald Reagan in a later State of the Union address, insisted that "poverty won."[1] As we know from the year-long hearings, program-slashing budget, and recently released report sponsored by the House Budget Committee, chaired by Representative Paul Ryan, Republican of Wisconsin, that attack—the war on the War on Poverty—is still being pressed today.[2]

Across the ideological spectrum, one thing that has figured prominently in the conflict over LBJ's signature domestic initiative is the large body of social science research and statistical data about poor people and social welfare spending that we have come to rely on for understanding poverty, and, at least ostensibly, for resolving political disputes about who is to blame. This, too, is a legacy of the War on Poverty, the product of a concerted effort led by government and foundations to create a field of research that would generate definitive knowledge about what officials at the OEO's research and planning division rather antiseptically referred to as poverty's "causes and cures." The impact of this effort has been lasting. For better or worse, it brought us the official poverty measures that few think are adequate—a four-person household in 2014 has to earn less than $23,850 to be considered poor—but that have become benchmark indicators of economic well-being nonetheless, and that do generate at least a modicum of news coverage when the Census Bureau releases them each year.[3] It gave rise as well to a loosely organized poverty research establishment, based in a number of specialized academic and contract research institutions and social policy think tanks, and linked by shared methodologies and networks of expertise. Although invested in an ideology of nonpartisan objectivity, the poverty research establishment has generally cast itself as a voice for the poor—actually, as a voice for decision making based on scientific evidence rather than Victorian-era ideas about pauperism and the poor—in policy and politics. Of late, poverty experts have found themselves spending inordinate amounts of time defending the very existence of a social safety net and, more generally, to offering empirically grounded correctives to pronouncements from various conservative politicians and the well-mobilized think tanks of the political right. Despite years of sniping about whether or not people who have big-screen televisions and access to air conditioning are really bad off enough to count among the poor, conservative ideologues now show few qualms about using data on rising poverty rates—albeit selectively, inaccurately, and out of context—to construct a narrative of the War on Poverty as a failure of the liberal welfare state.[4]

Paradox in the Midst of Plenty

Apart from the all-too-predictable political grandstanding inspired by the fiftieth anniversary, poverty research has over the decades generated an ever more sophisticated arsenal of methods for chronicling the changes in the size and demographics of the population in poverty, and the impact of the social programs that have made this cohort better off—or not—over time. These statistical trends alone provide support for two broad conclusions that defy currently reigning poverty myths. One is that the social policies that came out of the New Deal and Great Society welfare state have been generally effective, although hardly generous, in supplementing incomes and providing targeted benefits for low-income households. These policies include several of the Great Society programs anti-government conservatives love to hate, such as Medicaid and food stamps (the latter now formally known as the Supplemental Nutritional Assistance Program, or SNAP), of which, if anything, the problem is that they do not reach all of those eligible for benefits, let alone all in need of what these programs provide.[5] The other conclusion is that economic hardship turns out to be a strikingly widespread, diversified, and, as noted in a recent commentary by sociologist Mark R. Rank, "mainstream" experience that hits a majority of Americans over the course of their lives and that in the wake of the Great Recession has grown even more commonplace, sending the number of people in poverty to upward of forty-six million at last official count.[6]

And yet, we are still stuck in the outdated and even-then problematic idea of poverty that animated LBJ's declaration of war in 1964, before this swelling tide of research was produced: as something that happens to *other people* and has little to do with us; as a problem of people left out of the benefits of an otherwise well-functioning, affluent economy; as the proverbial "paradox in the midst of plenty" that makes a statement about the failings of poor people rather than about the failures, or the prevailing features, of prosperity. Metaphors, even estimates of the number of poor Americans, may have shifted in political discourse over the decades—from LBJ's "forgotten fifth" to Mitt Romney's "47 percent"—but the myth of otherness associated with being poor in America persists and cuts across ideological lines. This is not just a problem of political discourse. It is ingrained in the dominant tradition of poverty research and in the core concepts and practices that sustain it as a specialized subfield, both of which treat poverty as a condition exclusive to poor people and look for its "cure" in the measurable outcomes of anti-poverty policies. Although invented to make poverty more visible and tractable for policy purposes, these conventions have served instead to keep its deeper and more troubling implications out of view. As a result, poverty research has become caught up in a paradox of its own making—of diminishing insight into the problem of poverty amid more, and more intimately detailed, data about the poor. This situation has important consequences for our capacity to know, let alone respond to, the challenges poverty presents, most visible among them the rapid growth of inequality that has been a signal feature of the American—and global—economy since the 1970s.

Defining Poverty

To understand the roots of the paradox in poverty research, it is important to recognize how much of its conceptual and institutional edifice can be traced to a series of political decisions made in the early stages of the War on Poverty. One set of decisions had to do with how poverty would officially be defined. Following the initial lead of the Council of Economic Advisers, whose 1964 Economic Report of the President had characterized the poor as inhabiting "a world apart, whose inhabitants are isolated from the mainstream of American life and alienated from its values," the research establishment would define poverty narrowly, as a characteristic of individuals and households rather than social relations or political economy, and an absence of income rather than political and economic power.[7]

It would be measured absolutely, with a sharp line of demarcation between poor and non-poor, and with no assessment of distance from average standards of living or relative standing within the broader income distribution. And it would be defined penuriously, with the bare minimum standards of subsistence as a benchmark. These decisions were institutionalized in 1965, with the adoption of a method for "counting the poor" developed by Social Security Administration analyst Mollie Orshansky, who used a poverty line developed from Department of Agriculture economy food plans for families. Although Orshansky herself presented it as a matter of pragmatism and common sense, her measure was in fact a more sophisticated variation on an early-twentieth-century practice of turning to the then-new technology of calorie counting to establish "scientific" standards of deprivation based on how much—or how little—it would take to maintain working-class households at a subsistence level.[8]

Fighting the War by Breaking the Cycle

A second set of formative decisions had to do with how the War on Poverty would be fought. True to its title, the Economic Opportunity Act of 1964 would offer poor people "opportunity, and not doles," as LBJ insisted when he signed it. But the administration's program would also eschew direct job creation or major structural interventions in favor of more remedial measures that aimed, in the slogan adopted by the OEO, to help poor people "break the cycle" of deprivation and social alienation through education, training, and social rehabilitation. As part of an initiative premised on the fundamental soundness, and promise, of the existing economy, poverty research would confine itself to the study of people and places left behind, without questioning whether and how, to quote language embedded in the Economic Opportunity Act itself, "the well-being and prosperity of the United States have progressed to a level surpassing any achieved in world history."[9]

The notion that poverty is generated within a self-reproducing "cycle" of material deprivation and behavioral or cultural dysfunction was itself an expression of a way of thinking that had deep roots and many variations in eighteenth- and nineteenth-century Anglo-American social thought and has been the source of a disproportionate amount of theorizing ever since. Despite considerable change over the course of centuries, this theorizing has consistently centered on the most thoroughly subordinated or socially "submerged" segments of industrial and postindustrial working-class populations—Marx's *lumpenproletariat*, the Victorians' "dangerous" or "vicious" classes, the ghettoized American "underclass," Ronald Reagan's "welfare queen"—and on the behavioral pathologies that, even when understood to be adaptive to circumstances, supposedly perpetuate these groups' marginality. The War on Poverty helped to institutionalize such theorizing, but also to embed it within a consciously developmentalist, putatively sympathetic frame: Liberals embraced deeply flawed ideas about a "culture of poverty" as a rationale for remedial intervention, and not, as such ideas quickly became for their conservative critics, as an explanation for why intervention would only make things worse. The War on Poverty was an especially important venue for cultivating and trying out theories about how to help the "culturally deprived" children of poverty that were emerging within the specialized field of child development—in particular, ideas about the imperatives of early intervention that would quickly be embraced as gospel truth.

A Cold War Model for Research

A third set of formative decisions had to do with the organization and production of government-funded research, which by design would emulate the much-admired Cold War defense research industry in its heavily quantitative orientation, fascination with measurable outcomes and cost-benefit analysis, and dedication to a politically neutralized vision of mission-oriented knowledge. Research would be detached from action in this approach, segmented off in agency-based research offices and in independent think tanks that, although set up to "think for the poor," would frequently find themselves at odds with community-based activists and service providers over questions of desirable program outcomes and measures of success, and, more fundamentally, over the idea that social change could somehow be effectively engineered through applied expertise. Less relevant, in the resulting hierarchy of poverty knowledge, would be the political insights about the nature of poverty and the challenge of fighting it that were coming from the frontlines of community action.

But more than any particular set of decisions, poverty research reflected the influence of a way of thinking that, although elsewhere contested, was widely embraced within Great Society research and policy offices. Leading the way here were the Keynesian economists at the Council of Economic Advisers who were deeply invested in an ideology of democratic capitalism built around mass prosperity, specifically working- and middle-class and embedded in the New Deal welfare state. Full employment and economic growth would be powerful tools of liberal social politics in this way of thinking. These objectives would also be translated into numerical targets the economists felt confident they could achieve. On a pragmatic level, extending this logic meant defining the poverty problem in terms of concrete, achievable economic goals: Although a war against absolute deprivation could be declared over and won—as OEO planners projected when they presented Congress with a budget for ending poverty by 1976—a war against inequality would never be over. On a deeper political level that involved all sorts of assumptions about the political possibilities that would be opened up by economic growth, the logic of growth called for pitching the War on Poverty as an appeal to mutual economic interests: "Humanity compels our action," the Council of Economic Adviser wrote in the 1964 report, pronouncing the elimination of poverty to be a national goal. "But," they added, doing so was "sound economics as well."[10] In either instance, it meant treating poverty as an issue that could be siphoned off from the more entrenched structures of racial and economic inequality with the promise that eliminating it would work to the economic benefit of all. Poverty, defined narrowly as a problem of bare-bones income deprivation, could be eradicated without threatening major redistributions of power and wealth.

Experience soon put that logic (along with other assumptions of Great Society poverty knowledge) to the test. The War on Poverty met with massive resistance, especially but not exclusively in the South, as locally entrenched power brokers—and their allies in Congress—fought ferociously to maintain control over how newly available federal funds would be spent and how programs would be implemented or whether, financial incentives aside, they would be implemented at all. In this reaction, local powers-that-be confirmed what movement activists had known all along: that the struggles for economic, political, and civil rights were inextricably intertwined; that deprivation was too powerful a tool of political and economic control to yield so easily to appeals to shared economic interest or promises of federal relief; and that the assumptions that had made winning a war on deprivation seem straightforward, if not easy, would not hold up in the face of the political and economic interests arrayed against the idea of shared prosperity.[11] The lesson was clear, although whether it would be absorbed into the canons of research was not: Poverty could not so easily be understood, or resolved, by reducing it to a problem of income deprivation, or without coming to terms with the structural inequities keeping it in place. The true "paradox" of poverty amid plenty had much more to do with the social and institutional foundations of American plenty than with the people who experienced its deprivations.

Other assumptions were challenged by realities on the ground, and in the statistical data as well. Poor people were not an isolated class stuck in a "world apart," but part of a large and shifting segment of the population living and working in a hierarchically stratified economy. Economic growth and full employment left far more workers below the "line" than originally anticipated. LBJ's proscriptions against an expanded "dole" aside, OEO economists were soon pushing for across-the-board minimum income guarantees (an idea also embraced by Milton Friedman and the US Chamber of Commerce, albeit in a highly minimalist form and principally as a replacement for the welfare state). The conceptual apparatus of poverty research would continue to reinforce the otherness of poverty and the poor nonetheless: by sticking to the fiction of the "line," even while exploring better ways of measuring it; by devising more and more intrusive ways to explore the internalized mechanisms—these days turning once again to the cognitive and genetic—through which poor people and places supposedly perpetuate their own oppression; and, most of all, by failing to recognize poverty as a condition not only of poor people but of the political and economic structures, institutions, social and cultural practices, and stratified social relations that are at the root of inequality and that perpetuate its effects. These same structures and practices have given rise to a deregulated market economy that has brought us what, with a nod to historian Eric Hobsbawm and the more recent work of Thomas Piketty, we might well think of as a new age of capital.[12]

The Biologistics of Poverty

Today, the paradox of poverty research finds its starkest expression in the sense of disconnect between all we are learning and documenting about four decades' worth of widening inequality and economic insecurity and the renewed fascination with understanding poverty as a special affliction, indeed, as an issue somehow separate from the inequality said to be hollowing out the middle class, and as a condition somehow embedded in individuals, families, and deeply impoverished communities. Lately, this project has taken on an increasingly biologistic cast, as poverty experts find more, and more innovative (from a research perspective), ways of measuring how the impact of material deprivation gets "under the skin" and into "blood, the brain, and the body," to use the words of one recent report on findings from cutting-edge research on poverty and early childhood development.[13] These studies incorporate technologies and methods from biogenetics and brain science to argue that the effects of income deprivation are life altering, and more dire than was once thought, and to redouble the case for the earliest possible interventions, starting in the womb. Recent studies in social psychology and behavioral economics follow suit with experimental and observational studies that show scarcity to leave poor people too cognitively impaired to make sound decisions about things like spending and borrowing and planning for the future, and to avoid making bad ones.[14] In these and other ways, the latest poverty science seeks to dig deeper and to bring new perspective to the presumably elusive "cycle" that keeps poor people in poverty, or keeps sucking them back into it: Poor people make bad decisions, these studies tell us, not because they lack character but because material deprivation robs them of cognitive capacity.

What these studies don't do is acknowledge or engage the political-economic dimensions of the issues, except possibly as afterthoughts. Poverty is life altering, long lasting, and intergenerational because of the way it gets wired into the individual brain, the stress hormone response system, and repeated patterns of bad decision making—not because of the way it has been structured into our economy, politics, and overlapping social stratification systems. Still less does this literature set out to engage a discussion of such principles of social citizenship as freedom from want, which democratic theorists and activists have long embraced as requisites of political freedom, and for which these studies, however distantly, can be construed to provide empirical support. Instead, cycle-of-poverty research confines its policy prescriptions to outcomes it can safely predict, with suggestions for interventions aimed at helping poor people better cope with their deprived circumstances and all the associated stresses—and ultimately at changing the behaviors said to perpetuate their own poverty.

Changing the Focus

"Our American answer to poverty is not to make the poor more secure in their poverty," LBJ said upon signing the Economic Opportunity Act into law, "but to reach down and to help them lift themselves out of the ruts of poverty and move with the large majority along the high road of hope and prosperity."[15] In the decades since the War on Poverty was declared, American social policy has in fact proved far more preoccupied with keeping the poor insecure than with providing adequate opportunities to get, and stay, ahead. The downsizing of welfare in 1996 was but one major step in the long-term, systematic dismantling of safety net entitlements and labor rights, and, more generally, of the institutions of economic regulation and progressive redistribution, that once anchored the American version of social democracy. Where social policy has succeeded is in creating devices that make some employers feel more secure, even unapologetic, about paying their workers poverty wages. These include the Earned Income Tax Credit (EITC), the one income supplement that for the moment has bipartisan support precisely because it hinges on recipients' participation in the low-wage labor force and is seen as an alternative to both "dependency-inducing" welfare and the minimum wage. Yet as long as poverty research remains stuck in its outdated conventions, it has no way of grappling with this simple, devastating fact: Working poverty is a feature of American political economy that has become more widespread in the decades since the War on Poverty and is now more deeply entrenched than the behavioral patterns attributed to any particular class of poor people. This, as much as the statistical measures that show a surprisingly large number of people falling below or hovering just above the line, is what makes poverty about *us*: the policies and politics that have paved the way to an economy divided by the power of concentrated capital and the relentless logic of low wages, and to the paradox of an ever-increasing plenty that thrives on, and justifies, the increase in want.

This is not an unfamiliar paradox, nor an unfamiliar subject of inquiry. The political economist Henry George wrote about it in *Progress and Poverty* (1879), at the height of what we've now taken to calling the first Gilded Age, when he argued that the vast wealth of the very few created the poverty of the many, and called for a massively redistributive tax on profits from private landownership in response. Writing about that paradox, for George as for a much wider cadre of organizers, intellectuals, and movement activists, helped to open the door to new ways of investigating and thinking about the problem of poverty, in no small part by turning the focus back on the problem of capitalism, in order to frame a conversation about democracy.[16] Now, more than ever, that's where the focus of poverty research belongs.

(Fall 2014, 16.3)

Notes

[1] Lyndon B. Johnson, "Annual Message to the Congress on the State of the Union," January 8, 1964, American Presidency Project, http://www.presidency.ucsb.edu/ws/index.php?pid=26787; Ronald Reagan, "Address before a Joint Session of Congress on the State of the Union," January 25, 1988, American Presidency Project, http://www.presidency.ucsb.edu/ws/index.php?pid=36035.

[2] US House of Representatives House Budget Committee Majority Staff, *The War on Poverty: Fifty Years Later*, March 3, 2014, http://budget.house.gov/uploadedfiles/war_on_poverty.pdf.

[3] The official poverty thresholds for 2014 can be found at US Department of Health and Human Services, *2014 Poverty Guidelines*, http://aspe.hhs.gov/poverty/14poverty.cfm.

[4] Robert Rector and Rachel Sheffield, *Air Conditioning, Cable TV, and an Xbox: What is Poverty in the United States Today?*, Heritage Foundation, July 19, 2011, http://www.heritage.org/research/reports/2011/07/what-is-poverty; Rob Garver, "Economists Say Paul Ryan Misrepresented Their Research," *Fiscal Times*, March 4, 2014, http://www.thefiscaltimes.com/Articles/2014/03/04/Economists-Say-Paul-Ryan-Misrepresented-Their-Research.

[5] Martha J. Bailey and Sheldon Danziger, ed., *Legacies of the War on Poverty* (New York, NY: Russell Sage Foundation, 2013).

[6] Mark R. Rank, "Poverty in America Is Mainstream," *New York Times*, November 2, 2013, http://opinionator.blogs.nytimes.com/2013/11/02/poverty-in-america-is-mainstream/?_php=true&_type=blogs&_r=0#more-150248.

[7] Council of Economic Advisers, *Economic Report of the President* (Washington: US Government Printing Office, 1964), 55; American Presidency Project, http://www.presidency.ucsb.edu/economic_reports/1964.pdf.

[8] Mollie Orshansky, "Counting the Poor: Another Look at the Poverty Profile," *Social Security Bulletin* 28, no. 1 (1965): 3–29; B. Seebohm Rowntree, *Poverty: A Study of Town Life* (London, England: MacMillan, 1901).

[9] Economic Opportunity Act of 1964, Pub. L. No. 88-452, 78 Stat. 508, § 2. For an interesting take on this passage, see Louis O. Kelso and Patricia Hetter, "Equality of Economic Opportunity through Capital Ownership," in *Social Policies for America in the Seventies: Nine Divergent Views*, ed. Robert Theobald (New York, NY: Doubleday, 1968): 133–48.

[10] Council of Economic Advisers, *Economic Report*, 56.

[11] Annelise Orleck and Lisa Gayle Hazirjian, ed., *The War on Poverty: A New Grassroots History, 1964–1980* (Athens, GA: University of Georgia Press, 2011).

[12] Eric Hobsbawm, *The Age of Capital: 1848–1875* (New York, NY: Vintage, 1975); Thomas Piketty, *Capital in the Twenty-First Century* (Cambridge, MA: Harvard University Press, 2014).

[13] David Grusky and Christopher Wimer, ed., "Does Poverty Get Under the Skin? The Effects of Deprivation on Blood, the Brain, and the Body," special issue, *Pathways* (Winter 2011), http://web.stanford.edu/group/scspi/media_magazines_pathways_winter_2011.html.

[14] Sendhil Mullainathan and Eldar Shafir, *Scarcity: Why Having Too Little Means So Much* (New York, NY: Macmillan, 2013).

[15] Lyndon B. Johnson, "Remarks on Signing the Economic Opportunity Act of 1964," August 20, 1964, American Presidency Project, http://www.presidency.ucsb.edu/ws/?pid=26452.

[16] Henry George, *Progress and Poverty* (New York, NY: Cambridge University Press, 2009). First published 1879.

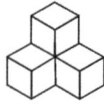

Falling

William McPherson

T he rich are all alike, to revise Tolstoy's famous words, but the poor are poor in their own particular ways.

Any reasonably intelligent reader could blow that generalization apart in the time it takes to write it. But as with most generalizations, a truth lies behind it. Ultimately, what binds the rich together is that they have more money, lots more. For one reason or another, the poor don't have enough of it. But poverty doesn't bind the poor together as much as wealth and the need to protect it bind the rich. If it did, we would hear the rattle of tumbrels in the streets. One hears mutterings, but the chains have not yet been shed.

I have some personal experience here. Like a lot of other people, I started life comfortably middle-class, maybe upper-middle class; now, like a lot of other people walking the streets of America today, I am poor. To put it directly, *I have no money*. Does this embarrass me? Of course, it embarrasses me—and a lot of other things as well. It's humiliating to be poor, to be dependent on the kindness of family and friends and government subsidies. But it sure is an education.

Social classes are relative and definitions vary, but if money defines class, the sociologists would say I was not among the wretched of the earth but probably at the higher end of the lower classes. I'm not working class because I don't have what most people consider a job. I'm a writer, although I don't grind out the words the way I once did. Which is one reason I'm poor.

My income consists of a Social Security check and a miserable pension from the *Washington Post*, where I worked intermittently for a total of about twenty-five years, interrupted by a stint at a publishing house in New York just before my profit-sharing would have taken effect. I returned to the *Post*, won a Pulitzer Prize, continued working for another eight years, with a leave of absence now and then. As the last leave rolled on, the *Post* suggested I come back to work or, alternatively, the company would allow me to take an early retirement. I was fifty-three at the time. I chose retirement because I was under the illusion—perhaps delusion is the more accurate word—that I could make a living as a writer and the *Post* offered to keep me on their medical insurance program, which at the time was very good and very cheap.

The pension would start twelve years later when I was sixty-five. What cost a dollar at the time I accepted the offer, would cost $1.44 when the checks began. Today, what cost a dollar in 1986 costs $2.10. The cumulative rate of inflation is 109.7 percent. The pension remains the same. It is not adjusted for inflation. In the meantime, medical insurance costs have soared. Today, I pay more than twice as much for a month of medical insurance as I paid in 1987 for a year of better coverage. My pension is worth half what it was. And I'm one of the lucky ones.

I was never remotely rich by what counts for rich today. (That requires a lot of zeroes after the first two or three digits.) But I look through my checkbooks from twenty-five and thirty years ago and I think, Wow! What happened? It was a long, slowly accelerating slide but the answer is simple. I was foolish, careless, and sometimes stupid. As my older brother, who to keep me off the streets invited me to live with him after his wife died, said, shaking his head in warning, "Don't spend your capital." His advice was right, but his timing was wrong. I'd already spent it. He sounded like the ghost of my father. Capital produces income. If you want to have an income, don't dip into your capital. I'd always been a bit of a contrarian, even as a child.

My money wasn't working hard enough to finance my adventures, which did, after all, come with a price. I wanted to explore and write about eastern Europe after the fall of the Wall, which I did for several years. It was truly a great adventure, it changed my life, and it was a lot more interesting than thinking about what it cost, which was a lot. There'd always been enough money. I assumed there always would be. (I think this is called denial.) So another dip into the well. In my checkbook, I listed these deposits as draws. That sounded very businesslike, almost as if I knew what I was doing. Sometimes I did. (It's hard to resist a little self-justification.)

Against the advice of people who thought they knew better, I bought shares in AOL before it really took off and in Apple when it was near its bottom. I figured Apple's real estate must be worth more than the value the market gave the company. I was right. Shares in both companies soared. If I'd shut up and stayed home…but I didn't. On the advice of these same people who advised me against AOL and Apple, I turned my brokerage account into a margin account for someone else to handle, and I left the country again. A few more dips into the well, a few turns in the market, a few margin calls, and when I went back for another dip, the well was empty. The old proverb drifts back to me on a wisp of memory. A fool and his money are soon parted. My adventures were over.

The story is, of course, more complicated than that—whose story isn't?—but these are the essentials. It's unlikely, and it's not intended, to evoke sympathy. I'd acted like one of those people who win the lottery and squander it on houses, cars, family, and Caribbean cruises. But I hadn't won the lottery; I'd fallen under the spell of magical thinking. In my opinion, I didn't squander the money, either; I just spent it a little too enthusiastically—not on Caribbean cruises but on exploring the aftermath of the fall of Communism in eastern Europe. I don't regret it. When my writing was bringing in a little money I had a Keogh plan, and when I was at the *Post* a 401(k) account. I'd made a little money in real estate and received a couple of modest but nice inheritances, which together, and with Social Security and the pension, would have given me enough income to live on, had I not felt I'd lost the ability to continue writing and had I forgone, or at least spent more modestly on, my work in Europe and related activities, avoided the margin account, and so on. The "so on," I should add, included a major heart attack that led to congestive heart failure, a condition that greatly reduced my physical resilience and taxed my already-limited income.

There are a lot of people like me, exiles from the middle class who suddenly finding themselves on Grub Street. Unless something truly awful has happened, they are not standing at the corner with a cup like my friend Kenny, whom I pass every Wednesday afternoon when I'm entering the farmers' market at Foggy Bottom. We chat. He's bent over a cane but always clean and nicely dressed. He tells me not to stay long, that it's too hot. Kenny is a genuinely compassionate man. I tell him I am writing an article on poverty, my own poverty, but I'd like to know about how he got where he is. Would he talk to me? Yes, he would, but our conversation hasn't happened yet. I feel guilty that I am shopping at this upscale market when I am wondering which medical bill I can postpone this month and, which, if any, I can pay. Meanwhile, Kenny stands at the corner with his cup. On my way out, I bring him a gelato. It's too hot to stand and talk.

Kenny looks poor. He looks weary. After it had been pointed out to me by a friend who has a brain in his head but once had no money in his pocket, I noticed that the truly poor often look weary. Dealing with the system—"the Man"—is frustrating, exhausting, and takes many hours of waiting for bus and subway, of shuffling back and forth from one office to the next, one building to the next, one bureau to the next, filling out forms and generating a growing stream of paper along the way. Fortunately, I haven't had to deal with government agencies very often, but once I took an addict, who was in dire straits, to an agency that might give him a referral for psychiatric treatment at a much reduced rate or even to a well-regarded clinic in another part of the city for free.

He'd need Medicaid, of course. It took the entire day, from eight in the morning to five at night. The waiting room was jammed. There must have been seventy-five people there, and for most of them it was not their first visit. When my friend was called to see a member of the staff who could pass him to another, and so on, I was the only white person in the room. But I was not the only poor person in the room. The only people who weren't were the two women behind the desk, probably hanging on by their teeth to the lowest rung on the middle-class ladder. Nice women, actually, patient and polite.

Poverty is a great leveler. There was camaraderie among those men and women in the waiting room. My awkwardness soon slipped away and I, too, became part of the group. I heard stories, I laughed, and we talked. It was interesting, an experience, as they say, like working on a freighter, which I did for a time. Only my experience as an able-bodied seaman in my youth was one of my attempts to try on a new identity and escape the world around me. This waiting room in a part of the District government most middle-class people never see was not an escape from the "real world"; it *was* the real world. All of us there had two things in common: None of us had any money, and all of us had time. That was good because, as I said, I was there all day. It's a common assumption that poor people don't have much need for time, but for rich people time is money. They have important things to do.

Poverty, my mother used to say, is a state of mind. She never stood in line to apply for welfare, or Medicaid, or food stamps. Then she would have learned, as I did, that it may be a state of mind—and to some degree I believe it is—but it is also a harsh daily reality for millions of her fellow citizens of this country and on this planet. And now for her son.

I am not trying to exaggerate my own particular plight. I've never had to apply for welfare, or Medicaid, or food stamps. I have asked the Department of Housing and Urban Development (HUD) to subsidize my rent and a District office to subsidize my medical insurance payments. That involved a lot of paperwork but not a lot of lines, and I am very glad to live in subsidized housing with a number of people who really run the gamut. One of them is the great-grandson of Leo Tolstoy. Another fled Bulgaria as the Communists were taking over, eventually came to the United States, speaks several languages, and worked for the Library of Congress. There are refugees from one regime or another, from all parts of the world. They come in all colors. Some were trained as lawyers, some have doctoral degrees, some were teachers. There are journalists and writers. What we have in common is we are all older, we are all poor, and each of us has, to a greater or lesser degree, the ailments that come with age. As everybody knows, if you don't have good insurance, medical bills can be catastrophic and have been for some of us here. But I think all of us would agree that living here beats living in a homeless shelter.

Compared with most poor people, I am fortunate. If you've got to be poor, finding yourself at the upper edge of poverty with a roof over your head and a wardrobe that doesn't look as if it came from the Salvation Army is as good as it gets. It also helps to be white.

An African-American trainer at a gym I used to go to before the well went dry had a lot of clients and must have made decent money, enough to support himself and his son, anyway. He was walking down Connecticut Avenue one day when he saw one of his female clients approaching.

"I don't have any," she exclaimed and turned abruptly away as he was opening his mouth to greet her. "I don't have any money!"

She didn't see my friend Jeff; she saw a black man in trainers about to ask her for a handout on one of the busier avenues in the city. Jeff doesn't look like a hustler. He doesn't look poor. I don't look poor, either, but I am white. So I never suffered that kind of demeaning slight.

By federal government standards, I'm not poor, but by any rational standard, I am. My income is above $11,670 annually, which, in 2014, puts me above the poverty line for a single person. My Social Security comes to more than that. The federal minimum wage in 2014 is $7.25 an hour, or $15,080 annually. When FICA taxes of 7.65 percent for Social Security and Medicare are deducted, that brings the income of a full time minimum-wage worker to $13,949. For a family of three, the poverty line is $19,790. This is not a joke. It doesn't leave much extra for an ice cream cone.

I have a roof over my head, thanks to the aforementioned HUD subsidy, which required hours of paperwork, signed affidavits from doctors, many duplicate copies, and a lot of running around. (The Paperwork Reduction Act was passed in 1980. How many trees, I wonder, has it saved?) The management of the building where I live used to deal directly with HUD. Now a company based in Alabama has been hired as a distant intermediary of sorts between the very capable management and HUD. I don't believe this was done in an attempt to reduce paperwork.

If you're poor, what might have been a minor annoyance, or even a major inconvenience, becomes something of a disaster. Your hard drive crashes? Who's going to pay for the recovery of its data, not to mention the new computer? I'm not playing solitaire on this machine; the hard drive holds my work, virtually my life. It is not a luxury for me but a necessity. I need dental work. Anybody got $10,000? Dentists are not a luxury. Dental disease can make you seriously ill. Lose your cellphone? What may be a luxury to some is a necessity to me. Without that telephone and that computer, my life as I have known it would cease to exist. Not long after, so would I. I am not eager for that to happen. Need to go to a funeral hundreds of miles away? Who pays for the plane ticket? In the case of the funeral, my nephew paid for the plane ticket. My daughter and son-in-law paid for the dental work. Sometimes, I find it deeply humiliating that I am dependent on such kindnesses when I would prefer that the kindnesses flow the other way. Most of the time, though, I am just extremely grateful for the help of family and friends. It's not so much humiliating as it is humbling, which is a good thing.

I am ashamed to have gotten myself into this situation. Unlike many who are born, live, and die in poverty, I got where I am today through my own efforts. I can't blame anyone else. Perhaps, it should be humiliating to reveal myself like this to the eyes of any passing stranger or friend; more humiliating to friends, actually, some of whom knew me in another life. Most of my friends probably don't realize or would rather not realize just how parlous my situation is. Just as well. We'd both be embarrassed.

Although I am embarrassed by my condition, and ashamed of myself for putting myself there, I feel grateful to have had some of these experiences and even more grateful to have survived them.

I am glad that none of my friends has ever found himself sitting on a bench in a park with a quarter in his pocket, as I once did, and nothing in the bank; in fact, no bank account. It's a very lonely feeling. It gives new meaning to the sense of loneliness and despair.

I wallowed in that slough for a bit. It was not, after all, a happy situation and I am not a dim-witted optimist. But I had two choices, die in the slough or move on. I thought of the last two lines of Milton's *Lycidas*,

> At last he rose, and twitch'd his mantle blue:
> To-morrow to fresh woods, and pastures new.

So I got up, forever grateful to Mr. Barrows, my college English instructor, for teaching me to study *Lycidas* seriously and realize what a great poem it is and why that matters.

(Fall 2014, 16.3)

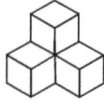

Saving the Soul
of the Smart City

Joshua J. Yates

In 1958, the year Americans became besotted by the tailfin, an editor at *Fortune* published a multi-authored work of cultural contrarianism titled *The Exploding Metropolis*.[1] William H. Whyte's team of writers included four other *Fortune* editors, among them Jane Jacobs. Their subject was the emerging suburban and auto-centric format of postwar metropolitan life, first pictured in General Motors' Futurama exhibit at the 1939 New York World's Fair and largely realized by the late fifties. Swimming against the dominant urban-planning wisdom of the time, Whyte and his coauthors argued that the accelerating suburbanization of American life represented a fundamental misunderstanding of the nature of the city, and that its chief architects and promoters were driven by a profoundly anti-urban spirit. Most of the renovation and new construction was, Whyte wrote, "being designed by people who don't like cities. They do not merely dislike the noise and dirt and the congestion. They dislike the city's variety and concentration, its tensions, its hustle and bustle. The new development projects will be physically in the city, but in spirit they deny it."[2] Looking hard at the transformations then underway, the critics offered dire warnings about what these changes would mean for people and cities over the long run—warnings that have since proven keenly prescient.

We, too, stand on the cusp of a revolutionary new urban form: "the smart city." That form emerges from a new wave of intensive urbanization and the proliferating uses of information technology to "optimize" the city's functioning. It takes shape not uniformly or seamlessly but in fits and starts—in a handful of places all at once, incrementally in others. As was the case with the commuter suburb before it, a potent combination of institutional interests, technological innovations, and cultural appetites fuels the smart city's rise. But this fact only raises the stakes, demanding that we look as hard at the coming of the smart city as Whyte, Jacobs, and their colleagues looked at the suburban efflorescence.

Shanghai: Circa 2030

I first encountered the city of tomorrow in Shanghai—at the 2010 World Expo, where I chanced upon Cisco's Smart + Connected Life pavilion. The central attraction was a giant LED screen featuring a video of Shanghai in the year 2030.[3] In this imagined near future, smart technology is integrated into the everyday existence of the city's residents. The video centers on a special occasion in the life of one Shanghai family—the celebration of a golden wedding anniversary. As the story unfolds, we gradually meet members of the family in their various stages of life—the grandparents preparing for their big day by videoconferencing with loved ones, a pregnant daughter-in-law who uses a smart watch to send real-time vital signs of her baby-in-utero to her doctor, who in turn dispatches an ambulance to bring her to the hospital for an unexpected early delivery, and so on.

Meanwhile, a typhoon is barreling down upon the city and threatening to disrupt the anniversary celebration and inflict severe damage. But not to fear: All of the smart technologies embedded in the buildings, transportation systems, critical infrastructure, and communications networks are in sync and under the watchful, all-seeing eyes of a city command center and its expert administrators. As the drama intensifies, we see how technologies, all presumably created by Cisco, are seamlessly optimizing ordinary events, even in extreme weather. This was Cisco's smart city version of the Shanghai Expo's motto: "Better City—Better Life." Much as GM's Futurama did in 1939, the Cisco pavilion prefigures a future that lies just around the corner and, in many ways, has already arrived.

The City of Tomorrow Is Here Today

Having already traveled some way down the road to the smart city, we are in a position to make out some of its initial tendencies, even while only dimly descrying its possible trajectories. What we see defies easy judgment. Looking at its potential, we find much to recommend about the smart city. Far from being anti-urban, for example, it is a vision that doubles down on the idea of the city, returning the center of gravity to the urban cores and reversing the development patterns of the past half-century. In doing so, the smart city promises to create built environments that are more human-centric, equitable, and environmentally resilient. To the extent that *this* vision is realized, there will indeed be much to celebrate about a smarter urban future.

But the smart city as it is actually coming into being raises a darker question: What would we be willing to trade for a cleaner, safer, more efficient, more sustainable, and even more pleasurable urban existence? For cities across the world, this is the overwhelming challenge of daily governance. Closer to home, we confront this question in our worries over the loss of autonomy and privacy amid the technological web of surveillance and interconnectedness we are spinning for ourselves. We confront it in the ways such smart technologies are already optimizing the quality of life for some while only intensifying inequality for others. At the deepest cultural level, we confront the question of autonomy versus convenience in the ways such technologies generate new forms of social control that are accepted because they appear to be backed by the authority of science and have been proven effective at improving our aggregate well-being. Taking a hard look at the smart city requires that we ask not only where it might fail to live up to the promises of its boosters, but also where it is successful and how it might nonetheless still fail us as citizens and as human beings.

The Optimizing Metropolis

We can begin taking a hard look at the smart city paradigm by examining its organizing concept: *optimization*. This term is ubiquitous in discussions about smart cities, and it provides a key to understanding the cultural reasoning behind this new urban form and what that reasoning might be committing us to, morally and civically, over the long run.

By definition, *optimization* simply means the act of making the most of a process, situation, or resource. It is maximizing potential in light of given circumstances. Facing situations of fiscal austerity, as many of them are, cities are drawn to optimization in their quest to economize. This much is easy to understand. But it is optimization in a more triumphant, maximizing register that underwrites the unquestioning optimism of boosters of the smart city and its potential. For instance, here is how Y Combinator, the Silicon Valley "accelerator" that created Airbnb, recently announced that it was getting into the smart city business: "We want to study building new, better cities. The world is full of people who aren't realizing their potential in large part because their cities don't provide the opportunities and living conditions necessary for success. A high leverage way to improve our world is to unleash this massive potential by making better cities."[4]

Having already disrupted entire industries in other fields, Y Combinator believes it can do the same for cities. To lead the way, it raises a set of "high-level" orienting questions:

- What should a city optimize for?
- How should we measure the effectiveness of a city (what are its KPIs [key performance indicators])?

- What values should (or should not) be embedded in a city's culture?
- How can cities help more of their residents be happy and reach their potential?

With many more years of experience working in real cities, IBM is confident that it knows the answers to Y Combinator's high-level questions. In "How Smart Is Your City?," issued by Big Blue's Institute of Business Value, the advice is simple and straightforward:

- Develop your city's long-term strategy and short-term goals.
- Prioritise and invest in a few select systems that will have the greatest impact.
- Integrate across systems to improve citizen experiences and efficiencies.
- Optimize your services and operations.
- Discover new opportunities for growth and optimization.[5]

IBM, in short, has the platform to help you optimize it all.

Optimization is not simply a for-profit enterprise aimed at a city's strategic functions. It is also meant to boost human welfare. In 2016, a smart city collaborative made up of the Barcelona Institute for Global Health (ISGlobal), in partnership with the Barcelona Agency for Urban Ecology and the Barcelona City Council, committed to redevelop 503 city blocks using human health and well-being as the primary design driver. "Over the next three years," the collaborative claims, "ISGlobal will provide scientific evidence and expertise in epidemiology, health impact assessment modeling, and impact assessment indicators *to optimize* the initial 46 Superblocks as models for population health, ultimately impacting more than 23,000 city residents"[6] (italics added). From Y Combinator's vision of disrupting the "city" itself to the Barcelona collaborative's efforts to improve human health and welfare, optimization is the smart city's first goal.

The rhetoric of optimization expresses the priorities of those who stand to benefit most from the world they describe, and that group stretches beyond Silicon Valley and the business technology world where it originated. It also reflects the aspirations of the highly educated professional and managerial stratum of society alternately referred to as "knowledge workers" (Peter Drucker), "symbolic analysts" (Robert Reich), and the "creative class" (Richard Florida). Florida maintains that this so-called new class makes up nearly a third of the work force in the United States—and considerably more than that in certain US communities.[7] Of course, this means that two-thirds of the workforce (as well as all those who have dropped out of it) are presumably outside the discourse of optimization, though they may still be subject to its demands.

The new class comprises the academics, public relations consultants, venture investors, artisans, designers, architects, planners, data analysts, artists, and others who today are both catalysts and leading indicators of urban revitalization all over the country. They are the purveyors and customers of the new urban chic that is transforming the look and feel of cities. Wherever they congregate, bike lanes, coffee shops, brew pubs, farm-to-table restaurants, farmers' markets, makers' spaces, and tech hubs are sure to arise. The members of the new class are also both the creators and denizens of digital urbanism, early adopters of the most popular technologies, and the people at whom the most popular city-focused apps are aimed, from Yelp to Foursquare to Uber to Kickstarter.

This professional-managerial stratum is as conspicuous for its energetic entrepreneurial outlook as it is for its socially expressive consumption patterns. In virtually every American city, an effervescence of social innovation and collaboration is reconfiguring how cities work. Traditional nonprofits and government agencies are starting to be run like businesses, while business startups are beginning to take on missions once reserved for nonprofits and government agencies. All of this entrepreneurial energy is channeled through a host of digital applications and Web-based platforms that are revolutionizing everything from how we eat, move, create, recreate, socialize, and volunteer to how we mobilize, share, search, and congregate in cities.

For the most part, the members of the professional-managerial stratum are both the subjects *and* the agents of optimization. As subjects, they are already feeling the multifarious incremental effects of optimization in their daily and personal lives. These people already interact with goods and services in ways that almost always include or depend on a digital dimension in the realm of what is now commonly called the Internet of Things. The ever-multiplying applications on offer provide an expanding range of "on-demand" amenities, more highly personalized services, and more "peer-to-peer" interactions. Whatever else these offerings might signify, they are all intended to boost quality of life through the optimization of lifestyle choices, experience, and convenience.

Live, Work, Measure

The ways our smartphones change our interactions with one another and our environment is a much-covered subject. Less familiar is the first generation of smart homes, which are interesting microcosms of—even precursors to—the smart city. According to one industry report, "By 2022, a family home in an affluent, mature market will contain more than 500 smart devices," all interacting with one another and with vendors and services outside the home.[8] Think of the refrigerators that already come with sensors that can determine when the milk is running low and then automatically order a delivery from Amazon. In the near future, human-machine interactions will be transformed from the voice-activated, mostly passive interactions we now have with (for instance) Amazon's Echo to more machine-initiated interactions.

Cities, too, are now counseled to optimize themselves in order to hold their own in what Jim Clifton, CEO of Gallup, calls the "all-out global war on good jobs." Pointing to places like San Francisco and Silicon Valley as the model, Clifton contends that not just any job will do. "The jobs war is won by knowledge jobs.... Good jobs are created by entrepreneurs working with innovators creating a winning business model."[9] In its "Smarter Cities for Smarter Growth" study, IBM warns cities that to compete in the twenty-first century, they

> will need to better apply advanced information technology, analytics and systems thinking to develop a more citizen-centric approach to services. By doing so, they can better attract, create, enable and retain their citizens' skills, knowledge and creativity.[10]

In short, cities must attract and retain Richard Florida's highly skilled, often highly educated creatives. Cities from Green Bay to Rochester have followed Florida's advice in redesigning their smart growth strategies around the "three T's" of urban success: technology, talent, and tolerance. Addressing talent and tolerance, cities spend millions developing cultural amenities, from the arts to recreation to entertainment. Simultaneously, they spend even more upgrading to the latest technological apparatus that will support innovation and spur economic growth. In a world where one city has to be smarter than the next to stay competitive, both Florida and IBM are there to help cities, in the words of the subtitle of the IBM study, "optimize their systems for the talent-based economy."

Finally, even where this class of urbanites does not explicitly employ the term, the spirit of optimization animates their expert discourse and professional practice. Never far from the concern with innovation and creativity is the language of measurement, return-on-investment scores, rankings, performance indicators, and social impact metrics. The drive to quantification and assessment is pervasive. Nothing is spared its calculating powers, including things once thought unmeasurable such as happiness or quality of life. Never before have so many people been so committed, or equipped, to track and measure as many facets of their lives and communities. The force and focus of optimization here is on our agency in making improvements in the social world—making a better life. In this register, optimization is how the charisma of creativity and innovation become instrumentalized through calculation for maximum impact.

Lifestyles increasingly enabled by smart tech, the pressures cities are under to attract and keep highly skilled creatives, and the drive toward quantification that animates expert discourse and professional practice—all of these show how the logic and rhetoric of optimization are already widely at work in this economically and culturally powerful class of urban elites. Moreover, because of their disproportionate cultural power, the ways they are imagining, and thus building, the smart city is affecting us all.

To be sure, the smart city is still an emergent urban form. It is open to many possible futures and trajectories. But the logic of optimization already exerts a powerful force on the smart city's *likely* futures. It also has implications for things more humanly basic and immediate—in particular, how we feel, how we know, and how we behave.

Don't Worry, Be Happy

A University of Vermont research team created a software program in 2009 to measure the hour-by-hour, day-by-day, month-by-month fluctuations of "happiness" among Twitter users. The team was able to assign a happiness score to 4.6 billion tweets by measuring the frequency of use of more than 10,000 words signifying emotion or a positive or negative experience.[11]

Viewed historically, this rather astonishing technological feat shows how far we have come in our ambition to measure features of human life that for so long seemed beyond calculation. It also signals the latest step in the evolution of our thinking about human well-being itself. From the introduction of social indicators in the 1960s and quality of life measures in the 1970s through the explosion of interest in happiness metrics during the past decade, it appears that we are finally in a position to move beyond gross domestic product and crude econometrics to measure what matters most, what many believe we should have been measuring all along.

We see analogues of this quest for a fuller, richer, more holistic picture of human well-being at work in nearly every economic sector and field of knowledge. The watchwords may be different, but they tell the same tale. "Sustainability" and "resilience" are terms of choice in energy and environmental circles, while "wellness" and the "social determinants of health" are common in the realm of medicine. In the arts, the discourse of "creative placemaking" and "livability" is popular, and in business, the idea of social impact and multiple bottom lines has a growing following. Taken together, these terms give expression to a culturally comprehensive drive toward a more human-centered understanding of well-being, and nowhere is that collective drive being given focus with greater fervor than in cities.

There is a complicated intellectual and social history behind this collective effervescence around well-being and happiness, from Jeremy Bentham's hedonic utilitarianism to what today is called the New Science of Happiness. Since antiquity, we have asked what human flourishing is, and, especially since the Enlightenment, how it can be measured. This latter question was Bentham's obsession, and although he failed to find a way to quantify happiness, utilitarianism has largely won the day in terms of how we think and talk about human well-being today.

To return to the University of Vermont researchers: They have arguably developed the first modern-day "hedonometer." Such a device was first conceptualized by Francis Edgeworth in 1881 as a psychophysical instrument that would count the numbers of "hedons," or units of subjective enjoyment, generated by an individual's experience. What is crucial here for the present discussion of the smart city is how this technology maps the terrain of happiness. Coding ten million tweets for words associated with positive feelings (*love, hope, wonderful*), on the one hand, and words associated with negative feelings (*hell, no, damn, sucks*), and looking at their relative frequencies in 373 urban areas, researchers discovered that Napa, California, was the happiest city in America, while Beaumont, Texas, was the unhappiest.

There are all sorts of reasons to be cynical about whether this research is really getting at happiness, but one should be mindful that it represents only a peek into the advancing world of hedonic analytics. National and city governments from Britain to Bhutan to Dubai now routinely collect data, mainly through surveys, on their citizens' feelings of happiness, life satisfaction, anxiety, and the meaningfulness of life. Since 2008, the Gallup-Healthways Well-Being Index has surveyed 1,000 people every day on their well-being and happiness. The research and methodology underlying the Well-Being Index are based, according to its website, on the World Health Organization's definition of health as "not only the absence of infirmity and disease, but also a state of physical, mental, and social well-being."[12]

But as the hedonometer example illustrates, we are also rapidly advancing beyond the survey into a post-statistical world of Big Data and physiological monitoring that circumvents self-reports of our happiness altogether.[13] This is all being made possible by cutting-edge technologies, including sentiment analysis such as that featured in the Twitter-based hedonometer, or mood-tracking algorithms derived from analysis of the faces of people in crowds (which has already been done in Britain by means of surveillance cameras in public places), or biomedical technologies like functional magnetic resonance imaging that can scan physio-chemical biomarkers associated with different subjective states of well-being.

As our digital, physical, and psychological worlds continue to converge, we can see how the growing interest in fuller pictures of human well-being is being fueled by both the new technological forms of measurement and by the insights such technologies are helping to generate out of the new science of happiness. Together, they are forming a powerful force for reimagining and redesigning our cities, and for optimizing the means of making us happier in the smart city.

One Big Math Problem

Ground was broken in New York City in 2012 for Hudson Yards, a $20 billion, twenty-eight-acre, mixed-use development on the west side of Manhattan. According to its website, "Hudson Yards is a triumph of culture, commerce and cuisine; a technological marvel that pairs style with sustainability; a convergence of parks and public space." But what makes Hudson Yards noteworthy is its proclaimed status as the nation's first "quantified community."[14] While there are other examples of "smart from the ground up" around the world—Songdo, South Korea, for example—Hudson Yards offers the first opportunity to design and build what its developers claim will be the "most connected, measured, and technologically advanced digital district in the nation."[15]

The excitement surrounding the construction of Hudson Yards demonstrates our ubiquitous demand for measurement and data. In 2012, the authors of an article in the *Harvard Business Review* declared that "data scientist" was the "sexiest job of the twenty-first century,"[16] and today we see a proliferation not only of data scientists in virtually every sector but also of chief technology officers across the corporate world. From the soup kitchen to the concert hall, all our inherited institutions must now establish their social value through numbers.

No one has done more to bring cities into the era of Big Data than former New York City mayor Michael Bloomberg. He is famous for articulating the core sentiment of this data-driven era: "I have a rule of thumb: If you can't measure it, you can't manage it."[17] Not surprisingly, Hudson Yards is a Bloomberg-era development plan, what one writer has described as "the capstone" of the former mayor's outcome-based urban and economic development strategy.[18]

But Bloomberg is not alone in his obsession with bringing data and measurement into the study and management of cities. Once again, long-standing intellectual aspirations are finding renewed vigor in the new science of cities. Quantitative urbanism, as it has come to be known, is focused on discovering the deep, universal laws of urban life and reducing what once seemed irreducible—the buzzing chaos of cities—to mathematical formulas by which to better manage its key functions.

The intellectual vanguard of this movement emerged at the Santa Fe Institute, where, mathematicians and theoretical physicists began turning their attention to cities in the early 2000s. Their initial work has since help launched a fast-growing field that challenges the more conventional intuitive and often aesthetic methodologies of urban planners and urban studies experts. The goal is to create what physicist Luís Bettencourt, one of this movement's leading lights, describes as "a new unified model of urbanization."[19]

This is no dismal science. On the contrary, it is a remarkably optimistic one, motivated by a genuine desire to overcome "wicked problems," avoid systemic blind spots, and better understand and manage complexity through a more mathematical and evidence-based program of urban science. Such a science will deliver a new era of policy insight and effectiveness and of more accountable and responsive governance. Open data, 311 call services, citizen smartphone applications: These are all believed to be but a small taste of what is to come. "We have within sight," Bettencourt proclaims, "age-old human aspirations, such as to eliminate extreme poverty, to end most injustice, to gain access to good health for all. All of this will have to happen in cities and it can now happen very quickly." How? While he is careful to qualify it, his answer is that bigger data and a more scientific approach to cities will be the game-changing element.[20]

This brings us back to the promise of Hudson Yards and what it represents as a prototype of the smart city. This smart community will be a platform for unprecedented data generation and measurement. Embedded smart tech will continuously collect and relay streams of informatics through arrays of sensors measuring everything from operational efficiency to productivity to quality of life. Every time residents use the public transportation system, walk through public space, operate a waste disposal unit, or activate any of the scores of apps on their smartphones, data will be collected from the objects surrounding them, while those objects will in turn be continuously communicating with one another. There to ensure that none of this data is lost will be New York University's Center for Urban Science and Progress (CUSP). Today, CUSP is home to a broad network of top universities and corporations that includes Carnegie Mellon University, the University of Toronto, IBM, Microsoft, Xerox, Cisco, Siemens, Arup, IDEO, and Lockheed Martin. It is the epicenter of what media theorist Shannon Mattern refers to as "the academy-industry-government complex" forming around cities.[21]

Yet, as machine learning and the Internet of Things come online over the next few decades, we can also expect that much that goes on in this quantified community will be watched by intelligent machines rather than by human experts in observation towers. The built environment itself will not just capture our individual data signatures passively. It will respond to and even anticipate our activities. "The city is becoming not just a collection of places and bodies," writes urban historian Leo Hollis, "but a living and connected network in which buildings, signs, users, and vehicles communicate with each other in real time."[22] All of this will generate massive quantities of data for real (and digital) data scientists to mine, scrape, and cache for both public and commercial purposes.

This "living network" is also a platform for a growing array of personalized data and self-measurement. To take just one area, our health, it is reported that 69 percent of Americans already "track their diet or exercise, while a third track their blood pressure, sleep patterns, and headaches." This health monitoring can now be done automatically through smartphones, but its use and incorporation into these devices has been encouraged explicitly by a "Quantified Self" movement that promotes wearable devices to track everything from steps per hour to caloric intact per meal to the number of daily meaningful social interactions. Far from vanity, this is, according to its promoters, "self-knowledge through numbers."[23] Self-knowledge through personalized data, however, does not refer *only* to personal knowledge privately accrued and retained. To make all of this self-knowledge possible, the platform must be ubiquitous. Almost by definition, optimizing what and how we know is one of the central premises of the smart city.

Better Living through Nudging

In the summer of 2010, British prime minister David Cameron established something quite novel in his cabinet office. Bringing together a small band of academic psychologists and economists, he created a behavioral insights team that has since come to be known as the "Nudge Unit" (taking its nickname from the 2008 book *Nudge: Improving Decisions About Health, Wealth, and Happiness* by Richard Thaler and Cass Sunstein). Having overcome a great deal of initial skepticism, the unit has been wildly successful. On topics ranging from pensions to army recruitment to foster care, its advice has become highly sought after not just in Britain but by governments and organizations around the world. Today, governments from Germany to Singapore to the United States are establishing their own "nudge units."

The core idea behind the "nudge" is that people do not always act in their own best interest, and consequently need help choosing better options for themselves. Whether failing to save for retirement, succumbing to impulse buying at the supermarket, or filing taxes late, people all too commonly make poor decisions (often by making no decision at all). In a society like that of the United States, which prizes choice above all else, this can come as a very inconvenient truth. The "nudgers" point out that poor decision-making by individuals also leads to all kinds of deleterious consequences for society. The compounding of poor decisions about one's personal health or spending habits, for example, can add up to enormous impacts on health care or on the collective risk of financial bubbles, both of which can end up costing taxpayers exorbitant amounts of money.

Rhetorically, at least, the attraction of the nudge seems to be that it approaches policy-making like a scientist rather than a bureaucrat or even a businessperson. It uses policy as a literal testing ground for the best way to present decisions to the public, thereby trying to nudge citizens toward leading better lives while saving taxpayers' money. "If the nudge unit has discovered anything," explains David Halpern, the British unit's CEO, "it's that an understanding of human behavior is vital for almost all public policy."[24]

It is perhaps not surprising that this kind of scientific approach to changing how people act is finding fertile ground in cities. Indeed, it seems a perfect complement to the rise of quantitative urbanism already discussed. So it is no coincidence that the British Nudge Unit has teamed up with Bloomberg Philanthropies to tackle endemic urban problems such as crime and homelessness in US cities. As we have seen, the "city as platform" offers unparalleled access to data and information that can be used not only to understand the challenges better but also to test better solutions.

As this suggests, the city is also becoming a vast, all-encompassing laboratory, the likes of which were once confined to totalizing institutions like prisons, army barracks, and mental hospitals. Cities, of course, have long been used as sites for studying the various facets of social life, but never with tools enabling such complete surveillance and such extensive control of the human environment. Prototypes of the smart city such as Hudson Yards have already generated exuberant optimism about what we will be able to learn, predict, and, increasingly, control. As the sociologist William Davies points out, the last hundred years have seen periodic surges of confidence in our ability "to acquire hard objective knowledge regarding individual decision-making, and then to design public policy (or business practices) accordingly."[25] But what might ultimately set the present surge of optimism apart from even that which attended the rise of "scientific management" in the 1920s or of new statistical approaches to management in the 1960s is the unprecedented compass it has set for itself: behavior modification not within a single organization, or even within an entire institution, but within and across a whole city. Never before has there been such an enthusiastic embrace of mass surveillance on such a broad or penetrating scale, nor such overweening confidence in the solutions we will be able to design because of it.

The convergence between Big Data and the nudge is spreading well beyond the wonky world of urban policy, with an emphasis on design that is no coincidence. During the past decade, design has quickly become one of the master disciplines of the knowledge economy. Indeed, while the "manager" was once a defining character type of twentieth-century modernity, the "designer" is as good a candidate as any for the defining type of the twenty-first. This is not to talk of design traditionally understood, as a principally aesthetic craft limited to the form and function of physical objects or the built environment. I am referring to a set of competencies that blends the affective, aesthetic, physical, and technical dimensions of things with the objective of finding creative solutions to human-centered problems. Design has thus become a transdisciplinary practice and form of thinking that can be equally applied to complex technical systems, organizational processes, or human communities. It is through design that we build the human interfaces that connect us to the vast digital and physical systems that constitute the smart city.

The Deeper Power of Design

At a surface level, design allows us to humanize the processes of optimization. The deeper power of design, however, lies in its capacity to connect with and give expression to our most basic motivations, and thus channel or redirect them to some end. In this way, it can do what data by itself cannot. But this makes design especially vulnerable to abuse, as the history of consumer marketing has made abundantly clear. The temptation in the age of Big Data and the nudge is for design to become another method of optimization rather than individual and collective reflection. Ostensibly, design can help cities provide citizens with tools helpful for making better choices for better lives. But leaving aside what constitutes "better" here, what if we take behavioral science seriously and begin to question whether people have the rationality to use these tools to make better decisions? What if it is more expedient—in terms of taxpayer savings or some collectively defined good—to make those decisions for them through design?

We do not have far to look to see how this is already occurring. Right now, many of us are subject to this kind of logic from our insurance providers. Premiums rise or fall depending on a number of factors connected to people's lifestyle choices and living environments. The actuarial choice architecture is simple: If you are overweight or if you smoke, you incur higher costs. But this logic appears to be shifting from a causal to a more interventionist mode. If you work in a large organization or institution, chances are you are already being nudged in areas related to your health and well-being—presumably for your own good, but most certainly for the good of the institution's productivity levels and bottom line.

253

Employees are routinely incentivized to make better decisions by enrolling in wellness class-es, joining a gym, or counting their steps per day—activities that are now all tracked and assessed by human resources departments and employers' insurance providers.

As the smart city comes online, we can expect this logic to become more compelling, and possibly more encompassing, as the urban environment becomes a living laboratory for both researching and designing the most effective nudges for bringing about desired behavioral outcomes.

Beyond Smart

In a time of surging populism, in part a backlash against technocratic elites, it may seem odd to focus so much concern on optimization. It will no doubt strike some as missing the real challenge and drama of the present "post-truth" moment. As one friend recent-ly exclaimed, "Please, please, bring back the technocrats!" Fair enough, though we might consider whether the populism of the present moment isn't better understood as an epi-sodic reaction to a deeper and more durable trend. As Shannon Mattern points out, it was instructive that while "everyone was watching the drama at Trump Tower, the world's largest searching-mapping-driving-advertising-information-organizing company [Google's parent company, Alphabet] was throwing its resources behind a 'fourth revolution' in urban infrastructure."[26] This suggests the future Google is betting on.

If we take that image of the future seriously, we may be inclined to see an Orwellian dystopia on the rise in the optimizing logics of Big Data and the nudge. This would be a mistake. While there are real worries about government abuse of the new surveillance tech-nologies, the more likely scenario, at least in the cities of the advanced industrial world, is a Huxleyan future in which citizens willingly trade away certain aspects of their freedom and autonomy for increases in material and subjective well-being—for a world engineered to enhance comfort, convenience, safety, even innovation and sustainability. This is precisely the world the optimizing metropolis promises to deliver. And short of massive political, economic, or environmental disruption, we have no reason to believe that the emerging smart city will not be moderately, if unevenly, successful. Where it is successful, it will be as transformative as the mid-twentieth-century regime of suburbanization and the automo-bile-based commute, potentially more so, since most people now live in urban environments and are thus subject to the forms of life these settings make possible.

Ever since Plato, we have understood that there is some reciprocal relationship between the nature of our cities (politically and physically) and those forms of life connected to our own self-images and identities. We might then ask ourselves not only what kind of people will be able to flourish in the smart city but what kinds of people we will need to become in order to flourish there. Moreover, what is the nature of flourishing that is on offer? It is hard to believe we could be satisfied with the likely answers. To borrow the words of political philosopher Wendy Brown, the optimization of well-being pushed by today's purveyors of the smart city represents "a steroidally charged form of Weberian instrumental rationality wrapped in Aristotelian ethics and Kantian legal rectitude."[27] It sells us the happy vitalism of the Romantics built upon the moral vision of Bentham, Comte, and Skinner.

The consequences this will have for civic life also raise hard questions. As more and more parts of our lives are made more convenient, comfortable, and enjoyable, what possible inducement could there be to do the difficult and often agonistic work of democratic deliberation? Might not the logic of the smart city simply reinforce the already existing geographic and virtual sorting and isolating that pervade our society as we opt for physical and digital environments that affirm our moral and political perspectives and lifestyle preferences? Moreover, will not our "intelligent" info-sphere be programmed and designed to continually anticipate and respond positively to those predilections, perhaps gently nudging us toward even more optimal states of mind and bodily well-being while minimizing hassle, inefficiency, and criticism? Likewise, will it not be part of optimization to make the user experience the primary goal, which by design means foregrounding consumer preference while backgrounding the structures of power and the distribution of the risk involved?

Given just how socially and economically stratified American society is at present, it does not seem too alarmist to raise such questions. At the very least, it seems reasonable to ask whether the kinds of civic skills and commitments we are likely to develop under the conditions of optimization will be adequate to an advancing future in which, by all counts, our society will be less demographically white, as or more politically fragmented, as or more geographically segregated, more economically unequal, and less socially trusting. Will we favored denizens of the smarter cities and metros be able or inclined to work across the deep differences of socioeconomic status and worldview that will continue to divide one neighborhood from another and threaten to intensify the social distances between urban centers and their suburban and rural satellites? It seems doubtful.

Toward Wisdom

Narrowing the horizon of living to one overriding register of value, a regime of optimization stamps out the broad, diverse array of conditions that make human life vital. It turns out that some of the things most necessary for human thriving cannot be optimized, and are greatly harmed to the extent that we try. Conviviality, family, friendship, serendipity, play, dependency, trust, calling, and yes, even happiness: These are just a few of the things that make life meaningful and which wither in the soil of optimization. Some of these qualities, as Jane Jacobs reminds us, are able to grow and blossom organically only from the self-organizing everyday forms of human contact that generate spontaneously from vibrant public places and street life. "The ballet of the good city sidewalk," Jacobs famously wrote, "never repeats itself from place to place, and in any one place is always replete with new improvisations."[28] Such emergence, as Hannah Arendt reminds us, can come only "against the overwhelming odds of statistical laws and their probability, which for all practical, everyday purposes amounts to certainty; the new therefore always appears in the guise of a miracle."[29]

Some, Jacobs and Arendt would agree, can come only through the civic friction that physical proximity and cultural particularity generate, and which can lead to genuine dialogue with our neighbors. But some, the philosopher Charles Taylor would remind us, come ultimately through the cultivation of the skills and virtues that power our commitments to working for the good of one another, even possibly at the expense of our own convenience and comforts. If the smart city is to contribute to a thriving human ecology oriented toward truth, justice, and goodness as well as prosperity, beauty, and sustainability, we stand in urgent need of a deep ethical and political turn that will help us cultivate the unoptimizable things for the purposes of making the city not just smart, but wise.

(Summer 2017, 19.2)

Notes

1. William H. Whyte Jr., ed., *The Exploding Metropolis* (Berkeley, CA: University of California Press, 1993). First published 1958.

2. Ibid., 7.

3. Spinifex Group, "Cisco Pavilion: Shanghai World Expo 2010" (video), accessed April 18, 2017, https://vimeo.com/12841328.

4. Adora Cheung, "New Cities," *Y Combinator* blog, June 27, 2016, https://blog.ycombinator.com/new-cities/.

5. Quoted in Leo Holis, *Cities Are Good for You: The Genius of the Metropolis* (New York, NY: Bloomsbury Press, 2013), 255.

6. "ISGlobal and BCNecologia Launch a Clinton Global Initiative Commitment to Action to Optimize the New 'Superblock' Model under Health Criteria," IS Global/Barcelona Institute for Global Health, September 20, 2016, http://www.isglobal.org/en/-/isglobal-y-bcnecologia-lanzan-un-commitment-to-action-de-la-clinton-global-initiative-para-optimizar-el-modelo-de-las-supermanzanas-bajo-criterios-de-.

7. Richard Florida, *The Rise of the Creative Class* (New York, NY: Basic Books, 2011), vii.

8. Nick Jones, "The Future Smart Home: 500 Smart Objects Will Enable New Business Opportunities," Gartner, Inc., July 9, 2014, https://www.gartner.com/doc/2793317/future-smart-home--smart.

9. Jim Clifton, *The Coming Jobs War* (New York, NY: Gallup Press, 2011), 66.

10. "Smarter Cities for Smarter Growth: How Cities Can Optimize Their Systems for the Talent-Based Economy," IBM Institute for Business Value, July 2010, https://www-935.ibm.com/services/us/gbs/bus/html/smarter-cities.html.

11. "Average Happiness for Twitter," University of Vermont Computational Story Lab, accessed April 18, 2017, http://hedonometer.org/index.html.

12 Gallup-Healthways Well-Being Index, accessed April 18, 2017, http://www.gallup.com/poll/106756/galluphealthways-wellbeing-index.aspx.

13 William Davies, "How Statistics Lost Their Power—and Why We Should Fear What Comes Next," *The Guardian*, January 19, 2017, https://www.theguardian.com/politics/2017/jan/19/crisis-of-statistics-big-data-democracy.

14 "A New Neighborhood for the Next Generation" (video), accessed April 18, 2017, http://www.hudsonyardsnewyork.com.

15 "NYU CUSP, Related Companies, and Oxford Properties Group Team Up to Create 'First Quantified Community' in the United States at Hudson Yards" (press release), New York University, Center for Urban Science + Progress, April 14, 2014, http://cusp.nyu.edu/press-release/nyu-cusp-related-companies-oxford-properties-group-team-create-first-quantified-community-united-states-hudson-yards/.

16 Thomas H. Davenport and D.J. Patil, "Date Scientist: The Sexiest Job of the Twenty-First Century," *Harvard Business Review*, October 2012, 70–76, https://www.tias.edu/docs/default-source/Kennisartikelen/harvard_data-scientist-the-sexiest-job-of-the-21st-century_2012.pdf?sfvrsn=0.

17 Stephen Goldsmith and Susan Crawford, *The Responsive City: Engaging Communities through Data-Smart Governance* (San Francisco, CA: Jossey-Bass, 2014), v.

18 Shannon Mattern, "Instrumental City: The View from Hudson Yards, circa 2019," *Places*, April 2016, https://placesjournal.org/article/instrumental-city-new-york-hudson-yards/.

19 Luís M.A. Bettencourt, "The Kind of Problem a City Is" (working paper), Santa Fe Institute, March 8, 2013, 3, http://uberty.org/wp-content/uploads/2017/01/city-problem.pdf.

20 Ibid., 11–12.

21 Mattern, "Instrumental City."

22 Holis, *Cities Are Good for You*, 251.

23 Bruce Feiler, "The United States of Metrics," *New York Times*, May 16, 2014, https://www.nytimes.com/2014/05/18/fashion/the-united-states-of-metrics.html.

24 Tamsin Rutter, "The Rise of the Nudge—the Unit Helping Politicians to Fathom Human Behaviour," *The Guardian*, July 23, 2015, https://www.theguardian.com/public-leaders-network/2015/jul/23/rise-nudge-unit-politicians-human-behaviour.

25 William Davies, *The Happiness Industry: How the Government and Big Business Sold Us Well-Being* (London, England: Verso, 2015), 235.

26 Mattern, "Instrumental City."

27 Wendy Brown, *Undoing the Demos: Neoliberalism's Stealth Revolution* (New York, NY: Zone Books, 2015), 140.

28 Jane Jacobs, *The Death and Life of Great American Cities* (New York, NY: Modern Library, 2011), 65–66. First published 1961.

29 Hannah Arendt, *The Human Condition* (Chicago, IL: University of Chicago Press, 1958), 177–178.

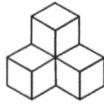

The New Political Economy and Its Culture

Richard Sennett

Democracy today takes form within a public culture that is profoundly influenced by the new political economy. In this economy, work and place are changing in ways that a mere twenty years ago seemed unimaginable. In the 1970s, the great corporate bureaucracies and government hierarchies of the developed world appeared to be securely entrenched, the products of centuries of economic development and nation-building. Commentators used to speak of "late capitalism" or "mature capitalism" as though earlier forces of growth had somehow entered an end-game phase. But today, a new chapter has opened. The economy is global and makes use of new technology; mammoth government and corporate bureaucracies are becoming both more flexible and less secure institutions. As a result, the ways we work have altered: short-term jobs replace stable careers, skills rapidly evolve, and the middle class experiences anxieties and uncertainties more confined in an earlier era to the working classes.

Place has a different meaning now as well, in large part thanks to these economic changes. An earlier generation believed that nations—and within nations, cities—could govern their own fortunes. Now, the emerging economic network is less susceptible to the controls of geography. A divide has thus opened between polity—in the sense of self-rule—and economy. This then raises the question, where can democracy really happen? What interests me in particular is the dramatic impact that underlying economic conditions have on the pursuit of democracy in the postmodern community and the postmodern workplace.

I look at the practice of democracy not so much as a fixed set of procedural requirements, but as a process that needs to have certain kinds of symbolic markers and consummations that define where people are in relation to each other. In other words, all democratic processes need to culminate in symbolic forms that are provisional but defined. And one of the ways that the postmodern economy is challenging democracy has to do with the destruction of those sign posts, especially those sign posts that mark how people are to make sense of their lives in terms of place and time. Postmodernity has managed to challenge the notion that time should have a coherent, narrative shape—it has had a disorienting effect. The flexible economy has not only fragmented workers' lives, but also made it very difficult for workers to understand how the project of survival itself has a history in time.

How do we experience institutional changes in work and place and, more generally, changes in our concept of time as a cultural shift? Old Marxist notions, which argued that the economy directly represents itself in consciousness, will not serve us. Allow me to put forward instead two simple propositions that seem to be emerging at the end of the twentieth century.

First, today's material conditions are impoverishing the value of work. Flexible, short-term work is ceasing to serve as a point of reference for defining durable personal purposes and a sense of selfworth. Sociologically, work serves ever less as a forum for stable, sociable relations. Second, the value of place has thereby increased. The sense of place is based on the need to belong not to "society" in the abstract, but to somewhere in particular. As the shifting institutions of the economy diminish the experience of belonging somewhere special at work, people's commitments increase to geographic places like nations, cities, and localities. The question is: commitments of what sort? Nationalism or ethnic localism can indeed serve as defensive refuges against a hostile economic order, but at a steep human price, fostering hatred of immigrants or outsiders.

These two propositions might suggest an unrelievedly bleak view of the culture of the emerging political economy. But this is not my view. Work is a problematic frame for the self, since it tends to equate worldly success and personal worth. Of more civic consequence is the fact that troubled fortunes might actually induce people to see themselves as other than economic animals. Rather than act defensively, they might instead put a certain distance between themselves and their material circumstances. They might recognize that their value as citizens is not dependent upon their riches. Such detachment could enrich the ways in which people use the places where they live. If work now restricts the self, place could expand it.

At least this was Hannah Arendt's hope a generation ago, when she articulated in *The Human Condition* her famous distinction between labor and politics.[1] She hoped in particular that in urban life, with its large scale and impersonality, people could conduct a civic existence that did not merely reflect or depend upon their personal fortunes. Today, the uncertainties of the new economy argue more than ever for a selfhood, as well as civic behavior, unchained from the conditions of labor. Yet, the places in which this might occur can neither be classical cities, like those Arendt admired, nor can they be defensive, inward-turning localities. We need a new kind of civic life to cope with the new economy.

Growth

To make sense of the culture of the emerging political economy, we might begin by defining its key word, "growth." Growth occurs, most simply, in four ways. The simplest is a sheer increase in number, an increase in supply (such as more ants in a colony or more television sets on the market). Growth of this sort appears in economic thinking among writers like Jean Baptiste Say, whose *loi des debouches* postulated that "increased supply creates its own demand." This increase in number can lead to an alteration of structure. This is how Adam Smith conceived of growth in *The Wealth of Nations*.[2] Larger markets, he said, trigger the division of labor in work. Growth in which size begets complexity of structure is familiar to us in government bureaucracies, as well as in industry. A third and quite different kind of growth occurs through metamorphosis. A body changes its shape or structure without necessarily increasing in number. A moth turning into a butterfly grows in this way, so do characters in a novel. Finally a system can grow by becoming more democratic. This kind of growth is anti-foundational. As John Dewey argued, the elements in a system are free to interact and influence one another so that boundaries become febrile, forms become mixed. The system contracts or expands in parts without overall coordination. Communications networks, such as the early Internet, are obvious examples of how growth can occur democratically. Such a growth process differs from a market mechanism, in which an exchange ideally clears all transactions and so regulates all actors in the system. Resistances, irregularities, and cognitive dissonances take on a positive value in democratic forms of growth. This is why subjective life develops through something like the practice of inner democracy—interpretive and emotional complexity emerges without a master plan, a hegemonic rule, and an undisputed explanation.

My own view is that the freedom and flexibility of democratic growth is not a matter of pure process, but gives rise to the need for signposts, defined forms, tentative rituals, and provisional decisions that help people to orient themselves and evaluate future conduct. Yet, the flexible economy is destroying exactly these formal elements, which orient people in the process of democratic growth. Put another way, what we need to cope with the emerging political economy is more democratic forms of flexible growth. The question is: where should such growth be promoted? At the workplace? In the community? Are they equally possible, or equally desirable, sites for democracy?

Smith's Paradox

Let me begin to look at these questions by examining the cultural deficits to the new capitalism. For example, one paradox of growth has dogged the development of modern capitalism throughout its long history. With material growth comes the impoverishment of qualitative experience.

The age of High Capitalism—which for convenience's sake can be said to span the two centuries following the publication of Adam Smith's *The Wealth of Nations* in 1776—was an era that lusted for sheer quantitative growth, of the first sort I've described, but had trouble dealing with the human consequences of the second sort, in which the increase in wealth occurred through more complex economic structures. Adam Smith argued that the division of labor, which was a structural complexity, was promoted by the expansion of free markets with ever greater numbers of goods, services, and laborers in circulation. To Smith, a growing society seemed like a honeycomb; each new cell was a place for ever more specialized tasks. A nail-maker doing everything himself could make a few hundred nails a day. Smith calculated that if nail-making were broken down into all its component parts, and each worker did only one task, a nail-maker could process more than 48,000 nails a day. Work experience, however, would become more routine in the process. Breaking the task of making nails into its component parts would condemn individual nail-makers to a numbingly boring day; hour after hour nail-makers would be doing the same small job.

I call this coupling of material growth with qualitative impoverishment "Smith's Paradox," after Adam Smith. Though Smith did not coin this term, he did recognize the existence of this paradox, which came down to us in what we call "Fordist Production," monotonous assembly-line work, the kind of assembly-line work prevalent in Ford's Highland Park plant in Michigan during the First World War. Today, proponents of the new capitalism claim that Smith's Paradox is now coming to an end. Modern technology promises to banish routine work to the innards of machines, leaving ever more workers free to do flexible, non-routine tasks. In fact, however, the qualitative impoverishment recognized by Smith has simply taken new forms. New technology frequently "de-skills" workers, who now tend to machines as electronic janitors. Meanwhile, the conditions of job tenure also compound de-skilling. Workers learn how to do one particular job well, only to find that work-task at an end. The reality now facing young workers with at least two years of college is that they will change jobs, on average, at least eleven times in the course of their working lives.

More brutally, the division of labor now separates those who get to work and those who don't. Large numbers of people are set free of routine tasks only to find themselves useless or under-used economically, especially in the context of the global labor supply. Geography no longer separates the skilled First World from the unskilled Third World. Computer code is written efficiently, for instance, in Bombay for a third to a seventh its cost in IBM home offices.

Statistics on job creation do not quite get at people's fear of uselessness. The number of jobs, even good skilled jobs, does not dictate who will have access to them, how long the jobs can be held, or, indeed, how long the jobs will exist. Ten years ago, for instance, the US economy had a deficit of computer systems analysts. Today, it has a surplus. And many of these highly skilled workers, contrary to ideology, do not retrain well. Their skills are too specific. In sum, the specter of uselessness now shadows the lives of educated middle-class people, and this specter now compounds the older experiential problem of routine among less-favored workers. The young suffer the pangs of uselessness in a particularly cruel way, since an ever-expanding educational system trains them ever more elaborately for jobs that do not exist.

The result of uselessness, de-skilling, and task-labor for the American worker is the *dispensable self*. Instead of the institutionally induced boredom of the assembly line, this experiential deficit appears more to lie within the worker—a worker who hasn't made him-or herself of lasting value to others and so can simply disappear from view. The economic language in use today—"skills-based economy," "informational competence," "task-flexible labor," and the like—shifts the focus from impersonal conditions like the possession of capital to more personal matters of competence. As this economic rhetoric becomes more personal, it gradually de-symbolizes the public realm of labor: economic inequality, power, and powerlessness are facts that are difficult to translate into self-knowledge. Similarly, the process of flexibilization in the workplace destroys permanent categories of occupation. Ironically, while work inequality has grown, the map for evaluating this inequality has been lost. While this shift in language seems personally empowering, it, in fact, can serve to increase the burdens on the working self.

This sense of "dispensability"—a sense of failing to be of much value in this economy—has great sociological implications. What Michael Young feared in his prophetic book, *The Rise of the Meritocracy*, has come to pass: As the economy needs ever fewer, highly-educated people to run it, the "moral distance" between the masses and the elite widens.[3] The masses, now comprising people in suits and ties, as well as those in overalls, appear peripheral to the elite, productive core. The economy profits by shrinking its labor base. Its emphasis on personal agency helps explain why welfare dependency and parasitism are such sensitive issues for people whose fortunes are now in doubt. Labor is disposable.

Some tough-minded economists argue that current forms of unemployment, under-employment, de-skilling, and parasitism are incurable in the emerging economic order, since the economy profits from doing "more with less." But this qualitative impoverishment, this re-organization that makes increasing numbers of people feel that they personally have no footing in the process of economic growth, poses a profound political challenge. There is no easy solution to Smith's Paradox, the problem of impoverished work experience. The postmodern vision of a project-less life is only for the elite. In the lives of most people, it is a form of oppression—a cultural ethos that is inhumane. There is a loss of the notion that you can guarantee something for your children, a profound loss of social honor. It is possible to live with a flexible self only if you are so empowered economically, culturally, and politically that "possibility" requires choices of the sort made by consumers in a mall.

Durable Time

Because sheer quantitative growth and the division of labor offer no remedy to the subjective, experiential problems of work, some policy makers have turned to the third model of growth, metamorphosis. In the political arena, such a form of development is called variously "auto-gestion," "self-management," or simply "change from within." The practical and worthy aim is to make work more humane by having workers themselves control their work. The goal is to have workers reform their institutions of work through a decisive act of collective will. In the political arena, metamorphosis occurs through rupturing established institutions. While management gurus practice rupture from the top down, socialists have aimed to remake work institutions from the bottom up. The practical record of such efforts at work re-organization is mixed. Some forms of change from within and workers' auto-gestion succeed, mostly in small, niche enterprises; others fail, overwhelmed by the larger currents of the global economy.

Change from within supposes order can be made out of chaos by an act of will; in political terms, the polity is self-creating. The social difficulty with the model arises, though, from the very act of will it supposes. Basic social bonds like trust, loyalty, and obligation require a long time to develop and have diminished as people do shifting, task-centered jobs. Loyalty requires that personal experience accumulate at an institution over time, but the emerging political economy will not let it accumulate. Personal time, like civic time, must possess duration and coherence. Workers form a sense of subjective strength and positive agency through making things last. But will alone is insufficient to accomplish that task.

Max Weber's famous image of modern life confined in an "iron cage" slights stability as a positive even in the lives of ordinary people. Weber feared the rise at the beginning of the twentieth century of large national bureaucracies and corporations that made use of the service ethic, earning the loyalty of those whom they made secure. Weber doubted that loyal servants make objectively-minded citizens. Yet petty bureaucrats, time servers, and the like derived a sense of status and public honor from their stations in bureaucracies. T.H. Marshall, the intellectual father of the modern British welfare state, understood this well: however static big institutions may be, however resistant to change from within, they provide their members a scaffolding of mutual loyalty and of trust that events can be controlled, which are prerequisites of citizenship. The bureaucrat as good citizen is not a pretty picture, but then, Jay Gould had no interest in the subject at all.

The current rush to take apart this institutional architecture is undoing the social, civic dimensions of durable time. Take loyalty, for example. When career paths are replaced by intermittent jobs, loyalties to institutions diminish. This generalization, of course, needs all sorts of qualification. For instance, one study of dismissed IBM programmers found that the people with more than twenty years of service remain enthusiastic about the company, while accepting their firing as a matter of fate. A more diminished sense of loyalty appears among younger workers, who have had more brutal dealings with the new economic order; many of these younger workers view the places where they work mostly as sites to make contacts with people who can get them better, or simply other, jobs.

In this, the young have not failed to do their duty, since new economic institutions make no guarantees in return. They routinely replace permanent workers with temporary workers, or "off-shore" work. Loyalty requires that personal experience accumulate in an institution, and the emerging political economy will not let it accumulate. Indeed, the profitable ease with which international capital today assembles, sells, and re-assembles corporations erases the durability of institutions to which one could develop loyalty or obligation.

Time, then, is everything in reckoning the social consequences of the new political economy. And as a cultural value, rupture—that favored child of postmodernism—is less politically challenging than the assertion that people ought to have the right to develop loyalty and commitment within institutions. If the dominant powers of the political economy violate durable time, can individuals provide for themselves—formally or informally—amongst one another the sign posts that institutions deny them?

This question is less abstract than it might seem at first. The modern economy did not simply wipe out the social struggles and personal values formed in an earlier phase of capitalism. What has been carried into the present from the past is a set of subjective values— values for making time coherent and durable, but in entirely personal terms. This personal, durable time intersects with the new economy of work in particularly disturbing ways.

The Coherent Self

The Victorians founded their sense of self-worth on life organized as one long project: the German values of *formation*, the English virtues of purpose, were for keeps. Careers in business, military, or imperial bureaucracies made the life-long project possible; these careers graded work into a clear sequence of steps. Such expectations devalue the present for the sake of the future—the present that is in constant upheaval and that may tempt the individual into byways or evanescent pleasures. Weber described future-orientation as a mentality of delayed gratification. Yet, this Victorian experience of cohering time has another side, which was subsumed under the ethical category of taking responsibility for one's life, though in a way quite opposite from the innovatory character of the will to change from within.

Today, late Victorian values of personal responsibility are as strong as a century ago, but their institutional context has changed. The iron cage has been dismantled, so that individuals struggle for security and coherence in a seemingly empty arena. The destruction of institutional supports at work, as in the welfare state, leaves individuals only their sense of responsibility; the Victorian ethos now often charts a negative trajectory of defeated will, of having failed to make one's life cohere through one's work. Take what happens when career paths are replaced by intermittent jobs. Many temporary workers are put in the unenviable position of knowing that their job insecurity suits obligation-resistant companies, yet these temporary workers none-the-less believe that they are themselves responsible for the mess made of their careers. This sense of personal responsibility deflects workers' anger away from economic institutions to themselves.

Meanwhile, the new economic map, which devalues the life-long career project, has shifted the optimal age curves of work to younger, raw employees (employees who range in age from the early twenties to early forties, instead of employees who range in age from the late twenties to middle fifties) even though adults are living longer and more vigorously. Studies of dismissed middle-aged workers find these workers both obsessed and puzzled by the liabilities of age. Rather than believing themselves to be faded and "over the hill," these older workers feel that they are more organized and purposeful than younger workers are. Even so, they blame themselves when they are perceived by management to be obsolete. Likewise, they blame themselves for not having prepared better for this contingency.

Workers' sense of personal responsibility and personal guilt is compounded by the rhetoric of modern management, which attempts to disguise power in the new economy by making the worker believe he or she is a self-directing agent—managers are now called "coaches," "facilitators," and the like. It is not the workers' "false consciousness" that makes these titles credible, but rather a twisted sense of moral agency.

In modernity, people take responsibility for their lives because the whole of their lives feels their making. But when the ethical culture of modernity—with its codes of personal responsibility and life purpose—is carried into a society without institutional shelters, there appears not pride of self, but a dialectic of failure in the midst of growth. Growth in the new economy depends on gutting corporate size, ending bureaucratic guarantees, and profiting from the flux and extension of economic networks. People come to know the resulting dislocations as their own lack of direction. The ethic of responsibility becomes, ironically and terribly, a subjective yardstick to measure one's failure to cohere.

In contrast, I would like to see discussions about democracy in the workplace enlarged beyond references to worker self-management. When we talk about democracy in the workplace, we must address the cultural dimensions of work, a different and literal kind of self-management in which coherence rather than rupture is a primary value. We must think through worker democracy in terms of this legacy of subjectivity. Is there some way to lighten workers' burden of self-responsibility, while acknowledging workers' desire for coherence and durability?

Place

The city is democracy's home, declared Hannah Arendt, a place for forming loyalties and practicing responsibilities. It also is a social setting in which personal attributes fade somewhat in a milieu of impersonality. Thus, Arendt imagined that the city—or more properly, "urbanity"—could relieve burdens of material circumstances in the social relations between people. Could Arendt's vision somehow be combined with the ideal of democratic growth invoked by John Dewey—that of the city as a place of ever increasing complexity of values, beliefs, and cultural forms?

The cities, as well as the smaller communities, we know in America bear little relation to this ideal place. In communities, people do indeed try to compensate for their dislocations and impoverished experience in the economy, but often in destructive ways—through communal coercion and shared illusion. Many current building projects are exercises in withdrawal from a complex world, deploying self-consciously "traditional" architecture that bespeaks a mythic communal coherence and shared identity in the past. These comforts of a supposedly simpler age appear in the New Englandish housing developments designed by the American planners Elizabeth Platter-Zyberg and Andreas Duwany, among the architects in Britain working for the Prince of Wales to reproduce "native" English architecture, and in the neighborhood renovation work on the Continent undertaken by Leon Krier. All these place-makers are artists of claustrophobia, whose icons, however, do indeed promise stability, longevity, and safety.

In order to avoid place-making on these conservative terms, we need to clarify what signposts and markers of form might successfully orient an alternative, open, and democratic community life. Let me cite three.

First, communities must not shy away from confronting hostile forces. Communities can indeed challenge the new economy rather than react defensively to it. Modern corporations like to present themselves as having cut free from local powers—they may have a factory in Mexico, an office in Bombay, and a media center in lower Manhattan; these all appear as nodes in a global network. Today, localities fear that if they exercise sovereignty, as when they tax or regulate a business locally, the corporation could just as easily find another node. I believe, however, that we are already seeing signs that the economy is not as locationally indifferent as has been assumed. You can buy any stock you like in Dubuque, Iowa, but not make a market of stocks in the cornfields. The ivy cloisters of Harvard may furnish plenty of raw intellectual talent, yet lack the craziness, messiness, and surprise that makes Manhattan a stimulating if unpleasant place to work. Similarly, in South-East Asia, it is becoming increasingly clear that local social and cultural geographies indeed count for a great deal in investment decisions. And because the new political economy is not, in fact, indifferent to location, there exists the possibility for making communal demands—contracting with corporations to assure jobs for a certain number of years in exchange for tax relief, or enforcing strict work-place rules on age discrimination. What matters is the will to confront. Up until now, polities have tended to behave like weak supplicants rather than necessary partners. Put simply, place has power.

Second, strong communities need not turn inward in a repressive fashion. Planning, especially in large-scale environments, can avert this and open groups up to one another by focusing on the borders of local sub-communities as active zones. For instance, "active edge" planners today seek to direct new building away from local centers and toward the boundaries separating communities. In East London, for example, some planners are working to make the edge of distinct communities into a febrile zone of interaction and exchange between different groups. Yet another strategy is to diversify central spaces, so that different functions overlap and interact in geographic centers. Planners in Los Angeles are seeking ways to put clinics, government offices, and old-age centers into shopping malls, which formerly were devoted solely to consumption activities. Planners in Germany are similarly exploring how to get light manufacturing back into the pedestrian zones in city centers.

In honor of Arendt, many of these planners call themselves members of the "New Agora" movement. They don't see planning as the attempt to determine a specific outcome, but they do make assumptions about the form in which interaction and process should occur. In the case of active-edge planners, the animating belief is that the more people interact, the more they will become involved with those unlike themselves. In the case of the central zone planners, the animating belief is that the value of a place will increase when it is not simply commercial. Such planning is "democratic" in my own use of the word. The agora has a defined shape that can open up the possibility of complexity rather than hegemony. Again, part and parcel of this complexity of place is the diversification of a place's purpose. For instance, you can make shopping malls into places where people actually hang out, not just places for consumption. If you make malls more like town centers, you can draw people out of the network of their intimate neighborhood.

When I say "intimate," I am not speaking of a psychological intimacy, but of exposure to your neighbors—such as knowing whether and how they are employed. Did they use credit to buy that Ford Windstar? America exposes people economically to each other in ways that enter social discourse as measures of relative personal merit. The reason I have focused my work on impersonality as a political project is that I believe that if we can provide more places in which that exposure is obscured, we can create the preconditions for a more just political discourse and interaction. Granted, you cannot force people to treat each other just as plain citizens, but at least you can provide the sites in which that kind of interaction might occur. And that is why cosmopolitanism (in a non-Kantian sense) can be a political project. My emphasis on the shaping of community is not, as it were, that such veiled communal relations would triumph over capitalism. That would give to place an absurd power. But *where* democracy occurs does matter in *how* democracy occurs.

Places, especially urban places, have the capacity to help people to grow out of themselves into a more impersonal citizenship, and so to relieve themselves of their own subjective burdens. This may seem abstract, but we experience one of its elements whenever we plunge into a crowded street. A hoary cliché views impersonal crowds as an evil. Throughout the history of the city, people have voted otherwise with their feet. And one great theme in the literature of modern urban culture—from Baudelaire to Aragon to Benjamin to Jane Jacobs—finds in crowds a peculiar antidote to selfhood with all its burdens, a release into a less personalized existence. When she moved to Washington Square in 1906, beginning an affair with another woman, Willa Cather declared, "At last I can breathe," by which she meant that her erotic life no longer defined the terms of her social existence—at least in the dense, impersonal place to which she had moved.

Impersonality does more than shelter outsiders or members of sub-cultures; it offers the possibility for what Stuart Hall calls "hybridity," a mixture of social elements beyond any single definition of self. Impersonal release has a particular value in terms of social class and material fortune. Various studies of existing mixed-class areas of big cities like New York and London yield an interesting portrait; intimate "neighborliness" is weak, but identification with the neighborhood is strong. The poor are relieved of social stigma; those who are rich in comparison—contrary to common sense, that most fallible of all guides—find daily life in a diverse neighborhood more stimulating than in places that serve only as private mirrors. These studies exemplify the sociological proposition advanced by Durkheim that impersonality and equality have a strong affinity.

The relief of self found in dense streets, mixed pubs, playgrounds, and markets thus is not inconsequential. Such dense forms of civil society affect how people think of themselves as citizens. As the late Henri Lefebvre put it, sensing one's "right to the city" helps people feel entitled to other rights, rights not based on personal injuries or on victimhood. As I say, no one could argue that an impersonal city life will extinguish either the reality or the sentiments aroused by economic failure. But "extinguish," like "rupture," belongs to the sphere of growth envisioned through metamorphosis. I imagine instead a more realistic democratic project, one which develops a kind of concurrent consciousness, in which a middle-aged, supposedly "over the hill" worker can also think of him-or herself in an entirely different way, by virtue of where he or she lives. This doubleness of self seems to be more practicable than the striving for rebirth, as in a metamorphosis.

To conclude, whether we seek for democracy in workplaces or in cities, we need to address the culture of the new capitalism. The economy does not "grow" personal skills and durable purposes, nor social trust, loyalty, or commitment. Economic practice has combined, however, with a durable cultural ethic, so that institutional nakedness co-exists with the will to take responsibility for one's life. The forms of polity we need to invent must help people transcend both elements of that combination: we need a model of growth that helps people transcend the self as a burdensome possession. Placemaking based on exclusion, sameness, or nostalgia is poisonous medicine socially, and psychologically useless. A self weighted with its insufficiencies cannot lift that burden by retreat into fantasy. Place-making based on diverse, dense, impersonal human contacts must find a way for these contacts to endure. The agora has to prove a durable institution. This is the challenge that urbanists like myself now confront.

Baudelaire famously defined modernity as experience of the fleeting and the fragmented. To accept life in its disjointed pieces is an adult experience of freedom, but still these pieces must lodge and embed themselves somewhere, hopefully in a place that allows them to grow and endure.

(Spring 2000, 2.1)

Notes

1   See Hannah Arendt, *The Human Condition* (Garden City, NY: Doubleday, 1959).

2   See Adam Smith, *An Inquiry into the Nature and Causes of the Wealth of Nations* (London, England: Strahun and Cadell, 1776).

3   See Michael Dunlop Young, *The Rise of the Meritocracy, 1870–2033: The New Elite of Our Social Revolution* (New York, NY: Random House, 1959).

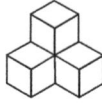

Seeing the Invisible Poor
A Conversation with Mike Rose

Jay Tolson

Jay Tolson (JT): You've written very eloquently about the challenges facing people who live and work at the bottom of our socioeconomic ladder, and one of the things you've noticed—something you claim is greatly complicating their plight—is how many, if not most, of them are becoming invisible to the rest of society. What do you mean by this? How did it happen, and is it getting worse?

Mike Rose (MR): Well, they're not literally invisible, of course. There are more than 46 million people in the United States living at or below the poverty line. But they are close to absent from public and political discourse, except as an abstraction—an income category low on the SES [socioeconomic status] index—or as a negative generalization: The poor are dependent on the government, the "takers," a problem. Consider Congressman Paul Ryan's recent comments about generations of men in the inner city "not even thinking about working." Neither the abstractions nor the generalizations give us actual people trying to live their lives as best they can.

Because of the various layers of segregation in our society—from work to schools to places of worship—those of us who are relatively socially mobile have few opportunities to live and work closely with people who are at the bottom of the income ladder. We don't know them. And because we don't know their values and aspirations, the particulars of their daily decisions, and the economic and psychological boundaries within which those decisions are made, the poor easily become psychologically one-dimensional—intellectually, emotionally, and volitionally simplified, not quite like us.

JT: Despite the growing gulf between the poor and "the rest," you've been pretty successful in staying in touch with what might be called the invisible class. What's given you this access, this connection?

MR: Well, I wouldn't want to claim any exceptional access or broad-scale knowledge. There are many poor communities—most, really—that I don't know much about at all. I grew up poor—my father was chronically ill and my mother worked long hours as a waitress—so I have a personal, intimate sense of economic hardship and insecurity. And a significant amount of work I've done over the years, both my own teaching and mentoring and my research, has involved people who are behind the economic eight ball. That work has taught me a lot. It has also enabled me to develop some relationships in which people have opened up parts of their lives to me. And I suspect the knowledge I gained from my family's own difficulties helps foster those relationships.

JT: How do we almost reflexively diminish the capacities, ambition, imagination, and determination of the poor—and thereby add to the distance that separates the well-off from the less well-off?

MR: It's a complicated business, to be sure, but I think our separation, our increasing economic segregation contributes to the diminishment. With segregation comes ignorance and apprehension. Part of the way we establish our shared humanity is by what we imagine goes on inside the head and the heart of others. If we are separated from a group not only physically but psychologically, then it becomes all the easier to attribute to them motives, beliefs, thoughts—an entire interior life—that might be deeply inaccurate and inadequate. And it's from those attributions we develop both our personal and public-policy responses to poverty.

JT: How do we even begin to break down barriers, or bridge the gulf, between the poor and the rest of society?

MR: There are so many structural impediments, from residential patterns that have developed partly out of housing policy to income inequality and the shredding of the social safety net. So, for starters, if we want to address the isolation I'm talking about, we need to do things that simply help poor people live a decent life: a higher minimum wage, tax credits, jobs programs, childcare, housing and transportation assistance. It's hard to participate in society when you're scrambling for your next meal or being booted out of your apartment. I'm not optimistic, given the focus on austerity and the terribly ungenerous cast to so many public policy deliberations.

We also need opportunities for people to develop and grow: educational and cultural programs, apprenticeships and job training, civic organizations. I'm thinking about places or occasions where poor people become more fully present actors on the societal stage, where their thoughts and feelings play out in ways that can have a positive effect on the direction of their lives. Social movements for civil rights or economic justice provide such a space. Cultural projects do as well—in churches and community centers, women's shelters, prison art programs. And, in my experience, second-chance educational programs and institutions—literacy centers, adult schools, many community colleges—can also play this role.

But these are complex institutions. Given the intricate relation in our country among social class, educational resources, and academic achievement, the adult school and community college reflect educational inequality and can contribute to it. A lot of students never complete a certificate or degree. Some institutions do better than others with similar populations, so the quality of governance, services, and teaching matters. These institutions are among the few places in mainstream society where poor people can become more publicly visible and display to their advantage multiple dimensions of their lives.

JT: Can you tell us how some of your own experiences in these places led to new understandings of the poor and their various plights?

MR: Let me give you a recent one. I spent several years studying a community college that serves one of the poorest populations in Southern California. Many of the students are older, coming back to school once their children are grown, or after a series of dead-end jobs, or having spent time in prison. Those coming straight from high school typically went to underperforming schools. Most students have to take remedial English or math. The majority of students are on financial aid and are burdened with health, housing, or transportation problems. They've got a lot on their shoulders.

One of the things that struck me—and it happened in stages, as I saw one example, then another, then another—was the powerful desire that being at the college unleashed in these students. Parents wanted to improve their economic prospects and do better by their kids. People who hadn't been in a classroom in decades spoke passionately about wanting to learn math this time or to become better readers and writers. Burly, trash-talking guys in a welding class were complimenting each other on welds being "beautiful" or "pretty," and, in their math class, were arguing about the correct solution to a problem. From physics to fashion design, students were beginning to redefine themselves, to envision a future of possibility. As one young woman said, "You will grow in a way that you never in your mind would imagine."

Of course, not all students at the college are affected so powerfully, and too many leave out of discouragement or because of financial burdens. But to witness repeatedly the mental vitality, the hope, the redefining of one's sense of self, makes you realize what is possible when the conditions are right.

JT: So, in addition to its practical economic value, college for these students yields other benefits as well?

MR: Absolutely. Even for the most occupationally oriented students. One of the things that concern me about current education policy aimed at students like these is its strict economic focus. We need to get more people into college to enhance their economic prospects and to secure the nation's economic future. Fine and true enough. The students want an economic boost, too. As one guy said bluntly in an orientation session, "I'm here because I don't want to work a crappy job all my life."

But so much else typically happens along the way. Students comment on how good it feels to learn new things, or to overcome old insecurities, or to have new intellectual and social as well as occupational avenues open up to them. If we don't acknowledge and try to foster this rich dimension of their education, then we're just repeating a long and troubling tendency in American education policy. Working-class students get a strictly functional education, heavy on job training and thin on everything else.

JT: Could you say something about another important, but often overlooked, institution that is important to people with relatively few resources? I mean the public library.

MR: When I was visiting public schools in small rural communities, I was struck by the role played by the local library. In addition to housing books and some films and music, it's an information resource, a meeting place, an Internet outlet. And in places where the population is sparse and widely distributed, the traveling library is a godsend. I spent a week at a one-room schoolhouse in Montana's Beaverhead Valley community, and there was a tiny library attached to the school, the only library around. It was the place kids got their books—and there were several intense readers in the class of fifteen, always hunched over a book. What a resource!

Rural or urban, libraries are a national treasure, and it's easy in these days of connectivity and constantly streaming media to forget how important they are to so many who can't afford all the technological bells and whistles. It's shocking, I think, that libraries are being forced to reduce hours and staff and close local branches. And this is at a time when only about two-thirds of the nation's libraries provide the only free Internet access in their communities—and when government and employment information and forms are increasingly going online.

JT: There've been many debates over the touchy subject of intelligence, what it is, how we measure it, and how such conceptions and measurements affect life chances and opportunities. How does what you call "a reductive view of intelligence" stand in the way of appreciating the inner lives of individuals who are often dismissed as society's less able or less gifted—and who are undercompensated as a result?

MR: As a country, we seem to be obsessed with intelligence, with measuring it, with boosting our kids' intelligence through products like *Baby Einstein*, with getting "smarter" workers into the new "smart" workplace. But the odd thing is that we tend to rely on a fairly narrow way of determining intelligence: We identify it with a score on a standard intelligence test (an IQ score) and with the traditional school-based tasks.

If one does well on an intelligence test or in school that clearly indicates some kind of cognitive competence. But if one doesn't do well—and, historically, poor performers include many low-income people—then the meaning of the score is much less clear. To do well tells us something about intelligence—and, usually, schooling—but not to do well provides much less information about intellectual capacity…though that poor performance may speak volumes about educational opportunity.

What struck me as I did the research for *The Mind at Work* was the number of instances of reasoning, of problem solving, of learning and applying that learning that fell outside what gets assessed in an intelligence test or the traditional school curriculum. There is the waitress at rush hour prioritizing on the fly a number of demands from customers, the kitchen, and the manager. And the plumber diagnosing a problem by feeling with his hands the pipes he can't see behind an old wall. And the hair stylist figuring out the style a customer wants through talk and gesture. This kind of brainwork surrounds us, yet might not be considered when we talk about intelligence.

JT: You've talked about some of the ways the lives of the poor are made harder by their growing "invisibility," but how is the rest of society, including the better off, made worse—and even impoverished—by the "disappearance of the poor"?

MR: Poverty represents a society's moral and civic failure. It also constricts our collective intelligence and creativity as so many people's potential is squelched. Thank goodness, the notion of an "opportunity gap" is finally making its way into public discussion. That gap hurts all of us.

One more thing: The marginalization that poverty begets keeps from the mainstream entire categories of experience and points of view that can enrich our culture and the way we understand and try to solve a whole range of problems. I don't want to romanticize the kinds of students I spent time with at that community college or claim that as a group they have superior gifts or insights. But some of them, because of their backgrounds, ask different kinds of questions, draw on fresh illustrations, come at problems in unusual ways. Nurturing that kind of intellectual and social diversity benefits us all.

(Fall 2014, 16.3)

IV.
Religion and Society

We Have Never Been Disenchanted

Eugene McCarraher

"Beautiful demon of Money, what an enchanter thou art!"

—Mark Twain and Charles Dudley Warner, *The Gilded Age*

One of the stories modernity tells about itself is titled "The Disenchantment of the World." Friedrich Schiller coined the phrase while lamenting the demise of the gods of Greek antiquity, but it was Max Weber who turned it into melancholy shorthand for the modern condition of secularity.[1]

The broad outlines of the tale are familiar to most educated people in the contemporary world: Before the Protestant Reformation, the earth was suffused and enveloped by "enchantment," an invisible universe of spirits and deities who inhabited the natural world and could shape the course of human affairs. These spirits animated objects, dwelled in mountains or forests, and delivered messages through dreams, oracles, and prophets. Whether they were capricious or governed by providential design, these forces could be mastered or entreated through practices of magic, divination, and prayer. The medieval Church built a Christian enclave for these beings in its system of saints, holy places, and sacraments, but its Protestant (and especially Calvinist) antagonists—suspicious, in Weber's words, of "magical and sacramental forces"—commenced the demolition of the enchanted sanctuary. And with the victories of science, technology, and capitalism, we discovered that the cosmos of enchantment was unreal, or at best, utterly unverifiable; we cast most of the spirits into oblivion, and made room for their withered but venerable survivors in our chambers of private belief.[2]

Among the North Atlantic intelligentsia, at least, this story in some form is so widely hegemonic that even religious intellectuals accept it. For instance, in *A Secular Age* (2007), Charles Taylor—a practicing Catholic—affirms, albeit in his own peculiar way, the consensus of "disenchantment." In the pre-modern epoch of enchantment, Taylor explains, the boundary that separated our world from the sacred was porous and indistinct; traffic between the two spheres was frequent, if not always desired or friendly. "Disenchantment" began with the church's rationalization of doctrine and the growing awareness that Christianity was not the world's only religion. Now, having left the enchanted universe behind, we disenchanted dwell within the moral and ontological parameters of an "immanent frame": the world as apprehended through reason and science, bereft of immaterial and unquantifiable forces, structured by the immutable laws of nature and the contingent traditions of human societies.[3]

What Taylor calls the "buffered self" is a kind of "immanent frame" that insulates the inner from the outer world, thus precluding any sense of the numinous or any notion that "nature has something to say to us." Although attempts to re-enchant the world have surfaced periodically—Romantic poetry and philosophy, "New Age" spirituality, various religious fundamentalisms—none of these bids to revitalize enchantment has succeeded in wrecking the "immanent frame."[4]

So goes the consensus. Yet Weber himself left clues for a rather different account of our condition. In this story—adumbrated in "Science as a Vocation" (1917)—we abide between two eras: "We live as did the ancients when their world was not yet disenchanted of its gods and demons," Weber speculated—"only we live in a different sense." Antiquity witnessed a long twilight of the gods, only to be followed by the dawn of a new one—whose own demise appeared to be the final senescence and annihilation of all enchantment from the world. Indeed, Weber observed, while "many old gods ascend from their graves," they are quickly "disenchanted," taking "the form of impersonal forces."[5]

But is that the only way to understand the "different sense" to which Weber alluded so nebulously—that modernity marks the crossing of the Rubicon of disenchantment? Perhaps the sociologist who considered himself "religiously unmusical" heard faint notes of enchantment in modernity; perhaps, despite their wounds, the old divinities had not risen to give consent to their deaths. Were they really "disenchanted" when they assumed their "secular" form? Or do they still roam among us in the guise of "secularization"?

There are good reasons to think so, and some of them lie within one of the more tumultuous and aggressive of the allegedly "disenchanting" forces of modernity: capitalism, whose "laws of the market" Weber had identified as one refuge for the phantoms of divinity. Of course, capitalism has long been presumed to be a powerful solvent of enchantment. "All that is solid melts into air; all that is holy is profaned," as Marx and Engels proclaimed in

The Communist Manifesto. Far from being bastions of piety, the bourgeois masters of capitalism have "drowned the most heavenly ecstasies of religious fervor…in the icy water of egotistical calculation." What if those waters of pecuniary reason constituted a baptismal font, a consecration of capitalism as a covert form of enchantment, all the more beguiling on account of its apparent profanity?

The Fetishized World

I want to explore two ideas in this essay that amount to a claim that *we have never been disenchanted.* (That's a deliberate echo of Bruno Latour, who once argued that "we have never been modern"—that we have never differentiated nature and society as clearly and rigidly as we believe.) First, capitalism has been a form of enchantment, a metamorphosis of the sacred in the raiment of secularity. With money as its ontological marrow, it represents a moral and metaphysical imagination as well as a sublimation of our desire for the presence of divinity in the everyday world. Second, the most incisive forms of opposition to capitalist enchantment have come in the form of what I will call "the sacramental imagination," a conviction that the material of ordinary life can mediate the supernatural.[6]

In this view, capitalism perverts both the sacramental character of the world and our consciousness of that quality—neither of which can ever be extinguished, only assaulted, damaged, and left in ruins. As Gerard Manley Hopkins summarized it so well in the Romantic idiom of the sacramental imagination, "the world is charged with the grandeur of God…. There lies the dearest freshness deep down things"—a freshness spoiled, he ruefully added, "seared with trade, bleared, smeared with toil." The world does not need to be *re*-enchanted; its enduring and ineradicable enchantment requires our belated recognition and reverence.

One source of the idea that capitalism is a metamorphosis of the sacred is the Marxist tradition, which has always been nonetheless ambivalent, if not contradictory, about the secular and the sacred in modern economic life. As Terry Eagleton writes in *Culture and the Death of God* (2014), his recent survey of "surrogate forms of transcendence" in the wake of God's (alleged) demise, capitalism is "fundamentally irreligious…and totally alien to the category of the sacred"—yet "the only aura to linger on" in our postmodern era "is that of the commodity or celebrity." In the *Manifesto* itself, capitalism is a ruthless assassin of enchantment, drowning ecstasy in a pool of mercenary rationality. But the capitalist himself is also "a sorcerer, who cannot control the powers of the nether world he has called up with his spells." Rhetorical flourish, to be sure, but it also reflected Marx's reading in ethnographical literature on "fetishism," the attribution of magical or supernatural powers to natural or fabricated objects.[7]

Fetishism is "a religion of sensuous desire," Marx had written in 1842, in which the worshipper fantasizes that an "inanimate object will give up its natural character in order to comply with his desires." In his unpublished "1844 manuscripts," Marx linked fetishism to "alienation"—the social process by which people lose control of their own labor and products, which is to say, to Marx, the sources of their own selfhood. Under capitalism, where the wage laborer is divorced both from the means of production and from control over his own actions and products, alienation takes a fetishistic form, an ascription of life to objects produced by none other than the worker himself. "The life which he has given to the object sets itself against him as an alien and hostile force," Marx mused. "If the product of labor does not belong to the worker, but confronts him as an alien power, this can only be because it belongs to a *man other than the worker*." The domination of labor by capital took the form of a modern animism, a capitalist variety of enchanted objects—"enchanted" by the worker's own powers.[8]

During the next two decades, the *anima* of capitalist animism in Marx's anatomy of enchantment shifted from estranged labor to money, even as both continued to represent the unresolved alienation of human agency. In the 1844 manuscripts, as well as in the unfinished *Grundrisse* (1857) and in the first volume of *Capital* (1867), Marx portrays money as the ontological foundation of a uniquely pecuniary way of being in the world—a metaphysics of money that resembles and supplants traditional forms of enchantment. On one level, money is another marker of alienation: Like divinity, it betokens "the alienated ability of mankind."[9]

Here, as elsewhere in Marx, rhetorical brio serves philosophical insight. Having drowned religious faith in the arctic of pecuniary reason, money becomes "the almighty being," the "truly creative power," the *de facto* ontological basis of reality in capitalist civilization. "The power of money in bourgeois society" extends farther and deeper than the market in commodities; like the God of Genesis, it brings things into being from nothing, and consigns all indigent objects and desires to the void of nonexistence. "If I have the *vocation* for study but no money for it, I have *no* vocation for study—that is, no *effective*, no *true* vocation. On the other hand, if I have really no vocation for study but have the will and the money for it, I have an *effective* vocation for it."[10]

As the metaphysical common sense of market society, money defines and even bestows all manner of qualities. "I am *stupid*, but money is the *real mind* of all things and how then should its possessor be stupid?" Money can even buy you love: "I am *ugly*, but I can buy for myself the most *beautiful* of women. Therefore I am not *ugly*, for the effect of *ugliness*—its deterrent power—is nullified by money." Like the fetishes of tribal peoples, money confers extraordinary powers once believed to belong to shamans, priests, and gods.[11]

Money's enchanting powers are even more evident in Marx's analysis of "the fetishism of commodities, and the secret thereof," one of the more trenchant passages in *Capital*. From the sardonic opening of the chapter—the commodity is "a queer thing, abounding in metaphysical subtleties and theological niceties"—through the exposure of "all the magic and necromancy that surrounds the products of labor as long as they take the form of commodities," Marx maintains that commodity fetishism amounts to the sacramental system of capitalism. (At one point, Marx compares the commodity fetish to the Eucharist.)[12]

The "secret" of fetishized commodities lies in their twofold character as "use-value" and as "exchange-value." The *use*-value of objects resides in their particular, qualitatively different uses—shoes for feet, food for eating, shirts for adornment. Their *exchange*-value rests in their status *as commodities*, objects produced for sale in the market for the purpose of capital accumulation. In order for these commodities to be exchanged for money, their incommensurable use values must be obscured; they must somehow be rendered qualitatively identical to other commodities.

The "universal equivalent" of money—"the god among commodities," as Marx had dubbed it in the *Grundrisse*—performs this act of ontological prestidigitation. Objects become "worth" so much in money; their value is defined in terms of money, not in terms of their utility for human purposes. In the market, this pecuniary alchemy induces the spell of "fetishism," by which people attribute a kind of agency and independence to commodities, the products of their own labor. Pervaded and commanded by the "god among commodities," objects are enchanted, enlivened, by money—the metaphysical substratum of capitalist society. Thus commodity fetishism is a specifically capitalist form of alienation, a modern recipe for the opium of the people.[13]

Despite the allures of capitalist enchantment, Marx was confident that revolutionary theory and practice would dispel the sacramental glamour of capitalism. When money and commodity fetishism were finally exposed as the lustrous guise of alienation, workers would retrieve the means of humanity, and the communist society of the future would have no need for magical compensations.

Yet Marx provided ample reason to doubt that what he called the "pre-history" of the species would end in a *Götterdämmerung* of disenchantment. It was never clear that the reduction of workers to industrial servitude would lead eventually to revolution, as money, that "god among commodities," exercised an increasingly potent and untrammeled authority in capitalist society. If capitalism enervates or demolishes all traditional sources of moral and ontological truth—if indeed, as proclaimed in the *Manifesto*, "all that is solid melts into air, all that is holy is profaned," all that is enchanted is disenchanted—nothing but capitalism could generate resistance to the rage to accumulate.

But as the metaphysical regime of capitalism, monetary and commodity fetishism was at least as beguiling as any previous order of enchantment, especially as all its rivals were evaporating. If the proletariat is thoroughly permeated by pecuniary enchantment, why would the oppressed ever desire the transcendence of alienation and servility? With sufficient technical and political ingenuity—mass production, consumer culture, the welfare and regulatory policies of modern liberalism and social democracy—the sacramental tokens of commodity fetishism could retard and even extinguish the growth of revolutionary consciousness.

A Sacramental Alternative

Yet if Marxism accounts for the persistence of enchantment in a scientific and technological age, it does so in large measure, as Simone Weil once remarked, because it is also "the highest spiritual expression of bourgeois society." It always bears repeating that capitalism, in Marxist eschatology, is a necessary stage in historical development, and that it shares with its nemesis a commitment to expanding productivity as a vehicle of "progress"—defined as the achievement of material abundance through the technological exploitation of nature. For both the bourgeoisie and its revolutionary antagonists, progress is fuelled, under capitalism, by the rage to accumulate through commodity production; if capitalists do not see "fetishism" or "enchantment" in the primacy of money or the circulation of commodities, Marxists who (rightly) see both must nonetheless consider them progressive in character, aiding in that "development of the productive forces" that must precede the construction of socialism and communism.[14]

Thus the progress of history is driven by enchantment; money's moral and ontological charms sanction "primitive accumulation," the dispossession of producers from the means of production and their conversion into wage laborers; the industrial division of labor and the ecological despoliation of the planet; the proletarianization of agricultural, artisanal, and eventually professional skills, all increasingly monopolized by a techno-managerial elite beholden only to capital; and the construction of a gorgeous symbolic universe of advertising, marketing, and entertainment, the arsenal of what David Graeber has characterized as capital's "war on the imagination." If Marxism demonstrates that we have never been disenchanted, it would also seem to prove that the enchantments of capitalism will be well-nigh impossible to eradicate.[15]

Weil traced the failure of the Marxist revolutionary imagination to its species of materialism. Like other nineteenth-century materialists, Marx conceived of matter as an inert and lifeless ensemble of forces; however "historical" his materialism claimed to be, the inertia of matter entailed subjection to the inviolable laws of the natural—and only—world. But if matter—including historical matter—is governed only by force, then the mechanisms of capitalist matter were, on Marx's own terms, invincible. "Marx's revolutionary materialism," Weil observed, "consists in positing on the one hand that everything is exclusively regulated by force, and on the other that a day will come when force will be on the side of the weak. Not that certain ones who were weak will become strong…but that the entire mass of the weak, while continuing to be such, will have force on its side." While Weil praised Marx for his acute portrayal of the apparatus of capitalist domination, she realized that the political implications of inanimate materialism were anything but emancipatory.[16]

Rather than reactively dismiss materialism altogether in favor of some "spiritual" ontology of politics, Weil hinted at a *sacramental* alternative. Shortly before her untimely death in 1943, Weil—by then what could be described as a fellow-traveler of Christianity, someone lingering in the vestibule but never entering the sanctuary—speculated that just as "yeast only makes the dough rise if it is mixed with it," so in the same way "there exist certain material conditions for the supernatural operation of the divine that is present on earth." The knowledge of those "material conditions" for "supernatural operation" would, Weil surmised, constitute "the true knowledge of social mechanics." If matter is not exactly "animate," the material world of society and history could be a conduit for divinity. Because we have "forgotten the existence of a divine order of the universe," we fail to see that "labor, art, and science are only different ways of entering into contact with it."[17]

Weil's gesture toward a "true knowledge of social mechanics" suggested a politics of the sacramental imagination. "Sacramentality" is a key but somewhat amorphous and elusive concept in Christian theology, referring not only to the official roster of sacraments but to the character of created reality as well. Just as a sacrament is a visible, material sign and vessel of divine grace, so matter itself is similarly "trans-corporeal," as theologian Graham Ward puts it. As Rowan Williams explains, sacramentality entails the belief that "material things carry their fullest meaning…when they are the medium of gift, not instruments of control or objects for accumulation." In what I am calling the sacramental imagination, "the corporeal and the incorporeal do not comprise a dualism," as Ward asserts; the visible, material realm "manifests the watermark of its creator."[18]

This sacramental critique of Marxist metaphysics would not be that it is "too materialist" but rather that *it is not materialist enough*—that is, that it does not provide an adequate account of matter itself, of its sacramental and revelatory character. Sacramentality has ontological and social implications, for the "gift" that Williams identifies is "God's grace and the common life thus formed."[19]

Theologians concerned with consumer culture employ sacramentality as a critique of commodification. "Commodities are transubstantiated into sacraments…in a world empty of the presence of God," Terence Tilley contends, becoming Williams's "instruments of control" and "objects of accumulation." Yet this way of putting it may concede too much to the conventional narrative of disenchantment—God, if not dead, has been eclipsed. But if the world is never "empty of the presence of God," commodification—and the fetishism from which it is inseparable—might better be characterized as a perversion or parody of the sacramental nature of material life.[20]

Since the Enlightenment, the hegemony of modern scientific and technological rationality has rendered belief in the "sacramentality" of the world, at best, a beautiful article of private faith. But even after the triumph of disenchantment among those Friedrich Schleiermacher dubbed the "cultured despisers" of Christianity, a sacramental imagination endured among its cultured, if not necessarily orthodox, admirers, especially among Romantic writers and intellectuals.

An Aesthetic Asylum

As the doyen of scholars of Romanticism, M.H. Abrams, explained, secularization has not been "the deletion and replacement of religious ideas" but rather their "assimilation and reinterpretation." Romantics, in his view, provided an aesthetic asylum for the spirits of pre-modern enchantment. Like Thomas Carlyle's Professor Teufelsdröckh, the philoso-pher-prophet of *Sartor Resartus* (1831), they longed to "embody the divine Spirit" of the gospel "in a new Mythus, in a new vehicle and vesture, that our Souls...may live." But Romanticism did more than preserve an interior enclave for the supernatural; as Bernard Reardon perceived, it also named "the inexpungeable feeling that the finite is not self-ex-plaining and self-justifying" and that "there is always an infinite 'beyond'"—a beyond that lived in the midst of us, leaving numinous traces in the world of appearance. In other words, Romanticism is the modern heir to the Christian sacramental imagination.[21]

Conveyed in a poetic rather than a theological idiom, Romantic ontology envisioned a reality that both transcended and pervaded the sensible world. Some of the signature passag-es of Romantic poetry are modern sacramental epiphanies. In his "Auguries of Innocence" (c. 1803) William Blake beckoned us

> To see a world in a grain of sand,
> And a Heaven in a Wild Flower,
> Hold Infinity in the palm of your hand,
> And Eternity in an hour.

Later, in "Tintern Abbey" (1798), William Wordsworth reported

> A presence that disturbs me with the joy
> Of elevated thoughts; a sense sublime
> Of something far more deeply interfused,
> Whose dwelling is the light of setting suns,
> And the round ocean and the living air,
> And the blue sky, and in the mind of man:
> A motion and a spirit that impels
> All thinking things, all objects of all thought,
> And rolls through all things.

The sacramental rapture of those passages might serve to reinforce the caricature of Romantic hostility to reason. Yet for Romantics the enemy was not reason *per se*, but rather what Blake cursed as "single vision": the occlusion of sacramental sight, the optics of mastery and exploitation, the inability to see the world as anything more than material resources.

Although divorced from orthodox theology, Romantic humanism echoed the traditional harmony of reason, love, and reality. When Romantics praised "enthusiasm," "reverence," and "imagination," they restated the venerable Christian wisdom that reason is rooted in love, that full and genuine understanding precludes a desire to possess and control. Against the imperious claims of "Urizen"—Blake's fallen "Prince of Light" and *your reason* reduced to measurement and calculation—Blake countered that "Enthusiastic Admiration is the First Principle of Knowledge & its last." "To know a thing, what we can call knowing," Carlyle surmised in *Heroes and Hero-Worship* (1840), we "must first *love* the thing, sympathise with it." Arising from a sacramental sense of the world as a "region of the Wonderful," Carlyle's incessant admonitions to "reverence" and "wonder" were, at bottom, exhortations to love.[22]

"Imagination" was the name Romantics gave to this erotic and sacramental consciousness. Yet imagination was not only a subjective enchantment; in the Romantic sensibility, imagination was the most perspicuous form of *vision*—the ability to see what is really there, behind the illusion or obscurity produced by our will to dissect and dominate. To Samuel Taylor Coleridge, if reason is "the power of universal and necessary convictions, the source and substance of truths above sense," then imagination is its vibrant sacramental partner, "the living Power and prime Agent of all human perception...a repetition in the finite mind of the eternal act of creation in the infinite I AM." For Romantics, imagination did not annul but rather completed rationality. During the French Revolution, Wordsworth observed, reason seemed "most intent on making of herself / A prime Enchantress." Though warning of the brutality of instrumental reason—"our meddling intellect / Mis-shapes the beauteous forms of things; / We murder to dissect"—Wordsworth described imagination as "Reason in her most exalted mood." Imagination was, for the Romantics, the ecstasy of reason.[23]

As the sacramental imagination in its most reputable form after the Enlightenment, Romanticism has been, as Robert Sayre and Michael Lowy have argued, "a vital component of modern culture," pervading an extraordinary array of aesthetic, political, and religious figures and movements—some of which were explicitly opposed to capitalism, though not necessarily from what we call "the Left." Indeed, the fondness for the Middle Ages displayed by some Romantic intellectuals has led to dismissal of Romanticism as a lovely incubator of irrationalism, reaction, and even fascism. But many other Romantic anti-capitalists did not seek to resurrect the past; they invoked the past for a critical perspective on the present more ontologically penetrating and politically promising than the futures held out by the disenchanted heirs of the Enlightenment. Though in no way systematic, the sacramental imagination of Romantic social criticism—better described, perhaps, as Carlyle did, as "Prophecy"—began from an ontology of sacral materialism, in terms of which the injustice and indignity that attended the accumulation of capital comprised a desecration.[24]

The lineage of Romantic anti-capitalism is too long and motley to delineate here, but its first representatives, Carlyle and John Ruskin, sketched the outlines of a prophetic sacramental imagination for subsequent critics of capitalist enchantment. In *Sartor Resartus*, "wonder" is Carlyle's term for both the awareness and the ontological condition of sacramentality. "The Universe is not dead," he declares, but rather "godlike," pervaded by "an Invisible, Unnameable, Godlike, present everywhere in all that we see and work and suffer." Against this sacral materialism Carlyle poses the "Gospel of Mammonism" in his indictment of industrial England, *Past and Present* (1843). Mammonism is the good news that money possesses and bestows a trove of "miraculous facilities." Money conjures a "horrid enchantment"—"enchantment," to Carlyle, is the counterfeit of wonder—in which owners and workers walk "spell-bound" in the midst of "plethoric wealth."[25]

While Ruskin's contemporaneous prominence as an acerbic critic of industrial capitalism is being recalled today by many on the post-Marxist Left, his sacramental conception of reality and especially of human beings is usually overlooked. First exhibited in his renowned work on art history and criticism, Ruskin's sacramental imagination soon embraced his social and ecological concerns as well. In the fifth volume of *Modern Painters* (1860), Ruskin declared that the "directest manifestation of Deity to man is in His own image, that is, in man." Earlier, in a passage in the fourth volume of *Modern Painters* (1856), he had mused that "in the midst of the material nearness of these heavens" God desires that we "acknowledge His own immediate presence."[26]

Ruskin's eloquent critiques of industrial capitalism were embedded in this sacramental ontology and humanism. His condemnation of mechanization—that it "unhumanizes" human beings of their creative skills—stemmed from his conviction that the industrial division of labor was a sacrilege against "His own image." The broadside against what he called the "nescience" of economics in *Unto This Last* (1862) reflected Ruskin's "amazement" at a world that "reaches yet into the infinite." His celebrated maxim, "there is no wealth but life," arose from this sense of an "infinity" that cherished and enlivened the whole of creation—a creation that mercenary plunder was reducing to a disenchanting wasteland. In *The Storm-Cloud of the Nineteenth Century* (1884), Ruskin's eerie premonition of ecological calamity, capitalist depredation corroded and perverted the planet's sacramental character. Because of industrial pollution, the climate exuded "iniquity"; the clouds announced "bitterness and malice"; smoke and sludge befouled "the visible Heaven" of nature.[27]

The Dustbin of Disenchantment

Well after the classic age of Romanticism, its sacramental dialect shaped the vernacular of a host of non-Marxist radicals in Europe and the United States. Before the success of the Bolshevik Revolution gave Marxism a near-monopoly on the radical imagination, Romanticism flourished among a motley range of critics. It animated the transatlantic Arts and Crafts movement, one of whose American devotees described craftsmanship as "the sacrament of common things." God, another artisanal ideologue put it, is "woven in tapestries and beaten in brasses and bound in the covers of books."[28]

A disciple of nature in the California redwoods, John Muir saw "sparks of the Divine Spirit variously clothed upon with flesh, leaves, rock, water"; the human body was a "flesh-and-bone tabernacle." Developers who wanted to ravage the landscape for profit were "temple-destroyers, devotees of ravaging commercialism." In search of what he called a "passionate vision," William James affirmed "saintliness" as a human ideal in *The Varieties of Religious Experience* (1905) on account of the saint's "rapture" and "ontological wonder." Contemptuous of capitalist society's reduction of life to moneymaking, James upheld the saint as an emissary from "another kingdom of being"—*this* world, apprehended in rapturous ontological wonder. Our proper attitude, as James wrote in "What Makes a Life Significant" (1900), is to be "rapt with satisfied attention...to the mere spectacle of the world's presence." The Christian socialist Vida Dutton Scudder outlined a sacramental counter to Marxist materialism in *Socialism and Character* (1912), arguably an early document of liberation theology. "The material universe," Scudder contended, "is a sacrament ordered to convey spiritual life to us." Since work and technology were material vessels of grace as well as forces of production, class struggles were conflicts over the means of beatitude.[29]

After World War I, the sacramental critique of capitalism abided, fraying or severing its connection to socialist politics and linking up with a more freelance radicalism. James Agee, for instance, considered his report on Alabama sharecroppers beaten down by the Great Depression, *Let Us Now Praise Famous Men* (1941), a meditation on the "predicaments of human divinity." Only a recollection of the image and likeness of God, Agee thought, could reveal "the true proportions of the savageness of the world." Agee's description of one family's house—a "tabernacle," he wrote, a sacred space "not to me but of itself"—conveyed the intrinsic, indestructible sacramentality of even the most wretched of the earth. Later, Allen Ginsberg exclaimed in "Howl" (1956) of the "heaven which exists, and is everywhere around us" being consumed by "Moloch," a behemoth of mercenary and technological nihilism:

> Moloch whose mind is pure
>   machinery! Moloch whose blood is running money! ...
> Moloch whose love is endless
>   oil and stone! Moloch whose soul is electricity and banks! ...

Kenneth Rexroth—anarchist, grey eminence of American bohemia, and syncretist of Catholicism and Buddhism—wrote of "the world as streaming / In the electrolysis of love." In both *The Making of a Counterculture* (1969) and *Where the Wasteland Ends* (1972), Theodore Roszak praised the Romantics for their "sacramental consciousness," which he hoped to enlist against a technocratic capitalism that now enjoyed a perverse "monopoly of the sacramental powers." Consigning Marxism and other secular revolutionary theories to the dustbin of disenchantment, Roszak called on a new generation of radicals who knew that "politics is metaphysically grounded" to draw upon "primordial energies greater than the power of our bombs."[30]

As the Trappist monk Thomas Merton realized, those "primordial energies" could be as gentle as the rain. In "Rain and the Rhinoceros," a haunting essay in *Raids on the Unspeakable* (1966), Merton imagined the sad perversity of a world reduced to inventory. As he listened to showers in the forest near Gethsemani, the Kentucky abbey where he lived, Merton hastened to convey the beauty of the rain before it "becomes a utility that they can plan and distribute for money"—they meaning business, determined to take everything free and incalculable and make it a paying proposition.[31]

To Merton, this insatiable avarice indicated an evil much deeper than moral perversion; it emanated from a capitalist enchantment that only masqueraded as secularity. Business was launching an ontological regime in which "what has no price has no value, that what cannot be sold is not real"; in the cosmology of capital, "the only way to make something *actual* is to place it on the market." Graphing the rain on the commercial axis of effective demand and scarcity of supply, the alchemists of commerce cannot "appreciate its gratuity." Yet for those who saw the world as the lavish largesse of a loving and prodigal God, "rain is a festival," a celebration of its own gifted and gloriously pointless existence. "Every plant that stands in the light of the sun is a saint and an outlaw," he exulted. "Every blade of grass is an angel in a shower of glory."[32]

Who are the acolytes of Romantic sacramentalism in our own age of mercenary enchantment, when the specter of ecological catastrophe forms a global storm-cloud of the twenty-first century? Pope Francis I, for one, who in his recent encyclical, *Laudato Si'* (2015), provides an erudite and often moving manifesto of the sacramental imagination. Opening with his namesake's "Canticle to the Creatures," the Pope proceeds to excoriate the economic system for pillaging the earth and its inhabitants; the biosphere "groans in travail," as he cites Paul's warning to the Romans.[33]

But as Francis insists in his own epistle to the disenchanted, the root of the violence wrought upon the planet lies in an ontological blindness. Divine love is "the fundamental moving force in all created things," Francis writes; the world is "illuminated by the love which calls us together into universal communion."[34] No doubt this will all seem foolish to the shamans and magicians of neoliberal capitalism, whose own imaginations are lavishly imprisoned in the gaudy cage of disenchantment. The Romantics would remind us that our capacity to act well relies on our capacity to see what is really there. For there are more things in heaven and earth than are dreamt of on Wall Street or in Silicon Valley.

(Fall 2015, 17.3)

Notes

1. Schiller referred to the "de-divinizing of the world" in "The Gods of Greece" (1788); Weber used the phrase in "Science as a Vocation" (1917–1919), *From Max Weber: Essays in Sociology*, ed. H.H. Gerth and C. Wright Mills, (New York, NY: Routledge, 2009 [1946]), 155.

2. Max Weber, *The Protestant Ethic and the Spirit of Capitalism*, trans. Talcott Parsons (New York, NY: Routledge, 2005), 61. Originally published 1905.

3. Charles Taylor, *A Secular Age* (Cambridge, MA: Harvard, 2007), 539–93.

4. Ibid., 37–42, 358, 711–72.

5. Weber, *Essays in Sociology*, 148–49.

6. Bruno Latour, *We Have Never Been Modern*, trans. Catherine Porter (Cambridge, MA: Harvard, 1993), esp. 32–35. Originally published in 1991 as *Nous n'avons jamais été modernes*.

7. Terry Eagleton, *Culture and the Death of God* (New Haven, CT: Yale University Press, 2014), ix, 8, 192.

8. Karl Marx, "The Leading Article in No. 179 of the *Kölnische Zeitung*" (1842), in Marx and Engels, *Collected Works*, Vol. 1 (New York, NY: Lawrence and Wishart, 1975), 189; "Economic and Philosophic Manuscripts" (1844), *The Marx-Engels Reader*), ed. Robert C. Tucker (New York, NY: Norton, 1978), 70–72.

9. *The Marx-Engels Reader*, 104.

10. Ibid., 104–05.

11. Ibid.

12. Karl Marx, *Capital* (Oxford, England, and New York, NY: Oxford, 2008), 42, 26. Originally published 1867.

13. Karl Marx, *Grundrisse: Foundations of the Critique of Political Economy*, trans. Martin Nicolaus (New York, NY: Penguin, 1993), 139. Translation originally published 1973. On the process of fetishization, see Marx, *Capital*, 42–50.

14. Simone Weil, "Fragments, 1933–1938," in *Oppression and Liberty*, trans. Arthur Wills and John Petrie (New York, NY: Routledge, 2013), 124. Translation originally published 1973.

15. David Graeber, *Revolutions in Reverse: Essays on Politics, Violence, Art, and Imagination* (New York, NY: Dubois, 2011), 6.

16. Weil, "Fragments," 183.

17. Ibid., 157, 159.

18. Graham Ward, *Cities of God* (London, England, and New York, NY: Routledge, 2000), 81–96, 157; Rowan Williams, *On Christian Theology* (Oxford, England: Oxford 2000), 218.

19. Williams, *On Christian Theology*, 218.

20. Terrence Tilley, *Inventing Catholic Tradition* (Maryknoll, NY: Orbis Books, 2000), 131.

21. M.H. Abrams, *Natural Supernaturalism: Tradition and Revolution in Romantic Literature* (New York, NY: Norton, 1973), 13; Thomas Carlyle, *Sartor Resartus* (London, England: Chapman and Hall, 1872), 134; Bernard M. G. Reardon, *Religion in the Age of Romanticism: Studies in Early Nineteenth-Century Thought* (New York, NY: Cambridge, 1985), 3.

22. William Blake, "Annotations to the Works of Sir Joshua Reynolds," in *The Complete Poetry and Prose of William Blake*, ed. David V. Erdman (New York, NY: Anchor Books, 1982), 647; Carlyle, *Heroes and Hero-Worship* (London, England: Chapman and Hall, 1840), 99; *Sartor Resartus*, 187.

[23] Samuel Taylor Coleridge, "Aids to Reflection" (1825) in *The Complete Works of Samuel Taylor Coleridge* (New York, NY: Harper, 1884), 241; William Wordsworth, "The French Revolution as It Appeared to Its Enthusiasts at Its Commencement," in *Selected Poetry of William Wordsworth*, ed. Mark Van Doren (New York, NY: Modern Library, 1956), 58; "A Few Lines Written Above Tintern Abbey," in *William Wordsworth: The Major Works*, ed. Stephen Gill (New York, NY: Oxford University Press, 2008), 131; "The Prelude," *Selected Poetry*, 583.

[24] Robert Sayre and Michael Lowy, "Figures of Romantic Anti-Capitalism," *New German Critique* 32 (Spring-Summer 1984), 42; Carlyle, *Sartor Resartus*, 130.

[25] Carlyle, *Sartor Resartus*, 99; *Past and Present* (London, England: Chapman & Hall, 1843), 2, 4, 7, 124, 166.

[26] John Ruskin, *Modern Painters*, Vol. V (London, England: Smith, Elder and Co., 1860), 202; *Modern Painters*, Vol. IV (London, England: Smith, Elder and Co., 1856), 89.

[27] Ruskin, excerpt from *The Nature of Gothic* in *Unto This Last and Other Writings*, ed. Clive Wilmer (New York, NY: Penguin, 1985), 84; *Unto This Last*, 222, 226; *The Storm-Cloud of the Nineteenth Century* (New York, NY: J. Wiley and Sons, 1884), 34, 43, 71.

[28] Quoted in T.J. Jackson Lears, *No Place of Grace: Antimodernism and the Transformation of American Culture, 1880–1920* (Chicago, IL: University of Chicago, 1981), 73. Horace Traubel quoted in Michael Robertson, *Worshipping Walt: The Whitman Disciples* (Princeton, NJ: Princeton, 2008), 264.

[29] John Muir, *The Unpublished Journals of John Muir*, ed. Lianne Wolfe (Madison, WI: University of Wisconsin Press, 1979), 138; *Muir: Nature Writings* (New York, NY: Library of America, 1997), 161; William James, *The Varieties of Religious Experience* (New York, NY: Longmans, Green, and Co., 1928 [1902]), 254–369; Vida Dutton Scudder, *Socialism and Character* (New York, NY: Houghton Mifflin Company, 1912), 147.

[30] James Agee, *Let Us Now Praise Famous Men* (Boston, MA: Houghton Mifflin Harcourt, 2001 [1941]), x, 94, 117, 121; Allen Ginsberg, *Howl and Other Poems* (San Francisco, CA: City Lights Books, 1956), 21; Kenneth Rexroth, "The Signature of All Things," in *The Collected Shorter Poems* (New York, NY: New Directions, 1967), 177; Theodore Roszak, *The Making of a Counter Culture: Reflections on the Technocratic Society and Its Youthful Opposition* (Garden City, NY: Doubleday, 1969); Theodore Roszak, *Where The Wasteland Ends: Politics and Transcendence in Postindustrial Society* (Garden City, NY: Doubleday, 1972), 277–465.

[31] Thomas Merton, "Rain and the Rhinoceros," in *Raids on the Unspeakable* (New York, NY: New Directions, 1966), 9.

[32] Ibid., 106.

[33] Pope Francis I, *Laudato si'* [Encyclical on care for our common home], sec. 1–2. http://w2.vatican.va/content/francesco/en/encyclicals/documents/papa-francesco_20150524_enciclica-laudato-si.html.

[34] Ibid., sec. 76–77.

Globalization and Religion

Peter L. Berger

G lobalization is a worldwide process, driven by economic and technological forces. It brings with it a multitude of social and political developments, some benign, others anything but benign (as recent events have made clear in a compelling way). But globalization has also had massive consequences in the area of culture, including the central cultural phenomenon of religion. It is this latter phenomenon that is the subject of this paper. Given our present situation, it is tempting to concentrate on the manner in which religion serves to legitimate the most horrendous acts of violence (and perhaps tempting to agree with those Enlightenment thinkers who saw all religion as a very bad thing). Let me suggest, however, that this would lead to a very distorted picture. Religion is above all a constituent in the ordinary lives of millions of ordinary people far removed from acts of violence. In order to get the picture right, we must cultivate a measure of detachment from the screaming headlines of the day, difficult though this is in our present circumstances.

The research center that I direct at Boston University recently completed its most ambitious project, a ten-country study of the cultural impact of globalization. In most of the countries studied, religion is an important area in which this impact is felt. It cannot be the purpose of this paper to give a summary of the study, but the picture that comes out is reasonably clear: There is indeed an emerging global culture. It has both elite and popular dimensions. It is mostly Western and especially American both in origin and content. Its *lingua franca* is English, and American English to boot. It is perceived as a great promise by some, as a great threat by others, both outside and within the West. But that is not the whole picture. The emerging global culture is not an irresistible juggernaut. It is neither uniform nor unchallenged. It is differently received in different countries, and it is modified, adapted, and synthesized with local cultural traditions in many, often startlingly innovative ways. What is more, there are cultural movements, many of them religious, that originate outside the West and that have an impact on the West. These movements constitute alternative globalizations, opening up the intriguing possibility of alternative modernities. Put simply, it is very unlikely that over time most of the world will look like Cleveland.

Social scientists and historians frequently differ in their assessment of the novelty of modern developments. The former tend to think that this or that development is an absolute novum; the latter can be relied upon to come up with a remarkably similar thing centuries ago. A correct assessment, of course, is usually somewhere in the middle. A useful parallel to contemporary globalization has been proposed by my colleague, the Chilean historian Claudio Veliz, who has described the present situation as "the Hellenistic phase of Anglo-American civilization." The Hellenistic era, like our own, was marked by a luxurious pluralism, especially in the area of religion, but also by the dominance of a Greek-derived and Greek-speaking culture. In this view, American English is the equivalent of the *koiné*, a somewhat vulgarized Greek ("basic Greek," as it were)—the language in which, not so incidentally, the New Testament was written. But there are significant differences, both in the scope and the pace of cultural penetration. I think it is safe to say that Hellenistic culture was mainly dominant in the urban centers of the Mediterranean world, in places like Alexandria or Antioch. A few miles away from these centers—say, in villages in Upper Egypt or in rural Syria—indigenous cultural life was largely unaffected. And, of course, modern means of communication have enormously accelerated the speed with which cultural influences can penetrate societies. To stay with the aforementioned metaphor, today bits and pieces of Cleveland can be found almost everywhere, and ever more so.

All of this is very pertinent as one turns one's attention to religion. For historical reasons that are not difficult to specify, the United States is in the vanguard of the contemporary "Hellenistic" pluralism. Diana Eck has called the United States the most religiously diverse society in history—a slight exaggeration, perhaps, but plausible all the same. I invite anyone who doubts this to get into a car and drive north on 16th Street in Washington, DC, from the White House toward Walter Reed Hospital. There is a religious edifice on almost every block. There are churches of every major Protestant denomination, a large Catholic church, synagogues of the various branches of American Judaism, a Greek Orthodox church and a Serbian Orthodox church, a Buddhist center, a Bahai center, and a large temple of a Vietnamese sect that I could not identify. As far as I can recall, there is no mosque, but only a short distance away is a splendid Islamic center. If America is the "vanguard society" of religious pluralism (Talcott Parsons' term is rather apt here), it is not the only place in which this phenomenon can be observed. A recent study has suggested that more people in England attend mosques every week than attend services in Anglican churches. In some English schools Sikh children outnumber Christian ones. Muslims now constitute the largest religious minority in France, out-numbering Protestants and Jews. When I visited

Buenos Aires for the first time recently, eagerly looking forward to experiencing the city celebrated in the writings of Jorge Luis Borges, the first thing I saw upon leaving the airport was a huge Mormon temple, topped by a golden statue of the Angel Moroni (who might well have found a place in one of Borges' stories).

If we are to acquire a valid picture of the global situation of religion today, one of the conventional ideas we must give up is the idea that our age is one of secularization. Put differently, we must give up the idea that modernity and a decline of religion are inexorably linked phenomena. I shared this idea in my earlier work as a sociologist of religion. Along with most people in the field, I had to give it up under the sheer pressure of empirical data. (Curiously, the idea is still held by many theologians, who regard it as an urgent task to accommodate Christianity to the alleged worldview of "modern man.") Our age is *not* an age of secularization. On the contrary, it is an age of exuberant religiosity, much of it in the form of passionate movements with global outreach.

This does not mean that secularization is not there at all. It is an important, but *limited* phenomenon. I would say that a delineation of these limits is one of the important tasks of the sociology of religion today. While I am ready to modify my view of this as new data come in, I would suggest the following picture: Most of the world today is as religious as it ever was, and in some places is more religious than ever, though there are two exceptions to this. One exception is sociological, the other geographical. The sociological exception is a cross-national cultural elite, consisting mostly of people with Western-style higher education, especially in the humanities and social sciences. Let me call this the "faculty-club culture." The geographical exception is western and central Europe. I have called this "Eurosecularity." Both behavioral and subjective data (that is, data about religious practices and about expressed religious beliefs) indicate that those European regions are exceptional. It also seems that secularization is part of the package of a common European culture, as it has spread from north to south (dramatically in Spain and Italy in the postwar years) and from west to east (in the wake of the demise of Communism). Ireland, once arguably the most Catholic country anywhere, is a fascinating case in point, as its "Europeanization" has brought with it a dramatic decline in the cultural dominance of the Catholic church. The very vortex of this European secularity may be located in eastern Germany and in the Czech Republic. Paul Zulehner, an Austrian sociologist of religion, has described these two territories as the first societies in which there has been a cultural establishment of atheism. There are a few other interesting locales, such as Australia and Quebec; perhaps they may be described as cases of "Europeanization at a distance." In any case, the comparison between Europe and America is very important in this connection: If modernity and secularization go hand in hand, how does one explain the United States? It is a vibrantly religious society, yet it is difficult to maintain that it is less modern than, say, the Netherlands. One often hears about an American "exceptionalism." This may be a useful term in many areas, but definitely not in the area of religion: it is Europe, not America, that is "exceptional" when it comes to religion.

If the equation "modernity equals secularization" does not hold up, there is another proposition that holds up much better: modernity fosters pluralism. There is no great mystery about this. It is the result of the breakdown of isolated cultural communities, as people and ideas move freely and massively across all cultural borders. Pluralism has one very important consequence: it undermines the taken-for-granted status of beliefs and values, a process that affects religion as much as any other component of culture. This does not mean (as secularization theory maintained) that people *give up* beliefs or values, but rather that these are now *chosen* rather than taken for granted. Put differently, pluralism does not necessarily change *what* people believe, but how they believe. Again, America, with its long experience of pluralism, is in the vanguard of this change. It is beautifully expressed in the very American term "religious preference." Contrast this with the traditional term "confession": "My religious preference is Catholic," versus "I am of the Catholic confession." There is a world of difference between these two terms, and the core of the difference is, precisely, choice. If one wants to dignify my proposition here with the title "pluralism theory," then its difference from secularization theory can be summarized rather neatly: What characterizes our era is not that there is too little religion, but rather that there is too much of it. This is a formidable challenge to theology and, more importantly, to the religious beliefs of ordinary people.

Arguably the two most dramatic cases of globalizing religion are Evangelical Protestantism, especially in its Pentecostal form, and renascent Islam. The two are obviously different in terms of their religious and moral contents, but they also differ significantly in their relations to the emerging ("Hellenistic") global culture. Evangelical Protestantism, I would propose, is an expression of the new global culture on the popular level. Renascent Islam is definitely not such an expression, representing at least a deliberate modification of that culture, in the form of an alternative route to global modernity, and at most a determined opposition to "Hellenism."

Pentecostalism

Evangelical Protestantism in various forms has expanded worldwide for the last half-century, but Pentecostalism probably accounts for some eighty percent, if not more, of this expansion. It is by far the most dynamic form of globalizing Protestantism. David Martin, the British sociologist who has studied this phenomenon for many years, estimates that there are at least 250 million Pentecostals in the world today, and possibly considerably more, since we know that there has been a growing Pentecostal movement in China, which is largely underground and thus difficult to enumerate. Outside the United States, where modern Pentecostalism originated about one hundred years ago, the great majority of Pentecostals are new converts. The most explosive growth has been in Latin America, where Martin estimates there are about 50 million Pentecostals. The movement has different dimensions in different Latin American countries, with Guatemala being the foremost case (for reasons that are unclear to me), with about 25% of its population now Protestant, and an even higher percentage in the capital area. These numbers, however, give an inadequate picture of the impact of Pentecostalism on what many still think of as a Catholic continent. Most Pentecostals are very active in their churches; most Catholics are not. Thus, research in Chile has shown that, although Pentecostals are still a minority of somewhere between 10% and 15%, the number of actively practicing Pentecostals is about the same as the number of *actively practicing* Catholics. No wonder that a Catholic bishop exclaimed some years ago: "What has democracy brought to Chile? Pornography, prostitution and Protestantism!" (In his mind, I suspect, the third is the worst of the three.) What is very important to understand is that this religious transformation has brought with it a cultural revolution. The new Protestants evince to an astounding degree the values that Max Weber called "the Protestant ethic," which played an important role, he claimed, in the development of "the spirit of capitalism" in Europe and North America. This has far-reaching social, economic, and even political consequences in a number of Latin American countries, notably in the emergence of an entrepreneurial and increasingly vocal Protestant middle class in several of them (Brazil is probably the most important case). I may sum this up by suggesting that Max Weber is alive and well, and living in São Paulo.

But if Latin America is the most important region for this religious explosion, it is not the only one. Pentecostalism has been rapidly spreading in sub-Saharan Africa, sometimes by itself, often in a synthesis with indigenous religious traditions, as in the so-called African Independent Churches. There has been significant growth in all overseas Chinese communities, in addition to whatever may be going on in China itself, and in the societies of the South Pacific. Pentecostalism has made inroads in eastern Europe, including Russia, where the Orthodox church, with the support of the state, is trying to repress it. Pentecostalism is also spreading in the most unlikely places, typically among marginalized people—among the Dalits (formerly known as Untouchables) in India, among the people of Nepal, and (most astounding of all) among European Gypsies. In sum, Pentecostalism is a truly globalizing movement.

I would contend that, as such, Pentecostalism has a positive relationship with the emerging global culture. It is, if you will, "vulgar Hellenism," as distinguished from elite "Hellenistic" movements such as feminism or environmentalism. It has shown remarkable adaptability to local conditions. Thus, in Latin America it uniformly uses Spanish and Portuguese, even if some of the texts used are translations from English, and almost all of its ministers are natives of the respective countries (indeed, Latin American Pentecostals are now routinely sending missionaries to Latinos in the United States). There is a lot of interaction between American Pentecostals and their coreligionists elsewhere—an emerging Pentecostal internationale, if you will. There is also the interesting phenomenon of what has been called the "Pentecostalization" of mainline Protestant churches, for example in Korea, where formerly staid Presbyterians are breaking out into glossolalia.

Historically, of course, all of this has its origins in the United States and thus represents a global outreach of a distinctly Western form of religion. I think, however, that there is a more important reason for seeing Pentecostalism as having a positive relation to the emerging global culture, namely in its psychological and moral consequences. The most important of these is an *individualized* religiosity, pitting itself against traditional hierarchies and collectivities. Pentecostalism thus has the character of a cultural dynamite, which is very reasonably feared by those who would uphold traditional culture. At least in Latin America, Pentecostalism arguably constitutes a "school for capitalism" (and thus a vehicle for social mobility in a modernizing economy), and perhaps even a "school for democracy" (here are people, most of whom have never had a voice of their own, creating and maintaining institutions of their own making). Thabo Mbeki, the president of South Africa, has been speaking of an "African Renaissance." It would be an intriguing turn of history if this renaissance were to be significantly shaped by a religion that started out in Los Angeles.

Renascent Islam

Renascent Islam has an equal dynamism, although it is somewhat less global in its scope. It is mainly located in populations that have been traditionally Muslim, such as the Islamic countries from North Africa to Southeast Asia and the Muslim diasporas in Europe and, to a lesser extent, in North America. There are some conversions, to be sure, notably among African Americans and to some extent among the peoples of sub-Saharan Africa, a region in which Islam clashes directly with the new Protestantism, but the phenomenon is mainly one among people who were already Muslim, but whose faith is being invigorated and activated by new religious movements. Unlike Pentecostalism, which mainly erupts among poor and marginalized people, renascent Islam is both a popular and an elite phenomenon. One obvious reason for this, of course, is the fact that Islam can look back on a civilizational history of immense cultural riches and intellectual sophistication, which Pentecostalism totally lacks. Thus, it is often the children of Westernized, secularized elites who take on a passionate Islamic identity, as in the Arab world, Turkey, and the former Soviet republics in Central Asia. Here, too, the religious transformation has far-reaching cultural consequences, as when the daughters of Harvard- or Oxford-educated intellectuals put on the veil to manifest Islamic modesty and the sons grow beards to symbolize Islamic manhood, typically to the great chagrin of their parents. It is accurate to say that no Muslim society between the Atlantic Ocean and the China Sea has remained untouched by this development.

It hardly needs saying these days that there are elements within renascent Islam that are fanatically opposed to everything associated with the West and with Western-tainted global culture. Such passionate anti-"Hellenism" was not invented by the current crop of homicidal terrorists. Some decades ago the Ayatollah Khomeini already inveighed against America as "the Great Satan," and there were passionately anti-Western Muslim movements at least as far back as the nineteenth century (one may recall, for instance, the Mahdist insurrection in the Sudan). It also does not need saying that this form of Islamism is enormously important politically, providing at least a partial verification of Samuel Huntington's thesis about a "clash of civilizations." It is all the more important, especially these days, to emphasize that this type of extremism does not represent the totality of renascent Islam. There are different voices, different movements in the Muslim world, even if for the moment they appear overwhelmed by the turbulence of extremism. Thus, Robert Hefner has shown in his recent work how a very different version of Islam—moderate, pacifist, open to pluralism and democracy—has developed in Indonesia. It was represented very impressively by Aburrahman Wahid and his movement, and one of the tragedies of his failed presidency is the weakening of this movement, which would have gained in influence throughout the Muslim world if Wahid had succeeded in leading Indonesia, the most populous Muslim country, into a period of prosperity and democracy.

However, even in its more moderate forms, renascent Islam represents a very real alternative to the emerging global culture. Inevitably, it posits alternative visions of social and political life, of the relation of religion and the state, and very significantly of the proper roles of women and men. It thus intends what the Israeli sociologist Shmuel Eisenstadt and the Harvard Sinologist Tu Wei-ming have called an "alternative modernity"—a modernity, that is, which will differ in important ways from the modernity represented by the Western-inspired global culture. Whatever else it may turn out to be, it will certainly not be secularized. The political developments of the near and not-so-near future will determine whether this vision will be capable of realization.

Other Western Religious Globalizers

While Pentecostalism is the most visible case of a Western-derived religious movement with a global reach, it is not the only one. In a broader sense of the term, of course, "global" has always described the reach of the Roman Catholic Church. It does so today in the context of contemporary globalization. Increasingly, the demographic profile of the Church has shifted to regions outside Europe and North America, a fact reflected very clearly in the geographical distribution of the College of Cardinals, as well as the Curia. This fact is important if one is to understand the policies of the Vatican. Positions and actions that embarrass many educated Catholics in Western countries are exactly those that are popular among masses of people in less developed countries. The global activities of the church occur on both elite and popular levels. Thus, on the elite level, there is the impressive program of Opus Dei, which has attained considerable influence in several Latin American countries and in the Philippines. On the popular level, there are movements such as the Legionnaires of Christ and Liberation and Communion, again evoking widespread interest and support.

The demographic shift away from the West also affects other Christian communities, such as the Anglican community, whose Lambeth Conferences are increasingly attended by bishops whose faces are not white and whose views differ sharply from those of progressive Anglicans in England or the United States. The Mormons, too, have been very successful in recruiting new adherents in regions far removed from Salt Lake City, particularly in the South Pacific region. Judaism, while in the main continuing a long tradition of not seeking converts among non-Jews, has its own global outreach, very noticeably in the influence in Israel and the ex-Communist countries in Europe of Orthodox movements with headquarters in the United States.

From East to West

As I have stressed before, globalization not only proceeds "from the West to the rest." There are also important movements going in the other direction, which Colin Campbell has described with the apt term "Easternization." Islam is undoubtedly the most important case of this, but there are others. Buddhism has made significant inroads in Western countries, especially in the United States. Estimates about religious groups here are unreliable, since the official census is legally prohibited from asking questions about religion, a fact that may please constitutional lawyers but is quite frustrating to scholars of American religion. The estimates of Buddhists in the United States rest somewhere around five million. The majority consists of immigrants and their children from Buddhist regions of the world, but it is estimated that there are some 800,000 converts. This includes people whose understanding of Buddhism is quite idiosyncratic, if compared with the traditional schools in Asia. It also includes people who are serious adherents of this or that school (mostly Mahayana in character). In all of these groups, there are interesting attempts to "Americanize" Buddhism, not only in the outward forms of organization, which often resemble those of Protestant denominations, but also in terms of religious and moral content (for example, with regard to reincarnation, rejected by some, and the attempt to find a Buddhist rationale for social and political engagement). The work of my colleague Stephen Prothero has been pioneering in describing the cultural adaptations and modifications of Buddhism, as well as Hinduism, in the United States. The latter tradition is less represented in this country (estimates hover around the figure of two million), but is very visible in Britain, where there is also a significant number of Sikhs. It is probably too early to tell, as it is in the case of Islam, whether distinctively Western versions of these religions will eventually emerge. Such versions will not only constitute cases of "alternative modernity," but alternative definitions of national identities that have traditionally been largely Christian. In 1955 Will Herberg published his influential book *Protestant-Catholic-Jew*, in which he argued that the range of socially accepted religions has steadily expanded from its original Protestant base to include Catholics and Jews. Since then, the range has widened. When Herberg was writing, the conventional view had become that American democracy was based on "Judaeo-Christian values." More recently there has been the so-called "Abrahamic" proposition, including Islam in a triumvirate of religions all worshipping one God and as such providing legitimacy to the American regime. Whether this proposition will survive the present crisis is uncertain. But even if it does, this does not answer the question of how to include those who adhere to the non-monotheistic traditions of southern and eastern Asia. How can one reconcile the Buddhist view that the self is an illusion with the idea of the rights of the individual? Or the Hindu valuation of caste with American egalitarianism? Add to this the enormous differences in the understandings of gender roles and sexual freedom. Mutatis mutandis, similar questions about a redefinition of national identity and political legitimacy are raised in Europe, especially in connection with Islam.

But, as Campbell points out, "Eastern" influences in the West are not circumscribed by formal adherence to non-Western religions. There is the very significant phenomenon of so-called New Age religiosity, which has been present in Western countries for a long time but which has gained a sharp ascendancy since the 1960s. It is a diffuse cultural phenomenon, rarely manifest in organizational forms, but nonetheless bringing about important changes in the lives of many people, especially in the United States. There are probably millions of Americans who regularly meditate, who try to establish a distinctly non-Western relationship to their own bodies and to nature, who believe in reincarnation, and whose political views are shaped by a Gandhian ideal of non-violence. And here, of course, there are innumerable cultural adaptations. For example, Asian meditational techniques originally designed to make contact with metaphysical realities (such as the cosmic Buddha or the Brahman) are instrumentalized to provide better mental health or even economic productivity ("yoga for stockbrokers," say). For another example, while reincarnation has been perceived as an endless horror to be escaped from in the religious imagination of India (the origins of Buddhism and Upanishadic Hinduism are incomprehensible apart from this perception), reincarnation now makes an American reappearance as yet another opportunity for a second chance. We don't have a clear picture as yet of the degree to which New Age ideas and practices have advanced in Western cultures, but where they have advanced there have been significant "Easternizing" changes in these cultures.

Challenges to the West

It seems to me that the developments I have described present Western societies with two challenges, one civic and the other religious. In principle, both challenges have considerable positive potential. I have already touched on the civic challenge, which is a challenge to the definition of national identity. What does it mean to be a German with dark skin, who kneels to pray in the direction of Mecca five times a day? What is a Sikh Irishman? Let me put this in American terms by taking an example recently used by Stephen Prothero: Imagine that you are a civics teacher at a high school in Honolulu. The majority of your students are of Asian ethnic backgrounds, many of them non-Christians. Do you still say that American society is based on Judaeo-Christian values? If so, how do you explain this to these kids? If not, what do you say? Will you include non-Christian, non-Jewish religious values as having something to do with the moral foundation of American society, and how will you do this? Or will you have to fall back on a purely secular view of how American society is to be morally legitimated? The example of a high-school civics class is useful, because it underlines the fact that these are not just academic questions, to be dealt with in academic colloquia, but are questions relevant to the ordinary lives of ordinary people. I believe that the future character of Western democracies will at least partially be shaped by the answers given to these questions, in Europe as much as in America.

The religious challenge is to the self-understanding of Christian and Jewish religious communities. It is, *au fond*, the great challenge of pluralism, which, as I have suggested earlier, is more important than the challenge of secularization. The Jewish response is complicated by the nature of Judaism as both a religious and an ethnic identity, and in this respect at least, the Jewish confrontation with pluralism resembles that of Eastern Christian Orthodoxy, (an issue that I cannot address here). For the churches of the Christian West, Protestant as well as Catholic, something like a paradigm shift will have to take place in the way they understand their contemporary situation. For nearly two hundred years that situation has been interpreted as existence in an age of secularity with which the churches have had to come to terms both theologically and in practice. An empirically more plausible paradigm puts pluralism at the core of the situation in which the churches find themselves. There is now a growing body of Protestant and Catholic thinkers who have understood this, and it has motivated the growing dialogue with non-Christian religions. Needless to say, different theological positions have emerged in this development, and very interesting insights have come out of this widening dialogue.

The challenge of religious pluralism is not just a concern to be addressed by academic theologians; it is very much a concern of lay people, and not least of their children, as they rub elbows in school and elsewhere with children of other religious traditions. As with the civic challenge, this religious challenge, too, should be seen in positive terms. It provides a fertile occasion for a re-examination of the grounds of faith and of the identity of believers and their communities, and very importantly for an assessment of what is central to their faith and what is not. Put differently, this concerns what might be "surrendered" in the dialogue with other faiths and what must be held onto, even if one has to say "no" to the interlocutors from other traditions. In the historical development of Christianity, for example, there have been a number of defining confrontations: at its very beginnings with official Judaism; then with the culture and thought of the Graeco-Roman world; in the Middle Ages, with the then superior civilization of Islam; and most recently, with modernity. Today the confrontation with the great religions of southern and eastern Asia will be an equally important occasion for a renewed understanding of both the Christian and Jewish faiths.

(Summer 2002, 4.2)

The Witness of Literature
A Genealogical Sketch

Alan Jacobs

My story is important not because it is mine, God knows, but because if I tell it anything like right, the chances are you will recognize that in many ways it is also yours. Maybe nothing is more important than that we keep track, you and I, of these stories of who we are and where we have come from and the people we have met along the way because it is precisely through these stories in all their particularity, as I have long believed and often said, that God makes Himself known to each of us most powerfully and personally. If this is true, it means that to lose track of our stories is to be profoundly impoverished not only humanly but also spiritually.

—Frederick Buechner[1]

Long ago at Calvin College's Festival of Faith and Writing—an enormous biennial gathering of writers, would-be writers, and passionate readers, most but not all of them Christians—I had a curious and memorable experience. The featured speaker that year was Frederick Buechner, a novelist and memoirist whose general fame was greatest at the beginning of his career, in the 1950s, and who, since then, had produced a series of well-reviewed but not especially popular books. His 1981 novel *Godric* was a finalist for the Pulitzer Prize in fiction; this is as close as he has come to winning a major literary award. Yet among those attending the Festival of Faith and Writing, Frederick Buechner was simply a rock star.

My wife and I had known Buechner for many years, and we arranged to meet him for coffee and a talk, before having dinner later in a larger group. But this private meeting proved difficult to arrange. So many people wanted to see him, to thank him, to get him to sign their often-re-read copies of his books—it was more than Buechner, or anyone else, could handle, and he had to be kept out of sight. So we were ushered in cloak-and-dagger fashion to a small, out-of-the-way room where the author was ensconced, so we could recall old times and catch up a bit.

An awkward situation ensued. The kind and efficient people running the festival clearly expected us to have five minutes with the great man and then depart; Buechner equally clearly expected to spend some time chatting. So when another visitor came in and we rose to leave, Buechner insisted that we sit back down. As it turned out, then, we spent most of the afternoon there, having our conversation regularly interrupted by new visitors. Some of these were other festival speakers—for instance, Alfred Corn, the distinguished poet and critic, dropped by, and he and Buechner compared notes for a few moments on shared friends and acquaintances in New York—but most were simply lovers of Buechner's work who had managed through some means unknown to us to gain brief admission to his presence. And almost all of them told the same story: *Your writing has meant everything to my Christian faith. I don't think I could be a Christian without your books.*

Throughout that afternoon—rising to greet strangers, then sitting down and striving to remain inconspicuous as they poured out their hearts—I couldn't help reflecting on the sheer oddity of the situation. These were people, by and large, who knew the Bible, who attended church, who had the benefits of Christian community. Yet they testified, almost to a person, that Christian belief would have been impossible for them without the mediation of the stories told by Frederick Buechner. I know literary history fairly well, especially where it intersects with Christian thought and practice, and it seemed to me that such radical dependence on literary experience would have been virtually impossible even a century earlier. But I also knew that Buechner's role was anything but unique, that other readers would offer the same testimony to the fiction of Walker Percy or Flannery O'Connor or C.S. Lewis.

How did such a state of affairs come about? How did literary writers come to be seen by many as the best custodians and advocates of Christian faith? It is a question with a curious and convoluted genealogy, one worth teasing out.

* * *

HUMANITIES: grammar, rhetoric, and poetry…for teaching of which, there are professors in the universities of Scotland, called humanists.

—*Encyclopaedia Britannica* (1768)

303

Cicero, in his *Pro Archia*, refers to the *studia humanitatis ac litteratum*: humane and literary studies. This phrase caught the eye of some early Renaissance scholars, especially the Tuscan Coluccio Salutati, correspondent of Petrarch, and his student Leonardo Bruni; it encapsulated their understanding of what education at its highest level should be. In the Italian universities of the fifteenth century, one who advocated this model and taught according to it was known as an *umanista*—an inevitable coinage, since a teacher of jurisprudence had long been known as a *jurista*, a teacher of canon law a *canonista*, and so on. So the term *humanist*, from which *humanism* in turn derives, was originally the product of student slang.

As Paul Oskar Kristeller explained long ago in what remains a useful treatment of the history, in the early modern period and especially in Italy, "the *studia humanitatis* came to stand for a clearly defined cycle of scholarly disciplines, namely grammar, rhetoric, history, poetry, and moral philosophy," pursued primarily by reading the greatest Latin writers, though eventually, in a secondary way, the major Greek figures were also included. Other philosophical subdisciplines that had their own professors, such as logic and metaphysics, played no part in the humanists' project. The *studia humanitatis* therefore were "concerned…neither with the classics [as such] nor with philosophy [as such]"; their focus "might roughly be described as literature. It was to this peculiar literary preoccupation that the very intensive and extensive study which the humanists devoted to the Greek and especially to the Latin classics owed its peculiar character, which differentiates it from that of modern classical scholars since the second half of the eighteenth century."[2]

Kristeller's use of "peculiar" twice in that last-quoted sentence is a stylistic infelicity, but a telling one. The *umanistas* were doing something unprecedented in keying the search for wisdom—including, as we shall see, specifically Christian wisdom—to the study of literature. This was, to put the point mildly, not in keeping with the dialectical approach of the medieval scholastic tradition, which they scorned. How this literary approach to the moral and social education of young men emerged is not, I think, perfectly understood, but some of the groundwork for it may have been laid by Boccaccio, writing in his *Life of Dante* in 1374. In the passage that follows, Boccaccio uses the term "theology" to mean "Holy Scripture":

> The subject of sacred poetry is divine truth, while that of the ancient poets is men and the gods of the pagans. They are opposite in so far as theology proposes nothing that is not true; poetry supposes certain things as true which are most false and erroneous and contrary to the Christian religion.… I say that theology and poetry may be said to be almost one thing when the subject is the same; and I say further that theology is nothing else than the poetry of God.… The sense of our *Comedy*…whether you call it moral or theological…is, at whatever part of the work most pleases you, the simple and immutable truth, which not only cannot receive corruption,

but, the more it is searched, the greater odor of incorruptible sweetness it emits to those who regard it.[3]

It is hard to imagine a scholastic dialectician not being utterly scandalized by Boccaccio's claim that "theology is nothing else than the poetry of God": Literature, and not philosophical theology, becomes the foundational genre of God's revelation. And of course poetry demands to be read as poetry, not as philosophy. So if Boccaccio is right, then a wholly different intellectual toolbox from that provided by Scholasticism is required for the one who seeks Holy Wisdom.

If I am right in thinking that the *Life of Dante* was a key text in the emergence of literary humanism, it is noteworthy that Boccaccio makes his case for the wisdom-giving power of poetry through a recent text written in the Italian vernacular—after all, this is not the direction the *umanistas* would take. But soon after he wrote about Dante, Boccaccio worked on a far larger and more ambitious project, the *Genealogia deorum gentilium*, or *Genealogy of the Pagan Gods*, in which he showed that the then-standard model of biblical exegesis—with its identification of four distinct levels of meaning, the literal, moral, allegorical, and anagogical—could usefully be applied by the Christian interpreter to pagan myths. So, for example, the story of how Perseus killed the Gorgon Medusa and then flew away on winged sandals becomes, on the moral level, "a wise man's triumph over vice and his attainment of virtue"; on the allegorical level, "the pious man who scorns worldly delight and lifts his mind to heavenly things"; on the anagogical level, "Christ's victory over the Prince of this world and his Ascension."[4]

Boccaccio thus shows in his *Life of Dante* how a great Christian writer can use poetry to convey to us "the simple and immutable truth," and in his *Genealogy of the Pagan Gods* how shrewd Christian readers can use interpretative methods originally developed for the study of the Bible to liberate the wisdom hidden in pagan texts. It is a strategy encompassing the Christian and the non-Christian, the writerly and the readerly.

Boccaccio died in 1375; twenty years later, another important development in this story was marked by the election of thirty-two-year-old Jean Gerson as chancellor of the University of Paris. In a superb work of scholarship on Gerson and—in the words of the book's subtitle—"the transformation of late medieval learning," Daniel Hobbins shows how the French academic gradually distanced himself from scholastic dialectical procedure and sketched out a new direction for Christian intellectual writing. Gerson was himself formed by scholastic education, and warmly commended its emphasis on sound logic: "We can never speak truly and properly without correct use of logic." But he also came to believe that the ways the scholastics deployed their logic had become stultifyingly rigid, and he constantly sought alternative means of organizing and presenting ideas. Some of Gerson's devices, Hobbins acknowledges, "may seem puzzling or contrived to modern tastes, but they are evidence of a creative mind at work striving for new forms of presentation." It is noteworthy that in the many dialogues Gerson composed for varying contexts, including even sermons, an especially prominent character is *Studiositas speculatrix* (Earnest Investigator), whose questions seem never to end. How to satisfy this relentless inquirer—this is a problem Gerson thought the traditional scholastic models failed to solve.[5]

Gerson was especially frustrated by the scholastic habit of addressing a disputed question merely by piling up citations to authorities, a habit already mocked by his older contemporary Geoffrey Chaucer in *The Canterbury Tales*—for instance, in the "Nun's Priest's Tale," where Chaunticleer the rooster uses a barrage of references to out-argue his consort, Pertelote: "Oon of the gretteste auctours that men rede/Seith thus…. And certes, in the same book I rede/Right in the nexte chapitre after this…. Lo, in the lyf of Seint Kenelm I rede…. And forther-moore I pray yow looketh wel/In the olde testament of Daniel." It is far too easy, Gerson came to believe, for the point of the discourse to be lost in the apparatus. Hobbins again: "Abandoning unnecessary citations and 'coming to the point and the heart of the matter as it seems to me,' as he says in a French sermon—this direct and personal approach is perhaps the most distinctive trait of Gerson's style."[6]

For Gerson, the problem was that the scholastics had paid but lip service to rhetoric as one of the foundational disciplines of the *artes liberales*: "We write, but we give no weight to our sentences, no number and measure to our words. Everything we write is flaccid, coarse, and sluggish. We write not new things but old, and when we try to pass them off as our own by recycling them, we deform them and render them absurd."[7]

It might appear that Gerson is merely another of the *umanistas* discussed earlier, with whom he was roughly contemporary, but he differs from them in certain significant ways. First of all, he retains far more respect for dialectical method and logic than they did, which is precisely why he soon became a marginal figure and was almost forgotten after his death: For the *umanistas* he was too scholastic, for the schoolmen too humanistic. He tried to be a mediating figure in a time of intellectual war. But second, and more important for my purposes here, Gerson's approach to rhetoric is not driven by a reverence for the unique greatness of classical authors, but rather by a desire to reach and move his audiences, whether in pastoral or academic contexts. Rhetoric for him is not a matter of conformity to incontrovertible Ciceronian norms, but rather the concern to find words that will stir people's hearts as well as their minds. Hobbins notes Gerson's great reverence for the Italian theologian and philosopher Bonaventure, who a century earlier had written in his *Collationes in Hexaemeron* (*Talks on the Six Days of Creation*) that "not through hearing alone but through heeding [*observando*] is one made wise."[8]

If we combine Boccaccio's insistence on the theological power of poetry with Gerson's desire to find a rhetoric that will move hearers and readers toward godly obedience, we end up with something like the argument Sir Philip Sidney makes in one of the great documents of the English Renaissance, *An Apologie for Poetrie* (c.1579)—which nevertheless is to be distinguished from those predecessors in important ways as well. At a crucial stage of his argument, Sidney places his apologia within a general account of the purposes of education:

> This purifying of wit, this enriching of memory, enabling of judgment, and enlarging of conceit, which commonly we call learning, under what name soever it come forth, or to what immediate end soever it be directed, the final end is, to lead and draw us to as high a perfection, as our degenerate souls made worse by their clayey lodgings, can be capable of.

What studies can bring about the "perfection" of which Sidney writes, can help our souls acquire "true virtue"? Sidney answers that though "some…thought this felicity principally to be gotten by knowledge," they disputed *which* knowledge was the most valuable: astronomy, natural philosophy, metaphysics, or music. Sidney rejects all of these as "but serving sciences," only truly useful if they "serve" the greater end, "the mistress knowledge, by the Greeks called *architektonike*, which stands, as I think, in the knowledge of a man's self, in the ethic and politic consideration, with the end of well-doing, and not of well-knowing only." In the art of *moving* men to "well-doing," "the poet is worthy to have it before any other competitors."

Here is a strong commendation, but again, although Sidney's identification of literature's power to move its audience to "virtuous action" echoes some of the beliefs of Boccaccio and Gerson, surely both of them would have found his formulation woefully lacking in theological specificity. And so as Renaissance humanism comes into its pedagogical and literary maturity, it simultaneously sheds its distinctively Christian character; it seeks a language that transcends—or, some might say, evades—theological detail. Surely this was a natural enough response to a century that had seen the rise of violent religious controversy that would not subside for many more decades.

This process of moving beyond—or away from—theology was not smooth and unruffled. Almost a century after Sidney, John Milton would strive for a more distinctively Christian account of what education should do: "The end then of Learning is to repair the ruins of our first Parents by regaining to know God aright, and out of that knowledge to love him, to imitate him, to be like him, as we may the nearest by possessing our souls of true virtue, which being united to the heavenly grace of faith makes up the highest perfection" (*Of Education*, 1644). It seems likely that Milton's definition is meant to extend and correct Sidney's: While Sidney speaks of "degenerate souls" in "clayey lodgings"—a formulation more Platonic than Christian—Milton identifies our problem in the specific terms of the biblical narrative, according to which Adam and Eve brought "ruin" into the world through disobedience. Sidney's model of education is ethical and in a certain sense spiritual, but there is nothing specifically Christian about it, and it may even run counter to Christian orthodoxy, even though Sidney himself was an earnest Christian.

So in the transition from Boccaccio to Gerson to Sidney, we see an intellectually powerful, literarily sophisticated Christian humanism arise, only to clip its own wings lest it contribute to a continent's discord. Milton's rearguard action, in his verse as well as his prose—*Paradise Lost* would form the last great monument of early modern Christian humanism—had little chance of achieving great influence. *Paradise Lost* is as theologically and biblically specific a poem as one can imagine, but its great fame in the two centuries following its publication in 1667 was perpetuated by many a poet who either ignored Milton's theology or, as William Blake famously did—"Milton was of the Devil's party without knowing it"—set it at odds with the poem.

* * *

There in the desert I lay dead,
And God called out to me and said:
"Rise, prophet, rise, and hear, and see,
And let my works be seen and heard
By all who turn aside from me,
And burn them with my fiery word."

—Alexander Pushkin, "The Prophet" (translation by D.M. Thomas)[9]

It would seem, then, that the story of Christian humanism was effectively over, especially given the general decline of orthodox (or even unorthodox) Christian belief among the learned in the eighteenth and nineteenth centuries. But with the advent of Romanticism, matters took an interesting turn, not because the Romantics were (by and large) either Christian or humanist in the senses in which I have been using those terms, but because they provided, whether they meant to or not, a new way in which a reconstituted humanism, simultaneously Christian and literary, could reform itself.

The "way" I speak of here is a literary one, but it is not the only such point of reentry. A distinctively philosophical Christian humanism also arises in the nineteenth century, largely at the instigation of Pope Leo XIII in his 1879 encyclical *Aeterni Patris*, which led to the enthronement of Thomas Aquinas as a model of Christian thought and the subsequent claim, made by many Catholic thinkers, most notably Jacques Maritain, that Christianity is the only genuine humanism. That new philosophical humanism overlaps with the literary one to some degree—certainly Maritain tries to draw them together, as does Flannery O'Connor in her frequent references to Aquinas in her correspondence—but, practically speaking, they develop as largely separate trends.

The renewal of a literary Christian humanism is illustrated by a highly representative Victorian book, *The Autobiography of Mark Rutherford* (1882). Recounting an episode from his university days, the author writes,

But one day in my third year, a day I remember as well as Paul must have remembered afterwards the day on which he went to Damascus, I happened to find amongst a parcel of books a volume of poems in paper boards. It was called *Lyrical Ballads*, and I read first one and then the whole book. It conveyed to me no new doctrine, and yet the change it wrought in me could only be compared with that which is said to have been wrought on Paul himself by the Divine apparition.

"Mark Rutherford" is the pseudonym of William Hale White, an English civil servant who had been raised in a Nonconformist home and studied to become a Congregationalist minister, but abandoned that plan when he lost his faith. It was William Wordsworth who restored that faith—or gave him a new one: White's rhetoric is richly ambiguous on this point, as we can see by continuing to read from the same passage:

God is nowhere formally deposed, and Wordsworth would have been the last man to say that he had lost his faith in the God of his fathers. But his real God is not the God of the Church, but the God of the hills, the abstraction Nature, and to this my reverence was transferred. Instead of an object of worship which was altogether artificial, remote, never coming into genuine contact with me, I had now one which I thought to be real, one in which literally I could live and move and have my being, an actual fact present before my eyes. God was brought from that heaven of the books, and dwelt on the downs in the far-away distances, and in every cloud-shadow which wandered across the valley. Wordsworth unconsciously did for me what every religious reformer has done—he re-created my Supreme Divinity; substituting a new and living spirit for the old deity, once alive, but gradually hardened into an idol.

On the one hand, White wants to say that Wordsworth gave him "no new doctrine"; on the other hand, he claims to have had a dramatic road-to-Damascus conversion from "the God of the Church" to "the God of the hills." The God of the Church had become an idol; now, thanks to the poetry of Wordsworth, White has a living God to whom he can give true worship. This is a step significantly greater than the one White's older contemporary John Stuart Mill took when he supplemented the dry rationalism of his Utilitarian upbringing with the reading of Wordsworth's poems: That had merely been, as Mill put it in his *Autobiography* (1873), "a medicine for my state of mind" insofar as those poems "expressed, not mere outward beauty, but states of feeling, and of thought coloured by feeling, under the excitement of beauty. They seemed to be the very culture of the feelings, which I was in quest of." Mill takes pains to insist that this encounter with Wordsworth did not change in any fundamental way his commitments or practices: "I never turned recreant to intellectual culture, or ceased to consider the power and practice of analysis as an essential condition both of individual and of social improvement. But I thought that it had consequences which required to be corrected, by joining other kinds of cultivation with it. The maintenance of a due balance among the faculties now seemed to be of primary importance."[10] White, by contrast, was given not just a renewed "culture of the feelings," but a divinity whom he could truly worship.

It is noteworthy that White's mediator is Wordsworth, because Wordsworth's friend and sometime collaborator Samuel Taylor Coleridge had also articulated, in his *Biographia Literaria*, a theological defense of poetry—but had done so in a more emphatically orthodox manner, in implicit and sometimes explicit dissent from Wordsworthian devotion. When Coleridge writes, "The primary IMAGINATION I hold to be the living Power and prime Agent of all human Perception, and as a repetition in the finite mind of the eternal act of creation in the infinite I AM," he is drawing a very clear line between poetic making and the *biblical* God—the one who says to Moses, "I AM THAT I AM"—not "the God of the hills."[11] Coleridge's linkage of poetry and divinity was often accepted in his time and after, but his orthodoxy was generally deemed optional or undesirable.

In light of this history, we might compare White's self-accounting to one made some years later by William Butler Yeats, who wrote, "I am very religious, and deprived by Huxley and Tyndall, whom I detested, of the simple-minded religion of my childhood, I had made a new religion, almost an infallible church, out of poetic tradition: a fardel of stories, and of personages, and of emotions, a bundle of images and of masks passed on from generation to generation by poets and painters with some help from philosophers and theologians." The dogma of this church Yeats states in these terms: "Because those imaginary people are created out of the deepest instinct of man, to be his measure and his norm, whatever I can imagine those mouths speaking may be the nearest I can go to truth."[12]

Thomas Henry Huxley and John Tyndall are often referred to as atheists, inaccurately: Huxley coined the term "agnostic" to describe his position, and Tyndall never specified his religious views. But both of them insisted that the claims of religion had to be subordinated to those of science—that only science was productive of knowledge, although religious faith could be a strong support of morals. In any event, to the arguments of Huxley and Tyndall against traditional religion, Yeats had no answer—just as William Hale White had no answer to the doubts that assailed him—until literature and the other arts came to the rescue. But what they rescued was something very different from Trinitarian Christianity, or any such "simple-minded religion" that a poet might associate with childhood.

We have come a long way here from Boccaccio and Gerson and even Sidney, and yet there are genuine continuities to be noted and accounted for. In the aftermath of Romanticism, with its cult of intuition and imagination as reliable pathways to truth, and its skepticism about the desiccating effects of reason as defined by the chief figures of the Enlightenment, we hear an echo of the humanist reinstatement of rhetoric, first as supplemental to and then as superior to dialectic. Only now, it is the aesthetic that complements (in Mill) and then transcends (in White and Yeats) the narrowly rational. The access to religious truth that philosophy and science seal off is re-enabled by aesthetic, and especially literary, experience.

This development seems to happen throughout Europe in the latter half of the nineteenth century. It is responsible for the founding of Browning Societies even during Robert Browning's lifetime, based largely on the belief that the true religious spirit might be breathed in, with unique ease and comfort, through poetry. In a typical passage from the early papers of the London Browning Society, an admirer wrote, "I must claim for Browning the distinction of being pre-eminently the greatest Christian poet we have ever had. Not in a narrow dogmatic sense, but as the teacher who is as thrilled-through with all Christian sympathies as with artistic or musical."[13] It is striking how strongly this assertion resembles the claims made in Russia for the novels of Fyodor Dostoevsky—claims that Dostoevsky himself endorsed by linking himself with Pushkin's poem "The Prophet"—even though the history of Christianity and Christian thought in Russia is so dramatically different from its English counterpart. Thus, Vladimir Solovyev, in a eulogy delivered just after Dostoevsky's death in 1881, wrote that "just as the highest worldly power somehow or other becomes concentrated in one person, who represents a state, similarly the highest spiritual power in each epoch usually belongs in every people to one man, who more clearly than all grasps the spiritual ideals of mankind, more consciously than all strives to attain them, more strongly than all affects others by his preachments. Such a spiritual leader of the Russian people in recent times was Dostoevsky."[14] The Victorian era was one dominated by sages of all kinds, but this is an especially peculiar one: the poet as prophet, as comforter, as vehicle of the sacred.

* * *

No eye his future can foretell
No law his past explain
Whom neither Passion may compel
Nor Reason can restrain.

—W.H. Auden, libretto to *The Rake's Progress*

For Victorian intellectuals, the versions of the Christian faith that could not be taken seriously were those of the previous generation: The faith of one's parents, whether biological, intellectual, or aesthetic, will inevitably seem "simple-minded." But children eventually become parents. The early-nineteenth-century Russian liberals whom Peter the Great had done so much to create, who looked back with scorn on traditional Orthodoxy, themselves came to seem absurdly naive to Dostoevsky, who satirized them mercilessly, especially in the character of Peter Verkhovensky in *Demons* (also known as *The Possessed*). Something similar came to befall the English Victorian advocates of an enlightened religion, or no religion at all.

Consider, for example, a story related by C.S. Lewis, who lost his faith in early adolescence and then went on to be tutored for some years by "a 'Rationalist' of the old, high and dry nineteenth-century type," a man named Kirkpatrick. "At the time when I knew him, Kirk's Atheism was chiefly of the anthropological and pessimistic kind. He was great on *The Golden Bough* and Schopenhauer."[15] But while Lewis was studying with Kirkpatrick, something happened: He started reading the fiction of George MacDonald, who, though a Victorian and not by every standard orthodox in his theology, was nevertheless the kind of person Lewis called "a thoroughgoing supernaturalist." Lewis's account of this experience is extremely telling:

> What *Phantastes* [MacDonald's 1858 novel] actually did to me was to convert, even to baptize…my imagination. It did nothing to my intellect nor (at that time) to my conscience. Their turn came far later and with the help of many other books and men. But when the process was complete—by which, of course, I mean "when it had really begun"—I found that I was still with MacDonald and that he had accompanied me all the way and that I was now at last ready to hear from him much that he could not have told me at that first meeting. But in a sense, what he was now telling me was the very same that he had told me from the beginning.[16]

We might usefully compare this with Lewis's recollection of encountering, a few years later, the essays of G.K. Chesterton: "I had never heard of him and had no idea of what he stood for; nor can I quite understand why he made such an immediate conquest of me," since, Lewis wrote, "my pessimism, my atheism, and my hatred of sentiment [should] have made him to me the least congenial of all authors." But without agreeing with Chesterton ("I did not need to accept what Chesterton said in order to enjoy it"), the young Lewis was "charmed" by him. He concludes this account by commenting, "In reading Chesterton, as in reading MacDonald, I did not know what I was letting myself in for."[17]

To grasp the import of this statement, one must take it literally: Lewis *did not know* what he was letting himself in for. What he had acquired was not knowledge of or even mere knowledge *about* Christian belief and practice, but, rather, a disposition to openness, a willingness to be charmed. This is why he says that reading MacDonald *baptized* his imagination: Baptism is the Christian rite of initiation, the beginning of new life in Christ, and, in Lewis's Anglican tradition, something that typically happens to infants. Through

MacDonald, he had been initiated into habits of aesthetic experience that would later make him receptive to Chesterton for reasons he could not then have stated: Only later ("when it had really begun") would come the knowledge that enabled him to give an account of what had happened to him when he read those books.

A quarter-century after Lewis underwent his imaginative baptism, a Frenchwoman of Jewish parentage but no religious upbringing would have an experience that bears notable structural similarities to his, but through an encounter with a seventeenth-century poet rather than a Victorian writer of fantasy. In 1942, Simone Weil wrote to the priest who had become her informal counselor—informal because she refused to be received into the Catholic Church—that in 1938 she had spent Passion Week at the monastery of Solesmes, where she attended services every day. There, she met a young Englishman whose face seemed to register some extraordinary experience when he received Communion, and who "told me of the existence of those English poets of the seventeenth century who are named metaphysical." George Herbert's "Love III"—a kind of allegory of the Lord's Table—struck her with particular force, and she memorized the poem. Weil told her counselor, Father Perrin, that "often, at the culminating point of a violent headache, I make myself say it over, concentrating all my attention upon it and clinging with all my soul to the tenderness it enshrines." But she did not know what she was letting herself in for by reciting such a poem. "I used to think I was merely reciting it as a beautiful poem, but without my knowing it the recitation had the virtue of a prayer. It was during one of these recitations that, as I told you, Christ himself came down and took possession of me."[18]

Here again, the imaginative or aesthetic experience precedes and paves the way for intellectual understanding. The way of reason is not rejected—indeed, the opposite is true—but the reason has to be released from its bondage in order to function properly. To borrow language from the philosopher Charles Taylor in *A Secular Age* (2007), the buffered self must become in some respect porous, and the most vulnerable buffer is the one that protects the imagination.

To use the language of "imagination" is to employ a post-Romantic concept, one that Boccaccio or Gerson or Sidney would have found baffling. (In early modern translations of the Bible, the word "imagination" is, without exception, used in a highly pejorative way: "Yet they obeyed not, nor inclined their ear, but walked every one in the imagination of their evil heart," from Jeremiah 11:8, is typical.) The twentieth-century British thinker Owen Barfield best understood the recuperation and elevation of the term: Its rise marks "the transition from a view of art which beholds it as the product of a mind, or spirit, not possessed by the individual, but rather possessing him; to a view of it as the product of something in a manner possessed by the individual though still not identical with his everyday personality."[19] My imagination, then, is not identical with my conscious mind—it works in some sense on its own, independent of my volition—but it does not come from without, it does not and cannot *possess* or (in older senses of the term) *inspire*. But it is precisely because imagination does not present itself as transcendent, and therefore does not put up the buffers, raise the shields, that it can become a *vehicle* of the transcendent. It constructs a back door to God.

I should note that imagination creates this door for readers more than for writers, at least in some cases. Writers may indeed dissent from the model of reception I have described. Flannery O'Connor, a lifelong Catholic rather than a convert or returnee like Weil, Lewis, and Coleridge, placed dogmatic belief front and center in her own thinking: "Your beliefs will be the light by which you see, but they will not be what you see and they will not be a substitute for seeing"[20]—a point of view rather different from the one that makes imagination the light by which dogma is seen, and recognized as desirable. But the key point for the reader is not *how* the writer sees but *that* the writer sees. All those who are led to and strengthened in religious faith by writers must believe that writers have, at the very least, superior powers of perception enabled by superior imagination. Percy Shelley's claim that "poets are the hierophants of an unapprehended inspiration" merely states in extravagant terms what all believers in the salvific witness of literature must affirm.

For this reason, it is typically sufficient that the writer *reveal* the conditions against which he or she dare not and need not *preach*. O'Connor again: "We are now living in an age which doubts both fact and value. It is the life of this age that we wish to see and judge."[21] Likewise, Walker Percy, a physician by training, found commonality between the doctor and the writer in the act of diagnosis: "To the degree that a society has been overtaken by a sense of malaise rather than exuberance, by fragmentation rather than wholeness, the vocation of the artist, whether novelist, poet, playwright, filmmaker, can perhaps be said to come that much closer to that of the diagnostician rather than the artist's celebration of life in a triumphant age."[22] The diagnostic novelist or poet—Auden comes to mind as a poet with this kind of forensic and etiological temperament—certainly "judges," but judges by portrayal and implication. And this is certainly for the best, if one would avoid triggering the powerful buffers and shields of modernity.

"Tell the truth but tell it slant," Emily Dickinson famously counseled, and throughout the long and meandering history of Christian humanism we see an increasingly strong preference, among a certain kind of reader, for the slanted truth. A defense of the powers of poetry (what we would call "literature") to carry Christian truth faithfully and vividly—a defense that arose in a period when dialectical method dominated European universities—underwent a series of transformations that seemed, at one point, to culminate in the victory of a Wordsworthian "God of the hills," a deity composed wholly of affect. At the end of the Victorian era, few could have imagined that in the next century literature would become, for many readers, not just the preferred but the only vehicle for conveying and commending a strongly traditional form of Christianity. But that is precisely what occurred. When institutional Christianity came increasingly to be despised, when preaching acquired a largely negative connotation, stories and poems took both their places. Perhaps no one from

Boccaccio to William Hale White would have known quite what to make of this. I confess that I myself do not know quite what to make of it, especially since I do not see any obvious heirs to Buechner—who himself is both less orthodox and far less popular than Lewis, O'Connor, or Percy. Perhaps the kind of thing I witnessed that day at Calvin College—*Your writing has meant everything to my Christian faith. I don't think I could be a Christian without your books*—will prove to have been merely a local and temporary phenomenon, a curious sideshow in twentieth-century Western Christianity. I hope not.

(Summer 2015, 17.2)

Notes

1   Frederick Buechner, *Telling Secrets* (San Francisco, CA: HarperSanFrancisco, 1991), 30.

2   Paul Oscar Kristeller, *Renaissance Thought: The Classic, Scholastic, and Humanist Strains* (New York, NY: Harper, 1961), Chapter 1.

3   Boccaccio, *Life of Dante*, trans. G.R. Carpenter (New York, NY: Grolier Club, 1900), 142.

4   *Boccaccio on Poetry: Being the Preface and the Fourteenth and Fifteenth Books of Boccaccio's Genealogia Deorum Gentilium*, trans. and ed. Charles G. Osgood (Indianapolis, IN: Library of Liberal Arts, 1956).

5   Daniel Hobbins, *Authorship and Publicity before Print: Jean Gerson and the Transformation of Late Medieval Learning* (Philadelphia, PA: University of Pennsylvania Press, 2009), 106.

6   Ibid., 109.

7   Ibid., 120.

8   Ibid., 120.

9   Cited as the epigraph to Joseph Frank, *Dostoevsky: The Mantle of the Prophet, 1871–1881* (Princeton, NJ: Princeton University Press, 2003).

10 John Stuart Mill, *Autobiography* (1873), Chapter V; http://www.gutenberg.org/cache/epub/10378/pg10378.html. Accessed March 23, 2015.

11 Samuel Taylor Coleridge, *Biographia Literaria*, ed. James Enell and W. Jackson Bate (Princeton, NJ: Princeton University Press, 1983), ch. 13.

12 *The Collected Works of W.B. Yeats Vol. III: Autobiographies*, ed. William H. O'Donnell and Douglas N. Archibald (New York, NY: Simon and Schuster, 2010).

13 *The Browning Society's Papers, Parts 1–3* (London, England: Browning Society, 1881); http://books.google.com/books?id=sWc4AAAAYAAJ. Accessed March 23, 2015.

14 Quoted in Joseph Frank, *Dostoevsky: The Mantle of the Prophet*, 756.

15 C.S. Lewis, *Surprised by Joy: The Shape of My Early Life* (New York, NY: Houghton Mifflin Harcourt, 1955), 139.

16 C.S. Lewis, Preface to *George MacDonald: An Anthology* (San Francisco, CA: HarperSanFrancisco, 2001). Originally published 1946, xxxviii.

17 Lewis, *Surprised by Joy*, 191.

18 Simone Weil, "Spiritual Autobiography," in *Waiting for God*, trans. Emma Craufurd (New York, NY: Harper Perennial, 2001), 27. Originally published 1951.

[19] Owen Barfield, *Speaker's Meaning* (Middletown, CT: Weslayan University Press, 1967); https://www.google.com/search?sourceid=navclient&ie=UTF-8&rlz=1T4MXGB_enUS524US554&q=Owen+Barfield+.

[20] Flannery O'Connor, *Mystery and Manners: Occasional Prose* (New York, NY: Macmillan, 1969), 91.

[21] Ibid., 117.

[22] Walker Percy, "Diagnosing the Modern Malaise," *Signposts in a Strange Land: Essays* (New York, NY: Macmillan, 2000), 206. Originally published 1991.

The Protestant Structure of American Culture

Robert N. Bellah

L et me begin with a passage that expresses in a few highly condensed words why
I believe Protestantism has provided the fundamental structure of American culture. It is a warning from a Unitarian leader, Henry W. Bellows, to his fellow
Unitarians in the middle of the nineteenth century. Historically Unitarianism is an offshoot
of Congregationalism and carries tendencies within Congregationalism, and Protestantism
more generally, to a kind of logical conclusion. Bellows named that conclusion "individualism." As he put it, writing in 1859,

> ...the sufficiency of the Scriptures turns out to be the self-sufficiency
> of man, and the right of private judgment an absolute independence of
> Bible or Church.... No creed but the Scriptures, practically abolishes all
> Scriptures but those on the human heart; nothing between a man's con-
> science and his God, vacates the Church; and with the church, the Holy
> Ghost, whose function is usurped by private reason; the Church lapses into
> what are called Religious Institutions; these into Congregationalism, and
> Congregationalism into Individualism—and the logical end is the aban-
> donment of the Church as an independent institution...and the extinction
> of worship as a separate interest.[1]

That Bellow's comments were prescient is indicated by a 1995–96 survey, which found that one third of Americans believe that "people have God within them, so churches aren't really necessary."[2] I hope to show the price we pay for that ever more prevalent idea.

Andrew Delbanco's recent book *The Real American Dream* has greatly helped me clarify the American situation by showing how our religious culture has changed over time.[3] Delbanco organizes his small book into three chapters entitled "God," "Nation," and "Self." These he sees, using Emersonian terminology, as "predominant ideas" that have successively organized our culture and our society, providing a context of meaning that can bring hope and stave off melancholy. Delbanco sees American Protestantism as leading first to nationalism, and then to individualism. In speaking of God as the predominant idea that first organized our culture, Delbanco is thinking primarily of the New England Puritans of the seventeenth and eighteenth centuries. Nation became the predominant idea from the time of the Revolutionary War until well into the twentieth century. Most recently self seems to have replaced, or if not replaced, subordinated, God and nation as the predominant idea of our culture. Delbanco argues for three loosely chronological epochs, though seeing many overlaps, but I will argue that all three ideas were present at the very beginning, and that, although changing in degree of dominance ever since, some of our deepest problems arise from the form of Protestant Christianity that first put its stamp on colonial culture.

Certainly the Puritans were focused on God; indeed they were God-obsessed. But from the beginning both nation and self were significant sub-texts. If one takes even so great a document as John Winthrop's 1630 sermon, "A Model of Christian Charity," preached on board the *Arbella* in Salem harbor just before the landing, we find a fusion of church and nation that leads Winthrop to a conscious identification of the Massachusetts Bay Colony with ancient Israel. If Winthrop took Moses's farewell sermon (Deuteronomy 30) as his basic text, he had copious New Testament allusions to strengthen his case, perhaps the most famous (notorious?) being the metaphor of a city on a hill: "[W]e shall be as a City upon a Hill [Matthew 5:14]; the eyes of all people are upon us...."[4] It took Ronald Reagan to embellish the city with the adjective "shining," found neither in Matthew nor in Winthrop, but suggestive of the long-lasting tendency to identify America with the City of God.

It has often been pointed out that the Protestant Reformation paved the way for modern nationalism by breaking the hold of the international church and replacing it with state churches instead. "The glory of God was replaced by the glory of the nation; by a curious dialectic the Reformation paved the way for this development," as it was put in one essay.[5] But the American case was extreme in fusing the glory of God with the glory of the nation in a sense of millennial hopes fulfilled: America as redeemer nation for all the world. A sense of the judgment of God hanging over the nation was evident in the closing lines of Winthrop's sermon where he warned that we will "perish out of this good land" if we do not obey God's commandments.[6] A sense of God's judgment was never more evident than in Lincoln's Second Inaugural Address, where he attributed the sufferings of the war to the judgment of God against slavery and quoted Psalm 19:9 as saying "the judgments of the Lord, are true and righteous altogether." But, as Roger Williams pointed out in criticism of the views of Winthrop, the problem came not from the absence of a sense of judgment (though that would be an often realized temptation), but from the confusion of the nation with the communion of the saints. For Williams the error was to confuse "a *people*, naturally considered," with the millennial ark of Christ, which as a result would be "to pull *God* and *Christ* and *Spirit* out of Heaven, and subject them unto *naturall*, sinful, inconstant men...."[7] Although Williams had a very problematic view of the church, still he knew it could not be identified with a nation. For Lincoln, as far as we know, the church had lost all significance. It was only the nation that had to bear, unworthy though it was, the great mission.

The Protestant temptation to confuse church and nation was linked to the very same conception of the church that would open the door to the confusion of God and self. On the face of it nothing could be further from the Puritan mind. The conquest of the self so as to make oneself transparent to God was the center of Puritan piety. And yet the very focus on the individual struggle was, as Sacvan Bercovitch points out in his book *The Puritan Origins of the American Self*, finally a form of self-assertion:

> ...the individual affirming his identity by turning against his power of self-affirmation. But to affirm and to turn against are both aspects of self-involvement. We can see in retrospect how the very intensity of that self-involvement—mobilizing as it did the resources of the ego in what amounted to an internal Armageddon—had to break loose into the world at large.[8]

Just as Lincoln represents a critical step toward a nation that has replaced the church, so Emerson represents a critical step toward a self that has replaced the church, one ratified by William James in his *Varieties of Religious Experience*, which is Puritan in its fascination with individual religious experience, and not only free from, but inimical to, any "institutional form" that that religious experience might take.[9]

James divides religion into two "branches," the personal and the institutional. He chooses to focus entirely on personal religion, leaving institutional religion aside as it lives "at second hand upon tradition."[10] Yet in this case, too, the Puritans foreshadowed later developments. Delbanco quotes John Cotton in the seventeenth century as saying: "If...the Papists aske, where was the Church visible, before *Luther*? The answer is, it was visible, not in open Congregations...but in sundry members of the church," that is, individual members who were persecuted by the church in their day.[11] When John Donne said in a sermon that every believer "hath *a Church* in himself," he was certainly not speaking of the natural self, but of the converted self.[12] Yet the locus of the church in the individual, with the church as an association only coming into existence through the voluntary action of the already converted, was the very notion that opened the door not only to the elevation of the self, but of the nation, to transcendent status. With respect to the fatal notion that the church consists only of the already converted, Roger Williams was, if anything, even more extreme than John Winthrop, however right he was to reject the conflation of church and nation.

Delbanco sums up his story about America near the end of his book:

> The history of hope I have tried to sketch in this book is one of diminution. At first, the self expanded toward (and was sometimes overwhelmed by) the vastness of God. From the early republic to the Great Society, it remained implicated in a national ideal lesser than God but larger and more enduring than any individual citizen. Today, hope has narrowed to the vanishing point of the self alone.[13]

What I am arguing, moving beyond Delbanco's argument though stimulated by it, is that the entire story of declension, that good Puritan word, is present in germ, so to speak, in the very form of Protestant Christianity of the first colonists. A fundamental critique of the premises of American society and culture, then, would require not only a critique of ontological individualism and its strange complementarity with the confusion of God and nation, but a critique of the Protestant Reformation itself, at least in its most influential American forms. That critique would be at the same time theological, ethical, and ecclesiological. My point of entry, as I have already indicated, is the Protestant doctrine of the church—from problems there, I think, flow the correlative theological and ethical problems that haunt not only Protestantism, but any culture, certainly American culture, that has developed from a Protestant basis.

I don't want in any simple sense to paint Protestants as the bad guys and Catholics, the obvious contrast term, as the good guys. In the history of religion one finds much to praise and much to blame but no one completely innocent or completely guilty. In particular I want to emphasize that the achievements of Protestantism have been major, and that, whatever the mistakes, the Reformation was, in my view, a necessary movement in the spiritual history of humanity, although I think ultimately it needs to be transcended.

Among the many contributions of Protestantism, I have only learned recently of the relation of Protestantism and environmentalism. David Vogel, my colleague in the Haas School of Business at Berkeley, in an as yet unpublished paper, has looked at the twenty-one richest nations in today's world. The purpose of his study was to understand why, although all rich nations have embraced the cause of environmentalism, some have done so much more enthusiastically than others. He divided the twenty-one nations into two groups: eleven he denominated as light green, concerned mainly with the quality of air and water that directly affect their population; and ten he denominated as dark green, concerned with the whole ecosphere, with endangered species, rain forests, ozone holes, and all the rest. Now his stunning discovery was that all but one of the ten dark green countries (the exception is

Austria) are of Protestant heritage, and none of the eleven light green countries is. The latter include six Catholic countries, one Greek Orthodox country (Greece), one Jewish country (Israel), and three Confucian/Buddhist countries (Japan, Korea, and Taiwan). But the correlations don't end there. Vogel found that, compared to the non-Protestant countries, the Protestant countries are the richest (Japan is an exception here) and have been rich the longest, are the most modern and have been modern the longest, are the most democratic and have been democratic the longest, and in addition have the most vibrant civic cultures. So it seems Max Weber's argument was even more general than he thought: there is a correlation of Protestant heritage not only with modern economic prosperity, but also with successful democracy, and, as Vogel discovered, strong environmentalism as well.[14]

Vogel's discovery led me to take the next step in my argument, namely the recognition that there are *cultural codes* embedded in national cultures and that those cultural codes, however transformed over time, are ultimately derived from religious beliefs. The language of cultural code is not uncommon today, but I have not previously used it. I'm not sure of the derivation of the phrase, but perhaps it can be traced back to Clifford Geertz's argument that culture patterns operate something like genetic programs.

I want to push beyond Geertz and use a dangerous analogy from Chomsky to argue that there are "deep" cultural codes and surface ones, and that the deep cultural codes, the ones most likely to be derived from religion, are far less malleable than the fads and fashions that inundate us daily. This is because deep cultural codes are so taken for granted, and operate at such a level of generality, that they may be effective even when, perhaps especially when, they are not recognized as such.

I want to illustrate my point by drawing further on Vogel's article and on the environmental historian, Donald Worster, whom he cites. It is important not to confuse a Protestant heritage country with a Protestant country. Vogel argues that historically Protestant culture overrides religious pluralism: "for the purpose of this analysis *all* Americans are Protestants regardless of what particular religion they do or do not practice, just as are all Germans...." Vogel seems to be confirming G.K. Chesterton's famous remark that "in America, even the Catholics are Protestants."

But the relation between Protestantism and "dark green" ideology gets even more interesting when we learn that the religious group least concerned with the environment in America today is Evangelical Protestants, from whose tradition Vogel argues, such ideology derives. Evangelical Protestants are more likely to evince an older Protestant mastery-over-nature orientation. How then does Vogel explain the correlation of Protestantism and dark green environmentalism? He does so in two ways. Following Worster he shows that the origin of modern American environmentalism was in Evangelical Christianity. Worster has a fine essay on John Muir, tracing his development from fervent Evangelical Protestant to pantheistic environmentalist.[15] But even more important to Vogel's point is the structural continuity even when explicit religious connection is disavowed:

Contemporary dark green environmentalism should be understood, in part, as [a] secularized version of Protestantism. Without necessarily making or acknowledging any explicit connection to religious beliefs or practices, it draws on the rhetoric and imagery of Protestantism.

Vogel points to several structural similarities:

First, both dark green environmentalism and Protestantism can be said to share a relatively pessimistic view of the world, one in which man is wicked and has committed multiple sins. For Protestants, the sins are against God; for environmentalists, they are against nature. For the former, the "wages" of this sin are eternal damnation; for the latter, it is the impending destruction of the eco-sphere. Both share an essentially apocalyptic vision. Thus if we continue in our present behaviors and values we are doomed. It is only by radically changing our ways—which include both our behaviors and our values—that we can possibly be "saved." The notion of Calvin and other Protestant reformers that we live in a depraved world filled with sinners bent on their own destruction is echoed in much contemporary "dark green" environmental rhetoric.

Second, Vogel notes the common importance of asceticism, expressed by the environmentalists in a concern for recycling, walking rather than driving, and so forth. Third is moralism: both Protestants and environmentalists are quick to make strong moral judgments. "By contrast," he writes, "non-Protestant cultures tend to exhibit a higher degree of tolerance for inconsistency." Fourth, he notes, Protestantism is a "highly egalitarian religion." This is a feature that links Protestantism to democracy. What the environmentalists do is extend the concept of the rights of man to include the rights of nature: "If people are equal in God's eyes, then so are natural objects such as whales, trees, animals, and rivers." Fifth, Vogel argues, just because Protestantism has a weakened sense of liturgy and sacramentalism, it is open to an aesthetic appreciation of nature. Indeed, it is largely on Protestant soil that Romanticism as an aesthetic movement has evolved. Environmentalism clearly has inherited the nature mysticism to which Protestants have been prone. Finally, and ironically, Protestantism and environmentalism are connected in that they both share an ethic of mastery, the very ethic that, Vogel says, "has, correctly, been associated with the ruthless subjugation of nature." But environmentalism gives the notion of mastery a new twist, or, we might say the cultural code undergoes a mutation. As Vogel puts it, "if one believes that control or mastery of the world is possible, one can just as readily choose to treat it well as dominate over it. In any event, it is people who are ultimately responsible for nature."

To sum up what I think the connection between Protestantism and environmentalism means for the understanding of how cultural codes operate, let me quote Donald Worster:

> Protestantism, like any religion, lays its hold on people's imagination in diverse, contradictory ways and that hold can be tenacious long after the explicit theology or doctrine has gone dead. Surely it cannot be surprising that in a culture deeply rooted in Protestantism, we should find ourselves speaking its language, expressing its temperament, even when we thought we were free of all that.[16]

But much as I want to recognize the positive contributions of Protestantism, I do not intend to preach American triumphalism and to laud the beneficence of Protestantism for giving our country wealth, democracy, and environmentalism. Instead I intend to put a twist on the idea of a deep cultural code. Just as a genetic code can produce a highly successful species, successful because specialized for a particular environment, but then, perhaps at its moment of greatest success, because of a dramatic change in that environment, the code can lead to rapid extinction; so a cultural code, which has long enjoyed remarkable success in many fields, can lead a civilization into abrupt decline if it disables it from solving central problems, perhaps problems created by its own success. And yet the cultural code, however deep, is not a genetic code: it can be changed, although sometimes it takes a catastrophe to change it.

So far I have focused on the positive contributions of the Protestant tradition. Let me now begin to assess the costs that have been exacted. The costs became increasingly evident when, to put it in Delbanco's terms, the self began to become the dominant idea in American culture, and the mitigating idea of the nation, in the absence of strong challenge from without, weakened. In his sobering book *Bowling Alone*, Robert Putnam gives an incisive analysis, based on an extraordinarily extensive collection of data of what we have come to in our society today.[17]

In the book Putnam describes the sharp decline of what he calls "social capital" in just about every sphere of American life for the last 30 years or more, all the more remarkable since the first 60 or 70 years of the twentieth century saw a significant increase in social capital. By social capital Putnam means social connectedness of almost every sort and finds all of them—from voting, to political activism, to membership in a wide variety of civic organizations (he takes his title from the stunning decline of bowling leagues), to informal socializing (including even having dinner with one's own family), to church-going, membership, and giving—weaker today than they have been for decades. But more is changing than a decline in belonging of all sorts. Social capital also consists in norms and expectations—that we stop at boulevard stops, for example, or that we expect that most people can be trusted—and all those measures are dramatically down as well. Anyone serious about understanding our society today will have to read *Bowling Alone* carefully to find out how we have changed in each different sphere. In a nutshell I can summarize it by saying we live in a very different society from the one I grew up in. Loyalty to others is not high on the agenda of most younger Americans, who can, not entirely inaccurately, be caricatured as sitting alone at their computers calculating how to maximize their self-interest. Rather than give the bad news across the board, let me turn to the most relevant field for our topic, the field of religion. For a long time many people, including me, thought that religion was relatively immune to these trends, that both church membership and church attendance were remarkably stable except for the unusual bump up in the 1950s, but, as it turns out, both membership and attendance have been in decline over the same period as other forms of engagement, that is, since 1960. Though a wide variety of groups, for example the PTA and the League of Women Voters, but also the Jaycees, the Kiwanis, and the Shriners, have been in precipitate decline in this period, the decline in the churches has been more gradual and has taken a bit longer to become evident. In fact, church giving has declined more sharply than church membership or church attendance, but all have steadily fallen for 40 years.

While it is the quantitative data that are most reliable, there are some things we can say about the quality of participation as well. We can discern in the life of religious communities something that is going on in the society in general: participation is less about loyalty and a strong conviction of membership and more about what one will get out of participating. Even evangelical churches that used to be able to count on their members now have to offer incentives, to "sell" their programs as adding value to the participants. Attachment to all groups, including churches, but even families, is increasingly evaluated in the following terms: What will I get out of it? What's in it for me? Before making the connection between all this and my theme of the Protestant structure of American culture, which I think is a close one, I want to look at Putnam's effort to explain what has happened to us in the last 30 or 40 years.

Putnam's primary explanation is generational change. On almost every variable in which he is interested, each generation starts lower than the one before and stays lower. On the other hand, those who started high have stayed high. My generation (note: not Putnam's generation—he is not just an old man being nostalgic), that is, those born between 1925 and 1930, which Putnam calls the most civic generation in American history, started out voting and we still vote, started out going to church and we still go to church, started out reading newspapers and we still read newspapers, and so on down the line, but each succeeding generation has started lower and remains lower. Another important variable in Putnam's analysis, one that overlaps with generation, is television watching. The number of hours spent watching television per person has gone up through the whole period when almost every form of participation has been declining, and again, the increase by generation is clear. But the correlation is not just general, it is quite specific: that is, within every generation, those who watch more television participate less in politics, civic life, informal socializing, and religion. Looking more closely, not all television watching has these negative effects.

Watching educational television or network news (network news now has a largely geriatric audience) is not negatively correlated with participation, but, like newspaper reading, is positively correlated. The kind of television that is negatively correlated with participation, and is by far the most common type, is television as entertainment, television for its own sake, simple channel hopping to find something to watch. Thus, I think what we can say is that *attentive* watching, or reading in the case of newspapers, does not undermine social connectedness. But it is the decline of attentiveness across the board that is problematic.

What I am suggesting is that the kind of people Americans are becoming, and increasingly so with each succeeding generation, makes it ever more difficult for them to sustain commitments to religious communities, to understand ritual, to organize their lives around sacred texts, and even to understand why some texts are sacred at all. (Let me remind you that we are talking about statistical trends here—among every generation, including the youngest, there are many civically minded, socially responsible, and religiously active people; there are just fewer of them.) Dense, multistranded commitments to many kinds of communities are being replaced, as Putnam puts it, with "single-stranded, surf-by interactions" so that "more of our social connectedness is one shot, special purpose, and self oriented."[18] This shift obviously is closely related to the dramatic change in the economic orientation of our society from an inadequate welfare state in the early postwar period to an increasingly marketized, privatized society at the end of the century. Someone recently asked a group of college students what makes their generation different, and their response was "we're more entrepreneurial than our parents." That says it all. If everything is commodified, if even religion is just one more consumer preference, then why do we need churches? Why not just buy our religious goodies on the web?

If we see a variety of symptoms that all is not well in our society, in spite of surface appearances, what is there about our deep cultural code that might be a significant part of the problem? Just when we are in many ways moving to an ever greater validation of the sacredness of the individual person, our capacity to imagine a social fabric that would hold individuals together is vanishing. This is in part because of the fact that our invincible individualism, deriving as I have argued from the Protestant religious tradition in America, is linked to an economic individualism which, ironically, knows nothing of the sacredness of the individual. Its only standard is money, and the only thing more sacred than money is more money. What economic individualism destroys and what our kind of religious individualism cannot restore is solidarity, a sense of being members of the same body. In most other North Atlantic societies, including other Protestant societies, a tradition of an established church, however secularized, provides some notion that we are in this thing together, that we need each other, that our precious and unique selves aren't going to make it all alone.

Roger Williams was a moral genius, but he was a sociological catastrophe. After he founded the First Baptist Church, he left it for a smaller and purer one. That, too, he found inadequate, so he founded a church that consisted only of himself, his wife, and one other person. One wonders how he stood even those two. Since Williams ignored secular society, money took over in Rhode Island in a way that would not be true in Massachusetts or Connecticut for a long time. Rhode Island under Williams gives us an early and local example of what happens when the sacredness of the individual is not balanced by any sense of the whole or concern for the common good.

Let me make two suggestions about how certain central Protestant beliefs have been vulnerable to distortion. Max Weber credited the great universalistic religions that arose in the first millennium B.C.E. with a strong rejection of magic. The Jewish prophets taught us that no worship of idols, no propitiation of spirits with sacrifice or incense, would save us. As Micah says "And what doth the Lord require of thee, but to do justly, and to love mercy, and to walk humbly with thy God?" (Micah 6:8). The Reformers took the opposition to magic very seriously, attacking the doctrine of transubstantiation and other Catholic practices that they deemed magical. In their fear of idolatry, they, in effect, pushed God out of the world into radical transcendence. With the doctrine of predestination, Calvin (or if not Calvin, as some scholars now believe, then some of his followers) described a God who had preordained everything that can occur before the beginning of time. It was natural for some philosophers and scientists to move from that idea to a deterministic physical universe without a personal God at all: "I have no need of that hypothesis," as one of them said. So Calvin's powerful doctrine of divine transcendence paradoxically opened the door to atheistic naturalism. Even more ominously, into the empty space left by the absence of God came first, as we have seen, the idea of the nation replacing the idea of God as the sovereign, and then an understanding of the self as absolutely sovereign that applies an essential attribute of God to the self. Since Calvinism as a consistent doctrine hardly survived the eighteenth century, I am arguing for this aspect of the Protestant cultural code as having made its ambiguous contribution quite some time ago.

There is a second Protestant source of our problem that is, however, very much alive and well today not just as part of the cultural code but as part of contemporary piety. This is the near exclusive focus on the relation between Jesus and the individual, where accepting Jesus Christ as one's personal Lord and Savior becomes almost the whole of piety. When this happens the doctrine of the God-Man can slip into the doctrine of the Man-God. The divinization of the self is often called Gnosticism, and Harold Bloom in his interesting book *The American Religion*, sees Gnosticism as the quintessentially American religion.[19] He says so not as a critic but as a believer, for he proclaims himself a Gnostic. He sees the Evangelical Protestant focus on the personal relation of the believer to Jesus as one of the major sources of American Gnosticism. If I may trace the downward spiral of this particular Protestant distortion, let me say that it begins with the statement "If I'm all right with Jesus, then I don't need the church," which we heard from some of the people we interviewed for *Habits of the Heart*. It progresses, then, to the Sheilaism that we described in that book. A woman named Sheila Larson defined her faith as: "It's Sheilaism. Just my own little voice."[20] But

Sheilaism seems positively benign compared to the end of the road in this direction, which comes out with remarkable force in an interview recounted in Robert Wuthnow's book *Loose Connections*: A man in his late twenties, who works as a financial analyst, describes the individualism that "you're just brought up to believe in" as follows:

> The individual is the preeminent being in the universe. There's always a distinction between me and you. Comity, sharing, cannot truly exist. What I have is mine, and it's mine because I deserve it, and I have a right to it.[21]

Let us hope he knows not what he says. The general tendency of American Evangelicalism toward a private piety pulls everyone influenced by it very much in this direction. Some may think that Jesus-and-me piety is very different from the individual as the preeminent being in the universe, but I am suggesting that they are only a hair apart.

If I have located our problem rightly, then religious faith has a particularly central responsibility for the present state of our common life. Especially when combined with the ideology of economic freedom with which it has long been linked, religious faith has contributed the deep cultural code that has led us into our present perilous situation. The connections I am trying to make are so deeply embedded in our history, so unconscious and even counter-intuitive, that I think it is a major task of religious intellectuals to uncover them and then to suggest a possible transformation, dare I say "reformation," of the deep cultural code. For if I am right, and our present deep cultural code is leading us toward grave catastrophes, such a transformation may be our most urgent necessity. I must also caution, however, that the code has escaped the control of religious groups, as I have suggested, and so a transformation of the deep cultural code at the religious level would be only the beginning—though I think it to be the most important beginning—of the transformation of our American code altogether.

So far I have assumed the answer to the question that my title asks—"multiculture or monoculture?"—and I have come down pretty firmly on the monoculture side. Does that mean I think cultural pluralism doesn't exist in America? I am not so foolish, but I am also convinced that the ideology of multiculturalism is much stronger than multiculturalism itself, and that the ideology of multiculturalism operates primarily as an agent of assimilation into dominant American culture. I would argue that genuine cultural pluralism is difficult to sustain in America and badly needs to be nurtured. It is the strength of our common culture that we need to worry about, not the allegedly disintegrative consequences of our cultural diversity.

For a talk I gave at the American Academy of Religion's annual meeting in 1997, I was given the title, "Is There a Common American Culture?" I began by asking the question not whether there is a common American culture but rather how it is that a plenary session of the American Academy of Religion could be devoted to this question in a society with so powerful and monolithic a common culture as ours. The answer, I said, is obvious: it has become part of the common culture to ask whether there is a common culture in America.

In a review of Nathan Glazer's book *We Are All Multiculturalists Now* (whose very title makes the point), K. Anthony Appiah quotes the book as saying, "The Nexis data base of major newspapers shows no reference to multiculturalism as late as 1988, a mere 33 items in 1989, and only after that a rapid rise—more than 100 items in 1990, more than 600 in 1991, almost 900 in 1992, 1200 in 1993, and 1500 in 1994...."[22] Appiah adds, "It seems that when it comes to diversity, we all march to the beat of a single drummer."[23]

It is important to understand the sociological reason why there not only is but has to be a common culture in America: culture does not float free from institutions. A powerful institutional order will carry a powerful common culture. The United States, surely, has an exceptionally powerful institutional order. The state in America, even though it is multi-leveled and, to a degree, decentralized, has an enormous impact on all our lives. The state is even responsible to a degree for the construction of multiculturalism through the little boxes that must be checked on a myriad of forms.

If the state intrudes in our lives in a thousand ways, the market is even more intrusive. There is very little that Americans need that we can produce for ourselves anymore. We are dependent on the market not only for goods but also for many kinds of service. Our cultural understanding of the world is shaped every time we enter a supermarket or a mall. I taught a senior seminar of about 20 students during the last semester before I retired, roughly divided into one-fourth Asian-American, one-fourth Hispanic-American, one-fourth African-American, and one-fourth Anglo-American. What was remarkable was how easily they talked together because of how much they shared. Beyond the ever-present state and market, they shared the immediate experience of coping with a vast state university, with its demands and its incoherence.

Education, which is linked largely though not exclusively to the state, and television and increasingly the Internet, which are linked to the market, are enormously powerful purveyors of common culture, socializers not only of children but of all of us most of our lives. Not only are we exposed from infancy to a monoculture, we are exposed to it monolingually. The cultural power of American English is overwhelming, and no language, except under the most unusual circumstances, has ever been able to withstand it, which is what makes the English Only movement such a joke. As Appiah notes, 90 percent of California-born Hispanic children of immigrant parents have native fluency in English, and in the next generation only 50 percent of them still speak Spanish.[24] One more generation and you can forget about Spanish. When third generation Asian Americans come to college, they have to learn Chinese or Japanese in language classes just like anyone else—they don't bring those languages with them. When language, which is the heart of culture, goes, then it becomes extremely difficult to sustain genuine cultural difference. Serious multicultural education would begin by teaching native English speakers a second language, but that, unlike most of the rest of the world, almost never happens in the United States. The half-hearted effort to teach Spanish in California public schools results in very few native English speakers with a secondary fluency in Spanish. Why don't most Americans speak another language? Because we don't have to—everyone in the world speaks English, or so we think.

If I am right, there is an enormously powerful common culture in America, and it is carried predominantly by the market and the state and by their agencies of socialization: television and education. What institutions might withstand that pressure and sustain genuine cultural difference? Immigrant communities have been able to sustain genuine cultural difference for a generation or so, but the power of American institutions leads to rapid cultural assimilation in the second and third generations, even when a significant degree of identity difference is sustained. But, I want to argue, culture in the strong sense is not the same thing as identity.

In spite of the tendency of the advocates of multiculturalism to ignore it, the only institution that can sustain strong cultural pluralism over the generations, and that only with great difficulty, is religion. For example, African Americans have distinct traditions of cuisine and music, but I would argue that the black church is the heart and soul of any lasting African-American culture. I would argue that religion is the only sustainable basis for cultural pluralism in America and that the church or its equivalent in other religions is the only institution capable of sustaining such pluralism. Since I have argued that American culture is Protestant to the bone and has affected every cultural and religious group more than they realize, I am putting a special burden on all non-Protestant groups, and particularly on the largest one, namely Catholics, to nurture a genuine multiculturalism in a very hostile environment.

It is with this background in mind that I think we can understand why multiculturalism as an ideology is so appealing to Americans today, but why the reality is so problematic. In a culture that tends to eliminate all genuine difference and assert the autonomy of the radically independent individual, but that still demands to know who each distinct individual is, it is tempting to assert an identity even with little actual content, and then to claim the right to equal respect in the name of that identity, which we imagine is cultural. I think Appiah gets it right when he says:

> But if we explore these moments of tension [between groups in contemporary America] we discover an interesting paradox. The growing salience of race and gender as social irritants, which may seem to reflect the call of collective identities, is a reflection, as much as anything else, of the individual's concern for dignity and respect. As our society slouches on toward a fuller realization of its ideal of social equality, everyone wants to be taken seriously—to be respected, not "dissed." Because on many occasions disrespect

still flows from racism, sexism, and homophobia, we respond, in the name of all black people, all women, all gays, as the case may be.... But the truth is that what mostly irritates us in these moments is that we, as individuals, feel diminished.

And the trouble with appeal to cultural difference is that it obscures rather than diminishes this situation. It is not black culture that the racist disdains, but blacks. There is no conflict of visions between black and white cultures that is the source of racial discord. No amount of knowledge of the architectural achievements of Nubia or Kush guarantees respect for African-Americans. No African-American is entitled to greater concern because he is descended from a people who created jazz or produced Toni Morrison. Culture is not the problem, and it is not the solution.[25]

If the problem is disrespect for the dignity of the person, then the solution is to go back to that deepest core of our tradition, the sacredness of the conscience and person of every individual. And that is what a great deal of the ideology of multiculturalism is really saying: We're all different; we're all unique. Respect that. But if this is true, then multiculturalism is more of an expression of the common culture—the common culture at its best to be sure—than a challenge to it. I am certainly not the first to say that multiculturalism, which has become so widely accepted in America, is part of the process of assimilation into the dominant culture, is indeed the very mechanism of the assimilation into the dominant culture today, and thus not in any real sense the expression of a genuine cultural pluralism.

The effort to invigorate a genuine cultural pluralism is part of the search for the common good in America, something we have almost lost, because, paradoxically, the common culture that we have inherited doesn't even know that the common good exists. Without a deep understanding of the common good, even the idea of the dignity of and respect for the individual, critically important though that is, will not be able to sustain itself. Without solidarity, loyalty, civic friendship in Aristotle's terms, without a conception of the church as something much more than a voluntary association, the dignity of the individual is swept away in a jumble of isolated, fragmented individuals, ruled only by the market, which doesn't understand the dignity of anything but money.

I am arguing that something is wrong not on the surface of American life but deep in the core of our common culture. So the real mission of cultural pluralism would be to offer an alternative to the radical Protestant individualism that has dissolved the Church into the messianic nation, such that once the messianic mission is lost, there is nothing left but the individual as the preeminent being in the universe, nothing left but "What I have is mine, and it's mine because I deserve it, and I have a right to it." We need the non-Protestant traditions, and the most thoughtful and self-critical sector of the Protestant tradition, to remind us that we are citizens of a deeply flawed city of man and that we badly need to recover an idea of the common good toward which we can aspire in the face of the disintegrative tendencies not of cultural pluralism but of radical individualism. Breaking the hold of the monoculture is, in my opinion, our greatest and most urgent challenge. A fundamental turn of direction would involve changes in our economy, our institutions, our culture, and in the core of our religious faith. There are not many signs at the moment that Americans are prepared to rise to that challenge.

(Spring 2002, 4.1)

Notes

[1] Henry W. Bellows, as quoted in Conrad Wright, *Walking Together: Polity and Participation in Unitarian Universalist Churches* (Boston, MA: Skinner House, 1989), 156.

[2] Wade Clark Roof, *Spiritual Marketplace: Baby Boomers and the Remaking of American Religion* (Princeton, NJ: Princeton University Press, 1999), 318.

[3] Andrew Delbanco, *The Real American Dream: A Meditation on Hope* (Cambridge, MA: Harvard University Press, 1999).

[4] John Winthrop, "A Model of Christian Charity," *Winthrop Papers*, vol. 2 (Boston, MA: Massachusetts Historical Society, 1931), 295.

[5] Francisco O. Ramirez and John Boli, "On the Union of States and Schools," *Institutional Structure: Constituting State, Society, and the Individual*, ed. George M. Thomas, John W. Meyer, et al. (Newbury Park, CA: Sage, 1987), 194.

[6] Winthrop, "A Model of Christian Charity," 295.

[7] Sacvan Bercovitch, *The Puritan Origins of the American Self* (New Haven, CT: Yale University Press, 1975), 110.

[8] Ibid., 20.

[9] William James, *The Varieties of Religious Experience, in Writings, 1902–1910* (New York, NY: The Library of America, 1987), 34.

[10] Ibid., 35.

[11] As quoted in Delbanco 27.

[12] Bercovitch, 11.

[13] Delbanco, 103.

[14] David Vogel, "The Protestant Ethic and the Spirit of Environmentalism: A Comparative Study of Environmental Policies and Politics" (Haas School of Business, University of California at Berkeley), unpublished manuscript.

[15] Donald Worster, "John Muir and the Roots of American Environmentalism," *The Wealth of Nature: Environmental History and the Ecological Imagination* (New York, NY: Oxford University Press, 1993), 184–202.

[16] Worster, 200.

[17] Robert D. Putnam, *Bowling Alone: The Collapse and Revival of American Community* (New York, NY: Simon and Schuster, 2000). Claude Fischer, perhaps the ablest quantitative sociologist in my department, affirms the validity of Putnam's analysis. The picture is not entirely news; in one sense it is a massive empirical confirmation of the argument of Robert Bellah, et al., *Habits of the Heart: Individualism and Commitment in American Life* (Berkeley, CA: University of California Press, 1985), although it is more than that.

[18] Putnam, *Bowling Alone*, 183–4.

[19] Harold Bloom, *The American Religion: The Emergence of the Post-Christian Nation* (New York, NY: Simon and Schuster, 1992).

[20] Bellah, 221.

[21] Robert Wuthnow, *Loose Connections: Joining Together in America's Fragmented Communities* (Cambridge, MA: Harvard University Press, 1998), 250, n. 25.

[22] Nathan Glazer, as quoted in K. Anthony Appiah, "The Multiculturalist Misunderstanding," review of *On Toleration* by Michael Walzer and *We Are All Multiculturalists Now* by Nathan Glazer, *The New York Review of Books* (9 Oct. 1997): 32, n.5.

[23] Appiah, 32, n.5.

[24] Geoffrey Nunberg, as quoted by Appiah, 30–1.

[25] Appiah, 35–6.

The Theological Roots of Liberalism in Turkey
"Muslimism" from Islamic Fashion to Foreign Policy

Neslihan Cevik

Many social theorists, especially in international relations and sociology, assume that there is a divide both between religion and modernity and between politics and culture. These divides are then used in depictions of Islamic revivalism, portraying Islam as intrinsically anti-modern and Islamic movements as reactions against modernity, in the form of either private cultural escape or violent political mobilization. This is not only a Western perspective; it is shared by elites in the Muslim world, most ambitiously by Turkish elites.

Given this interpretive frame, it is not surprising that the rise of the Justice and Development Party (JDP) in Turkey, along with a national assembly that started to look more and more religious (the president and prime minister had veiled wives and a majority of congressmen defined themselves as observant Muslims), was alarming for secularist Turks and Western observers, who fully expected the party to infuse religiosity inside the state, eventually leading to a Sharia state, and to seek intra-Umma alliances internationally, leading to an overall Islamization.

Contrary to these expectations, the JDP, rather than pumping Islamic blood into the society, promoted a liberal, national polity (from minority rights to gender politics to civil-military relations) and developed a foreign policy that gave more or less equal effort to deepening relations with the West (the EU and the U.S., and new allies such as Greece and Russia) and to repairing its relations with its Muslim hinterland and expanding its reach to North Africa and Caucasia.

Watching these developments, scholars and pundits labeled Turkey a "moderate Islamist country" and the JDP as "moderate Islamists" (albeit with up-and-down tensions produced by the flotilla events, Turkey's position in the UN on Iran, and the arrests in the Ergenekon case). This label has been helpful to differentiate Turkey and the JDP from Islamic expressions that reinforce a secularism-versus-Islam divide.

However, while the term "moderate" is helpful, what constitutes "moderate," how it is different from "radical," who formulates it, and what it includes (or excludes) remain undefined. Answers to these questions are becoming more and more urgent since Turkey and the JDP's so-called "moderate Islamism" are suggested as a potential model for the Muslim world in the face of the democratic uprisings in the Middle East and North Africa.

The prevalent interpretations for the rise of moderate Islam, as well as its content, tend to focus mainly on political mechanisms: national party politics and foreign policy. Where the JDP separates its Islamic ideology from foreign relations, this mildly Islamic Turkish foreign policy is explained through regional dynamics and strategic, material, or security concerns. The JDP's mildly Islamist national politics is also explained as strategic adaptations, where, through half a century of experience, Islamic actors are argued to have learned how to play the democratic game, or even pose a "modern outlook" (with the help of the efficient state-management of Islam).

These interpretations fail to recognize the broader and deeper transformations that preceded the JDP's rise and that underlie its so-called "moderate" national and foreign policy. They start with the assumption that Islam is essentially anti-Western and anti-modern; thus if Islam, even slightly, informs a national or foreign policy, the outcome must be anti-modern and anti-Western. Starting with this assumption, these interpretations fail to capture the emerging linkages between Islam and modernity that are generating a new Islamic expression in Turkey, which has inspired the JDP's domestic and international policies. The broader problem is the marginal place culture is given in these interpretations. The fixation on the political prevents many from connecting the changes in Turkish national and foreign policy to changes in theological perceptions of the individual, faith, and lifestyle.

A New Islamic Expression: Muslimism

> Don't use bright colors; otherwise, you would look like a walking ball of fabric.... If you have an orange veil and orange shoes, no way you would look aesthetic; unless you want to look like a fruit! Wear the bone so your

hair won't show. But loosen the scarf to lessen the claustrophobic effect. Instead of square scarves, prefer rectangular scarves. Hang down your scarf underneath your jacket and create a Grace Kelly effect.[1]

These are the rules for the new, chic wearing of the *tesettur* (female Islamic covering) suggested by Rabia Yalcin, a veiled Turkish woman and the owner of Rabia "Haute Couture."

By articulating Islamic principles of covering with modern rules of fashion, a chic wearing of the *tesettur* fashionably challenges the secularist conception of a separation between Islam and modernity. It also challenges Islamists for whom the same style of covering is the "work of the devil." In the Qadimayya neighborhood in Iraq, for example, four mannequins dressed in the Turkish style of the *tesettur* are displayed as examples of "degenerate Muslim women who will eternally burn in hell for turning men into voracious monsters."[2]

How do we explain the difference between these views, each claiming to be equally Islamic? Could this simply be global consumerism making pious Turks bourgeois, where the Iraqi mannequins are a wakeup call for Turks to go back to authenticity?

I think not. Pious Turks have not only launched Islamic fashion shows, following the neoliberal transition, an emerging Muslim middle class has also established human rights organizations that articulate Islamic references of human rights with Western references (for example, linking the farewell speech of the prophet Mohammad with United Nations conventions); businessmen organizations that embrace the free market, while moralizing its principles with Islamic ethics (for example, competition, pragmatism, individual enterprise, and liberty are related to *helal* [permissible] versus *haram* [impermissible] gain, *israf* [prodigality], individual-profit versus *infak* [spending to please God] and to do *hayir* [blessed/goodness]; and women's associations that retrieve progressive Islamic concepts (for example, *ijtihad* and *masalih*, both referring to adaptation to the social currents) to challenge male dominant exegesis of Islamic theological sources and traditional practices such as polygamy or laws of inheritance.

These new everyday life institutions are embodiments of a new Islamic orthodoxy— what I term "Muslimism"—that engages modernity in an alternative, novel way. Encounters between religion and modernity have historically taken two forms: religions either reject modernity or fully adapt to it (liberalization or secularization). Differing both from fundamentalist rejection and liberal accommodation, Muslimism embraces many aspects of modern life while submitting that life to a sacred, moral order.

More specifically, Muslimism is a hybrid identity frame empowering engagements between Islam and secular modernity in novel and innovative ways. These engagements go beyond the "hardware imports" (what Olivier Roy has previously called "Sharia plus electricity"). Instead, Muslimists reposition Islam vis-à-vis global modernity and world cultural principles such as universal rights, international law and institutions, individuation, multiculturalism, liberalism, the free market, and democracy. This repositioning is pervasive among the areas of theology and faith (*din* [religion]); everyday life, economics, and lifestyles (*dunya* [world]); and politics and political participation (*deylet* [state])—that is, among the three d's of *din*, *dunya*, and *deylet*. This reframing, nonetheless, is not secularization; Muslimism, differing from liberal theologies, submits these engagements to an "objective truth" and an "objective" separation between *helal* [permissible] and *haram* [impermissible].

What Do Muslimists Want?

For Muslimists, the main aim is not capturing the state to Islamize the community (as in fundamentalism), nor Islamizing the community to eventually bring in an Islamic state (as in neo-fundamentalism). Muslimism is neither state centered nor community centered. Instead, the main zeal of Muslimism is to contrive a lifestyle in which the "Muslim individual" can be modern while preserving proper Islamic living. Thus, Muslimism is individual oriented.

This individual orientation is found in theology, social relations, and politics.[3] It is rooted in a theological empowerment of *iman* [inner ethics] over externally imposed control by the state or community. *Iman* acts as a constant and ever-present guide directing the Muslim individual towards *hayir* [blessed/goodness] and away from *şer* [enormity] regardless of whether external control is present, thus undermining the theological function of a policing state or a gazing community. Within this framework, faith is a matter of individual choice, and "faith as choice" is more meaningful and valuable than "faith as forced."

Sociologically, the emphasis on *iman* empowers the self, increases individual autonomy (at the expense of community), and hence allows self-expression and personalism (at the expense of homogeneity). New veiling styles and civil association memberships replace following *cemaat/tarikat* [religious orders], as aspirations for self-development and education make strong statements about individuality, self-expression, and individual autonomy.

As this individual-oriented Islamic expression becomes more and more prevalent in the society, scholars too quickly associate this new form with a shift from "political Islam" to "cultural Islam." While effectively challenging the conventional fixation on the political, it has done so at the expense of the political, by completely taking it out of the picture. In other words, it reduces the flourishing of civil associations or new veiling styles to mere cultural expressions, overlooking the transfusions from cultural into political.

From Cultural to Political: Muslimism and the JDP

The realization of the Muslimists' theological and cultural demands requires a political frame that guarantees individual choice and autonomy. Such a political frame can neither be entertained under a Sharia state, which eliminates choice by imposing religion (for example, compulsory veiling) nor under a strictly secularist one, which equally eliminates choice by preventing religious freedoms (for example, banning the veil).

Muslimists have engaged in the political space to bring about a state model that will frame their demands in a liberal, pluralistic polity. However, until the turn of the century, Muslimists did not have a political outlet that was in line with their peculiar designs of the three d's or that could institutionalize their demands at the political level.

As center-right parties weakened, the Muslimists were left with two options, the secularist or the Islamist political parties. Neither discourse could attract the Muslimists, as they both have been equally state centered and commensurate with an authoritarian view of society—either based on a bureaucratic order or an Islamic communitarian one. Moreover, neither discourse could absorb the increasingly globalizing world cultural principles of liberalism and individual enterprise. Each resisted global modernity—one through a religious reaction and the other through a statist and nationalist resistance.

In the 1990s, the Muslimists embraced the Islamist Welfare Party (even though they had already started to separate themselves from its grassroots, most notably *cemaat(s)* [religious orders] as it was the only party, at the time, open to religious sentiments, yet this relationship was only temporary and was marked by tension. This alliance was broken by the 1997 postmodern coup, which closed off the Welfare Party to halt Islamist political mobilization, but which also unintentionally cleared the political arena of Islamist power structures, creating a vacuum for the articulation of a new Islamic expression by new religious actors.

It was the founders of the JDP, after breaking off from the Islamist political establishments, who took advantage of this vacuum and filled it in with a party politics that realigned Islamic sentiments along Muslimist attitudes and values.

The JDP pursues a liberal and democratic national polity and uses the universalistic language of human rights, particularly on issues that relate to terror law, capital punishment, censoring, ethnic minority and religious minority rights, torture and prisons, institutional gender discrimination, and military and civilian relations. The JDP government also has drawn legal boundaries for social issues, some of which intertwine with Islamic morality (for example, regulations on alcohol), but parallel to Christian Democratic Parties in Europe, the JDP attempts to sharply distinguish such actions from a desire to establish religious law. For example, regulations on alcohol resemble ones found in Western countries rather than the Islamic regulations found in Iran or Saudi Arabia. Similarly, regulations are based not on a religious language but a secular one relating to health concerns and social hazards.

Whether it pertains to moral [*din*], social [*dunya*], or political [*devlet*] issues, most importantly, the party expresses its discourse in line with the attitudes expressed by Muslimists in balancing state, society, and individual choice. It articulates freedoms within a liberal state, thus appealing to Muslimists.

Similar to its national polity, Muslimist sentiments for conciliatory politics and demands for further integration into the global system are also played out in the party's foreign policy.

The party calibrated a foreign policy that is both Westward and Eastward—where previously West weighed more heavily for secularist parties and East for the Islamist ones. But by aggressively promoting membership in the EU and simultaneously looking Eastward, the party took one step further and clearly claimed a special calling for Turkey to provide a new model of conciliation for the world. This way the party bridges, on the one hand, civilizational divides and, on the other, nationalistic objectives (ascribing Turkey a special place) with globalist ones (conciliation between Muslims and the West).

Consequently, the JDP's Islamic politics are, under the current conditions, informed or inspired by Muslimist impulses. The party managed to articulate Muslimist impulses to a great extent gaining significant electoral support from Muslimists. It is important to note, this does not mean the party itself is Muslimist or that it will keep moving in this direction. Any number of scenarios might lead the JDP to move toward a more statist or Islamist approach and forsake liberal policies and globalist objectives. External threat, regional dynamics, European exclusion, and harsh secularist responses (including military intervention) could effect such changes. But, one would also expect that if the JDP moves towards either a more statist or an Islamist frame, it would lose the support of Muslimists and likely would vindicate those who argue that it is essentially Islamist.

So far, I have attempted to illustrate that the "moderate Islamist" domestic and foreign policies of the JDP and the JDP itself are actually rooted in broader cultural transformations that find expression in a new religious orthodoxy. What seemed to be an apolitical, cultural Islam translates its theological/cultural demands into political involvement by getting linked to certain political parties that are in line with its demands. Therefore, while Muslimism is not state centered, it is not a mere cultural expression, either. It engages the political space and has significant political implications, challenging the divide between "politics" and "culture." This also shows that associating the emergence of moderate Islamic politics in Turkey with the emergence of the JDP, seeing the party as the ultimate actor producing a new Islamic expression is reductionistic, ignoring the underlying civil roots and theological basis of "moderate Islam" in Turkey.

Muslimism as Change and Change as a Regional Cultural Demand

The Muslimist orthodoxy, more broadly, is a response to a quest among the pious for a "better life." In the Muslimist context, this "better life" is not equated with an Islamic order that would convert the world (community/state) into a God-observant place. Instead, it is built upon everyday life solutions that would allow pious Muslims to be incorporated into modernity and enjoy its promises to the utmost (from extended political rights to economic and social upward mobility to leisure) while remaining within the limits of *helal* [permissible] and *haram* [impermissible].

Muslimism challenges both the Islamist definitions of who is a good Muslim and how to be one and the secularist definition of how to be modern. It cracks the binaries between the two. More concretely, for example, within the Muslimist frame, being veiled or devout no longer prevents women from promoting women's rights, becoming active in voluntary associations, owning a business, preferring career over marriage, or getting plastic surgery. Similarly, Islamic sentiments no longer prevent advocating a liberal, democratic national polity or becoming an EU member.

While this particular reframing of Islam and modernity is unique to Turkey, the demand for change and the desire for better lives are broader; we find them recently in others parts of the Muslim world in an epidemic-like form.

The current uprisings in the Middle East and North Africa initially looked like economic reactions, but soon enough it became obvious that economic demands are only part of a broader political march under the demands for democratization, and this political march is itself part of a broader cultural march demanding better lives. This "better life" includes not only democratic states but also promises for "not littering streets or bribing officers." Interestingly, these micro aspects (clean streets, halting patronage) were also seen as cooperating in good and piety instead of sin and transgression.[4] Piety, in this context, is not sought through suicide bombings in an attempt to convert the world, but, as is the case for Muslimists, it is sought through Muslims embracing aspects of modernity from political values to economy to everyday life.

(Summer 2011, 13.2)

Notes

[1] Ayse Arman, "Interview with Rabia Yalcin: What is Worn at Home is Offside for Outside," *Hurriyet Newspaper* (15 July 2009), http://www.hurriyet.com.tr/yazarlar/ 12072960.asp. Translation by author.

[2] John Leland and Duraid Adnan, "Mannequins Wear a Message for Iraq's Women," *The New York Times* (8 February 2011), http://www.nytimes.com/2011/02/09/ world/middleeast/09baghdad.html.

[3] My choice of conceptualizing this new orthodoxy as "Muslimism" aims to reflect its layered individual orientation. The concept "Islamism" cannot describe this new form. Linguistically, Islamism describes a set of actions and ideas oriented towards Islam itself. Paralleling this, the academic use of Islamism refers to an ideology aiming to retrieve an Islamic order, either through the *Umma* [community] or the state. But, more than a new label, Muslimism is an analytical category; it brings with it a certain methodological thinking and suggests that we focus our attention on the Muslim subject and his or her actions, rather than assuming religious texts (or Islam more broadly) will produce homogenous ideas, aims, and actors, as if Islam is independent of Muslims and the contexts surrounding it.

[4] See the Tahrir Square document "Start with Yourself First" (14 March 2011), http://www.tahrirdocuments.org/2011/03/start-with-yourself-first/#more-161.

Religion and Violence
A Conversation with Veena Das

Thomas Cushman

Thomas Cushman (TC): One of the more interesting ideas in human rights these days is the idea that the goal of the human rights movement is to provide agency to those who don't have it, presumably because of cultural repression. This seems to me to be a loaded idea of what agency means within culture. I am thinking of a recent photograph from Iraq that showed a Shiite brigade of militant, veiled women marching in protest against the U.S. occupation. You might, for instance, interview one of these women, who appear to the average Western observer to be repressed, and she might tell you: "I am free as a bird. I love my life." The Westerner, with her human rights ideology of agency as individual freedom from culture, might dismiss this as "false consciousness." She might say, "You are not really free: you are marching in formation; you are veiled." What seems to be lacking in the Western ideology of human rights, and what anthropologists seem to have always understood (which explains some of the hesitance of some anthropologists toward the universalism of human rights), is the idea that freedom can come from within culture. And in cases where one sees religiously grounded expressions of violence that look like instances of cultural repression, one can surmise that for participants these mighty actually be experiences of freedom.

Veena Das (VD): That is such an important point that you're making, because how and where you locate freedom is not a very simple task. A lot of people presume that there is a universal list that you can use to go and say, this is a "local sighting" of this or that idea of freedom in this local idiom. There might, however, be a very different way of constructing freedom.

340

TC: In my view, this is partially due to the heritage of Marx hanging over the interpretation of culture and religion rather than Durkheim. If you're Durkheim, you don't necessarily start with the view of culture as repression, but as "becoming."

VD: Well, you would see it as both, of course: repression and "becoming."

TC: Yes, since a Durkeimian view would see culture as constraining, but also constitutive of individuality and individual freedom, or as "freedom within culture." Historically speaking, religion has been a major cultural form from within which people have expressed agency.

VD: I'm very hesitant to engage in any kind of totalizing, because it's the ambiguity that I find interesting. The most important idea regarding religion is that it is not just a domain of oppression or freedom. People have the possibility of being able to move between religious and secular realms. In March of 2002, there were terrible riots against Muslims in the state of Gujarat in India. These were not only expressions of religious violence but also state-sponsored violence. But while some Hindus were motivated by Hindu symbols to kill, maim, and rape, others found this to be a desecration of religious symbols.

I was particularly moved by some paintings I saw done by an artist who paints in the Madhubani style that uses primarily Hindu religious and mythological symbols. He made a series of paintings in which he took primarily religious iconography and converted it into a powerful criticism of what happened in the riots and the pogroms against the Muslims. What I found very interesting is that his paintings are deeply religious; they weave in figures like the present Chief Minister of Gujarat, who takes on demonic proportions recognizable to those familiar with Hindu mythology. He also had the figure of Gandhi. The series is a lament and a critique but this becomes sayable for the painter with a religious iconography. He couldn't have painted this critique outside of religious language. This kind of work is an expression of many different regions of the self that any complex tradition allows and even enables.

TC: There is a tendency, I think, for people to think that religion is either violent or pacific in its essence. I'm thinking of some recent rightwing Christian fundamentalists in the U.S., who have created a binary opposition between Christianity and Islam.

At a certain level, though, one can make sociological observations about the structural relationship between religion and violence. I'm thinking here of an excellent book by David Martin called *Does Christianity Cause War?*[1] Martin argues that Christianity, when tied closely to the state in earlier historical periods, did serve more strongly as a legitimating ideology for war and violence. He notes that as Christianity became more autonomous from the state, it actually became a more pacific force. So that, for instance,

Christianity was deeply implicated in the violence of colonialism, but became precisely a major force which drove the anti-slavery movement and anticolonial movement in Britain. Similarly, in the United States, in spite of the quasi-religious rhetoric of George Bush, Christianity has been a strong force behind the anti-war movement.

I wonder if you could comment on the present relation between Islam and violence more generally, obviously not in the sense of some kind of essentialist view, but in terms of the close relationship between Islam and the state in what some authors (such as Paul Berman and Christopher Hitchens) have referred to as "Islamofascism."

VD: The relation between religion and state raises very important issues, and I am glad that you pointed to the transformations in Christianity. My first observation is that we would need to look at the global processes and the geopolitical contexts in which new state forms emerged in the Muslim world. The growth of authoritarian regimes in the Middle East is closely tied to colonial interests and now to the alliance between global capital and political regimes in these regions.

My second observation is that there are enormous differences in the way that Islam is anchored as ideology to state formation and state legitimacy in say Pakistan or Malaysia, on the one hand, and in Saudi Arabia, on the other. The last Malaysian Prime Minister, Mahathir Mohamad, wanted to lead the whole of Asia into regimes that addressed questions of poverty and development, as his 2020 plan showed. He claimed this to be part of the Islamic character of Malaysia. He made anti-Western and anti-Semitic statements, but also was tough in his criticisms of many Islamic states and of terrorist tactics of warfare. So clearly a formulation like "Islamofascism" is simply a lazy formulation that manages to obscure these complex developments within Islam. Finally, the critiques of authoritarian rulers have also come from followers of Islam within these countries and not only from Western critics, and many have paid a heavy price for criticizing the lack of civil liberties within such regimes.

TC: My more specific point is that contemporary Christians are less likely to be suicide bombers, for example.

VD: They may not be suicide bombers, but they may be party to the whole idea of just punishment, which can be as violent. There is a very interesting difference over here in the U.S., in the sense that many are more comfortable with violence from a distance. Dropping a cluster bomb from above is seen somehow as a "civilized" way of doing warfare, and suicide bombing is seen as an "uncivilized" way of doing warfare. But, in both cases, it's warfare.

TC: Might it be, then, that Christianity is linked to violence in a different way than Islam?

VD: That certainly is a very interesting question, because remember that in the international press you never get anything on the pacifist, pietistic, non-violent, and non-cooperating movements within Islam. So we know very little about the way in which people might have resisted or might have thought of alternate ways of doing politics.

TC: Is there a pacifist movement within Islam? And, if so, is its invisibility purely due to lack of press coverage?

VD: It's a question of how you word it. Pietistic movements within Islam have a long history. In my own country, India, there are tireless scholars and activists like Asghar Ali Engineer who are completely against violence in any form. In Indonesia there is a new Islamic university that is dedicated to serious dialogue between various forms of Islam and other religions. One question is whether the state form can embody those particular traditions of Islam. So there is a very interesting question that many states face: how can we be modern Muslims? It seems to me very often that we block those kinds of pathways for peoples and states to think of themselves in new ways. There is a presumption that any aspirations to the modern must mean that tradition will be compromised. So, both from the traditionalists and the so-called modernists, that particular area becomes an area of suspicion. So you might get people thinking, "Well that's not truly Islam because they are being unduly influenced by the West," which puts into circulation a very difficult idea of authenticity, as if to say, traditions don't have a right to grow and change. We need to think much more about those kinds of experiments.

TC: In terms of the modern consciousness of Islam, the ordinary modern Muslims who are going about their modern business, while also being good Muslims, are not newsworthy. There is very little cognizance of what might be called "quotidian Islam." What's newsworthy is the violent Shiite brigade or seemingly religiously inspired crowds hanging burned corpses from bridges. This strikes me as very important, since the media representation of Islam defines the "essence" of Islam for many people who are completely unfamiliar with it.

VD: But actually, I'm saying more than that. I'm saying not just that Muslims in their ordinary lives might be going about their ordinary business. I think there are other processes at work. There simply isn't enough appreciation that people in these countries write books, paint, and make films. Who are the publics who are consuming these? Neither do we see that the forms of politics that are being engaged in are varied. For instance, Palestinians are engaged in a certain kind of warfare for survival, but students who participated in protests in Iran were also engaged in politics. So one has to look at this diversity of experimentation and see what other kinds of assemblages are there within which people get placed.

343

TC: I wonder, then, how does one carry forth the complexity of those kinds of things in public consciousness when the only thing that gets attention is religious violence. Since mass communication seems intimately tied to covering almost exclusively religious violence, the public sphere is thus colonized by such images.

For me, one way around this is to enhance the experiences of intersubjective communication between religious peoples. So, for instance, you could develop a program in which you could take a devout Muslim from, say, Iraq, and bring him into contact with a fundamentalist American Christian in the American South. They might be completely at odds theologically, in terms of the content of their religious belief, but in each case, the form of religious experience is *pious*. They might recognize and appreciate each other's piety. The normal, not-violently-disposed Muslims and Christians don't connect. The entire connection between the West and Islam is made through mediated images of violence, so that at a distance the American Christian sees the essence of Islam as embodied in the violent mob, whereas the Iraqi Muslim sees the American Christian behind the imperial political project of the American state. There is no intersubjective communication about the experience of the sacred, the everyday forms of piety that are almost always pacific.

VD: There have been all of these efforts by the World Council of Churches, for instance, to promote religious dialogue and so on. But again, it always becomes a question of a dialogue about theological premises. Whereas it seems to me that what you are saying, and what is very interesting, is that there is a different way of connecting, which is not based on some kind of a cognitive understanding, but on some kind of affective connection that people could make, and it doesn't have to be a complete commitment to each other, but it can be a particular point at which we connect.

TC: It seems to me that everyone is impressed by other peoples' rituals, for instance. On my first visit to a mosque, I was struck not by the content of Islam, since it is not apprehendable in that instance to me either theologically or linguistically, but by the form of the sacred, a sense of the numinous that transcends any theological content. The same sense is evident in a Russian Orthodox ceremony, or a high mass in a Catholic cathedral. There is a tendency, I think, to focus on the conflicts in cultural forms rather than on the resonances.

VD: What I would say is that you could have a kind of horizontal connection, which is not brought about through leaders, but is a particular point of connection. It is not even a commitment like a friendship but presents the possibility of something like a resolution in the future, not necessarily now.

TC: In your essay, "Violence and Translation," you write about difference, diversity, and "the withdrawal of recognition to the other." You note that "difference, when it is cast as non-criterial, becomes untranslatable precisely because it ceases to allow for a mutual future in language."[2] You remind us that the problem isn't just the closing off of the present in intersubjective communication that is the problem, but the closing off of the future in such communication. I imagine that there are some times when mutual futures together must be closed off, in cases, for instances when one or both parties lose complete trust in one another, or inflict irreconcilable trauma on a relationship. It is illusory to imagine that all relationships can be open to a mutual future in language.

One of my criticisms of the sacralization of difference and diversity in contemporary multicultural movements is that, despite good intentions, by stressing difference and diversity (which is essentially to objectify otherness), mutual futures in language are made more difficult. I would prefer a modality which stresses some shared ideals, or some common recognition of our humanity, as well as our frailty and vulnerability.

If we get back to the intensifying violence today, it seems to me that the forms of violence based on difference are becoming more fixed and settled more deeply into the fabric of culture, and as a result, the crisis is not only about the conflicts in the present, but the closing off of mutual futures. I'm not only talking about conflicts between Bush and the Shiites in Iraq. Now the left intellectuals are battling with the neoconservatives, and you see the development of critiques of America and "Empire" that are of a distinctly quasi-religious nature and converse reactions that put forth an idolatry of America that is a new form of civil religion, which is quite pronounced in America. Perhaps I'm being too pessimistic!

VD: Well, I think that the world is chaotic, but for me this is a good thing because it allows me to think that even small groups of people thinking differently can change something. I think this is of the utmost importance that this should happen. I'm really encouraged by examples such as this painter that I mentioned earlier, or the rallies for peace, or small communities refusing to pay taxes to protest that their money should not go to support warfare.

TC: I'm going to persist somewhat with my pessimism, or perhaps a better way of putting it is my tragic sense of contemporary history. Your painter expresses a nice idea, but he strikes me as quixotic, since the monsters are so much bigger than his paintings.

VD: But I think of Gandhi and of the fact of daring to have a different kind of politics. Nobody thought that this "naked fakir," as Churchill called him, could actually take on something like the British Empire. But he was able to mobilize the energies and the discontent of the subaltern populations. I'm pessimistic at times, but I don't know how to live that pessimism. And you're not living that pessimism!

TC: Well, of course, I take an existential response to the *Weltschmerz*, or world-weariness, caused by living in history, by retreating to the quotidian and enchanting forms of existence: family, children, and what have you. And I imagine that even those who commit religiously inspired violence are not very happy with their violence (although some, to be sure, are) and also have spheres of affection and enchantment in their otherwise turbulent lives. But, still, it is the intensification of violent language and its assumption of quasi-religious forms, which is perhaps our most central reality, that is worrisome. And this always intensifies in wartime.

In order to try to understand the discourse surrounding the war in Iraq, I've found John Dewey's writings before and during World War I to be extremely useful. Dewey was extremely concerned about the intensification of language during the war and what might be called "linguistic violence." He supported the war on the grounds that Germany was a distinct threat to world peace, but he also argued vociferously against essentializing the Germans as beasts. This bestialization of the "Hun" was predominant in public discourse, and he argued that it was not necessary to the winning of the war. The consequence would be that, long after the war, the violent images would continue to negatively affect social relations. There might be pragmatic reasons for disarming Iraq, which are valid on utilitarian grounds, but they get hedged about by all of these cultural constructions and the situation escalates, producing the same kind of symbolic reaction on the "other side." Together these take on a kind of self-generating life of their own, which comes to be independent and perhaps even counterproductive to the pragmatic task at hand.

VD: That's why this particular point about keeping open the possibility of futures is very important. I'm not saying that everything can be resolved right now, but we have to be placeholders for a different kind of future. One of the most disturbing things to me is the problem in India of when Islam or Hinduism, which are really complex civilizations, gave up on the ambition of understanding their own complexity. Those who become the spokesmen of Hinduism against Islam, or who posit that Muslims are the major problem in India today, are often people who have absolutely no sense of the complexity of their own traditions or the history of their own civilizations. I will not go into the so-called pragmatic reasons of going into war in the case of Iraq because it would take too long to show the falseness of the many analogies used.

TC: In many cases, the truncated sense of cultural complexity leads to a similarly non-complex sense of the self as well. People come to see themselves in the banal terms of a simplified culture and history. This happened in Bosnia. At the beginning of the war, Bosnia was perhaps the most liberal and secular republic of the former Yugoslavia. Bosnian Muslims were highly secular and religious mostly in name. As the war and genocide progressed and the Bosnians became more and more isolated by the indifference of the world to their plight, they took on increasingly Muslim identities, which were based on a quite simplistic and even caricaturish understanding of Islam in Bosnia, crafted by nationalist Muslim elites. And many of them ended up assuming an identity that was similarly simplistic and even in accordance with the stereotypical and essentialist constructions of Serbian nationalists.

VD: I'm thinking of Croatia, which had a wonderful scholarship on other religions, but ended up expelling those kinds of intellectuals. There were violent reactions against women intellectuals, for instance, who were arguing for more complex, hybrid identities. What is interesting to me is that those who confuse these simplistic categories are the ones who are excluded most violently.

TC: I reread your essay on the anthropology of pain and have a question for you based on that.[3] As you noted, some of the most intense forms of social solidarity are based on common experiences of pain. What you have now in the current world context, especially in Iraq, is a kind of mutual infliction of pain, which serves to deepen the solidarity of conflicting parties against each other. For instance, I was listening to Colin Powell's response to the violence in Iraq against Americans, and he noted that this only served to strengthen the resolve of the United States, which, in turn, leads to the infliction of more pain on certain groups of Iraqis, which strengthens their own solidarity and resolve. As I think about your work in relation to the problem of religious violence, it occurs to me that perhaps religious language is an attempt to articulate experiences of pain, but not simply in a passive way, but as a vocabulary of action which itself can come to serve as a cultural template for violence itself. So my question is: how do you counter the collective solidarities produced by the infliction of pain?

VD: My fundamental premise in that essay was that there are no standing languages of pain. Standing languages of pain fail us. The ambiguity around pain is precisely that you can get, at one level, the most fantastic forms of human solidarity, which are brought about because we learn to respond to the other's suffering, so that we acknowledge the other as someone with a soul. But simultaneously, you also get the possibility of creating the most violent forms of rejection, also premised upon the notion of pain. So you can have pain as creating communities of sympathy but also creating communities of *ressentiment*. It's interesting to think about the mediatization of pain. There is also the interesting question about the ways in which you might have circulations that move beyond the immediate context of pain. Some of the most violent forms of oppression are premised on somebody's capacity to inflict pain on someone else. This might be the basis upon which future memories are created, and these memories might be created around *ressentiment*, which is a great danger. That's why my sense is to always engage in what I would call a "descent into the ordinary."

I have a different way of thinking about religion. I don't think of religion as something which is only about the transcendent. In my sense, the idea of religion and spirituality as self-formation is very closely related to these possibilities of the everyday and recognition of the everyday, rather than some grand projects of remaking mankind or something like that. There is a great danger in the flight from the everyday. As I say in "Violence and Translation," we have to live with some forms of uncertainty and violence. To accept that is not to be fatalistic. Thinking that we are going to somehow exclude every form of pain seems to me to be a very dangerous way of thinking. I am for a version of moral perfectionism that is rooted in acknowledging the flesh and blood character of our being in the world.

(Spring 2004, 6.4)

Notes

[1] David Martin, *Does Christianity Cause War?* (Oxford, England: Clarendon, 1998).

[2] Veena Das, "Violence and Translation," *Anthropological Quarterly* 75.1 (2002): 107.

[3] Veena Das, "The Anthropology of Pain," *Critical Events: An Anthropological Perspective on Contemporary India* (Oxford, England: University Press, 1995), 175–96.

V.
The Self and Self-Making

Get a Life
Illusions of Self-Invention

Wendy Kaminer

It is probably easier to become a celebrity in America today than to find something new—or something nice—to say about celebrity culture. We are all experts in this culture. It is our habitat, as inescapable as the weather; and like the weather, insistent and occasionally oppressive, celebrity culture demands attention but exhausts imagination. It's like a hot August day when all people can say is "Hot enough for you," and they say it repeatedly. Google the phrase "celebrity culture," and you'll find about 38,000 hits; bloggers, reporters, columnists, and academics are all pondering the phenomenon of fame and what people do to achieve it. You'll find disquisitions on celebrity and consumerism, celebrity and victimization, celebrity and sex, celebrity and gender, celebrity and literature, celebrity and politics, celebrity and the visual arts, celebrity and exhibitionism, celebrity and ritual, celebrity and crime, celebrity and selfhood, and, of course, celebrity and moral decline. (I have yet to find an article on celebrity and moral uplift.)

I wondered how to approach this very familiar topic, and then, last fall, something entirely unfamiliar occurred: the Red Sox won the World Series. Baseball is not exactly emblematic of celebrity culture; it preceded modern celebrity and the celebrity athlete. Still, the business of sports depends on star players with star salaries, corporate endorsements, and even some high profile owners. As many have observed, professional sports is show business. The Red Sox World Series win will not, like Paris Hilton's cell phone, provide you with a direct line to the epicenter of celebrity culture, but it can help you make a few connections.

The Sox last won the series in 1918, a few years after D.W. Griffith's film *The Birth of a Nation* helped launch the modern film and propaganda industry, but a few years before the birth of celebrity, as we know it. (Celebrity is hardly a new phenomenon, but it is a changing one. Consider that Charles Lindbergh has been described as our first modern celebrity.) So the 86-year drought endured by generations of Red Sox players and fans was a fertile period for celebrityhood. You no longer have to traverse the Atlantic alone in a marathon flight in a primitive plane to achieve it.

It is worth noting perhaps that for many faithful Sox fans the long awaited win was both astonishing and inevitable, as was Lindbergh's flight nearly 80 years ago. That the Red Sox's conquest of the Cardinals, and even the yankees, was somewhat less impressive than Lindbergh's conquest of the Atlantic did nothing to diminish the joy of it for fans; and the victory extravaganzas in Boston dramatized at least one important dynamic of celebrity worship—the intense vicarious pleasures of it.

Perhaps the wishful identification of idolizers with their idols has always been obvious, especially in spectator sports, where fans are expected to enjoy and exhibit team spirit. "We won!" the fans exclaim, and I always want to respond, "Who's we? Exactly how did you contribute to this victory, while you watched it from the sidelines, the sports bar, or the comfort of your den?" But I never quite realized the power or content of that "we" until the Sox won the series. After the final out of the final game, the Red Sox rushed out of the dugout and joyously piled on top of each other, as winning teams are apt to do. At about the same moment, it seems, fans in sports bars starting piling on top of each other as well.

Their behavior was so clearly, and apparently so unselfconsciously, imitative. The fans seemed intent on experiencing exactly what the players were experiencing, and not just vicariously. They could only imagine actually playing in the series, but they didn't have to imagine being part of a victory pile. They could form one of their own. The trouble is that the fans hadn't exactly earned the victory, no matter how important they imagined their support for it. They had been watching the game, not playing it, although many were probably wishing or imagining that they were playing, not watching. It is a common, harmless fantasy, in moderation, but sometimes you have to wonder about the reality this fantasy displaces. When a 23-year-old watching the victory parade declares, "This is the best day of our lives," all you can say is, "I hope not."[1]

I don't discount the enthusiasm of youth or the influence of alcohol on the behavior of sports fans, whose post-game celebrations sometimes turn riotous and violent. But while occasional celebratory riots may be influenced by alcohol, they may be caused, in part, by the intense identification of fans with players and the desire to share in the catharsis of victory in a battle hard-fought. I suspect that the essential falseness of the feeling that "we," not "they," win ball games partly accounts for those victory celebrations that turn into victory mobs. The wildness of the mob looks like overcompensation.

Imitation is not, of course, the only form of flattery for fans; some offer infatuation, which players, like other pop stars, are apt not to discourage: Red Sox heartthrob Johnny Damon, who recently published a book, contracted not to cut his hair during his book tour. Most of the team enjoyed iconic status, at least temporarily, and some share of sex appeal. People wanted to touch them or see them up close. They yearned for some semblance of a personal connection. As *The Boston Globe* noted, in its special supplement on the victory parade (which you can purchase on its website along with Red Sox memorabilia):

Most fans waited hours for a moment that, in the end, was merely a glimpse of the team. But few seem disappointed. In one electric moment at Government Center, Santa Lopez made eye contact with slugger David Ortiz, who pointed at her with both index fingers while she played a guira, a musical instrument from their native Dominican Republic. "I feel crazy," Lopez, a preschool teacher from Boston, said after the board carrying Ortiz passed.[2]

Still, the fans' identification with their team can't simply be dismissed as a trigger for either sophomoric carousing or imaginary romances. It may also be a symbol or even a medium for essential, actual relationships. As the Red Sox victory celebration showed, for many Sox fans, the "we" who won the Series spanned several generations of friends, parents, and grandparents, some of whom didn't live to see the Sox prevail. Fans were not simply wishfully identifying with a baseball team or fantasizing about their connections to particular players. They were celebrating or commemorating intense emotional bonds forged by actual, not vicarious relationships. Some attended the parade with their families; some were accompanied by memories of deceased family members. The victory parade was also a memorial service.

One website created by fan Shaun Kelly asked the Sox to win the series for the sake of his late father.[3] The site became a memorial page for innumerable fans and led to a book, by Eric Christensen, called *Win It for...: What a World Championship Means to Generations of Red Sox Fans.* "It's our fathers and our mothers and our grandparents," Kelly wrote in his posting. "It's our next door neighbors and our baseball coaches and our aunts. These are the ghosts that matter to us." *The Boston Globe* described some of the elegies posted on Kelly's site:

Postings recalled the grandmother who stayed awake until 2 a.m. to hear Sox games on the West Coast. Or the uncle who coached Little League for 40 years. Several varied on the theme of lazy afternoons when their fathers let them play hooky from school and treated them to a game.... "Win it for my grandfather who died five hours before we beat the Yankees last week," one fan wrote. "For my mother who had to tell me with two outs in the ninth as my friends were bursting into cheers. And for all of us."[4]

Shaun Kelly offered this explanation for the popularity of his site: "While we've all come to grips with our loved ones' deaths, there was always this unfinished business about the Red Sox winning. Now we can put that to bed." Some fans imagined that the dead were celebrating too: "Hopefully wherever she is, she was able to get a good view of the game," one fan posted, recalling a recently deceased friend. "you wish she could be here to experience it. But you also take comfort in knowing that she must be jumping for joy."[5]

You may doubt the existence of an afterlife; or if you believe in the afterlife, you may doubt that the spirits or souls who inhabit it continue to care about baseball. You may lack the fervent love for a team that was harbored by these faithful Red Sox fans. You may find their love perplexing. But it can't be easily dismissed or lamented as just another delusion of a vicarious celebrity culture. The relationship between celebrity and audience is falsely intimate, of course, and it is disturbing when a fan declares her love for celebrities who don't even know she exists. Fans imagine themselves on a firstname basis with celebrity players—Pedro, Nomar, or Manny—while for the players, any particular fan is merely a category, not an individual. But the relationship between fans may be profoundly intimate, and professions of love for a team of strangers may, in part, be expressions of love for families and friends.

One fan drove down from New Hampshire with his nine-year-old son to watch the victory parade because "he wanted to relive what he called 'one of the best experiences of my life,' sitting in center field with his son during game 2 of the World Series."[6] A 27-year-old woman reported flying up from Virginia to watch the parade with her father, who took her to Red Sox games when she was little: "Every time I think about this it makes me want to cry," she said. "It's more for my dad than anything." This was a familiar refrain: a 45-year-old man who watched the parade with his father (who'd flown in from Colorado to attend) said, "I became a Red Sox fan because of my father. That's why this is so special to me. I was hoping they'd do it before he died."[7]

In the end, what was most surprising about the Red Sox victory was not the team's startling comeback in the fourteenth inning of the fifth game of the American League play-off, or the six-game winning streak that followed, or the mere fact that the Red Sox finally won the Series after 86 years. What was most surprising about this victory was the perspective it offered on the fans' heartfelt connections with each other.

But people can bond over torturing cats. If the relationships between people with common interests or obsessions can be productive, benign, or nobody else's business, the occasion for their relationships may be worth critiquing. The effect of fandom on individual fans is hard to characterize, however, like the effect of religion on co-religionists. "Religion is only good for good people," Mary McCarthy said.[8]

We might view celebrity culture similarly, noting that its individual effects are contingent. It is facile to note that "love" for a pop star or athlete may compensate for the absence or inadequacy of genuine romantic attachments or other actual, intimate relationships (although facile statements are not necessarily false); and it is important to remember that when love for a celebrity is shared, it may become a basis for friendship. But put aside the bathos of shrieking, lovelorn fans; their hysteria remains disturbing.

You might discern similar hysteria in the crowds at a revival meeting when higher deities than pop stars are invoked. Worship is often a collective exercise, whether the objects of adoration are secular or religious, and fervently worshipful crowds seem easily transformed into mobs. The effect of the Red Sox win on fans was contingent too. Relief, if not surprise, greeted the happy ending provided by rejoicing fans. So while the Sox fans' intense identification with the team was not exactly a tale of moral uplift, it was a welcome occasion for peaceful, emotional catharsis. As one man observed, "I'm letting go of a lot of baggage, a lot of bitterness. I feel like I want to see Grady Little, I want to see Bill Buckner, and I want to apologize to them."[9]

You can regard this statement as evidence of either the uses or the abuses of fandom. Either you focus sympathetically on the release of "baggage" and "bitterness" afforded by a World Series win, or you wonder that so much baggage and bitterness was generated by a World Series loss. You might respond critically to this man, noting that a World Series or play-off game, even against the yankees, is only a game; or you might value his ability to use the game as a relatively harmless vehicle for existential angst. You might want to tell this man to "get a life," or you might welcome the possibility of experiencing and releasing potentially destructive emotions through baseball.

Spectator sports are theatrical entertainments, after all. Should we view the larger spectacle of celebrity positively, as another form of theater and opportunity for catharsis? Or is Western civilization declining when people vicariously experience the break-up of Brad and Jen with the same emotional intensity with which they might experience the tragedy of Romeo and Juliet?

It is fair to worry about the decline of literacy, if not civilization, when tabloids replace Shakespeare; but highbrow and lowbrow entertainments—tragedy and slapstick—have long co-existed. (We study popular culture, in part, to have an excuse for wallowing in it.) The important difference between the Brad and Jen break-up and Romeo and Juliet's tragic romance as spectacle or entertainment is not the difference between *People* magazine and Shakespeare's plays. It is the difference between fictional characters and actual human beings.

People have long lost themselves in books; they have fallen in love with fictional heroes, or emulated them, or imagined their own lives would conform to their favorite fictional narratives. Indeed, the protagonist, male or female, whose ideals and expectations derive from popular fiction is a familiar literary character. Think of Catherine Morland in Jane Austen's *Northanger Abbey*. When she first ventures out into the world, young, unsophisticated, and besotted with gothic novels, Catherine mistakes innocent, actual events for sinister plot turns. Since *Northanger Abbey* is a comic tale, some embarrassment, but no harm comes to Catherine as she learns that life does not read like her favorite books. Catherine is a well-intentioned ingénue, and her confusion of real life with fiction is merely immature, not pathological, or malevolent; it poses a threat only to her pride, and she learns quickly from her folly when it is exposed to her. Imagine how differently she would fare if she continued to resist reality (she might end up like Madame Bovary). Imagine how differently we would view her if she regarded other people as mere fictions, or objects or extensions of her own desire.

At best, she would be a pest, an irritant, to the object of her fantasies or obsessions. At next best, she would be an unwelcome intruder, if she actively coveted her idol's status, possessions, or relationships. Consider the battle between starlet and star in the classic 1950 film, *All About Eve*. The starlet, played by Anne Baxter, flatters and serves the star, played by Bette Davis, so that she can effectively obliterate her, by appropriating her career, as well as her husband. (She gets the former, not the latter.) At worst, a groupie, acolyte, or fan can be a stalker; not content merely to admire, a stalker essentially wants to appropriate the object of her obsession. She exhibits a proprietary interest in her idol and a belief that the idol has a concomitant obligation to respond with affection, desire, or an admission that the idol is one with the fan. She wants either to *be* her idol or to enjoy an intimate relationship with her, to see herself reflected and confirmed in the idol's eyes.

So while efforts to appropriate fictional characters may be benign and amusing (assuming the fictional role model is not one of Patricia Highsmith's sociopaths), efforts to appropriate the characters of real people are inherently malevolent. Indeed, the fear of being subsumed by another person or entity seems primal. Consider the emotional resonance of two, mid-twentieth-century horror films about theft of the self: *Invasion of the Body Snatchers*, with its nightmare vision of pod people, and *The Fly*, in which a scientist turns into a fly. Or consider David Cronenberg's terrifying 1986 remake of *The Fly*, which focuses not on the fantastical bodily transformation into another species but on the destruction of personality, self, and soul.

Outside the realm of science fiction, nature offers a tragically common version of this progressive destruction of selfhood, in Alzheimer's and other brain disorders. "Consciousness virtually disappears in advanced states of Alzheimer's," neurologist Antonio Damasio observes in *The Feeling of What Happens*:

> The decline first affects extended consciousness by narrowing its scope progressively to the point in which virtually all semblance of autobiographical self disappears. Eventually it is the turn of core consciousness to be diminished to a degree in which even the simple sense of self is no longer present.[10]

We like to think of our selves as somehow inalienable, inviolate, or maybe even immortal, but the self can be destroyed by the same body that houses and nurtures it.

I don't want to exaggerate the threat of appropriation posed by celebrity worship; I simply want to identify the potential horror lurking in the proprietary relationships that some fans imagine they enjoy with celebrities. We can't dismiss as harmless the fantasy that we can "love" celebrities who remain strangers to us and that they can love us back—a fantasy encouraged by pop stars who declare their love for fans. "I love you all," some stars assure their audiences, on leaving the stage. I doubt they expect to be taken seriously, but in professing their love, they assume some responsibility for the imaginary relationships fans form with them.

"You Made Me Love You," a young Judy Garland famously sings to a photo of Clark Gable in one of her early films (*Broadway Melody of 1938*). Her love song might be an indictment of celebrity as well as a tribute to it. The image of Garland singing to a movie star's photograph has its charms, but only because it is fictive. When real-life fans convince themselves that their love for a star is real and perhaps ought to be requited, they begin to seem dangerously deranged. Fortunately, the vast majority of fans are content to imitate, not stalk, the objects of their appropriative desires, perhaps, in part, because celebrities actively enable imitation and profit from it greatly. Many fans are followers who want to look or smell like their favorite celebrities; that's what makes J.Lo rich. But the imitative impulse is often mutual: celebrities are sometimes fashioned to reflect the conventional dreams and desires of their target audiences. Ashlee Simpson is perhaps most accurately described as a famous version of her fans; her most salient characteristic is banality.

The most charismatic celebrities combine banality with hints of divinity, like Princess Diana; they satisfy the paradoxical desire for accessible deities, inviting both identification and idolatry. Diana was indeed the "people's princess," as Tony Blair declared after her death, although her bond with the "people" was not forged by egalitarianism, as he implied; it reflected her un-exceptionalism. Like Ashlee Simpson, Diana was, in part, a follower and product of pop culture; her persona seemed borrowed from popular therapies, romance novels, soap operas, and conventional notions of feminine nurturance and victimization. Beautiful, glamorous, aristocratic, and not averse to being revered (she aspired to be the "queen of people's hearts"), the Princess of Wales was also a strikingly ordinary woman who suffered from the ordinary syndromes and sicknesses diagnosed by pop therapists and, once upon a time, regularly dissected on *Oprah*. Diana was not just a fairytale princess; she was also a woman wronged, a single mother with an eating disorder, insufficient self-esteem, and a history of familial dysfunction.[11]

It is not surprising that, like Elvis, Princess Diana was virtually deified after her premature death, as she became a goddess of pop theologies, celebrated for her loving nature and ability to transcend the weaknesses and struggles that she shared with other mortals. "Diana won the hearts of people across the globe for her great capacity to love and her unashamed openness…," one website paying tribute to the "Goddess" Diana proclaims.

The world related to Diana's tragedies of rejection, betrayal and devastation; her struggles with negative emotions and related illness; and the eventual championing over the emotional turmoil. Diana managed to successfully conquer her own identity bringing out the "Warrior Goddess" within.[12]

The cult inspired by Diana was extraordinary, in scope if not intensity: if the Beatles were more famous than Jesus Christ, as John Lennon once remarked, Diana was arguably more famous than the Beatles; and, like Lennon, she was a martyr to her own celebrity. But celebrities don't have to enjoy or endure her level of renown, or suffer selfsacrifice, in order to be sanctified. Celebrity culture draws a very fine line between the ridiculous and the sublime: Compared to Jesus Christ, Red Sox centerfielder Johnny Damon responded with enthusiastic modesty, noting that the comparison was "incredible.... What more can you ask for? Even being mentioned in the same sentence as Jesus or God.... I mean, those guys are awesome."[13] Indeed. But the denizens of celebrity culture are easily awestruck. Television shows are promoted in somber reverential tones, as if watching were a sacred ritual. The market in celebrity memorabilia is flourishing, thanks to fans willing to purchase whatever their favorite celebrities have touched. Recently, fans of film director Tim Burton flocked to his ex-girlfriend's garage sale.[14] A pair of dirty socks allegedly worn by Bryan Adams was auctioned off on eBay for more than $1,000 last year.[15] Some socks, however, are priceless: The bloody sock injured Red Sox pitcher Curt Schilling wore in Game 2 of the World Series is enshrined in the Baseball Hall of Fame. Schilling's in-laws drove from Maryland to Cooperstown, New york to deliver the sock because "they didn't trust the U.S. mail," *The Boston Globe* reported. Ted Spencer, curator of the Baseball Hall of Fame, wondered how to display the sock: "Do we just lay it out," he asked, "or do we stuff it in a shoe like a foot."[16]

Celebrity culture may reflect the religious impulse, which gives rise to this sort of fetishism, at its most amusing or ridiculous; but it reflects that impulse nonetheless and illustrates the relationship between the accessibility of idols and their promise of transcendence: How can people know or be inspired by gods or saints with whom they can't identify? "All religion must begin with some anthropomorphism," Karen Armstrong observes in *A History of God*. "A deity which is utterly remote from humanity...cannot inspire a spiritual quest."[17]

The fans' need to bond or identify with idealized celebrities probably inspires their delight in occasionally glimpsing the reality masked by the ideal. If the cosmetic surgery boom reflects, in part, our desire to look like celebrities, the market for candid photos of celebrity cellulite reflects our desire to see celebrities look like us. It is not meanness or schadenfreude so much as the desire for intimacy that seems to underlie the appeal of reality photos of stars.

This oxymoronic faith in the possibility of intimacy between strangers is characteristic not just of celebrity worship (and the illusion of intimacy provided by the camera). It is also an adaptation to the loss of privacy; if you can't keep secrets you might as well devalue secrecy and reveal yourself to strangers. The exhibitionism so essential to celebrity is, in part, a subversion of surveillance. But it is also a hallmark of the cloying, confessional, therapeutic culture that flourished in the 1990s and dates back at least to the late 1960s, although aficionados of the counterculture who exhorted us to let it all hang out were amateurs compared to contemporary exhibitionists who populate reality television and individual webcasts.

With some measure of fame so easily attainable, you might expect its value to decline; but instead of devaluing fame generally, the market tends to create hierarchies of renown, as it creates hierarchies of other commodities. The ubiquity of counterfeit luxury goods—Rolex watches, Burberry scarves, or Louis Vuitton bags—doesn't seem to have much effect on the status or price of the "real" things. The celebrities of reality television are knock-offs, like faux Chanel accessories sold on the street. "Real" celebrities—movie stars, athletes, evangelists, or talk show hosts—retain their cachet, not to mention their wealth and their numbers of fans.

The trouble with contemporary celebrity culture is its tendency not to cheapen fame but to make it more accessible: as the accessibility of celebrity increases, so does the obligation to achieve it. Celebrity, once conferred on a relative fortunate few, now seems within reach of the many who believe they deserve it. So the aura of failure that attaches to people who remain poor in a supposed meritocracy now threatens to attach to the growing number of people who seek fame but remain anonymous. Reality television is populated by positive thinkers, most of whom are destined for disappointment:

> "I'm psyched," people say, confronting a plate of worms or a panel of judges. "I'm definitely going to win this thing."

Like the manufactured pop stars or recording artists they emulate, most would-be American idols of reality television talk alike, dress alike, pose alike, and sing alike. Uniqueness is not rewarded in this culture; it tends to select contestants who are most attractively or skillfully familiar. Self-actualization is invoked but not practiced. This is a culture of self-censorship. Fluent in cliché and focused on embodying common ideals, aspiring idols apparently want not to be themselves; success lies in most convincingly being someone else.

Celebrity impersonators proliferate, devoid of any satiric intent. But celebrity culture can't be credited or blamed for the triumph of appropriation; it dates back to the early 1900s when Marcel Duchamp exhibited common, "ready-made" objects—most famously a urinal—as art. (Duchamp's urinal, shown in 1917, was recently rated the most influential work of modern art in a poll of 500 art experts, the BBC reported.)[18] Whether or not contemporary artists exhibit similar objects, like soup cans, more satirically or cynically than would-be pop stars exhibit themselves as "ready-made" celebrities, their work expresses a questionable notion of individual inventiveness characteristic of copycat celebrity culture.

The constraining of individualism by the desire to conform is a familiar theme in American culture that long predates contemporary celebrityhood, or contemporary art, and is hardly uniquely American. "Society has now fairly got the better of individuality," John Stuart Mill said of mid-nineteenth-century England. The "danger which threatens human nature is not the excess, but the deficiency, of personal impulses and preferences."[19] Celebrity culture, so closely tied to consumption, may be rightly condemned for acquisitive self-centeredness, but it is wrongly confused with individualism. It lacks the "individual spontaneity" that Mill considered essential to liberty.[20] Conformity or the rejection of eccentricity reflected an antipathy to freedom or, at least, a crabbed notion of it, Mill suggested.

Generally, people don't make choices or decisions by consulting their own preferences or the demands of the "best and the highest" in themselves, he charged. They consult what he considered the "despotism" of custom:

> They ask themselves, what is suitable to my position.... I do not mean that they choose what is customary in preference to what suits their own inclination. It does not occur to them to have any inclination except for what is customary. Thus the mind itself is bowed to the yoke; even in what people do for pleasure, conformity is the first thing thought of; they like in crowds; they exercise choice only among things commonly done; peculiarity of taste, eccentricity of conduct are shunned equally with crimes; until by dint of not following their own nature they have no nature to follow; their human capacities are withered and starved....[21]

Was Mill over-generalizing? Of course—it is an occupational hazard for philosophers and social critics. But his impassioned accusation, or lament, aptly describes the vice that derives from the "virtue" of appropriation. It is perversely satisfying to note that our own imitative celebrity culture is essentially nothing new. The culture of celebrity is a familiar culture of confinement, self-imposed. Most of us participate in this culture, and many of us feel diminished by it, as we collaborate in the impoverishment of our own imaginations.

(Spring 2005, 7.1)

Notes

[1] Brian MacQuarrie, "Thank You," *The Boston Globe* (31 October 2004).

[2] Ibid.

[3] Peter DeMarco, "A Site Where Prayers Were Answered," *The Boston Globe* (29 October 2004): F14. You can find the site at sonsofsamhorn.com, which bills itself as "one of the most well-informed and introspective Red Sox discussion communities on the net."

[4] Ibid.

[5] Ibid.

[6] Michael Levenson, "Celebration Bringing Fans From All Over," *The Boston Globe* (29 October 2004).

[7] Bella English, "After Decades of Longing, Generations Can Rejoice," *The Boston Globe* (31 October 2004).

[8] Mary McCarthy, *Memories of a Catholic Girlhood* (New York, NY: Harcourt Brace, 1946), 23.

[9] MacQuarrie, "Thank You." Grady Little was the Red Sox manager in 2003, blamed for losing the American League play-off to the Yankees. Bill Buckner was a Red Sox first baseman who missed a ground ball in an infamous play in Game 6 of the 1986 World Series against the Mets.

[10] Antonio Damasio, *The Feeling of What Happens* (New York, NY: Harcourt Brace, 1999), 104.

[11] I've remarked on this cult of Diana previously in *Sleeping with Extra-Terrestrials: The Rise of Irrationalism and the Perils of Piety* (New York, NY: Pantheon, 1999), 130–34 .

[12] See www.splash.net.au/goddess2/goddessDiana/goddess.html.

[13] Sean Flynn, "Heeere's Johnny," *Boston Magazine* (February 2005).

[14] Sharon Waxman, "Rummaging for a Piece of Tim Burton," *The New York Times* (12 March 2005).

[15] Marie Puente, "The Sweet Smell of Excess," *USA Today* (4 February 2005).

[16] Carol Beggy and Mark Shanahan, "Schilling Sock in the Hall," *The Boston Globe* (10 February 2005).

[17] Karen Armstrong, *A History of God* (New York, NY: Ballantine, 1993), 48.

[18] See http://news.bbc.co.uk/2/hi/entertainment/4059997.stm.

[19] J.S. Mill, *On Liberty* (Middlesex, England: Penguin, 1985), 125.

[20] Ibid., 120.

[21] Ibid., 125–6.

The Strange Persistence
of Guilt

Wilfred M. McClay

Those of us living in the developed countries of the West find ourselves in the tightening grip of a paradox, one whose shape and character have so far largely eluded our understanding. It is the strange persistence of guilt as a psychological force in modern life. If anything, the word *persistence* understates the matter. Guilt has not merely lingered. It has grown, even metastasized, into an ever more powerful and pervasive element in the life of the contemporary West, even as the rich language formerly used to define it has withered and faded from discourse, and the means of containing its effects, let alone obtaining relief from it, have become ever more elusive.

This paradox has set up a condition in which the phenomenon of rising guilt becomes both a byproduct of and an obstacle to civilizational advance. The stupendous achievements of the West in improving the material conditions of human life and extending the blessings of liberty and dignity to more and more people are in danger of being countervailed and even negated by a growing burden of guilt that poisons our social relations and hinders our efforts to live happy and harmonious lives.

I use the words *strange persistence* to suggest that the modern drama of guilt has not followed the script that was written for it. Prophets such as Friedrich Nietzsche were confident that once the modern Western world finally threw off the metaphysical straitjacket that had confined the possibilities of all previous generations, the moral reflexes that had accompanied that framework would disappear along with them. With God dead, all would indeed be permitted. Chief among the outmoded reflexes would be the experience of guilt, an obvious vestige of irrational fear promulgated by oppressive, life-denying institutions erected in the name and image of a punitive deity.

Indeed, Nietzsche had argued in *On the Genealogy of Morality* (1887), a locus classicus for the modern understanding of guilt, that the very idea of God, or of the gods, originated hand-in-hand with the feeling of indebtedness (the German *Schuld*—"guilt"—being the same as the word for "debt," *Schulden*).[1] The belief in God or gods arose in primitive societies, Nietzsche speculated, out of dread of the ancestors and a feeling of indebtedness to them. This feeling of indebtedness expanded its hold, in tandem with the expansion of the concept of God, to the point that when the Christian God offered itself as "the maximal god yet achieved," it also brought about "the greatest feeling of indebtedness on earth."

But "we have now started in the reverse direction," Nietzsche exulted. With the "death" of God, meaning God's general cultural unavailability, we should expect to see a consequent "decline in the consciousness of human debt." With the cultural triumph of atheism at hand, such a victory could also "release humanity from this whole feeling of being indebted towards its beginnings, its *prima causa*." Atheism would mean "a second innocence," a regaining of Eden with neither God nor Satan there to interfere with and otherwise corrupt the proceedings.[2]

This is not quite what has happened; nor does there seem to be much likelihood that it will happen, in the near future. Nietzsche's younger contemporary Sigmund Freud has proven to be the better prophet, having offered a dramatically different analysis that seems to have been more fully borne out. In his book *Civilization and Its Discontents* (*Das Unbehagen in der Kultur*), Freud declared the tenacious sense of guilt to be "the most important problem in the development of civilization." Indeed, he observed, "the price we pay for our advance in civilization is a loss of happiness through the heightening of the sense of guilt."[3]

Such guilt was hard to identify and hard to understand, though, since it so frequently dwelled on an unconscious level, and could easily be mistaken for something else. It often appears to us, Freud argued, "as a sort of *malaise* [Unbehagen], a dissatisfaction,"[4] for which people seek other explanations, whether external or internal. Guilt is crafty, a trickster and chameleon, capable of disguising itself, hiding out, changing its size and appearance, even its location, all the while managing to persist and deepen.

This seems to me a very rich and incisive description, and a useful starting place for considering a subject almost entirely neglected by historians: the steadily intensifying (although not always visible) role played by guilt in determining the structure of our lives in the twentieth and twenty-first centuries. By connecting the phenomenon of rising guilt to the phenomenon of civilizational advance, Freud was pointing to an unsuspected but inevitable byproduct of progress itself, a problem that will only become more pronounced in the generations to come.

Demoralizing Guilt

Thanks in part to Freud's influence, we live in a therapeutic age; nothing illustrates that fact more clearly than the striking ways in which the sources of guilt's power and the nature of its would-be antidotes have changed for us. Freud sought to relieve in his patients the worst mental burdens and pathologies imposed by their oppressive and hyperactive consciences, which he renamed their superegos, while deliberately refraining from rendering any judgment as to whether the guilty feelings ordained by those punitive superegos had any moral justification. In other words, he sought to release the patient from guilt's crushing hold by disarming and setting aside guilt's moral significance, and re-designating it as just another psychological phenomenon, whose proper functioning could be ascertained by its effects on one's more general well-being. He sought to "demoralize" guilt by treating it as a strictly subjective and emotional matter.

Health was the only remaining criterion for success or failure in therapy, and health was a functional category, not an ontological one. And the nonjudgmental therapeutic worldview whose seeds Freud planted has come into full flower in the mainstream sensibility of modern America, which in turn has profoundly affected the standing and meaning of the most venerable among our moral transactions, and not merely matters of guilt.

Take, for example, the various ways in which "forgiveness" is now understood. Forgiveness is one of the chief antidotes to the forensic stigma of guilt, and as such has long been one of the golden words of our culture, with particularly deep roots in the Christian tradition, in which the capacity for forgiveness is seen as a central attribute of the Deity itself. In the face of our shared human frailty, forgiveness expresses a kind of transcendent and unconditional regard for the humanity of the other, free of any admixture of interest or punitive anger or puffed-up self-righteousness. Yet forgiveness rightly understood can never deny the reality of justice. To forgive, whether one forgives trespasses or debts, means abandoning the just claims we have against others, in the name of the higher ground of love. Forgiveness affirms justice even in the act of suspending it. It is rare because it is so costly.

In the new therapeutic dispensation, however, forgiveness is all about the forgiver, and his or her power and well-being. We have come a long way from Shakespeare's Portia, who spoke so memorably in *The Merchant of Venice* about the unstrained "quality of mercy," which "droppeth as the gentle rain from heaven" and blesses both "him that gives and him that takes."[5] And an even longer way from Christ's anguished cry from the cross, "Forgive them, for they know not what they do."[6] And perhaps even further yet from the most basic sense of forgiveness, the canceling of a monetary debt or the pardoning of a criminal offense, in either case a very conscious suspension of the entirely rightful demands of justice.

We still claim to think well of forgiveness, but it has in fact very nearly lost its moral weight by having been translated into an act of random kindness whose chief value lies in the sense of personal release it gives us. "Forgiveness," proclaimed the journalist Gregg Easterbrook writing at *Beliefnet*, "is good for your health."[7] Like the similar acts of confession or apology, and other transactions in the moral economy of sin and guilt, forgiveness is in danger of being debased into a kind of cheap grace, a waiving of standards entirely, standards without which such transactions have little or no moral significance. Forgiveness only makes sense in the presence of a robust conception of justice. Without that, it is in real danger of being reduced to something passive and automatic and flimsy—a sanctimonious way of saying that nothing really matters very much at all.

The Infinite Extensibility of Guilt

The therapeutic view of guilt seems to offer the guilt-ridden an avenue of escape from its power, by redefining guilt as the result of psychic forces that do not relate to anything morally consequential. But that has not turned out to be an entirely workable solution, since it is not so easy to banish guilt merely by denying its reality. There is another powerful factor at work too, one that might be called the *infinite extensibility of guilt*. This proceeds from a very different set of assumptions, and is a surprising byproduct of modernity's proudest achievement: its ceaselessly expanding capacity to comprehend and control the physical world.

In a world in which the web of relationships between causes and effects yields increasingly to human understanding and manipulation, and in which human agency therefore becomes ever more powerful and effective, the range of our potential moral responsibility, and therefore of our potential guilt, also steadily expands. We like to speak, romantically, of the interconnectedness of all things, failing to recognize that this same principle means that there is almost nothing for which we cannot be, in some way, held responsible. This is one inevitable side effect of the growing movement to change the name of our geological epoch from the Holocene to the Anthropocene—the first era in the life of the planet to be defined by the effects of the human presence and human power: effects such as nuclear fallout, plastic pollution, domesticated animals, and anthropogenic climate change. Power entails responsibility, and responsibility leads to guilt.

I can see pictures of a starving child in a remote corner of the world on my television, and know for a fact that I could travel to that faraway place and relieve that child's immediate suffering, if I cared to. I don't do it, but I know I could. Although if I did so, I would be a well-meaning fool like Dickens's ludicrous Mrs. Jellyby, who grossly neglects her own family and neighborhood in favor of the distant philanthropy of African missions. Either way, some measure of guilt would seem to be my inescapable lot, as an empowered man living in an interconnected world.

Whatever donation I make to a charitable organization, it can never be as much as I could have given. I can never diminish my carbon footprint enough, or give to the poor enough, or support medical research enough, or otherwise do the things that would render me morally blameless.

Colonialism, slavery, structural poverty, water pollution, deforestation—there's an endless list of items for which you and I can take the rap. To be found blameless is a pipe dream, for the demands on an active conscience are literally as endless as an active imagination's ability to conjure them. And as those of us who teach young people often have occasion to observe, it may be precisely the most morally perceptive and earnest individuals who have the weakest common-sense defenses against such overwhelming assaults on their over-receptive sensibilities. They cannot see a logical place to stop. Indeed, when any one of us reflects on the brute fact of our being alive and taking up space on this planet, consuming resources that could have met some other, more worthy need, we may be led to feel guilt about the very fact of our existence.

The questions involved are genuine and profound; they deserve to be asked. Those who struggle most deeply with issues of environmental justice and stewardship are often led to wonder whether there can be any way of life that might allow one to escape being implicated in the cycles of exploitation and cruelty and privilege that mark, ineluctably, our relationship with our environment. They suffer from a hypertrophied sense of guilt, and desperately seek some path to an existence free of it.

In this, they embody a tendency of the West as a whole, expressed in an only slightly exaggerated form. So excessive is this propensity toward guilt, particularly in the most highly developed nations of the Western world, that the French writer Pascal Bruckner, in a courageous and brilliant recent study called *The Tyranny of Guilt* (in French, the title is the slightly different *La tyrannie de la pénitence*), has identified the problem as "Western masochism." The lingering presence of "the old notion of original sin, the ancient poison of damnation," Bruckner argues, holds even secular philosophers and sociologists captive to its logic.[8]

For all its brilliance, though, Bruckner's analysis is not fully adequate. The problem goes deeper than a mere question of alleged cultural masochism arising out of vestigial moral reflexes. It is, after all, not merely our pathologies that dispose us in this direction. The pathologies themselves have an anterior source in the very things that make us proudest: our knowledge of the world, of its causes and effects, and our consequent power to shape and alter those causes and effects. The problem is perfectly expressed in T.S. Eliot's famous question "After such knowledge, what forgiveness?"[9] In a world of relentlessly proliferating knowledge, there is no easy way of deciding how much guilt is enough, and how much is too much.

Stolen Suffering

Notwithstanding all claims about our living in a post-Christian world devoid of censorious public morality, we in fact live in a world that carries around an enormous and growing burden of guilt, and yearns—sometimes even demands—to be free of it. About this, Bruckner could not have been more right. And that burden is always looking for an opportunity to discharge itself. Indeed, it is impossible to exaggerate how many of the deeds of individual men and women can be traced back to the powerful and inextinguishable need of human beings to feel morally justified, to feel themselves to be "right with the world." One would be right to expect that such a powerful need, nearly as powerful as the merely physical ones, would continue to find ways to manifest itself, even if it had to do so in odd and perverse ways.

Which brings me to a very curious story, full of significance for these matters. It comes from a *New York Times* op-ed column by Daniel Mendelsohn, published on March 9, 2008, and aptly titled "Stolen Suffering."[10] Mendelsohn, a Bard College professor who had written a book about his family's experience of the Holocaust, told of hearing the story of an orphaned Jewish girl who trekked 2,000 miles from Belgium to Ukraine, surviving the Warsaw ghetto, murdering a German officer, and taking refuge in forests where she was protected by kindly wolves. The story had been given wide circulation in a 1997 book, *Misha: A Mémoire of the Holocaust Years*, and its veracity was generally accepted. But it was eventually discovered to be a complete fabrication, created by a Belgian Roman Catholic named Monique De Wael.[11]

Such a deception, Mendelsohn argued, is not an isolated event. It needs to be understood in the context of a growing number of "phony memoirs," such as the notorious child-survivor Holocaust memoir *Fragments*, or *Love and Consequences*, the putative autobiography of a young mixed-race woman raised by a black foster mother in gang-infested Los Angeles.[12] These books were, as Mendelsohn said, "a plagiarism of other people's trauma," written not, as their authors claimed, "by members of oppressed classes (the Jews during World War II, the impoverished African-Americans of Los Angeles today), but by members of relatively safe or privileged classes." Interestingly, too, he noted that the authors seemed to have an unusual degree of identification with their subjects—indeed, a degree of identification approaching the pathological. Defending *Misha*, De Wael declared, astonishingly, that "the story is mine...not actually reality, but my reality, my way of surviving."[13]

What these authors have appropriated is *suffering*, and the identification they pursue is an identification not with certifiable heroes but with certifiable victims. It is a particular and peculiar kind of identity theft. How do we account for it? What motivates it? Why would comfortable and privileged people want to identify with victims? And why would their efforts appeal to a substantial reading public?

Or, to pose the question even more generally, in a way that I think goes straight to the heart of our dilemma: How can one account for the rise of the extraordinary prestige of *victims*, as a category, in the contemporary world?

I believe that the explanation can be traced back to the extraordinary weight of guilt in our time, the pervasive need to find innocence through moral absolution and somehow discharge one's moral burden, and the fact that the conventional means of finding that absolution—or even of keeping the range of one's responsibility for one's sins within some kind of reasonable boundaries—are no longer generally available. Making a claim to the status of certified victim, or identifying with victims, however, offers itself as a substitute means by which the moral burden of sin can be shifted, and one's innocence affirmed. Recognition of this substitution may operate with particular strength in certain individuals, such as De Wael and her fellow hoaxing memoirists. But the strangeness of the phenomenon suggests a larger shift of sensibility, which represents a change in the moral economy of sin. And almost none of it has occurred consciously. It is not something as simple as hypocrisy that we are seeing. Instead, it is a story of people working out their salvation in fear and trembling.

The Moral Economy of Sin

In the modern West, the moral economy of sin remains strongly tied to the Judeo-Christian tradition, and the fundamental truth about sin in the Judeo-Christian tradition is that sin must be paid for or its burden otherwise discharged. It can neither be dissolved by divine fiat nor repressed nor borne forever. In the Jewish moral world in which Christianity originated, and without which it would have been unthinkable, sin had always had to be paid for, generally by the sacrificial shedding of blood; its effects could never be ignored or willed away. Which is precisely why, in the Christian context, forgiveness of sin was specifically related to Jesus Christ's atoning sacrifice, his vicarious payment for all human sins, procured through his death on the cross and made available freely to all who embraced him in faith. Forgiveness has a stratospherically high standing in the Christian faith. But it is grounded in fundamental theological and metaphysical beliefs about the person and work of Christ, which in turn can be traced back to Jewish notions of sin and how one pays for it. It makes little sense without them. Forgiveness, or expiation, or atonement—all of these concepts promising freedom from the weight of guilt are grounded in a moral *transaction*, enacted within the universe of a moral *economy* of sin.

But in a society that retains its Judeo-Christian moral reflexes but has abandoned the corresponding metaphysics, how can the moral economy of sin continue to operate properly, and its transactions be effectual? Can a credible substitute means of discharging the weight of sin be found? One workable way to be at peace with oneself and feel innocent and "right with the world" is to identify oneself as a certifiable victim—or better yet, to identify oneself with victims. This is why the Mendelsohn story is so important and so profoundly indicative, even if it deals with an extreme case. It points to the way in which identification with victims, and the appropriation of victim status, has become an irresistible moral attraction. It suggests the real possibility that claiming victim status is the sole sure means left of absolving oneself and securing one's sense of fundamental moral innocence. It explains the extraordinary moral prestige of victimhood in modern America and Western society in general.

Why should that be so? The answer is simple. With moral responsibility comes inevitable moral guilt, for reasons already explained. So if one wishes to be accounted innocent, one must find a way to make the claim that one cannot be held morally responsible. This is precisely what the status of victimhood accomplishes. When one is a certifiable victim, one is released from moral responsibility, since a victim is someone who is, by definition, not responsible for his condition, but can point to another who is responsible.

But victimhood at its most potent promises not only release from responsibility, but an ability to displace that responsibility onto others. As a victim, one can project onto another person, the victimizer or oppressor, any feelings of guilt he might harbor, and in projecting that guilt lift it from his own shoulders. The result is an astonishing reversal, in which the designated victimizer plays the role of the scapegoat, upon whose head the sin comes to rest, and who pays the price for it. By contrast, in appropriating the status of victim, or identifying oneself with victims, the victimized can experience a profound sense of moral release, of recovered innocence. It is no wonder that this has become so common a gambit in our time, so effectively does it deal with the problem of guilt—at least individually, and in the short run, though at the price of social pathologies in the larger society that will likely prove unsustainable.

Grievance—and Penitence—on a Global Scale

All of this confusion and disruption to our most time-honored ways of handling the dispensing of guilt and absolution creates enormous problems, especially in our public life, as we assess questions of social justice and group inequities, which are almost impossible to address without such morally charged categories coming into play. Just look at the incredible spectacle of today's college campuses, saturated as they are with ever-more-fractured identity politics, featuring an ever-expanding array of ever-more-minute grievances, with accompanying rounds of moral accusation and declarations of victimhood. These phenomena are not merely a fad, and they did not come out of nowhere.

Similar categories also come into play powerfully when the issues in question are ones relating to matters such as the historical guilt of nations and their culpability or innocence in the international sphere. Such questions are ubiquitous, as never before.

In the words of political scientist Thomas U. Berger, "We live in an age of apology and recrimination," and he could not be more right.[14] Guilt is everywhere around us, and its potential sources have only just begun to be plumbed, as our understanding of the buried past widens and deepens.

Gone is the amoral Hobbesian notion that war between nations is merely an expression of the state of nature. The assignment of responsibility for causing a war, the designation of war guilt, the assessment of punishments and reparations, the identification and prosecution of war crimes, the compensation of victims, and so on—all of these are thought to be an essential part of settling a war's effects justly, and are part and parcel of the moral economy of guilt as it now operates on the national and international levels.

The heightened moral awareness we now bring to international affairs is something new in human history, stemming from the growing social and political pluralism of Western democracies and the unprecedented influence of universalized norms of human rights and justice, supported and buttressed by a robust array of international institutions and non-governmental organizations ranging from the International Criminal Court to Amnesty International.

In addition, the larger narratives through which a nation organizes and relates its history, and through which it constitutes its collective memory, are increasingly subject to monitoring and careful scrutiny by its constituent ethnic, linguistic, cultural, and other subgroups, and are responsive to demands that those histories reflect the nation's past misdeeds and express contrition for them. Never has there been a keener and more widespread sense of particularized grievances at work throughout in the world, and never have such grievances been able to count on receiving such a thorough and generally sympathetic hearing from scholars and the general public.

Indeed, it is not an exaggeration to say that one could not begin to understand the workings of world politics today without taking into account a whole range of morally charged questions of guilt and innocence. How can one fully understand the decision by Chancellor Angela Merkel to admit a million foreign migrants a year into Germany without first understanding how the powerfully the burden of historical guilt weighs upon her and many other Germans? Such factors are now as much a part of historical causation and explanation as such standbys as climate, geography, access to natural resources, demographics, and socioeconomic organization.

There is no disputing the fact, then, that history itself, particularly in the form of "coming to terms with" the wrongs of the past and the search for historical justice, is becoming an ever more salient element in national and international politics. We see it in the concern over past abuses of indigenous peoples, colonized peoples, subordinated races and classes, and the like, and we see it in the ways that nations relate their stories of war. Far from being buried, the past has become ever more alive with moral contestation.

Perhaps the most impressive example of sustained collective penitence in human history has come from the government and people of Germany, who have done so much to atone for the sins of Nazism. But how much penitence is enough? And how long must penance be done? When can we say that the German people—who are, after all, an almost entirely different cast of characters from those who lived under the Nazis—are free and clear, and have "paid their debt" to the world and to the past, and are no longer under a cloud of suspicion? Who could possibly make that judgment? And will there come a day—indeed, has it already arrived, with the nation's backlash against Chancellor Merkel's immigration blunders?—when the Germans have had enough of the Sisyphean guilt which, as it may seem to them, they have been forced by other sinful nations to bear, and begin to seek their redemption by other means?

Who, after all, has ever been pure and wise enough to administer such postwar justice with impartiality and detachment, and impeccable moral credibility? What nation or entity at the close of World War II was sufficiently without sin to cast the decisive stone? The Nuremberg and Tokyo war crimes trials were landmarks in the establishment of institutional entities administering and enforcing international law. But they also were of questionable legality, reflecting the imposition of ad hoc, ex post facto laws, administered by victors whose own hands were far from entirely clean (consider the irony of Soviet judges sitting in judgment of the same kinds of crimes their own regime committed with impunity)— indeed, victors who might well have been made to stand trial themselves, had the tables been turned, and the subject at hand been the bombing of civilian targets in Hiroshima and Dresden.

Or consider whether the infamous Article 231 in the Treaty of Versailles, assigning "guilt" to Germany for the First World War, was not, in the very attempt to impose the victor's just punishment on a defeated foe, itself an act of grave injustice, the indignity of which surely helped to precipitate the catastrophes that followed it. The assignment of guilt, especially exclusive guilt, to one party or another may satisfy the most urgent claims of justice, or the desire for retribution, but may fail utterly the needs of reconciliation and reconstruction. As Elazar Barkan bluntly argued in his book *The Guilt of Nations*, "In forcing an admission of war guilt at Versailles, rather than healing, the victors instigated resentment that contributed to the rise of Fascism."[15] The work of healing, like the work of the Red Cross, has a claim all its own, one that is not always compatible with the utmost pursuit of justice (although it probably cannot succeed in the complete absence of such a pursuit). Nor does such an effort to isolate and assign exclusive guilt meet the needs of a more capacious historical under-standing, one that understands, as Herbert Butterfield once wrote, that history is "a clash of wills out of which there emerges something that no man ever willed."[16] And, he might have added, in which no party is entirely innocent.

So once again we find ourselves confronting the paradox of sin that cannot be adequately expiated. The deeply inscribed algorithm of sin demands some kind of atonement, but for some aspects of the past there is no imaginable way of making that transaction without creating new sins of equivalent or greater dimension. What possible atonement can there be for, say, the institution of slavery? It is no wonder that the issue of reparations for slavery surfaces periodically, and probably always will, yet it is simply beyond the power of the pres-ent or the future to atone for the sins of the past in any effective way. Those of us who teach history, and take seriously the moral formation of our students, have to consider what the takeaway from this is likely to be. Do we really want to rest easy with the idea that a proper moral education needs to involve a knowledge of our extensive individual and collective guilt—a guilt for which there is no imaginable atonement? That this is not a satisfactory state of affairs would seem obvious; what to do about it, particularly in a strictly secular context, is another matter.

Again, the question arises whether and to what extent all of this has something to do with our living in a world that has increasingly, for the past century or so, been run according to secular premises, using a secular vocabulary operating within an "immanent frame"—a mode of operation that requires us to be silent about, and forcibly repress, the very religious frameworks and vocabularies within which the dynamics of sin and guilt and atonement have hitherto been rendered intelligible. I use the term "repress" here with some irony, given its Freudian provenance. But even the irreligious Freud did not envision the "liberation" of the human race from its religious illusions as an automatic and sufficient solution to its problems. He saw nothing resembling a solution. Indeed, it could well be the case, and paradoxically so, that just at the moment when we have become more keenly aware than ever of the wages of sin in the world, and more keenly anxious to address those sins, we find ourselves least able to describe them in those now-forbidden terms, let alone find moral release from their weight. Andrew Delbanco puts it quite well in his perceptive and insightful 1995 book *The Death of Satan*:

> We live in the most brutal century in human history, but instead of step-
> ping forward to take the credit, the devil has rendered himself invisible.
> The very notion of evil seems to be incompatible with modern life, from
> which the ideas of transgression and the accountable self are fast receding.
> Yet despite the loss of old words and moral concepts—Satan, sin, evil—we
> cannot do without some conceptual means for thinking about the univer-
> sal human experience of cruelty and pain.... If evil, with all its insidious
> complexity, escape the reach of our imagination, it will have established
> dominion over us all.[17]

So there are always going to be consequences attendant upon the disappearance of such words, and they may be hard to foresee, and hard to address. "Whatever became of sin?" asked the psychiatrist Karl Menninger, in his 1973 book of that title. What, in the new arrangements, can accomplish the moral and transactional work that was formerly done by the now-discarded concepts? If, thanks to Nietzsche, the absence of belief in God is "the notional condition of modern Western culture," as Paula Fredriksen argues in her study of the history of the concept of sin, doesn't that mean that the idea of sin is finished too?[18]

Yes, it would seem to mean just that. After all, "sin" cannot be understood apart from a larger context of ideas. So what happens when all the ideas that upheld "sin" in its earlier sense have ceased to be normatively embraced? Could not the answer to Menninger's question be something like Zarathustra's famous cry: "Sin is dead and we have killed it!"?

Sin is a transgression against God, and without a God, how can there be such a thing as sin? So the theory would seem to dictate. But as Fredriksen argues, that theory fails miserably to explain the world we actually inhabit. Sin lives on, it seems, even if we decline to name it as such. We live, she says, in the web of culture, and "the biblical god…seems to have taken up permanent residence in Western imagination…[so much so that] even nonbelievers seem to know exactly who or what it is that they do not believe in."[19] In fact, given the anger that so many nonbelievers evince toward this nonexistent god, one might be tempted to speculate whether their unconscious cry is "Lord, I do not believe; please strengthen my belief in your nonexistence!" Such was Nietzsche's genius in communicating how difficult an achievement a clean and unconditional atheism is, a conundrum that he captured not by asserting that God does not exist, but that God is dead. For the existence of the dead constitutes, for us, a presence as well as an absence. It is not so easy to wish that enduring presence away, particularly when there is the lingering sense that the presence was once something living and breathing.

What makes the situation dangerous for us, as Fredriksen observes, is not only the fact that we have lost the ability to make conscious use of the concept of sin but that we have also lost any semblance of a "coherent idea of redemption,"[20] the idea that has always been required to accompany the concept of sin in the past and tame its harsh and punitive potential. The presence of vast amounts of unacknowledged sin in a culture, a culture full to the brim with its own hubristic sense of world-conquering power and agency but lacking any effectual means of achieving redemption for all the unacknowledged sin that accompanies such power: This is surely a moral crisis in the making—a kind of moral-transactional analogue to the debt crisis that threatens the world's fiscal and monetary health. The rituals of scapegoating, of public humiliation and shaming, of multiplying morally impermissible utterances and sentiments and punishing them with disproportionate severity, are visibly on the increase in our public life. They are not merely signs of intolerance or incivility, but of a deeper moral disorder, an *Unbehagen* that cannot be willed away by the psychoanalytic trick of pretending that it does not exist.

The Persistence of Guilt

Where then does this analysis of our broken moral economy leave us? The progress of our scientific and technological knowledge in the West, and of the culture of mastery that has come along with it, has worked to displace the cultural centrality of Christianity and Judaism, the great historical religions of the West. But it has not been able to replace them. For all its achievements, modern science has left us with at least two overwhelmingly important, and seemingly insoluble, problems for the conduct of human life. First, modern science cannot instruct us in how to live, since it cannot provide us with the ordering ends according to which our human strivings should be oriented. In a word, it cannot tell us what we should live for, let alone what we should be willing to sacrifice for, or die for.

And second, science cannot do anything to relieve the guilt weighing down our souls, a weight to which it has added appreciably, precisely by rendering us able to be in control of, and therefore accountable for, more and more elements in our lives—responsibility being the fertile seedbed of guilt. That growing weight seeks opportunities for release, seeks transactional outlets, but finds no obvious or straightforward ones in the secular dispensation. Instead, more often than not we are left to flail about, seeking some semblance of absolution in an incoherent post-Christian moral economy that has not entirely abandoned the concept of sin but lacks the transactional power of absolution or expiation without which no moral system can be bearable.

What is to be done? One conclusion seems unavoidable. Those who have viewed the obliteration of religion, and particularly of Judeo-Christian metaphysics, as the modern age's signal act of human liberation need to reconsider their dogmatic assurance on that point. Indeed, the persistent problem of guilt may open up an entirely different basis for reconsidering the enduring claims of religion. Perhaps human progress cannot be sustained without religion, or something like it, and specifically without something very like the moral economy of sin and absolution that has hitherto been secured by the religious traditions of the West.

Such an argument would have little to do with conventional theological apologetics. Instead, it would draw from empirical realities regarding the social and psychological make-up of advanced Western societies. And it would fully face the fact that, without the support of religious beliefs and institutions, one may have no choice but to accept the dismal prospect envisioned by Freud, in which the advance of human civilization brings not happiness but a mounting tide of unassuaged guilt, ever in search of novel and ineffective, and ultimately bizarre, ways to discharge itself. Such an advance would steadily diminish the human prospect, and render it less and less sustainable. It would smother the energies of innovation that have made the West what it is, and fatally undermine the spirited confidence needed to uphold the very possibility of progress itself. It must therefore be countered. But to be countered, it must first be understood.

(Spring 2017, 19.1)

Notes

[1] The discussion that follows is drawn from the second essay in Friedrich Nietzsche, *On the Genealogy of Morality*, ed. Keith Ansell-Pearson, trans. Carol Diethe (Cambridge, England: Cambridge University Press, 2006), 35–67. First published 1887. I here take note of the fact that any discussion of guilt per se

runs the risk of conflating different meanings of the word: *guilt* as a forensic or objective term, *guilt* as culpability, is not the same thing as *guilt* as a subjective or emotional term. It is the difference between *being* guilty and *feeling* guilty, a difference that is analytically clear, but often difficult to sustain in discussions of particular instances.

[2] Ibid., 61–62.

[3] Sigmund Freud, *Civilization and Its Discontents*, trans. James Strachey (New York, NY: Norton, 2005), 137, 140. First published 1930.

[4] Ibid., 140.

[5] William Shakespeare, *The Merchant of Venice*, Act 4, Scene 1, lines 184–205; see e.g., Stanley Wells and Gary Taylor ed., *The Oxford Shakespeare: The Complete Works*, second edition (Oxford, England: Oxford University Press, 2005), 473.

[6] Luke 23:34 (Revised Standard Version).

[7] Gregg Easterbrook, "Forgiveness is Good for Your Health," *Beliefnet*, n.d., http://www.beliefnet.com/wellness/health/2002/03/forgiveness-is-good-for-your-health.aspx. Accessed 5 January 2017.

[8] Pascal Bruckner, *The Tyranny of Guilt: An Essay on Western Masochism*, trans. Steven Rendall (Princeton, NJ: Princeton University Press, 2010), 1–4.

[9] T.S. Eliot, "Gerontion," line 34, in *The Complete Poems and Plays: 1909–1950* (Orlando, FL: Harcourt Brace Jovanovich, 1971), 22. The poem was first published in 1920.

[10] Daniel Mendelsohn, "Stolen Suffering," *New York Times*, March 9, 2008, WK12, http://www.nytimes.com/2008/03/09/opinion/09mendelsohn.html?_r=0.

[11] The book was *Misha: A Mémoire of the Holocaust Years* (Boston, MA: Mount Ivy Press, 1997), and the author published it under the name Misha Defonseca. According to the Belgian newspaper *Le Soir*, De Wael was the daughter of parents who had collaborated with the Nazis: see David Mehegan, "Misha and the Wolves," *Off the Shelf* (blog), *Boston Globe*, March 3, 2008, http://www.boston.com/ae/books/blog/2008/03/misha_and_the_w.html.

[12] Binjamin Wilkomirski, *Fragments: Memories of a Wartime Childhood* (New York, NY: Schocken, 1997); Margaret B. Jones, *Love and Consequences: A Memoir of Hope and Survival* (New York, NY: Riverhead, 2008).

[13] In a final twist of the case, in May 2014 the Massachusetts Court of Appeals ruled that De Wael had to forfeit the $22.5 million in royalties she had received for *Misha*. Quotation from Lizzie Dearden, "Misha Defonseca: Author Who Made Up Holocaust Memoir Ordered to Repay £13.3m," *The Independent*, May 12, 2014, http://www.independent.co.uk/arts-entertainment/books/news/author-who-made-up-bestselling-holocaust-memoir-ordered-to-repay-133m-9353897.html; additional details from Jeff D. Gorman, "Bizarre Holocaust Lies Support Publisher's Win," *Courthouse News Service*, May 8, 2014, http://www.courthousenews.com/2014/05/08/67710.htm.

[14] Thomas U. Berger, *War, Guilt, and World Politics after World War II* (New York, NY: Cambridge University Press, 2012), 8.

[15] Elazar Barkan, *The Guilt of Nations: Restitution and Negotiating Historical Injustices* (Baltimore, MD: Johns Hopkins University Press, 2000), xxxiii.

[16] Herbert Butterfield, *The Whig Interpretation of History* (New York, NY: Norton, 1965), 45–47.

[17] Andrew Delbanco, *The Death of Satan: How Americans Have Lost the Sense of Evil* (New York, NY: Farrar, Straus and Giroux, 1995), 9.

[18] Paula Fredriksen, *Sin: The Early History of an Idea* (Princeton, NJ: Princeton University Press, 2012), 149.

[19] Ibid.

[20] Ibid., 150.

Moodiness
The Pathos of Contemporary Life

Harvie Ferguson

Modernity has never been fully comprehensible. Since its European emergence, around 1600, a distinctive sense of *newness* has become a characteristic feature of human experience quite generally. Modern society and modern life, in all its aspects, were experienced as radically different from, and not just the development out of, older forms. Yet the real nature of that experience, and what it reveals about both the object and subject of modern life, has remained obscure. The radical origin of modernity, as Frank Ankersmit has shown in an impressive study, required a moment of oblivion, a trauma in which the complex global interrelatedness of the present to the past and everything it stood for was effaced.[1] The modern was an assertion of the essential freedom of humanity to become itself through the creation of its own future. As increasing numbers of people became conscious of the radical implications of its Copernican moment of self-creation, modernity established its vision of autonomy—withdrawn from god, cut off from nature, and remote from the Past.

Pathos

Modernity arose in the transformation of reality into the *experience* of reality. But experience had no sooner emerged as the decisive qualification of reality than it broke up, differentiated, fragmented, and dissolved into a multiplicity of particularities, aspects, and processes.

376

In the revolutionary moment of self-consciousness—the sense of experiencing the world as well as the world revealed in that experience—reason and madness, desire and despair, pleasure and disgust entered in distinctive and incommensurable ways into the constitution of the *multiple worlds* of modernity. Between the world and the bewildering variety of its depictions, representations, and figurations, experience found itself caught in the ebb and flow of impenetrable moods. In the continuous interplay of these social processes of construction and deconstruction, which are in principle unlimited in their subdivision and variety, a series of significant *modalities* of experience were established as significant and ontologically distinct regions. The world was not one but many, but the confusion of the many fell effortlessly into a seemingly prearranged tripartite order defined by qualitatively distinct and mutually exclusive media of experience. The premodern unity of being, that is to say, was transformed into the qualitatively distinctive worlds of thinking, willing, and feeling. Broadly speaking, the earlier period of modernity was dominated philosophically by the thematic discourse of thinking, the mid-period by the dynamics of willing, and the later, contemporary period by the access of feeling.

Metaphysical theories of modern experience, thus, arose initially in response to the radical separation of the human subject from the sheer exteriority of the world of objects that stood over against it. Our cognitive relation to the world was viewed as decisive for every aspect of life, and, in particular, epistemological issues inherent in this perspective conditioned all philosophical reflection on a representation of the world within which all experience is confined. However, the process of representation is subject to an immanent *logos* (reason) that, ultimately and obscurely, provides an adequate navigational aid for the human subject in the midst of impenetrable objects. Indeed, the interconnection of doubt and reason serve continually to undermine and rebuild knowledge as the fundamental human relation to the world. Reason is understood as the mechanism that adequately orders and makes coherent the world open to the senses; it makes the world intelligible. In the process, reason is made abstract and hypostasized as a normative, regulatory principle to which human subjectivity is subordinated. But reason, unable finally to clarify either the nature of the world or the mechanism of its own operations, was continually undermined by ever-renewed doubt.

In a somewhat later, parallel development, modern Romanticism grasped reality in terms of the inner life of the subject and elevated its active self-development through willing and striving into a fundamental principle of development and growth governing nature as well as humanity. The immediate sense of subjective presence was constituted experientially, and progressively made transparent, through the operation of will and intention. In positing the world, the subject came into its own as a self-conscious being. Selfhood, in other words, was the regulatory principle inherent in the immediacy of inner experience. However, just as reason became an imperious and abstract norm standing above all actual life, so selfhood was projected into the future as the *telos* of all striving and willing. Selfhood became a demanding, and ultimately self-defeating, struggle to actualize and express unique individuality in its full authenticity. Selfhood could never wholly disclose itself, and the failure of authentic self-expression resulted in various forms of despair.

In contrast to the evidently central roles of thinking and willing in the construction of modern experience, feeling, until quite recently, apparently played a minor role. The passions lay outside the modalities of comprehension born with modernity. neither explicable in terms of reason, nor understandable in terms of selfhood, the passions were rejected and suppressed as inherently disruptive, discontinuous, and disorderly. Against the spirit of modernity, passion overcame and overwhelmed the subject newly constituted as rational and self-conscious. The *logos* of the passions (pathology) constituted a disorderly succession of irresistible and fundamentally alien states of being. It was only with the late nineteenth-century crisis in bourgeois self-confidence that the passions were again acknowledged and recognized as an integral aspect of the continuously transforming character of modern experience.

Pleasure emerged as the immanent regulatory principle of a region of experience hitherto regarded as radically antinomian. Rather than being suppressed outright, the passions could be contained and subject to the constraining possibility of pleasure. As Freud, wholly in tune with the times, demonstrated, pleasure depended on a self-limiting mechanism of restraint and moderation. However, as Kierkegaard writing in the early 1840s had foreseen, the pursuit of pleasure and its transformation into the uniquely modern life-value, had the perverse effect of tainting every potentially enjoyable experience with boredom and disgust.

Everydayness

We never lived through the ideal categories of modernity; the time and space of the philosopher and scientist—empty, continuous, infinite—bear little relation to the qualitatively varied spatial experiences of home, neighborhood, city, countryside, wilderness, and so on, or the equally diverse temporalities of, for example, waking and sleeping, workdays and holidays, or childhood and old age. It was only in terms of the wholly abstract idea of modernity that Reason and Selfhood emerged as immanent self-regulatory principles of, respectively, cognitive and conative regions of experience. Actual life satisfied itself with thoroughly incoherent but livable compromises, common sense, and respectability. Similarly the life of the passions conceptualized in terms of a self-regulatory mechanism of pleasure made sense for the new philosophical discourses of aesthetics and psychology, but remained alien to everyday life for which *comfort* emerged as a modest goal.

With respect both to everyday life and its theoretical model, however, the history of modernity can be read as, firstly, the suppression, followed by the slow re-emergence, and now the increasing dominance of the passions as the primary modality through which reality is given. Whereas for the period of classical modernity, distinctive feeling-tones accompanied the vivid presentation of exterior objects and interior intentions, more recently the typical construction of experience in terms of well-defined foreground forms and indefinite background features has dissolved into the turbulence of continually changing states and conditions of life in general. We no longer experience a world, or sense ourselves as the subject of that experience; we are, rather, shrouded and carried along in the moodiness of the present.

In a challenging way, the philosophical conundrums of modernity, the separation of subject and object, self and other, being and world, have been finally resolved—not in a moment of clarifying synthesis but in the enigmatic character of life itself. We are daily seized, and often in small ways, by excitement and fear; we are possessed by anxiety, sadness, anger, and regret; experience comes to us, first of all, in an access of feeling. The succession of moods, the undramatic swell of affect as well as the periodic intensification of varied emotions, comes over us in an obscure manner. Contemporary life *is* moodiness, the immediate feeling of the moment. experience no longer comes tinged with feeling; it comes *as* feeling and often, it seems, without regard to its cognitive and/or active content.

The puzzling exteriority of the world becomes characteristic also of immediate and intimate experience. We inhabit *its* moodiness; *our* mood is simultaneously an aspect of the world. We are in the spontaneous flow of life and, in a peculiar sense, therefore outside ourselves. *Alterity* rather than *identity* is the conspicuous feature of contemporary experience. The exteriority of experience, its baffling outwardness, and the frustrating sense in which it is elusively "somewhere else" is manifest in every aspect of contemporary life. Whereas sociology, in a variety of classical and contemporary formulations, thought through the experience of the world as remote, unreachable, and strange, we now find ourselves ambiguously implicated in a banal and familiar reality. We are now ourselves, other than ourselves, and other than selves. This is the pathos of immediacy. We are *beside ourselves* with contemporary life, subject to, and subjects of, *its* moodiness.

Atmosphere

The exteriority of mood, however, is not over against us in the way in which, for Modernity, reality was constituted as a collection of "things." The impenetrable objectivity and remoteness of all objects gives way here to the engulfing closeness and familiarity of the atmosphere. Mood is atmosphere. It is background, the most general affect-tone characterizing ordinary experience.[2] Moods are "in the air." We breathe the mood of the moment and, inspired by its vitality, are attuned (to use Heidegger's uniquely felicitous term) to its reality. We are by turns excited, angered, consoled, sorrowful, and so on; alternatively, we are drained of life and bored. There is always something, or nothing, "in the air." We do not yet know what it is, but we are alert, ready to catch it, to catch on to it, to go with it, and keep abreast of it. now, of course, the air is alive with invisible messages and images; we are continually oriented and "plugged into" the live "stream" of the present. Contemporary technology here facilitates and organizes a form of life that had already become well established. The mobile, hand-held, wireless-free device is, perhaps, the best example of the way in which contemporary technology and design becomes successful by "catching on" to the present mood and provides new means of detecting, receiving, and living through whatever is "in the air."

Everything now is "up in the air." In the tumult of contemporary life, ideas, images, intentions, decisions, values, personalities, memories, hopes, and events are all thrown into the meteorological chaos of the present. Life is "in the air," as if we had finally defeated gravity and realized the centuries-old dream of unaided flight. Reality is "in the air," continually changing in terms of visibility, humidity, temperature, mobility, and so on. We frequently refer to mood in terms of weather: dull, stormy, breezy, sunny, cold, warm, and so on. In passing moods, we are dissolved into currents of air, and, at the same time, moods are embodied in quite precise physical forms. Contemporary illnesses of various sorts, for example, are "in the air" and "going around." Mood, medium, and mode—contemporary life is everywhere an atmospheric phenomenon.

The history of Modernity, in fact, can be glimpsed in the darkening sky and thickening atmosphere of some of its most striking artistic imagery. The sharply defined object and lucid atmosphere of both Italian and Flemish Renaissance painting was already turning vague and cloudy in Giorgione's *Tempest* (1505). The clarity of the Renaissance image, through which we have learned to grasp reality, here gives way to an obscure and even opaque indeterminacy. Everything is seemingly held in abeyance; a hushed atmosphere of the uncanny shrouds the world, and rather than appearing in luminous but distant objects, a new reality is presaged in a dark and turbulent sky.

For the Renaissance, atmosphere is primarily light. The air is the medium of Divine luminosity. The tradition continued into the modern period and reached new perfection in Vermeer's captivating interiors, and most recently in the tangible light of Edward Hopper's remarkable depiction of contemporary American life. But the cloudiness of Romanticism, as well as the huge skies of the Dutch landscapes, announced a new concern with the obscurity and indefiniteness of atmospheric forms.[3] Seized upon by the great painters of modern moods, Caspar David Friedrich and J.M.W. Turner, clouds, mist, fog, and vapor became the very stuff of existence.

Mood is no longer the accompanying tone of experience that has its focus in precisely delimited objects and subjects—the background radiation, so to speak, of the social cosmos. It is, rather, the medium of reality, our reality, the immediate here and now of everyday life. nor is mood only the ambient air, as distinct from the indrawn breath; it is, in Zygmunt Bauman's evocative term, the *liquidity* of contemporary life.[4] And it is the moodiness of contemporary life that confers reality on the atmosphere in a peculiar and significant way. In Karl Marx's memorable phrase, "everything solid melts into air"; the sense of the real, that is to say, has been dislodged from the earth, from the solidity and sheer *thingness* of its formed objects, and turned the limpid air dark with menacing vapor.[5]

This view cannot easily be written off as the fanciful image of some artists and writers. Quite apart from the validity of such images in their own context, modern science, which had provided the most compelling account of reality consecrated as objects, abandoned all the most central and significant concepts of mechanical philosophy. The "point-mass" realism of Galileo and Newton was transformed by James Clerk-Maxwell into a dispersed and continuous field of force.[6] The hitherto "obvious" localization of matter-in-space gave way to an energized medium: the ether.

Mood is background with which all foregrounding has merged; atmosphere is the dispersal of subjectivity into currents of life.

Feeling Loss

What *is* the mood of contemporary life? What is the something that is "in the air"? Of course mood is mobile, changeable, and unsettled; all moods are aspects of a general moodiness, a continuous process of transformation. It nonetheless makes sense to describe a predominant or general mood that constitutes something of an undertow to the affective currents of everyday life. What is the atmospheric condition that marks the "current climate"? In contemporary terms we might ask, "what is the default position of the passions?" Both as the recurrent theme of, and background swell to, electrifying bursts of feeling, contemporary life is characterized by a curious sense that life is elsewhere; life is characterized, that is, by a ubiquitous sense of loss.

Something of value has vanished, but what? The peculiar feeling tone of the present, the diffuse ache of existence, somehow eludes particularity and pervades the atmosphere with the strange vapor of loss. A miasma of absence is draped over the excited, restless movement of contemporary life. The overwhelming frenzy of social life; the ceaseless pursuit and accumulation of possessions; the continuous development of science, knowledge, and art; and the extraordinary wealth of entertainments and diversions of all kinds that now force themselves upon us do nothing to dispel the fog of melancholy. Loss is generic and essential to modernity and has found innumerable expressions in modern western philosophy and literature: the withdrawal of Being, the concealment of Reality behind appearance, the substitution of experience for truth, the conversion of the world into a picture of the world. We live in the deceptive and unreliable medium of representations, confined within a consciousness that, maddeningly, makes us conscious of its own limits.

Sociology developed, in part, as a response to, and an attempt to explain and exorcise, the specter of loss haunting modernity. The experience of loss was grasped in terms of the actual passing of community, authority, certainty, security, tradition, intimacy, and so on that, it was claimed, had been striking features of premodern western society. It is perhaps surprising, therefore, that until recently feeling was of marginal interest to sociologists, who were concerned primarily with the structural features of modern society and its institutional culture. Thus, while forms of knowledge, aesthetic movements, and images of collective life and its history have been exhaustively described and analyzed, and in spite of the general recognition of its recalcitrant ubiquity in modern society, the feeling of loss and more generally the character of feeling as such, have been neglected. Feeling was grasped as a mystery: internal, subjective, private, and, above all, inscrutable. Feeling was a region of experience into which even sociologists should not venture.

Now, as if making up for lost time, the passions threaten to displace long-established analytical, institutional, historical, and cultural preoccupations of the human sciences. It no longer strikes anyone as odd that academics should write social histories of anger, fear, envy, hope, or any other feeling, or that particular social groups, periods, movements, and events can be characterized in terms of their emotional content as much as, or more than, their purpose, intention, or composition.[7] This interest serves, first of all, to uncover an alternative history of modernity, one that begins with Spinoza rather than Descartes, and through suggestive reinterpretations of classical texts, brings to light the transformation of its passions.

A striking contradiction is already evident, not only from academic studies, but in more general commentaries on contemporary passions. On the one hand, feeling is publicly far more evident and is more readily manifest than until recently was commonly the case, and, on the other hand, it seems increasingly difficult adequately and legitimately to express our own personal and immediate feelings. There is an abundance, perhaps superabundance, of public demonstrations of grief, love, rage, excitement, and so on. Public reaction to the death of Michael Jackson is only a recent and striking example of a widespread current tendency to open emotionality. Sporting stars cry with joy or disappointment, equally tearful politicians and preachers confess to deceit, and ordinary people are roused to hatred. Public life is bathed in banal sentimentality. At the same time, and notwithstanding successive waves of liberation that have opened some, if not many, to new experiences and acknowledgement of hitherto suppressed feelings in themselves and others, it seems as difficult as ever to communicate genuine feelings and establish meaningful relationships through them.

How has this contradiction arisen? And how, more generally, has feeling come to occupy such a prominent but indeterminate place in contemporary life? This question arises only from the perspective of an academic philosophy of Modernity. For all such philosophies, both classical and romantic, the construction of modern experience is the experience of the world. In relation to the world, and particularly as it arises through the active will and agency of the subject, experience is focused and defined through self-experience. All experience, that is to say, is simultaneously the self-experience of the world, and thus of its world. From the perspective of ordinary life, however, modernity was the practice of how *not* to be myself—of how, in fact, to avoid altogether the heavy obligation of authenticity and self-development.[8]

For ordinary life, however, experience no longer serves as the immediate "proof" of our existence any more than it provides indubitable knowledge of the world. now "I" am aware of myself as dissolving and flowing outward. It is not that we sense the loss of the world as loss of feeling, or the feeling of loss; now we directly and immediately feel loss as self-surrender to the stream of life. And this, after all, is not only or merely evident in the ubiquity of a sense of loss but also manifests itself as a process of social formation in which life finds itself once again the collective subject.

Feeling is a wound, the outflow of self; the reverse movement of the entire history of modernity that consisted in energy coming from outside, "fixing" the interior, and holding it in tensed, energetic readiness. Reality now is present in a sense of dissolution and loss; a bewildering intuition of life flowing outward, ebbing away, and finding itself in the abundant flow of life in relation to which we jog along or run along to keep "in touch" with ourselves.

Feeling loss is neither an emotional anesthesia, nor nostalgia for an imagined past; it is simply a sense of draining away. An old world slips away and with it the sense of everything real, but this is the prelude to a new reality, sustained by and sustaining, nothing more (or less) substantial than a mood. The intermingling co-presence of myself as an inner life and the moody collective subjectivity of contemporary life are apprehended first of all as feeling loss. But this feeling leads outwards. I am "beside myself" with grief, desolation, boredom, and loss. It is not "in me" or "just me"; the "beside myself" of feeling loss is a penumbra of being that floats in the air and draws me into the collective Being of (an unhappy) collective life.

Beside Myself

What do people do all day? They "keep in touch" with one another, with events; they "keep up with" and "abreast of" news; they become part of "breaking news," the wave form of emergent time that, always keeping just ahead of the formed objectivity of events themselves, remains forever and eternally breaking, emerging, and trembling still with potentiality. It is as if coming into existence was a kind of death. The trick is to "stay ahead." The contemporary "beside myself" is just what happens to be going on at the time; it is fashionable, and everything can be considered from the standpoint of the fashionable. Reality, as it were, intensifies at the moment of its appearance, bursting forth with the all the energy of new life. But, in the very moment of its appearance, the fashionable decays into the merely conventional.[9] The truly fashionable is not yet visible; it is the emerging moment, the "now" moment of what were at one time popularly known as "happenings."

Passions overwhelm; they happen *to* us and take us *out of* ourselves. I am beside myself *with* anger, glee, excitement, grief, love, and so on. These states stand alongside and *separate* from the "me" that is invaded by unruly and disorienting bursts of passion for which it disclaims all responsibility. Here Hume, surely, is on the right track. The ungovernability of the passions, their peculiar irresponsibility and irrationality, not only define their specific character; they ultimately wreck every self-conscious effort towards the construction of a rational and just world. *Beside* myself is distinct from *in* myself (I feel well "in myself "), but it is not *other* than myself or even *outside* myself. "I" become angry or fall in love, but do not, and cannot, do so at will. Yet the most intense feeling "comes to me" and "comes over me," overwhelms and "sweeps me away." It is nothing other than self, but that self is now the collective subject rather than the individuated and interiorized ego. Passion is self-surrender to a collective subjectivity and, thus, in a different sense to that invoked by Hume, eminently, and even pre-eminently, social in character.

Beside myself is the mood of the immediate present; the mood that settles over and engulfs me is the same mood in which others are carried along and carried away. Mood cannot be grasped, that is to say, in a conventional sociological framework of interactive agency; it is the collective subject. The immediacy of mood is quite unlike the inner individuality of subjective agency. Mood, which is the opening of the passions, arrives unbidden and often unwelcome; it rarely responds to deliberation or effort. to "get into" a good mood, as much as to "throw off" a bad mood, remains one of the great psychological tricks of everyday life. In fact, mood responds immediately to the present and, thus, properly speaking belongs to a region of sublimity, the "now moment" that resists figuration as experience. even where it qualifies (as in fact is always the case) uniquely individual life forms, the "beside myself " of moodiness is never truly private. The isolation of depressive states, the grip of an anxious moment, the rapture of love, draw on, and indeed *are*, collective moods of the age. In this context, it is worth noticing that boredom and depression, which are asocial in that they cut people off from one another, are the new, contemporary forms of what Kant termed "unsocial sociability": a collective sentiment felt uniquely as a singular and internal affect.

Feeling is exterior not because it is projected or externalized in some way. It is, rather, the case that the collective subjectivity of passion, after a lengthy period of repression in the modern era, now appears openly and on its own behalf. Passion no longer needs to be interiorized and hidden; it remains on the outside, and that is now, consequently, where *we* are. And the "we" of collective life, which is felt in the immediacy of the passions, cannot be explained in terms of determinate sequences of cause and effect, nor can it be rendered meaningful in terms of values or goals imposed upon it or retrospectively read into it. The collective, the passionate, cannot be narrated; quite literally it does not make sense. Passion is the pure social phenomenon, the ontological region of being in which society shows itself as *social* in an absolutely free way.

Passion, thus, is properly construed as eternal, rather than fashionable. Passion does not measure or notice time; as it is without cause, effect, intention, or significance, duration and succession do not enter directly into its constitution. Passion arises from its own dead zone, boredom, for which it provides the ideal solution to the problem of "passing the time." The "beside myself " of mood carries the self away—away from itself into the ungraspable fluidity that Gilles Deleuze recognized as the pure immanence of collective life.[10]

This is an unexpectedly comfortable world. Currents of life arise in us as the varied moods of collective subjectivity. This relation, which, reviving a phrase from Lucien Lévy-Bruhl, might be called "the participatory consciousness of contemporary passions," transforms the object world.[11] Ordinary objects, of course, still exist. A general sense of dissolution does not imply the actual disappearance of objects. They remain themselves but, open to the same currents of life that register in us as moods, objects also participate in the passions of contemporary life. The remoteness of objects gives way to an intimate relation with things in the world. A multiplicity of things shares our moods; things are cool, *chic*, sexy, brutal, charming, and so on. Objects are not dead matter. Many people name their motorcars. Uniform, mass-produced commodities take on personal qualities that distinguish them from others. And never quite predictable, they manifest "a mind of their own." We cannot resist touching things and, in this way, participate in their mood. And it is through touching, that is, through feeling, that we become acclimatized to contemporary moodiness.

For the philosophical culture of modernity, reality was grasped in terms of individuated, interior experience that implied an alienated, externalized, and estranged relation to the object world. But now the uncomfortable homelessness of human subjectivity in the modern world is mitigated in the participatory consciousness of moods that includes within it the entire world of objects. The contemporary world, far from being a strange and unknown landscape, is altogether familiar and, to that extent, comforting.

May-Be

As distinct from the orthodox division of modern experience into subject and object, that is to say, mood is both "extended subject" and "intensive object," and mysterious only to the extent that an older philosophical orthodoxy persists. Mood is subjective, collective exteriority; it is the propensity of the passions, a tendency towards the differentiation and forming of feeling into distinct and characteristic affective states. In moodiness, everything is held in abeyance.

Mood is background into which all foregrounding has merged; atmosphere is the dispersal of subjectivity into currents of life. This world is familiar, comfortable, friendly, and incomprehensible: the extended subject, the exteriority of immediate self presence without objectification, alienation, the "may-be" of everything, even that which has happened or is just now actually taking place. On the screen we watch the "live" event simultaneously with its description, its commentary, its parallel and related occurrences. The subjunctive mood, the peculiar being of may-be, is no philosophical conceit.[12] It is, for example, the common grammatical form of speech for ordinary Glaswegians for whom almost every statement is delivered with an implicit question mark, inciting the common response: "aye, mibbe" or "mibbe-no."

In a striking way contemporary moodiness, which has grown directly out of european Modernity, resonates with Oriental and particularly modern Japanese culture. We are now becoming sensitive, for example, to what the Japanese refer to as "the pathos of things" (*mono no aware*).[13] More generally, and over a longer period, Japanese culture has recognized the emotional import of objects and insisted on the exterior character of feeling. And in the many remarkable works of François Jullien, we find, not only a vivid account of the hidden, indefinite, unformed, temporary, and endlessly ambiguous character of classical Chinese culture but, surprisingly though quite unmistakably, the most subtle and compelling account of *our* moodiness.[14]

(Spring 2011, 13.1)

Notes

[1] Frank Ankersmit, *Sublime Historical Experience* (Stanford, CA: Stanford University Press, 2005).

[2] Stephen Strasser, *Phenomenology of Feeling: An Essay on the Phenomena of the Heart*, trans. Robert T. Wood (Pittsburgh, PA: Duquesne University Press, 1977).

[3] Hubert Damisch, *A Theory Of /Cloud/: Toward a History of Painting*, trans. Janet Lloyd (Stanford, CA: Stanford University Press, 2002).

[4] Zygmunt Bauman, *Liquid Modernity* (Cambridge, England: Polity, 2000).

[5] Karl Marx, *The Communist Manifesto*, trans. Samuel Moore (1848; Harmondsworth, England: Penguin, 2004).

[6] Bruce Clarke and Linda Dalrymple Henderson, ed., *From Energy to Information: Representation in Science and Technology, Art, and Literature* (Stanford, CA: Stanford University Press, 2002).

[7] William M. Reddy, *The Navigation of Feeling: A Framework for the History of Emotions* (Cambridge, England: Cambridge University Press, 2001); Martha Nussbaum, *Upheavals of Thought: The Intelligence of the Emotions* (Cambridge, England: Cambridge University Press, 2003); Thomas Dixon, *From Passions to Emotions: The Creation of a Secular Psychological Category* (Cambridge, England: Cambridge University Press, 2006).

[8] Alain Ehrenberg, *The Weariness of the Self: Diagnosing the History of Depression in the Contemporary Age* (Montreal, Canada: McGill-Queens University Press, 2010).

[9] Gilles Lipovetsky, *The Empire of Fashion: Dressing Modern Democracy*, trans. Catherine Porter (Princeton, NJ: Princeton University Press, 2002).

[10] Gilles Deleuze, *Pure Immanence: Essays on a Life*, trans. Anne Boyman (New York, NY: Zone, 2005).

[11] Lucien Lévy-Bruhl, *Primitive Mentality*, trans. L.A. Clare (Boston, MA: Beacon, 1966).

[12] Rodolphe Gasché, *Of Minimal Things: Studies on the Notion of Relation* (Stanford, CA: Stanford University Press, 1999).

[13] Steve Odin, *Artistic Detachment in Japan and the West: Psychic Distance in Comparative Aesthetics* (Honolulu, HI: University of Hawaii Press, 2001).

[14] François Jullien, *The Propensity of Things: Toward a History of Efficacy in China*, trans. Janet Lloyd (New York, NY: Zone, 1995); *Detour and Access: Strategies of Meaning in China and Greece*, trans. Sophie Hawkes (New York, NY: Zone, 2000); *Vital Nourishment: Departing from Happiness*, trans. Arthur Goldhammer (New York, NY: Zone, 2007).

Ladies in Waiting

Becca Rothfeld

Your absence has gone through me
Like thread through a needle.
Everything I do is stitched with its color.

—W.S. Merwin[1]

In the most memorable scene of the 2002 film *Secretary*, nothing happens. The protagonist, Lee, sits as still as possible, her hands planted firmly on the desk in front of her. She has been instructed by her lover, who is also her sexually sadistic employer, to hold this position until he returns. For over ten minutes, a period that represents entire days in the movie's internal timeline, Lee remains faithfully immobile, wetting herself in the process.

Lee offers up her violent passivity as proof of her love, and her physical humiliations are like religious devotions. Hoping to gratify her lover by depriving herself of food, she declines into hunger-induced delirium in which she experiences a hallucinatory vision of her therapist. He explains, "There's a long history of this in Catholicism. The monks used to wear thorns on their temples, and the nuns wore them sewn inside their clothing."[2] Like centuries of monks, nuns, and mystics before her, Lee transforms her inertia and hunger into an active occupation through the performance of sacrificial pain.

Hunger is a particularly intensified iteration of waiting: acute wanting directed toward a palpably absent object. The literal hunger of mystics like Catherine of Siena, who famously fasted for much of her life, corresponds to a greater hunger, necessarily insatiable, for communion with God. When Lee's lover comes to her rescue, he resuscitates her with a protein shake, and their relationship adopts the familiar, flagellatory rhythm of feeding and hungering, deprivation and indulgence. Lee's grand gesture, the gift of her famished waiting, is its origin and its core.

Waiting seems central to the experience and practice of masochistic piety's messianic successor, romantic love, the force that is supposed to redeem twenty-first-century women as religious salvation once redeemed their forebears. But how exactly does waiting figure into contemporary romance? In his 1977 treatise *A Lover's Discourse*, Roland Barthes argues that waiting is constitutive of love:

> "Am I in love?—Yes, since I'm waiting." The other never waits. Sometimes I want to play the part of the one who doesn't wait; I try to busy myself elsewhere, to arrive late; but I always lose at this game: whatever I do, I find myself there, with nothing to do, punctual, even ahead of time. The lover's fatal identity is precisely: *I am the one who waits.*[3]

In Barthes's view, love is centrally defined by the transfiguration of neutral lack into conspicuous vacancy, of emptiness into absence: Love is waiting, and waiting is love. For Catherine of Siena, perennially ravenous, the absence is God's. For Lee, delectably paralyzed with submission, it is her boss's. For the lover, the beloved's absence is always acute. Distance is not a redistribution of presence but an evasion or a thwarted expectation, like a phantom limb.

In *Secretary*, Lee has fled the premise of what would have been her wedding to a banal boyfriend, and as she awaits her boss's return she wears a crumpled wedding dress. This image might seem to undermine the usual marital tropes: A sort of inverse Miss Havisham, Lee deserts her conventional lover at the altar in favor of a sexually deviant relationship. She is the abandoning, not the abandoned, party, and her passivity is chosen, not imposed.

But despite this, she represents yet another variation on the familiar figure of the woman waiting. Initially, this woman wove while her husband went off to war; later, she donned a wedding dress and waited at the altar for a man who would never come; finally, she settled behind her telephone or her mailbox, first analog, then digital, to wait for men who would probably never call or write. As Barthes elaborates,

> Historically, the discourse of absence is carried on by the Woman.... It is Woman who gives shape to absence, elaborates its fiction, for she has time to do so.... It follows that in any man who utters the other's absence *something feminine* is declared: this man who waits and who suffers from his waiting is miraculously feminized. A man is not feminized because he is inverted but because he is in love.[4]

Barthes suggests that waiting is constitutive of love—the lover is "the one who waits." If waiting, even for men, is an essentially female posture, then love proves to be a fundamentally feminine exercise. The figure at the desk, with her tattered wedding dress, her throbbing hunger, her clenched hands, could only have been a woman.

The Day-After Text

At first, everything was good, as it tends to be in the early stages, after the first bouts of effortless intimacy, when your body fits so neatly into a foreign body that it seems to have returned to a familiar place. I received his day-after text promptly, approximately seven hours after I left his bed. The text was a ritual gesture, and its content mattered less than its arrival within the allotted twenty-four hours, before the possibility of future interaction expired. In its immediate aftermath I did not wait. But as our conversation acquired momentum and settled into a comfortable cadence, I found the distribution of my attention shifting. Some part of it was withheld, repurposed, devoted to measuring the increasing lengths of his silences. He was beginning to recede, and I was beginning to wait.

As long as he was the unanswered party and I could imagine *him* in a state of painful expectation, I felt invulnerable. I fantasized about never replying, about savoring my silence and his presumed anxiety for the rest of my life, but I never managed to go very long without answering and reverting to my habitual state of waiting. ("I try to busy myself elsewhere, to arrive late; but I always lose at this game....")

Before I met him, I spent most of my time at the British university where I was studying "abroad" taking prolonged showers, checking Facebook in the library, and thinking haltingly about the essays I was writing for my master's program. In the library, I sat next to a young man with preternaturally red cheeks—they looked painful, scraped—who seemed to be conducting a survey of eighteenth-century botanical atlases. For hours, he sat hunched over his laptop, scrutinizing archival documents that somebody, perhaps he, had laboriously scanned. Sometimes he took notes by hand. Not once did I ever see him check his e-mail or Facebook, as I often did, only to find that no one had contacted me since the last time I checked, five minutes before.

At the pub, where the beleaguered members of my course congregated once a week to "talk about their 'work,'" no one talked about their work. The botany boy, to whom I had never spoken, was never in attendance. Maybe these sessions occurred when he did his laborious scanning. I lamely sipped sparkling water while my peers, who drank beer, speculated endlessly about the weather, which was so stubbornly noncommittal (never torrential but never fully sunny) that it left little to the predictive faculties.

After I met him, however, I spent much of my time waiting for him. This was more engaging than one might imagine. Immediately after receiving messages from him, I felt a sense of amazed, vertiginous relief that he had answered—yes, he had answered—and this lasted for several seconds at a time before it reverted to muted panic that soon he would answer at greater and greater intervals and then would cease to answer at all. I experienced a cumulative total of maybe five minutes of joy during the week before I saw him again, not counting sleeping hours.

There is an eroticism to waiting: Sexual fulfillment requires that one urgently desire what is necessarily, torturously delayed. Romantic waiting is, like certain shades of pain, delicate enough to hint teasingly at future gratification but never disagreeable enough to preclude it. But at a certain point, gratification has been so thoroughly warded off that waiting becomes unendurable, and it wasn't long after our second meeting that I began to wait in earnest. What had at first been surprised delight that he existed was transformed, without my noticing it, into fear that his privacy would close back over him. His silences began to stretch longer and longer, often for days. I wondered, relentlessly and futilely, what this portended. When I confronted him about what I could only describe as a "tonal shift"—what seemed to me to be a cruel infliction of waiting—he purported to have no idea what I was talking about.

This shift (tonal or otherwise) in patterns of waiting represented a shift in power: Expectation is a form of subjugation. What is the opposite of waiting: the imposition of waiting on someone else? I wished it on him, ineffectually, like a curse. As his communications petered out, I felt increasingly powerless, besieged. I recalled the medieval conception of God as sustaining us, actively willing us into existence second by second, and I felt that his silence was at every moment draining me of myself.

Depression, Too, Is a Form of Waiting

In *Iris*, the literary critic John Bayley's tragic account of his brilliant wife, the novelist and philosopher Iris Murdoch, and her descent into the fog of Alzheimer's, he quotes clergyman Sydney Smith's advice to a depressive: "Take short views of the human life—never further than dinner or tea."[5] Depression, too, is a form of waiting, for deliverance or vindication or a sudden onslaught of meaning that fails, devastatingly, to arrive. Waiting is a manipulation of time—it is "enchantment," as Barthes writes, a spell that stills and silences its victims—and its antidote is to make time pass at the usual rate once again. (In *Great Expectations*, Miss Havisham's abandonment and subsequent waiting arrest time completely: She stops the clocks at 8:40, the moment at which she received the letter breaking off her engagement.)

Smith exhorts the depressive to throw herself entirely into some proximate thing, to repopulate the vast stretches of undifferentiated blankness with something like events. One tries to foist sequences back onto a slop of time that has come to consist in the recurring, harping note of absence. So one lives, one tries to inhabit the minutiae of the activities one performs, one tries to externalize oneself and ultimately to lose one's sense of one's selfhood altogether, so that one can become the objects one rearranges on the dresser and forget that one is waiting, that none of one's activities are complete without some additional element that is wretchedly, unforgettably elsewhere.

Why did I obey the unspoken imperative to wait? Was I trying, like Lee, to prove my affection through my mute endurance? Was my inability to revert my experience of duration to its former state, when his silence was not perceived as a continual laceration, indeed was not perceived at all, somehow masochistic? Or perhaps I felt waiting was better than mourning.

"The woman was then lied to, cheated on, tormented, and often not called. She was intentionally left up in the air about his intentions. One or two letters went unanswered. The woman waited and waited, in vain. And she did not ask why she was waiting, because she feared the answer more than the waiting," writes Austrian author Elfriede Jelinek in *The Piano Teacher*.[6] To be "not called," this phrasing intimates, is to be actively wounded: "Not calling" is a transitive offense, like "tormenting." But Jelinek's conclusion seems wrong: Waiting, which renders everything provisional, which suspends progress or conclusion of any kind, is worse than clarity. It is waiting that keeps one captive at the desk, determined to see things through until he returns or one starves, whichever comes first.

Waiting Is the Rule

There is, of course, a simpler answer to the question of the role waiting plays in contemporary courtship than Barthes's convoluted philosophical one. It is that women wait for men: They wait for their Tinder matches to initiate contact, for men to propose to them after years of dating or to ask them on dates at all, for the decisive day-after text (a custom that I realized with some surprise has antecedents in classical Japan; in *The Tale of Genji*, noblewomen anxiously await morning-after haikus in the wake of their nocturnal exploits).

The messages that I answer immediately, without inserting a buffer of delay calculated to give the (erroneous) impression that I'm busy or unavailable, come from my female friends, and they often constitute an agonized refrain: How soon should I reply? Can I say something yet? Should I call? I know I shouldn't text him, but.... My advice, ingrained in me by years of comparable counsel from comparably responsive female friends, is always to wait. Waiting is the rule, the convention, tacitly enforced by men who retreat from female aggression and actively perpetuated by women who self-police. This is the agreement we opt into when we receive the first day-after texts with such awed gratitude, as if we didn't deserve them.

Literature bears out Barthes's claim and my experience: In books, it is always women who wait. In the *Odyssey*, Penelope awaits the return of her husband for twenty years, weaving a funeral shroud for her father during the day and unraveling it during the night to put off intermediary suitors, one of whom she will wed when the interminable tapestry is finally complete. Penelope is the product of an oral lyrical tradition that excluded women, and it is only fitting that a male authorship relegated her to the sort of maddening inactivity that waiting so often entails. Like Miss Havisham, condemned to tread the same obsessive mental routes over and over again, Penelope is doomed to weave and unweave the same tired designs to no discernable end.

Centuries later, Walt Whitman would open his 1856 poem "A Woman Waits for Me" with a succinct expression of breathtaking entitlement: "A woman waits for me" as if it were simply and irrefutably so. Later still, in Raymond Carver's poem "Waiting," a male speaker makes his way to

> the house where the woman
> stands in the doorway
> wearing the sun in her hair. The one
> who's been waiting
> all this time.
> The woman who loves you.
> The one who can say,
> "What's kept you?"[7]

There is a fond condescension to this poem: It is tender, but it takes the woman's love and patience—her presence in the door, her mounting fear—for granted. To the male narrator, the waiting woman is a comforting inevitability. The woman's anxious and vaguely accusatory question does not come from a comparable place of security—not that Carver bothers to investigate.

Of course, waiting women have also spoken for themselves. Gaspara Stampa, a sixteenth-century Italian poet often regarded as the iconic jilted lover, anticipates Barthes's equation of waiting with love in her seminal poem "By Now I Am So Tired of Waiting":

> By now I am so tired of waiting,
> so overcome by longing and by grief,
> through the so little faith and much forgetting
> of whom of whose return I, weary,
>   am bereaved,
>
> that she who makes the world pale, whitening
> it with her sickle, and
>   claims the final forfeit—

I call on her often for relief,
so strongly sorrow wells within
    my breast.

But she turns deaf ears unto my plea,
scorning my false and foolish thoughts,
as he to his return stays also deaf.

And so with weeping whence
    my eyes are filled,
I make piteous these waters and this sea;
while he lives happy there upon
    his hills.[8]

Stampa's poem is, at its core, an indictment of indifference: She denounces the man to whom it is addressed because he fails to suffer from her absence, and thus fails to conceive of the passage of their time apart as an exercise in waiting. Stampa, in contrast, is excruciatingly aware of her lover's absence, and she can be described as *waiting* precisely because she experiences separation as pain. This is what waiting is: the transformation of time into misery.

Dorothy Parker's short story "A Telephone Call," a two-thousand-word exercise in agonized anticipation, echoes Stampa's initial figuration of apathy as the inverse of waiting. The work follows a woman waiting for a telephone call (not, we presume, forthcoming) from a man she loves:

I mustn't. I mustn't do this. Suppose he's a little late calling me up—that's nothing to get hysterical about. Maybe he isn't going to call—maybe he's coming straight up here without telephoning. He'll be cross if he sees I have been crying. They don't like you to cry. He doesn't cry. I wish to God I could make him cry. I wish I could make him cry and tread the floor and feel his heart heavy and big and festering in him. I wish I could hurt him like hell.[9]

The story ends inconclusively, as it must. Resolution would be too relieving: It is inimical to the uncertainties and frustrations of waiting. With a gesture that mirrors Penelope's in its contrived futility, the narrator begins to count by fives, hoping that her beloved will call her before she reaches five hundred. "Five, ten, fifteen, twenty, twenty-five, thirty, thirty-five...." "A Telephone Call" concludes without concluding.

Waiting is sustained by the possibility of fulfillment yet to be decisively precluded. The woman in Parker's story is capable of waiting because she is capable of hope. If she believed with any certainty that the call in question would never come, then her orientation would change: She might grieve, but she would no longer wait. The man who neglects to telephone is certain that a woman is waiting on the other end of the line, and this is why he is not waiting, why he feels no urge to confirm that she is still there with her hands placed, as instructed, on the desk.

As in *Secretary*, waiting—a nonevent—constitutes the crucial narrative force in "A Telephone Call." Parker eschews conventional plot arcs, in which ends represent marked departures from beginnings. The woman waiting by the phone follows Penelope in performing activities that represent a particularly poignant kind of stasis. For every image she weaves, there is a countervailing un-weaving: for every advance, a retreat. There is no progression, just endless circling around the same fixed point of obsession. Waiting itself is her occupation and preoccupation. "Absence becomes an active practice, a *business* (which keeps me from doing anything else)," writes Barthes.

If women historically have been the ones who wait, it is at least in part because most cultures have confined them to state of involuntary idleness. (Penelope is not permitted to leave home to participate in the war effort, and Lee is the secretary, not the boss.) The gendered distribution of waiting assumes a hierarchy of time and activity in which men set the terms and fix the schedules. To be waited for is to assert the importance of one's time; to wait is to occupy a position of eternal readiness in which one can be called on at male convenience. Waiting amounts in this sense to "waiting on": Waiting women exist provisionally and subserviently, in the service of an absent element.

In his book *Interruptions*, the critic Hans-Jost Frey writes, "To understand waiting as expectation is to think of it from the point of view of totality. One who waits is in a state of incompleteness and waits for completion."[10] (This formulation vindicates Jelinek's cleverly transitive phrasing: If waiting is an active occupation, then absence is an active cruelty.) There emerges a metaphysical dependence: If togetherness is completion, then separation is fragmentation. The integrity of the lover is conditional upon the beloved, the eternally awaited. If waiting constitutes love, as Barthes suggests, it is because waiting is the ultimate act of vulnerability: It requires a willingness to endanger one's wholeness, to halve oneself.

Jolted Out of the Self

Barthes makes two suggestions, both radical. First, he suggests that love is a question of waiting, and second, that waiting is essentially feminine. From this it follows that to fall in love is to become "feminized"—to wait, and thereby take up a traditionally and stereotypically feminine project. But Barthes goes further, proposing that the object of love is absent in a stronger sense: What it means to love, he writes, is for "an always present *I*" to be defined "only by confrontation with an always absent *you*." *A Lover's Discourse* is structured as a series of one-sided declarations, "the site of someone speaking within himself, *amorously*, confronting the other (the loved object), who does not speak."[11] The lover waits, speaks, entreats, but the beloved is constitutionally silent.

To love is to be jolted out of the self by the strangeness of another person, and the beloved entrances precisely because of his unutterable difference—the most basic and insuperable absence. He is absent even when he is present because he is other, situated outside of myself: "But isn't desire always the same, whether the object is present or absent? Isn't the object *always* absent?" As Barthes reminds us, there are two concepts in Greek for desire, one for the missing someone who's left, and a second for the more curious sensation of missing someone beside me, someone who is with me but who remains less than fully accessible to me: "*Pothos*, desire for the absent being, and *Himéros*, the more burning desire for the present being."[12]

Maybe love is the recovery of some former, half-remembered unity, and what we experience is just the aftermath of a prior separation. In the poem "Misery and Splendor," Robert Hass writes of a couple mid-coitus that "they are trying to become one creature, and something will not have it."[13] But do they really want to become "one creature," to collapse into each other? Wouldn't this just expand the sphere of a single loneliness? Love and sex must honor difference: The beloved must continue to resist assimilation into the self, must remain apart, elusive, an adored, if tonally inconstant, mystery.

The Art of Elective Waiting

Waiting is consuming. At times it is terrible, a wound that cannot be mitigated but must instead be mutely survived. There are days when making it to dinner or tea, as per Sydney Smith's sage advice, is a feat. And sometimes waiting is an insult, an indignity, as pointlessly pathetic as refusing to take off the wedding dress in which you were abandoned years ago by someone who no longer cares and probably doesn't remember.

But waiting in some form is necessary. In his essay "Penelope Waiting," literary critic Harold Schweizer argues that narrative itself is a specialized kind of waiting: "What constitutes a literary text or a work of art," he writes, "is not its formal closure or sensuous completeness but rather its complicated extension in our own time of waiting."[14] Stories require displaced elements, problems that plague us enough to keep us reading and caring. Investment is diffuse, and present enjoyment is predicated on the projection of future fulfillment. Narrative obeys erotic laws: This is why the seeming non-stories of *Secretary* and "A Telephone Call" absorb us. Just as delay intensifies narrative and deferral intensifies orgasm, difference intensifies love.

The alternative to dejected waiting, then, is patience, the art of elective waiting: a capitulation that women author, a passivity over which we assert ownership and which we might come to more comfortably inhabit. When we identify with it, even the worst of it, waiting becomes an end in itself. Frey writes, "There is a waiting without expectation. It can set in when one has waited for something for so long, without seeing any signs of imminent fulfillment, that the object of expectation gradually begins to fade, and yet one does not stop waiting."[15] Waiting without expectation is like prayer, devotion undertaken without the expectation of immediate reward or acknowledgment.

There is no true not-waiting, anyway. What seems like fullness is just an intimation of filling, a preview of a more complete dissolution. What I want—to not wait, to converge—is impossible. I want everything, all at once, every part of myself touching every part of you at every moment. An intimacy as absolute as this could only be violent, a rupture. It would conceive of flesh as no more than barrier. It would hurt. I have wanted to admit you into my privacy: I have craved a feast of trespass and violation. And at times I have wanted you to wrench me apart and enter into me until the only life I remember is your life and the only word I remember is your name.

But this isn't possible, and I don't really want it, anyway. If I were a part of you, I would not be apart from you and there would be no me in opposition to you, no you to elude me. Instead, I choose my waiting and the joy I find in surrender, in flinging myself at everything I encounter with the brutality of adoration. Catherine of Siena understood this: The whole purpose of adoring God to the point of such delicious abjection is that he is by nature unattainable. He never arrives with a protein shake, prizing hunger apart from filling, or pleasure apart from pain. He never defiles the purity of agony with the weakness of relief. He hurts without mercy. He is a story that never ends.

(Fall 2016, 18.3)

Notes

1   W.S. Merwin, "Separation," in *The Second Four Books of Poems* (Port Townsend, WA: Copper Canyon Press, 1993), 15. Retrieved from Poetry Foundation website: https://www.poetryfoundation.org/poetry-magazine/poems/detail/28891.

2   Steven Shainberg (director), Erin Cressida Wilson (screenwriter), *Secretary* (motion picture), distributed by Lions Gate Films (2002).

3   Roland Barthes, *A Lover's Discourse*, trans. Richard Howard (London, England: Vintage Classics, 2002), 40.

4   Ibid., 14.

5   John Bayley, *Iris: A Memoir of Iris Murdoch* (London, England: Duckworth, 1998), 44.

6   Elfriede Jelinek, *The Piano Teacher*, trans. Joachim Neugroschel (London, England: Serpent's Tail, 2009), 75.

7   Raymond Carver, "Waiting," in *All of Us: The Collected Poems* (New York, NY: Vintage Books, 2000). Retrieved from *Writer's Almanac*, http://writersalmanac.publicradio.org/index.php?date=2001/05/25.

8   Gaspara Stampa, "By Now I Am So Tired of Waiting," in *The Defiant Muse: Italian Feminist Poems from the Middle Ages to the Present*, ed. Beverly Allen, Muriel Kittel, and Keala Jane Jewell (New York, NY: Feminist Press, 1986), 15.

9   Dorothy Parker, "A Telephone Call," in *The Portable Dorothy Parker*, intro. Brendan Gill (New York, NY: Viking Press, 1973), 121.

10 Hans-Jost Frey, *Interruptions*, trans. Georgia Albert (Albany, NY: State University of New York Press, 1996), 57.

11 Barthes, *A Lover's Discourse*, 3.

12 Ibid., 15.

13 Robert Hass, "Misery and Splendor," in *Human Wishes* (New York, NY: HarperCollins, 1989). Retrieved from Poetry Foundation website: https://www.poetryfoundation.org/poems-and-poets/poems/detail/49593.

14 Harold Schweizer, "Penelope Waiting," *Soundings: An Interdisciplinary Journal* 85, nos. 3–4 (2002): 280.

15 Frey, *Interruptions*, 57.

On Being Midwestern
The Burden of Normality

Phil Christman

After my Texas-born wife and I moved to Michigan—an eleven-hour drive in the snow, during which time itself seemed to widen and flatten with the terrain—I found myself pressed into service an expert on the region where I was born and where I have spent most of my life. "What is the Midwest like?" she asked. "Midwestern history, Midwestern customs, Midwestern cuisine?" I struggled to answer with anything more than clichés: bad weather, hard work, humble people. I knew these were inadequate. Connecticut winters and Arizona summers are also "bad"; the vast majority of humans have worked hard, or been worked hard, for all of recorded history; and *humility* is one of those words, like *authenticity* or (lately) *resistance*, that serves mainly to advertise the absence of the thing named.

I soon learned that I was hardly the only Midwesterner left tongue-tied by the Midwest. Articulate neighbors, friends, colleagues, and students, asked to describe their hometowns, replied with truisms that, put together, were also paradoxes: "Oh, it's in the middle of nowhere." "It's just like anywhere, you know." "We do the same things people do everywhere." No-places are as old as Thomas More's *Utopia*, but a no-place that is also everyplace and anyplace doesn't really add up. Nor, at least in my experience, does one hear such language from people in other regions—from Southerners, Californians, Arubans, Yorkshiremen. Canadians live in a country that has been jokingly described as America's Midwest writ larger—Canada and our Midwest share, among other things, manners, weather, topography, and a tendency among their inhabitants to downplay their own racism—yet they are hyperspecific in their language, assuming a knowledge of local landmarks that it never occurs to them non-Canadians may not possess. They assume that whatever their setting is, it is *a setting*, not, as Midwesterner-turned-expatriate Glenway Wescott once wrote of Wisconsin, "an abstract nowhere."[1]

When pressed, a person might explain these tropes of featurelessness by pointing out the similarities imposed across the Midwestern landscape by capitalism. Boosters sometimes still call the region "America's breadbasket," and for much of the late nineteenth and twentieth centuries it was also, to a large degree, America's foundry, and, during World War II, its armory.[2] (Such is the extractive quality of Midwestern economic history that some historians have proposed that we take seriously the painter Grant Wood's irritated description of the region, in his 1935 pamphlet *Revolt against the City*, as a colony of the East.)[3] What all of this means in practice, of course, is vast visual repetition: mile upon mile of cornfields, block upon block of crumbling factories. (Willa Cather: "The only thing very noticeable about Nebraska was that it was still, all day long, Nebraska.")[4]

But even used and battered landscapes have their particularity. Detroit's blight isn't Cleveland's blight, any more than Manchester's is Birmingham's. Nor are any two cornfields truly exactly alike, despite Monsanto's best efforts. The British cultural imagination has been formed by writers such as Thomas Hardy and D.H. Lawrence who are perfectly capable of distinguishing among bleaknesses; there's no reason the American imagination should not pay the Midwest the same tribute. Especially in a period when some of the more interesting art and music consists of similar procedures repeated on a massive canvas, when cultured people are trained to find meaning in the tiny variations of a Philip Glass symphony or an early John Adams tape piece, you'd think we could learn to truly *see* Midwestern flatness as something richer than mindless repetition. (Willa Cather again: "No one who had not grown up in a little prairie town could know anything about it. It was a kind of freemasonry.")[5]

Even if we insist, wrongly, on seeing the Midwest's physical geography as featureless, there's no reason to extend the mistake, as many even within the region do, to its cultural landscape. In a 2015 essay for *Slate*, "The Rust-Belt Theory of Low-Cost High Culture," reporter Alec McGillis marveled at the cheapness—and, it seems, the mere presence—of good orchestra and museum tickets in interior cities:

> The Cleveland Orchestra, one of the best in the world, offers a "young professional package," with regular concerts and special events, for a mere $15 per month—$20 for a couple. When I visited the St. Louis Art Museum, a monumental building deep within verdant Forest Park, I was stunned by its wealth of German expressionists (it has the world's largest collection of Max Beckmanns)—all for the entrance fee of $0. In Milwaukee, I spent hours with my laptop at the cafe in the art museum's Calatrava-designed wing....

> In Detroit, friends and I got a prime table at Baker's Keyboard Lounge, its oldest jazz club, for a $10 cover.[6]

I appreciate McGillis's enthusiasm, but why on earth was he so surprised? This is a part of the country where, the novelist Neal Stephenson observes, you can find small colleges "scattered about…at intervals of approximately one tank of gas." Indeed, the grid-based zoning so often invoked to symbolize dullness actually attests to a love of education, he argues:

> People who often fly between the East and West Coasts of the United States will be familiar with the region, stretching roughly from the Ohio to the Platte, that, except in anomalous non-flat areas, is spanned by a Cartesian grid of roads. They may not be aware that the spacing between roads is exactly one mile. Unless they have a serious interest in nineteenth-century Midwestern cartography, they can't possibly be expected to know that when those grids were laid out, a schoolhouse was platted at every other road intersection. In this way it was assured that no child in the Midwest would ever live more than $\sqrt{2}$ miles [i.e., about 1.4 miles] from a place where he or she could be educated.[7]

Minnesota Danish farmers were into Kierkegaard long before the rest of the country.[8] They were descended, perhaps, from the pioneers Meridel LeSueur describes in her social history *North Star Country*:

> Simultaneously with building the sod shanties, breaking the prairie, schools were started, Athenaeums and debating and singing societies founded, poetry written and recited on winter evenings. The latest theories of the rights of man were discussed along with the making of a better breaking plow. Fourier, Marx, Rousseau, Darwin were discussed in covered wagons.[9]

If you've read Marilynne Robinson's Gilead trilogy, you know that many of these schools were founded as centers of abolitionist resistance, or even as stops on the Underground Railroad.

When, looking in your own mind for a sense of your own experiences in a region, you find only clichés and evasions—well, that is a clue worth following. So I began, here and there, collecting tidbits, hoarding anecdotes, savoring every chance piece of evidence that the Midwest was a distinctive region with its own history. In doing so I noticed yet another paradox: If the Midwest is a particular place that instead thinks of itself as an *anyplace* or *no-place*, it is likewise both present and not present in the national conversation. The Midwest is, in fact, fairly frequently written about, but almost always in a way that weirdly disclaims the possibility that it has ever been written or thought about before. The trope of featurelessness is matched by a trope of neglect (for what can one do with what is featureless but neglect it?). Katy Rossing, a poet and essayist, has described the formula:

1. Begin with a loquacious description of the Euclidean-flat homogeneity of the landscape. This place looks boring. It looks like there's nothing here worth thinking about. Example: "The sins of the Midwest: flatness, emptiness, a necessary acceptance of the familiar. Where is the romance in being buried alive? In growing old?" (Stewart O'Nan, *Songs for the Missing*)

2. In fact, it seems no one has really thought about it before, they all write. What IS the Midwest? The West, South, and East all have clear stories, stories that are told and retold in regionally interested textbooks, novels, movies. The Midwest? It's a humorously ingenuous, blank foil for another region. Example: *Fargo, Annie Hall.*

3. But wait a minute, the writers tell you, it turns out this place isn't empty at all! They spend the remainder of the article crouched in a defensive posture.[10]

Rossing misses one or two tricks—there must also be a resentful invocation of the term *flyover country* ("a stereotype," as one lexicographer points out, "about other people's stereotypes").[11] And one must end self-refutingly, by pointing out a number of example of Midwestern distinctiveness or high achievement, all of which—the frontier, Abraham Lincoln, populism, the Great Migration, Chicago, the growth and decline of manufacturing—are so thoroughly discussed as to bring the article's initial premise into question.[12] The density of these evocations of let's-stop-ignoring-the-Midwest only increased after the 2016 election,[13] as national newspapers, ignoring the dozens of articles they had already published on the region, pledged themselves to the Rust Belt as though to a strict Lenten discipline.[14]

Actually, there is no dearth of commentary upon the Midwest, once you begin to look for it. Historian and politico Jon Lauck points to the region's rich historiographic tradition in *The Lost Region*; journals devoted to the region's history and literature come and go (*MidAmerica*; *Midwestern Gothic*); the Society for the Study of Midwestern Literature sponsors superb, if frequently ignored, scholarship; regional independent presses win awards and capture attention (Coffee House, Greywolf, Dzanc, Belt, Two Dollar Radio); writers as major as Toni Morrison, Louise Erdrich, Marilynne Robinson, David Foster Wallace, and Richard Powers set book after book in the region. (Morrison in particular is so identified with the South—because, to be blunt, she's black—that people forget she's from Ohio. *The Bluest Eye, Sula,* and *Beloved* are set there, *Song of Solomon* in Michigan.) If you took English in high school, you read—or pretended you read—Cather, Scott Fitzgerald, Ernest Hemingway, Sherwood Anderson, Sandra Cisneros, and Theodore Dreiser, all of whom wrote of the region lovingly or ambivalently;

if you took it in graduate school, you may also have read Wescott, William H. Gass, Saul Bellow, Jaimy Gordon, Dinaw Mengestu. The situation resembles nothing so much as the episode of the television show *Louie* in which the main character, stricken with guilt over his lapsed friendship with a less successful comedian, appears at the man's house and demands a reunion, a reckoning; whereupon the old friend, after a meaningful silence, remarks that Louie has delivered the same speech twice before: He'd forgotten each time. Our reckoning with the Midwest is perpetually arriving, perpetually deferred.

Andrew R.L. Cayton, one of the foremost historians of the region, gives a partial explanation for this neurotic repetition: Much of the discourse about the Midwest is mentally filed under the heading "local," not "regional."

> Historically, when people in the Midwest argue with each other over questions of identity, they fight over issues on universal, national, or local levels. They talk about what it means to be an American, a Lutheran, a farmer, a woman, a lesbian, a feminist, a black man; they almost never talk about what it means to be Midwestern, except in the most cursory fashion. In trying to locate a "heartland code," one ethicist found that residents of the St. Louis area invoked generalities, such as "respect for family," "respect for religion," "respect for education," "honesty," "selflessness," and "respect for the environment." They rarely got more specific than that.... In virtually all the recent work on the Midwest, it remains a setting, not a particular constellation of attitudes or behaviors.[15]

We Midwesterners talk about ourselves, and we are talked about by others, but in terms either universal or local: Abe Lincoln of the log cabin, or Abe Lincoln of world history, but not, despite the movie, Abe Lincoln of Illinois, who was formed in part by that "great interior region" he lauded in his 1862 Annual Message to Congress.[16] A Midwesterner may be a human, an American, a Detroiter, at most a Michigander, but a "Midwesterner" only when reminded of the fact. Cayton blames this lack of "regional consciousness" in part on geography: "Regional identity—the creation of an imagined community—requires a strong sense of isolation. And the Midwest is not, strictly speaking, isolated. It is in the middle." More important, however, is the intensity of local attachment: "But it is less regional *rootlessness* than local *rootedness* that makes the construction of a regional identity so difficult in the Midwest.... Localism, this pride in family, town, and state, leaves little room for interest in a coherent regional identity. In general, Midwesterners want to be left alone in worlds of their own making."[17]

Cayton's last remark, in particular, throws light on the way the Midwest is often depicted in American art, and the way Midwestern artists tend to function. Think of Grant Wood's farm couple, posted like sentries; of the intensely self-aware little Midwestern scenes that dot the landscape of American popular-music history like a series of private kingdoms: Motown in the '60s, Ann Arbor-Detroit in the late '60s and early '70s, Cleveland in the mid-'70s, Minneapolis in the early '80s. Think of Prince, who famously shot down Matt Damon's attempt at conversation—"I hear you live in Minnesota"—with that wonderful remark, at once quintessentially Prince and quintessentially Midwestern: "I live inside my own heart, Matt Damon."[18] From Prince in his private Paisley Park kingdom in the middle of Minnesota; to Robert Pollard in Dayton, with his one-person record industry; to Bob Dylan, cloistered in his private languages and allegories; from William H. Gass's novels and stories, walled and defended in purple prose and private grudges like old Michigan fort towns; to Marilynne Robinson's elaborately homemade worlds and worldview; to Gwendolyn Brooks's lifelong loyalty to Chicago, the Midwestern artist hunkers down on the landscape; she lives in her own heart. We remember her, then, as the artist of that patch of landscape, not as a "Midwestern artist."

If it is not the Midwest that is missing from American history or culture, or even from the national conversation, but simply a Midwestern "regional consciousness," as Cayton puts it, one naturally wonders whether such a category is important in the first place. Do Midwesterners need another "grid" (to borrow a term from the social critic George W.S. Trow) on which to plot their own lives? We already have families, towns and cities, a country, a species. Perhaps we are simply Americans, with no need for further differentiation.

It's certainly tempting to think so—because this idea is actually the one that gives the Midwest its most persistent self-understanding, the frame in which we see ourselves and through which others see us. We think of ourselves as basic Americans, with no further qualification. "The West, South, and East all have clear stories," as Katy Rossing puts it. But in the Midwest, we don't. We're free. And that *is* our story.

The authors of this story are not terribly hard to name. One of them is Lincoln, who, in his 1862 address to Congress having already labeled the Midwest the "great interior region," went even further, commending it as "territorially speaking...the great body of the republic."[19] It's a part of the country, but also, give or take, the country. Another author was Frederick Jackson Turner, whose *The Frontier in American History* (1920) characterizes the Middle West (as the slightly more dignified phrase of his day had it) as follows:

> Both native settler and European immigrant saw in this free and competitive movement of the frontier the chance to break the bondage of social rank, and to rise to a higher plane of existence. The pioneer was passionately desirous to secure for himself and for his family a favorable place in the midst of these large and free but vanishing opportunities. It took a century for this society to fit itself into the conditions of the whole province.... Little by little, nature pressed into her mold the plastic pioneer life.... From this society, seated amidst a wealth of material advantages, and breeding

individualism, energetic competition, inventiveness, and spaciousness of design, came the triumph of the strongest. The captains of industry arose and seized on nature's gifts. Struggling with one another, increasing the scope of their ambitions as the largeness of the resources and the extent of the fields of activity revealed themselves, they were forced to accept the natural conditions of a province vast in area but simple in structure. Competition grew into consolidation.[20]

Turner's Middle West is a sort of buffer zone between capitalism and the democracy of yeoman farmers, the straw mattress on which Hamilton lies down with Jefferson. "The task of the Middle West is that of adapting democracy to the vast economic organization of the present," he writes.[21] One might have thought this was everybody's job. By tasking the Midwest in particular with the work all citizens of a developed democracy must do, Turner cannot help suggesting that the region is defined solely by a sort of extra degree of Americanness, by being American to the nth power. (Wescott again: "What seems local is national, what seems national is universal, what seems Middle Western is in the commonest way human.")[22] As the geographer James Shortridge puts it, "The Middle West came to symbolize the nation…to be seen as the most American part of America."[23] Nor is average Americanness quite the same as average Russianness or average Scandinavianness, for the United States has always understood itself, however self-flatteringly, as an experiment on behalf of humanity. Thus, Midwestern averageness, whatever form it may take, has consequences for the entire world; what we make here sets the world's template. The historian Susan Gray has even detected echoes in Turner's language of Lamarckian evolution, a theory dominant among biologists a century ago, when Turner was writing. The new characteristics that the "old" races of the world acquired in their struggle to build a world among the prairies and forests would create an actual new, American race.[24]

Small wonder, then, that Midwestern cities, institutions, and people show up again and again in the twentieth-century effort to determine what, in America, is normal. George Gallup was born in Iowa, began his career in Des Moines at Drake University, and worked for a time at Northwestern; Alfred Kinsey scandalized the country from—of all places—Bloomington, Indiana. Robert and Helen Lynd, setting out in the 1920s to study the "interwoven trends that are the life of a small American city," did not even feel the need to defend the assumption that the chosen city "should, if possible, be in that common-denominator of America, the Middle West." They chose Muncie, Indiana, and called it Middletown.[25] We cannot be surprised that the filmgoers of Peoria became proverbial, or that newscasters are still coached to sound like they're from Kansas.[26] Nor that a recent defender of the region's distinctiveness feels he must concede, in the same breath, that it "was always less distinctive than other regions,"[27] or that a historian can call "ordinariness" the Midwest's "historic burden."[28] If it is to serve as the epitome of America for Americans, and of humanity for the world, the place had better not be too distinctly anything. It has no features worth naming. It's anywhere, and also nowhere.

What does it do to people to see themselves as normal? On the one hand, one might adopt a posture of vigilant defense, both internal and external, against anything that might detract from such a fully, finally achieved humanness. On the other hand, a person might feel intense alienation and disgust, which one might project inward—*What is wrong with me?*—or outward, in a kind of bomb-the-suburbs reflex. A third possibility—a simple, contented *being normal*—arises often in our culture's fictions about the Midwest, both the stupid versions (the contented families of old sitcoms) and the more sophisticated ones (*Fargo*'s Marge Gunderson, that living argument for the value of banal goodness). I have yet to meet any real people who manage it. A species is a bounded set of variations on a template, not an achieved state of being.

I took the first option. As a child, I accepted without thinking that my small town, a city of 9,383 people, contained within it every possible human type; if I could not fit in here, I would not fit in anywhere. ("Fitting in" I defined as being occupied on Friday nights and, sooner or later, kissing a girl.) Every week that passed in which I did not meet these criteria—which was most of them—became a prophecy. Every perception, every idea, every opinion that I could not make immediately legible to my peers became proof of an almost metaphysical estrangement, an oceanic differentness that could not be changed and could not be borne. I would obsessively examine tiny failures of communication for days, always blaming myself. It never occurred to me that this problem might be accidental or temporary. I knew that cities existed, but they were all surely just Michigan farm towns joined together *n* number of times, depending on population. Owing to a basically phlegmatic temperament, and the fear of hurting my parents, I made it to college without committing suicide; there, the thing solved itself. But I worry what would have happened—what does often happen—to the kid like me, but with worse test scores, bad parents, an unlocked gun cabinet.

But I also worry about the people who *can* pass as Midwestern-normal. At its least toxic, this can lead to a kind of self-contempt: the nice, intelligent young women in my classes at the University of Michigan who describe themselves and their friends, with flat malice, as "basic bitches." In artists, it can lead to self-destructive behavior, to the pursuit of danger in the belief that one's actual experiences have furnished nothing in the way of material. It also leads us to one of the other great stereotypes of Midwesterners, one that I think has a little more truth to it than the nonsense about hard work and humility: We are repressed. Any emotion spiky or passionate enough to disrupt the smooth surface of normality must be shunted away. Garrison Keillor, and in some ways David Letterman, made careers from talking about this repression in a comic mode that both embodies it and transmutes it into art. The Minnesota writer Carol Bly finds it less amusing:

> [In the Midwest] there is a restraint against *feeling in general.* There is a restraint against enthusiasm ("real nice" is the adjective—not "marvelous"); there is restraint in grief ("real sober" instead of "heartbroken"); and always, always, restraint in showing your feelings, lest someone be drawn closer to you.... When someone has stolen all four wheels off your car you say, "Oh, when I saw that car, with the wheels stripped off like that, I just thought ohhhhhhhh."[29]

Critiques of emotional repression always risk imposing a single model for the Healthy Expression of the Emotions on a healthy range of variations. But anyone who has lived in the Midwest will recognize the mode Bly describes, and if you've lived there long enough, you'll have seen some of the consequences she describes:

> You repress your innate right to evaluate events and people, but…energy comes from making your own evaluations and then acting on them, so… therefore your natural energy must be replaced by indifferent violence.[30]

Donald Trump won the Midwestern states in part because he bothered to contest them at all, while his opponent did not. But we cannot forget the *way* he contested them: raucous rallies that promised, and in some views incited, random violence against a laundry list of enemies. Since his victory, the Three Percent Militia has become a recurring, and unwelcome, character in Michigan politics.

A regional identity built on its own denial, on the idea of an unqualified normality: This sounds, of course, like whiteness—a racial identity that consists only of the absence of certain kinds of oppression. (White people can, of course, be economically oppressed, though if the oppression goes on in one place long enough they tend to lose some of their whiteness, to be racialized as that Snopes branch of the human family, the white trash.) And here we hit upon the last major stereotype of the Midwest, its snowy-whiteness.

If the South depends on having black people to kick around, Midwestern whites often see people of color as ever new and out of place, decades after the Great Migration. The thinking goes like this: America is an experiment, carried out in its purest form here in the Midwest; people of color threaten the cohesion on which the whole experiment may depend. Thus, while Southern history yields story after story of the most savage, intimate racist violence—of men castrated and barbecued before smiling crowds, dressed as for a picnic—Midwestern history is a study in racial quarantine.[31] Midwestern cities often dominate in rankings of the country's most segregated. And though the region has seen its share of Klan activity and outright lynchings—I write this days after the acquittal of the St. Anthony, Minnesota, police officer who killed Philando Castile—the Midwest's racism most frequently appears in the history books in the form of riots: Detroit, 1943; Cleveland, 1966;

Milwaukee, Cincinnati, and Detroit again, 1967; Chicago, Cincinnati again, and Kansas City, 1968; Detroit again, 1975; Cincinnati again, 2001; Ferguson, 2014; Milwaukee again, 2016. A riot is, among other things, a refusal to be quarantined. And the Midwest quarantines its nonwhite immigrants, too—the people from Mexico and further south, from the hills of Laos or the highlands of Somalia, and from the Middle East, who commute from their heavily segregated neighborhoods to harvest the grain, empty the bedpans, and drive the snowplows. This is not to mention the people whose forced removal or confinement gave rise to the notion of the Midwest as an empty canvas in the first place. The twentieth-century history of racism in the Midwest is, on the whole, both a terrible betrayal of the abolitionist impulse that led to the settlement of so much of the region and a fulfillment of the violence inherent in the idea of "settling" what was already occupied.

Our bland, featureless Midwest—on some level, it is a fantasy. The easiest, most tempting tack for a cultural critic to take with fantasies is to condemn them. Given what ideas of normalness, in particular, have done to this country, to its nonwhite, nonstraight, non-middle-class, nonmale—and also to those who are all of those things, and are driven slightly or fully crazy by the effort to live up to the norm that is their birthright—it is tempting simply to try to fumigate the myth away.

Tempting, but probably not possible. As the English moral philosopher Mary Midgley argues, myths are "organic parts of our lives, cognitive and emotional habits, structures that shape our thinking."[32] Since thinking cannot be structureless, a frontal attack on one myth usually leaves us in a state of uncritical, unnamed acceptance of a new one. Self-conscious attempts to create new myths, meanwhile, are like constructed languages; they never quite lose their plastic smell. We should ask instead whether our story of the Midwest—this undifferentiated human place—contains any lovelier, more useful, or more radical possibilities. At the very least, we should try to name what there is in us for it to appeal to.

Marilynne Robinson's Gilead trilogy has been read so often as to be reduced to a gingham study in Americana, and Robinson, a complex and in some ways cranky thinker, to "an Iowa abbess delivering profundities in humble dress."[33] This is a strange way to think about the story of a man dying before his son's tenth birthday; of an emotionally distant drifter who fails at prostitution and eventually marries a pastor; of an Eisenhower Republican family that loses its chance at partial redemption because the kindly dad is a racist. If conflating Marilynne Robinson with cozy regionalists like Jan Karon gets more people to buy Robinson's books, I suppose I can't object too strenuously, but it may lead some readers to miss the strangeness of passages such as this one in *Home* (2008):

> In college all of them had studied the putative effects of deracination, which were angst and anomie, those dull horrors of the modern world. They had been examined on the subject, had rehearsed bleak and portentous philosophies in term papers, and they had done it with the earnest suspension of

> doubt that afflicts the highly educable. And then their return to the *pays natal*, where the same old willows swept the same ragged lawns, where the same old prairie arose and bloomed as negligence permitted. Home. What kinder place could there be on earth, and why did it seem to them all like exile? Oh, to be passing anonymously through an impersonal landscape! Oh, not to know every stump and stone, not to remember how the fields of Queen Anne's lace figured in the childish happiness they had offered to their father's hopes, God bless him.... Strangers in some vast, cold city might notice the grief in her eyes, even remember it for an hour or two as they would a painting or a photograph, but they would not violate her anonymity.[34]

This passage offers a stunning inversion of the trope of featurelessness. While acknowledging that the place (in this case Gilead, Iowa) has a history ("the childish happiness they had offered to their father's hopes"), Glory Boughton, the narrator, longs for the "anonymity" and "impersonal landscape" of a "vast, cold city" (Chicago, Minneapolis, Milwaukee). She longs for "deracination," for the sense of being an anyone moving through an anyplace. Why should a person long for this? Anonymity is usually felt as a burden, and the sense that one is a mere "basic person" can imprison as much as it liberates.

Yet the passage resonates, because we humans need to feel that we are more than our communities, more than our histories, more even than ourselves. We need to feel this because it is true. The cultural conservative ideal, with its deeply rooted communities—an idea that finds a strange echo in the less nuanced kinds of identity politics—is a reduction as dangerous to human flourishing and self-understanding as is the reduction of the mind to the brain or the soul to the body. The "deeply rooted community" is, in reality, at least as often as not, a cesspit of nasty gossips, an echo chamber in which minor misunderstandings amplify until they prevent people from seeing each other accurately, or at all. As for the identities that drive so much of our politics, they are a necessary part of the naming and dismantling of specific kinds of oppression—but we've all met people for whom they become a cul-de-sac, people who ration their sympathy into smaller and smaller tranches of shared similarity until they begin to resemble crabbed white men. Moral imaginations, like economies, tend to shrink under an austerity regime.

Every human is a vast set of unexpressed possibilities. And I never feel this to be truer than when I drive through the Midwest, looking at all the towns that could, on paper, have been my town, all the lives that, on paper, could have been my life. The factories are shuttered, the climate is changing, the towns are dying. My freedom so to drive is afforded, in part, by my whiteness. I know all this, and when I drive, now, and look at those towns, those lives, I try to maintain a kind of double consciousness, or double vision—the Midwest as an America not yet achieved; the Midwest as an America soaked in the same old American sins. But I cannot convince myself that the promise the place still seems to hold, the promise of flatness, of the freedom of anonymity, of being anywhere and nowhere at once, is a lie all the way through. Instead, I find myself daydreaming—there is no sky so conducive to daydreaming—of a Midwest that makes, and keeps, these promises to everybody.

And then I arrive at the house that, out of all these little houses, by some inconceivable coincidence, happens to be mine. I park the car. I check the mail. I pet the cat. I ready myself for bed. I can't stay up too late. Between the Midwest that exists and the other Midwest, the utopic no-place that I dream of, is hard work enough for a life.

(Fall 2017, 19.3)

Notes

1 Glenway Wescott, *Good-Bye, Wisconsin* (New York, NY: Harper, 1928), 39. Quoted in Richard Nelson Current, *Wisconsin: A History* (Urbana, IL: University of Illinois Press, 2001), 161.

2 See C.K. Hyde, *Arsenal of Democracy: The American Automobile Industry in World War II* (Detroit, MI: Wayne State University Press, 2013).

3 Edward Watts, *An American Colony: Regionalism and the Roots of Midwestern Culture* (Athens, OH: Ohio University Press, 2001), xii. See also Watts's "The Midwest as a Colony: Transnational Regionalism," in *Regionalism and the Humanities*, ed. Timothy Mahoney and Wendy J. Katz (Omaha, NE: University of Nebraska Press, 2009), 166–89.

4 Willa Cather, *My Ántonia* (Boston, MA: Houghton Mifflin, 1954), 5. First published 1918.

5 Ibid., 1.

6 Alec McGillis, "The Rust-Belt Theory of Low-Cost Culture," *Slate*, January 1, 2015, http://www.slate.com/articles/arts/culturebox/2015/01/cheap_high_culture_in_baltimore_buffalo_detroit_and_other_midsize_cities.html.

7 Neal Stephenson, "*Everything and More* Foreword," in *Some Remarks* (New York, NY: HarperCollins, 2012), 273.

8 See Thomas Wetzel, "A Graveyard of the Midwest," *MidAmerica* 26 (1999): 10–24.

9 Meridel LeSueur, *Ripening: Selected Work, 1927–1980* (Old Westbury, NY: Feminist Press, 1982), 36.

10 Katy Rossing, "Smothered: American Nostalgia and the Small Wisconsin Town," *Hypocrite Reader*, January 2012, http://hypocritereader.com/12/smothered-american-nostalgia.

11 This supposed pejorative appears to have been popularized by Midwesterners reacting defensively to the region's supposed unpopularity in the coastal mind. See Gabe Bullard, "The Surprising Origin of the Phrase 'Flyover Country,'" *National Geographic*, March 14, 2016, http://news.nationalgeographic.com/2016/03/160314-flyover-country-origin-language-midwest.

12 For two examples, see Matthew Wolfson, "The Midwest Is Not Flyover Country," *The New Republic*, March 22, 2014, https://newrepublic.com/article/117113/midwest-not-flyover-country-its-not-heartland-either, and Michael Dirda's review of Jon Lauck's *The Lost Region*, *Washington Post*, February 4, 2014, https://www.washingtonpost.com/entertainment/books/the-lost-region-toward-a-revival-of-midwestern-history-by-jon-k-lauck/2014/02/05/55e90e08-8a90-11e3-833c-33098f9e5267_story.html?utm_term=.62c430eef907. Or, one might simply Google the phrase "Not just flyover country."

[13] Eric Schulzke, "The One County That Tipped Michigan to Trump," *Deseret News*, November 16, 2016, http://www.deseretnews.com/article/865667328/The-one-county-that-tipped-Michigan-to-Trump-and-why-ignoring-it-is-not-an-option.html.

[14] See Anne Trubek, "The Media Didn't Forget the Rust Belt—You Did," *Refinery29*, November 17, 2016, http://www.refinery29.com/2016/11/130147/rust-belt-trump-voters-election-media-issues.

[15] Andrew R.L. Cayton, "The Anti-Region," in Cayton and Susan E. Gray, *The American Midwest: Essays on Regional History* (Bloomington, IN: Indiana University Press, 2001), 148.

[16] Abraham Lincoln, "Second Annual Message to Congress," in *Lincoln: Political Writings and Speeches*, ed. Terence Ball (New York, NY: Cambridge University Press, 2013), 157.

[17] Ibid., 149, 150.

[18] Kenzie Bryant, "Prince Had No Time for Matt Damon's Small Talk," *Vanity Fair*, July 18, 2016, http://www.vanityfair.com/style/2016/07/matt-damon-prince-small-talk.

[19] Lincoln's delimitation of a "great interior region"—"bounded east by the Alleghenies, north by the British dominions, west by the Rocky Mountains, and south by the line along which the culture of corn and cotton meets"—doesn't exactly conform to the US Census Bureau's definition of the Midwest, nor to any of a half-dozen other common definitions. (Lincoln, "Second Annual Message," www.presidency.ucsb.edu/ws/?pid=29503.) Referring to the West, which at that time included Michigan, the nineteenth-century novelist Caroline Kirkland wrote, "How much does that expression mean to include? I never have been able to discover its limits." Me neither. (Kirkland is quoted in Edwin S. Fussell, *Frontier in American Literature* [Princeton, NJ: Princeton University Press, 1954], 3.)

[20] Frederick Jackson Turner, *The Frontier in American History* (New York, NY: Holt, 1950), 154. First published 1920.

[21] Ibid., 155.

[22] Quoted in Ronald Weber, *The Midwestern Ascendancy in American Writing* (Bloomington, IN: Indiana University Press, 1992), 7.

[23] James Shortridge, *The Middle West* (Lawrence, KS: University of Kansas Press, 1989), 33.

[24] Susan E. Gray, "Stories Written in the Blood: Race and Midwestern History," in Cayton and Gray, *The American Midwest*, 127.

[25] Robert S. Lynd and Helen Merrell Lynd, *Middletown: A Study in American Culture* (New York, NY: Harcourt, Brace, 1959), 7–8. First published 1929. The identification of Middletown and Muncie is attested in a number of places; see the chapter on Middletown in Sarah E. Igo, *The Averaged American: Surveys, Citizens, and the Making of a Mass Public* (Cambridge, MA: Harvard University Press, 2008).

[26] See Edward McClelland's delightful *How to Speak Midwestern* (Cleveland, OH: Belt Publishing, 2016), 9–10.

[27] Wolfson, "The Midwest Is Not Flyover Country."

[28] Nicole Etcheson, "Barbecued Kentuckians and Six-Foot Texas Rangers: The Construction of Midwestern Identity," in Gray and Cayton, *The American Midwest*, 78.

[29] Carol Bly, "From the Lost Swede Towns," in *Letters from the Country* (New York, NY: Harper and Row, 1981), 4.

[30] Ibid., 5–6.

[31] I mean this more or less literally. The book exists; see Thomas J. Sugrue, *The Origins of the Urban Crisis* (Princeton, NJ: Princeton University Press, 1997).

[32] Mary Midgley, *Myths We Live By* (London, England: Routledge Classics, 2014), 7.

[33] Mark Athitakis, *The (New) Midwest* (Cleveland, OH: Belt Publishing, 2017), 9.

[34] Marilynne Robinson, *Home* (New York, NY: Farrar, Straus & Giroux, 2008), 282.

Love and Its Discontents
Irony, Reason, Romance

Eva Illouz

...in my experience poetry speaks to you either at first sight or not at all. A flash of revelation and a flash of response. Like lightning. Like falling in love.

Like falling in love. Do the young still fall in love, or is that mechanism obsolete by now, unnecessary, quaint, like steam locomotion?... Falling in love could have fallen out of fashion and come back again half a dozen times, for all he knows.

—J.M. Coetzee[1]

...for it is weakness not to be able to countenance the stern seriousness of our fateful times.

—Max Weber[2]

Reflecting on the impact of the French Revolution on social mores, Edmund Burke mused on what was in store for humanity:

All the pleasing illusions that made power gentle, and obedience liberal, which harmonized the different shades of life...are to be dissolved by this new conquering empire of light and reason. All the decent drapery of life is to be rudely torn off. All the super-added ideas, which the heart owns, and the understanding ratifies, as necessary to cover the defects of our weak and shivering nature, and to raise it to a dignity in our own estimation, are to be exploded as a ridiculous, absurd and antiquated fashion.[3]

Burke anticipates what would become one of the chief sources of the dynamism and discontent of modernity, namely the fact that beliefs—in transcendence and authority—become accountable to Reason. And, for Burke, far from auguring a progress in our condition, "the Empire of light and reason" exposes us to truths we cannot bear. For, Burke says, as power withers away, our illusions will also fade, and this new nakedness will leave us immensely vulnerable, exposing and revealing both to ourselves and to others the true ugliness of our condition. The scrutinizing of social relations by the implacable gaze of Reason can only tear down the harmonious web of meanings and relationships on which traditional power, obedience, and fealty rested. For only lies and illusions can make the violence of social relationships bearable. To be tolerable, human existence requires a modicum of myths, illusions, and lies. Put differently, Reason's indefatigable attempts to unmask and track down the fallacies of our beliefs will leave us shivering in the cold, for only beautiful stories—not truth—can console us.

Marx, the most forceful heir and defender of the Enlightenment, curiously concurred with the ultra-conservative views of Burke in his famous dictum: "all that is solid melts into air, all that is holy is profane, and men at last are forced to face with sober senses the real conditions of their lives and their relations with their fellow men."[4] Marx, like Burke, views modernity as a "sobering of the senses," as a violent arousal from a pleasant if numbing slumber and a confrontation with the naked, bare, and barren conditions of social relationships. This sobering realization may make us more clever and less likely to be lulled by the fanciful and vain promises of the Church and of the Aristocracy, but it also empties our lives of charm and mystery, and of a sense of the sacred. Knowledge comes at the price of desecrating that which we revered. Thus Marx, like Burke, seems to think that cultural fantasies—not truth—make our lives meaningfully connected to others and committed to a higher good. Although Marx neither rejected the new empire of light nor longed to return to the defunct rituals of the past, we can detect in him the same Burkean dread of what lies ahead for a humanity in which nothing is holy and everything is profane.

What makes Marx distinctly and profoundly modernist was not his endorsement of modernity (progress, technology, reason, economic abundance), but precisely his ambivalence toward it. From the start, modernity involved the uneasy and simultaneous acknowledgment of the extraordinary energies unleashed by Reason and of the danger such exercise of Reason may entail. At the very same time that moderns declared themselves free of the shackles that had fogged the mind and consciousness, they longed for that from which they had proudly claimed to release themselves: a sense of the sacred and transcendent and the very capacity to believe. The triumphant call of Reason dissecting myths and beliefs became properly modern when it was intertwined with the mournful longing for transcendent objects to believe in and be swayed by. Modernity is defined by its ambivalence toward its legitimating cultural core, by a sense of dread of the powers it may unleash.

Max Weber famously lent this ambivalence its most poignant pathos with his famous view of modernity as characterized by "disenchantment." Disenchantment does not mean simply that the world is no longer filled with angels and demons, witches and fairies, but that the very category of "mystery" comes to be disparaged: for, in their impulse to control the natural and social world, the various modern institutions of science, technology, and the market, which aim at solving human problems, relieving suffering, and increasing wellbeing, also dissolve our sense of mystery. The vocation of scientific work is to solve and conquer mysteries, not to be under their spell. Similarly, capitalists whose principal wish is to maximize their gains, often disregard and undermine those values—religious or aesthetic—that limit economic activity. Precisely because science and economics have considerably expanded the limits of our material world, helping us to resolve the problem of scarcity and making Nature yield to human needs, the gods have deserted us. What in an earlier age was governed by faith, personal fealty, and charismatic heroes, becomes a matter of calculable means. But this process toward rationalization does not eliminate all manifestations of passion; rather, it generates attempts to restore, even if vicariously, orders of experience dominated by fervor and passion.

What makes Weber's diagnosis of modernity so full of pathos is the fact that he did not think moderns could ever overcome their longing for meaning and fervor. That is why modernity would offer occasional flights from the realm of Reason, but these flights would remain just that, temporary, partial, and thus could not open up to wholeness and the totality of transcendence.[5] This is why Weber's epistemology was a reflection of the only recourse left to Reason: that of Stoic neutrality in the face of the warring gods of values. Contrary to the "prophets of the classroom," he could not and would not take a position, and preferred to adopt the stoic and self-abnegating heroism of the modern man of science, who observed the loss entailed by modernity yet forbade himself to mourn it; who contemplated the lost fervor of the past and the glorious promises of the future, yet refused to be either a prophet of doom or a clarion for utopias. Rejecting the left-wing, liberal, un-ambivalent endorsement of progress and emancipation, as well as any conservative longing for the past, Weber offered a position of *intellectual stoicism* in which one had to forego the urge to take sides, and one had only to take stock of the irreconcilable, self contradictory, and even self-defeating tendencies at work in modernity.

It is *intellectual stoicism* we may have to adopt when evaluating the drastic transformation and rationalization of love in modernity. Indeed, the history of love is far from being a story of progressive emancipation from the shackles of economic rationality. Instead of assuming—as historians have—that modernity simply "liberated" the romantic sentiment from the economic necessity of merging and expanding capital and property, love—both as a cultural ideal and as a cultural practice—has incorporated the very aporias of modernity, its built-in contradictions, which do not allow us to trumpet victories or mourn the past.

Disenchanting Love

A widely accepted view opposes premodern marriage—determined according to criteria of social rank, status, and wealth—to the modern mode of mate selection, in which love as a spontaneous emotion presumably now plays a primordial role in mate selection. Yet, while more emancipated and more egalitarian, and thus, more free and unconstrained, modern love is also counter-intuitively more rationalized than its premodern counterpart. The modern romantic condition more often resembles the process of "sobering up" described by Marx than the fervor and frenzy of premodern lovers. This change is paradoxically caused by—or at least concomitant with—the fact that there is no longer a strong institutional distinction between interest-driven and purely romantic decisions, indeed because these two modes of action have become closely intertwined.

The cultural model of "love at first sight" provides the most ready illustration of what might be dubbed an "enchanted" version of love, a view of love as an intensely meaningful experience that opens up the self to a quasi-religious sense of transcendence. "Love at first sight" contains a few consistent characteristics: It is experienced as a unique event, unexpectedly erupting in one's life. It is inexplicable and irrational. It is incited upon the first encounter and therefore not based on cognitive and cumulative knowledge of the other; rather, it derives from a holistic and intuitive form of experience. It disturbs one's daily life and provokes a deep commotion of the soul. The metaphors used to describe that state of mind often indicate a force that is overwhelming and overpowering (heat, magnet, thunder, electricity). The object of love elicits overwhelming sentiments beyond the control of the lover; the value of the object of love is so high that he or she becomes incommensurable, and it is impossible to substitute another for the loved one. The absoluteness and un-conditionality of the commitment are thus total.

"Enchanted" love is simultaneously spontaneous and unconditional, overwhelming and eternal, unique and total. This approach to romantic love thus affirms the radical uniqueness of the object of love, the impossibility of substituting one object of love for another, the incommensurability of its object, the refusal (or impossibility) to submit feelings to calculation and Reason, and the total surrender of the self to the loved person. Such a view of love has traversed the cultural history of the West, but it has several secular cultural variants. For example, in the Middle Ages, religious rhetoric was often mixed with amorous rhetoric, presenting the loved one as a divinity, which had the effect of strengthening further the view of love as a total experience, in which the lover aims to fuse with and even be absorbed in and by the object of love. Compare this model with the following quip by Candace Bushnell—the celebrated author of the column that inspired the worldwide famous television series *Sex and the City*:

> When was the last time you heard someone say, "I love you!" without tagging on the inevitable (if unspoken) "as a friend." When was the last time you saw two people gazing into each other's eyes without thinking, Yeah right? When was the last time you heard someone announce, "I am truly, madly in love," without thinking, Just wait until Monday morning?[6]

Candace Bushnell expresses here a thoroughly self-conscious, supremely ironic, and disenchanted approach to love. As witnessed by the emergence of the genre of "chick-lit"—literature geared to women about the difficulties of relationships—modern love has become the privileged site for the trope of irony. The rationalization of love is at the heart of the new ironic structure of romantic feeling, which marks the move from an "enchanted" to a disenchanted cultural definition of love.

Structures of feeling, the highly felicitous expression coined by Raymond Williams, designate social and structural aspects of feelings and the feelings of social structures. They are "social experiences in solutions."[7] An ironic structure of feeling has come to pervade romantic relationships because of the "disenchantment" or "rationalization" of love.

What is disenchantment? Weber was never entirely clear about it, but we may grasp it *a contrario*, by reflecting on what enchantment is. An enchanted experience is mediated by powerful collective symbols that key one to a sense of the sacred. It is based on beliefs and feelings that involve and mobilize the totality of the self; these beliefs and feelings are not processed in second-order cognitive systems and are ultimately unjustifiable. These symbols constitute and overwhelm the experiential reality of the believer. In enchanted experiences, there is no strong distinction between the subject and object. Thus, the object of the belief has an ontological status for the believer that cannot be put into question. Disenchantment is both a property of belief that becomes organized by knowledge systems and expert cultures (as opposed to hot symbols), and a difficulty in believing. This is because both the cognitions and emotions organizing belief become rationalized.

According to Weber, what makes conduct rational is the fact that it is "methodical," that it is systematic, that it calculates means to achieve ends, and is in Weber's words, "controlled by the intellect." Rational action is consciously regulated, not random, habitual, or impulsive. A rational attitude undermines enchantment because in order to know and approach an object it uses systematic rules and codes, independent of the subject and object of knowledge, thus separating the subject and object of knowledge and delegitimizing knowledge gained in an epiphanic, intuitive, or irruptive mode. A number of massively powerful cultural forces can be said to have refashioned the sentiment and experience of love, and to have contributed to its rationalization and thus to a profound change in the way in which we experience it: science, technologies of choice, and political values. The convergence and confluence of these three forces, I argue, have been responsible for the creation of an ironic structure of feeling in the romantic experience.

Making Love into a Science

First, and perhaps foremost, is the prevalence of scientific explanations of love, which have been disseminated widely through the institutions of the university and the mass media. Throughout the twentieth century and into the twenty-first, psychology, psychoanalysis, biology, and evolutionary psychology have explained the feeling of love by subsuming it under such categories as "the unconscious," "sex drive," "hormones," "survival of species," or "brain chemistry." Under the aegis of scientific explanations, these frameworks undermine the view of love as an ineffable, unique, and quasi-mystical experience, ultimately undermining both its absoluteness and uniqueness.

Although psychoanalysis and dynamic psychology put love at the center of the constitution of the self, they undermine its cultural status by viewing it as the result of psychic processes, such as those of "psychic trauma," "Oedipal conflict," or "repetition compulsion." The Freudian popular culture in which most modern polities have become steeped has made the forceful claim that love is a reenactment of early childhood conflicts and that it is often nothing but the repetition of a drama with other early protagonists who are the true origin, and even the cause, of the present object of love.

This has the simple effect of countering the idea that love is ineffable and mystical. Instead, psychoanalysis claims, love is caused by the ways in which we form attachments to early parental figures, and by the ways in which our psyche faces and processes the Oedipus complex. Love is thus reduced to a universal psychic structure.

In creating a straight narrative line and coherence between childhood and adult romantic experiences, psychological culture encourages an ongoing process of self-understanding and careful self-monitoring of the psyche, and an intellectualization of romantic relationships, through the systematic labeling of emotions, and their regulation and monitoring by techniques of self-awareness and self-transformation. Moreover, in prescribing models of intimacy based on negotiation, communication, and reciprocity, the *psy*sciences make intimate relationships highly *plastic*, to be fashioned out of the design and reflexive monitoring of an autonomous will and tailored to the particular needs and psychological make-up of an individual, thus liquidating the association of love with an absolute form of transcendence. Love becomes an emotion to be tailored to the needs of individuals, and in its affirmation of individual wellbeing, psychology defuses the ideals of sacrifice and self-abandonment.

Autonomy is at the center of the model of selfhood advocated by psychology, and the practice of autonomy transforms the ideal of emotional fusion into an ideal of negotiation between two fully mature selves. Finally, psychology also makes the experience of romantic suffering into yet another symptom of an insufficiently mature psyche. In psychological culture, suffering does not signal an emotional experience stretching above and beyond the boundaries of the self. Romantic suffering is no longer the sign of selfless devotion or of an elevated soul; such love—based on self-sacrifice, fusion, and longing for absoluteness—is viewed as the symptom of an emotional dysfunction. The former cultural equation of love with suffering—with a kind of consummatory, self-wasting experience in which the self can affirm its love in its ostentatious display of self-loss—becomes deeply suspicious in the new therapeutic culture.[8]

The model of health that massively penetrates intimate relationships demands that love be aligned along definitions of wellbeing and happiness and submitted to the iron law of utility. For example, unreciprocated love is reinterpreted as a sign that the individual needs to repeat an experience of abandonment. The emotional experience of love becomes harnessed to a utilitarian project of the self, a project in which one has to secure maximum pleasure and wellbeing, thus making love into an experience in which one should count his/her utilities.

Biology has had a slightly different impact on the cultural frames through which love is understood. Biologists typically explain love through chemical processes that, even more than psychology, reduce love to factors that are entirely extraneous to the sentiment of love itself. Studies in neuroscience have suggested that a consistent number of chemicals are present in the brain when people testify to feeling love. These chemicals include: testosterone, estrogen, dopamine, norepinephrine, serotonin, oxytocin, and vasopressin. For example, a dramatic increase in the amount of dopamine and norepinephrine is said to be present in the brain when one is infatuated with another person. More specifically, higher levels of testosterone and estrogen are present during the lustful phase of a relationship. Dopamine, norepinephrine, and serotonin are more commonly found during the attraction phase of a relationship. The serotonin effects of being in love have a similar chemical appearance to obsessive-compulsive disorder, which in turn would explain why we seem not to be able to think of anyone else when we are in love. Serotonin levels are also significantly higher in the brains of people who have recently fallen in love than in the brains of others. Oxytocin and vasopressin seem to be more closely linked to long-term bonding and relationships characterized by strong attachments. In the February 2006 issue of *National Geographic*, Lauren Slater's cover page article "Love: The Chemical Reaction" discusses love strictly as a chemical reaction. Both attraction and attachment are viewed as being triggered by different chemical components. The euphoria or exaltation we may feel as a result of being in love are nothing but a chemical and involuntary reaction of the brain. Research also emphasizes that these symptoms tend to disappear after two years on average. The result of this reduction of love to brain chemistry is to dispose of a mystical and spiritual view of love and to substitute for it a new form of materialism that has the effect of discounting the intensity and feeling of uniqueness when falling in love.

While offering a different view, evolutionary psychologists similarly attribute the feeling of love to an extraneous factor that serves the human species. According to Dylan Evans, in evolutionary terms, emotions like love (or guilt or jealousy) are thought to have helped resolve the "problem of commitment."[9] Given that people must cooperate with each other, how will they commit themselves to another and/or insure another's commitment? The answer, evolutionary psychologists say, is through emotions. Romantic love in particular may have served the purpose of instilling a desire to reproduce and to ensure that men and women will not walk out on each other on a whim. Here again, the interpretive shift operated by evolutionary psychology has had the effect of deflating the felt uniqueness and transcendent character of love, making it a mere functional necessity to insure cooperation at the level of the species. Love becomes nothing more than the blind necessity of nature and of the social group.

Scientific modes of explanation—psychological, biological, evolutionary—by their nature tend to be abstract and extraneous to the categories of felt and lived experience. In contrast, premodern religious explanations that viewed intense love as the manifestation of spirit possession or as a temporary loss of Reason still resonated with the felt experience of the subject. Scientific explanations reduce love to an epiphenomenon, a mere effect of prior causes that are unseen and unfelt by the subject, and that are neither mystical nor singular but rather located in involuntary and almost mechanical—psychic or chemical—processes. With the prevalence of scientific modes of explanation, it is difficult to hold onto the view of love as a unique, mystical, and ineffable feeling. In that sense, love has undergone the same process of disenchantment as Nature: it is no longer viewed as inspired by mysterious and grand forces but rather as a phenomenon in need of explanation and control, as a reaction determined by psychological, evolutionary, and biological laws.[10]

Scientific interpretations of love do not replace traditional romantic conceptions of love, but rather compete with them, and in fact *undermine* them. Science tends to subsume particular experiences under general and abstract categories, thus doing away with their particularity. Because scientific frameworks aim to explain and find causes, they naturally undermine any experience based on the ineffable and the irrational. The overall effect of scientific interpretive frameworks on love is both deflationary and reflexive. They dethrone love of its transcendental status, making it instead a psychological or physical force, working beyond and beneath the concrete particular experiences of specific individuals. They also create a strong "unreality effect," making actors doubt love's reality and explicitly attend to the underlying "real" causes for their love.

Weber did not think that an increase in scientific understanding brought about a greater understanding of the concrete conditions of our lives. In a lecture, he noted:

When we spend money today I bet that even if there are colleagues of political economy here in the hall, almost every one of them will hold a different answer in readiness to the question: How does it happen that one can buy something for money—sometimes more and sometimes less? The savage knows what he does in order to get his daily food and which institutions serve him in this pursuit. The increasing intellectualization and rationalization do not, therefore, indicate an increased and general knowledge of the conditions under which one lives.[11]

More than that, as Nicolas Gane suggests, non-scientific explanations might be superior to the scientific ones because they account for the totality of our lived experience.[12] Nonscientific explanations are superior to the scientific ones in that they are holistic and more organically connected to the totality of our experiences. Scientific explanations of our experience make us more distant from that experience, both cognitively and emotionally. According to Weber, there is a way in which science makes our experience less intelligible, for there is an incompatibility between existential frames of meaning and abstract, systematic ones.

Technologies of Choice

Another cultural force that has contributed to the rationalization of love has been the overlap of Internet technology with psychological knowledge and the ideology of choice that derives from the market.[13] That the choice of a mate has become more rational than ever before has often been misperceived because love as a pure emotion has become a far more important dimension in mate selection than ever before in history.

What was a premodern rationality? A premodern actor looking for a mate was notoriously rational: s/he typically considered criteria such as dowry size, a candidate's personal or family wealth and reputation, education, and family politics.[14] But what is often omitted in these discussions is the observation that the calculation stopped here. Given the limited options, beyond general and rudimentary requirements of character and appearance, actors made very few demands from prospective partners, and more often than not, settled for the *first available* satisfactory *good enough* marriage prospect. Thus, in arranged marriage, choice involved little reflexive calculation as people had few emotional, educational, and lifestyle prerequisites.

Two main differences in the modern situation strike even the casual observer: the premodern actor looking for a mate seems a simpleton in comparison with today's actors, who from adolescence to adulthood develop an elaborate set of criteria for the selection of a mate. Such criteria are not only social and educational, but also physical, sexual, and perhaps most of all emotional. Psychology, Internet technology, and the logic of the capitalist market applied to mate selection have contributed to create a self-conscious, manipulable personality, who uses an increasingly refined and wide number of criteria, presumably conducive to greater compatibility. Psychology in particular has greatly contributed to defining persons as sets of psychological and emotional attributes, themselves submitted to the imperative of compatibility. Thus what has become a hyper-cognized, rational method of selecting a mate goes hand-in-hand with the expectation that love provide authentic, unmediated emotional experiences.

These characteristics of modern partner selection are most patently illustrated in the realm of online dating.[15] Internet dating sites have become highly popular and profitable enterprises. According to researchers of digital technology at comScore Networks, in December 2006 the leading US online dating site was Yahoo! Personals with more than 4.5 million hits, and US online dating sites received a total of 20 million hits from US visitors per month. With monthly packages costing between $10 and $50, online dating is also a lucrative business.[16] Indeed, in 2006 online dating was the second largest online, paid content category, with revenues of over $1 billion for the year.[17] While market growth seems to be slowing down, Jupiter Research has predicted that revenues for US online dating sites will be $932 million in 2011. Clearly online dating represents a significant trend in modern courtship.

By enabling users to investigate a vast number of options, the Internet encourages the maximization of partner selection in unprecedented ways, in stark contrast to the methods of premodernity. Maximization of outcome has become a goal in and of itself.[18] For example, many respondents to an open-ended questionnaire about the uses of Internet dating sites declared the choices available were so large that they would get in touch only with people who corresponded very precisely to their diverse aspirations. Moreover, the majority of respondents reported that their tastes changed in the course of their search and that they aspired to "more accomplished" people than they did at the beginning of the search. Clearly the case of online dating shows that actors use elaborate rational strategies to achieve their romantic desires, thus confirming the claims of Smelser and Alexander that computer technology has a strong rationalizing effect: "the gradual permeation of the computer into the pores of modern life deepened what Max Weber called the rationalization of the world."[19]

Like no other technology, the Internet has radicalized the notion of the self as a "chooser" and the idea that the romantic encounter should be the result of the best possible choice. That is, the virtual encounter has become hyper-cognized, the result of a rational method of gathering information to select a mate. It has literally become organized as a market, in which one can compare "values" attached to people, and opt for "the best bargain." The Internet places each person searching for another in an open market of open competition with others, thus radicalizing the notion that one can and should improve one's romantic condition and that (potential or actual) partners are eminently interchangeable.

This marks the move to *technologies of interchangeability*, that is, technology that expands the pool of choices, enables the rapid move from one partner to another, and sets up criteria for comparing partners and for comparing oneself to others. The Internet enables the development of a comparative mindset, made possible (or "afforded" in the language of sociologists of technology) by the fact that technology lays out choices and offers tools (such as "score cards") to measure the relative merits of each potential partner. Partners become eminently interchangeable, and given they can be evaluated according to a certain metric, they can be improved on. That is, the Internet, combined with the ideologies of psychology and the market, reinstitutes a process of *commensuration* between potential partners. Wendy Nelson Espeland and Mitchell L. Stevens define "commensuration" as follows: "Commensuration involves using numbers to create relations between things. Commensuration transforms qualitative distinctions into quantitative distinctions, where difference is precisely expressed as magnitude according to some shared metric."[20] The combined effects of psychology, the Internet, and the capitalist market have the cultural effect of making potential partners commensurable, measurable, and comparable to each other according to new techniques and cognitive tools of evaluation. These cognitive tools constitute, one more time, new principles of equivalence.

Political Emancipation as Rationalization

The norms of equality, consensuality, and reciprocity, which have come to dominate the moral vocabulary of our polities, have rationalized love and profoundly transformed the terms within which relationships are negotiated. In his *Politics of Authenticity*, Marshall Berman suggests that "it is only in modern times that men [sic] have come to think of the self as a distinctly *political* problem."[21] Given the gender used by Berman, it is ironic that this sentence has been particularly and spectacularly applicable to women in the twentieth century. Indeed, feminism has exerted perhaps the single most significant influence on women's subjectivity and on the relations between the sexes. Second-wave feminism has profoundly transformed our understanding of the emotion of love.[22] More than any other political or cultural formation, feminism importantly influenced the cultural history of love because it tore down the veils of male chivalry and the feminine mystique. In calling on women and men to debunk power, feminism also called on them to adopt ideals of equality, reciprocity, and fairness; the feminist movement, as a *cultural* formation, introduced rules of conduct that rationalized love and sexual relations in two important ways: it called on women to become aware of power relations inside intimate bonds and thus fostered a new way of thinking reflexively about romantic practices, of attending to their rules and cultural presuppositions; it further instilled rules of interaction to secure symmetrical exchange, thus introducing greater predictability and uniformity in the romantic bond. From a sociological standpoint, "power" is a cultural frame that helps conceive, organize, and thereby generate social relationships. That is, if we suspend our commitment to gender equality, we may perceive the ways in which the cultural categories of "power," "reciprocity," and "equality" have reorganized romantic relationships, driving them to become predictable and controllable.

Moreover, the demand that language be neutral and purged of its gender biases, that sexual relationships be cleansed from the long shadow of power, that mutual consent and reciprocity be at the heart of intimate relationships, and finally that impersonal procedures secure such consent—all of these have had the effect of undermining the cultural practice of "seduction," as a semi-conscious practice of playing with one's body and language in order to arouse desire in another.

In characterizing the perfect seducer, Robert Greene indicates the importance of maintaining the incomplete nature of the romantic interaction, including increasing ambiguity, sending mixed signals, mastering the art of insinuation, confusing desire and reality, mixing pleasure and pain, stirring desire and confusion, toning down the sexual element without getting rid of it, refusing to conform to any standard, delaying satisfaction, and not offering total satisfaction.[23] In other words, seduction requires a capacity to play with and twist the rules of ordinary interactions that require clarity and truthfulness. As Shadi Bartsch and Thomas Bartscherer put it: "ambivalence is built into the erotic phenomenon."[24] Seduction is ambivalent, and it is their ambivalence that makes the prototypical seducers of Western culture exemplary of a certain form of freedom from morality. Don Juan, Casanova, and Cleopatra embody a kind of sovereignty and self-possession that are not easily bound by rules. In his/her desire to seduce without commitment, the seducer uses ambiguity. Ambiguity is essentially a way of maintaining uncertainty with regard to the meaning and intention of a speaker, it also enables both power and freedom, that is, the capacity to say something without meaning it, the capacity to imply several meanings at once, and most importantly, the capacity not to be accountable to moral principles. Such freedom, while always problematic from a moral and political standpoint, is also a precondition for playfulness because playfulness is synonymous with the crossing of boundaries, which in turn produces uncertain and ambiguous meanings. Thus, as the philosopher Robert Pippin suggests: "there is something about eros that cannot be accommodated easily within Christian or liberal-egalitarian humanism."[25]

Indeed, I would argue that irony has replaced playfulness and has become the dominant trope and tone of our times. Irony is inimical to love and playfulness because, as David Halperin writes,

> Some experiences…are incompatible with irony. In order to have them at all, it is necessary to banish any hint of irony. Conversely, the arrival of irony signals the end of the experience, or its diminution. Irony's opposite is intensity. In moments of intense, overwhelming sensation, we have little awareness of context and no attention to spare for more than one set of

meanings. In such states, we become literalists: we can experience only one kind of thing. The three cardinal experiences that demand the elimination of irony, or that cannot survive irony, are raw grief or suffering, religious transport, and sexual passion.[26]

Irony is a figure of speech that feigns ignorance; it feigns ignorance but counts, for its effect, on the knowledge of the hearer. It is the trope of the person who knows too much but refuses to take reality seriously. Modern romantic consciousness has the rhetorical structure of irony because it is saturated with knowledge, but it is a disenchanted knowledge that prevents full belief and commitment. Thus, if love is a modern religion, as has often been claimed, it is a peculiar one indeed, for it is a religion that cannot produce belief, faith, or commitment.

(Spring 2010, 12.1)

Notes

[1] J.M. Coetzee, *Disgrace* (New York, NY: Penguin, 1999) 13.

[2] Max Weber, "Science as a Vocation," *From Max Weber: Essays in Sociology* (London, England: Routledge, 2001) 149.

[3] Marshall Berman, *All That Is Solid Melts Into Air* (Gloucester, MA: Peter Smith, 1988) 109.

[4] Berman, 95.

[5] Lawrence A. Scaff, *Fleeing the Iron Cage: Culture, Politics, and Modernity in the Thought of Max Weber* (Berkeley, CA: University of California Press, 1989).

[6] Candace Bushnell, *Sex and the City* (New York, NY: Atlantic Monthly Press, 1996) 2.

[7] Michael Payne, ed., *Dictionary of Cultural and Critical Theory* (Blackwell Reference Online, 1997): http://www.blackwellreference.com/public/tocnode?id=g9780631207535_chunk_g978063120753522_ss1-37.

[8] As William Wordsworth put it in *Influence of Natural Objects* (unpublished, 1799) (emphasis added): "By day or star-light, thus from my first dawn / Of childhood didst thou intertwine for me / The passions that build up our human soul; / Not with the mean and vulgar works of Man; / But with high objects, with enduring things, / With life and nature; purifying thus / The elements of feeling and of thought, / *And sanctifying by such discipline / Both pain and fear,—until we recognize / A grandeur in the beatings of the heart.*"

[9] Dylan Evans, *Emotion: The Science of Sentiment* (New York, NY: Oxford, 2001).

[10] One should perhaps nuance this claim because psychology still viewed the experience of love as singular, and somehow tried to explain it in terms of the private history of the subject.

[11] Quoted in Nicholas Gane, *Max Weber and Postmodern Theory: Rationalization versus Re-enchantment* (London, England: Palgrave, 2002) 53.

[12] See Gane, *Max Weber and Postmodern Theory*.

[13] Eva Illouz, *Cold Intimacies* (Cambridge, England: Polity, 2007).

14 As the existing literature on modernization shows, it is difficult to define the parameters of socio-cultural periods such as "premodern" and "modern"—unlike periods of political history, they are not clearly marked by discrete events. For the purposes of this paper, I use "premodern" to refer to the period that extended roughly from the fifteenth century through the late seventeenth/early eighteenth century. In contrast to Herman R. Lantz, in "Romantic Love in the Pre-Modern Period: A Sociological Commentary," *Journal of Social History* 15.2 (1981): 349–70, I do not use the term "premodern" to mean "early modernity," rather, to indicate the period immediately preceding modernity. As I see it, modernity began with the onset of the Industrial Revolution, but my discussion of the modern situation focuses specifically on developments within the past few decades. Further study of the intervening period, examining nineteenth-century English novels and early dating practices in the twentieth century might help to understand the gradual development of modal configurations.

15 For examples of other rational methods of modern partner selection, see Richard Bulcroft, et al., "The Management and Production of Risk in Romantic Relationships: A Postmodern Paradox," *Journal of Family History* 25.1 (January 2000): 63–92; Stanley B. Woll and Peter Young, "Looking for Mr. or Ms. Right: Self-Presentation in Videodating," *Journal of Marriage and Family* 51.1 (February 1989): 483–8; and Aaron C. Ahuvia and Mara B. Adelman, "Formal Intermediaries in the Marriage Market: A Typology and Review," *Journal of Marriage and Family* 54.1 (February 1992): 452–63.

16 See http://www.onlinedatingtips.org.

17 A. Wharton, "The Dating Game Assessed," *Reviewtoday.org* (May/June 2006).

18 Barry Schwartz, *The Paradox of Choice: Why More is Less* (New York, NY: Ecco, 2003); Sheena S. Iyengar and Mark R. Lepper, "When Choice is Demotivating: Can One Desire Too Much of a Good Thing?" *Journal of Personality and Social Psychology* 79.6 (December 2000): 995–1,006.

19 Neil J. Smelser, *Problematics of Sociology* (Berkeley, CA: University of California Press, 1997); and Jeffrey C. Alexander, *The Meanings of Social Life: A Cultural Sociology* (New York, NY: Oxford University Press, 2003).

20 Wendy Nelson Espeland, "Commensuration and Cognition," *Culture in Mind: Toward a Sociology of Culture and Cognition*, ed. Karen A. Cerulo (New York, NY: Routledge, 2002) 64. See also, Wendy Nelson Espeland and Mitchell L. Stevens, "Commensuration as a Social Process," *Annual Review of Sociology* 24 (1998): 313–43.

21 Marshall Berman, *The Politics of Authenticity: Radical Individualism and the Emergence of Modern Society* (New York, NY: Atheneum, 1970) xvi.

22 This paper deals with heterosexual love. Unless otherwise specified, our use of the term "love" should be understood in this sense.

23 Robert Greene, *The Art of Seduction* (New York, NY: Viking, 2001).

24 Shadi Bartsch and Thomas Bartscherer, "What Silent Love Hath Writ: An Introduction to Erotikon," *Erotikon: Essays on Eros, Ancient and Modern*, ed. Shadi Bartsch and Thomas Bartscherer (Chicago, IL: University of Chicago Press, 2005) 7.

25 Robert B. Pippin, "*Vertigo*: A Response to Tom Gunning," *Erotikon: Essays on Eros, Ancient and Modern*, ed. Shadi Bartsch and Thomas Bartscherer (Chicago, IL: University of Chicago Press, 2005) 280.

26 David M. Halperin, "Love's Irony: Six Remarks on Platonic Eros," *Erotikon: Essays on Eros, Ancient and Modern*, ed. Shadi Bartsch and Thomas Bartscherer (Chicago, IL: University of Chicago Press, 2005) 49.

Adolescents and the Pathologies of the Achieving Self

Joseph E. Davis

Growing up, I've always had a lot of pressure to do well in school and things like that and be like—you know how your parents always want you to be better than them?... It's just like so much pressure, and I think that's a lot of it, that's why I get really nervous speaking in front of people or doi...projects when the grade is dependent on them or things like that. That always makes me nervous because maybe I'm not going to do as [well]...and then it's going to mess [up] my grades, and then I'm not going to be able to be this person I'm supposed to be.

—Sarah, college freshman, age 19

Young people like Sarah, from well-to-do suburban families, live in a world of high expectations that often includes enormous pressures to be successful.[1] I have changed the names of my interviewees and any other details necessary to protect their anonymity. Like many of her classmates at the very competitive college where she is now a freshman, she has long felt that she needs to "get straight A's," "do everything perfectly," and have just the right, outgoing personality. Part of the performance pressure comes from her family. Her parents have high standards, and her father sometimes states them in no uncertain terms. The weight of responsibility, however, according to Sarah, arises from her parents' hopes for her. "They just hope," she says, "for better for you and for you to be all you can be." Her mother, professionally quite successful, "never has directly told me I have to be this person, but it's just like I think I definitely just look at her and I'm like, oh my gosh…. How am I not doing as well as her?" Additional pressures to perform—to be "this person"—come from the school environment, which Sarah characterizes as a "ruthless competition" both socially and academically, from her status-conscious friends, and from the foreboding sense that "everything I'm doing now is going to determine my life." Trying to live up to expectations is a constant source of stress.

Sarah was one of two dozen college students, aged 18–22, we interviewed as part of my larger study on the use of psychoactive medications to deal with everyday life problems. More than half of these young people were taking a medication for problems with anxiety, sadness, and distractibility, many since high school. The rest of the students, describing very similar problems as the medication-takers, were coping in other ways. Sarah was in the latter category. As early as middle school, her mother took her to see a therapist because she was "nervous and anxious about things." Although the subject of medication was discussed, neither Sarah nor her mother thought it necessary. Sarah still doesn't. Compared to those taking medication, Sarah, like others in the non-medication group, is more likely to draw distinctions between external pressures and her own sense of how she is internally constituted. In reflecting on the causes of her nervousness and anxiety, she points to the expectations and competitiveness of her social environment. At the same time, she also recognizes that she has, at least in part, internalized the expectations. She does not believe that it is possible for her "to do everything that my parents want—or my father wants me to do," yet "even though I think I'm not able to do it, it's like I'm still going to keep pushing myself." She knows she shouldn't let "other people's pressures become a big issue" for her, that she "can't do everything perfectly," but she feels as if she has to "do it perfectly." So she worries not just that underperformance will let others down but also that she is failing in important ways to reach her own "full potential."

All the striving comes at a cost. The gap between lived experience and self-image is a source of pain. "And every single time I feel it," Sarah states, "it just puts me down more." She experiences intense anxiety around exams and presentations, discomfort in many social situations, and general feelings of inadequacy. Ashamed of her nervousness about school performance and unwilling to appear weak, she hides her feelings from both her family and her friends. She worries that even her close friends might "judge me and think I'm weird or something." When friends notice that she is on edge, she feels compelled to act like nothing is wrong and tries "extra hard" to hide her nervousness. This isolation also contributes to Sarah's conviction that her struggles are somehow unique, that something "deeper in myself," and not just external pressures, is at root. Sarah believes that "a lot of people have pressures from their parents and from society and stuff like that, but I just don't think they react to it the same way that I do, or with so much intensity." She is certainly right about the pressures, but interviews with young people in similar circumstances suggest her reactions are only too common.

Under Pressure

Adolescents can and often do live under considerable stress. Some well-documented "stressors" include family problems, like divorce; interpersonal difficulties with peers; illness; and the very common personal concerns with how they act and look. The list also includes achievement expectations, which have grown dramatically in the past two decades.[2] In the postindustrial economy, a college degree is now widely regarded as essential to occupational success. Most schools, in the interest of fostering open social mobility, have eliminated defined educational tracks and redesigned the curriculum on a decentralized, course-by-course basis. Support for vocational programs has dried up as resources have been shifted to college preparatory, honors, and Advanced Placement courses.[3] According to sociologists of education, these changes and the "college for all" norm they reflect have played an important role in the "soaring" educational and occupational achievement expectations of adolescents.[4] Borrowing a page from the "status attainment" model of earlier sociological theory, these rising ambitions are sometimes hailed as an unalloyed good. Ambitious plans, according to the theory, serve as a source of motivation that leads young people to more successful educational and occupational outcomes. There is evidence, however, that the rising expectations are increasingly disconnected from what can be realistically achieved and, in fact, go unfulfilled for many.[5] As has long been recognized, the inability to realize important goals produces high rates of distress.[6]

Another effect of the "college for all" norm has been to greatly increase competition for admission to prestigious colleges and universities, whose value as markers of achievement and future success has intensified as the general value of a college education has been diluted. If the adverse consequences of frustrated educational expectations fall disproportionally on the disadvantaged, the stress of competition for spots in elite colleges falls disproportionally on the privileged. In many places, middle- and upper-middle-class schools have become a "pressure-cooker environment," as one of the students we interviewed, Dan, 21, describes his high school. These schools are characterized by demands for high performance and individual achievement, constant comparison and competition, and extensive homework and high-stakes exams.[7] The college application process is particularly fraught, but the whole environment can have a driven quality. "We got to school an hour early," Dan recalls and not without pride, "and finished up the last work [we] were doing. Everyone stayed until 5:00 or 6:00 at night playing sports and then went home and worked until 10:00 p.m. or 11 or 12 or 1 or 2...."

Parenting priorities have shifted with the educational competition and the larger status anxieties that fuel it. Professional, upper-middle class, and immigrant parents are especially likely to transmit high expectations, exert pressures to succeed, and carefully manage their children's lives. A new term has been coined, "helicopter parents," to describe those who hover over and obsess about the achievements of their children. These parents have been criticized for producing anxious, over-scheduled, and sleepdeprived teens, good at conforming to expectations but lacking in independence and skills for coping with adversity.[8] Such criticisms certainly have merit, and both journalistic accounts and research studies document the stress that such family environments can produce.[9] At the same time, negative critiques of "hyper-parenting" and "pressurecooker" schools are easily overdrawn.[10] Both reflect and reproduce new and larger cultural ideals about individuals as enterprising—as entrepreneurs of the self—who strive economically and efficiently for fulfillment, excellence, and success.

The words "enterprise" and "entrepreneur," of course, are business terms. Their meaning has been shifting over the past few decades as both a reaction to bureaucratic organizational forms believed to be inefficient and as a necessary response to new rules of competition in a global economy.[11] The corporate ideal, in the words of one observer, is now to mobilize the "enterprising capacities of each and all, encouraging them to conduct themselves with boldness and vigor, to calculate for their own advantage, to drive themselves hard, and to accept risks in the pursuit of goals."[12] This powerful ethic has subsequently been generalized not only to all types of organizations and more and more social contexts (for example, the family, schools) but to all forms of individual conduct. People themselves are to make an enterprise of their lives and conduct their activities with energy, initiative, and calculation, seeking to maximize their own human capital, project a future, and act upon themselves in order to better achieve their goals.[13] For the students we interviewed, the source of keenest distress was not parental pressure or schools but the failure to meet the obligations of such a personal ethic.

Diffuse Demands

Of the two dozen students we interviewed, half discussed their problems with sadness, anxiety, or lack of concentration without making reference to parental expectations or demands. A few students in this group, like Ryan, 19, whose father suddenly abandoned the family after 25 years of marriage, characterize their parents as having problems of their own and not at all hovering or micro-managing. However, for most of these students, parents play a very active and involved role in their lives. Some describe their parents as benevolently "overprotective" or, as with Rachel, 20, who is having trouble staying organized in college, they were there in high school "to do a lot of tasks for me" and "keep track of the work I had to do." Others emphasize their close and emotionally dependent relationships with their mothers.

Katie, 22, happily recounts how she still calls her mother every day: "just like every little problem I call her…." In these cases, parental involvement in helping to manage their daily lives is viewed positively, as the normal and expected type of support that parents provide.

The other half of the students, including Sarah discussed above, describe their parents as having high or very high educational expectations for them. All of the students in this group attend selective colleges and universities, and almost all are the children of immigrant parents and/or from relatively affluent families. They did not express any one view or experience of parental expectations. A few viewed their parents' expectations more or less positively. Dan, who attended the pressure-cooker high school, feels that his parents are satisfied by his solid school performance and is pleased that their high expectations have also "become my own." Those expectations have driven him to work hard, he explains, and have helped make him "a high achiever in the academic aspects of my life," which "is an important thing to me." Kim, 20, whose parents immigrated from the Philippines, observes that "I have been really harsh on myself" for a long time and thinks she "picked that up" from her parents who always focused on the one B+ on her report card rather than the balance of A's. They "had really high expectations of me," she says, but "I don't think it is necessarily a bad thing. I mean, it has definitely helped me to drive myself and to motivate myself to improve things."

Most of the students are less sanguine and characterize their parents' expectations and performance demands as more of a burden. Megan, 19, daughter of very successful Chinese immigrants, tells a common story. Her parents, she says, especially her father, have "very, very high expectations" for her. Though "I know my dad's expectations are unrealistic," she says, "at the same time, if someone sets a bar for me, it's a personal disappointment if I don't reach it or if I disappoint. Regardless of how unrealistic my dad's expectations are, those are his expectations, and if I can't meet them, why can't I meet them?" "I guess," she continues, "by proxy I adopted those same expectations for myself." Together with the high demands of school and her friends, which she also emphasizes, the pressures "combine and then I need to be superhuman and then I'm not and then life sucks." Still, Megan does not otherwise describe her parents as hovering and stresses how much she loves them and how they are "the people that I cling to."

Perhaps the clearest account of over-parenting comes from Anna, 21. Always a very good student, she did not begin to feel the pressure of her high-achieving parents' expectations until her older sister left for college. When her sister was applying, Anna recounts, "they were always getting on her about everything, about what colleges to apply to, taking her to everything," and after she left, Anna's parents bore down on her and her preparation for college. At 15, for instance, her mother took her to see a neurologist about possible attention deficit/hyperactivity disorder (ADHD). Although she had only gotten one "bad grade" in school, she notes, she "was always bad at standardized tests," had recently taken the PSAT, and sometimes did not pay attention in school. "I can concentrate really well," she explains, "when I'm interested in something, but if I'm not interested in a subject, my mind wanders a lot." The neurologist diagnosed her "pretty fast" with ADHD and wrote a prescription for Adderall. Her mother, who Anna feels, "was really gung-ho about getting me diagnosed," in fact, "kind of got scared" and did not fill the prescription. Anna continued to do "really well" in school, but her grades were a constant topic of discussion. Now a student at a very selective university, her parents call her all the time, and her grades are "the only thing they talk to me about. Not the only thing, but the main thing." Despite her performance, Anna does not feel she's meeting their expectations and resents their constant surveillance.

As noted above, the students who draw a distinction between external pressures, parental or otherwise, and their own sense of their inner workings are the *least* likely to be taking a medication. This does not necessarily mean that the parents of students taking a medication have any different educational expectations or are any less involved in their children's lives. Virtually all of the students on medication describe similar high school experiences to those not taking a medication, similar ambitions, and seemingly similar family relationships. In several of the cases, the students describe being taken to the doctor while in middle or high school because their parents perceived them as performing below their potential or because of their own school performance anxieties. John, 18, for example, was taken by his physician mother, who had devoted long hours to helping him with his work in elementary school, to a neurologist because his "grades started dropping in sixth or seventh grade." John believes he was just bored, but the doctor "said I had a slight ADHD" and wrote a prescription for Ritalin. Unlike with Anna, the prescription was filled. While there are other similarities between the two groups, the difference is that the students taking medication view their problems as primarily, though not exclusively, arising from *within* themselves.

Jennifer, 19, for example, began taking Paxil for Generalized Anxiety Disorder the very day in the tenth grade that she "just started freaking out" about a B+ on a calculus test. Since the third grade, she had, with "all of my friends," been "in the advanced, the talented and gifted program" and calculus was her "first really hard class." It had not started well. On the initial quizzes, she recounts, "I didn't get grades that I wanted," that is, "grades up to my standard." Then came the B+, the "mini panic attack," and a trip to the family doctor. Unlike the students, such as Sarah or Megan, who see their own high expectations as partly an internalized reflection of the expectations of others, Jennifer believes her "very high standards" are simply "who I am." She also believes that she is by nature "a very anxious person," although she is quick to point out that her anxiety is "not social" and "only for school." "I do not want to get a bad grade," she explains, and "that's basically the overwhelming factor of my life." Her anxiety motivates her to study constantly, but it also produces worry and physical symptoms (sweaty hands, a racing heart) come test time. Jennifer, an only child, identifies other stresses in her life and even characterizes her sophomore year as the "year of anxiety" at home because of her parent's separation and emotional problems. Nonetheless, she believes that her test anxiety, must, in part, have a biological basis because her parents haven't worried about her grades, and she "can't figure out where I would have gotten the behavior from if it wasn't" from them. Initially angry and resistant to the medication, she acquiesced, and found, after some trial and error with brand and dosage, that it eased her anxiety. She took it for about a year and then stopped as a "defiance thing" toward her mother, only resuming, of her own volition, in college.

There is clear evidence in the interviews to suggest that the tendency to view problems as internal to the person or as biological is conditioned by the fact of taking medication for them.[14] In describing her thinking about the medical encounter, first in high school and then in college, Jennifer suggests such recoding. She characterizes her initial high school doctor visit as very frustrating because while she was angry and "didn't want to actually talk about it [her anxiety]," she also "wanted someone that wanted to know...someone who was actually interested in and kind of personally invested in how you felt," who "would actually just sit down with you and ask, 'well, why are you feeling this?'" She wanted the doctor to understand and acknowledge that "I wasn't just flipping out for no reason, and that I was a smart kid. I wasn't just any kid that's getting B's and is worried about that." Her anxiety had a reason: "I was like, it's the tests. I need to do this...I need to study more or get better grades, or why did I do this? I'm so dumb." Rather than take the time to listen, to perhaps explore how Jennifer's learning environment was making her feel inadequate, the doctor had her fill out symptom questionnaires, talked mainly with her mother, and then "just gave me some medicine."

When explaining her later decision to restart medication, Jennifer's language is different. A grade of B- on a freshman-year, midterm exam got her worried; she "was really not okay with that," cried a lot, and doggedly pursued remedial help from the instructor. She also knew that sophomore year would bring more hard classes. And so, without prompting from her parents, she returned to the doctor. Earlier, she strongly resisted the implications of a diagnosis and medication. Now all resistance was gone.[15] She wanted the drug, and she was pleased that the doctor agreed immediately and was "like, okay, I'll write you a prescription for it." Now, she describes the drug as a kind of prophylactic ("like a helmet when you ride a bike") that she takes to keep her anxieties "at bay," where they do not challenge, as she put it, "how you think about yourself...or how people see you because people don't see that side also." The beauty of the medication is that it does not interfere with her understanding of herself, that "part of me that's like, I have to do well, I have to do well, I have to get good grades," her good anxiety, if you will, but blunts and prevents others from seeing the "really high levels" of her "biological anxiety." Recognizing that she has changed her view since high school, she now attributes her earlier and different understanding to her age and rebelliousness.

Talk of expectations, whether from parents, school, or peers, or generated from within, raises an obvious question: expectations for what? Toward the end of each interview, we asked students about the American Dream, how they define it, and how they see themselves in relation to it. Almost everyone defined it as including career success and some affluence and material comfort, in addition to a family. In a very general way, each embraced the dream, but was also quick to reject its materialist and statusclimbing aspects and emphasize instead good family relationships, or happiness, or the freedom to do what you want. No doubt, the ladder they have been climbing—achieving good grades, demonstrating leadership and well-roundedness, getting into a competitive college—and that their parents and schools have encouraged (or pushed), has aimed toward, has been seen as essential to, securing this future. In terms of the stresses students feel in their daily lives, however, achieving specific future goals seems to play a role for only a few, and these identify adjusting their expectations as helpful for coping with the stress. They have made peace with not being a doctor, for example, or have found their true passion. For others, their sadness or anxiety, their perception of themselves as abnormal or disordered, appears linked to a different kind of ambition, less directed to specific goals as to signaling that one is a particular sort of person. In Jennifer's story and in many of the other students we interviewed, being smart, being outgoing, being a leader—being what I'll call an "achieving self "—are ends in themselves and a yardstick by which they measure themselves and rate their potential. Coming up short can be deeply disorienting.

Achieving Full Potential

Jennifer's identity, as we saw, is deeply entwined with an image of herself as smart, and her sense of success and potential is linked with that image. Michelle, 22, the daughter of parents from Asia, has a similar vision. She is one of the students whose family has "really high expectations" for her and who feels a lot of pressure to do well. Unlike other such students, she describes a troubled home and difficult family relationships and characterizes her separated parents as "really absent" from her life and her relationship with them as "really not close…at all." Her case is also different in that she has been diagnosed with two different disorders and takes medications for both. In the interview, she expressed considerable ambivalence about one of the diagnoses and was rather indifferent to the drug she was taking for it. She underscored the other diagnosis, for ADHD, and the other medication, Ritalin. This priority was also reflected in the symptom checklists that we asked her to fill out for both diagnoses: she scored herself very high for ADHD, moderate to low for depressive symptomatology.[16] About the ADHD and Ritalin, she expressed no ambivalence. In her self-narrative, her experiences of family problems, sadness, and loneliness were marginalized, and primary emphasis was placed on her intellectual ability and challenges to it.

More than once, Michelle asserted that "I know that I'm smarter than 99 percent of people, or especially in my schools" and that until some problems arose, "school was obviously really easy for me." She stresses that she studies very hard, is very competitive, and gets really nervous during testing situations. If she "got an A- on something, I would just cry." Throughout high school, her combination of hard work, a careful system of rechecking test answers, and a "lot of caffeine pills," helped compensate for the fact that "reading always took me so long" and "I was always staying up really late." Despite normally performing very well on standardized tests, she found her performance on the SAT "really frustrating." On the math section, "I didn't even finish," and on the math SAT2, "I fell asleep." In fact, she says, "I scored pretty high, but I think I could have gotten it almost perfect.... I could be completely wrong, but that's what I think." She likes the selective college she attends, but "there's just no doubt in my mind that I'm smart enough to go to somewhere better than here." Nonetheless, college has been a struggle and, she recounts, "I haven't done really well at school...." A pivotal moment came when she decided to go to her college's Student Health Center. There, they got things "figured out."

At the Center, Michelle saw a therapist who, she says, "taught me ways to be organized and stuff like that," as well as a psychiatrist. Though she characterizes the experience as "really awesome" and "probably the greatest moment of my life," it was not without its own frustrations. At the Center, she was first put through an extensive battery of tests for learning disabilities and a general psychological evaluation. "They really devoted a lot of time to me," she reports, "and made a really, really big effort." However, Michelle was already convinced that "I'm very clearly ADHD," and was therefore incredulous when she was told that "you're kind of on the borderline, the tests aren't really coming out one way or the other." She speculates that "maybe the bar is set higher because it's through the school. Like maybe you would get more attention from a private practitioner, but they also wouldn't be as scrutinizing...." She also wonders if perhaps her intelligence is part of the problem. "This is actually going to sound really, really awful," she says, "but I think I'm smarter than other people are, and I think that, I don't know, not that I need separate tests, that's not what I was saying, but I don't know...I don't know how I could have come out as borderline."

Borderline or not, the psychiatrist diagnosed Michelle with ADHD and prescribed Ritalin. Michelle, who takes the Ritalin on an "as-needed basis," finds it very helpful. "I do better in school," she reports, "because of being on medication." Seeing its effect now, she says, "kind of makes me angry because I went through a lot of really unnecessary hurdles, especially in high school." Now she reads "really fast," stays awake, is better organized, and "everything comes so easily to me when I take it." In fact, easily enough that taking the medication also represents a threat to her self-conception. So, "I just kind of always have to tell myself, no, you actually are that smart. You're just like, well, like my doctor always [tells] me, it's like, no, you really are that smart, it's just you are taking it to be at your full potential." It doesn't help, she argues, that neither her parents nor her best friend—she no longer talks with any of them about her problems—think she should be on Ritalin. Just to be sure that she is not gaining an "unfair advantage," she tests herself: "I'll do it maybe once every two weeks where I just won't take it and have a day of class, just to remind myself of how things used to be, to justify the fact that it's okay that I'm taking it." She also emphasizes that she still works very hard: "I'm in the library probably more than 65 percent of people, 70 percent I want to say."

Together with the medication, the ADHD diagnosis helps Michelle order and explain her experience. Now she understands why her world was coming apart. "I think," she says, "the medication and the revelations that came with it, I know myself a lot better now. There were all these questions and things I didn't understand before, and it's helped me figure them out. And that's awesome, that's the fun part." If not exactly at peace, Michelle does feel that, at least for the time being, the winds buffeting her vision of herself, of her intellectual capacity and potential, have been quieted.

For other students, the demands of their "full potential" leave them in serious doubt about whether they are "up to par." Megan, who we met above, also wants to be "the person" but perceives herself to be falling short. The problem began in high school. She attended a very elite school, and there she began "to feel like I was mediocre or below average." Earlier, she "was the smartest person in the class" and had been on the gifted and talented track since the fifth grade. It made her feel special: "When I was younger, people would be like, 'Oh, you learn so well.' That's a big reason why some people made fun of me when I was younger; they were like, 'You're such a dork, why do you do multiplication tables in 30 seconds,' I was very smart when I was younger." As discussed earlier, she also believes her parents' high expectations contributed to this image of herself, which she took to heart. But then came high school, and she was surrounded by very bright, high-achieving kids. She began to "feel marginalized" and yearned to "feel special again." In ninth grade she "started to feel very different from the people around me," to "drift away from people," and by the twelfth grade "felt very isolated." All of these feelings carried over into college.

Although she is a scholarship student at a first-rate university, she is disappointed. It was her "safety school." In coming to this college, she says, "I was very angry and then I started thinking…'my God, I'm like smarter than everyone here,' which is not true, but please indulge me because not only do I have an inferiority complex, I also apparently have a superiority complex." She now wants to "show that I don't deserve to be here or I should be somewhere better by acing all my classes and being president of 40 organizations. And that is really not happening. I am, if anything, a mediocre student…and that just makes me so angry or so angry at the world and then me for not being the person." She is "frequently plagued by regret" that she isn't more active in student organizations, doesn't "do all these extraordinary things" and doesn't "distinguish [herself] in some way. "I want to impress someone," she says, and "I don't; I end up being impressively unimpressive," which "crushes me." She is worried that "I'm becoming the exact type of person that I thought I was not."

Whereas students like Jennifer and Michelle turned to medication and the narratives of Generalized Anxiety and ADHD to address the gaps between their vision of themselves and their experience of their social environment, Megan cannot do so. She describes herself as "chronically sad," and her life "as a chore" and "a to-do list." And "that's the feeling I've had for so long, like years, that it's become my default." She recognizes this is not "healthy" and "I really, really, really want this to change…." But she rules out categorically calling herself depressed, which she believes medically indicates "there is something chemically wrong" and the "only way it can be fixed is chemically." To call herself depressed would be to admit being "cosmically screwed." To do so would be to surrender any sense of agency, to give up the belief that you can "think yourself out of it," and to accept being "thought of as weak" and "get pity and that's gross" [laughs]. It's "horrifying to me," she says, "that there would be something so wrong with me that I would have to resort to needing something to make me into a normal human being. I feel like when people take drugs, they're not even themselves anymore, they're an artificial version of themselves." Rather than "clinically depressed," she argues, "I tend to just think of myself as sad because then I can do it. I can get myself out of it." So Megan acknowledges that she needs to "do something," but, ironically, like Jennifer and Michelle who take medication, resists any alteration of her self-image. On that, she says, "I'm very stubborn."

Pathologies of the Achieving Self

The students we interviewed feel compelled to strive for and to realize their "potential." Throughout their young lives, parents, teachers, and others in their social milieu have continually incited them to action, choice, and self-improvement. They have been encouraged to take full advantage of the many opportunities available to them, to set goals and deadlines, to work hard and overcome obstacles, to discover and develop their natural talents, and to refine and express their personality. The motivation, to be sure, is to promote their freedom and personal fulfillment, to help them develop the resources necessary to gain a competitive advantage, to go far and thrive in the very fluid, individualistic, and demanding structures of late modern life. This freedom brings obligations, including an obligation to strive for success and responsibility for whatever outcomes ensue, but the content or form of success remains open. Very few students said they felt any pressure to make specific career choices; none said that they were expected to follow in their parents' footsteps. The achievement ladder they are on reaches up into an open sky. What they did express—and not as attributable to any specific source and sometimes imaged as arising from within themselves—was powerful pressure to conform to certain abstract imperatives of the achieving self.

The imperatives are a set of normative attributes, behaviors, and personality features. They are manifested as contrasts with the fears and challenges to self-image that the students report—fears that they might not be "ridiculously smart" but "mediocre," not impressive or interesting but "weird" or "boring," not confident but "awkward" and "self-conscious," not self-disciplined and productive but a "slacker" and "unmotivated," not strong but "weak"

435

and "pitiable," not self-sufficient but "dependent," not perfect but a "loser." The imperatives can also be observed through the emotional experiences that students seek to regulate with drugs or control by some other means: discouragement and loneliness, nervousness and insecurity, jealousy and emotional vulnerability, shame and humiliation, regret and self-blame. In their effort to blunt these emotions, students convey additional norms of the achieving self. While proactive, aggressive, and impressive, this self is also easy-going, non-defensive, flexible, resilient, and resourceful. Like the entrepreneurial ideal of the successful corporation, the achieving self is energetic, efficient, focused, and competitive.[17]

The pathologies of the achieving self—its sadness, anxiety, and obsessiveness—are the reciprocal of these normative imperatives and can only be understood in terms of them. Granted, the direct pressures of over-involved parents and pressure-cooker schools can be a significant source of stress for some. But what stands out clearest in the interviews is how punishing deviations from the normative imperatives of the achieving self can be. Against these often contradictory norms—aggressive and competitive, yet laid back and funny; driven while effortless—failures are read as personal flaws or weaknesses of moral character. One can see why being told, as the medication takers have been, that one's problems are the result of a chemical imbalance, comes as a relief. Chemical imbalances (in this view) are fixable; a flawed self is not. Certainly the achieving self has many satisfactions, and when smoothly ascending the ladder of achievement, its burdens weigh lightly. The suffering comes at those moments when the ascent is threatened or interrupted. Then comes the disappointment, the fear, even terror, that, as Sarah put it, "I'm not going to be able to be this person I'm supposed to be."

(Spring 2009, 11.1)

Notes

[1] I have changed the names of my interviewees and any other details necessary to protect their anonymity.

[2] Kimberly A. Goyette, "College for Some to College for All: Social Background, Occupational Expectations, and Educational Expectations Over Time," *Social Science Research* 37 (2008): 461–84.

[3] See, for example, Goyett; and Alan Kerckhoff, "The Transition from School to Work," *The Changing Adolescent Experience: Social Trends and the Transition to Adulthood*, ed. Jeylan T. Mortimer and Reed W. Larson (New York, NY: Cambridge University Press, 2002), 52–87.

[4] Chardie L. Baird, Stephanie W. Burge, and John R. Reynolds, "Absurdly Ambitious? Teenagers' Expectations for the Future and the Realities of Social Structure," *Sociology Compass* 2.3 (2008): 944–62; Patrick West and Helen Sweeting, "Fifteen, Female and Stressed: Changing Patterns of Psychological Distress Over Time," *Journal of Child Psychology and Psychiatry* 44.3 (2003): 399–411.

[5] John Reynolds, Michael Stewart, Ryan Macdonald, and Lacey Sischo, "Have Adolescents Become Too Ambitious? High School Seniors' Educational and Occupational Plans, 1976 to 2000," *Social Problems* 53.2 (2006): 186–206; see also Goyette.

[6] Iain Walker and Heather J. Smith, "Fifty Years of Relative Deprivation Research," *Relative Deprivation: Specification, Development, and Integration*, ed. Iain Walker and Heather J. Smith (Cambridge, England: Cambridge University Press, 2002) 1–9; Carsten Wrosch, Gregory E. Miller, Michael F. Scheier, and Stephanie Brun de Pontet, "Giving Up on Unattainable Goals: Benefits for Health?" *Personality and Social Psychology Bulletin* 33.2 (2007): 251–65.

[7] See, for example, Alexandra Robbins, *The Overachievers: The Secret Lives of Driven Kids* (New York, NY: Hyperion, 2006); Carl Honoré, *Under Pressure: Rescuing Our Children from the Culture of Hyper-Parenting* (New York, NY: HarperOne, 2008).

[8] See, for example, Honoré; Madeline Levine, *The Price of Privilege: How Parental Pressure and Material Advantage Are Creating a Generation of Disconnected and Unhappy Kids* (New York, NY: HarperCollins, 2006); Denise Clark Pope, *Doing School: How We Are Creating a Generation of Stressed-Out, Materialistic, and Miseducated Students* (New Haven, CT: Yale University Press, 2001); Alvin Rosenfeld and Nicole Wise, *The Over-Scheduled Child: Avoiding the Hyper-Parenting Trap* (New York, NY: St. Martin's Griffin, 2000).

[9] See, for example, Victor R. Wilburn and Delores E. Smith, "Stress, Self-Esteem, and Suicidal Ideation in Late Adolescents," *Adolescence* 40.157 (Spring 2005): 33–45; Ellen Greenberger, Jared Lessard, Chuansheng Chen, and Susan P. Farruggia, "Self-Entitled College Students: Contributions of Personality, Parenting, and Motivational Factors," *Journal of Youth and Adolescence* 37.10 (2008): 1193–1204.

[10] See, for example, Joseph L. Mahoney, Angel L. Harris, and Jacquelynne S. Eccles, "Organized Activity Participation, Positive Youth Development, and the Over-Scheduling Hypothesis," *Social Policy Report* 20.4 (2006).

[11] Paul du Gay, "Against 'Enterprise' (But Not Against 'Enterprise,' for That Would Make No Sense)," *Organization* 11.1 (2004): 37–57.

[12] Nikolas Rose, *Inventing Our Selves: Psychology, Power, and Personhood* (Cambridge, England: Cambridge University Press, 1996) 154.

[13] Rose, 154. See Colin S. Cremin, "Profiling the Personal: Configuration of Teenage Biographies to Employment Norms," *Sociology* 39.2 (2005): 315–32; Joseph E. Davis, "The Commodification of Self," *The Hedgehog Review* 5.2 (Summer 2003): 41–9; and du Gay.

[14] David A. Karp reports a similar finding in his interviews with individuals suffering from depression; see his *Speaking of Sadness: Depression, Disconnection and the Meanings of Illness* (New York, NY: Oxford University Press, 1996).

[15] Lawrence H. Diller suggests that such a shift may be fairly common; see his *Running on Ritalin: A Physician Reflects on Children, Society, and Performance in a Pill* (New York, NY: Bantam, 1998), 294.

[16] All of the people we interviewed filled out one or more symptom checklists: "The Adult ADHD Self-Report Scale (ASRS-vl.l) Symptom Checklist"; the "Quick Inventory of Depressive Symptomatology (Self-Report) (QUIDS-SR 16)"; or the "Social Phobia Inventory."

[17] The connection of self to business norms is suggested in a recent *Washington Post* article. A business psychologist argues that if the Internet company Google "were a person, it would be the model of a psychologically healthy adult." Its "corporate culture and management practices," he continues, "depend upon cooperation, collaboration, non-defensiveness, informality, a creative mind-set, flexibility and nimbleness, all aimed at competing aggressively for clear goals within a constantly changing environment" (Douglas LaBier, "You've Gotta Think Like Google," *Washington Post* [11 November 2008]: http:// www.washingtonpost.com/wp-dyn/content/article/2008/11/07/AR2008110703319.html).

Evil, Pain, and Beauty
A Conversation with Elaine Scarry

Jennifer L. Geddes

Jennifer L. Geddes (JLG): *The Body in Pain: The Making and Unmaking of the World* focuses both on the infliction of pain and on creativity. It's a jarring combination, and yet, you see a connection between them. You argue that the infliction of pain reverses the process of creation, suggesting that it undoes or deconstructs the victim's world and his or her ability to make a world. Could you say more about this?

Elaine Scarry (ES): When I talk about pain and creation, I really do mean in the most literal way possible that they are opposites and opposites that are, as you say, jarring in their relationship. When I started writing the book, I actually had begun by thinking that if I wanted to write about pain, I should not begin to talk about creation. As a student and young teacher of literature, I knew that often in literary realms we refer to the fact that out of suffering comes creation, and I had originally felt resistance to that idea just because the relentless nature of cancer pain, or burn pain, or pain inflicted in political contexts, never has any room in it for creation and, therefore, to imagine that great acts of creativity could come about seemed to excuse and apologize for the existence of suffering in the world. So my original intention was to write only about pain and not to stray into creation. And, then, as I began to work on the question of torture—and I can almost remember the moment in which this happened, as I sat there reading piles and piles of Amnesty International materials—I suddenly saw that the structure of cruelty that I was observing was actually a kind of standing of creation on its head. Not only were suffering and creation not in league with one another; they were radical opposites.

The work of pain is to deconstruct or unmake objects of consciousness, as we can see if suddenly you accidentally slam a hammer on your hand and your mind goes blank or you see stars. You can literally see the unmaking of the objects of consciousness in front of the mind's eye. So too with language. If one is suddenly put in pain for a moment or an hour or a day or, in a worse situation, several days or even longer, you can watch language deteriorate. One's ability to say sentences, and then even one's ability to say words, disappears. In the initial moment of pain, someone might say an expletive, and then a cry; these are half-way points in the disintegration of language until, finally, one just surrenders and is quiet. That is the rude physical fact of pain.

In the cultural context I was looking at, in documents from the '70s, there was a literal acting out of the unmaking of the objects of consciousness and the unmaking of the objectifying power of language. For example, in torture not only did the torturer inflict pain, but there was actually a kind of miming of the unmaking of the world by enlisting all the objects of the world into the act. Even if the torturer was using a mechanism such as, let's say, a way of inflicting electrical discharge into the person, he would also refer to chairs and tables and windowsills and baskets and blankets and telephones and all kinds of cultural artifacts, and in that way made the body of the prisoner somehow a kind of agent for not only experiencing its own pain, but for witnessing the dissolution of the made world.

Sometimes people say to me that bodily experiences are always language-destroying, that pain is language-destroying, but so is pleasure. I think that that's not correct. There are places where we can see that pleasure can interfere with language. Lovers, for example, in the moment of making love may begin to speak baby talk. But, lovers are also able to call on the greatest powers of language-building. They write hymns to one another and write poems and romances, and so we have a huge linguistic celebration of love. So, too, the pleasure of eating, which is a very physical act, is very compatible with conversation, with dinner parties, and that's been true from Plato's symposium forward, or actually much earlier, when the assemblies of people in Homer are sitting around feasting and talking. Physical pain is not just language-destroying, it also destroys the objects of consciousness, and conversely, pleasure is world-building, or, to put it the other way, world-building is pleasurable. I really do see them as opposed.

JLG: How are good and evil related to creation and injury?

ES: The word "evil" isn't one that I spontaneously think of when I'm thinking about this, and yet, it certainly has many features in common with what I'm talking about when I describe cruelty or injustice. One of the virtues of using the vocabulary of good and evil is that it does register an oppositional ground—that is, it does state the fact that there are two alternatives, which is something I very much believe. My book is divided into Part I on unmaking and Part II on making, so that I place injury or the willful infliction of injury in opposition to creation. In our own intellectual time, I think we've been very discouraged from ever wanting to say: "Look, there are two distinguishable things." Instead, we've been asked again and again to say

"Everything is just a version of its opposite; and it may seem that these things are different, but really they're just the same in the end." And I don't think that's true. Injustice or (using the word you introduced) "evil" not only likes to ape creation and turn it on its head, but also very much profits from our getting confused about whether what we're looking at is creation or cruelty. Whereas I think that genuine acts of making and creation, which are normally on the side of diminishing pain, have to, among other things, continually keep sorting out and de-coupling creation from its appropriative and opposite counterpart of cruelty.

JLG: One definition of evil might be "using the language-destroying power of pain to unmake someone's world intentionally." Pain can be caused by unintentional actions, but the *intentional* use of that attribute of pain to unmake someone's world could be a definition of evil. What do you think about that?

ES: I think that that's right. The pain that has no human agent, such as certain forms of cancer pain or burn pain, are every bit as horrible for the person who suffers them, and yet, we can at least work to heal that pain, and no one's confused about whether it's a good or not. The idea that actually willfully inflicting those kinds and levels of pain—if there is such a thing as evil, then that is what it is. If I hesitate at all about the word "evil"—let me insert a parenthesis in here as to why I hesitate—in some ways "evil" is a very resonant term, and I'm sure that for some people it conveys a kind of absolute quality that explains why the cruel acts that it holds within it have to be absolutely prohibited. For me, for some reason, the word "evil" doesn't work in my intuitive, everyday world, to carry with it that absolute prohibition in the way that "injustice," or a more neutral-sounding word like "cruelty," does. It may be because "evil" sounds theological and, therefore, may have a slight feeling of excusing the human actors involved, as though it was a force beyond them, that they couldn't help participating in. But, I'm just saying that as a parenthesis, because I think, for the most part, what you mean by "evil" and what I mean by "injustice" or "willful infliction of cruelty" or "willful infliction of injury" are very close to one another.

JLG: How does the idea of injury fit into your understanding of the relationship between evil and suffering?

ES: Whereas there are a lot of things in the world that are morally ambiguous, the willful infliction of injury is not ambiguous, and normally one can take that as a kind of center of gravity for understanding what's to be aspired to and what's to be avoided. And so I think that the language of evil absolutely should have the infliction of injury associated with it, if we use it at all. It has the benefit of asserting that there is a double ground. It's not that everything blends into, or smudges into, each other and that things that are good can't be differentiated from things that are evil.

JLG: Some people claim that suffering is the result of evil. Others suggest that suffering is the evil against which we should fight. How do you see the relationship between evil and suffering?

ES: I certainly think that suffering that is not willfully inflicted is as hateful—as horrible and hateful and to be dreaded—as suffering that is willfully inflicted. I think, though, that there is a certain advantage in holding out the word "evil" to describe acts of agency, that is, acts that are intentional. If what the word "evil" does is to mark out something that we plan to work together to eliminate or avoid, then that's a virtue of the language. That is, it designates something against which we will stand.

JLG: Your work is focused on pain as injury, with torture and war being the two primary situations of pain that you discuss. What do you think of those instances in which pain is not the infliction of injury, for example, the pain associated with medical operations in which the goal is the alleviation of an illness or a wound that has caused pain, or childbirth, or extreme physical exertion? How does the intention of the inflictor of pain relate to whether we view this infliction as injury or as evil?

ES: I think that at the very heart of pain is the felt experience of aversiveness. It is something that is immediately palpable as something we don't want or one doesn't want. Here again, is something that people sometimes get very confused about. They'll say: "Well, pain is neutral. It can either be positive or negative." No, that's not correct. Pain is negative. It's the felt experience of aversiveness. It's something that in the most vivid way possible one doesn't want and doesn't want it with all one's being; and therefore, it really is a kind of acting against one's will—both because one feels the helplessness of one's own will in getting rid of it and because, even before one's attempt to get rid of it, the mere fact of its existence seems to call into question the power of one's own volition, or the power of one's own will.

So, to go on to your question: what about those situations in which there is some voluntary control on the individual's part? I think those situations are very different. If I will myself into a situation of pain such as a medical therapy, and I agree to go to a doctor and let her do something to me that hurts, then it's already very different. And it's not just different as an interpretative act, but, rather, to say that more clearly, the act of interpretation is so deeply grounded in the felt experience itself that if I am actually seeking it, it already has a kind of power to transform the pain. That is, it is no longer pain, since pain is centrally the felt experience of aversiveness. So it may have unpleasant sentient characteristics associated with it, but it doesn't fundamentally insult my whole being the way physical pain which is unwanted does. If you watch any child go into a medical office and watch his or her face as the needle or the scalpel approaches, it's a reminder that being able to willingly take on pain, as we do when we go to the physician, is a learned experience. It is deeply counter-intuitive.

JLG: Isn't it the case that the pain is still unwanted, that there's still an aversiveness to pain, but that there's a greater good that makes the individual willing to bear it, in which case it's still physical pain and still has aversiveness at its core?

ES: I think that's right. It's certainly the case that one undergoes terrible pain by agreeing, say, to chemotherapy. It's just unquestionable. And it's certainly the case that childbirth involves extremely high levels of pain. But, in both of those cases, as you said, there's a good outcome, very great outcome, and also there's some recognition that the amount of time involved is limited, which it isn't if it's certain other forms of pain. The kind of repudiation that would be involved in unwanted pain is not the same.

Now, here's another crucial element in all these situations: The person who's experiencing the pain is also the person who gets the benefits of the greater good. It's the person who's chosen the medical therapy who will derive the benefits, if there are benefits to be derived, from the medical therapy. And it's the person undergoing childbirth who will have this wonderful new creature in the world with her soon. The problem with these instances being cited is that they then get used by people to say that sometimes pain leads to a greater good, where it's one person who's being put in pain and somebody else who's getting to determine what the greater good is. And, of course, this is very clearly true in regimes that torture. I'm sure they're telling themselves that they don't really want to inflict pain, but for the good of the regime, they have to do it. What is absolutely crucial is that the location of sentience for the pain and for the assessment of the pleasure or what the good is to be derived have to be in the same location. And if they're not, then the thing is a very great falsification.

JLG: Torture is one of the most extreme examples of the situation in which the suffering of one person is used for the supposed good of another: the pain of the victim of torture is directly inverse to the good for which the torturer claims he is doing this torturing. Is that why you see torture as "close to an absolute immorality"?

ES: I think you're exactly right that one person's pain is being appropriated and its attributes are being objectified and falsely conferred on someone else or something else. And, therefore, it does represent an absolute of immorality. That's my judgment, but it's also a widely shared judgment. It's why international prohibitions on torture are stated in unqualified form, and it's why torture has extra-territorial jurisdiction in the United States where, unlike any other political crime, it doesn't have to have happened on our soil or even to involve a U. S. citizen for it to be tried in the country. Those are, legally, very unusual circumstances. But it is just for the reason you point to: there is a complete lack of consent in the situation so that the location of the pain and the location of the asserted good to be derived are wholly severed from one another. The example of torture shows this in its global features and also in the minute workings of it. Very literally you can watch in slow motion this transfer across the two locations, so that, for example, certain features of pain, like its totalizing power, are transferred over to the regime; in this mime that's going on in the prison room, it seems to be the regime that's total. Well, the regime isn't total at all. It's usually because the regime's in a lot of trouble and doesn't have ordinary forms of popular verification and authorization that it's resorting to torture, and, yet, for the duration of the act of torture, it seems as though the regime is total and totalizing because the felt experience of pain is total and totalizing. But it does seem to me an absolute standard.

Once in a while, you'll hear somebody try to make an argument like: "Let's imagine a situation where we would all agree to torture. Imagine someone has a key secret to some kind of terrible weapon, like a nuclear bomb, and only by torturing him or her do you find out where it is." Leaving aside the fact that it's been demonstrated over and over again that torture leads to a mountain of false information, not to true information—even if we can allow that it leads to true information, it doesn't change the fact that there's no reason to want to change the fact that torturing the person is wrong. It's just that in that situation one would be willing to accept carrying out a very wrong act in order to do something else. But to say that as though what you really want is to absolve somebody—I mean, why would anyone in that situation even want to absolve themselves in wrongdoing? Presumably they're going to do something for humanity. They are not going to ask to be absolved from that.

JLG: There's no reason to try to say that torture is a good thing—even if, for example, it does save the world from this nuclear bomb. It's still a very bad, destructive thing to torture someone, but you might say it was a necessary evil for that particular situation.

ES: I think that's exactly right.

JLG: Let's talk about beauty and evil, which is a strange combination, but you went from writing a book about pain and to writing a book about beauty and justice. How do you understand the relation between injury and beauty?

ES: I think the whole sequence of questions you've been asking me underscores the bridge, the structure, that connects the earlier work I did on pain and the more recent work on beauty. It's in part because *The Body in Pain* is so much about the opposition between pain, on the one hand, and creation, on the other, so that creation, which is very bound up with beauty, really does stand in opposition to pain. Some people who have read the book, *On Beauty and Being Just*, even when they've been incredibly generous to the book, have said: "Well, she never talks about ugliness." But, beauty, like anything else, can have many different opposites. And the thing that, for me, is the opposite of beauty is injury. There is a straightforward continuity between the two works. Beauty makes us want to diminish injury in the world. When I say that beauty makes us feel adverse to injury, what I'm trying to say is that one never wants to cease being opposed to injury.

The felt experience of standing in the presence of beauty is life-affirming; it both makes us salute the aliveness (or if it's an artwork, the kind of life-likeness) of the thing before which we stand, and ignites or vivifies our awareness of our own aliveness, making the pleasurable facts of sentience more emphatic. It's always the work of creation to diminish pain, but not to diminish sentience. It's the work of creation to amplify the pleasurable forms of sensation, such as seeing. Creation helps us see farther, or hear better, or with more acuity, or to touch better, but it's only the adversity of sentience, of physical pain and injury, that creation opposes. Beautiful things incite in us the desire to do one of two things: to protect and take care of beautiful things that are already existing in the world, to engage in acts of stewardship, and to perform new acts of creation. When you're in the presence of something beautiful, it often leads you to want to bring yet more beauty into the world. So you see a beautiful tree, and now you want to take a photograph of the tree, or make a drawing of the tree. The tree is already beautiful and yet, now it's going to be supplemented with one more beautiful thing, this sketch or this photograph. And the outcome may be incredibly great, as is the case if you're Leonardo doing this sketch, or it may be something as modest as just the fact of staring. When one stares at a beautiful building or a beautiful flower or stares acoustically at a beautiful piece of music by playing it again and again and again, what one is doing is perpetuating its existence in the world, that is, perpetuating, giving it more standing, giving it more ground to stand on. And, therefore, that act, though it seems very ordinary—the act of staring either with your ears or your eyes or your hands or whatever—is very closely bound up to the act of creating, since what it tries to do is bring about more of this thing that already is.

JLG: I was thinking about your descriptions of pain as the shrinking of the world to just the body or the part of the body that is in pain, and of seeing beauty or experiencing beauty as a sort of duplication or reproduction—there's a certain fecundity to it that is a multiplier of sensations, a desire to reproduce the beautiful object or to share it or to insure its existence along with one's own.

ES: I think that that's true: beauty really is distributive in nature; pain and injury do throw you back on yourself. One thinks of that great definition of aging by Stravinsky as the ever-shrinking perimeter of pleasure, where there's only the felt fact of aversiveness. And yet, beauty wholly carries one out of oneself, as in the descriptions given by Simon Weil and by Iris Murdock as a kind of de-centering, in which your own preoccupations about yourself fall away. You're actually in the very unusual position of being willing to be secondary to or adjacent to or lateral to the figure, and yet being at the same time in a great state of pleasure.

There are lots of things in the world that can make us feel secondary or tertiary or lateral, and there are lots of things in the world that can make us feel acute pleasure, but usually they don't happen simultaneously, and in beauty, they really do. But I hadn't quite seen it so clearly in the way that you've just made me see it, as really clearly the opposite of the soul-destroying throwing back on the adversity of the body that can happen in the brute forms of extreme and sustained physical pain.

(Summer 2000, 2.2)

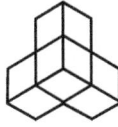

Contributors

Helen Andrews is a Robert Novak Journalism Fellow and has worked as an editor and a think tank researcher.

Robert N. Bellah (1927–2013) was Elliott Professor of Sociology Emeritus at the University of California at Berkeley. His works include *Beyond Belief, Emile Durkheim on Morality and Society, The Broken Covenant, The New Religious Consciousness, Varieties of Civil Religion, Uncivil Religion, Imagining Japan* and, *The Robert Bellah Reader*. The latter reflects his work as a whole and the overall direction of his life in scholarship "to understand the meaning of modernity."

Seyla Benhabib is the Eugene Meyer Professor of Political Science and Philosophy at Yale University. She is the author most recently of *The Rights of Others: Aliens, Citizens and Residents* (2004, winner of the Ralph Bunche award of the American Political Science Association) and *Another Cosmopolitanism: Sovereignty, Hospitality and Democratic Iterations* (2006), based on her Berkeley Tanner Lectures, with commentaries by Jeremy Waldron, Bonnie Honig, and Will Kymlicka. She was awarded the 2009 Ernst Bloch Prize of the city of Ludwigshafen for her contributions to analyzing the conflicts of a multicultural global world.

Philippe Bénéton is professor emeritus of political science, University of Rennes, France. His books include *Equality by Default* and *The Kingdom Suffereth Violence: The Machiavelli/ Erasmus/More Correspondence and Other Documents*.

Professor, sociologist, and theologian, **Peter L. Berger** (1929–2017) was the author of several influential books, including *The Social Construction of Reality: A Treatise in the Sociology of Knowledge with Thomas Luckmann; Invitation to Sociology: A Humanistic Perspective; A Rumor of Angels: Modern Society and the Rediscovery of the Supernatural;* and *The Sacred Canopy: Elements of a Social Theory of Religion.*

Talbot Brewer, a faculty fellow at the Institute for Advanced Studies in Culture, is professor of philosophy and chair of the department of philosophy at the University of Virginia and author of *The Retrieval of Ethics*.

Neslihan Cevik is a Turkish sociologist of religion and the author of *Muslimism in Turkey and Beyond: Religion in the Modern World* as well as an associate fellow at the Institute for Advanced Studies in Culture.

Phil Christman teaches first-year writing at the University of Michigan and is the editor of the *Michigan Review of Prisoner Creative Writing*. His work has appeared in *The Christian Century*, *Paste*, *Books & Culture*, and other publications. The essay published here has been expanded to book form in *Midwest Futures*.

Matthew B. Crawford is a senior fellow at the Institute for Advanced Studies in Culture at the University of Virginia. His books include *Why We Drive: Toward a Philosophy of the Open Road*, *The World Beyond Your Head: On Becoming an Individual in an Age of Distraction* and the best-selling *Shop Class as Soulcraft: An Inquiry into the Value of Work*.

Thomas Cushman is Deffenbaugh de Hoyos Carlson Professor in the Social Sciences and Professor of Sociology at Wellesley College, general editor for the series "Post-Communist Societies and Cultures," and editor of *Human Rights Review*. He has published numerous papers and books on Soviet society and the Balkans and has co-edited, with Stjepan G. Mestrovic, *This Time We Knew: Western Responses to Genocide in Bosnia*.

Veena Das is the Krieger-Eisenhower Professor of Anthropology at the Johns Hopkins University. She has written widely on Indian ethnography and anthropology. Among her books are *Life and Words: Violence and the Descent into the Ordinary*, *Affliction: Health, Disease, Poverty*, and three co-edited volumes, *The Ground Between: Anthropologists Engage Philosophy*, *Living and Dying in the Contemporary World: A Compendium*, and *Politics of the Urban Poor*.

Lorraine Daston is director emerita of the Max Planck Institute for the History of Science, Berlin, and a visiting professor in the Committee on Social Thought, University of Chicago. Her many books, authored, coauthored, and edited, include *Objectivity*, *How Reason Almost Lost Its Mind: The Strange Career of Cold War Rationality*, and *Science in the Archives*. The essay that appears here was adapted from her 2016 Page-Barbour Lectures at the University of Virginia.

Joseph E. Davis is Research Associate Professor of Sociology at the University of Virginia and moderator of the Picturing the Human colloquy at the Institute for Advanced Studies in Culture. He is editor (with Ana Marta González), most recently, of *To Fix or To Heal: Patient Care, Public Health, and the Limits of Biomedicine.*

Mark Edmundson is University Professor in the Department of English at the University of Virginia. His books include *Why Write? A Master Class on the Art of Writing and Why It Matters* and *Self and Soul: A Defense of Ideals.*

Jean Bethke Elshtain (1941–2013) was an American ethicist, political philosopher, and public intellectual. Her books included *Sovereignty: God, State, Self; Just War against Terror: The Burden of American Power in a Violent World; Jane Addams and the Dream of American Democracy; Who Are We? Critical Reflections and Hopeful Possibilities. Politics and Ethical Discourse; New Wine in Old Bottles: International Politics and Ethical Discourse; Real Politics: Political Theory and Everyday Life; Augustine and the Limits of Politics; Democracy on Trial,* among others.

Harvie Ferguson is a professor of sociology at the University of Glasgow. He has written extensively on the development of cultural, philosophical, and psychological aspects of the development of western modernity.

Jennifer L. Geddes is an associate professor of Religious Studies at the University of Virginia. Her areas of research include evil and suffering, the Holocaust, ethics, critical theory, twentieth-century literature, and religion and culture. Previously, she was the editor of *The Hedgehog Review.*

John Gray is a political philosopher and author of *Seven Types of Atheism; Endgames: Questions in Late Modern Political Thought; After Social Democracy;* and *False Dawn: The Delusions of Global Capitalism.*

James Davison Hunter is the founder and executive director of the Institute for Advanced Studies in Culture and LaBrosse-Levinson Distinguished Professor of Religion, Culture, and Social Theory at the University of Virginia. He is also the publisher of *The Hedgehog Review.* His many books include *Science and the Good: The Tragic Quest for the Foundations of Morality* (with Paul Nedelisky), *Culture Wars: The Struggle to Define America,* and *The Death of Character: Moral Education without Good or Evil.*

Louis Hyman is an associate professor of history in Cornell University's School of Industrial and Labor Relations. He is the author of *Temp: How American Work, American Business, and the American Dream Became Temporary*, *Debtor Nation: The History of American in Red Ink* and *Borrow: The American Way of Debt*.

Eva Illouz is a professor of sociology at the Hebrew University in Jerusalem. Her books include *Why Love Hurts: A Sociological Explanation*, Cold Intimacies: The Making of Emotional Capitalism, *Consuming the Romantic Utopia: Love and the Cultural Contradictions of Capitalism*, *Saving the Modern Soul: Therapy, Emotions, and the Culture of Self-Help*, among others.

Alan Jacobs is a distinguished professor of humanities in the honors program at Baylor University. A prolific essayist, reviewer, and blogger, he is the author of *The Year of Our Lord 1943: Christian Humanism in an Age of Crisis*, *"The Book of Common Prayer": A Biography*, and *The Pleasures of Reading in an Age of Distraction*, among others.

Russell Jacoby is a professor of history at the University of California, Los Angeles, an author and a critic of academic culture. His book *The Last Intellectuals: American Culture in the Age of Academe* chronicled the disappearance of the public intellectual in America.

Wendy Kaminer, a lawyer and social critic, writes about law, liberty, feminism, religion, and popular culture.

T.J. Jackson Lears, a visiting fellow at the Institute for Advanced Studies in Culture, is a professor of history at Rutgers University and the editor of Raritan. He is the author of *Rebirth of a Nation: The Making of Modern America, 1877–1920*, among other books.

Rebecca Lemov is an associate professor of the history of science at Harvard University and the author of *World as Laboratory: Experiments with Mice, Mazes, and Men* and *Database of Dreams*. She is also a coauthor of *How Reason Almost Lost Its Mind: The Strange Career of Rationality in the Cold War*.

Eugene McCarraher is an associate professor of humanities at Villanova University and author of *The Enchantments of Mammon: Capitalism as the Religion of Modernity*.

Wilfred M. McClay is G.T. and Libby Blankenship Chair in the History of Liberty and director of the Center for the History of Liberty at the University of Oklahoma. His latest book is *Land of Hope: An Invitation to the Great American Story*.

William McPherson (1933–2017), a novelist, critic, and journalist, was the editor of the *Washington Post Book World* and was awarded the Pulitzer Prize for Criticism. His first novel, *Testing the Current*, was republished by New York Review Books Classics in 2013.

Martha C. Nussbaum is an American philosopher and the current Ernst Freund Distinguished Service Professor of Law and Ethics at the University of Chicago, where she is jointly appointed in the law school and the philosophy department. Her books include, among others, *The Monarchy of Fear: A Philosopher Looks at Our Political Crisis*, *Upheavals of Thought: The Intelligence of Emotions*, and *Not for Profit: Why Democracy Needs the Humanities*.

Alice O'Connor, professor of history at the University of California, Santa Barbara, is the author of *Poverty Knowledge: Social Science, Social Policy, and the Poor in Twentieth-Century U.S. History* and *Social Science for What? Philanthropy and the Social Question in a World Turned Rightside Up*.

John M. Owen IV is Ambassador Henry J. Taylor and Mrs. Marion R. Taylor Professor of Politics at the University of Virginia and Faculty Fellow at the Institute for Advanced Studies in Culture.

Mike Rose is the author of many books, including *The Mind at Work* (tenth anniversary edition, 2014), *Back to School*, and *Why School?* (revised edition, 2014). He is a research professor in the UCLA Graduate School of Education and Information Studies.

Becca Rothfeld is a doctoral candidate in the department of philosophy at Harvard University.

Elaine Scarry is an American essayist and professor of English and American Literature and Language. She is the Walter M. Cabot Professor of Aesthetics and the General Theory of Value at Harvard University. Her books include *The Body in Pain: The Making and Unmaking of the World* and *On Beauty and Being Just*.

Richard Sennett trained at the University of Chicago and at Harvard University, receiving his Ph.D. in 1969. He divides his time between New York University and the London School of Economics, as well as maintaining informal connections to MIT and to Trinity College, Cambridge University. His books include *The Craftsman* and *The Corrosion of Character*.

Jay Tolson is editor of *The Hedgehog Review*.

Michael Walzer is an American political theorist and public intellectual. He is a professor emeritus at the Institute for Advanced Study in Princeton, New Jersey, and co-editor of *Dissent*. He is the author of, among others, *A Foreign Policy for the Left*, *In God's Shadow: Politics in the Hebrew Bible*, and *The Paradox of Liberation: Secular Revolutions and Religious Counterrevolutions*.

Leif Weatherby is an assistant professor of German at New York University and the author of *Transplanting the Metaphysical Organ: German Romanticism between Leibniz and Marx*.

Chad Wellmon is an associate professor of German studies at the University of Virginia and principal of UVA's Brown College. His books include *Organizing Enlightenment: Information Overload and the Invention of the Modern Research University* and *The Rise of the Research University: A Sourcebook*, which he co-edited with Louis Menand and Paul Reitter.

Joshua J. Yates holds a position at Duke Divinity School and is a Fellow at the Institute for Advanced Studies in Culture. He is a former research assistant professor at the University of Virginia.